THE WILL OF THE PEOPLE

THE WILL
OF THE
PEOPLE

How Public Opinion Has Influenced

the Supreme Court

and Shaped the Meaning

of the Constitution

BARRY FRIEDMAN

Farrar, Straus and Giroux / New York

FARRAR, STRAUS AND GIROUX
18 West 18th Street, New York 10011

Library of Congress Cataloging-in-Publication Data
Friedman, Barry, 1958–
  The will of the people : how public opinion has influenced the
Supreme Court and shaped the meaning of the Constitution / Barry
Friedman.
    p. cm.
  Includes bibliographical references and index.
  ISBN: 978-0-374-22034-1 (hardcover : alk. paper)
  1. United States. United States—Public opinion. 2. Judicial
process—United States—Public opinion. 3. Public opinion—United
States. I. Title.

KF8748.F79 2009
347.73'12—dc22

                                                    2008054247

Designed by Abby Kagan

www.fsgbooks.com

1 3 5 7 9 10 8 6 4 2

To Jill

CONTENTS

THE WILL OF THE PEOPLE

INTRODUCTION

"[T]o decide upon the meaning of the constitution"

I n the first half of the 1930s, the American people faced two seemingly intractable problems. The first was the Great Depression, the country's worst-ever economic downturn. Desperate for a leader, if not a savior, the people elected Franklin Roosevelt President and gave him a strong Democratic majority in Congress. Following Roosevelt's inauguration, Congress began adopting New Deal measures with alacrity; the pace of legislation was simply breathtaking. Many today dispute how effective these measures ultimately were, but at the time, Roosevelt's program offered something people sorely needed: hope.

The second problem was the Supreme Court. In case after stunning case the justices struck down New Deal legislation, ruling that it violated the Constitution. To Roosevelt and the millions who supported him, the Supreme Court's persistent veto was an unfathomable breach of the democratic principle: that the will of the people should govern.

In the winter of 1937, Roosevelt struck back at the Court. Fresh from a landslide victory that *The New York Times* dubbed "a political Johnstown flood," Roosevelt determined that the justices would no longer stand in the way of his popular agenda.[1] He asked Congress to give him the power to add an additional appointee to the Court for every justice over the age of seventy who refused to retire. Should the elderly and recalcitrant justices not yield, Roosevelt planned to "pack" the Court with as many as six new members of his choosing.

For five anxious months, the question of whether or not Congress should approve Roosevelt's dramatic plan gripped the country. In the very thick of it *Newsweek* reported that "state legislators, public officials, editors, and millions of plain John Does had joined in a furious debate." Gallup polling, still in a relatively primitive state, showed voters shifting to and fro in response to the latest development. "Street-corner discussions, arguments at restaurant tables, a seemingly endless stream of radio addresses and newspaper reports, protracted hearings before the Senate Judiciary Committee and animated congressional debates" convinced Merlo Pusey, a prominent historian and editorialist who chronicled the fight and went on to write the Chief Justice's biography, that "our national conscience has been deeply stirred."[2]

How Congress voted on Roosevelt's plan would say much about the future of the Supreme Court. But it would say far more about the American people and the sort of government they preferred. To hear it told, they faced a stark choice: either demand the triumph of the popular will and approve FDR's proposal to subjugate the Court, or insist that even a democratic government must operate within the limits of the Constitution and reject the plan.

As it happened, the country and the Court found a way out of the seeming dilemma, a solution that has influenced the nature of American government ever since. Congress rejected Roosevelt's plan. But it did so only after the Court signaled its capitulation and began to approve New Deal measures, at which point public opinion turned squarely against the plan. In effect, a tacit deal was reached: the American people would grant the justices their power, so long as the Supreme Court's interpretation of the Constitution did not stray too far from what a majority of the people believed it should be. For the most part, this deal has stuck.

Roosevelt's attack on the Court was brazen, but it was only one of many that have occurred throughout the nation's life. What follows is the chronicle of the relationship between the popular will and the Supreme Court as it unfolded over two hundred–plus years of American history. It reveals how the Supreme Court went from being an institution intended to check the popular will to one that frequently confirms it. And it explains that this occurred as the American people gradually came to understand and then to shape the role played by the justices, thus defining the terms of their own constitutional democracy.

JUDICIAL REVIEW AND DEMOCRACY

The specific target of Roosevelt's ire was the power of judicial review, the practice by which courts, and particularly the Supreme Court, determine whether government actions are consistent with the Constitution. In American life, the Constitution reigns supreme. Exercising judicial review, courts have the power to strike down even congressional statutes and acts of the President when they are found out of keeping with constitutional standards.

Throughout history, the chief complaint against judicial review has been that it interferes with the right of the people to govern themselves. After the Supreme Court struck down yet another New Deal measure in 1936, the *New York Daily News*, the country's first tabloid, with a circulation at the time of well over one million, thundered: "We do not see how old judicial gentlemen . . . can forever be permitted to override the will of the people as expressed through the people's own elected Legislatures, Congress and President."[3] A union official, expressing support for Roosevelt's plan, explained the problem: "Unless all branches of our national government are made responsive to changing conditions and thereby truly democratic, popular elections are turned into a farce. The judiciary is no exception."[4] The President, the members of Congress, and the states' chief executives and legislators all are accountable to the people through regular elections. Not so the justices of the Supreme Court, who are appointed (not elected) and who—short of removal by impeachment, which has never happened—serve for life. Yet when the justices base a ruling on the Constitution, the country must live with that decision unless and until the Court reverses itself or the rare constitutional amendment is adopted. There is no overriding the Court otherwise.

This extraordinary power was a rather uniquely American innovation, emerging without plan or design in the period prior to the Constitutional Convention as a means of checking the excesses of democracy.[5] In the years following independence, increasing numbers of Americans watched with apprehension as legislative assemblies trampled fundamental rights. Gradually, almost imperceptibly, judges answered the call of lawyers to refuse to enforce such laws on the ground that they were "repugnant to" the state constitutions. Then the framers of the United States Constitution adopted the innovation of judicial review to solve a problem of their own: how to ensure that the state governments followed national authority. James Madison, one of our most revered founders, suggested that Congress have a veto over every state law, but few of his colleagues were willing to go that far. Instead, they left it to the judges to decide if particular state laws (and perhaps federal laws as well) conflicted with national authority, and in particular with the Constitution.

Although few in the early days of American democracy recognized the full potential of judicial review, some who did were alarmed. As the struggle over ratification of the Constitution entered its most heated days, the Anti-

Federalist (i.e., anti-ratification) pamphleteer "Brutus" weighed in, express-ing grave concern about the proposed federal judiciary. He thought it almost unimaginable to give judges the power "to decide upon the meaning of the constitution."[6] Brutus pointed to Great Britain, where "I believe [the judges] in no instance assume the authority to set aside an act of parliament under the idea that it is inconsistent with their constitution." Brutus reminded his readers that the judges possessing this extraordinary authority "cannot be removed from office or suffer a diminution of their salaries." "The supreme court under this constitution," Brutus predicted—some would say quite accurately—"would be exalted above all other power in the government, and subject to no control." No fewer than four times he intoned: *"[T]here is no power above them."*[7]

When Roosevelt defended his Court-packing plan, he joined hands across the ages with Brutus in condemning the Supreme Court's unaccountability to the popular will. Devoting one of his legendary fireside chats to the plan, Roosevelt described American government as a "three horse team provided by the Constitution to the American people so that their field might be plowed. . . . Two of the horses [the Congress and the executive] are pulling in unison today; the third is not." Roosevelt stressed that this was not as it should be: "It is the American people themselves who are in the driver's seat. It is the American people themselves who want the furrow plowed. It is the American people themselves who expect the third horse to pull in unison with the other two."[8] Many at the time were of like mind.

These sorts of challenges to the Supreme Court's power should sound extremely familiar. Throughout the course of American history, many of the United States' most revered public figures have expressed similar sentiments. Like Roosevelt and his followers in the 1930s, Thomas Jefferson, Abraham Lincoln, and Theodore Roosevelt before them all struggled with the judi-ciary, and all said essentially the same.[9] Jefferson, who fought history's first great battle against the Court, complained that "our judges are effectually independent of the nation."[10] In its notorious 1857 decision, in *Dred Scott v. Sandford*, the Supreme Court denied Congress had the constitutional author-ity to resolve the question of slavery in the territories. Lincoln responded: "[I]f the policy of the government, upon vital questions affecting the whole people, is to be irrevocably fixed by the decisions of the Supreme Court . . . the people will have ceased, to be their own rulers."[11] In his 1912 third-party bid for the presidency, Theodore Roosevelt concurred: "The American people and not the courts are to determine their own fundamental policies."[12]

The current mantra against "activist judges" is simply the latest incarna-tion of this persistent complaint about judicial accountability. If anything is new today, it is only that, for the first time in American history, the Supreme Court's power of judicial review has come under siege simultaneously from both sides of the ideological spectrum.[13] Modern-era critics on both the political left and the right paint a picture in which Brutus's worst nightmare has come true in spades. The problem is no longer judicial review, they say; it is "judicial supremacy"—on issue after issue of grave public concern the justices insist on having the last word, if not the only one. Critics who agree on little else now unite in decrying the Court's all-powerful approach.

DEBATING CONSTITUTIONAL MEANING

There is a weighty response to this complaint about judicial hegemony. In the American system of democracy, the popular will nonetheless is subject to those boundaries specified in the Constitution. What is the point of having a written Constitution if government officials can transgress it at will?

When the justices strike down laws, they are quick to offer reassurance that they are not imposing their own will on the American people; rather, they simply act in the name of the Constitution. "There should be no misunderstanding as to the function of this court," urged Justice Owen Roberts, one of the men in the middle on a divided Supreme Court during the New Deal struggle. "This court neither approves nor condemns any legislative policy. Its delicate and difficult office is to ascertain and declare whether the legislation is in accordance with, or in contravention of, the provisions of the Constitution; and, having done that, its duty ends."[14]

Roberts's absolution—"the Constitution made us do this"—reverberates throughout history's most famous decisions, both those reviled and those admired. When the Supreme Court limited Congress's power over slavery in *Dred Scott*, it was (naturally) offered as a necessary interpretation of the Constitution. When the Supreme Court struck down school segregation in *Brown v. Board of Education*, the reason was that the Constitution's Equal Protection Clause demanded it. When the Court protected the right of Jehovah's Witnesses children who refused to salute the flag in public schools because their religion forbade it, the First Amendment to the Constitution was determinative. "The very purpose of a Bill of Rights was to withdraw certain subjects from the vicissitudes of political controversy, to place them beyond the reach of majorities," explained the Court majority.[15]

Anytime the Supreme Court is under attack, its defenders will quite naturally brandish the Constitution, insisting that those who govern must play by its rules. Opponents of the Court plan—and in the 1930s this included many of FDR's political supporters—argued that threatening the Court effectively threatened constitutional government itself. Frank Gannett owned a chain of newspapers in the Northeast; he favored Roosevelt early on but came to have a change of heart and ultimately led the attack against the Court plan through his National Committee to Uphold Constitutional Government. Gannett and many others saw Roosevelt's proposal as a giant end run around the Constitution. Gannett penned an open letter to the American people in which he said: "If it is necessary to change the Constitution it should be done in the regular way." [16] The respected historian James Truslow Adams, one of a flood of notables who took to the radio to debate Roosevelt's proposal, worried aloud that "if the Constitution is to be changed by packing the Court, then that same method might some day be used to alter those parts which guarantee us our religious and other liberties." [17]

The great problem, of course, is that when the issue is fraught, the American people typically disagree over what the Constitution means. So do the justices themselves. That is why judicial decisions interpreting the Constitution become so controversial.

Roosevelt did not challenge the Supreme Court merely by relying on the election returns (though he surely did allude to the strength of his popular majority). Instead, he argued that the justices' understanding of the Constitution was wrong. During his fireside chat on his plan to reorganize the judiciary, Roosevelt pointed to vehement dissent within the Court itself over the proper outcome of New Deal cases. "In the face of these dissenting opinions, there is no basis for the claim made by some members of the Court that something in the Constitution has compelled them regretfully to thwart the will of the people." His plan, Roosevelt explained, was simply a way "to take an appeal from the Supreme Court to the Constitution itself." He insisted that if read properly, the Constitution provided ample power to address the problems of the Depression. Roosevelt urged the American people to read the Constitution for themselves: "Like the Bible, it ought to be read again and again." [18]

As often as not, fights over judicial power really are fights over the meaning of the Constitution. This is not to say that judicial power isn't an issue in and of itself; it is always a fair question in a democracy whether a public official has too much power, or is insufficiently accountable to the people. But judicial power becomes an issue precisely because judges interpret the Constitution and because judicial decisions seem so very final. This has been the case from the start. Brutus did not challenge the authority of the Supreme Court in the abstract. Rather, he opposed adoption of the Constitution because he feared the power of a strong central government. Brutus believed the Court inevitably would side with the national government against the states, and so he fretted over the extent of judicial power. The very same was true of Jefferson, Lincoln, and Theodore Roosevelt: each attacked the Court precisely because he had a very different understanding of the Constitution from the one held by a majority of the justices.

Caught up in immediate controversy, Americans can overlook this point. They fail to see that what looks to be a roaring battle over judicial power is simply the latest round in a much broader struggle over the proper interpretation of the Constitution. In a constitutional democracy, majority will regularly is pitted against minority rights. This tension, which is at the heart of constitutional democracy, would exist even if there were no judges. It is the meaning of the Constitution itself that is up for grabs, and judicial power is nothing more than a pawn in that battle.

In a sense, the history of the relationship between judicial review and the popular will has been one of great continuity. The justices decide cases involving constitutional questions of substantial importance to the American people. Given the seeming finality of judicial decisions, those who disagree with the justices lash out at the Court and the power of judicial review. Those who agree with the justices jump to their defense, waving the Constitution. And a fight over the Constitution becomes one about the judges.

CONSTRUCTING JUDICIAL POWER

Although this is a story of continuity, it also is one of fundamental change. The nature and extent of the Supreme Court's authority have plainly grown over time, in ways that are both unmistakable and undeniable. The power the Court wields is the product of a lengthy evolution in American political thought. In the course of struggling over judicial review as a proxy for their greater constitutional disagreements, the American people came to tailor, and then ultimately to accept, the role of the Supreme Court.[19] We have the Court we do because the American people have willed it to be so.

History makes clear that the classic complaint about judicial review— that it interferes with the will of the people to govern themselves—is radically overstated. The American people have always had the ability to limit judicial review—or even to eliminate it entirely. The persistent question throughout history has been whether, and to what extent, they should exercise this power. In the course of answering that question, the American people have confronted, and given meaning to, the idea of democratic government under a constitution.

During the debate over ratification of the Constitution, Alexander Hamilton, writing as "Publius" in *The Federalist Papers*, rejected Brutus's prediction that the judiciary would prove all powerful. Hamilton's "Federalist No. 78" remains today one of history's great defenses of judicial independence. But the most memorable part of Hamilton's tract was his point that there was no need to worry about the judges because they had little capacity to threaten democratic principles.

Judges, Hamilton explained, lacked both the executive's control over the "sword" and Congress's control over the "purse." Possessing "neither FORCE nor WILL, but merely judgment," the judiciary "must ultimately depend upon the aid of the executive arm even for the efficacy of its judgments." For this reason, he assured his readers, the judiciary would be "the least dangerous" of the three branches of government.[20] It turned out that Hamilton was at least as prescient as Brutus about judicial power.

It is difficult to appreciate today the devastating nature of some of the early challenges to judicial authority. In the aftermath of the Civil War, Congress had the task of "reconstructing" the southern states as part of restoring the Union. Many at the time believed that given the chance, the Supreme Court would render a decision invalidating continued military rule of the South before Congress could consolidate the gains the Union had achieved on the battlefield. But quite unlike all the hand-wringing we hear today, judicial supremacy did not trouble members of Congress then. Listen to Representative John Bingham of Ohio, a Republican leader of the Congress:

> If . . . the court usurps power to decide political questions and def[ies] a free people's will it will only remain for a people thus insulted and defied to demonstrate that the servant is not above his lord by procuring a further constitutional amendment and ratifying the same, which will defy judicial usurpation by annihilating the usurpers in the abolition of the tribunal itself.[21]

As it turned out, Bingham's colleagues did not have to go nearly so far as "annihilating" the Supreme Court to ensure they controlled it. Rather, Congress simply withdrew the Court's jurisdiction at a critical moment, and the justices bowed to a greater power. So much for Brutus's worries.

The irony of the defeat of Roosevelt's Court-packing plan is that the very weapon denied him in his struggle against judicial authority was used freely by Abraham Lincoln's generation. Lincoln and his fellow Republicans swept into power as the Civil War began. The *Dred Scott* decision having made the potential dangers of judicial review perfectly clear, the newly Republican Congress was hardly going to stand pat and allow the justices to threaten its efforts to hold the Union together. Three times during the Civil War and its aftermath, Congress altered the number of justices who sat on the Supreme Court. In each instance, proponents of enlarging or reducing the number of justices offered a reason that had nothing to do with ensuring political control of the Court, just as Roosevelt wrapped his own plan in the flimsy gauze of an argument that the elderly justices were behind in their work and needed help. But those watching were perfectly aware that by altering the number of justices, Congress ensured that the Court majority rested in hands that could be trusted.[22]

Roosevelt failed where the Civil War Congress succeeded in part because Americans' understanding of the Supreme Court and its role had changed between 1868 and 1937. This was not history's first change of attitude toward judicial review. When the Supreme Court decided the *Dred Scott* case, holding that Congress could not regulate slavery in the territories, many of Lincoln's generation feared the decision would ultimately tear the country asunder. Yet very few of them said that *Dred Scott* should simply be ignored or defied. This may not be surprising to us today, when talk of defying the Supreme Court is taboo, a signal that one is unwilling to play by the basic rules of American governance. It was apparently unsurprising to many Americans in 1857 as well. Nonetheless, a generation or two earlier, defiance of the Supreme Court by state governments was the order of the day.[23]

Some prominent works of political science and history have taken into account the relationship between the popular will and judicial power, but they fail to capture how that relationship has evolved throughout the course of American history. This is unfortunate, because it is only through observing this evolution that we can begin to really understand the authority the Supreme Court wields today. In 1960, Harvard political scientist Robert McCloskey published a wonderful, engaging history entitled *The American Supreme Court*, in which he argued that the justices ignore public opinion at their peril. For this reason, he concluded, the Court "seldom strayed very far from the mainstreams of American life and seldom overestimated its own power resources."[24] Despite its remarkable insight, McCloskey's justly famous history failed to grapple with just how judicial power had been sculpted by those very instances in which the justices did in fact overestimate their own power. The justices today unequivocally exercise more authority than they did at the founding. But that authority exists as it does today only because through a process of trial and error, step and misstep, the country came to understand what it wanted out of the Supreme Court, as well as what it would tolerate.

THE CONTOURS OF THE HISTORY

There have been four critical periods in the American people's changing relationship with judicial review and the Supreme Court. The lines between the periods are hardly distinct. History resists easy categorization; major developments come in fits and starts. Still, attention to these periods allows us to see how American thought about the role of judicial power has evolved over time.[25]

The first period—from the time of independence until the early 1800s—saw the remarkably quick acceptance of judicial review, followed by grave threats to the independence of the judiciary as the implications of the practice became evident. It was in this period that judges began to strike state legislative measures and the Constitutional Convention in Philadelphia adopted judicial review as a means of keeping the states in line with national authority. Soon enough, though, the country saw the danger of unaccountable judges with the power to interpret the Constitution. In the late eighteenth century, the country split into two political parties, which had great enmity for each other. Following the "Revolution of 1800," in which Thomas Jefferson's Republicans captured the executive branch and the Congress, the Federalist Party tried to fight a rearguard action from the judiciary. The newly empowered Republicans were not prepared to accept such partisan conduct on the bench. Congress abolished some of the judgeships created by the Federalists and threatened the impeachment of Supreme Court justices, acts that were criticized by the Federalists as a grave disregard for the independence of the judiciary. This first period came to a close in the early 1800s only after a tacit deal had been reached by which judicial independence was guaranteed so long as the judges refrained from engaging in blatant partisan politics from the bench.[26]

The second period, which ran from roughly the War of 1812 until the Nullification Crisis of 1832–1833, was characterized by frequent, officially sanctioned defiance of judicial decrees. Most of the Supreme Court's constitutional decisions in this period were aimed at state governments. Yet in the states' rights environment in which the Court was operating, the states would regularly fail to show up when haled before the justices and would often defy orders the Court issued. Virginia's highest court refused to concede that the Supreme Court had the authority to review its decisions. Georgia actually hanged a man in the face of a Supreme Court order to the contrary.[27]

This period of defiance came to a gradual close only when the national leaders recognized they needed the Supreme Court to help keep the states in line. President Andrew Jackson had no particular fondness for the Su-

preme Court, whose rulings often conflicted with his policies. In 1832, however, when South Carolina claimed the power to nullify federal laws and
threatened to secede from the Union, Jackson did an abrupt about-face. He
in turn threatened to use force against South Carolina and placed the authority of his office squarely behind the Supreme Court as an arbiter of
constitutional disputes.[28]

The Supreme Court's reviled decision in *Dred Scott* ushered in the third
period of judicial authority, that of controlling the courts. Though the nation
had come gradually to reject official defiance of Court decisions, what was
to be done if the Court put the country into a seemingly impossible situation, as it seemed to many to have done in *Dred Scott*? If judicial decisions
were going to stick, in ways potentially in conflict with the popular will, then
the answer was to exercise control over the courts to make sure the judges
handed down only those decisions the people were prepared to accept. It
was in this period that John Bingham uttered his threat to annihilate the
Court, while his colleagues manipulated the size of the Court thrice and
stripped it of jurisdiction.[29]

The third period continued until 1937. During this time the Supreme
Court learned the importance of playing to a constituency, of having a patron that could protect it. Between the end of Reconstruction and the Great
Depression, the judiciary grew in power by offering its backing to corporate
and commercial interests that exercised enormous authority throughout the
country.[30] In the late 1800s, the federal judiciary eliminated state laws that
interfered with interstate commerce. In the early 1900s, the courts struck
down progressive legislation adopted to ease the plight of workers caught
up in America's industrial revolution. Throughout this long period there
were many attempts to control the judges; some were successful, but many
failed. Although the reasons why it proved so hard to control the judges in
struggle after struggle were complex, the impact of the failure was not. The
result was a great loss of faith in the objectivity of the judiciary and of law
itself.[31]

The Court fight of 1937 served as the threshold to the modern era. Central to the importance of these events was Roosevelt's success in assembling
a coalition of the common people of the country. With Roosevelt's chief
constituency signaling its disapproval of the Court-packing plan, the idea of
control gave way to the seeming supremacy for which the Court is noted today. In retrospect, the Supreme Court's breathtaking 1954 decision in *Brown
v. Board of Education* barring segregated public schools was but the opening
salvo in what has been sweeping judicial intervention in some of the country's most controverted issues. Since the 1950s, the Supreme Court has

granted women equality, legalized abortion, expanded the rights of criminal defendants, taken control over imposition of the death penalty, recognized gay rights, banned prayer in schools, limited Congress's power to regulate as it sees fit, and even decided one of history's closest presidential elections.

No wonder that today the Supreme Court is described as practically impregnable. Politicians decry the justices; scholars condemn them. Remedies for judicial power are sought. Yet year after year, the nine members of the Court take their seats on the nation's highest bench and continue to tell Americans what the Constitution means, seemingly aloof from the controversy that swirls about them.

THE MODERN ERA

Still, appearances can be deceiving. In a sense, today's critics of judicial supremacy are right: the Supreme Court does exercise more power than it once did. In another sense, though, they could not be more wrong. The Court has this power only because, over time, the American people have decided to cede it to the justices. The grant of power is conditional and could be withdrawn at any time. The tools of popular control have not dissipated; they simply have not been needed. The justices recognize the fragility of their position, occasionally they allude to it, and for the most part (though, of course, not entirely) their decisions hew rather closely to the mainstream of popular judgment about the meaning of the Constitution. It is hardly the case that every Supreme Court decision mirrors the popular will—and even less so that it should. Rather, over time, as Americans have the opportunity to think through constitutional issues, Supreme Court decisions tend to converge with the considered judgment of the American people.

In rejecting the Court plan, but only after the justices' turnabout, the American people defined the modern era. They would support the exercise of judicial review so that the Court could do precisely what its New Deal defenders said it would—specify and enforce constitutional liberties—but they would offer this support only so long as the Court's decisions did not stray far, and for long, from the heart of what the public understood the Constitution to mean. And this, to a remarkable extent, is what has happened. On issue after contentious issue—abortion, affirmative action, gay rights, and the death penalty, to name a few—the Supreme Court has rendered decisions that meet with popular approval and find support in the latest Gallup Poll.

In short, the modern era is one of a symbiotic relationship between popular opinion and judicial review.[32] The Court will get ahead of the American people on some issues, like the death penalty or perhaps school desegregation itself. On others, such as gay rights, it will lag behind. But over time, with what is admittedly great public discussion, but little in the way of serious overt attacks on judicial power, the Court and the public will come into basic alliance with each other.

In the course of acting thus, the Supreme Court has made itself one of the most popular institutions in American democracy. The justices regularly outpoll the Congress and often even the President in terms of public support or confidence. When the Supreme Court decided the contested presidential election of 2000 in *Bush v. Gore*, many saw this as a low point for the justices. Yet prior to the decision more than 60 percent of the country said it was the Court's job to resolve the matter, compared with only 17 percent for Congress! And within a year of the decision in *Bush v. Gore* the Court again was running at high levels of support among Republicans and Democrats alike.[33]

These facts profoundly call into question the image of the Supreme Court as an institution that runs contrary to the popular will. In the modern era, the supposed tension between popular opinion and judicial review seems to have evaporated. The Court certainly is under persistent attack. Those who lose fights over the meaning of the Constitution are never happy and rarely go down quietly. Still, the more salient Supreme Court decisions generally meet with great public approval.[34] And even when they do not, the public supports the Court's right to decide the cases nonetheless.

The ultimate question, of course, is whether this is a good thing. Though the developments of the last half century may seem to put to rest the tension between judicial review and the popular will that Roosevelt and many others have felt so acutely, they actually serve only to raise a set of questions that are crucial to a full understanding of American constitutional democracy. The popularity of the Court and its decisions notwithstanding, it remains the case that the Constitution was supposed to be a shoe that pinches. The Constitution was intended to serve as a limitation on the popular will, at least at certain times. If judicial decisions are running in popular traces, has the Constitution been abandoned? What does it mean to have a Constitution that is regularly interpreted to mean what the American people want it to mean? Is popularity what we really desire from the justices—and should we? Perhaps most important: What is the capacity of the Court to stand up for the Constitution at times when constitutional values are threatened precisely because they are unpopular with the American people? Is there any hope in the Supreme Court for the protection of constitutional liberty?

Although these are the right questions to ask, even tentative answers necessarily await the conclusion of the story. The framers and their successors would have scoffed if they had been told that the judges were to follow the popular will. For generations, the Supreme Court seemed at best a nettlesome thorn in the side of the American people, not their walking companion. Before we even begin to answer these questions, then, it is necessary to understand the events that brought us to the modern state of affairs—and the changes in American thought that went along with them. It is nearly impossible to evaluate the Court's present symbiotic relationship with the American people without a full picture of how that relationship evolved and how it operates today.

The short answer, though, rests in distinguishing the passing fancy of the American people from their considered judgment. Judicial review would indeed be a puzzling addition to the American system of government if all the Supreme Court did was mirror transient public opinion. The value of judicial review in the modern era is that it does something more than that. It serves as a catalyst for the American people to debate as a polity some of the most difficult and fundamental issues that confront them. It forces the American people to work to reach answers to these questions, to find solutions—often compromises—that obtain broad and lasting support. And it is only when the people have done so that the Court tends to come into line with public opinion.

This, then, is the function of judicial review in the modern era: to serve as a catalyst, to force public debate, and ultimately to ratify the American people's considered views about the meaning of their Constitution. Admittedly, this was hardly the framers' vision for the Supreme Court, nor is it one that most Americans, scholars of the Court included, believe the Court plays. Yet given that constitutional meaning cannot remain entirely stable over the entire course of American history, and given the incredible difficulty of the constitutional amendment process the framers bequeathed us, this role has proven to be one we could hardly live without.

THE AMERICAN PEOPLE AND THE CONSTITUTION

Typically, histories of the Supreme Court focus on the justices and their decisions. Here, however, the chief protagonists are the American people. This is a chronicle of their shifting attitudes toward the Supreme Court, judicial review, and constitutional government. If anything should be evident by the conclusion, it is that the Supreme Court exercises the power it has precisely because that is the will of the people.

Claiming to capture the evolving views of the American public is something any author ought to do with enormous trepidation. Public opinion is an enormous force in the United States, as many famous visitors to our shores, such as Alexis de Tocqueville and Lord James Bryce, have noted with wonder.[35] Yet anyone who spends time in this country knows equally well there is no single American voice. Public opinion is a collage of ever-shifting views.

For these reasons and more, giving expression to the popular will can indeed seem a daunting task. At the least, history privileges elite voices.[36] The words of members of Congress and Presidents are recorded for posterity. The publishers of journals and authors of books have the means to ensure what they think, and their thoughts remain available to the ages.[37] Not so, necessarily, of the many "John Does"—to use the words of the 1937 *Newsweek* story about the fight over Roosevelt's plan—whose views often seem to slip unheard or unheeded beneath the ocean of time. It is a fact worthy of note that the voices of prominent women and people of color are so few in this story, at least until its later years.

Indeed, something as seemingly clear as a tally of votes, or a poll, can misrepresent the views of the American people in important ways. African-Americans did not receive the franchise until after the Civil War, and during the following decades it was stripped of many of them once again through the calculated machinations of state officials. The Nineteenth Amendment, giving women the franchise, was not ratified until 1920. Nor are vote tallies necessarily representative of the views of those Americans who can vote. Voter turnout has risen and fallen throughout American history, in ways both provocative and puzzling. During the end of the nineteenth century, upward of 80 percent of the electorate would turn out to vote in some elections; by the 1920s, following all the Progressive Era "reforms," participation plummeted sharply.[38] Even during times of high turnout, corporate influence and machine politics have played distorting roles.[39]

Still, capturing and writing about American public opinion toward the judiciary are not as daunting as they might appear. Despite all these quite reasonable cautions, which many historians face, there is very good reason to have faith in the possibility of chronicling changes in public attitudes toward the idea and the institution that is judicial review.

For one thing, controversies in American politics often replicate the adversarial form of the courtroom. By the time matters reach the boiling point, the American people are frequently asked to come down for or against some very basic proposition. At least with the luxury of hindsight, it is possible to see what the issues were and which side prevailed.

For another, it is wrong to say the voices of the vast majority of Americans are not preserved to us. Many of the elites whose views are recorded here were chosen or retained their places precisely because of their ability to give voice to the sentiments of their constituents and audiences. That is what long-serving politicians and successful journalists do. Sometimes they mold public opinion; more often they mirror it. In either case, they can be its embodiment.[40]

Perhaps most important, in some of the most crucial moments in the struggle over judicial review there was an extraordinary engagement of the American people.[41] That is precisely what Merlo Pusey was capturing when he described "[s]treet-corner discussions, arguments at restaurant tables," and the like. The Jane and John Does of the era *did* stand up to be noticed; they wrote letters, held meetings, and organized civic responses in a way that, quite frankly, might seem remarkable today. We do have access to their views.[42] One of the noteworthy aspects of this story is the way in which the role of the judiciary often was defined most by those—the composite groups and individuals—who in fact opposed it.

This struggle over judicial power has been of the greatest consequence, for through it the American public has come to work out the deepest underlying tension in their form of government, the tension between a democratic government and a Constitution that limits what popular majorities and their elected officials may do. How is it possible to reconcile a belief that the people should at any moment be permitted to find their own way with a set of rules that limits what it is the people can do? Even as some of our greatest thinkers have struggled with the question at a theoretical level, the American people have managed to work it out as a matter of daily practice. This is the story of how they did so.

I

CONCEPTION

"It is their province to decide upon our laws"

I n 1789, just three months into the First Congress of the United States, a momentous debate took place in the House of Representatives. The question before the House was whether the President should have to obtain the Senate's approval before removing cabinet officials. The text of the Constitution provides no certain answer to the question, stating only that the President "shall appoint" such officials "with the Advice and Consent of the Senate."[1] The question was a fraught one: the Americans were still smarting from their treatment as subjects of the British crown and continued to harbor deep fears of a President with monarchical authority. Members of Congress noted the "importance and magnitude" of the issue, one on which, as Representative James Madison put it, "the genius and character of the whole Government" would depend.[2] After long and heated debate the question was resolved, by a vote of 34–20, in favor of sole presidential removal power.[3]

For present purposes, the truly stunning aspect of the debate over presidential removal of cabinet officials was the wide-ranging consensus in the House—among those both for and against the bill—that it would ultimately be for the judiciary to decide the constitutional question. Representatives who were trying to take sole presidential removal authority out of the pending bill may only have been seeking tactical advantage when they said they "would rather the Judiciary should decide the point, because it is more properly within their department."[4] Yet even those who favored granting removal power to the President agreed that the judges would have the last word on the subject. "Gentlemen say it properly belongs to the Judiciary to decide this question," said Representative Abraham Baldwin of Georgia. "Be it so. It is their province to decide upon our laws; and if they find this clause to be unconstitutional, they will not hesitate to declare it so."[5]

If the revolutionaries of 1776 had been told that a legislative body soon would be assigning primary, perhaps sole, responsibility for determining constitutional meaning to the judges, they would have been shocked. So too would their British counterparts. Whatever their other disagreements, few on either side of the Atlantic at that time would have advocated the power of judicial review this represented. Even five years prior to the removal debate such widespread agreement in favor of judicial review was unimaginable.[6]

How, then, did the judiciary experience this remarkable rise?

Judicial review emerged as a solution to two very different problems that presented themselves in the early years of the new United States. First, as the Americans made the transition from conducting a revolution to running their state governments, respected members of the community came to experience grave misgivings about the kinds of laws being passed by popular assemblies. "The acts of almost every legislature have uniformly tended to disgust its citizens, and to annihilate its credit," protested one Maryland pamphleteer.[7] In a small number of cases scattered throughout the states, judges gradually asserted the authority to declare laws inconsistent with constitutional guarantees null and void. Then the members of the Constitutional Convention of 1787, well aware of this development, seized on judicial review to solve a problem of their own: ensuring that the states did not stray from national authority. Rejecting a veto of state laws in the national legislature, the delegates decided instead to require state judges to ensure that state measures conformed to national law, including the Constitution itself. The early exercises of judicial power invariably occasioned dissent, but the strength of these twin rationales put judicial review on a course toward rapid acceptance.

LEGISLATIVE SOVEREIGNTY AND JUDICIAL POWER

"[T]he omnipotence of parliament"

In England, the very notion of a judge's striking down a legislative enactment would have been practically unthinkable, running afoul of "the omnipotence of parliament." On the eve of the American Revolution, William Blackstone published his *Commentaries on the Laws of England*. Though by all accounts only an average lawyer, Blackstone possessed the gift of synthesis. His *Commentaries* persuasively captured the essence of British law and legal thought at the time he wrote. In them, Blackstone described the vast power of Parliament, saying it "can . . . do every thing that is not naturally impossible."[8]

Sir Edward Coke's opinion in the 1610 *Bonham's Case* attained renown precisely because it seemed a rare judicial challenge to parliamentary omnipotence. Thomas Bonham had been fined and imprisoned by the Royal College of Physicians, acting pursuant to an act of Parliament, for practicing medicine without a license. Because the Royal College received any fine it imposed, Coke ruled for Bonham, holding that the Royal College's action violated the rule against parties being judges in their own case.[9] In language that appeared to foreshadow the possibility of judicial review, Coke wrote: "[W]hen an Act of Parliament is against common right and reason, or repugnant, or impossible to be performed, the common law will controul it, and adjudge such Act to be void."[10]

As Blackstone explained it, however, Lord Coke had done nothing other than engage in an ordinary and uncontroversial act of interpreting a legislative statute to make sense of it—because that was all he was allowed to do. English judges, Blackstone readily acknowledged, were free to interpret parliamentary acts so as to avoid "any absurd consequences, manifestly contradictory to common reason." But if Parliament spoke clearly, that was the end of the matter; no judge could intrude. Taking Coke's own example, Blackstone said that though it was a rule that no man should act as a judge in his own cause, if a parliamentary statute said otherwise, "there is no court that has the power to defeat the intent of the legislature."[11]

Parliament was not at liberty to ignore the English constitution; there simply was no higher power to hold it accountable. England's constitution, though unwritten, was very much a real thing. It rested on custom reaching back across the ages, as well as on various writings, such as the Magna Charta of 1215.[12] The unwritten nature of the English constitution made it particularly susceptible to shifting arguments regarding its meaning.[13] It was subject to being reinterpreted in light of changing practice or overwhelming expressions of the popular will.[14] Despite the malleability of the unwritten constitution, however, Parliament still could step outside constitutional bounds by enacting a law plainly contrary to long and clearly settled usage.[15] Nonetheless, Blackstone explained, what Parliament chose to do, "no authority upon earth can undo."[16]

In sharp contrast with their English counterparts' notions of parliamentary sovereignty, the American revolutionaries chose to place their faith in the people.[17] Virginia's Declaration of Rights of 1776 made very clear who was doing the ruling on their side of the Atlantic: "[A]ll power is vested in, and consequently derived from, the people."[18] Similarly, the first provision of North Carolina's Declaration of Rights of 1776 read, "[A]ll political power is vested in and derived from the people only," while that of Maryland indicated that "all government of right originates from the people."[19]

If anything, though, the idea of popular sovereignty initially served only to reinforce legislative authority in the states. The young Americans consolidated power in their legislatures, which were seen as the best embodiment of the people's will. Having had enough of the crown's heavy-handedness, the Americans cut their newly elected chief executives down to size. State governors, largely chosen by the legislative body, had no hand in making legislation and often were hobbled with executive councils. Pennsylvania's constitution—the most radical of the founding documents—actually did away with a chief executive altogether, in favor of a popularly elected governing council.[20]

Prior to the Revolution, colonial judges had been subject to both executive and legislative authority.[21] Appointed by crown officials and often viewed as part of the executive arm, judges were frequently beholden to the legislative assemblies for their salaries.[22] There was a long tradition of legislators exercising judicial authority themselves, particularly when it came to adjudicating claims against the government.[23] Both juries (which at the time decided not only the facts but legal questions as well) and the insistence that judges adhere strictly to case precedents helped control judicial discretion.[24]

Following independence, state legislatures came to exercise even greater authority over the judiciary. The legislators usually chose the judges themselves, sometimes in conjunction with an executive who was also dependent on the legislature. Judges were appointed for fixed terms, and their salaries and perquisites of office were subject to legislative manipulation. Some legislatures felt free to remove judges; others abolished entire courts at will. Legislative bodies regularly exercised judicial functions, including serving as the court of last resort or overturning judicial determinations. In some states, such as New Hampshire, the judiciary was not considered an independent branch of government at all.[25]

This was hardly an intellectual or political environment in which one would have expected judicial review to appear, and yet it did. As the 1789 congressional removal debate indicates, a fairly dramatic transformation in thinking about judicial review took place in the thirteen short years after 1776. The change was hardly deliberate. Like much else in this period, it was the result of improvisation, a response to events.

THE IMPETUS FOR JUDICIAL REVIEW

"[T]he vilest collection of trash ever formed by a legislative body"

Judicial review first emerged as a response to the excesses of democracy. During the 1770s and 1780s, the new American legislative bodies went on a binge of lawmaking. On the eve of the Constitutional Convention, James Madison penned a set of notes on the "Vices of the Political System of the United States." Madison, thirty-six at the time he wrote, had made politics his life, serving as a representative in both the Virginia legislature and the Continental Congress. In "Vices," Madison observed that "[a]mong the evils, then, of our situation, may well be ranked the multiplicity of laws, from which no State is exempt."[26] The problem was not just the number of laws. Connecticut's Noah Webster, an educator and the father of American dictionaries, writing in *The American Magazine* in 1788 under the pen name "Giles Hickory," decried those measures that seemed to threaten basic rights: "[S]o many *legal infractions* of sacred right—so many public invasions of private property—so many wanton abuses of legislative powers!"[27]

Drafters of the early state constitutions had foreseen, and tried to protect against, legislators overstepping their constitutional bounds. The chief safeguard of legislative fidelity was to be frequent elections. Most of the early constitutions also contained a bill of rights or similar declaration. These were included to provide a benchmark against which the people could measure the laws. If the legislative body transgressed these limits, or so the theory went, the people would respond by removing their faithless representatives.[28] In a later round of constitution writing, executive and judicial authority was strengthened as well. Judges were appointed to serve during "good behavior" rather than for limited terms, and some constitutions prohibited cutting judicial salaries. States experimented with councils of "censor" or "revision," whose task it was to alert the people to legislative violations or to provide an executive veto.[29] Pennsylvania's censors were charged "to enquire whether the constitution has been preserved inviolate in every part" or "whether the legislative and executive branches [had] . . . assumed to themselves, or exercised other or greater powers than they are intitled to by the constitution."[30] The Pennsylvania council was to censure unfaithful acts and to recommend calling a constitutional convention if necessary, while New York's Council of Revision actually possessed a veto on laws, which could be overridden only by a two-thirds legislative vote.[31]

As it happened, these measures to ensure that legislatures kept within constitutional limits were not very successful. The three state councils that actually operated—in Pennsylvania, New York, and Vermont—often did so dysfunctionally and were eventually eliminated.[32] As for the bills of rights, Madison himself derided them as "parchment barriers," too easily overcome by legislators.[33] In the Virginia convention debating ratification of the federal Constitution in 1788, one delegate drove the point home by noting how ineffective Virginia's bill of rights had been: "But sir, this bill of rights was no security. It is but a paper check. It has been violated in many other instances."[34]

Prominent members of the community began to express disgust as state legislatures regularly enacted laws that were seen as violating fundamental rights. Among the more frequent and troubling abuses were paper money and tender laws, debtor relief laws, and violations of the common law right to a trial by jury.[35] James Iredell was a highly regarded North Carolinian who had emigrated from Great Britain as a teenager. He became a leading revolutionary and held many important legal posts in North Carolina government; in 1790, George Washington appointed him one of the first justices to the Supreme Court.[36] Serving as North Carolina's attorney general in 1780, Iredell complained to his wife about the work of North Carolina lawmakers, calling it "the vilest collection of trash ever formed by a legislative body."[37] William Plumer, who was to hold every high political office in New Hampshire, including governor and United States senator, issued a similar warning in 1787: "Our liberties, our rights & property have become the sport of ignorant unprincipled State legislators!"[38]

The problem, as it fell particularly to James Madison to recognize, was not the legislators so much as their constituents, the people themselves. The original constitutional drafters had assumed the people would hold their representatives to account for violating constitutional principles. But as Madison explained in "Vices," the legislators too often were only doing what the people demanded.[39] This led Madison to question "the fundamental principle of republican Government, that the majority who rule in such Governments are the safest guardians both of public good and of private rights."[40] Iredell made much the same point, writing to his friend Richard Spaight, who was attending the Constitutional Convention: "The majority having the rule in their own hands, may take care of themselves; but in what condition are the minority, if the power of the other is without limit?"[41] Speaking at the convention, Governor Edmund Randolph of Virginia told delegates, "Our chief danger arises from the democratic parts of our constitutions. . . . None of the constitutions have provided sufficient checks against the democracy."[42]

It was in this environment that judicial review emerged as yet one more means of dealing with troubling state legislation.[43] In a small handful of cases in the 1780s, judges began to refuse to enforce laws found to violate fundamental liberties.[44] Given the controversy that inevitably attended exercise of the practice, judges were understandably tentative and circumspect, careful to cast no unnecessary aspersion upon the legislature. It was not until 1795, when the practice of judicial invalidation was gaining wider acceptance, that a judge explicitly lowered a scathing finger at the sort of legislation that occasioned its necessity. In that year Supreme Court Justice William Paterson was "riding circuit," i.e., traveling to the lower federal courts to hold trials and hear appeals. In the circuit court of Pennsylvania, he presided over *Vanhorne's Lessee v. Dorrance*, a case involving conflicting claims of title to land. At issue was a Pennsylvania statute that took property from one group of claimants, forcing the ousted parties to accept other lands in return. Comparing American government favorably in theory with that of England, "where the Parliament is omnipotent, and can mould the Constitution at pleasure," Paterson nonetheless was appalled that in England "a more sacred regard should have been paid to property." "Shame to American legislation!" he exclaimed to the listening jurors.[45]

THE PRECURSORS OF JUDICIAL REVIEW

"[B]ee not contrary and repugnant"

Although the exercise of judicial review itself was something of a novelty, the tools for holding legislation void were not; they could be found in two basic well-recognized and long-established principles of judging. First, there was the problem of conflict. A judge faced with two inconsistent rules, both of which seemed to govern a case, had to resolve the conflict. Second, there was the idea of hierarchical authority. When a judge resolved such a conflict of laws, inferior law necessarily yielded to that which was superior.[46]

Blackstone discussed both these concepts in his *Commentaries*. For example, one of "the rules to be observed with regard to the construction of statutes" was *"leges posteriors priores contrarias abrogant"*: where two statutes are in conflict, the later in time controls. Blackstone similarly emphasized the importance of hierarchy in resolving a conflict between common law—the decisions of judges—and a law of Parliament. Given parliamentary supremacy, "[w]here the common law and a statute differ, the common law gives place to the statute."[47]

These twin concepts played a central role in Great Britain's control over its colonies. The colonists elected their own legislative assemblies, but their laws were supposed to remain as consistent as possible with acts of Parliament as well as colonial charters and decisions of the Privy Council. Legislating for different peoples in different places might require some variation, but there were limits. Colonial charters granted colonial bodies the authority to make their own laws so long as they were not "repugnant to" English law.[48] There is, in fact, some evidence that the word "unconstitutional" was used to describe such repugnance.[49] Rhode Island's charter included the requirement that its "lawes, ordinances and constitutiones . . . bee not contrary and repugnant unto, butt, as neare as may bee, agreeable to the lawes of this our realme of England, considering the nature and constitutione of the place and people there."[50] The New York proprietor was permitted as well to make law "not contrary to but as near as conveniently may be agreeable to the Laws, Statutes & Government of this Our Realm of England."[51] In Rhode Island, civil litigation frequently made its way to the Privy Council for repugnancy review, and Pennsylvania's attempt to create a court system of its liking was overturned repeatedly on this basis.[52]

The concept of hierarchical authority retained its significance even after the colonies declared independence. In 1787 the Continental Congress, then called the Congress of the Confederation, relied on the concept in its effort to ensure that the states complied with treaty obligations.[53] John Jay, serving at the time as Secretary of Foreign Affairs, reported to Congress on the difficulties in relations with the British caused by states violating the terms of the Treaty of Peace. A unanimous Congress responded by passing a resolution declaring that all state laws that interfered with national treaties should be repealed.[54] Congress recommended that the states accomplish this by setting out the repealing principle in general terms, leaving it to the "proper Department, viz, the Judicial" to decide "whether any particular Act or clause is or is not contrary to the treaty."[55]

One of the most renowned of the early "judicial review" cases, *Rutgers v. Waddington*, was of just this nature, a claimed conflict between state legislation and treaty obligations. Elizabeth Rutgers, an elderly widow, owned a brewery that Joshua Waddington, a British loyalist, occupied while New York City was under British control. Rutgers sued Waddington for back rent owed under New York's Trespass Act, passed specifically to permit recovery for property used by loyalists during the British occupation.[56] The case attracted huge attention; Alexander Hamilton, who represented Waddington, referred in his brief to the "*public clamour* which makes a difficulty in the present case."[57] Hamilton's argument in *Rutgers* recognized the importance of maintaining consistency between national treaties and state laws. He maintained that Rutgers's demand for rent in this case—particularly when Waddington had held the property under proper British authority and paid rent to the British—violated the law of nations and obligations under the Treaty of Peace.[58]

City mayor James Duane rendered a decision in *Rutgers* that was practically taken off the pages of Blackstone.[59] Rather than invalidate the statute as repugnant to higher law, he simply interpreted the statute's "general words" as yielding an "unreasonable" result in this "collateral matter," one "not foreseen by the legislature."[60] In this way Duane could, strictly speaking, avoid any claimed authority to strike laws off the books entirely. But in deciding the case, Duane displayed keen awareness of the problem of reconciling state laws with the higher national authority. He said that to allow any state "to abrogate or alter any one of the known laws or usages of nations" would be "contrary to the very nature of the confederacy . . . as well as dangerous to the union itself."[61]

THE THEORY OF JUDICIAL REVIEW

"[C]annot admit any act of the Legislature as law,
which is against the constitution"

The next move—judges actually holding a legislative statute void because of its inconsistency with fundamental law—was a big step. Still, when American lawyers urged judges to do so, the lawyers' reasoning possessed a certain irrefutable air. This was because it drew directly from the logic of the Revolution itself.

From town assemblies and public meetings across the colonies in the run-up to the American Revolution, there came remarkable consensus that parliamentary acts exceeding Parliament's constitutional authority were null and void.[62] The most famous reliance on that idea may have been in the controversy over parliamentary legislation authorizing the use of writs of assistance. The writs were legal orders permitting officials to conduct searches for customs violations even if they had no specific reason to believe a violation had occurred.[63] In his 1761 argument in the *Writs of Assistance Case*, James Otis argued that "an Act [of Parliament] against the Constitution is void."[64] Parliament's imposition of the Stamp Tax roused similar claims. Seeking to raise funds, the English Parliament in 1765 imposed a tax on certain documents, represented by a tax stamp. The tax was bitterly opposed in the colonies. Responding to the royal governor's claim that as an act of Parliament, the Stamp Act had to be followed, the House of Representatives of Massachusetts demurred: "[T]here are certain original inherent rights belonging to the people, which the Parliament itself cannot divest them of, consistent with their own constitution."[65] In 1765, Massachusetts Chief Justice Thomas Hutchinson reported the colonists' resistance to the Stamp Act: "The prevailing reason at this time is that the Act of Parliament is against Magna Charta, and the natural Rights of Englishmen, and therefore, according to Lord Coke, null and void."[66]

After the Revolution, some American lawyers began to urge judges not to enforce legislative acts that violated constitutional guarantees. Given his previous comments about legislative "trash," it comes as little surprise that one of the most eloquent early arguments in favor of judicial review was that of James Iredell. Iredell was prompted to write on the subject by the case of *Bayard v. Singleton*.[67] Singleton held some property acquired from the state of North Carolina that Bayard claimed as his own. Bayard's father-in-law had refused to take an oath of loyalty to the United States and, fearing his property would be confiscated as a result, conveyed the property to his daughter (Bayard's wife) before going into exile. Singleton's lawyer moved to dismiss Bayard's suit, pointing to a North Carolina statute that required dismissal upon a showing that the property was acquired from a "commissioner of forfeited estates."[68] In other words, the statute effectively commanded the courts to dismiss any suit seeking the return of lands confiscated on account of their association with British loyalists. This brought on an argument from Bayard's lawyers that the statute was unconstitutional because, among other things, it denied the claimant a jury trial.

While the *Bayard* case was pending, Iredell published an anonymous letter, "To the Public" from "An Elector," setting out at length the case for judicial review, grounding it firmly in the idea of popular sovereignty. He then expanded upon those reasons in a letter to his friend Richard Spaight (later the governor of North Carolina), who had written from the Constitutional Convention to complain about the *Bayard* court's decision to invalidate the law.[69] Iredell argued that the exercise of judicial review was a necessary counter to the governing power of the state assembly. "We had not only been sickened and disgusted for years with the high and almost impious language from Great Britain, of the omnipotent power of the British Parliament, but had severely smarted under its effects," he wrote. Americans "were not ignorant of the theory *of the necessity of the legislature being absolute in all cases*" but had expressly rejected it. "Other governments have been established by chance, caprice, or mere brutal force. Ours, thank God, sprang from the deliberate voice of the people."[70] Popular sovereignty necessarily implied limits on the legislative branch.[71] "I have . . . no doubt," continued Iredell, "that the power of the Assembly is limited and defined by the constitution. It is a *creature* of the constitution."[72]

This very same concept—that popular sovereignty actually required judicial review as a check on the legislature—was central to the 1786 argument of James Varnum in *Trevett v. Weeden*, one of the earliest and most renowned cases of judicial review.[73] Rhode Island had passed a statute that compelled merchants to accept paper money as legal tender. Merchants were loath to accept the paper tender, which devalued quickly. In response, the legislature passed a "force" law: if merchants failed to take the paper money, a summary action could be brought to discharge the debt they were owed. John Trevett, a cabinetmaker, went to John Weeden, a butcher, to buy a joint of meat. When his money was refused, Trevett sued.[74] Weeden's lawyer, James Varnum, argued that the force act was unconstitutional because it denied the defendant a jury trial. The case attracted attention near and far.[75] Varnum, a distinguished Revolutionary War general, highlighted the importance and novelty of his claim that the judges should strike the law as unconstitutional: "[F]rom the first settlement of this country until the present moment, a question of such magnitude as that upon which the judgment of the Court is now prayed, hath not been judicially agitated."[76] Not one to hide his light under a bushel, Varnum published his argument in a pamphlet that was for sale in Philadelphia at the time of the Constitutional Convention.[77]

In his argument to the court, Varnum emphasized the legislature's necessary subordination to the people's will as reflected in their constitution. This claim of Varnum's was particularly remarkable given that Rhode Island had not adopted a new constitution upon independence. Instead, the state continued to rely on its colonial charter.[78] But according to Varnum, the customary constitution still governed, and under it the legislature was accountable to the people's superior will. "Have the citizens of this State ever entrusted their legislators with the power of altering their constitution?" Varnum asked the court. "If they have, when and where was the solemn meeting of all the people for that purpose?"[79]

The argument for judicial review was made all the easier when unlike the situation in England, the state had a written constitution. In the 1793 case of *Kamper v. Hawkins*, Virginia judges invalidated a state law passed to save money by combining judicial duties and powers in one office.[80] Each of the five judges in *Kamper* wrote a separate opinion explaining his vote to strike down the law. One of those judges, St. George Tucker, later became famous for publishing an Americanized version of Blackstone's *Commentaries*. Tucker's opinion in *Kamper* relied heavily upon the importance of a written constitution: "[W]ith us, the constitution is not an 'ideal thing, but a real existence: it can be produced in a visible form': its principles can be ascertained from the living letter."[81] As Varnum's argument in *Trevett* demonstrated, a written constitution was not essential. Still, it plainly helped to have one's rights in writing. Iredell explained in a letter to Spaight: "Without an express Constitution the powers of the Legislature would undoubtedly have been absolute (as the Parliament in Great Britain is held to be)."[82]

Recognizing that striking a legislative statute nonetheless would be controversial, the early supporters of judicial review explained the practice with reference to the familiar obligation of a judge to resolve a conflict between competing sources of authority. The commands of the constitution and the legislative statute differed with each other, and so one must yield. Varnum told the Rhode Island court that judges have no power "to repeal, to amend, to alter laws, or to make new laws . . . God forbid!" But when the legislators "proceed no farther than merely to enact what they may call laws, and refer those to the Judiciary Courts for determination, then . . . the Judges can . . . decide upon them." And when they do, the judges "cannot admit any act of the Legislative as law, which is against the constitution."[83] This was how the North Carolina judges in *Bayard* also saw it. "[T]he judicial power was bound to take notice of" the constitution "as much as of any other law whatever."[84] Writing in *Kamper*, St. George Tucker put the matter succinctly: "[T]he *judiciary* are *bound* to take notice of the constitution, *as the first law of the land*; and that whatsoever is contradictory thereto, it [sic] *not* the law of the land."[85]

As St. George Tucker's opinion in *Kamper* made clear, under the ordinary rule of hierarchical authority the constitution trumped the statute because it, as a representation of the popular will, was "fundamental" law.[86] One of St. George Tucker's colleagues on the bench in *Kamper*, Spencer Roane, emphasized that the legislature was "subordinate to the great constitutional charter, which the people have established as a fundamental law." Roane conceded initial misgivings on the existence of the power of judicial review but after consideration concluded that "the judiciary may and ought to adjudge a law unconstitutional and void, if it be plainly repugnant" to the constitution.[87] Iredell had made much the same argument in his letter to Spaight written six years earlier, stating that the constitution, "*being a fundamental law*, and a law *in writing* of the solemn nature I have mentioned . . . the judicial power, in the exercise of their authority, must take notice of it."[88] Although the plaintiff in *Bayard* ultimately failed to acquire the property he sought, on this point the North Carolina court agreed with Iredell. The judges concluded that the inconsistent statute must fall before the constitution, "standing in full force as the fundamental law of the land."[89]

Though distant from one another in space and time, these early arguments for the power of judicial review shared a remarkably similar logic. In the case of a conflict between a legislative statute and the people's constitution, the former necessarily must give way to the latter. Instances in which judges actually struck down laws were very few—admittedly no more than a handful of cases occurred prior to the Constitutional Convention of 1787—but it was a beginning.

THE PUBLIC'S RESPONSE TO JUDICIAL REVIEW

"[A] decision acquiesced in by the legislative body of the state"

These early instances of judicial review hardly passed unnoticed. To the contrary, the judges often experienced a backlash from angry citizens and legislators. Many of the invalidated laws were harsh measures aimed at British loyalists; others were economic relief measures during hard times.[90] Striking down such laws understandably aroused the citizenry. Judges, sensitive to the possibility of public discontent, were slow to rule against a law unless absolutely necessary. Once they had, they usually felt the brunt of public dissatisfaction.[91]

Quite remarkably, however, in each of the cases the judges ultimately prevailed. Although there was grumbling—loudly at some times, less so at others—legislators regularly conformed the law to judicial dispositions, either by repealing the offending statute or by modifying it. In only one instance is it even arguable that the judges paid a price for their actions. Judicial review, when it happened, tended to stick.

A case in point is the 1780 decision of the New Jersey Supreme Court in *Holmes v. Walton*. *Holmes* involved a law that confiscated property believed to have been taken across enemy lines, a measure intended to put a halt to trading with the enemy. The constitutional problem was that the statute allowed for only a six-person jury (rather than the traditional twelve). John Holmes had property seized by militia major Elisha Walton; the jury gave judgment to Walton, and Holmes appealed, claiming a jury of six people was unconstitutional. The New Jersey Supreme Court delayed resolution of the case for ten months, apparently hoping the legislature would solve the problem for it. The two houses of the New Jersey legislature struggled with each other, eventually agreeing to a compromise that allowed (but did not require) a twelve-person jury. Apparently deeming the legislative compromise insufficient, the New Jersey Supreme Court rendered judgment for Holmes.[92]

After the judges ruled against the New Jersey law, a petition was filed with the legislature from sixty angry residents of the county of Monmouth, "complaining that the Justices of the Supreme Court have set aside some of the Laws as unconstitutional, and made void the Proceedings of the Magistrates, though strictly agreeable to the said Laws, to the Encouragement of the disaffected, and great Loss of the loyal Citizens of the State, and praying Redress."[93] The issue was understandably a sensitive one for patriots eager to stop trading with the enemy. More petitions followed from Monmouth, as well as from Middlesex and Essex, including a demand that the New Jersey Supreme Court be denied the right to review seizure cases altogether.[94]

Despite these protests, a new legislature, chosen but a month after the *Holmes* decision, passed a law entitling either party in a seizure action to a twelve-person jury on request. The legislature instructed that the act be circulated in the newspaper.[95] Some years later the New Jersey Supreme Court's chief justice referred to *Holmes* as "not only a judicial decision [exercising the power of judicial review], but a decision recognized and acquiesced in by the legislative body of the state."[96]

Judge Duane's 1784 decision in *Rutgers v. Waddington* occasioned a similar howl. After the Mayor's Court ruled against the widow Rutgers, nine prominent men published a four-column response in *The New-York Packet* inveighing against the decision. "This proceeding, in the opinion of a great part of the citizens of this metropolis, and in our opinion," the writers contended, "is an assumption of power in that court, which is inconsistent with the nature and genius of our government, and threatening to the liberties of the people."[97] At a large public meeting several days after *Rutgers*, an address to the people was adopted, calling for the election of senators who would protect them from judicial tyranny.[98]

Ultimately, though, acquiescence again followed. Two months later, strong opposition to the *Rutgers* decision still remaining, the assembly issued a resolution condemning the decision as "subversive of all law and good order . . . because, if a court instituted for the benefit and government of a corporation may take upon them to dispense with, an act in direct violation of a plain and known law of the state, all other courts either superior or inferior may do the like."[99] Nonetheless, another motion, recommending appointment of a mayor and recorder "as will govern themselves by the known laws of the land," was defeated by a vote of 31–9.[100]

Only after *Trevett v. Weeden* did the judges appear to suffer any penalty, and even that is subject to some uncertainty. When the Rhode Island court dismissed the case against Varnum's client, the butcher Weeden, for refusing to accept paper money, the judges "were thanked by the Spectators in an almost universal Plaudit." So recounted *The Boston Gazette*, one of several distant newspapers to report on the case.[101] (Given what was about to happen, one suspects the audience was packed with merchants unhappy about the paper money laws.) An angry legislature responded with the demand that the judges appear and explain themselves. Following a two-month delay (during which time some of the judges claimed illness), the judges appeared and took the position that they could not be questioned about their legal reasoning—"for the reasons of their judgment upon any question judicially before them, they were accountable only to God, and their own consciences."[102] The assembly voted its dissatisfaction with the judges' answers and took up the question of "dismissing the Judges from their office." In the face of great disagreement, the assembly sought legal advice from the attorney general and others. The attorney general told assembly members that the judges could not be dismissed from their positions unless they had engaged in criminal conduct, and they had not. The assembly then relented and released the judges.[103]

When they next came up for reappointment, four of the five judges who decided *Trevett* were not retained. Only the chief justice, who apparently never publicly stated reasons for his decision in the case, kept his position.[104] At the Constitutional Convention, Madison told his colleagues that "[i]n R. Island the Judges who refused to execute an unconstitutional law were displaced."[105] Madison might have been right, but it was only speculation. Rhode Island regularly replaced its judges. Indeed, four of the justices who ruled in *Trevett* were new themselves.[106] Though many have joined Madison in asserting that the *Trevett* justices were not reappointed because of their decision, it is simply impossible to know.[107]

So this is where matters stood as the delegates to the Constitutional Convention moved toward Philadelphia in 1787: in a tiny number of cases in the 1780s, judges actually refused to enforce legislation deemed to violate constitutional guarantees. The judges plainly were reluctant; the public in response often aroused. Yet once faced with the decisions of the judges, legislatures, despite their ready accountability to the public, demurred.

JUDICIAL REVIEW AT THE CONSTITUTIONAL CONVENTION

"[T]his Constitution . . . shall be the supreme Law of the Land"

Throughout history—typically when the Supreme Court is causing controversy—questions have been raised about whether the framers of the

Constitution intended judges to have the power of judicial review over state and federal laws. The delegates had no cause to resolve definitively the question of whether judges would review the laws of Congress for consistency with the Constitution, though many delegates clearly believed they would. The unmistakable intention of the convention, however, was to have courts review state laws to ensure their conformity with national law, including the Constitution of the United States.[108]

Although the instances of judicial review were still few by the summer of 1787, the delegates who gathered in Philadelphia were plainly aware of the practice. *Holmes v. Walton* and *Trevett v. Weeden* were decided prior to the convention, while *Bayard v. Singleton* and some additional cases from New Hampshire were to be handed down during the proceedings. Both James Madison and Massachusetts's Elbridge Gerry referred to past cases at key moments of debate, and more than a few delegates had firsthand knowledge of those cases through their individual participation.[109] Several had been counsel—among them Alexander Hamilton (*Rutgers*), William Davie (*Bayard*), and Edmund Randolph (who served as Virginia's attorney general and briefed the question of judicial review in another Virginia case, *Commonwealth v. Caton*)—while others (David Brearley in *Holmes* and George Wythe and John Blair in *Caton*) were judges. John Francis Mercer wrote a brief on the "great Constitutional question" in *Caton*, while Gouverneur Morris of Pennsylvania was but one of the delegates who had publicly indicated familiarity with the idea prior to the convention.[110]

Judicial review emerged at the convention as the solution to the problem of how to ensure that the willful, and often recalcitrant, states complied with the law of the Union. The second and third items on Madison's list of "Vices" were "Encroachments by the States on the federal authority" and "Violations of the law of nations and of treaties."[111] Governor Edmund Randolph of Virginia kicked off the formal business of the convention by enumerating the failures of the Confederation. "*It cannot defend itself against incroachments,*" he told the delegates. "To What expedient can congress resort, to compel delinquent States to do what is right[?]"[112]

The delegates rejected Madison's preferred solution: "that the National Legislature . . . be impowered . . . to negative all laws passed by the several States, contravening in the opinion of the National Legislature the articles of Union."[113] Madison's enthusiasm for a veto by the national legislature over state laws reflected not only his concern for the problem of a uniform national law but his increasing dissatisfaction—evident in his "Vices" paper—with state lawmaking in general. Other delegates, most likely focused only on the problem of preserving the Union, believed the negative would be too

strong a medicine.[114] As Gouverneur Morris observed on the day the negative was finally rejected in the convention, "[t]he proposal of it would disgust all the States."[115] Responding from Paris to Madison's complaints that
the negative had been rejected in Philadelphia, Thomas Jefferson would say
that he too disapproved of it, because "the hole & the patch should be
commensurate."[116]

Most delegates who spoke to Madison's proposed negative believed that
it was unnecessary, given that another tool was readily at hand, judicial review of state laws to ensure consistency with the Constitution and national
law. Roger Sherman of Connecticut argued that "the Courts of the States
would not consider as valid any law contravening the Authority of the
Union."[117] This did not satisfy Madison, who responded, "Confidence can
[not] be put in the State Tribunals. . . . In all the States these are more or
less dependt. on the Legislatures." It was here that Madison alluded to the
dismissal of the judges following *Trevett v. Weeden*.[118] Nonetheless, the delegates were unyielding, and Madison's negative failed. Later, in a philosophical letter to Jefferson, Madison continued to press his point: "[I]t is more
convenient to prevent the passage of a law, than to declare it void after it is
passed."[119]

The text the delegates settled upon to establish judicial review of state
laws can be found in Article VI of the Constitution. The Supremacy Clause,
which figures heavily in later controversies over judicial review, has two
parts. First, it declares that "[t]his Constitution, and the Laws of the United
States which shall be made in Pursuance thereof; and all Treaties made, or
which shall be made, under the Authority of the United States, shall be the
supreme Law of the Land." Then it goes on to bind state judges to apply this
"supreme Law" in cases that they hear, "any Thing in the Constitution or
Laws of any State to the Contrary notwithstanding."[120]

Though it was the state courts that were charged as an initial matter
with determining whether state law was consistent with federal law, the national Supreme Court was understood to possess the ultimate say on the
matter. Madison's skepticism about trusting state courts to be faithful to
federal law had some weight to it and resonated in a related debate: whether
the national government ought to have its own set of courts. Failing the
negative, Madison and others preferred a strong federal judiciary to patrol
the states. Other delegates, more protective of state prerogatives, demurred,
believing that the "State Tribunals might and ought to be left in all cases to
decide in the first instance." The most opponents of a federal judiciary would
concede was "the right of appeal to the supreme national tribunal," this "being sufficient to secure the national rights & uniformity of Judgmts."[121] The

disagreement was resolved in what is sometimes referred to as the Madisonian Compromise. State courts were bound by the Supremacy Clause to apply the federal Constitution as superior law. The Constitution then created a Supreme Court with jurisdiction to review state court judgments but left it to Congress, in the future, to "ordain and establish" such inferior courts as it found necessary.[122]

In contrast with the focus on judicial review of state laws, the convention said nothing definitive about judicial review of congressional laws.[123] The record simply contains a collection of suggestive statements, largely made during the debate over Randolph's proposed plan for a national Council of Revision. The proposal envisioned a national body "with authority to examine every act of the National Legislature before it shall operate."[124] The council was to have consisted of the President and some number of federal judges. The idea of such a council was to rear its head almost to the end. Madison and his allies, notably James Wilson of Pennsylvania, were dogged in their support, believing that the "Judiciary ought to have an opportunity of remonstrating agst projected encroachments on the people as well as on themselves."[125]

It is patently clear from the criticisms leveled against the Council of Revision that many delegates assumed there would be judicial review of congressional laws. What troubled opponents was the idea of giving the judges two cracks at invalidating legislative enactments: once before they went into effect and once after. Thus Massachusetts's Elbridge Gerry said that judges "will have a sufficient check agst. encroachments on their own department by their exposition of the laws, which involved a power of deciding on their Constitutionality."[126] Others echoed the same sentiment; Massachusetts's Rufus King was of the view that "the Judicial ought not to join in the negative of a Law, because the Judges will have the expounding of those Laws when they come before them; and they will no doubt stop the operation of such as shall appear repugnant to the constitution."[127] Wilson, when he reintroduced the idea in late July, did so precisely because he believed that the power of judicial review "did not go far enough. Laws may be unjust, may be unwise, may be dangerous, may be destructive; and yet not be so unconstitutional as to justify the Judges in refusing to give them effect."[128]

Ironically, the only unequivocal statement against judicial review at the convention was made in support of the Council of Revision. John Mercer, who attended the convention briefly as a delegate from Maryland, and whose brother had been a judge in a Virginia case involving the question of judicial review, "disapproved of the Doctrine that the Judges as expositors of the

Constitution should have authority to declare a law void. He thought laws ought to be well and cautiously made, and then to be uncontroulable."[129] After Mercer spoke, Delaware's John Dickinson stated that he was "strongly impressed" with Mercer's remarks and also thought "no power ought to exist." But Dickinson was "at the same time at a loss what expedient to substitute."[130]

RATIFICATION OF THE CONSTITUTION

"Are you sure that your federal judiciary will act thus?"

Ratification of the Constitution provided the body of the American people with the opportunity to weigh in on the nature of their new government. In part because the proceedings of the convention were intended to be secret, and in part for reasons of democratic legitimacy, it is common today in seeking the "original meaning" of the Constitution to look beyond the discussion at the Constitutional Convention to the wide-ranging debate—in formal assemblies and by the people "out-of-doors"—over the Constitution's ratification.[131] Judicial review had somewhat greater prominence in the ratification debates than it did in the discussions at the Philadelphia convention. Some who disapproved of the power at the convention, like Connecticut's Oliver Ellsworth and Delaware's John Dickinson, switched to support it during the ratification debates.[132] Still, for all the divining on the subject afterward, the fact is that the commentary on judicial review during ratification was a small drop in a very large bucket. The debates over the Constitution largely were about more pressing topics, such as federalism and executive power.[133]

From the moment the Continental Congress—technically, at this point, the Congress of the Confederation—transmitted the proposed Constitution to the states, Federalists (the Constitution's supporters) and Anti-Federalists (its opponents) fought to sway popular opinion to their side. Anti-Federalists often attached ominous meanings to the provisions of the Constitution, while Federalists sought to reassure the people by dismisssing the Anti-Federalists' arguments as implausible and by pointing out the Constitution's virtues. Tellingly, however, the arguments of both sides assumed that judges would exercise the power of judicial review under the Constitution.[134]

Federalists offered up judicial review as one basis of reassurance to those worried about the power of the new national Congress. Judicial review would ensure that the national government would remain within bounds imposed by the Constitution. "If the general legislature should at any time overleap their limits," declaimed Oliver Ellsworth in the Connecticut ratifying convention, "the judicial department . . . will declare it to be void."[135] Pennsylvania delegate James Wilson, Virginia delegate John Marshall, and North Carolina delegate John Steele made similar statements.[136]

Anti-Federalists, who were indeed worried about the overweening authority of the national government, acknowledged the existence of the power of judicial review but fretted that it would prove too weak to provide a sufficient check on Congress. Patrick Henry, a delegate to the Virginia ratification convention, wondered if the federal judiciary would be sufficiently steadfast to do the job. Referring to prior decisions by the Virginia courts in regard to Virginia's constitution, he asked: "Are you sure that your federal judiciary will act thus?" "Is that judiciary as well constructed, and as independent of the other branches, as our state judiciary?"[137] John Smilie, a delegate to the Pennsylvania ratification convention, pointed out that Congress might impeach judges who declared laws unconstitutional, while Robert Whitehill, another Pennsylvania delegate, argued that the judiciary could simply be ignored when it attempted to void a law.[138]

Even as Anti-Federalists doubted that judicial authority would prove effective, they simultaneously feared the adverse effects of giving the power of judicial review to federal judges.[139] In making their arguments, Anti-Federalists sometimes exaggerated the power that the federal courts would have under the new Constitution. The Anti-Federalist pamphleteer "Federal Farmer" joined prominent Massachusetts politician Samuel Osgood in arguing that in cases in which the federal government was unconstitutionally infringing on the rights of the states, the federal judiciary naturally would rule in favor of the federal government and uphold the unconstitutional law.[140] Brutus, in his now-famous exchange with Hamilton, also claimed that federal courts would expand Congress's powers "by the liberal construction which the judges may give the constitution" and that accordingly "the states will lose their rights, until they become so trifling and unimportant, as not to be worth having."[141] Brutus expressed concern that the power of judicial review was too unbridled, investing courts with the last say on the meaning of the Constitution.[142]

Nowhere in here, notably, is there any doubt that judges would exercise the power of judicial review. Within the context of the broader contest over ratification, apparently no one was prepared to deny the practice. Federalists relied on it as a basis for restraining congressional power. And the Anti-Federalists, ironically, were led to argue both that the power might not be great enough and that it was dangerous nonetheless.

THE ARGUMENT AGAINST JUDICIAL REVIEW

"The legislature must be considered as the supreme branch of the government"

Judicial review had its opponents, of course, but in the early years of the Republic critics simply failed to persuade their fellow citizens. The issue was debated on various occasions, but on balance judicial review was seen to do more good than harm. It was not until trouble finally came, in the early 1800s, that these criticisms took on much greater weight.

The most famous exchange on the subject of judicial review and judicial independence today remains the one that took place between Brutus and Hamilton during ratification of the Constitution. The opponents of the *Rutgers* decision published their views, and so we know what they thought as well.[143] In their correspondence after *Bayard* was decided, Iredell's friend Spaight made the case against judicial review.[144] There also are some more obscure sources. Connecticut's *Middlesex Gazette* carried an extended newspaper debate in 1792 between the pseudonymous Hambden (who was for judicial authority) and Philopatriae (who was against).[145] In 1797, the students at Tapping Reeve's renowned law school in Litchfield, Connecticut, held a moot court on the issue of judicial review.[146] Zephaniah Swift apparently was the single treatise writer of the time who inveighed against the practice.[147] From these sources, a consistent argument against judicial review emerged.

The case against judicial review began, ironically enough, by conceding the problem of unconstitutional legislation that judicial review was meant to solve. Spaight stressed the "tyrannical and unjust proceedings of most of the State governments," including many that he thought were "of a more alarming and destructive nature" than the one set aside in *Bayard*.[148] "It may sometimes happen," Philopatriae acknowledged, "that the Legislature will enact a rule or ordinance, contrary to the good and happiness of their constituents."[149]

Even so, judicial review was unacceptable to these authors. The problem, as they saw it, was the independence of the judiciary. "If they possessed the power [of judicial review]," Spaight asked of Iredell, "what check or control would there be to their proceedings?"[150] It was precisely in this context that Brutus worried that "the supreme court under this constitution would be exalted above all other power in the government, and subject to no controul. . . . There is no authority that can remove them."[151]

Several observers pointed to the difficulty with inferring the power of judicial review when it was not stated expressly in a constitution. "The people have spoken by the constitution, in which it is not claimed there is any such authority given," the Litchfield student advocates argued. At least one of their moot court judges ruled squarely with them on this point: "[W]e can hardly suppose that if it had been designed to invest them with a power so great and important, it would not have been mentioned in the Constitution." [152]

The real problem, though, was of accountability to the popular will. Putting judicial review in the hands of independent judges threatened popular governance. This was the central claim against the practice. Legislators were accountable to the people; judges were not. "The legislature must be considered as the supreme branch of the government," declared Swift. "[W]here the judiciary are independent of the people . . . it is a total prostration of the government, to vest them with a power of deciding that legislative acts are null." [153] In the *New-York Packet* response to *Rutgers*, the authors protested: "That there should be a power vested in courts of judicature, whereby they might controul the supreme Legislative power we think is absurd in itself. . . . The design of courts of justice in our government, from the very nature of their institution, is to declare laws not to alter them." [154] Spaight too railed that "it would have been absurd, and contrary to the practice of all the world," to bestow the power of judicial review. "[T]he State, instead of being governed by the representatives in general Assembly, would be subject to the will of three individuals . . . which would be more despotic than the Roman Decemvirate, and equally as insufferable." [155]

Given that there remained the possibility of unconstitutional laws, what was to be done? Both the responsibility and the remedy for such laws, critics of judicial review argued, rested with the people. "Blame not [the legislators] for exercising their powers," Philopatriae argued, "but censure the people for suffering such powers to exist." [156] He explained, "The people are the proper centinels to guard against the encroachments of the Legislature . . . by procuring a repeal of the obnoxious law." [157] Alternatively, "the obvious remedy will be to change our legislators," a remedy that commended itself as well to Spaight, who wrote in a letter to Iredell: "[T]he only one that I know of, is the annual election." [158]

The problem was that arguments for and against judicial review ultimately worked their way into a deadlock. In his writings on the subject, Iredell examined the proposed alternatives to judicial review, explaining why none of them would suffice. He scorned the common practice of remonstrance or "humble petition" to the legislature as suggesting that "electors hold their rights by the *favor of their representatives*," the sort of thing that led the practice of petitioning to die out in favor of instructing legislators. Equally unappealing was relying on the "whole people [to] resist," a "dreadful expedient indeed." So terrible was revolution that Iredell believed many would suffer their rights be violated rather than resort to it.[159] Elections also were unsatisfactory, because they "only secure the views of a majority; whereas every citizen . . . should have a surer pledge for his constitutional rights than the wisdom and activity of any occasional majority of his fellow-citizens, who, if their own rights are in fact unmolested, may care very little for his."[160]

In truth, this was an irreconcilable tension. Judges endowed with the power of judicial review might prove unaccountable and go astray. But many saw no satisfactory alternative to the problem of unconstitutional legislation without judicial review. Spaight, even as he protested judicial authority, allowed that "our Constitution, unfortunately, has not provided a sufficient check, to prevent the intemperate and unjust proceedings of our Legislature, though such a check would be very beneficial, and, I think, absolutely necessary to our well-being."[161]

THE SWIFT RISE OF JUDICIAL REVIEW

"[A] remedy even for the failures of the supreme Legislature itself"

Following ratification, the practice and acceptance of judicial review by both the state and federal courts accelerated. There were no fewer than twenty state cases in the next fifteen years in which at least one judge wrote a decision relying on the power to strike down legislation as unconstitutional.[162] Many federal courts did the same, with little reaction.[163] One of the earliest cases in which a federal judge exercised judicial review over a state's enactment involved a Rhode Island law.[164] Though the substance of the decision received wide coverage in newspapers of the day, the fact that the judges had struck down a law was met with nary a whimper, in sharp contrast with the popular reaction in that state to *Trevett*.[165]

Learned legal scholars of the time recognized and often lauded the existence and importance of judicial review. During this period, the country saw the publication of some of its first treatises on the law and was treated to extended lectures on the legal system. These works were produced by individuals who already were prominent or were destined to become some of the leading lights of the American bar: James Wilson, St. George Tucker, James Kent. They praised the independence of American judges as one of the unique and most valuable aspects of American constitutionalism.[166] Though he denied the wisdom of the practice of judicial review, even Zephaniah Swift, a vocal naysayer, recognized that the idea was "very popular and very prevalent."[167]

Judicial review received repeated endorsement in Congress.[168] Time and again, as in the debate of 1789 regarding the President's sole power to remove cabinet officials, representatives acknowledged that courts would measure laws against the Constitution, striking those that fell short. Madison spoke in the House of Representatives in favor of adding a bill of rights to the Constitution: "If [the proposed amendments] are incorporated into the Constitution, independent tribunals of justice will consider themselves in a peculiar manner the guardians of those rights; they will be an impenetrable bulwark against every assumption of power in the Legislative or Executive." [169] In the debate over establishing the Bank of the United States, one representative brushed aside claims that the Supreme Court might find Congress's work unconstitutional, saying: "[I]t was the glory of the Constitution that there was a remedy even for the failures of the supreme Legislature itself." [170]

Clear confirmation that the First Congress anticipated judicial review can be found in one of its most important enactments, the Judiciary Act of 1789.[171] That act established the federal court system, including the creation of some "inferior" courts, pursuant to the compromise at the convention. Section 25 of the Judiciary Act, which, like the Supremacy Clause, was to become the topic of heated debate in the years to come, authorized the Supreme Court to review certain state court decisions, including those involving contests between federal and state authority.[172] When citizens of a state bridled under a federal law, they were free to argue that it violated the Constitution. Although the expectation may have been that the Supreme Court would generally uphold challenged federal laws, nothing compelled it to do so. In this way Congress effectively bestowed upon the Supreme Court the power to review state and congressional statutes alike.[173]

Still, there was some distance between accepting judicial review in theory and being comfortable with the practice when a favored law was struck down. This was apparent when federal judges called into question a congressional act for the first time. Congress had passed a statute requiring those judges to adjudicate claims for war pensions, obviously an important and sensitive matter. The justices of the Supreme Court, sitting in the lower judicial circuits, declined to do so on the ground that their decisions were improperly subject to revision by the Secretary of War and ultimately by Congress. The judges did not help the case for judicial review by choosing to assert their prerogative over congressional statutes for the first time with regard to a law aiding crippled veterans. (Recognizing their awkward position, some of the judges contrived ways to resolve the claims informally until Congress could solve the problem.[174]) "The decision of the Judges, on the validity of our pension law," Representative Fisher Ames from Massachusetts wrote a friend, "is generally censured as indiscreet and erroneous." [175] Some believed the judges had chosen a "singular occasion" on which to exercise such "extraordinary controul," given that it was "merely a personal duty which they avoid by the exercise of the right." [176] Philadelphia's *National Gazette* reported: "[N]ever was the word *'impeachment'* so hackneyed, as it has been since the spirited sentence passed by our judges on an unconstitutional law. The highfliers, in and out of Congress, and the very humblest of their humble retainers, talk of nothing but *impeachment! impeachment! impeachment!*" [177]

Nonetheless, as was becoming commonplace, the verdict of the judges stood. Congress responded with a measure that left "the question of the propriety or right of the court on neutral ground." [178] During congressional discussions of the pensions matter in 1792, one member suggested "the necessity of passing a law to point out some regular mode in which the Judges of the Courts of the United States shall give official notice of their refusal to act under any law of Congress, on grounds of unconstitutionality." [179] Nothing ever came of the idea.

From humble, one might even say virtually nonexistent, beginnings, judicial review appeared off to a strong start. True, the number of cases in which it was exercised remained small. And the judges had not done anything of grave consequence. Yet the practice seemed destined for longevity. While stating that "there is no adjudication of the Supreme Court itself upon the point," Justice Samuel Chase summed up the state of affairs in 1800 in a case called *Cooper v. Telfair*: "It is, indeed, a general opinion, it is expressly admitted by all this bar, and some of the Judges have, individually, in the Circuits, decided, that the Supreme Court can declare an act of congress to be unconstitutional." [180]

2

INDEPENDENCE

"Judges, created for political purposes, . . . from this day cease to exist"

The judiciary's rapid rise soon ran afoul of a superior force that was to dog it all its days: politics.[1] In the election of 1800, Thomas Jefferson's Republican Party captured control of Congress and the executive branch from the reigning Federalist Party, setting the stage for the nation's first transition of political power. Having lost their cause before the voters, the lame-duck Federalists withdrew to the judiciary as a haven. When it appeared as though the Federalists were prepared to use their judicial offices to harass their rivals, the Republicans launched American history's first great assault on the judiciary. They were determined to demonstrate that officials elected by popular vote held the upper hand over unaccountable judges.

Throughout the partisan battles of the early 1800s, the question of judicial review proved secondary to a much more fundamental challenge: whether the judiciary would manage to survive as an independent branch of government. In 1803, the Supreme Court's Chief Justice, John Marshall, authored his legendary opinion in *Marbury v. Madison*. *Marbury* is revered today both at home and abroad for establishing the Supreme Court's power of judicial review. In its day, however, *Marbury* was seen as a purely political ploy, one of little practical significance. Congress, by contrast, held rapt the attention of the entire country with two dramatic moves to deprive federal judges of their offices. In 1802, when Congress repealed a lame-duck Federalist measure that had created new circuit court positions, throwing out the recently appointed judges, the Federalist representative Benjamin Tallmadge of Connecticut marveled at the flagrant attack on the judiciary: "[W]e have now progressed thirteen years, under the auspices of a constitution, . . . and until very lately I have never heard the independence of your Judiciary called in question."[2] Three years later, as Congress began proceedings to impeach the Federalist Supreme Court justice Samuel Chase, the Federalist *New York Evening Post* condemned the move: "He must be wilfully blind indeed who does not see in the present attack on the S. Court the same spirit which led to the former attack on the circuit judges."[3]

The dramatic turnaround in the judiciary's fortunes can be marked in former supporters of judicial review and judicial independence who came to question the federal judiciary's role. This held particularly true for the Virginians, the most prominent of whom was Jefferson.[4] When Madison wrote Jefferson at the beginning of the Constitutional Convention urging that Congress have a negative over state laws, Jefferson replied suggesting the alternative of judicial review: "Would not an appeal from the state judicatures to a federal court in all cases where the act of Confederation controlled the question, be as effectual a remedy, and exactly commensurate to the defect?"[5] Similarly, in the debate over adding a bill of rights to the Constitution, Jefferson reminded Madison: "[Y]ou omit one [argument in favor of a declaration of rights] which has great weight with me, the legal check which it puts into the hands of the judiciary."[6] Yet following his taking office as President in 1801, Jefferson served as the whispering voice urging congressional attacks on the judiciary. For the rest of his life Jefferson condemned the federal judiciary as a "corps of sappers and miners" undermining democracy.[7]

In the charged political environment of the 1800s, partisans came to link arguments about judicial review with questions of judicial independence. Federalists argued that judicial independence was essential precisely because of the power of judicial review. "[T]he dependence of the judges upon the Legislature, and their right to declare the acts of the Legislature void, are repugnant and cannot exist together," maintained Delaware's Federalist representative James Bayard. But to Republicans, the combination of judicial review and judicial independence was unfathomable. "Give them the powers and the independence now contended for," declaimed Maryland's Joseph Nicholson in the House during the repeal debate, and "your Government becomes a despotism, and they become your rulers."[8]

The conflict between the Republican Congress and the Federalist judiciary abated only when a tacit deal emerged that set the judiciary on the course to the authority it maintains today. Called repeatedly on the carpet for nakedly partisan use of judicial offices, Federalists ultimately conceded that the judicial bench was no place for political activism. In exchange, Republicans acknowledged that an impartial judiciary must be granted some modicum of independence.

PARTISAN TENSIONS OF THE LATE 1790S

"[T]he baneful effects of the spirit of party"

When the Constitution was framed and the new government set in motion, political parties were not supposed to be part of the picture. Fear of faction played heavily in Madison's writing.[9] Jefferson said, in 1789, that if he "could not go to heaven but with a party," he would rather not go at all.[10] As late as 1796, Washington could still use his Farewell Address to warn his fellow citizens with a straight face about "the baneful effects of the spirit of party."[11]

Parties emerged as Federalists and Republicans (as they came to be known) differed over issues of domestic politics and foreign affairs. It is difficult to overstate the degree of party passion and mutual distrust, if not outright paranoia, that engulfed opposing camps during the 1790s and early 1800s.[12] Alexander Hamilton's management of the Treasury and plans for the national economy were the early catalyst. Hamilton, the first Secretary of the Treasury, was a brilliant man with a sweeping nationalistic vision. His plans for the assumption of the states' Revolutionary War debt, for resolving the problem of speculation in war bonds, and especially for the creation of the Bank of the United States, were deeply controversial. Although Hamilton's proposals were largely adopted by the Congress, substantial minorities opposed them, fearing consolidation of the national government at the expense of the states and the privileging of an urban and manufacturing economy over an agrarian and rural one.[13] As with much else in the period, the divisions were partly sectional (the North and East opposed to the South) and partly matters of class.[14]

In this partisan environment, debates over fundamental politically charged issues were readily tied to the Constitution. Such was the case with Hamilton's 1790 proposal for a national bank. While opponents doubted the "expediency" of the measure, they also argued that Congress lacked the power under the Constitution to charter a national bank.[15] Considering whether to sign the measure, President George Washington requested and received from Hamilton and from his Secretary of State, Thomas Jefferson, competing reports on its constitutionality. Washington ultimately sided with Hamilton, who argued that the bank was constitutional. The seeds of discord were sown.[16] Devout Federalist Fisher Ames observed: "The federalists have triumphed;

they have laid their own passions asleep; they have roused those of their adversaries."[17]

Perhaps no issue divided Americans throughout the 1790s more than whom to look to as allies and trading partners, the British or the French. America frequently found its formal policy of neutrality under pressure in the face of the vast wars sweeping the European continent in the wake of the French Revolution. Republicans shared feelings of fraternity with France, given that country's own democratic revolt. Federalists, in turn, sought accord with Britain, respecting its commercial might and horrified at the bloody turn taken by the French Revolution.[18] At times, partisans could be identified on the streets by the color of the badges or cockades they wore: black for the Federalists; red, white, and blue for the Republicans.[19]

The great glue that held the endeavor together dissolved when Washington chose to retire rather than be a candidate for president in the 1796 election. The Federalist John Adams was elected to succeed him; Jefferson came in second in the electoral college and was Vice President. There was a brief moment of possible amity between the two and their parties, but it quickly collapsed. The passions of Republicans were roused as Federalists brought the nation to the brink of war with France, called for a large standing army (which Republicans believed, and not entirely without foundation, might be aimed at them), increased the size of the navy, and raised taxes to pay for it all.[20]

The bizarre XYZ Affair yielded Adams and the Federalists political support for a time. Adams sent three commissioners—John Marshall, Charles Cotesworth Pinckney, and Elbridge Gerry—to France to negotiate an accommodation. The three were treated badly by France's foreign minister, Talleyrand, who, angry over perceived American provocations, refused to deal with the emissaries officially, demanded payments of great bribes through his agents, and intimated that war might be in the offing were the bribes not forthcoming.[21] When Adams reported to Congress that negotiations were failing, Republicans overplayed their hand by demanding release of the commissioners' dispatches, in which Talleyrand's emissaries were referred to anonymously as X, Y, and Z.[22] Publication of the dispatches sent the country into a frenzy of indignation at the French, and for that moment the Federalists' star was ascendant.[23]

Overplaying one's hand was not reserved to Republicans, however. Trying to seize the initiative and exploit patriotic fervor for partisan advantage, Federalists pushed through Congress the Alien and Sedition Acts.[24] The Alien Acts permitted the government to remove from the country foreigners deemed untrustworthy. The Sedition Act authorized the suppression of most criticism of the government. Although Federalists were careful to incorporate several progressive aspects of libel law into the Sedition Act, such as the ability to prove truth as a defense, the law still had an extraordinarily broad compass.[25] Some Federalists plainly intended to use these measures to suppress Republican electoral efforts and thus retain political power.[26]

JUDGES AS PARTISANS

"Is it for the public good or for party purposes?"

Enter the judges. For much of the partisan squabbling of the 1790s they had sat on the sidelines, relatively remote from politics.[27] The enforcement of the Sedition Act, however, brought the judges to center stage and in turn helped bring the Republicans to power. In ten notorious cases under the act, the Federalist judiciary acted in what looked to be a strongly political fashion.[28] One involved the trial of Matthew Lyon, a rough-hewn and outspoken Republican congressman from Vermont. Lyon was prosecuted for statements in print and speech that were critical of the Adams administration.[29] Justice William Paterson—the very judge who in *Vanhorne's Lessee v. Dorrance* had charged the jury on its responsibilities in considering the challenge to the constitutionality of a statute—told Lyon's jurors: "You have nothing whatever to do with the constitutionality or unconstitutionality of the sedition law. Congress has said that the author and publisher of seditious libels is to be punished; and until this law is declared null and void by a tribunal competent for the purpose, its validity cannot be disputed."[30] Paterson's conduct was mild compared with that of some of his colleagues, who presided over (or initiated) prosecutions with a heavy hand and often imposed harsh penalties. For this conduct Republicans called the Federalist judiciary to task.[31] Following his conviction and harsh treatment by partisan officials, Lyon was reelected to office by a huge margin.[32] Federalist enforcement efforts were garnering this sort of reaction everywhere.[33] If anything, the Sedition Act only helped spark the growth of the Republican press.[34]

Judges were partisan in even more obvious ways. It was common for judges charging grand juries to provide a sort of civics lesson, imparting their views regarding the operation of the constitutional system.[35] In the partisan fever of the times, these charges stepped easily beyond civics to politics.[36] In his charge to a New Hampshire grand jury, Justice Paterson derided "Jacobins" (read: Republicans) as the "disorganizers of our happy Country."[37] As related by a friendly newspaper, Justice Iredell similarly defended the Alien and Sedition Acts and, after calling the attention of the grand jury to the "present situation of the country," praised "the mild and virtuous administration of the [Federalist] government."[38] Nor was the partisanship of judges confined to the bench. Judges also served as presidential electors.[39] The Supreme Court's 1800 term was delayed because Supreme Court justice Samuel Chase was in Maryland stumping for Adams, leading *The Philadelphia Aurora*, the most prominent Republican publication of the 1790s, to decry "the Supreme Court adjourning from day to day, and the business of the nation hung up, until Chase shall have disgorged himself!!"[40]

Following the election of Jefferson in 1800, the Federalists took advantage of what was then a long lame-duck period prior to the transition of offices to turn the judiciary further to their purposes.[41] The position of Chief Justice had become vacant when Oliver Ellsworth, the nation's third, resigned on account of illness. Adams renominated the first Chief Justice, John Jay, for the job and had him confirmed by the Senate without his consent, but Jay turned the position down. (It was not prestigious enough.) Adams then tapped John Marshall for the job.[42] Marshall was sworn in on February 4, 1801, while continuing to hold his present office as Adams's Secretary of State.[43]

Next, the Federalists enacted the Circuit Judges Act, soon to become the center of enormous controversy.[44] It had long been a matter of some discontent that the Supreme Court justices had to ride circuit—travel from state to state to hear cases in the lower federal courts when the Supreme Court itself was not in session. This practice was one of the reasons that John Jay had retired from the Chief Justice post in the first place.[45] The circuit courts were reorganized under the Circuit Judges Act, and sixteen new circuit judge positions were established, relieving the Supreme Court of the necessity of riding circuit and providing prime judicial patronage for the outgoing Federalist administration. The Supreme Court's jurisdiction was also expanded, and the number of justices was slotted to be reduced from six to five when the next vacancy occurred, thereby denying Jefferson an anticipated early appointment.[46] Had it not been for partisan politics, many may have conceded the virtue of some of these judicial reforms.[47] Under the circumstances, though, the Republican *Aurora* reasonably asked: "Is it for the public good or for *party purposes*?"[48]

Federalists scurried to fill all the new judicial offices with Federalist judges.[49] Gouverneur Morris, a Federalist senator from New York, explained matter-of-factly that the Federalists "are about to experience a heavy gale of adverse wind; can they be blamed for casting many anchors to hold their ship through the storm?"[50] Jefferson was understandably furious. Writing to John

Dickinson, he accused the Federalists of having "retired into the Judiciary as a stronghold" and worried that "from that battery all the works of Republicanism are to be beaten down and erased."[51]

The Federalist judiciary soon proved Republican worries apt. In June 1801, by a 2–1 party line vote, Federalist judges on the new Circuit Court for the District of Columbia instructed the district attorney to bring libel charges against the editor of the mouthpiece of the Jefferson administration, *The National Intelligencer*.[52] One Republican editorialist asked, "Can any candid men have any further doubts as to the object which was intended by the new Judiciary system?"[53]

The most distressing event for Republicans, though, was Chief Justice John Marshall's issuance of a "show cause" order in the newly filed case of *Marbury v. Madison*. In addition to the new circuit judgeships, the lame-duck Federalist Congress created forty-two justice of the peace positions for the District of Columbia on February 27, 1801. Adams gave one of these to a Maryland gentleman named William Marbury. Marbury was confirmed for the position by the Senate on March 2, 1801, and his commission was signed by Adams on March 3. When the Adams administration expired on March 4, Secretary of State John Marshall had not yet delivered some of the newly minted judicial commissions. Among them was Marbury's. Upon taking office, Jefferson directed his Secretary of State, James Madison, not to deliver the commissions. Marbury sued Madison for his commission, part of a calculated Federalist effort to embarrass the Republicans.[54] In December 1801, Marshall's Supreme Court ordered Madison to appear and give reasons why Marbury's commission should not be ordered delivered to him.[55] The issuance of the show cause order gave every appearance of a Federalist judiciary preparing to meddle in the affairs of the newly elected administration.

THE NATURE OF THE PARTISAN STRUGGLE

"[A] set of people, known by the name of electioneering men"

What happened next reflected the sea change in politics that had taken place over the prior decade. The Republicans' triumph in 1800 was the result of a burgeoning popular political movement, fueled by growing voter participation.[56] Federalist maneuvering around the judiciary was seen as intransigent, a refusal to accept the verdict of the election returns, and an affront to the fundamental principle of popular rule. Some Republicans felt that if the Federalist judges would not subside, they would have to be taught where the true power in government rested.

In the many years before 1800, politics had been characterized by "deference." Elites governed by their own sensibilities; the people emerged from the background only for the cyclical election rituals in which candidates mingled among them and "treated" them to food and drink as part of the process of wooing their support. The characters of men, much more than political ideology, governed these contests.[57]

As differences drove Americans apart in the 1790s, Republicans created an entirely new kind of politics: popular, ideological, and party-driven. Writing in the early 1790s, Madison had reflected on the value of "a general intercourse of sentiments" brought about by, among other things, "a free press, and particularly *a circulation of newspapers through the entire body of the people, and Representatives going from, and returning among every part of them.*"[58] He, Jefferson, and others set out to make this happen. They created a network of party journals to engage public opinion and counter an already vibrant Federalist press. In 1790 there were roughly ninety regularly published papers; by 1800 that number had jumped to more than two hundred.[59] Though a paper was doing extremely well if it had as many as two thousand subscribers, its actual readership was much higher as journals were passed from hand to hand and read in coffeehouses and taverns.[60] Republican editors, who were often influential party leaders, worked to fashion the party line and brought it home to the people.[61] The national Congress became a place for representatives to develop party attachments, hold caucuses, select tickets, and enforce party discipline.[62]

Prominent Federalists viewed this new form of popular politics with alarm. Alexander Addison was a leading Federalist and Pennsylvania state judge whose grand jury charges were deemed pearls of wisdom among the faithful. Referring to the growing and rambunctious Republican press, he told one grand jury: "Speech, writing, and printing are the great direction of public opinion, and public opinion is the great director of human action. . . . Give to any set of men the command of the press, and you give them the command of the country; for you give them the command of public opinion, which commands every thing."[63] This was precisely why the Sedition Act was of such significance to Federalists and Republicans both.[64] Addison likewise condemned "the curse and calamity of this country . . . a set of people, known by the name of *electioneering men*, whose conduct, the whole year round, is constantly governed by prospect of influence on the day of election."[65]

Republican efforts at mobilizing and organizing the people paid off handsomely in the election of 1800. Partisan affiliations were not always clear in these days, so any count necessarily is an estimate. Still, prior to the 1800 contest the House of Representatives was roughly 63–43 Federalist to Republican;

after it the Republicans held the lead by about 66–41.[66] The Republicans won over an expanded electorate; approximately 20 percent of eligible voters cast ballots for President in 1796 compared with roughly 30 percent of eligible voters in 1800.[67] The vote in the electoral college provided stunning evidence of party discipline. In 1796, thirteen different candidates received at least one vote. In 1800, only one candidate outside the major parties received a vote.[68] Hamilton conceded after the election that the Federalists had focused too much on the propriety of what they were doing and had "neglected the cultivation of popular favor, by fair and justifiable expedients."[69]

Given that they had just won a heated election, recognized by all as registering the will of the people, the Republicans could hardly be expected to sit idly by in the face of Federalist shenanigans surrounding the judiciary. In his inaugural address, Jefferson had appeared conciliatory, saying: "We have called, by different names, brethren of the same principle. We are all republicans: We are all federalists."[70] Privately, though, he fumed about Federalist packing of the judiciary and the circuit judges legislation in particular.[71] Another Republican leader wrote James Madison: "The ground work laid for the future efforts of the [Federalist] Party—under a formidable and extended Judiciary wholly devoted to them—promises no peace."[72]

Any doubt about whether the Republicans would move against the Circuit Judges Act thus disappeared the instant the Supreme Court issued its show cause order in the *Marbury* case.[73] Even the cautious among them quickly overcame any reluctance about removing the newly appointed judges. "The conduct of the Judges on this occasion has excited a very general indignation," reported the Virginia senator Stevens Thomas Mason to Virginia's governor, James Monroe, "and will secure the repeal of the Judiciary Law of the last session about the propriety of which some of our Republican friends were hesitating."[74] Sure enough, in early January 1802 Kentucky's Senator John Breckinridge moved in the Senate for the repeal of the judiciary legislation.[75]

REPEAL OF THE CIRCUIT JUDGES ACT

"[I]t shakes questions that I thought were fixed"

For the next three months, the entire country was joined in a great spectacle and civics lesson, as the Senate and then the House debated the repeal of the Circuit Judges Act. The press brought home to its readers the great weight of what was occurring in Congress. "Nothing can or ought to be more interesting to every American," insisted Hamilton's *New York Evening Post*.[76] "Juris

Inconsultus," writing on the pages of the Republicans' *National Intelligencer*, said the debates over "the judicial power of the United States" that "are about to engage our public councils, and already engage the public mind" presented questions of "the first degree of importance" and urged that they be treated like "Solon's law, by which each citizen was required to take some side."[77] The author need hardly have worried.

Legislators on both sides played to the galleries and frequently invoked the broader public beyond.[78] Memorials flowed into Congress, initially opposed to the measure but eventually balanced by those in favor.[79] Newspaper coverage of the repeal debate was particularly prolix, often involving verbatim transcripts of hours-long floor speeches.[80] The *New York Evening Post* told readers that "no apology can be necessary for devoting the principal part of our paper to the debates on this all-important subject." Washington, D.C.'s *National Intelligencer* said the same when it finally deviated from its almost "exclusive" coverage. Partisan papers cheered the speeches of their heroes and derided those of their opponents.[81]

The Republicans' initial case for the bill was easy, albeit a little disingenuous. It was common in legislative debates during the early era of the Republic to distinguish arguments going to the "expediency" of a measure from those regarding its "constitutionality." The Republicans pressed "expediency." In his First Annual Message to Congress, in December 1801, Jefferson brandished statistics designed to call into question the need for the new judgeships. These statistics, which became the focus of close debate, turned out to be inaccurate.[82] Still, Republicans stuck to their guns. "[W]hile some few had the candor to acknowledge that the expence of the system was of no consequence," observed "A Ploughman, At his Desk" in New York's Federalist *Commercial Advertiser*, "the impudent and designing pretended that their only aim was to rid the people of their burthens."[83]

The Federalists staked their case on the Constitution. Article III of the Constitution states that judges are to "hold their Offices during good Behaviour" and may be removed only by impeachment. Because the new circuit court positions the Republicans sought to abolish had already been filled, Federalists argued, the move to repeal the Circuit Judges Act represented an unconstitutional removal of the judges.[84]

Although this "good Behaviour" argument was precisely what had given some Republican leaders and members of Congress initial pause about pursuing the repeal of the Circuit Judges Act, they now maintained that the provision applied only to removal of judges by the President, not the Congress.[85] Republicans found their own constitutional toehold in language that granted Congress the power to "ordain and establish" the lower federal courts.

If Congress could create the judgeships, or so the argument went, it could eliminate them.[86] Even out of the Republicans' own mouths, the distinction seemed a little drawn. "I do not admit the right of the Legislature to hurl these judges from their offices," acknowledged one Republican, who then turned right around to say: "[Y]et I must contend and shall ever contend for the right which Congress possesses to abolish an office."[87] Federalists mocked Republican claims that "though you cannot remove a judge from his office, you may take the office from the judge."[88] "[U]pon this principle, although you may not kill, by thrusting a dagger into the breast of your neighbor, yet you may compel your neighbor to kill himself by forcing him upon the dagger."[89]

For Federalists, the repeal legislation represented a grave attack on that holiest of holies, the independence of the judiciary. Bold metaphors tumbled from Federalist lips to describe the virtues of the system under attack: "fortress of the Constitution," the "ballast of the national ship," and—the most provocative and extended of the lot—"manly independence and firmness, so essential to an upright and good judge."[90] They pleaded to the point of hysteria regarding what was at stake. "[M]y mind recoils at the decision of the Constitutional question," Representative Samuel Dana of Connecticut explained, "because it shakes questions that I thought were fixed, and which were not to be discussed; because if decided one way, we shall be sent back to the first principles of society."[91]

The difficulty the Federalists faced was that despite their moral dudgeon, they hardly stood the debate's high ground. To hear Federalists tell it, said Breckinridge, "we are about to demolish the principal pillar in the fabric of our Constitution, and thereby dissolve the Union."[92] Rather, Republicans insisted, they only were fighting fire with fire, purifying a judiciary already prostrated to partisanship. The Circuit Judges Act, they said, "was passed for the sole purpose of embarrassing the new Administration." "[I]s it not just, is it not right, to repeal a law passed with views so wicked?"[93] Over and over Republicans reminded listeners: "Have we not heard judges crying out through the land, sedition!"[94] "If they wished the judges, like the tribe of Levi, to have been set apart from other men for the sacred purposes of justice," Virginia's fiery House Republican leader John Randolph lectured the galleries, "they should have considered well before they gave to publicans and sinners the privilege of the high priesthood."[95]

Given party discipline, it was the numbers, not the arguments, that ultimately mattered. Voting along party lines, Congress handily passed the repeal measure. The vote in the House was 59–32. It was closer in the Senate, 16–15, but as *The National Intelligencer* reminded its readers, this was because the Senate turned over more slowly than the House: only one-third of its membership stood for election at any time, and thus it had been more insulated from the upheaval of the 1800 election.[96]

The reaction of the party press was predictable. Federalist papers quickly condemned "the *fatal* effect of party rage which has succeeded in *beginning* the destruction of the Charter of our Liberties." "The Constitution—Gone Forever!" moaned the *New-York Spectator*.[97] For Republicans, though, this was "the final triumph of Republicanism." "The will of *the People*, when it is fully and clearly expressed, *shall* govern." So proclaimed Tom Adams's *Independent Chronicle*, in Boston, the leading voice of New England Republicanism and perhaps the most influential Republican journal of the time. Adams responded to Federalist arguments that the Constitution's letter had been violated by saying its "spirit" nonetheless was preserved.[98] *The National Intelligencer* simply exulted: "Judges, created for political purposes, and for the worst of purposes under a republican government, for the purpose of opposing the national will, from this day cease to exist."[99]

JUDICIAL INDEPENDENCE AND JUDICIAL REVIEW

*"Will you say . . . [t]hat the body whom they are
to check has the power to destroy them?"*

Where was judicial review in all this? The subject was omnipresent among Federalists. They repeatedly hammered home the point that dependent judges could not be trusted to rule on the constitutionality of congressional laws. Republicans were plainly loath to discuss the issue or respond. Given the practices of the preceding thirteen years, it would have been startling to find the Republicans denying the authority of judges to refuse to enforce laws deemed inconsistent with the Constitution.[100] Still, judicial review posed a very immediate threat for them; many wondered whether the judges would dare hold the repeal of the Circuit Judges Act itself unconstitutional. So Republicans simply shifted the conversation to their high ground, popular accountability, wondering aloud how any branch of government could remain independent of the people themselves.

Federalists offered judicial review as the primary reason for safeguarding judicial independence. Judicial review itself was essential to protect individual liberty and property rights, they maintained.[101] Yet how could judges be depended upon to rule honestly on these issues if they were beholden to legislative grace for their very survival? "Will you say . . . [t]hat the body whom they are to check has the power to destroy them?" asked Delaware's representative and leading congressional Federalist James Bayard. Bayard's colleague from North Carolina, Representative Archibald Henderson, elaborated: it simply would not matter "whether Congress sit in judgment upon their laws themselves, or whether they sit in judgment upon those who are appointed for that purpose."[102]

Federalists baited the Republicans with this point incessantly, daring them to deny the power of judicial review. They dwelt upon the "monstrous and unheard of doctrine which has been lately advanced, that the judges have not the right of declaring unconstitutional laws void."[103] They delighted in citing all the old cases and congressional statements in favor of judicial review, especially when the authors were Republicans: "[W]e have with us in opinion the whole choir of Virginia judges . . . among these I recognize the names of Pendleton, of Wythe, of Tazewell, of Tucker, of Tyler, and of others."[104]

For the most part, Republicans declined to take the bait. Judicial review, Republican representative Andrew Gregg of Pennsylvania explained, plainly protesting a bit too much, was "entirely irrelevant to the subject immediately before the Committee."[105] That is precisely why it was a moment of high drama when just at the end of the Senate debate, John Breckinridge took the floor to say: "I did not expect, sir, to find the doctrine of the power of the courts to annul the laws of Congress as unconstitutional, so seriously insisted on. . . . To make the Constitution a practical system, this pretended power of the courts to annul the laws of Congress cannot possibly exist."[106] The Federalist Gouverneur Morris was instantly out of his chair "to congratulate this House, and all America, that we have at length got our adversaries upon the ground where we can fairly meet. They have now, though late, reached the point to which their arguments tended from the beginning."[107] Republicans in the House learned from this exchange to avoid the subject of judicial review as much as possible. One Republican, John Bacon of Massachusetts, conceded the power of judicial review, for which, reported the Federalist *Green Mountain Patriot*, he received a "severe scolding" from party leaders "as soon as the Committee rose."[108] A very few others ran to the opposite extreme, such as a fired-up John Randolph, who insisted: "Here is a new power, of a dangerous and uncontrollable nature, contended for. The decision of a Constitutional question must rest somewhere. Shall it be confided to men immediately responsible to the people, or to those who are irresponsible?"[109]

To the extent that there was a party line on the issue of judicial review, however—and it was not much of one—Republicans seemed of the view that judges had the power to rule on the constitutionality of a law when resolving a case depended upon it, but that the other branches or "departments" of government were entitled to their constitutional views as well.[110] Senator Robert Wright of Maryland "admitted" "that judges ought to be the guardians of the Constitution, so far as questions were constitutionally submitted to them" but still believed "the Legislative, Executive, and Judiciary, each severally [were] the guardians of the Constitution, so far as they were called on in their several departments to act."[111] In this, their view accorded with Jefferson's. Jefferson explained his position in a note to John Adams's wife, Abigail, in the context of his pardon of those found guilty by Federalist judges of Sedition Act prosecutions:

> Both magistracies are equally independant in the sphere of action assigned to them. The judges, believing the law constitutional, had a right to pass a sentence of fine and imprisonment, because that power was placed in their hands by the constitution. But the Executive, believing the law to be unconstitutional, was bound to remit the execution of it; because that power has been confided to him by the constitution.[112]

The lurking problem, of course, was what should happen if the branches disagreed with each other. A few Republicans suggested it was for the people ultimately to decide. This presumably is what Representative Philip Thompson of Virginia meant when he said the judges "may, to be sure, for a while, impede the passage of a law, by a decision against its constitutionality; yet, notwithstanding the law is in force, is not nullified, and will be acted upon whenever there is a change of opinion."[113]

Federalists did not really disagree that ultimately questions of constitutionality were for the people. It was just that, as James Bayard pointed out in response, the popular verdict on legislation at periodic elections might not be enough to protect individual liberty. "I admit," he said, that "the power to decide upon the validity of our laws resides with the people."[114] But suppose, he suggested, Congress passes an unconstitutional law, and people are prosecuted under it anyway, over their resistance. "Deny to the courts of the United States the power of judging upon the constitutionality of our laws, and it is vain to talk of it existing elsewhere."[115]

Rather than engage on the question of judicial review, Republicans shifted the thrust of the conversation to the question of accountability. They could not comprehend how judges could possess the power to invalidate the legislature's laws yet remain unaccountable to the popular will. That was precisely what repeal of the Circuit Judges Act was about. "If the judges . . . are to be so independent . . . and if their power in deciding on the constitutionality of laws, is to be unlimited," reasoned Pennsylvania's Representative Andrew Gregg, "the Legislature is a subordinate branch of the Government—the Judiciary is paramount—the supreme power is in their hands."[116] Representative Joseph Nicholson, who later served as one of the House "managers" prosecuting the impeachment of Justice Samuel Chase in the Senate, warned that "these judges, thus rendered omnipotent, may overleap the Constitution and trample on your laws; they may laugh the Legislature to scorn, and set the nation at defiance." [117] "Do not the observations of gentlemen, who insist upon the permanent tenure of the Judicial office, place the creature above its creator, man above his God, the model above its mechanic?" asked another Republican senator. [118]

Yet again, the arguments for and against judicial review reached a stand-off. Federalists stressed the value of judicial review to individual liberty and the concomitant importance of judicial independence. Republicans insisted the government must be accountable in all regards to the people.

In part because the larger questions did not require answering, and in part because Federalists and Republicans alike were unsure what the popular verdict would be on their positions, both sides exercised some degree of caution in taking those positions to an extreme. In his first message to Congress, Jefferson initially included a paragraph outlining his view that each department remained free to interpret the Constitution for itself. Ultimately he withheld it as "capable of being chicaned, and furnishing the opposition something to make a handle of." [119] Federalists were similarly cagey about responding to the concerns about the popular accountability of judges put to them by the Republicans. When Federalists addressed the Republican challenge, it was to point out that judges were not entirely unaccountable to the people, but only "while they behave themselves well." [120] Tempting fate, Representative Bayard asked of the Republicans: If the judges "have offended against the Constitution or laws of the country, why are they not impeached?" [121]

MARBURY V. MADISON

"As it was born in death so it died in life"

It was well over a year before anyone heard what the Supreme Court had to say about any of this. Immediately following passage of the Repeal Act, Republicans, fearful of how the Court might rule on the act, hurriedly raced through Congress a bill canceling the Court's next term and delaying the one after that. [122] Delay, Republicans maintained, contrary to what anyone might think before or since, actually was good for litigants, as they would not be "hurried" to court. Apparently the more important the case, the more beneficial the delay: "[W]here the demand is great, the delay should be proportionably long."[123]

By the time the Court finally had a chance to speak (after the Republicans trounced Federalists again in the election of 1802, the repeal of the Circuit Judges Act apparently having hurt them not one whit), the justices were facing not one but two politically sensitive cases.[124] The first was Marbury's, which also had been delayed by the recent legislation.[125] The second was the anticipated challenge to the Repeal Act. Zealous Federalists had thought up a number of ways to make hay out of the repeal issue, persisting in their argument that the legislation violated the Constitution. They published a public "Protest" and petitioned Congress for relief, and some judges filed lawsuits challenging their dismissal.[126] But the case that made it to the Supreme Court—*Stuart v. Laird*—involved preexisting litigation that had been shuttled back and forth between courts as the new circuits were created and then abolished. Stuart's lawyer was Charles Lee, who had been Attorney General under the Washington and Adams administrations and who also was representing Marbury.

Whereas *Marbury* presented the question of whether the judges could issue orders to high executive branch officials, *Stuart* squarely posed the issue of judicial review: whether the judges could strike down an act of Congress if they found it unconstitutional. Lee made two broad constitutional arguments about the Repeal Act. The first was the familiar argument that it violated the "good Behaviour" clause. "So much has been recently said, and written and published upon this subject," Lee told the Court, "that it is irksome to repeat arguments which are now familiar to every one." By abolishing the new circuit courts, the Repeal Act also had restored the Supreme Court justices to circuit-riding activities. Lee raised a variety of arguments why this was unconstitutional as well.[127]

Despite the doubts some of the justices held about the constitutionality of the Repeal Act, most of them were not overly keen about being confronted with the issue. Corresponding with one another privately on the question, they decided to resume their circuit-riding activities rather than engage in public protest of the Repeal Act.[128] As Marshall delicately put it, the "consequences of refusing to carry the law into effect may be very serious."[129] Luck had it that Marshall was sitting on the lower court that heard *Stuart v. Laird*. He promptly ruled against the Federalist challenge, but the plaintiff (unwilling to take a hint) pursued the case to the Supreme Court.[130] Thus *Stuart* sat alongside *Marbury* on the docket when the justices returned from their forced recess in February 1803.

As they confronted these two blockbuster cases, the justices of the Supreme Court were hardly lacking for evidence of just how dicey things were. Madison, on direct orders from President Jefferson, had refused even to respond to the Court's show cause order, making clear their shared contempt for the entire *Marbury* proceeding.[131] Several senators made plain that they considered the *Marbury* litigation an unwarranted political attack on the President.[132] As for the Circuit Judges Act, when the dismissed Federalist judges petitioned Congress for relief, Representative Joseph Nicholson threatened direct action. "The resolution contemplated giving the power to try the right of the judges to their claims; but the great object in reality was to authorize the judges of the Supreme Court to decide upon the constitutionality of the repealing act. . . . If the Supreme Court shall arrogate this power to themselves and declare our law to be unconstitutional, it will then behoove us to act."[133] Lest this seem an idle threat, just days before the oral argument in *Marbury*, Jefferson sent to the House papers suggesting the impeachment of Federalist district judge John Pickering.[134] Pickering was mentally deranged and a drunk to boot, and in fairness Federalists had resisted entreaties for a more graceful resolution to a problem that required one.[135] Still, enough threats of impeaching Federalist judges were swirling about to lead Marshall to worry. If the justices had any lingering doubts, Pennsylvania's impeachment of the ardent Federalist judge Alexander Addison in January 1803 could not have been reassuring.[136]

The Supreme Court resolved the *Marbury* case first. Writing for the justices, Marshall cut right to the chase. William Marbury was entitled to his commission: he had been nominated by the President, his appointment was confirmed by the Senate, and that commission had been signed and sealed as the law required. This ruling brought to the fore the central issue in the case, the power of the judges over the executive branch. Marshall understood that Republican eyes were on him as he addressed the issue. "[I]t is not wonderful that . . . such a case as this . . . should at first view be considered by some, as an attempt to intrude into the cabinet, and to intermeddle with the prerogatives of the executive."[137]

Marshall's conclusion was that executive officials were answerable in court, though he was careful to draw a distinction between cases involving political issues that judges would not touch and those involving violations of legal rights that called out for judicial resolution. "Questions, in their nature political . . . can never be made in this court."[138] But the executive's autonomy ended "where a specific duty is assigned by law, and individual rights depend upon the performance of that duty. . . ."[139] Such was the case with Marbury's commission: because his legal right had been violated, he was entitled to come to the judiciary for help. "The very essence of civil liberty certainly consists in the right of every individual to claim the protection of the laws, whenever he receives an injury." Were this not the case, Marshall wrote, the United States would no longer deserve to be called "a government of laws, and not of men."[140]

In concluding that the executive was answerable in court for the violation of Marbury's legal rights, however, Marshall ran the serious risk of emphasizing just how impotent his Court was. In the ordinary course, a decision that Madison should have delivered Marbury's commission would be followed by an order for Madison to do so. Yet the justices could be certain that any order they issued in *Marbury* would be defied by Madison. If this happened, the inherent weakness of the judiciary would be on display for all to see.

Marshall wriggled out of this glaring problem by holding that despite Marbury's entitlement to the commission, the Court was without jurisdiction to give it to him. According to Marshall, Congress had by statute bestowed jurisdiction on the Court to issue the order against Madison. But such relief could be given only if that congressional statute itself was consistent with the Constitution. Marshall determined it was not, because the statute authorized the Supreme Court to hear a category of cases the Constitution assigned to the lower courts in the first place. Congress, Marshall concluded, lacked the power to move such cases from the Supreme Court's "appellate" to its "original" jurisdiction.[141]

In order to determine if the Supreme Court had jurisdiction over Marbury's case, Marshall thus found it necessary to tackle the question of judicial review: "whether an act, repugnant to the constitution, can become the law of the land."[142] This was precisely the question lurking in *Stuart v. Laird*, of course, where the constitutionality of the Repeal Act was pending. It was to become a signature move of John Marshall's to take a controversial question pending in one case and answer it in another, where he might dispose of it more easily. That is what he did here.

Though the question of judicial power was "deeply interesting to the United States," Marshall wrote, it was an easy one: he need only "recognize certain principles, supposed to have been long and well established, to decide it."[143] Obviously, Marshall began, any congressional statute contrary to the Constitution must be void. Central to his argument was the special nature of a written constitution. "Certainly all those who have framed written constitutions contemplate them as forming the fundamental and paramount law of the nation, and consequently the theory of every such government must be, that an act of the legislature repugnant to the constitution is void."[144]

Marshall then went on to ask, coming to the heart of the matter: "[D]oes it, notwithstanding its invalidity, bind the courts, and oblige them to give it effect?" In other words, even if a statute was unconstitutional, were courts compelled to apply it anyway? This was, to Marshall, "an absurdity too gross to be insisted on." After all, "[i]t is emphatically the province and duty of the judicial department to say what the law is." When confronted with two rules that "conflict with each other," a court must decide which governs. "This is of the very essence of judicial duty."[145] In this way Marshall handed down *Marbury*'s great ruling that courts could indeed refuse to give recognition to acts of Congress deemed unconstitutional.[146]

Having resolved the question of judicial review in *Marbury*, the Court then avoided further controversy in *Stuart v. Laird* by holding that there was no constitutional problem presented by the repeal of the Circuit Judges Act. The *Stuart* Court issued a terse decision dismissing Lee's arguments about the constitutionality of requiring Supreme Court justices to ride circuit, while ignoring altogether the claim that abolishing existing judgeships was unconstitutional.[147] Resting alongside the Court's expansive *Marbury* decision, *Stuart*'s cursory treatment of the issues that had gripped the country for months clearly conveyed the message that the justices had heard enough of the repeal of the Circuit Judges Act. "[T]he question is at rest, and ought not now to be disturbed."[148]

Marshall's deft move in all this, the one applauded by many in years hence, was in announcing fundamental principles of constitutional government and claiming great authority for the judiciary to enforce them, all the while managing to avoid requiring anyone to honor that authority in any tangible way.[149] In *Marbury*, he had answered not only the question of the courts' power over executive officials but also the question posed in *Stuart v. Laird*, that of judicial review. He had answered both questions in the judiciary's favor. Yet he had also avoided exposing the judiciary to reprisal, because neither decision ultimately required anyone to do anything. Madison did not need to deliver Marbury's commission, because the Court lacked jurisdiction.[150] And after *Stuart*, the Repeal Act lived.

Despite the fame Marshall's opinion in *Marbury* later achieved, nothing he said on the subject of judicial review was new. True, *Marbury* represented the first instance in which the full Supreme Court had unequivocally declared that it could refuse to follow an act of Congress.[151] The logic of Marshall's opinion, however, merely echoed what those such as Iredell and Hamilton had said years earlier.[152] Even the clever argument about why the Supreme Court's jurisdictional statute was unconstitutional was not Marshall's invention.[153] During the repeal debate, a Republican representative had made much the same argument, explaining why the *Marbury* case posed little threat.[154] One can almost imagine Marshall's glee at hearing the Republicans handing the Supreme Court a safe way out of the dilemma posed by the *Marbury* and *Stuart* litigations.[155]

While not new, much of what Marshall did in rendering the *Marbury* decision violated important norms of judging. Struggling to emphasize the separation between law and politics, Marshall ignored settled legal rules in such a fashion as to suggest that it was politics as much as law driving him. Given the ultimate conclusion that the Court lacked jurisdiction, Marshall's gratuitous tongue-lashing of Jefferson and Madison for failing to deliver Marbury's commission was entirely unwarranted. If the Court had no juris-diction, it should have said so and said nothing more.[156] Moreover, as Sec-retary of State, Marshall had participated in the very events being litigated before the Court in *Marbury*.[157] He ought to have removed himself from par-ticipating in the *Marbury* case, just as he did in *Stuart v. Laird* (where he had decided the case while sitting on the lower court).[158] Even the ruling on the jurisdictional issue was dubious: there were prior precedents suggesting the Court did in fact have jurisdiction and a variety of ways Marshall could have worked around the supposed conflict between the Constitution and the ju-risdictional statute.[159]

Marshall's decision in *Marbury v. Madison* makes the absolute best of a bad situation, in light of the justices' clear understanding of the limits of their power.[160] Marshall could not order relief from the Republicans and hope to see his will followed. Rather than simply capitulate and dismiss Marbury's case for lack of jurisdiction, therefore, the Court did the only thing it could: deliver a stout lecture on constitutional principles and the proper role of the judiciary and withdraw. It was a brilliant move, but it was clearly a political one.[161]

The reaction to *Marbury* in the press was strictly by party line. Federal-ists deemed *Marbury* "highly important," no doubt because it could be used to skewer Jefferson further still for "bursting asunder the limits prescribed by the constitution, and sacrificing on its more than cruel altar 'legal vested rights.'"[162] "Constitution violated by the President" was how Hamilton's *New York Evening Post* put it.[163] As for Republicans, at least in terms of the results, there was nothing with which they could disagree. (Several Republi-can papers actually congratulated the Court for the *Stuart* ruling.)[164]

To Republicans, *Marbury* represented more of the same partisan conduct they had come to expect from Federalist judges.[165] As the critic "Littleton" said in a multipart series that appeared in *The Virginia Argus* and was widely reprinted, "To decide upon the merits of a cause without jurisdiction to entertain it, I affirm to be contrary to all law precedent and principle."[166] There was only one extended critique of the judicial review portion of the *Marbury* opinion, by an "Unlearned Layman."[167] For the most part, Republicans appeared to recognize the Court had done nothing but deliver a sermon, albeit a strongly worded one, and like most sermons it could be forgotten rather quickly upon one's exiting the church.[168] Littleton likened the awkward and convoluted *Marbury* opinion to some frightful beast, "[i]ts head in the rear, its tail in front, its legs mounted on high to support the burthen [burden], while its back was destined to tread the earth its bowels in the exterior, and its hide in the interior." And he was prescient about its fate, at least if one did not look to the very distant future: "As it was born in death so it died in life."[169]

THE CHASE IMPEACHMENT

"[T]o exorcise from our courts the baleful spirit of party"

While future generations were to applaud Marshall's opinion, his near term was to be far more uncomfortable. The one (and perhaps only) clear immediate impact of the *Marbury* opinion was to anger the thin-skinned Jefferson yet further.[170] This alone might have mattered little. But then, shortly after *Marbury*, Marshall's colleague Justice Samuel Chase, unable to see when enough was enough, delivered a highly incendiary political grand jury charge in Baltimore. When Jefferson heard of this, he wrote Representative Joseph Nicholson, saying, "Ought this seditious and official attack on the principles of our Constitution, and on the proceedings of a State, to go unpunished?"[171] Soon enough, the House of Representatives impeached Chase. Continued partisanship had gotten the judiciary into yet further trouble. It took this last major battle to sort things out.

Chase had been in this position before. He had been a controversial figure in Maryland politics since the early 1770s, and when he angered political opponents there, they also had tried to remove him. In the winter of 1794, he was investigated by the Maryland House of Delegates for holding two offices at once: chief judge of the General Court of Maryland and judge on Baltimore's Court of Oyer and Terminer. Although the motion to remove Chase from office was easily defeated, a resolution asserting the unconstitutionality of his appointments was kept from a vote by a much narrower margin.[172] Given to strong emotions, and never a figure to shy from controversy, Chase had violently opposed British rule; next he fought *against* the Constitution;

then he belatedly joined on to fight *with* the Federalists, for whom he now displayed a fierce loyalty. The Republicans detested him.[173]

It is unclear how far the Republicans initially intended to take their program of impeaching Federalist judges. Pickering's impeachment had a sound enough nonpartisan justification, but even in that case Jefferson apparently sent the papers to Congress only after Pennsylvania's successful removal of Judge Addison.[174] Pennsylvania governor Thomas McKean subsequently wrote to Jefferson, approving Pickering's removal: "So you find sir we know how to get rid of obnoxious judges as well as the Congress."[175] As Republican impeachment efforts gained momentum, a friendly newspaper from Charleston, South Carolina, offered this anecdote: "'I don't know how to remove these large stones,' said a labourer on a turnpike road—'Call them federalists, and they will soon be *removed*,' replied a bystander."[176]

The Federalists certainly believed that Chase was the next step in an extended campaign.[177] Senator John Quincy Adams—John Adams's son and destined to become President himself—viewed the Pickering impeachment as "but a preparatory step to the assault upon Judge Chase," with the ultimate end to "have swept the supreme judicial bench clean at a stroke."[178] The only question, as New Hampshire's Federalist *Portsmouth Oracle* asked, was: "Which of the Judges of the Supreme Court or District Court will next have their turn at denunciation[?]"[179] Some supposed Marshall to be the Republicans' ultimate target.[180] So concerned was the Chief Justice by these doings that in a letter to Chase, Marshall proposed weakening the power of judicial review in exchange for keeping their jobs. Perhaps, he suggested, the "modern doctrine of impeachment should yield to an appellate jurisdiction in the legislature. A reversal of those legal opinions deemd unsound by the legislature woud certainly better comport with the mildness of our character than a removal of the Judge who has rendered them unknowing of his fault."[181]

As with the repeal of the Circuit Judges Act, Republicans initially were hesitant to embark upon their impeachment vendetta.[182] However, largely on the basis of the efforts of Representative John Randolph, in March 1804 the House voted articles of impeachment against Chase. Ultimately there were eight counts against Chase, most of which involved allegedly partisan conduct while presiding over high-profile sedition or treason cases.[183] The first article alleged misconduct in the treason trial of John Fries, who had led a hapless "rebellion" against federal taxes.[184] The next five articles related to partisan judging in the Sedition Act trial of James Callender, a scandalmongering journalist whom Jefferson had supported in attacking the Federalists (and who later turned viciously on Jefferson himself).[185] The final two articles involved Chase's overstepping bounds with grand juries, including the eighth article, which involved the Baltimore jury charge that had pushed Jefferson over the edge.[186] Troubled by the Repeal Act, Maryland legislation attacking judges, and the passage of universal suffrage, Chase had told the Baltimore grand jury:

> The independence of the national Judiciary is already shaken to its foundation, and the virtue of the people alone can restore it. The independence of the judges of this State will be entirely destroyed, if the bill for the abolition of the two supreme courts should be ratified by the next General Assembly. The change of the State constitution, by allowing universal suffrage, will, in my opinion, certainly and rapidly destroy all protection to property, and all security to personal liberty; and our republican constitution will sink into a mobocracy, the worst of all possible governments.[187]

The National Intelligencer, one of numerous papers that reported the event, opined that the charge "may be pronounced the most extraordinary that the violence of federalism has yet produced."[188] Chase was not without his defense. His lawyers relied on numerous precedents to show his conduct was warranted in law. The Baltimore grand jury charge appeared the most nakedly partisan of the counts, but Chase was hardly alone in this conduct. Republican House Speaker Nathaniel Macon, consulted before the effort began, had questioned if impeachment was appropriate "for expressing to a grand jury political opinions which every man was permitted to hold and express elsewhere."[189]

Chase's trial before the Senate gripped the attention of the nation for most of February 1805. The breadth and scope of newspaper coverage were staggering.[190] An advertisement by publishers of a volume on the proceedings bragged to have hired two full-time people, "one of whom is a professional stenographer," to produce a record of the trial.[191] Vice President Aaron Burr was the presiding officer. He had made such elaborate arrangements that Federalist senator Uriah Tracy, who was to be helped into the hall for the final vote while gravely ill from pneumonia, observed the Senate "was fitted up in a style beyond anything which has ever appeared in this country." More than a thousand spectators attended.[192] Representative Caesar Rodney, one of the impeachment managers, commented in closing arguments that the "novelty and magnitude have excited so much interest and attention, that it seems to have superseded for the moment, not only every other grave object or pursuit, but every other fashionable amusement or dissipation."[193]

There was every reason to expect Chase's removal. The charges and evidence against him had been disseminated in the Republican press long before the trial began.[194] Even if the impeachment was seen as partisan in nature, Chase still was widely believed to have engaged in serious misconduct.[195] John Marshall, called to testify at the impeachment trial, was forced to concede that some of Chase's conduct on the bench was irregular.[196] Massachusetts's Republican *National Aegis* pricked the Federalist press for viewing Chase's removal as almost certain: "The inference may be just, but it is not *kind* in the Honorable Judge's friends to trumpet it forth to the world."[197] All but four Republicans in the House had voted for the impeachment.[198] The Constitution required a two-thirds Senate majority to remove an impeached judge; if Republicans, who held twenty-five seats of the thirty-four Senate seats, voted along party lines, they had two votes to spare.[199]

As it happened, though, Chase was acquitted. The highest number of votes any count received was nineteen, four short of the constitutional majority required for conviction. The Federalists voted in Chase's favor on party lines. Yet at least six Republicans joined all the Federalists in voting against every count. The highest vote getters were the articles addressing partisan irregularities in the Callender trial and the Baltimore grand jury charge.[200]

Explaining precisely why Chase was acquitted has proven no easy task for historians. There exists surprisingly little information on why the six Republicans voted as they did. There are various theories of political intrigue offered to explain the votes, but each rests on conjecture to some extent and runs into conflicting evidence.[201] One of the Republican "no" voters, Senator Samuel Latham Mitchill of New York, wrote his wife after the decision to say: "On this occasion myself and my colleague Smith acted with the Federalists. But we did so on full conviction that the evidence, our oaths, the Constitution, and our consciences required us to act as we have done. I suppose we shall be libelled and abused at a great rate for our judgment given this day."[202] Taking Mitchill at his word, he still provides little information on why so many Republicans voted to acquit.

It is obvious that Chase's team outgunned their opponents. The leader of the House managers, John Randolph, was not a lawyer, putting him at a serious disadvantage against Chase's crack legal team.[203] Prosecution witnesses not infrequently supported the defense case, such as when John Taylor testified regarding the Callender trial that he did not "perceive[] any anger expressed by the court."[204] One observer of the trial commented: "I swear if they go on much farther, they will prove Judge Chase is an angel."[205] The managers could not seem to agree on a theory of the standard for impeachment, while Chase's team held reasonably firm to the principle that conviction was appropriate only if Chase's conduct constituted an indictable offense.[206]

Still, it is difficult to believe the quality of the lawyers standing alone made the difference. Party discipline can be a powerful engine.[207] It held during the Repeal Act vote, despite the misgivings of some members.[208] True, cracks were showing as the Republican majority in Congress grew. Still, it is hardly as though the Federalists' case on Chase prevailed. Their position that impeachment was proper only for indictable offenses was plainly rejected by the majority of the Republicans. The article that garnered the most votes, the Baltimore grand jury charge, was highly partisan but not indictable.[209] Many Republicans voted guilty on any number of the counts against Chase.

Although we may never have access to the secret and perhaps unknowable motives of participants to the Chase impeachment, it nonetheless is possible to identify the social understanding of events on the basis of the actions and words of the participants.[210] The "lesson" of the Chase impeachment—confirmed by history since—was twofold. Judges would refrain in the future from blatantly partisan use of their offices.[211] In return, Congress would grant the judiciary some modicum of independence. Certainly it would no longer use impeachment to attack judges for good faith actions on the bench.[212] Both halves of this deal are apparent from the arguments and actions of the participants at the trial, as well as some of the accompanying newspaper coverage. Critically, each side of the controversy effectively conceded the other's core point.

The central theme of the Republicans, a point they had made since 1800, was that partisan judging of the kind Chase appeared to have done was simply unacceptable. According to the impeachment managers, Chase's highest crime was "staining the pure ermine of justice by political party spirit."[213] Preparing senators to hear the witnesses against Chase, John Randolph told them what to look for: "Through the whole tenor of his judicial conduct runs the spirit of party."[214] After the witnesses had testified, another manager, Representative George Campbell of Tennessee, highlighted what the senators had heard: "The judicial authority was prostituted to party purposes, and the fountains of justice were corrupted by this poisonous spirit of persecution. . . ."[215] Chase had "turn[ed] the judicial power, with which he was vested, into an engine of political oppression."[216] The party press made much the same point repeatedly in its condemnation of Chase. "Plain Truth," in an open letter to Chase in Boston's *Independent Chronicle*, said: "Human nature is altogether incapable of supporting the proper character of a judge, under the keen and bitter contentions of political parties." The solution, one concurred in by others, was that "[j]udges and clergymen ought not to involve themselves in those party conflicts." [217]

Such partisan conduct was completely inappropriate for a judge, the managers argued. "Shall he not put off the political partizan when he ascends the tribune; or shall we have the pure stream of public justice polluted with the venom of party virulence?" [218] Joseph Nicholson told the senatorial jury that the whole case was about seeing this did not happen in the future: "It is our duty to prevent party spirit from entering into our courts of justice." [219] John Randolph's closing argument was famously bad. He was ill, wandering, histrionic. But he pulled it together at the very end, looked the Senate in the eye, and told the senators (intentionally echoing George Washington, one surmises): "We adjure you on behalf of the House of Representatives and of all the people of the United States, to exorcise from our courts the baleful spirit of party. . . ." [220]

But why would one read the impeachment trial and its result as prohibiting such partisan behavior? After all, Chase was *acquitted*. "If a man like Judge Chase can escape the punishment of his misdemeanours," asked the Republican *Richmond Enquirer* in the aftermath, "where is the judge . . . who *can* be made to expiate his offences in a court of impeachment . . . ?" [221] Jefferson too complained of the ineffectiveness of impeachment—"an impracticable thing, a mere scare-crow"—bemoaning how judges were independent even of public opinion. [222]

One must read the impeachment as a condemnation of judicial partisanship, because it was the one thing the Federalists did not defend in their labors for Chase. This had not been part of their arguments for judicial independence during the repeal debate, and it was not now. [223] Indeed, during the Chase proceedings the Federalist *New York Evening Post* used the occasion to condemn the "electioneering" conduct of some state judges: "If such conduct is to be tolerated, it is not difficult to perceive, that the time is fast approaching, when the sanctuary of Justice will be profaned . . . all men who have an interest at stake in the community, should make a solemn pause e'er it be too late." [224] The only time Chase's lawyers seemed to sanction anything approaching partisan conduct was with regard to the Baltimore grand jury charge, asking: "In what part of our laws or constitution is it written, that a judge shall not speak on politics to a grand jury?" (This of course was nothing more than the Republican Macon had asked.) Even yet, immediately after making this argument, Chase's lead attorney, Robert Goodloe Harper, conceded: "Such conduct may perhaps be ill-judged, indiscreet, or ill-timed.

I am ready to admit that it is so; for I am one of those who have always thought, that political subjects ought never to be mentioned in courts of justice."[225]

At the same time, Chase's defenders won their own war—over judicial independence. "[I]f through him, a wound is given to the Constitution and the Independence of the judiciary is destroyed, we may in vain lament over our fallen rights," the *Washington Federalist* commented, capturing the overtones of the defense.[226] This was the constant theme of Chase's lawyers throughout the case. Chase's counsel Charles Lee told the Senate it was about to set a precedent "which will have a most important influence in our country. . . . An upright and independent judiciary is all important in society."[227] Robert Harper reminded the senators that political power could shift, that those who wielded power today could be impeached tomorrow. "Need I," he asked, "urge the necessity of adhering to those principles, as it respects the independence of the judiciary department?"[228] "The independence of the judiciary, the political tocsin of the day, and *the alarm bell of the night*, has been rung through every change in our ears," Republican manager Caesar Rodney observed with some exasperation.[229]

As on the issue of partisanship, the defenders of judicial independence were helped in their cause by their opponents. In the early stages, the impeachment effort had taken on the character of a witch hunt by Republicans. John Quincy Adams, in his diary, captured the spectacle of William Branch Giles, a fervid Republican senator from Virginia, buttonholing a wavering colleague and explaining his theory of impeachment: "The Senate sitting for the trial of impeachments was not a court, and ought to discard and reject all process of analogy to a court of justice." As grounds for impeachment, it was quite sufficient for Congress simply to declare to judges: "*We want your offices*, for the purpose of giving them to men who will fill them better."[230]

Ultimately, the House managers had to come down as well on the side of judicial independence. Even Giles apparently felt compelled to act against his partisan theory of impeachment, voting to acquit on four charges. Manager Rodney, after expressing his frustration with how Chase's counsel had raised the issue of judicial independence repeatedly, still said: "To the rational independence of the judiciary I am, and ever have been a firm and uniform friend."[231] Chase's lawyers emphasized this point, contrasting the case of the House managers with those beyond, who were clamoring that judges should be accountable to the people.[232] Republicans simply thought partisanship was inconsistent with this admirable independence. "My desire," Rodney continued, "is that the laws, like the providence of the deity, should shed their protecting influence equally over all."[233]

Except for those most passionately involved, the Chase verdict signaled the end of the great struggle between the Federalists and Republicans over independence and partisanship. After the acquittal, Randolph and Nicholson stormed to the House chamber to denounce the Senate for its action. According to the *Washington Federalist*—admittedly not a neutral source—Randolph "more than once called the Judge an *acquitted Felon*" and made the House the "vehicle for envenomed spleen and mortified pride to vent themselves."[234] Randolph introduced a proposed constitutional amendment that would have made judges removable by the President on address by both houses of Congress.[235] Nicholson one-upped him and fingered the real villain, introducing another amendment that would have permitted state legislatures to recall their senators.[236] The House quietly shelved both amendments. Even this heavily Republican body had had enough.

The Federalist failure to defend partisanship, and the nature of the verdict, had sent the desired message. A chastened Chase remained on the bench following the trial but quieted down significantly. As Chase wrote fellow Federalist Rufus King, "[M]y age, infirmities & the wicked Prosecution I have suffered, have determined me never to take any Part in any public Measure whatsoever."[237] *The National Intelligencer* actually commented approvingly on a grand jury charge delivered shortly after the acquittal: "Judge Chase delivered a short and pertinent charge to the grand jury—his remarks were pointed, modest and well applied."[238] The justices had apparently learned their lesson. Indeed, in 1814, just as the next trouble was about to begin, *The National Intelligencer* praised the Supreme Court as "a branch of the Government which it is important to hold in due veneration, and whose decisions are entitled to the highest respect."[239]

Prior to the battles of the late 1790s, many Americans, Federalist and Republican alike, held an attachment to the idea of an independent judiciary. But Republicans found that attachment sorely tested by what they viewed as partisan judicial behavior. Ironically, judicial review had come to such quick acceptance that given the shenanigans of Federalist judges, Republicans were prepared to attack judicial independence itself. If judges possessed the power of judicial review and used it in partisan ways, they could not be left unaccountable to the people. Judicial independence ultimately prevailed, but only after the Federalists had signaled that they were prepared to abjure partisan judging.

3

DEFIANCE

"[O]bliged to decide constitutional questions,
which have encountered much opposition"

Independence is not the same as power. This was a lesson brought home
repeatedly to the justices of the Supreme Court over the next several
decades. The resolution of the partisan conflicts of the early 1800s provided the judiciary with a certain degree of autonomy and security, yet the
justices' authority remained profoundly open to question. State officials frequently thumbed their noses at the Court. They refused to appear when
summoned, denied that the Supreme Court was the arbiter of the constitutionality of state laws, and blatantly defied judicial orders.

There is no better example of the Supreme Court's woes in this period
than the trouble the justices encountered when they intervened in the state
of Georgia's conflict with the Cherokee tribes. Georgia wanted the tribes removed from its territory; the Cherokee sought legal recourse. Put on notice
of the Cherokee's intention to bring suit in the Supreme Court, *The Georgia
Journal* fumed, in a fashion representative of the times: "Has it come to this,
that a sovereign and independent state is to be insulted, by being asked to
become a party, before the supreme court, with a few savages, residing in her
own territory!!!—Unparalleled impudence." [1] The *Augusta Constitutionalist*
scoffed: "[T]o whom will the order be directed?—and let it be directed to
whom it may—can it ever be enforced?" [2] Georgia's subsequent disregard of
the Supreme Court's orders proved this to be no idle talk.

The difficulty the Court faced was that its decisions ran up against an
emerging states' rights ideology that threatened not only judicial authority but

the Union itself. Throughout the nation's first century, agreement often could not be reached on the seemingly most fundamental of constitutional questions, the nature of the American federal system.[3] Repeatedly states recurred to the argument that there could be no umpire in their disputes with the national government—and certainly not the Supreme Court. The states would never "have committed an act of such egregious folly," insisted "Amphictyon," in the *Richmond Enquirer*, "as to agree that their umpire should be appointed and paid by the other party."[4] Rather, state defenders maintained, the Constitution formed a compact among sovereign states, and each state party to the compact retained the power to "nullify" federal laws it believed unconstitutional.

Matters changed almost overnight, and the Supreme Court's authority was enhanced immeasurably, when in late 1832 the state of South Carolina strenuously asserted its right to nullify the federal tariff law and appeared ready to back up its claim with force. All of a sudden, the necessity of national supremacy meant more than rhetoric about state sovereignty. President Andrew Jackson was the towering figure of the period; he rode at the front of one of America's great popular movements and was not understood to be a particular friend of the judiciary. Jackson supported states' rights and had been quietly undermining the Court in its controversy with Georgia over the Cherokee. In the face of South Carolina's actions, however, Jackson took a firm position: he denied that states had a right to nullify federal law, threatened to use force to defend the Union, and affirmed the Supreme Court's role in arbitrating constitutional questions.

The framers of the Constitution had yoked together the authority of the Supreme Court and the supremacy of national institutions. If national leaders wanted to see their authority remain paramount over the states, they were compelled to support the national judiciary as well. This lesson, which became clear during the Nullification Crisis of 1832–1833, would be repeatedly reinforced thereafter. And as national voices rose to support the Supreme Court's role in arbitrating constitutional disputes, public tolerance for officially sanctioned defiance of Supreme Court decisions began to fade.

THE STATES IN THE CONSTITUTIONAL PLAN

"[T]he consolidation of our Union"

In the first half of the 1800s, the allocation of authority between the state and the national governments proved a persistent problem. This was because the framers of the Constitution, forced to perform a balancing act between those wary of national power and those eager to see greater control at the center, had left the boundaries of authority somewhat vague. Without a clear demarcation of the state and federal governments' respective roles, any institution attempting to umpire between them was bound to find its decisions subject to contest.

Following independence, states' concerns for their own prerogatives had led to a notoriously weak and ineffectual original Union.[5] George Washington called it "little more than a shadow without the substance." Under the Articles of Confederation that preceded the Constitution, the only branch of the central government was a Congress, which did not even have the power to tax. On major questions, nine of the thirteen states had to concur to get anything done. There was no executive or judicial branch. Lacking an enforcement sword, and with an often empty purse, Washington deemed "Congress a nugatory body, their ordinances being little attended to."[6] It was no small wonder that the entire endeavor found itself near collapse by the time the Constitutional Convention was called.[7]

In addressing the Confederation's shortcomings, the delegates to the Constitutional Convention had to tread a careful path. They knew they needed to strengthen the central government. At the same time, they risked alienating those protective of the states. The route they ultimately chose was dictated as much by the need to reach some accommodation as by any considered theory of government. It was agreed early on that the new government ought to possess the executive and judicial authorities the Confederation lacked.[8] But defining the extent of the national government's powers (and thereby the limits imposed on the states) proved more nettlesome. Though there undoubtedly were a few delegates who would have been happy to see the separate existence of the states eliminated, this option was not even remotely plausible.[9]

Transmitting the newly drafted Constitution to the Congress of the Confederation (which in turn submitted it to the states for ratification), the framers conceded that they had found it "difficult to draw with precision the line" between the powers of the state and national governments.[10] Under the Virginia Plan for the new Constitution, authored largely by James Madison, Congress would have had the power to "legislate in all cases to which the separate States are incompetent; or in which the harmony of the U.S. may be interrupted, by the exercise of individual legislation."[11] Rather than adopt this general principle, the convention opted instead to enumerate, in Article I, Section 8 of the Constitution, the specific powers that the national legislature could exercise. The idea was that Congress could enact legislation only in these enumerated areas, while all remaining legislative authority would remain in the states.[12] Even this illusory precision was blurred, however, because Congress was given additional authority to pass whatever other laws "shall be necessary and proper for carrying into Execution the foregoing Powers."[13]

The framers optimistically hoped that "the consolidation of our Union" would be in "the greatest interest of every true American," but "consolidation" quickly became—and long persisted as—the rallying cry of those jealous of state prerogatives.[14] "[T]he adversaries of the proposed Constitution," explained James Madison, writing as "Publius" in *The Federalist Papers*, say the convention ought "'to have preserved the *federal* form, which regards the Union as a *Confederacy* of sovereign states; instead of which, they have framed a *national* government, which regards the Union as a *consolidation* of the States.'"[15] The Anti-Federalists opposed ratification of the Constitution in no small part because they believed that the size of a governing body mattered; in a smaller Republic the people were more apt to participate and to have their voices heard. The Anti-Federalists feared that the accumulation of national power would threaten the most vital end of government, the preservation of human liberty.[16] Patrick Henry, Virginia's and perhaps the nation's leading Anti-Federalist, expressed his desire for union in terms that stated these priorities clearly: "The first thing I have at heart is American *liberty*, the second thing is American Union."[17]

Madison insisted the opponents of the Constitution put the cart before the horse when they asked not what powers the national government should have but "exhausted themselves in a secondary inquiry into the possible consequences of the proposed degree of power to the governments of the particular States." Because "the public good, the real welfare of the great body of the people, is the supreme object to be pursued," the proper question was what authority the national government necessarily must possess. Madison sought to reassure his audience that because of the selection process for the President and Congress, "each of the principal branches of the federal government will owe its existence more or less to the favor of the state governments." He went to some length to show that none of the powers granted to the national government "is unnecessary or improper." To the extent that these powers were essential to an effective national government, Madison nonetheless held firm: the authority of the states simply would have to give way. "[A]s far as the sovereignty of the States cannot be reconciled to the happiness of the people, the voice of every good citizen must be, Let the former be sacrificed to the latter."[18]

In "Federalist No. 46," Madison sought to reassure those nervous about the expansion of federal authority. Whether either government would grow in power at the expense of the other, he wrote, "will not depend merely on the comparative ambition or address of the different governments," but on how the people felt about those governments. In their calculations, he explained, the Anti-Federalists simply had forgotten that the "ultimate authority . . . resides in the people." Besides, the states themselves would serve to check the national government. "They would be signals of general alarm." If the federal government overstepped its bounds, Madison argued, the states would come together to address the problem. "Every government would espouse the common cause. A correspondence would be opened. Plans of resistance would be concerted." [19]

SHIFTING LOYALTIES TO NATION AND STATE

"FEDERALISTS TURNED ANTI-FEDERALISTS"

Madison proved right about one thing: the framers' federal structure quickly proved to be an effective way for those who lacked power at the national level—whoever they happened to be—to challenge policies they disliked. The states frequently sounded Madison's alarm, though often it was difficult to disentangle principled constitutional objections to national authority from the immediate desires of a state's inhabitants. As national political power shifted from one party to another, side switching was profound; even ardent states' rights advocates seemed to change their tune when they took the national helm, and those displaced from national power quickly found a new love for state authority. [20] This called into question whether the abstract principle of states' rights had any weight or instead was simply an opportunistic means for expressing dissent. [21]

Little could Madison have imagined, as he wrote "Federalist No. 46," that he and his allies would soon be the first to sound the alarm in just the manner he had recommended. When the controversy between Federalists and Republicans came to a head in the fight over the Alien and Sedition Acts, Madison and Jefferson arranged to have resolutions against the hated laws passed by the Virginia and Kentucky legislatures. Republicans were disappointed (though perhaps not surprised) that the courts had not acted to strike down the acts. The Virginia Resolution, ghostwritten by Madison, called upon "the like dispositions in the other states" to declare that the Alien and Sedition Acts "are unconstitutional; and that the necessary and proper measures will be taken *by each*" for state cooperation "in maintaining unimpaired the authorities, rights, and liberties, reserved to the states respectively, or to the people." [22]

As would so often be the case when a state challenged national policy, the reaction of the other states was significantly less supportive than Madison and Jefferson had hoped. Far from applauding the Virginia and Kentucky Resolutions, some of the (largely Federalist-controlled) state legislatures harshly condemned them. The Delaware House of Representatives, in words gentler than others used, criticized the "very unjustifiable interference with the General Government and constituted authorities of the United States. . . ."[23] A number of the responses made the point that "the State Legislatures are not the proper tribunals to determine the constitutionality of the laws of the general government." Rather, that responsibility rested in "the judicial department" or "in the Supreme Court of the United States, ultimately."[24] Stung by the hostile response of sister states, Madison authored a report defending Virginia's actions.[25] This report was destined to become the Magna Charta for those who subsequently opposed federal authority.[26] In the coming years, the opposition of Virginia and Kentucky (and Madison's defense of it) was referred to as the "spirit" or "principles of '98."

No sooner did the Republicans secure the national government in 1801, however, than Federalists claimed it was their adversaries who now were overstepping national authority. The immediate issue was the Louisiana Purchase, concluded in 1803. Americans, having set out to acquire New Orleans from the French, received a surprise offer from Napoleon that dropped the broader territory into their lap for a mere fifteen million dollars.[27] While most of the country applauded the Louisiana Purchase as a great accomplishment, New England Federalists were apoplectic, asking how Jefferson could square the acquisition with his prior understanding of the limited, specific nature of national powers.[28] Feeding New England's anxiety was concern about how the new southern and western lands would affect the balance of political power in the Union.[29] Jefferson personally favored a constitutional amendment to secure the purchase, but he put scruples aside, worrying that the delay necessary to do so, even assuming he succeeded, would cashier the deal. "[S]trict observance of the written laws is doubtless one of the high duties of a good citizen," Jefferson wrote, "but it is not the highest. The laws of necessity, of self-preservation, of saving our country when in danger, are of higher obligation."[30]

Federalists quickly came to understand the value of invoking state sovereignty against national power. In 1807, with American shipping at the mercy of the conflict between the British and French, Jefferson and Congress imposed an embargo on all American maritime foreign trade.[31] The economic impact of the embargo fell mostly upon the Federalist heartland of New England, where resistance to federal enforcement of the embargo mounted, leading to constitutional objections, claims of nullification, and even threats of secession.[32] Difficulties of enforcement eventually doomed the measure, but not before New Englanders invoked "the principles of '98" in challenging the validity of the laws enforcing the embargo.[33] The Massachusetts legislature referred to one of the enforcement acts as "in many respects, unjust, oppressive and unconstitutional, and not legally binding on the citizens of this state."[34] Connecticut's staunchly Federalist government forbade state officials to assist in enforcement, asserting "the unquestionable right of this State to abstain from any agency in the execution of measures, which are unconstitutional and despotic."[35]

The irony of New England Federalists invoking state sovereignty against national authority did not escape observers. The *Richmond Enquirer* was the chief voice of the Richmond Junto, a group of Virginia's leading Republican citizens and the central political force in the state. In response to the Massachusetts declaration, the *Enquirer* published a long article headlined "THINGS TURNED TOPSY-TURVY" OR *FEDERALISTS TURNED ANTI-FEDERALISTS.* Much of the article was an attempt to distinguish Massachusetts's conduct from that of Virginia in 1798. The *Enquirer* denied that states could simply "evade" federal laws and compel the federal government to "consult the wishes of each state." "If these doctrines go into effect, the chain that binds together these states, will soon be dissolved." Referring specifically to the Supremacy Clause, as well as Section 25 of the Judiciary Act—the provisions adopted by the framers of the Constitution and the First Congress to provide for judicial review of state laws—the *Enquirer* emphasized that the federal judiciary was the supreme interpreter of the Constitution.[36]

During the War of 1812, New England's ever-growing antipathy to the Republican administrations was received so poorly by the rest of the nation that ultimately it spelled the demise of the Federalist Party. New England governors refused to call the state militias to federal aid, and radical Federalists again talked of disunion.[37] "Mr. Madison has declared war, let Mr. Madison carry it on," preached the rector of Boston's Trinity Church. "The Union has long since virtually dissolved: and it is full time that this part of the Disunited States should take care of themselves."[38] Having had enough of embargoes and war, delegates from New England states gathered at the ill-starred Hartford Convention to discuss "means of security and defence . . . not repugnant to their obligations as members of the Union" and to consider "amendments to be affected in the national constitution."[39] The convention embraced a strict secrecy rule, shrouding the precise events in some mystery, but it unquestionably is the case that some of the Hartford delegates favored secession.[40] Just as the convention was concluding, the war came to a close with the signing of the Treaty of Ghent, and General Andrew Jackson had his great victory in the battle of New Orleans. Long afterward the Republicans claimed the Hartford Convention was treasonous.[41] Although it ultimately adopted a relatively moderate course, association with the convention and with the Federalist Party became fatal in national politics.[42]

THE SUPREME COURT AS FEDERAL ARBITER

"They strike at the roots of States-Rights and State Sovereignty"

In the aftermath of the War of 1812, the United States experienced a burst of what Albert Gallatin, who had served as Secretary of the Treasury under both Jefferson and Madison, called the "national feelings" of the Revolution: the people "are more American; they feel and act more like a nation."[43] It was during this period that the Supreme Court began to issue what to this day are acknowledged to be its great nationalizing opinions. Gallatin had hoped that with these national feelings "the permanency of the Union is thereby better secured," but by the 1820s national unity had given way to resurgent states' rights sentiments. The Court continued its nationalistic course, nonetheless, earning it the enmity of those whose loyalties leaned more to state than Union.

The postwar surge of nationalist sentiment led to adoption of what Kentucky senator and longtime Speaker of the House Henry Clay was to call, and champion as, the American System.[44] Madison laid out the three elements of that plan in his annual message to Congress following the war. First, Madison suggested the use of the tariff on imports, which to that point had been primarily a revenue raiser, to protect certain domestic manufacturing industries that had grown up during the war from international competition. Second, Madison indicated that a new Bank of the United States would "merit consideration." The first Bank's charter had lapsed in 1811, but the failure of the state banking system to provide a workable currency during the war had convinced even former opponents like Jefferson and Madison that a national banking institution was necessary.[45] Finally, Madison recommended a system of federally funded internal improvements: "[T]he occasion is a proper one for recalling the attention of Congress to the great importance of establishing throughout our country the roads and canals which can best be executed under the national authority." Besides their inherent utility, Madison lauded the "political effect of these facilities for intercommunication in bringing and binding . . . together the various parts of our extended" country.[46]

In the intervening years—dubbed the Era of Good Feelings because James Monroe (who succeeded Madison) was reelected in 1820 with all but one vote in the electoral college and party passions appeared to have subsided—the Supreme Court handed down decisions that later generations were to deem great for enhancing the authority of the national government.[47] It did so, remarkably, with the bench comprised mainly of judges who were appointed by Jefferson and Madison.[48] For example, in 1816, in *Martin v. Hunter's Lessee*, the Virginia Court of Appeals, led by its chief justice and Marshall's adversary, Spencer Roane, insisted that the Supreme Court lacked jurisdiction to review its decisions. In a strongly worded rebuttal authored by Justice Joseph Story, a Madison appointee, the federal Supreme Court scolded the Virginia court, explaining that Supreme Court review was both intended and essential to assure the uniformity and supremacy of federal law. "The constitution has presumed (whether rightly or wrongly we do not inquire) that state attachments, state prejudices, state jealousies, and state interests, might sometimes obstruct or control, . . . the regular administration of justice."[49] Similarly, in *Gibbons v. Ogden*, an 1824 decision involving Robert Fulton's steamboat monopoly, the Court gave expansive definition to Congress's enumerated legislative powers. The commerce power at issue in the case, Marshall wrote, "like all others vested in Congress, is complete in itself, may be exercised to its utmost extent, and acknowledges no limitations, other than are prescribed in the constitution."[50]

Though the many Marshall Court decisions of this period wove the basic rules that made the United States into a great nation, they often ran ahead of existing sentiments for union and eventually brought great wrath upon the justices. To be sure, some part of the country applauded each of the Court decisions, and *Gibbons* was almost universally admired.[51] John Quincy Adams, Monroe's successor, said Marshall "has done more to establish the Constitution of the United States on a sound construction than any other man living."[52] Unfortunately for the Court, however, it handed down a number of its most controversial decisions just as ardor for Congress's national program was cooling and states' rights feelings were emerging.[53] Writing in 1826, on the fiftieth anniversary of independence, the politician, scholar, and orator Edward Everett distinguished the "family feeling" people held toward the states from their "metaphysical and theoretical" connection to the Union. "Like the illimitable city, where its central point is fixed, [the Union] yet looks raw and new."[54] State attachments felt ever stronger.

Virtually all of the Marshall Court's nationalizing decisions provoked the anger of states' rights advocates, but nothing compared to the outrage triggered by the monumental decision in *McCulloch v. Maryland*, which allowed Congress to exercise broad "implied" powers.[55] Following Madison's recommendation, Congress had chartered a Second Bank of the United States.[56] Although it was nominally a national institution, most of the stock of the Bank was in private hands. The Bank's branches took business from state banks, evoking hostility. Maryland had imposed and sought to collect a tax from the Bank's Baltimore branch; the Bank argued that the Constitution prohibited states from taxing federal institutions. Given the importance of the case, the Court said it would hear from additional counsel and extended oral argument to nine days. When the argument began, Justice Story noted, the courtroom "was full almost to the point of suffocation, and many went away for lack of room."[57]

The central issue in *McCulloch* was whether Congress even had the power to charter the Bank, a question Chief Justice Marshall answered by granting Congress extraordinarily broad leeway. All conceded there was no specific enumerated congressional power in the Constitution to charter such institutions. The question, therefore, was whether or not the charter fell within the catchall grant of all powers "necessary and proper" to effectuate those that were granted. Maryland's lawyers argued for a narrow (and perhaps literal) interpretation of "necessary": because allowing the Bank would go beyond those powers specifically set out in the Constitution, any authority further "implied" by the Necessary and Proper Clause must be strictly limited to just those things without which the enumerated powers would be a nullity. Marshall opted for something far more capacious, stating famously that "[i]n considering this question, we must never forget that it is a *constitution* we are expounding." Given that the Constitution was "intended to endure for ages to come," it must be "adapted to the various *crises* of human affairs." In order to ensure this, Marshall interpreted "necessary and proper" in a sweeping way: "Let the end be legitimate, let it be within the scope of the constitution, and all means which are appropriate, which are plainly adapted to the end, which are not prohibited, but consist with the letter and spirit of the constitution, are constitutional."[58]

As generous as *McCulloch* was when it came to defining the powers of the national government, it was strict in limiting the powers of the states. The Constitution contained some explicit limitations on state powers, but the *McCulloch* Court found implicit limits as well. On the question of whether states could tax the Bank, even the Bank's lawyers conceded that "[t]here is no express provision for the case," and taxation plainly was a power Congress and the states held concurrently.[59] Still, the Court concluded, "the power to tax involves the power to destroy," and thus Maryland could not be tolerated to impose its tax on an instrumentality of the national government.[60]

The reaction to *McCulloch* was a harbinger of what was to come over the next decade. *The National Register* correctly predicted that *McCulloch* "will not fail to throw the friends of the state banks into a fever."[61] In part the Court was the victim of rotten luck as to timing.[62] The Panic of 1819 was believed by many to have been sparked by actions of the Bank of the United States.[63] Philadelphia's *General Advertiser* deemed Marshall's opinion "a most lamentable sophistry."[64] Newspaper coverage was virulently negative, especially in the South and West.[65]

But the truly consequential impact of *McCulloch* was that it fully raised the states' rights bear from its slumber. Many who did not have any particular issue with the Bank nonetheless bridled at the broad claims of national authority in Marshall's opinion. "It is not on account of the bank of the United States we speak thus," wrote Hezekiah Niles, whose *Niles' Register* was one of the country's most popular and respected periodicals; "it is but a drop in the bucket compared with the *principles* established by the decision."[66] "A deadly blow has been struck at the *sovereignty of the states,*" he explained, "and from a quarter so removed from the people as to be hardly accessible to public opinion."[67] The Court was subjected to an extended barrage of criticism for granting Congress such extensive powers at the expense of the states. The Frankfort, Kentucky, *Argus of Western America*, a leading regional voice, opined that the principles of *McCulloch* "must raise an alarm throughout our widely-extended empire. They strike at the roots of States-Rights and State Sovereignty."[68] Spencer Roane arranged for his cousin and fellow member of the Richmond Junto Thomas Ritchie, editor of the *Richmond Enquirer*, to publish pseudonymous essays by "Amphictyon" and "Hampden" (the latter being Roane himself), savagely attacking the reasoning and conclusion of *McCulloch*.[69] Even while accepting the Bank as an institution, these authors condemned the "danger arising from the implied powers," which could "sweep off every vestige of power from the state governments."[70] "That man must be a deplorable idiot," wrote Roane as Hampden, "who does not see that there is no earthly difference between an *unlimited* grant of power, and a grant limited to its terms, but accompanied with *unlimited* means of carrying it into execution."[71]

The Court—or its Chief Justice in any event—was not nearly as "removed" from public opinion as Hezekiah Niles believed. Marshall was greatly alarmed when he got word of the forthcoming *Enquirer* pieces. He wrote Justice Story shortly after the decision to say: "Our opinion in the Bank case has roused the sleeping spirit of Virginia, if indeed it ever sleeps."[72] The problem, Marshall explained to another colleague, Justice Bushrod Washington, was that "not a word will be said on the other side."[73] So concerned was

Marshall to leave the attacks unanswered that he published two sets of essays in response, under the pseudonyms "Friend of the Union" and "Friend of the Constitution."[74]

From the time of *McCulloch* forward the Court was under almost constant fire.[75] Following yet another decision emphasizing the Supreme Court's power over state courts—*Cohens v. Virginia*—Spencer Roane again went into action, this time under the pseudonym "Algernon Sydney."[76] Responding to a letter of Roane's following the decision in *Cohens*, Madison commented that "[t]he Gordian Knot of the Constitution seems to lie in the problem of collision between the federal & State powers, especially as eventually exercised by their respective Tribunals."[77] Roane's fellow Virginian John Taylor published three memorable, albeit rambling, tracts against the Court.[78] In the introduction to one—*Construction Construed*—the editor of the *Richmond Enquirer*, Thomas Ritchie, captured the prevailing sentiment: "We have been lately rushing rapidly towards the gulph of consolidation."[79] Just looking at the *Gibbons* case resting on the Court's docket had made Justice Story shudder. "We have already had our full share of the public irritations and have been obliged to decide constitutional questions, which have encountered much opposition—I had hoped for a little repose; but I perceive it is not to be allowed us."[80] He could hardly know.

THE STATES' RESPONSE

"[T]o refuse obedience to the decisions and mandates of the Supreme Court"

What made this period truly distinct in Supreme Court history was not that the Court was under attack—that proved common enough—but that in the face of disagreement, the states regularly denied the authority of the Court to decide and simply determined not to comply.[81] When popular with the state citizenry (and it often was), official defiance could prove difficult for the Court to overcome, unless the national executive was prepared to use force (and it seldom was). This reality proved the truth of Hamilton's observation in "Federalist No. 78" that the judiciary was "the least dangerous branch." Marshall, writing as the "Friend of the Constitution" in response to Virginia's attack on *McCulloch*, brought the poignancy of experience home to Hamilton's prediction: "[T]he judicial department, being without power, without patronage, without the legitimate means of ingratiating itself with the people, forms this weakest part."[82] Marshall's intellectual adversary John Taylor put it more crisply: "They could not make the militia march."[83]

From its first invalidation of a state law—an 1810 Georgia decision—the Court poked its constitutional stick in the eyes of New Jersey, New York, Virginia, Ohio, and Kentucky, among others.[84] "The infringement of the rights of the states by the judiciary," accused the *Washington Gazette* in the early 1820s, "is more likely to effect a consolidation of the Union, than any other excuse or causes which exist."[85] Criticizing the Court on the floor of Congress in 1826, Senator Martin Van Buren of New York (who became President a decade later) said: "[T]here are few States in the Union upon whose acts the seal of condemnation has not from time to time been placed by the Supreme Court."[86]

In response to the Supreme Court decisions, the states made defiance a fine art. In *New Jersey v. Wilson*, the Supreme Court required the state of New Jersey to put back in place a tax exemption it had withdrawn from certain Indian lands.[87] Years later it emerged that New Jersey had simply continued to collect the tax.[88] Similarly, all the attention in the *Martin* litigation was spent on the high-level dispute over whether the decisions of the Virginia Court of Appeals could be reviewed by the Supreme Court of the United States. But after the Supreme Court asserted its authority, the decision was ignored anyway.[89]

Pennsylvania's resistance to federal judicial authority, which surfaced in 1809 in the *United States v. Peters* litigation, highlighted the importance of having the national executive behind the Supreme Court if the Court's orders were to be enforced. During the height of the embargo controversy in New England, Pennsylvania found itself in a fight over proceeds from the sale of a prize vessel, a ship captured on the open seas during the American Revolution. Lengthy litigation ensued in the Pennsylvania courts, while the funds from the ship's sale remained in Pennsylvania's possession.[90] In 1802, suit was brought in the federal District Court of Pennsylvania to recover proceeds from the ship captured more than twenty years earlier. The federal court ordered Pennsylvania to turn over funds it held.[91] The Pennsylvania legislature commanded state officials to ignore the federal court order.[92] When the case finally made its way to the Supreme Court, John Marshall (his eye clearly on events in New England) chastised Pennsylvania severely: "If the Legislatures of the several States may, at will, annul the judgments of the Courts of the United States . . . the Nation is deprived of the means of enforcing its laws by the instrumentality of its own tribunals."[93] Pennsylvania, in a froth over state sovereignty, was unrepentant. "[A]s guardians of the state rights," the Pennsylvania legislature resolved, "they cannot permit an infringement of those rights, by an unconstitutional exercise of power in the United States' courts."[94]

As was the case in every federal district, the Pennsylvania federal court had a marshal to enforce its orders, but the marshal's enforcement power easily could prove toothless in the face of state-sanctioned defiance. The marshal was authorized to "execute throughout the district, all lawful precepts directed to him."[95] When the Pennsylvania federal court ordered the marshal to serve the necessary papers, the governor called out a brigade of the militia to oppose him. The federal marshal in Pennsylvania then proved to have more pluck than anyone expected and, using his authority to "command all necessary assistance," promptly swore out a warrant for a two-thousand-member posse comitatus to assist him.[96] "The Rebellion in Pennsylvania is assuming a more dangerous and threatening aspect," was the lead story in the *New-York Commercial Advertiser*, one of numerous national papers following details of the confrontation closely.[97]

The matter was resolved only when President James Madison indicated his intention to use federal force to bring Pennsylvania to heel. Viewing the escalating confrontation, the Pennsylvania legislature asked its United States senators to seek a constitutional amendment "that an impartial tribunal may be established to determine disputes between the general and state governments."[98] It also authorized the governor to work something out with the President of the United States. The governor wrote Madison asking him to "discriminate between opposition to the Constitution and law of the United States [i.e., what was going on in New England] and that of resisting the decree of a Judge . . . conceived, on a usurpation of power." Madison was unremitting in response: "[T]he Executive is not only unauthorized to prevent the execution of a decree sanctioned by the Supreme Court of the United States, but is especially enjoined, by statute, to carry into effect any such decree, where opposition may be made to it."[99] Pennsylvania capitulated.[100]

In sharp contrast with the resolution of the *Peters* affair, the controversy in Kentucky over the Supreme Court's decision in *Green v. Biddle* demonstrated how ineffective the Court could prove without the chief executive's support. Unfortunately for the justices, such support rarely was forthcoming in the 1820s. *Green v. Biddle* involved an interstate compact between Virginia and Kentucky, adopted when Virginia ceded land to Kentucky upon Kentucky's achieving statehood. The compact provided that the title of Virginia landholders would remain as secure under Kentucky law as it had been under Virginia's. In the intervening years, Kentucky residents had often squatted on land owned by Virginia citizens. Matters were not helped by often complicated and clouded land titles. Kentucky, in an effort to aid its residents, had passed "occupying claimant" laws, providing that before the holder of a land title could oust a squatter, he was required to pay the occupying claimant for improvements made to the land. The occupying claimant laws were challenged as a violation of the Constitution's prohibition on laws "Impairing the Obligation of Contracts." In *Green*, the Court invalidated the occupying claimant provisions, holding that the interstate compact was indeed "a contract" impaired by Kentucky law.[101]

The decision in *Green v. Biddle* was met in Kentucky with widespread dismay. "Kentucky has felt a shock more tremendous than the dreadful earthquake, in the destruction of her occupying claimant laws," cried the *Argus of Western America*.[102] Times were hard. Not only were occupying claimants faced with eviction from lands they had improved, but a substantial portion of Kentucky's population was being pressed to repay significant debts that it owed. To ameliorate the financial crisis, the Kentucky legislature enacted a series of debtor relief laws in 1821. Kentucky courts, however, following the lead of the Supreme Court, invalidated the laws as violations of the Constitution's Contract Clause. A Relief Party sprang up to oppose these court decisions and took control of the Kentucky legislature and statehouse.[103] Angry with state courts that adhered to federal decisions and invalidated relief measures, yet unable to muster a two-thirds vote to impeach the judges, the angry "Relief" legislature simply abolished the Kentucky Court of Appeals and replaced it with another. (Legal chaos broke out as the existing "Old Court" denied the validity of the measure abolishing it and continued to hold court.)[104] In 1825, Relief governor Joseph Desha devoted the better part of his annual message to "differences in our judiciary and the encroachments of the federal tribunals."[105] Kentucky's state legislature asked Governor Desha to assist in determining "the mode deemed most advisable . . . to refuse obedience to the decisions and mandates of the Supreme Court of the United States . . . and whether, in the opinion of the Executive, it may be advisable to call forth the physical power of the State to resist the execution of the decisions of the Court."[106]

The Kentucky courts could apparently hear the voice of the people and continued to enforce Kentucky's occupying claimant laws despite the Supreme Court's decision to the contrary in *Green v. Biddle*.[107] They justified this defiance on the ground that the Supreme Court technically had decided *Green* with only three of seven justices sitting.[108] Thus, stated the Kentucky Court of Appeals, the *Green* decision "cannot be considered as having settled any constitutional principle." That court nonetheless was unwilling "to admit the binding force of that decision . . . if it had been the unanimous opinion of all the judges composing the Supreme court."[109] Defiance remained the state of affairs in Kentucky until, in 1831, the Supreme Court approved a state law imposing a statute of limitations on any land claims by

Virginia landholders.[110] (The Court also changed its practice to avoid deciding constitutional cases by less than a majority of the full bench.)[111]

Ohio's defiance of the Supreme Court was, if possible, more raucous yet. A month before *McCulloch* was decided, Ohio had passed a law imposing a $50,000 tax on each branch of the Bank of the United States. One provision, referred to colloquially as the Crow-Bar Law, ordered the state auditor to go into each branch and seize assets needed to satisfy the tax if it had not been paid. Six months after the *McCulloch* decision, in September 1819, the auditor's agents forcibly seized from the bank's vault some $120,000, which state officials then refused to turn over despite a federal court injunction to do so.[112] *The National Register* expressed the horror of much of the national press: "If the example spreads, anarchy will follow, and add greatly to embarrassments which are already too prevalent."[113] Yet Ohio remained defiant. Ohioans argued that *McCulloch* was an "agreed" case and thus not binding upon them.[114] "The doctrine of unlimited sovereignty, set up in the Supreme Court of the United States in the case of *Maryland and McCulloch*, can now be fairly tested," argued an Ohio paper, "not by deciding a case made, but by enforcing those doctrines in an actual controversy for the money taken."[115] Unless the Bank of the United States withdrew from the state, one correspondent to the *Niles' Register* explained, "this state will proceed to collect the tax next year, in like manner, the case of McCulloch vs. the state of Maryland, to the contrary notwithstanding."[116] More than a year later the Ohio legislature adopted, by wide margins, resolutions sticking to its guns. The conflict came to an end only after Ohio had had an opportunity to take the issue of the tax on the Bank of the United States to the Supreme Court itself; by the time it lost its case there more than four years had passed, emotions had subsided, and compliance followed.[117]

The frequent claim of state officials during this period was that the Supreme Court simply lacked authority over them. The committee report to the Pennsylvania legislature in the *Peters* matter stated that "no provision is made in the Constitution for determining disputes between the General and State Governments."[118] The Virginia General Assembly said the same prior to the decision in *Cohens*: "[T]he Supreme Court of the United States does not possess appellete [*sic*] jurisdiction in any case decided by a State court."[119] Unwilling to concede anything even by appearing as a party before the Supreme Court, Virginia hired counsel who were instructed simply to argue that the Court lacked jurisdiction and then to depart.[120]

The states also repeatedly sought fundamental change from Congress regarding the authority of the Court. The first such proposal was made in 1821, when Kentucky suggested an amendment to the Constitution granting the Senate appellate jurisdiction over cases involving states or state laws.[121] Then, resentful of the close margin on the Court in *Green v. Biddle*, Kentucky instructed its representatives to seek a law requiring that "a concurrence of at least *two-thirds* of all the judges shall be necessary" for a state law to be struck down.[122] None of these measures was adopted, but they occasioned extended and heated congressional debate.[123]

The most dramatic state-organized congressional attack on the Court came in 1831, when the Judiciary Committee of the House of Representatives actually reported out a bill to strip the Court of its Section 25 jurisdiction altogether. Section 25 was the provision of the Judiciary Act of 1789 conferring jurisdiction on the Supreme Court to review cases coming from the highest state courts. There had been prior attempts to repeal Section 25, but surrounding events made the 1831 attempt appear more plausible.[124] The committee stated that "the Constitution does not confer power on the Federal Judiciary, over the judicial departments of the States, by any express grant" and that the First Congress, which concluded otherwise, was mistaken.[125] Marshall, after ruling against Missouri in one case, wrote Justice Story that "it requires no prophet to predict that the 25th Section is to be repealed."[126] Story and his "wisest friends" were gloomy too: "If the twenty-fifth Section is repealed, the Constitution is practically gone. . . ."[127] Following events, *The National Intelligencer* opined that without Section 25 the Constitution "will have become a dead letter."[128]

THE CHEROKEE CONTROVERSY

"[O]rders received from the supreme court . . . will be disregarded"

The 1831 challenge to Section 25 came amid the most flagrant and public defiance the Court faced during this period, from the State of Georgia in the Cherokee controversy. Georgia's recalcitrance captivated the country and set the stage for the grand conflict that followed. It raised the question whether, as the *Niles' Register* put it, there is "power in the Constitution to preserve itself."[129]

Georgia sought the removal of the Native American tribes to western lands. As early as 1802, the United States had committed to obtaining voluntary removal, but progress had been slow. Some tribes had withdrawn, but the Cherokee had opted to stay where they were. Thirst for expansion and discovery of gold on Cherokee lands made the state of Georgia impatient to see the Cherokee depart. In 1830 Congress passed the Indian Removal Act, explicitly authorizing the President to trade tribal land for new territory west of the Mississippi. As that accomplished too little too slowly for Georgia, the state enacted a number of measures denying Cherokee sovereignty over their lands and imposing Georgia law on them.[130] "Now, that the measures of the general government have resulted in failure," insisted the impatient editors of *The Georgia Journal*, published in the state capital city, "Georgia must act on her own responsibility."[131]

The controversy over removal of the Cherokee played out through three Supreme Court decisions, handed down between the end of 1830 and the spring of 1832.[132] The question lurking behind all the cases was whether Georgia legislation denying Cherokee sovereignty over their lands was consistent with the obligations of prior treaties between the tribe and the United States.[133] To press their case, the Cherokee had retained high-powered counsel, among them William Wirt, former Attorney General in the administrations of James Monroe and John Quincy Adams.[134]

Georgia made its defiant posture clear early in the litigation. Wirt wrote Georgia's Governor George R. Gilmer suggesting the parties resolve their differences though an agreed litigation. "In the supreme court of the United States, we shall find a tribunal as impartial and as enlightened as can be expected on this earth."[135] Gilmer's response (published along with Wirt's letter in the *Niles' Register*) was contemptuous. "You say that the supreme court of the United States is a high, impartial, and enlightened tribunal. Why such commendation?" Even the suggestion of going to court, Gilmer wrote, was "exceedingly disrespectful to the government of the state."[136]

As it happened, matters ended up in the Supreme Court before Wirt could even file his case. When a Cherokee named Corn Tassel was accused of killing someone on Cherokee lands, Georgia asserted its criminal jurisdiction over the lands, trying and convicting Tassel for murder. Tassel took an appeal to the Supreme Court under Section 25. Marshall issued a writ of error on December 12, 1830.[137]

Georgia's widely noted response to the Supreme Court's taking jurisdiction over the matter was stark defiance. Governor Gilmer forwarded to the legislature the Court's writ "purporting to be signed by the chief justice of the United States." He informed the legislature that "orders received from the supreme court . . . will be disregarded; and any attempt to enforce such orders will be resisted with whatever force the laws have placed at my command."[138] The legislature promptly authorized the governor to "disregard any and every mandate and process" from the Supreme Court and resolved that Georgia "will never so far compromise her sovereignty . . . to become a party."[139] A correspondent to *The Georgia Journal* noted the "unanimity manifested in the Legislature," that even those who had shown "their over-weaning attachment to the authority of the General Government" had gone along and that party spirit was "*almost* lost sight of in the effort to sustain the honor and dignity of the State."[140] The result: Corn Tassel was executed on December 24.[141] "Notwithstanding the great outcry about a Writ of Error in the Tassels [*sic*] case, and the promise of mighty things to be accomplished by 'the most distinguished Bench in the world,'" scoffed the *Augusta Constitutionalist*, "the culprit perished on the scaffold."[142] Editorialized Washington, D.C.'s *United States' Telegraph*: "[T]he position in which the supreme court is placed by the proceedings of Georgia, demonstrate the absurdity of the doctrine . . . that that court is clothed with supreme and absolute control over the states."[143]

Wirt's own legal case on behalf of the Cherokee proved futile, but events surrounding it demonstrated the extent to which the Chief Justice was playing to public opinion himself. Wirt filed suit directly in the Supreme Court under a jurisdictional grant that permits suits between a state of the United States and a "foreign state" to commence there. A heavily fractured bench ruled against Wirt.[144] Marshall wrote the opinion denying jurisdiction, one in which he nonetheless expressed considerable concern for the Cherokee. "If courts were permitted to indulge their sympathies," he began, "a case better calculated to excite them can scarcely be imagined."[145] Justices Joseph Story and Smith Thompson dissented (they would have heard the case then and there) but prepared no opinions. This was not uncommon; early in his tenure Marshall had put a stop to the prior practice of each judge's writing a seriatim, or separate opinion. Troubled in this case that the weight of the written opinions disfavored the Cherokee, however, Marshall suggested that Story and Thompson memorialize the grounds for their dissent after the decision was handed down.[146] "[N]either Judge T. nor myself contemplated delivering a dissenting opinion, until the Chief Justice suggested to us the propriety of it, and his own desire that we should do it," Story wrote to the Court's Reporter, Richard Peters.[147] Then Peters took the highly unusual step of publishing all the opinions as a pamphlet.[148]

Just as the Cherokee prepared to file suit elsewhere, the state of Georgia suddenly offered them a third crack at the Supreme Court. Georgia had passed a law requiring anyone living among the Cherokee to obtain a license. Two missionaries, Samuel Worcester and Elizur Butler, refused to do so, not wanting to concede Georgia's authority over the Cherokee lands. When imprisoned, the two appealed, again challenging Georgia's anti-Cherokee laws.[149]

In *Worcester v. Georgia*, the Supreme Court ruled for the missionaries in an opinion highly favorable to the Cherokee claims, but by now the question of the moment was whether the state would comply with any mandate of the Court.[150] As it had in the prior cases, the state declined to show up to argue its case. Its legislature adopted a resolution stating: "[T]he State of Georgia will not compromise her dignity as a sovereign State . . . as to appear in, answer to, or in any way become a party to any proceedings before the Supreme Court."[151] Well aware that compliance was going to be an issue, Wirt confronted the issue directly in his argument to the Court: "Shall we be asked (the question has been asked elsewhere) how this court will enforce its injunction, in case it shall be awarded?" Wirt insisted there "will be time enough to meet that question when it shall arise. . . . In a land of laws, the presumption is that the decisions of the courts will be respected."[152] After the decision, Justice Story wrote his friend Professor George Ticknor, of Harvard, "The Court has done its duty. Let the nation now do theirs."[153]

Georgia's reaction to the *Worcester* decision held the Court up to scorn. The new governor, Wilson Lumpkin, addressed the legislature, expressing his "great satisfaction to find that our whole people, as with the voice of one man, have manifested a calm, but firm and determined resolution to sustain the authorities and sovereignty of their state, against this unjust and unconstitutional encroachment of the federal judiciary."[154] Referring to the missionaries, the *Macon Advertiser* said, "They have been placed where they deserved to be," and cawed that "not all the eloquence of a Wirt, or [his cocounsel] a Sergeant, nor the decision or power of the Supreme Court can take them from it unless the State chooses to give them up."[155] The "feeling in Georgia, as shewn in the remarks in the newspapers, &c," wrote Hezekiah Niles, is "to go on—*let the consequences be what they may.* . . ."[156]

THE LACK OF EXECUTIVE SUPPORT

"The decision of the supreme court has fell still born"

The eyes of the nation shifted to the President of the United States, Andrew Jackson. Wirt had told the Court in the *Worcester* case that "it is part of the sworn duty of the President of the United States to 'take care that the laws be faithfully executed.'" "[I]s this Court to anticipate that the President will not do his duty"?[157] More rested on the answer to this question than the fate of the missionaries or even the Cherokee Nation. Hartford's *Connecticut Mirror*, one of many national papers fixated on the case, asked sharply: "What is the highest court in America worth, if its decisions may be contemned—disputed—resisted—and its authorized, delegated power set to naught?"[158]

In fact, there was nothing immediate for Jackson to enforce. The country was gearing up for the 1832 presidential election, and the Cherokee controversy played heavily in it. Jackson's opponents made much of the fact that he was allowing the missionaries to remain in prison and the Supreme Court's mandate to go unheeded.[159] "If he refuses to exercise the powers vested in him to execute the laws," insisted Jackson's antagonist, *The New-York Daily Advertiser*, somewhat hysterically, "either he must be impeached . . . or the Union of the States will be dissolved."[160] Under the law governing at the time, however, Jackson's responsibilities would not even kick in until the Georgia court refused to release the missionaries, the Supreme Court ordered the marshal to execute its order directly, and the marshal proved unable to do this with the force available to him. The Militia Act authorized the President to "call forth" the militias of any state "whenever the laws of the United States shall be opposed, or the execution thereof obstructed . . . by combinations too powerful to be suppressed by the ordinary course of judicial proceedings, or by the powers vested in the marshals. . . ."[161] An attempt was made to hurry the news of the Georgia court's refusal back to the Supreme Court, but the justices (who surely understood the politics and timing of the situation as well as anyone else) already had recessed and would not take the bench again until the 1833 term began—after the election.[162] "And so," sighed the *Niles' Register*, explaining the rules regarding enforcement to any who would listen (most apparently did not), "it appears, the matter must rest until January next."[163]

Still, if the judiciary was ultimately going to have to rely upon Jackson to resolve the Cherokee controversy, there was good reason to be concerned. The recalcitrance of Georgia might humiliate the Court and denigrate its authority, yet it was unclear whether Jackson would do anything about it. Story wrote Ticknor that Georgia, "full of anger and violence," would probably "resist the execution of our judgment" and "I do not believe the President will interfere, unless public opinion among the religious of the Eastern and Western and Middle States, should be brought to bear strong upon him. The rumor is, that he had told the Georgians he will do nothing."[164]

The Court's decision in *Worcester* was at odds with Jackson's own Indian policy, which from the outset had been Indian removal. Removal had been an issue in Jackson's 1828 election; he called for it in his First Annual Message; and he had pushed the Removal Act through a divided Congress in 1830 with brute force.[165] After Corn Tassel had been executed, John Quincy Adams called the Constitution "prostrate in the State of Georgia, complaining that "the Executive of the United States is in league with" the state.[166] History apocryphally reports Jackson's saying in response to *Worcester*, "John

Marshall made his decision, now let him enforce it."[167] Although it is unclear if the words are actually his, following the decision, Jackson, while still pressing for removal, observed to General John Coffee that "[t]he decision of the supreme court has fell still born, and . . . it cannot coerce Georgia to yield to its mandate."[168] Newspapers were rife with reports, true or not, that Jackson would not support the decision.[169] As one North Carolina member of Congress observed, "Gen. Jackson could by a nod of the head or a crook of the finger induce Georgia to submit to the law. It is by the promise or belief of his countenance and support that Georgia is stimulated to her disorderly and rebellious conduct."[170]

The twin poles of Jackson's political ideology—democracy and states' rights—also boded poorly for his supporting the Court against Georgia. Jackson sat at the head of a burgeoning popular democratic movement, as had Jefferson, and historically this sort of movement had shown little patience for the judiciary. Following the voice of the people was Jackson's creed.[171] "I know of no tribunal to which a public man in this country, in a case of doubt and difficulty, can appeal with greater advantage or more propriety than the judgment of the people," Jackson explained in his Second Annual Message.[172] The years prior to Jackson's first election in 1828 had seen a shift to universal (white male) suffrage, as well as intense political organization.[173] What remained of the Federalist spirit bemoaned giving the vote to "men with no property to assess and no character to lose."[174] Eventually Jackson's followers created an extensive political machine highly attuned to public opinion.[175] Martin Van Buren, who helped engineer Jackson's victory and became his Vice President (as well as heir apparent) in the second term, made an art of this. Van Buren's loose political organization, the Albany Regency, mastered use of the press, mass meetings, and city machines.[176] On inauguration day, one Jackson aide wrote: "It is a proud day for the people. General Jackson is *their own* president." (Justice Story, less enamored of the new President, feared that "[t]he reign of King 'Mob' seems triumphant.")[177]

Jackson's stout support of states' rights only compounded the problem. Although it is easy to see how support for majority will and states' rights might come into conflict—they were about to shortly—Jackson and his supporters saw the two as going hand in hand.[178] Any tension was smoothed by assigning most tasks of governance to the states. In his First Inaugural, Jackson said he "hope[d] to be animated by a proper respect for those sovereign members of our Union, taking care not to confound the powers they have reserved to themselves with those they have granted to the Confederacy."[179] (Take note of his last word.)

Jackson's conduct regarding the rechartering of the Bank of the United States led many observers to doubt he would lift a finger in support of the Supreme Court in the Cherokee litigation. An even greater issue in the election of 1832 than the Cherokee controversy was the brouhaha over rechartering the Bank of the United States. In the years following 1819, the Bank had lost favor with many, especially among Jackson's followers. Still, the country was split on the issue. The Bank's charter was not up until 1836, and Jackson hoped to delay action till his second term. Kentucky's senator and erstwhile presidential candidate Henry Clay, looking for an election issue, made a point of seeing to it that legislation rechartering the Bank was sent to Jackson prior to the 1832 contest.[180] Jackson vetoed the bill, arguing the Bank was both inexpedient and unconstitutional.[181] Conceding that Congress twice had chartered the Bank, Jackson said: "[M]ere precedent is a dangerous source of authority, and should not be regarded as deciding questions of constitutional power except where the acquiescence of the people and the States can be considered as well settled."[182]

Jackson's veto of the Bank stated a philosophy that, read literally, would justify his refusal to uphold Supreme Court orders. Earlier that year Jackson had told Nicholas Biddle, the president of the Bank, that he had "read the opinion of John Marshall [in *McCulloch v. Maryland*] . . . and could not agree with him."[183] In his veto message, Jackson acknowledged that the Supreme Court had upheld the constitutionality of the Bank in *McCulloch*, but he demurred nonetheless.[184] "If the opinion of the Supreme Court covered the whole ground of this act, it ought not to control the coordinate authorities of this Government. The Congress, the Executive, and the Court must each for itself be guided by its own opinion of the Constitution."[185] Martin Van Buren claimed Jackson shared the views expressed by Senator Hugh Lawson White of Tennessee in the fierce Senate debate over Jackson's veto. "If either of these co-ordinate departments is . . . called upon to perform an official act, and conscientiously believe the performance of that act will be a violation of the constitution, they are not bound to perform it, but, on the contrary, are as much at liberty to decline acting, as if no such decision had been made."[186] If these were Jackson's views about the effect of Supreme Court decisions, then they would seem to countenance not enforcing the edict in the *Worcester* case, even in the face of a Supreme Court order to do so.

Both Jackson's supporters and opponents read Jackson's Bank Veto Message on the rechartering as a clear indication of his willingness to part ways with the Court over the Cherokee.[187] One pro-Jackson newspaper urged ignoring the Court on the Cherokee issue in precisely the same terms that

Jackson was to adopt in his Bank veto. "He is a *co-ordinate* and INDEPEN-
DENT branch of the government, bound by his oath to support the constitution *as it is,* and not as it shall be *interpreted* by the federal judges."[188] But
Jackson's opponents likewise tied the fate of the Cherokee to the Bank. Pittsburgh's *National Gazette* parodied the Veto Message:

> There is a constitution of the US. But every man has a right to judge of it
> provisions and no one is bound to obey or enforce it if he believes it to be
> unconstitutional. Ministers of the Gospel are under the protection of the
> laws. But when falsely imprisoned the President is not bound to enforce a
> decision declaring them so—if it will in his opinion injure his re-election to
> office.[189]

The thought on all minds was that if Jackson believed he should exercise
judgment independent of the Court when deciding whether to use his veto
power with regard to the Bank, he might do the same with regard to his obligation to "take care that the laws are faithfully executed" in the Cherokee
litigation.[190]

THE NULLIFICATION CRISIS—AND ITS LOGIC

*"[W]hose prerogative is it to decide on the constitutionality
or unconstitutionality of the laws?"*

Jackson found his freedom of action in the Cherokee controversy constricted
when, in the interim, the country confronted a yet graver threat to the stability of the Union. Faced with a federal tariff law it considered intolerable
and unconstitutional, South Carolina claimed the right to "interpose" its authority and "nullify" the federal law. At the heart of South Carolina's claimed
right to nullify was a theory of the Union that gave to states, and explicitly
denied to the Supreme Court, the right to judge the constitutionality of certain congressional laws. Vice President John Calhoun was the intellectual
force behind his native South Carolina's theory of nullification. In January
1831, he wrote to his longtime political collaborator and friend Virgil Maxcy,
"The question is in truth between the people & the Supreme Court. We contend, that the great conservative principle of our system is in the people of the
States, as parties to the Constitutional compact, and our opponents that it
is in the Supreme Court."[191] This question, brewing since 1798, was given full
vent in 1830 in one of Congress's most important constitutional discussions

of all time, the Webster-Hayne debate. At the heart of that debate, Daniel Webster proclaimed, rested the "great question": *"[W]hose prerogative is it to decide on the constitutionality or unconstitutionality of the laws?"* [192]

By the mid-1820s, the southern states had come to view the federal tariff law as oppressive, favoring northern manufacturing interests at their expense. Hoping to defeat the tariff in 1828, southerners loaded the bill down with increased import taxes they thought would be unpalatable. [193] "Its enemies spiced it with whatsoever they thought would render it distasteful," Daniel Webster recounted once the great debate began; "its friends took it, drugged as it was." [194] The gambit failed, and Congress passed the "Tariff of Abominations," under which South Carolina in particular believed it suffered greatly. [195]

The attempt to defeat the 1828 tariff a failure, South Carolina published its Exposition and Protest. The document was drafted secretly by John Calhoun. [196] Calhoun served as Vice President under both John Quincy Adams and Andrew Jackson. He was an intense and deeply intellectual man whose life's blood was politics. Although he was a longtime nationalist with presidential ambitions, the fight over the tariff compelled the relatively moderate Calhoun to ally himself firmly with his native South Carolinians, becoming a partisan of states' rights and the leading theorist of the doctrine of nullification. [197]

The Exposition and Protest implored Congress to scale back the tariff and threatened nullification if it did not. South Carolina's argument was that the tariff was unconstitutional. Congress had the power to tax, the protest acknowledged, but only for the purpose of raising revenue. The power was being "abused by being converted into an instrument for rearing up the industry of one section of the country on the ruins of another." In such a case, South Carolina claimed, it had a right to "interpose her veto." [198] South Carolina traced its logic of nullification straight back to the "good old Republican doctrine of '98, the doctrine of the celebrated 'Virginia Resolutions.'" [199]

In 1830 the question of nullification erupted on the Senate floor. At that time, South Carolina hardly stood alone in its aggressive assertions of state sovereignty. [200] The debate began innocuously enough, as the Senate discussed a bill on land policy. The issue was whether to continue to survey western lands for sale to settlers. Arguably there already was sufficient land available on the market, though westerners saw opposition to further surveying as a ploy to retain laborers for eastern manufacturers. [201] Early in the debate, Missouri's Senator Thomas Hart Benton took the opportunity to reach out to the South on behalf of the West. Robert Hayne of South Carolina eagerly seized the invitation, offering support for the West on land policy, in exchange for western support on the tariff.[202] Sensing what was happening, Daniel Webster rose to his feet and in a brilliant maneuver shifted the entire course of the debate. He ignored Benton completely and turned all his legendary rhetorical skills on Hayne.[203] (Hayne complained of Webster's "losing sight entirely" of the "gentleman from Missouri" to "pour[] out all the vials of his mighty wrath upon my devoted head.")[204] So began the Webster-Hayne debate, which played out in the Senate between January and May 1830 and involved sixty-five speeches given by almost half the Senate's members. Thousands flocked to the galleries to listen; some hundred thousand copies of Webster's second reply to Hayne had circulated by the end of that year. Public interest underscored the vitality of these issues to the Union.[205]

At its most simple, the Webster-Hayne debate was about whether one's allegiances ran primarily to the states or to the national government. "I am one of those who believe that the very life of our system is the independence of the States," declared Hayne, raising his banner, "and that there is no evil more to be deprecated than the consolidation of this Government."[206] Webster thundered back: "Consolidation!—that perpetual cry, both of terror and delusion—consolidation! . . . Do they mean, or can they mean, any thing more than that the Union of the States will be strengthened, by whatever continues or furnishes inducements to the people of the States to hold together?"[207]

Fundamental to the debate was the nature of the American Union. Hayne advanced the view, common among states' rights advocates, that the Union was a "compact" among the various states.[208] Webster disagreed: the Union was formed not by the states but by the *people* of the United States. "It is, sir, the People's Constitution, the People's Government; made for the People; made by the People; and answerable to the People. The People of the United States have declared that this Constitution shall be the Supreme Law."[209]

This was no abstract disagreement; on its back rested the legitimacy of nullification. As Webster saw it, the states (and the people of any state) had but two choices: they could (and should) comply with federal law, or if they believed this law unconstitutional and felt mortally aggrieved, they could undertake "the unalienable right of man to resist oppression; that is to say, upon the ground of revolution." But, he insisted, "the right of a State to annul a law of Congress, cannot be maintained."[210] For Hayne and those in agreement with him, however, there was a third legitimate way. Precisely because they were founding parties to the compact, the states might simply withdraw their consent to a particular national law in the face of "a deliberate, palpable, and dangerous exercise of other powers not granted by the said compact."[211] While Webster would call such dissent "rebellion," said Hayne, "[a]ccording to my opinion it would be just, legal, and *constitutional resistance*."[212]

Central to the logic of nullification was that no part of the national government—including, or especially, the Supreme Court—could arbitrate questions regarding the allocation of power between the states and the federal government. "[T]he doctrine that the Federal Government is the exclusive judge of the extent as well as the limitations of its powers," Hayne argued, "seems to be utterly subversive of the sovereignty and independence of the States."[213] The denial of federal authority plainly included the Supreme Court. Hayne quoted Madison in his report on the Virginia Resolutions: "[I]t follows of necessity . . . that there can be no tribunal above their authority to decide in the last resort, whether the compact made by them be violated." Rather, Hayne concluded, it fell to the states to "decide, in the last resort, such questions as may be of sufficient magnitude to require their interposition."[214]

Ironically, given both the framers' design and modern understandings, those who denied the power of the Supreme Court over the states nonetheless typically conceded the Court had the authority to review the acts of the other federal branches. "The Supreme Court," said Hayne, "may nullify an act of Congress, by declaring it to be unconstitutional." This was a vital part of the system of checks and balances. "The House of Representatives checks the Senate, the Senate checks the House, the Executive checks both, the Judiciary checks the whole."[215] The question of the moment was about state power vis-à-vis Congress.[216]

If the Supreme Court did not have final authority over the states, how were disputes to be resolved? South Carolina realized it needed some answer, and it had devised an intricate one. As Hayne explained, "I would resort to a peaceful remedy—the interposition of the State 'to arrest the progress of the evil,' until such times as 'a Convention, (assembled at the call of Congress or two-thirds of the States,) shall decide to which they mean to give an authority claimed by two of their organs.'"[217] In other words, if a state disagreed with Congress over the meaning of the Constitution, Congress had to seek a constitutional amendment.[218] If this seemed to turn the Constitution on its head, to Hayne it made perfect sense because "the constitution does not permit a minority to submit to the people a proposition for an amendment of the constitution." "A *written Constitution* was resorted to in this country, as a great experiment, for the purpose of ascertaining how far the rights of a minority could be secured against the encroachments of majorities. . . ."[219]

For nationalists like Webster, however, to deny the authority of the Supreme Court over the states was inadmissible. Its role as arbiter of state power was confirmed, Webster argued, by the Supremacy Clause and the clause granting "the Judicial power" to "all cases arising under the Constitution and Laws of the United States. These two provisions, sir, cover the whole ground. They are, in truth, the key-stone of the arch. With these, it is a Constitution; without them, it is a Confederacy."[220] "It comes at last then to this," spelled out Webster's compatriot Delaware senator John Clayton: "we have no other direct resource . . . to save us from the horrors of anarchy, than the Supreme Court of the United States."[221]

BACKING UNION—AND THE COURT

"[T]he proper remedy is a recourse to the judiciary"

The Supreme Court was due to take the bench in early 1833 and to confront Georgia's continued intransigence in the *Worcester* case. Now, however, the question Jackson faced was defiance not only of the Court but of the Union itself. Disappointed that Jackson's first term did not spell relief from the tariff, in late 1832 South Carolina ratcheted up the stakes and actually nullified the federal tariff law. In response, the country's leadership moved quickly to support not only federal authority generally but that of the Supreme Court in particular.

Jackson understood the election of 1832 as a referendum on his policies—removal of the Cherokee, veto of the Bank bill, and but a slight adjustment of the tariff—and perhaps it was.[222] He won by a landslide. In the same month as he triumphed, however, South Carolina acted. In November 1832, South Carolina's duly convened convention of the people issued its Ordinance of Nullification. That ordinance declared the federal tariff "null, void, and no law"—and therefore not binding on state officials. It prohibited the appeal of any case challenging the ordinance to the Supreme Court. And it stated that any application of force or enactment of an enforcement act by Congress was "inconsistent with the longer continuance of South Carolina in the Union."[223] The gauntlet was down.

Jackson's response to nullification could hardly have been in doubt; he was, if nothing else, a Union man, having fought for it all his life.[224] "I had supposed that everyone acquainted with me knew that I was opposed to the nulifying [sic] doctrine," he wrote as early as 1830.[225] On April 13, 1830, Jackson attended a Jefferson Day dinner at which numerous toasts were being given suggesting support for South Carolina. When it was Jackson's turn, he uttered his famous riposte: "Our *Federal* Union; *It must be preserved*." (Calhoun followed Jackson, and replied: "The Union; Next to our liberty, the most dear; may we all remember, that it can only be preserved by respecting the rights of the States.")[226]

Nonetheless, there was a real tension between resolving the Nullification Crisis and blinking at Georgia's continued defiance of the Supreme Court. "[N]o person but a Jackson or a Van Buren man can see any essential difference between the cases of Georgia and South Carolina," editorialized the *United States' Telegraph*, at this point firmly in the Calhoun camp.[227] South Carolina agreed wholeheartedly. In response to Jackson's Anti-Nullification Proclamation, South Carolina said it was all "the more extraordinary, that he had silently, and as it is supposed, with entire approbation, witnessed our sister state of Georgia avow, act upon, and carry into effect, even to the taking of life, principles identical with those now denounced by him in South Carolina."[228]

Attempts to separate the Georgia and South Carolina cases only underscored the issue of whether the Supreme Court decisions would be treated as the law of the land and enforced as such.[229] "It cannot be believed," said Georgia's Governor Lumpkin, ". . . that any honest man of common sense will be at a loss to draw the proper distinction between the destructive heresies and acts of South Carolina . . . and those acts of Georgia."[230] That was all he said, though; he seemed incapable of drawing the distinction himself. A Savannah paper helped out, identifying the obvious distinction precisely. "The nullification of South Carolina declares acts of Congress unconstitutional which operate upon the whole UNION; the constituted authorities of Georgia declare a JUDGMENT OF THE SUPREME COURT an *usurpation*. . . ."[231] The heart of the issue was what a Supreme Court decision was worth.[232]

Perhaps that is why, as South Carolina threatened its defiant course, important voices came to be heard supporting the Court's role as federal umpire. Kentucky, its dispute over *Green v. Biddle* now behind it, immediately came to the Court's defense against South Carolina.[233] Questions of disputed power "have all been settled by the judicial power of the United States, and the decisions of that tribunal have been sustained by the intelligence and patriotism of the people."[234] Ohio too was quick to dismiss South Carolina, leading *The Cincinnati Gazette* to observe wryly that when Ohio "was enacting nullification and the Supreme Court was restraining her within her constitutional orbit," South Carolina and Georgia supported the Supreme Court, but "when South Carolina and Georgia wage the war, Ohio and Kentucky breast it."[235]

The bill to repeal Section 25 quickly came to naught. The simple fact that it was reported out of committee was noteworthy, and it certainly gave the justices a scare. The committee's majority was overrepresented by southerners, though. The vote against the repeal, in early 1831, was overwhelming.[236]

James Madison, now deeply into retirement, was compelled to clarify, if not recant, his prior views on the Supreme Court's authority.[237] As he observed the defiant attitudes of the states to federal authority throughout the foregoing years, Madison had been forced to rethink the position expressed in his Report on the Virginia Resolution. He already had told Jefferson of his present position in private correspondence.[238] As the prospect of nullification rose, Madison felt the need to go public. In a letter written for public consumption to Edward Everett, then the editor of *The North American Review*, Madison expressed his unequivocal disapproval of nullification, as well as his support for the binding effect of Supreme Court decisions on the states. "Those who have denied or doubted the supremacy of the judicial power of the U.S. & denounce at the same time nullifying power in a State, seem not to have sufficiently adverted to the utter inefficiency of a supremacy in a law of the land, without a supremacy in the exposition & execution of the law." Madison stressed that in accepting the Court's role as ultimate umpire, he did not necessarily agree with specific decisions: "[T]he power has not always been rightly exercised." "Still it would seem that, with but few exceptions, the course of the judiciary has been hitherto sustained by the predominant sense of the nation."[239]

As expected, Jackson came down squarely behind the authority of the Union. He issued a forceful proclamation condemning nullification. "The laws of the United States must be executed." The proclamation entreated South Carolina to reconsider, while making it clear that if it did not, he would fulfill his duty: the Constitution forms "a *government*, not a league," and whether it formed by compact or otherwise, no state could secede "at pleasure."[240]

Jackson also came out for the judiciary. This was essential inasmuch as South Carolina's nullification ordinances tried to shut off all access to the federal judiciary. "There are two appeals from an unconstitutional act passed by Congress—" Jackson responded, "one to the judiciary, the other to the people and the States." Adopting the precise reasoning of Daniel Webster (as had Madison in his letter to Everett), Jackson pointed to the Supremacy Clause and the jurisdiction of the federal courts to hear constitutional questions as the means of resolving federal-state disputes.[241]

To avoid any embarrassment to the administration in its strong Union stand, the matter of the Cherokee missionaries was quickly settled out of court. Jackson's supporters, apparently with his approval, appealed to Georgia to release the missionaries. "From the unpleasant agitations which, at the present time are convulsing . . . another of the independent states of the Union, we feel the deepest interest that all danger of conflict between the authorities of Georgia and any of the authorities of the General Government should be put to rest."[242] Governor Lumpkin, ready to be rid of the matter, and no doubt aware of the difficulties he now might face if he did not, invited the missionaries' wives to dinner and indicated that he would welcome applications for pardons; soon after, he signed a bill that repealed the law under which the missionaries were being held.[243] The removal issue apparently settled in the election, and with the authority of the Court so obviously at stake, the Missionary Board reversed its position on taking the case back up to the Court "in view of the changes in circumstances."[244] On January 8, 1833, the missionaries wrote Lumpkin saying they had withdrawn their appeal; Lumpkin ordered their release on January 14, 1833.[245]

With timing that seemed hardly coincidental, Jackson sent his Force Bill to Congress two days after the Cherokee matter had been resolved. The Force Bill requested specific congressional authorization to use the military in South Carolina. As such, it set off a firestorm. While all, including sister southern states, disapproved of South Carolina's nullification, large numbers throughout the country were equally uncomfortable with Jackson's strong threats of force.[246]

Passage of the Force Bill proved yet another victory for the Supreme Court. In transmitting the measure to Congress, Jackson clearly identified the judiciary as the proper site for resolving disputes over federal authority. In his message, Jackson criticized South Carolina for failing to exhaust "all constitutional remedies" before taking its drastic step. "[T]he proper remedy is a recourse to the judiciary."[247] The bill itself strengthened the judicial enforcement mechanisms along lines that had been recommended by William Wirt during the Cherokee controversy.[248] Although the debate revealed that the Court continued to have its detractors, a substantial proportion of Congress fell in with the Court. Section 25 of the Judiciary Act was praised as the "sheet anchor of the Constitution," and Representative Philip Doddridge of Virginia argued that a motion to repeal Section 25 is "equivalent to a motion to dissolve the Union."[249] When Webster concluded his rousing speech on behalf of Union and Court, the *Niles' Register* reported that "there was a spontaneous burst of applause from the galleries."[250]

The entire matter was finally resolved when in a compromise engineered by Clay, the tariff was lowered. The Force Bill then passed by telling margins. Though many southerners boycotted the vote, it passed by an overwhelming margin of 32–1 in the Senate. (For point of comparison, the tariff compromise passed in the Senate 29–16.) The vote was 149–48 in the House.[251] A popular novelist of the era remarked: "It is amusing to witness the unanimity of public opinion at this moment—to hear the old sober standard anti-Jackson men, who tho't the republic was lost if he were reelected say 'well: I really believe it is all for the best that Jackson is president.'"[252]

Jackson's turnaround on the states' rights doctrine and the Supreme Court was noted by all.[253] Many struggled to reconcile his well-known states' rights views with those expressed in the Anti-Nullification Proclamation.[254] One person described the proclamation as "just such a paper as Alexander Hamilton would have written and Thomas Jefferson condemned."[255] Nothing signified Jackson's change of heart more than the surprise Justice Story experienced at his own warm treatment by the President. Writing after a dinner at the White House on January 27, 1833, he said: "Notwithstanding I am 'the most dangerous man in America,' the President specially invited me to drink a glass of wine with him." Of course, the admiration was mutual. Story continued: "But what is more remarkable, since his last Proclamation and Message, the Chief Justice and myself have become his warmest supporters, and shall continue so just as long as he maintains the principles contained in them."[256]

Jackson's Farewell Address also contained a clear statement of support for the Court. Reflecting back on the crisis, he said that "in order to maintain the Union unimpaired it is absolutely necessary that the laws passed by the constituted authorities should be faithfully executed in every part of the country." Recognizing that "[u]nconstitutional or oppressive laws may no doubt be passed by Congress," "if they are within the reach of judicial authority, the remedy is easy and peaceful." "But until the law shall be declared void by the courts or repealed by Congress," no resistance is justified.[257]

It was particularly easy for Jackson to laud the Court as he left office, for by then he had remade it. All told, Jackson had six appointments to the Court, including the new Chief Justice, Roger Taney. Taney had served in Jackson's cabinet (as Attorney General and Secretary of the Treasury). He had played an instrumental and controversial role in withdrawing the government's funds from the Bank of the United States, provoking a financial crisis. When Jackson nominated him for an associate justice position, it created a furor, and opponents stalled the nomination. As fortune had it, John Marshall died shortly thereafter, and Jackson nominated Taney for the center chair instead (from which he was to preside over the *Dred Scott* case years later). In the interim the composition of the Senate had changed, and Taney was confirmed, along with Philip Pendleton Barbour, one of Virginia's lawyers in its conflicts with the Court, to fill the other chair.[258] Not long after filling these two vacancies, Jackson had Congress pass a bill creating two new federal circuit courts and two additional Supreme Court seats to go with them. Jackson filled one of the vacancies as he left office, leaving the other to his successor, Martin Van Buren.[259]

When historians tally the winners and losers of the nullification fight, the Supreme Court regularly ends up in the winner's column.[260] At the least, the Court avoided the embarrassment of further conflict with the state of Georgia, a conflict it could not help losing.[261] Much more was gained, however, as Jackson and other national leaders rallied behind the Court as the crisis was brought to a close. The framers had intended the judiciary as the means to keep the states in check, and the Nullification Crisis brought the country behind the Court in just that way.

4

CONTROL

"Have we not sought to mold and conform it . . . to our own will?"

During the autumn of 1858, Abraham Lincoln and Stephen Douglas made their way around the state of Illinois, engaging in a series of debates that brought listeners flocking to open fields and fair-grounds by the thousands. Their contest attracted the attention of the en-tire nation. Douglas, a Democrat who had represented Illinois in the United States Senate since 1847, was fending off a challenge from the man who was to defeat him for the presidency of the United States only two years later. Douglas explained to his audiences that "[p]rior to 1854, this country was divided into two great political parties, known as the Whig and Demo-cratic parties." While those parties "differed in regard to a Bank, and in re-gard to a Tariff," and the like, both parties nonetheless were "national and patriotic in their principles—both advocating principles which were univer-sal in their application." Since then, however, "a great revolution had taken place." The Whig Party had disintegrated, replaced by Lincoln's Republi-cans. And now the parties were "divided by a geographical line." [1]

The sectional issue that divided Douglas's Democrats from Lincoln's new Republican Party was slavery, of course. As Douglas put it, "the whole North, so far as it can be assembled under the Abolition or Republican banner," was "in hostility to the Southern States, Southern people, and Southern institu-tions." [2] And while Douglas was correct that only recently had the conflict torn the parties asunder, a lasting solution to the problem of slavery had evaded politicians for decades.

The year before the Lincoln-Douglas debates, in the case of *Dred Scott v. Sandford*, the Supreme Court tried its hand at resolving the slavery question.[3] By affording constitutional protection to slavery, the justices essentially disabled the political branches from any further attempt at compromise short of amending the Constitution. "We are now told . . . [t]he highest authority has spoken," pronounced the great African-American abolitionist Frederick Douglass in cadenced tones, his contempt barely concealed. "The voice of the Supreme Court has gone out over the troubled waves of the National Conscience, saying peace, be still." Yet, Douglass observed presciently, the Supreme Court's resolution was no more likely to stick than any that had preceded it: "[T]he more the question has been settled, the more it has needed settling."[4]

On several occasions between *Dred Scott* and the aftermath of the Civil War, the Supreme Court looked poised to take actions that might threaten the ability of national officials to save and restore the Union. With the stakes so high, it was hard to imagine the justices would be permitted by those in power to do so. *The New York Herald*, a newspaper that had supported *Dred Scott* and opposed Lincoln in 1860 and that enjoyed the largest circulation in the nation—in part because its pages were devoted to a vivid nationalism that resonated during the shared travail of the Civil War—put it this way:

> Shall the opinions of a bare majority of these nine old superannuated pettifoggers of the Supreme Court, left to the country as the legacy of the old defunct Southern slaveholding oligarchy, prevail, or shall these old marplots make way for the will of the sovereign people and the national constitution as expounded by Washington and Hamilton, and as established by a million of Union bayonets in a four years' civil war?[5]

The problem, though, was precisely what to do about the Court? Although the imperatives of war and of Reconstruction ensured that the justices would not be allowed to disable national decision makers, it was increasingly impermissible to engage in (or apparently even to suggest) the sort of naked defiance that had met Supreme Court rulings earlier in the century. The various responses of *Dred Scott*'s opponents, who accepted its authority yet sought ways to sidestep the decision or have the justices overturn it, signaled this change in attitudes toward Supreme Court rulings. But if defiance was moving off the table, what was to replace it?

Because the Supreme Court could not be ignored, it had to be controlled. It became essential to ensure that disfavored decisions were simply not rendered in the first place or, if rendered, were quickly reversed. Jurisdiction stripping and Court packing were two techniques frequently mentioned. Referring to the justices' anticipated ruling on the constitutionality of military rule during Reconstruction, the moderate Republican John Bingham (whom we met in the Introduction) said: "[I]f gentlemen are at all apprehensive of any wrongful intervention of the Supreme Court in this behalf, sweep away at once their appellate jurisdiction in all cases, and leave the tribunal without even color or appearance of authority for their wrongful intervention."[6] Concerned about a related ruling, the highly popular journal *Harper's Weekly* suggested that if "the Supreme Court undertakes to declare that the people . . . can do nothing to secure [their] Government from similar assaults . . . let the Supreme Court be swamped by a thorough reorganization and increased number of Judges."[7]

The era of Civil War and Reconstruction was transitional for the practice of judicial review. Public figures evidenced greater respect for judicial rulings than they had during prior periods of political pressure; in many regards the contrast with the defiant rhetoric and actions of the 1820s was telling. Yet throughout this period the justices often took actions that invited attacks and imperiled their autonomy. When necessity demanded it, inventive measures were employed to bring the Supreme Court to heel, and the justices invariably acquiesced in the face of Congress's greater power. Paradoxically, while respect for the rule of law was on the rise, the Court departed the era with its reputation in tatters.

THE SLAVERY ISSUE

"I am jealous of the power of the South"

At the Constitutional Convention, Madison had observed "the great division of interests among the states" over slavery, predicting that it, "more than anything else, would strain the bonds of union over time."[8] "I consider the Tariff, but as the occasion, rather than the real cause of the present unhappy state of things," Calhoun wrote privately during the Nullification Crisis, expressing what all recognized about the ongoing states' rights struggle of the mid-nineteenth century. The "real cause" was the "peculiar domestick institutions" of the South.[9] Abolitionist William Lloyd Garrison responded to the Cherokee controversy by changing the masthead of *The Liberator* to show a slave auction occurring while the Indian treaties were trampled underfoot.[10]

Without ever mentioning slavery by name, the Constitution recognized the practice and provided assurances to the South. Representation and direct taxation were to be determined according to the "whole Number of free Persons" and "three fifths of all other Persons." [11] Congress was deprived of the power to halt the "Migration or Importation of such Persons as any of the States now existing shall think proper to admit"—until 1808.[12] States were required to "deliver up" those "held to Service or Labour" and claimed by citizens of another state.[13] "[T]he thing is hid away, in the constitution," Abraham Lincoln was to say in his run against Douglas for Illinois's Senate seat, "just as an afflicted man hides away a wen or a cancer, which he dares not cut out at once, lest he bleed to death; with the promise, nevertheless, that the cutting may begin at the end of a given time." [14]

Violent disagreement broke out over slavery when the territory of Missouri sought admission to the Union as a slave state in 1818, and was quelled only by the fashioning of the Missouri Compromise of 1820. Maine was admitted as a free state, paired with Missouri to preserve sectional political balance. A boundary line was drawn across the nation at 36°30' of latitude. Slavery would be permitted below the line and prohibited above it.[15] The foremost goal of most national politicians at the time was to keep the lid on the pot. Debating Hayne in 1830, Daniel Webster made evident his dislike of the South's "peculiar institution." Still, "I do not complain. . . . [i]t is the original bargain—the compact—let it stand: let the advantage of it be fully enjoyed." "The Union," proclaimed Webster, "is too full of benefit to be hazarded in propositions for changing its original basis." [16]

The Missouri Compromise held until the 1840s, when it was threatened by the likely acquisition of new territory as a result of the Mexican-American War. Hostilities between the two countries broke out several months after the annexation and then admission of Texas into the Union in late 1845. Many Whigs opposed the war, seeing it as an effort to advance slavery. In 1846, Democratic representative David Wilmot proposed in the House that "neither slavery nor involuntary servitude shall ever exist in any part" of the territory acquired from Mexico.[17] Wilmot's Proviso, which was offered often but never passed, indicated the complexities of the slavery debate.[18] Some of Wilmot's northern supporters were moved by abhorrence of the practice, to be sure, but for many, the stronger impulses were economic and political.[19] Wilmot highlighted economic worries over "Free Labor" competing with slavery: "[T]he negro race already occupy enough of this fair continent; let us keep what remains for ourselves, and our children . . . for the free white laborer." [20] Sectional balance, however, was the primary political concern. "I am jealous," Wilmot explained at a later date, expressing the views of many, "of the *power* of the South." [21]

The Compromise of 1850 looked to contain sectional tensions but harbored the seeds of greater strife. The deal was conceived by Kentucky's Senator Henry Clay and maneuvered through Congress by the young and tactically adept Stephen Douglas. California would be admitted as free, and the remainder of the Mexico territories would come in without restrictions. However, the compromise also contained a strict provision enforcing the Constitution's guarantee that "fugitive" slaves would be returned to their owners.[22] Several high-profile "rescues" of runaway slaves followed, raising sympathies for abolition.[23]

Then the Kansas-Nebraska Act of 1854 shattered the Missouri Compromise and plunged the country into turmoil over the issue of slavery. The act, which was the brainchild of Douglas, declared the Missouri Compromise "inoperative and void." The territories of Kansas and Nebraska were organized along the new principle of "popular sovereignty"—what Lincoln derisively called "*squatter sovereignty*"—which left it to the people of the territories to make their own decisions regarding "domestic institutions."[24] "Whatever may be thought or said of it in other respects," Martin Van Buren wrote in his disquisition on political parties, the Kansas-Nebraska Act "excit[ed] sectional animosities to a far more perilous height than they had ever reached before."[25]

Passage of the Kansas-Nebraska Act effectively remade party lines, just as Stephen Douglas told the debate audiences.[26] Many northern Democrats deserted their party, believing passage of the Kansas-Nebraska Act a betrayal in that it allowed slavery above the familiar compromise line.[27] As a result, the northern Democrats went from having ninety-one seats in Congress to twenty-five after the midterm election of 1854.[28] The Whig Party also self-destructed; by 1860 it had disappeared completely.[29] The antislavery Republican Party was born, pledging to battle "for the first principles of republican government" and against "schemes of aristocracy the most revolting and oppressive with which the earth was ever cursed, or man debased."[30]

By 1856, the country was on fire over the slavery issue. The Kansas-Nebraska Act had failed to answer a critical question: whether the settlers of each territory would choose to be slave or free at statehood, or before. It thus created a footrace to control the decision. A terrific fight broke out in "Bleeding Kansas" over whether the territory would be admitted free or slave.[31] With party lines split apart, Democrat James Buchanan captured the White House in 1856 with less than a majority of the popular vote.[32] Massachusetts senator Charles Sumner gave a heated speech on "The Crime Against Kansas," in which he heaped opprobrium on (among others) South Carolina and its senator Andrew Butler. Butler's cousin, South Carolina congressman Preston Brooks, responded by caning Sumner badly on the Senate floor.[33] Even more appalling to the North than the caning itself was the warm reception it received in the South, a metaphor in their view for the violence required to maintain slavery.[34] Matters were at a boiling point.

THE *DRED SCOTT* DECISION

"[T]he tribunal to decide such questions"

With the country so deeply divided over slavery in the territories, politicians of various stripes had begun to look to the Supreme Court to resolve the issue.[35] The justices apparently believed they could succeed where others had failed. No fan of *Dred Scott*, Martin Van Buren conceded that "sincerely believing the safety of the Union endangered by continued agitation," the Court "hoped to arrest it."[36] "[T]here had become such a difference of opinion," wrote Justice James Wayne in his opinion, "that the peace and harmony of the country" required "settlement . . . by judicial decision."[37]

Willingness to turn the matter over to the judiciary can be understood in part by the relatively high place the Supreme Court had come to hold in the American mind.[38] Whigs had opposed Roger Taney's appointment as Chief Justice in 1836. Andrew Jackson's Attorney General had assisted in drafting the message accompanying Jackson's veto of the Bank bill; as Jackson's Acting Secretary of the Treasury he had dealt a severe blow to the Whigs' beloved Bank by withdrawing federal deposits. Whigs also were concerned about early Taney Court decisions that suggested a sharp change of direction from the Court under Marshall. It quickly became clear, however, that the Court under Taney was steering a relatively moderate course.[39] This brought Whigs and Democrats behind the Court: Whigs because they had long been supporters of the judiciary and were happily reassured; Democrats because the Court was now comprised of their appointees.[40] William Duer, one of many pro-Court treatise writers of the time, was engaging in only slight hyperbole when he said, "[W]herever the Supreme federal tribunal has pronounced its solemn decision, its authority must be deemed conclusive; because that Court, and that Court alone, possesses ultimate and final jurisdiction upon all points of controversy arising under the Constitution. . . ."[41]

In truth, though, politicians were desperate for anyone to save them the morass of the slavery issue, and the Court seemed as likely a prospect as any. The 1850 Compromise included a provision essentially referring the slavery question to the Court, leading Ohio senator Thomas Corwin to comment that the nation had enacted a lawsuit, not a law.[42] Though some, particularly antislavery northerners, feared resolution of the slavery question by the justices, many others seemed content to invite the Supreme Court in.[43] Clay himself, a perennial Whig candidate for President, proclaimed that the compromise left the question of slavery to the "only competent authority that can definitely settle it forever."[44] During the debate over the Kansas-Nebraska Act, Lewis Cass, a Michigan senator who had been the Democratic Party presidential nominee in 1848, acknowledged that no statutory language could resolve the dispute "until it is finally settled by the proper tribunal."[45] Even Lincoln said in Galena, Illinois, that "[t]he Supreme Court of the United States is the tribunal to decide such questions, and we will submit to its decisions."[46]

The lawsuit the nation ultimately got began in St. Louis, Missouri, in 1846. Dred Scott, a slave, sued his owner for his freedom and that of his family. He argued he had gained his liberty as a result of having been taken by his owner, a military officer, to the free state of Illinois, as well as to the northern territory free by virtue of the Missouri Compromise. He claimed he was entitled to that liberty despite voluntarily returning to Missouri. The Missouri Supreme Court ruled against Scott. Dred Scott would have won under prior decisions of that court because slaves were deemed free under Missouri law when they left the state for a free state or territory. Feeling pressed by national antislavery sentiments, however, the Missouri Supreme Court did a sudden volte-face, saying Missouri "is willing to assume her full responsibility for the existence of slavery within her limits."[47]

Dred Scott refiled his suit in federal court, in the case that was to make its way up to the Supreme Court.[48] He alleged the federal court had jurisdiction over the case under the Constitution's "diversity" provision, which applies to cases between parties who are citizens of different states. Dred Scott's then owner, who was from New York, denied such jurisdiction existed: "Dred Scott, is not a citizen of the State of Missouri . . . because he is a negro of African descent."[49] In other words, as the child of slaves the law denied him state citizenship for federal purposes. The district court ruled against Scott's owner on the jurisdictional question, but for him on the merits, holding itself bound by the Missouri Supreme Court ruling that Dred Scott was a slave under Missouri law.[50]

Although the justices initially intended to dispose of the case on narrow grounds, they were driven by forces internal and external to render the decision that subsequently caused so much controversy.[51] Incoming President James Buchanan wrote his friend Justice John Catron to inquire whether the Court would decide the case by the time of his inauguration in March 1857.

Buchanan had been elected as a peacemaker and undoubtedly hoped the Court could solve the slavery issue for him.[52] Catron, a Tennessean and supporter of slavery, responded to Buchanan on February 10 to say the Court would not resolve the question of Congress's power over slavery in the territories.[53] But Catron then wrote back to tell the President-elect that the justices had switched direction. He even suggested language for Buchanan to use in his inauguration address and enlisted Buchanan's help in persuading fellow justice Robert Grier, a Democrat from Pennsylvania, to join the five southern justices in holding that Congress lacked power over slavery in the territories. (Buchanan did as asked.)[54] At his inauguration, fully informed of the Court's intentions, Buchanan was able to instruct the country that "[this] is a judicial question which legitimately belongs to the Supreme Court of the United States before whom it is now pending, and will, it is understood, be speedily and finally settled."[55]

Two days after Buchanan's inauguration, the Court announced the decision that left contemporaries and posterity perplexed as to its precise holding. From the standpoint of legal craftsmanship, *Dred Scott* was a mess.[56] Each justice wrote his own opinion. An author, describing the decision in *The North American Review*, facetiously explained, "There is no majority in favor of anything; but a majority against everything suggested; unless it should be claimed that Judge Grier is in favor of something."[57]

There was, however, no mistaking the Court's thunderbolt ruling: the Missouri Compromise was unconstitutional.[58] Conventional understanding has it that the Court decided two things. The first was that "a negro, whose ancestors were imported into this country, and sold as slaves" could not be a citizen of the United States. Thus, Dred Scott was not entitled to invoke the jurisdiction of the federal courts. This holding undoubtedly would have engendered some opposition but may have been met with equanimity by most Americans.[59] Hardly so the conclusion about the Missouri Compromise: although the Kansas-Nebraska Act already had spelled an end to its operation, more was at stake here. According to the Court, slaves were property, and Congress was powerless to do anything about it.[60]

The Court's decision set off a firestorm of criticism, wounding the Court as it has not been since.[61] "If epithets and denunciation could sink a judicial body," wrote the *New-York Daily Tribune*, "the Supreme Court of the United States would never be heard of again."[62] A full two years after the decision was rendered, Senator John P. Hale finished a discussion of the Court saying, "I hope I may be excused if I have not denounced them sufficiently for the enormity of their decision; I will make it up on some other occasion."[63]

Long after, upon Taney's death, Senator Charles Sumner opposed a routine proposal to have a commemorative bust of him made, saying, "If a man has done evil during life he must not be complimented in marble." [64]

THE RESPONSE TO *DRED SCOTT*

"[W]e propose to have that decision reversed"

Despite the uproar over *Dred Scott*, the gradual rise of judicial authority was evident in the nation's reaction to the decision. It is no surprise that in the face of the country's greatest judicial calamity ever, strong things were said. Taken in full, though, the public's reaction to *Dred Scott* reflects the evolution in the nation's commitment to judicial review. In sharp contrast with the out-and-out defiance of the Court in the 1820s and the confrontational rhetoric that often met its decisions, the response to *Dred Scott* was largely comprised of a series of evasions and legalisms. Critics of the decision attempted to minimize its consequence without attacking the general authority of the Supreme Court to decide constitutional questions. The very nature of these arguments served only to underscore the growth of judicial supremacy, the notion that the justices' decisions bound not only those before the Court but all other actors in government as well.

Those who favored judicial resolution of the slavery question, and who could tolerate this one, insisted on adherence to the Court's decision. No surprise the South felt this way. "A prize, for which the athletes of the nation have often wrestled in the halls of Congress," crowed the *Richmond Enquirer*, "has been awarded at last, by the proper umpire." *The New York Journal of Commerce*, which, like many northern business publications, was sympathetic to the South and slavery, was even clearer: "It is now decided on authority which admits of no appeal or question, and which few will presume to dispute." [65]

But even some of those who detested the Court's decision recognized its weight. Declaiming the "wickedness" of the outcome, New York's vehemently antislavery *Independent* (edited by the abolitionist Henry Ward Beecher) regretted "the interpretation forced by a grave judicial court . . . almost invested, according to the doctrines of many, with the attributes of Jehovah himself." "What ought we to do? Shall we rebel?" asked Boston's *Zion's Herald and Wesleyan Journal*. "We answer, No. . . . Shall we repudiate the Court? If so, we might as well have none, which would be a greater evil." [66]

The nature of the Republican response was complicated by long-standing political and ideological commitments. Republicans were in some sense successors to the Whigs and before them the Federalists, all of whom had too long supported the rule of law to make a quick flip against judicial authority.[67] "If the doctrine of estoppel could be applied to politians [*sic*]," Martin Van Buren observed wryly, "it would certainly not be difficult to show that the Federal party and its successors are very clearly estopped from objecting to the action of the Supreme Court of which we have been speaking."[68]

Most of the arguments responding to *Dred Scott* amounted to claims that this particular decision—for one reason or another—lacked legal authority. The primary, and most plausibly legitimate of these, was the "dicta" argument.[69] Though most people could live with *Dred Scott's* citizenship holding, what was intolerable was the ruling that Congress had no power to resolve the slavery question in the territories.[70] The frequent response was that "every thing" subsequently said and done by the Supreme Court after the jurisdictional ruling "was extrajudicial—*obiter dicta* decisions, which, not affecting the merits of the case, are of no authority."[71] By this logic, the Court's ruling about Congress's power to contain slavery lacked any legal force. The widely respected *New York Evening Post* explained to readers that dicta "must be regarded as extra-judicial and as having no more authority than the conversations of the judges held in the street."[72] Several state legislatures passed resolutions making just this point.[73] Exhibiting the tension created by growing notions of judicial supremacy, Senator William Pitt Fessenden of Maine (a moderate Republican who was to chair the Joint Committee on Reconstruction after the war) acknowledged that "I am bound to render obedience to the Supreme Court of the United States" but quickly qualified his point: "[W]hen they undertake to settle questions not before them, I tell them those questions are for me as well as for them . . . they are men like myself and others. . . ."[74]

To similar effect, critics argued that the Court simply should not have ruled on a question that was "political" rather than "legal."[75] The "political question" doctrine had its roots in the Marshall and Taney Courts' struggle to separate political decisions from legal ones in the public mind.[76] The legal-political line played in popular rhetoric as well. Debating Webster, Senator Hayne had insisted that "questions of sovereignty are not the proper subjects of judicial investigation."[77] Now Republican opponents of the Court's decision enlisted the line to their own use. Hannibal Hamlin, Maine's other senator, who left the Democratic Party over the Kansas-Nebraska Act and was Lincoln's running mate in 1860, insisted, "It was a political question purely," while *The National Intelligencer* (a leading Whig paper) regretted the Court had been called upon to "pronounce upon questions involved in political controversy."[78] Capturing both the "dicta" and "political question" points concisely, former Democratic President Van Buren criticized the Court for resolving "a great political question by an extrajudicial decision." [79]

The third response was to seek to undermine the decision's legitimacy in the public mind by impugning the motives of the justices who rendered it. This was an inevitable reaction to a Supreme Court bench overpopulated with southern justices.[80] The *New-York Daily Tribune*, virulently antislavery and with roughly forty-five thousand subscribers, condemned the Court as "scandalously sectional, grossly partial, a mockery of the Constitution, a serf of the slave power, and a disgrace to the country." [81] "It is certainly a little curious," the *Tribune* observed, "that every measure of legislation which either directly or indirectly seeks to retard the spread of Slavery, is at once discovered by certain people to be unconstitutional." [82] Even Van Buren attributed the result to "the supreme bench . . . doubtless more or less under the pressure of an all-absorbing popular influence at the South, to borrow a leaf from the book of our political opponents." [83]

Dred Scott's opponents, especially Lincoln, argued at length that the decision was the result of a broad conspiracy to install slavery throughout the country. Though the nation long had been treated to claims of a conspiracy of the "slave power," the conspiracy argument was all the rage after *Dred Scott*, fueled by what participants observed at Buchanan's inauguration. Buchanan had said when taking office that he would "cheerfully submit" to the Supreme Court's judgment. The public did not know that Justice Catron had tipped Buchanan off, but they did see a whispered conversation between the Chief Justice and Buchanan on the inauguration stand. While there is nothing unusual about the Chief Justice and the President's speaking to each other at such a moment, members of the public were certain that Taney was informing Buchanan what to say just before he said it—evidence of an even more widespread collaboration.[84] That led the *Chicago Tribune* to conclude, "[T]here has been for long years a conspiracy against Freedom in this Republic, and that certain members of the Supreme Court were engaged in it, we do not doubt." [85] Lincoln made much of the conspiracy theory in his debates with Douglas, including an extended metaphor implicating Taney, Buchanan, Franklin Pierce, and Stephen Douglas:

> [W]hen we see a lot of framed timbers, different portions of which we know have been gotten out at different times and places, and by different workmen—Stephen, Franklin, Roger, and James, for instance—and when we see these timbers joined together . . . or if a single piece be lacking, we see the place in the frame exactly fitted and prepared yet to bring such piece in—in such a case we feel it impossible not to believe that Stephen

and Franklin, and Roger and James, all understood one another from the beginning, and all worked upon a common plan or draft drawn before the first blow was struck.[86]

Lincoln's emphasis on the conspiracy point fitted nicely with his political strategy. Once Stephen Douglas found a way to claim—disingenuously perhaps—that even under *Dred Scott* the territories still could determine the slavery question for themselves (i.e., that they could still decide to bar slavery), Lincoln's Republicans needed to find a way to distinguish their platform. Lincoln repeatedly suggested (however implausibly) that the Court was about to permit slavery in the free states as well.[87] There was a case pending, *Lemmon v. People*, that raised the question of whether slaveholders could bring their slaves into a free state without the risk of having them declared emancipated.[88] *Harper's Weekly*, a moderate voice at the time, dismissed the significance of the "Lemon case (all these slave cases are sour enough)," doubting that slavery could be prohibited in free states.[89] Lincoln, though, preyed on these fears. Seeing another unfilled "niche" in his frame, he suggested, "We shall *lie down* pleasantly dreaming that the people of *Missouri* are on the verge of making their State *free*; and we shall *awake* to the *reality*, instead, that the *Supreme* Court has made *Illinois* a *slave* state."[90]

Still, none of this explained precisely what was to be done about the *Dred Scott* ruling. This was a point on which Douglas prodded Lincoln repeatedly, calling into question Lincoln's fealty to judicial authority. Lincoln, he said, "makes war on the decision of the Supreme Court, known as the Dred Scott decision." Douglas, by contrast, proclaimed he was "content to take it as having been delivered by the highest judicial tribunal on earth; a tribunal established by the Constitution of the United States, and hence that decision becomes the law of the land, binding on you, on me, and on every other good citizen, whether they like it or not."[91] Once "the decision is made," Douglas insisted, "my private opinion, your opinion, all other opinions must yield to the majesty of that authoritative adjudication."[92]

Lincoln ridiculed Douglas for being so wed to the decision. "I cannot make the judge fall loose from his adherence to this Dred Scott decision . . . he is like some creature that will hang on which he has got his hold to a thing, you may cut his arms and limbs off, and still he is hanging on." Douglas, Lincoln chastised, unnecessarily treated the decision as a "thus saith the Lord."[93] "The sacredness that Judge Douglas throws around this decision is a degree of sacredness that has never been before thrown around any other decision."[94]

It is sometimes claimed that Lincoln's own view of *Dred Scott* was in accord with the departmental theory that each branch was entitled to interpret the Constitution for itself and thus as a denial of judicial supremacy.[95] In his widely quoted First Inaugural Address, Lincoln spoke of *Dred Scott*, saying:

> [T]he candid citizen must confess that if the policy of the government, upon vital questions, affecting the whole people, is to be irrevocably fixed by decisions of the Supreme Court, the instant they are made, in ordinary litigation between parties, in personal actions, the people will have ceased, to be their own rulers, having, to that extent, practically resigned their government, into the hands of that eminent tribunal.[96]

Lincoln recognized in his inaugural that despite adverse consequences, the decision "must be binding in any case, upon the parties to a suit, as to the object of that suit." But when it came to those beyond the original lawsuit, he allowed only that it was "entitled to very high respect and consideration, in all paralel [*sic*] cases, by all other departments of the government."[97] Add to that the fact that he more than once said, "If I were in Congress, and a vote should come up on a question whether slavery should be prohibited in a new Territory, in spite of the Dred Scott decision, I would vote that it should," and it looks as if Lincoln did in fact deny that Supreme Court decisions bound public officials who were not party to the case.[98]

Yet, seen in the context of all his remarks, Lincoln was hardly challenging judicial supremacy. Indeed, he recognized a broader binding effect to the decision than he generally is given credit for. On June 26, 1857, at Springfield, Lincoln plainly acknowledged: "We think [the Supreme Court's] decisions on Constitutional questions, when fully settled, should control, not only the particular cases decided, but the general policy of the country, subject to be disturbed only by amendments of the Constitution as provided in that instrument itself."[99] Then, in a speech in Chicago on July 10, 1858, he explained again that as a "rule of property" a judicial decision applies to all who stand in the same shoes as Dred Scott. "That is," the justices in effect say, "when a question comes up upon another person, it will be so decided again, unless the court decides in another way, unless the court overrules the decision."[100] It is possible that by the time of his inaugural Lincoln's views had moved away from these expressions of supremacy. Parsing his many statements on the case, however, suggests that he simply had a more nuanced understanding of judicial authority, one not so very different from that held today.

In Lincoln's view, because the *Dred Scott* decision had not "settled" the question of Congress's power in the territories, he could legitimately seek to have the decision "overruled." Lincoln pointed to all the reasons this particular decision was not settled: it was based "upon a mistaken statement of fact"; it was "made in a divided Court by a bare majority of the Judges"; the justices could not agree among themselves on the basis for the decision; and "it is so made as that its avowed supporters disagree with one another about its meaning."[101] The goal, therefore, was to do "what we can to have it overrule this"; "we mean to do what we can to have the court decide the other way."[102]

To fully understand Lincoln's remarks, it is essential to distinguish between legislative and executive responses to a determination by the justices. While the events of the 1830s demonstrated the difficulty that arises when executive officials refuse to enforce judicial orders, legislative response is an entirely different matter. As Lincoln explained, there must be some way to challenge a constitutional ruling, in order to see if the Supreme Court— on reflection—might reconsider. In practice, there often is no way to cause the justices to revisit a troublesome decision unless the legislature passes a law that can provide the basis for further litigation. Although the refusal of the executive to enforce a court order can leave legal rights without remedy, passage of a law by the legislature simply opens up those legal rights to new adjudication.[103]

What Lincoln finally proposed as a means of getting *Dred Scott* overruled was no more or less than what is widely recognized today as one of the legitimate ways to change a disfavored ruling by the Supreme Court. Lincoln's precise remedy was political action, which would ultimately result in a new ruling (rendered, one hoped, by some new justices). He explained that though *Dred Scott* was binding as a legal matter, it was not as "a political rule that shall be binding upon the man when he goes to the polls to vote, or upon the member of Congress, or upon the President [acting here in the capacity of signing or refusing to sign a bill], to favor no measure that does not actually tally with the principle of that decision."[104] Rather, a new law could be passed so the Court would have a chance to reconsider. In this specific way, "we propose to have that decision reversed, and to have a new true judicial decision spread upon the records of the country."[105] Lincoln's hope, as Stephen Douglas himself described it, was that the people would "elect a President who will appoint judges who will reverse the Dred Scott decision."[106]

DEFYING THE COURT?

"I raise no question upon the legal validity of the judgment"

Dred Scott was ultimately reversed not by the appointment of new judges, but by a constitutional amendment. Before that could happen, however, the country was forced to fight its bloodiest war ever. Some scholars have claimed that in this interval between *Dred Scott* and eventual amendment, Congress and the executive defied the Court's ruling.[107] To the contrary, it is clear once again from the combination of subterfuge and legalism employed to deal with *Dred Scott* that out-and-out defiance was becoming increasingly unacceptable. Legislators did offer up legislation that could have led to *Dred Scott*'s reversal—had it been challenged—but they did so all the while acknowledging that the Supreme Court would ultimately judge what they were doing.

When Congress passed a bill banning slavery in the territories in 1862, speakers conceded the Supreme Court authority as much as they challenged it.[108] Obviously the bill was in tension with *Dred Scott*, but congressional rhetoric in 1862 sounded nothing at all like the bygone days of Ohio over the Bank, Georgia over the Cherokee, or Virginia over the Supreme Court's jurisdiction itself. The 1862 measure was largely symbolic given that, as several representatives were at pains to point out, there were no longer any territories where slavery was legal.[109] Still, supporters said they wished "only . . . to prevent slavery where the Government has a right to prevent it . . . and nothing else."[110] Denying any intention of exceeding Congress's powers, speakers declared they wanted to march "up to that line squarely."[111] One representative argued that this "plain and simple bill . . . will not be open to criticism in courts of law."[112] But even if it were, Pennsylvania's William "Pig Iron" Kelley acknowledged that the law would stand only "until it can be tested before the Supreme Court of the United States; and if sustained as constitutional law by that court. . . ."[113] At most then, the bill provided a means to mount a challenge to *Dred Scott*, just as Lincoln had suggested the country might.

A number of scholars, typically those advancing a departmental theory of judicial review, have asserted that the executive branch declined to follow the *Dred Scott* ruling during the war; they are wrong if by this they mean executive officials blatantly refused to abide by it.[114] Lincoln's Attorney General Edward Bates issued a legal opinion that limited the impact of *Dred Scott* severely, not by defying it but by engaging in a concededly sharp, lawyer's interpretation. The specific question was whether free blacks could serve as ship captains in the coastal trade, given that Congress had limited the privilege to citizens and that *Dred Scott* had denied slaves and their descendants citizenship.[115] In answering the question, Bates assured his audience: "I raise no question upon the legal validity of the judgment in Scott vs. Sandford."[116] Rather, he explained, given the procedural posture of the *Dred Scott* case, the Supreme Court could rule on nothing other than what Sandford had alleged: "[T]he said plaintiff, Dred Scott, is not a citizen of the State of Missouri . . . *because he is a negro* of African descent; his ancestors were of pure African blood."[117] Anything else that "was said in the long course of the case, as reported, (240 pages) respecting the legal merits of the case, and respecting any supposed legal disability resulting from the mere fact of color, . . . was '*dehors the record*,' and of no authority as a judicial decision."[118] So limited, Bates argued, only a small number of individuals could be barred by *Dred Scott* from the privileges of citizenship: "They must be of *African* descent, not Asiatic, even though they come of the blackest Malays in southeastern Asia . . . [and their] ancestors . . . must have been of *pure* African blood, not mixed with the tawny Moor of Morocco, or the dusky Arab of the desert, both of whom had their origin in Asia." And so on.[119]

Bates's colleague, Secretary of State William Seward, engaged in even more of a charade but also demonstrated no outright defiance. Apparently Seward issued passports to free blacks. This began when Senator Charles Sumner asked Seward to do so on behalf of a young man whose "complexion was said to be 'colored' and his hair 'short and curly.'" Seward refused but said he would issue a passport for anyone whom Sumner "certified to be a citizen, without description." When Sumner so certified, the passport was issued. (Subsequently, Sumner tells us, Seward awarded passports to blacks on the basis of Bates's opinion regarding blacks acting as ship captains in the coastal trade.)[120]

Congress ultimately resolved *Dred Scott*'s holding regarding congressional power to ban slavery by proposing the Thirteenth Amendment. Lincoln had emancipated the slaves in rebel states as a wartime measure, but that was not beyond reproof and did not cover the entire country.[121] The Thirteenth Amendment mandated the end of slavery throughout the country. In debates over the amendment, congressional speakers made clear this was how they intended to overrule *Dred Scott*.[122]

As for *Dred Scott*'s other holding, concerning the citizenship of slaves and their descendants, Congress tried to resolve it by ordinary legislation but in the face of opposition ultimately opted for yet another amendment. Immediately after the war Congress passed civil rights legislation that, among other things, declared that "all persons of African descent born in the United States are hereby declared to be citizens of the United States."[123] Objection was made that the law was invalid and bound to be struck down. "If the Supreme Court decision is a binding one and will be followed in the future, this law which we are now about to pass will be held of course to be of no avail," declared Maryland's Democratic senator and respected constitutionalist Reverdy Johnson.[124] Some in Congress thought there was a simple solution: because slavery was no longer constitutional (given the Thirteenth Amendment), "[i]f they are not citizens, may we not naturalize them?"[125] Nonetheless, in order to respond to this and other objections that the 1866 law was unconstitutional, Congress proposed what became the Fourteenth Amendment, the passage of which would, as will be apparent shortly, engage the Court in yet further controversy.[126]

WARTIME MEASURES AND JUDICIAL AUTHORITY

"[A]re all the laws, but one, to go unexecuted . . . ?"

As is often the case, the government's wartime measures frequently threatened individual rights in ways that created the potential for conflict between the executive and the judiciary. Here, again, issues were raised regarding judicial supremacy and the legality of defying Court rulings. Unsure of each other's response, both Lincoln and the Supreme Court labored to avoid any collision. In one famous instance, though, Lincoln's and Taney's decrees crossed each other. Although the event provided a grand challenge to judicial authority, Lincoln was careful to argue the lawfulness of his conduct.

Throughout the war, Lincoln justified executive measures as no more than necessary to save the Union.[127] His authority, he said, "has purposely been exercised but very sparingly."[128] "I can no more be persuaded that the government can constitutionally take no strong measure in time of rebellion, because it can be shown that the same could not be lawfully taken in time of peace," Lincoln wrote, "than I can be persuaded that a particular drug is not good medicine for a sick man, because it can be shown to not be good food for a well one."[129] Still, people were detained, the writ of habeas corpus was suspended, military trials were held, courts and clergy interfered with, and newspapers shut down.[130]

Not looking to buy trouble, the administration simply avoided the Supreme Court whenever possible with regard to these wartime measures, while the Supreme Court did its best to stay out of harm's way.[131] When the Wisconsin Supreme Court issued a decision (apologetically) calling into question Lincoln's authority to suspend the writ of habeas corpus, the government chose not to appeal. Edward Bates wrote to Secretary of War Edwin Stanton say-ing that he feared the Supreme Court would not vindicate them.[132] Like-wise, when overly zealous officials seized a noted Ohio politician for antiwar efforts and tried him in front of a military tribunal, the Court dismissed the case for lack of jurisdiction. Later decisions suggest this dismissal was trans-parent avoidance on the justices' part.[133] "[D]uring the war the most strenu-ous efforts were made to use the court in such a way as to embarrass the Government," Supreme Court Justice Samuel Freeman Miller told an audi-ence several years afterward, discussing his own efforts to see that the Court steered clear of conflict with the administration.[134] All this was probably to the good. Taney, it turns out, was secretly preparing decisions against the gov-ernment on the issues of confiscation, emancipation, and conscription.[135]

Nonetheless, Lincoln did have one legendary run-in with Taney during the war. With the corridor to Washington through Maryland jeopardized by rebel activities, Lincoln authorized his generals to suspend the writ of habeas corpus.[136] Habeas corpus is an ancient common law remedy, much admired by the colonists and throughout American history, used to free individuals from executive detention and to bring them before courts to ensure the law-fulness of confinement. The Constitution plainly permits suspending the writ "when in Cases of Rebellion or Invasion the public Safety may require it."[137] The problem is that the Constitution is silent about which branch can suspend the writ, though the Suspension Clause resides in Article I of the Constitution, suggesting only Congress possesses the power. Facing a dire situation, this did not stop Lincoln.[138]

When the Chief Justice issued a decision challenging Lincoln's suspen-sion of the writ of habeas corpus, Lincoln simply ignored him. The military had arrested John Merryman, a well-to-do Baltimore resident, who was a lieutenant in a disloyal militia unit that was bent upon wreaking havoc. Merryman applied for a writ of habeas corpus. Taney, who was sitting as the circuit justice (and who happened to be from Baltimore himself), ordered military officials to produce Merryman. They refused, relying on the claim that Lincoln had validly authorized the suspension of the writ.[139] When the military refused to produce Merryman so that the Court could inquire into the legality of his confinement, Taney delivered a powerful opinion condemn-ing the suspension of the writ. "I have exercised all the power which the constitution and laws confer upon me, but that power has been resisted by a force too strong for me to overcome."[140] He shipped a copy of his order off to the President, who, pursuant to his power to "take care that the laws be faith-fully executed," ought to "determine what measures he will take to cause the civil process . . . to be respected and enforced."[141] Lincoln did nothing.[142]

Although Lincoln obviously defied Taney's order, he went to great efforts after the fact to justify his legal right to do so. Lincoln subsequently sought (and eventually obtained) congressional ratification of his actions.[143] In his address to Congress, Lincoln argued that the framers could not have intended to deny the President power to suspend the writ at times when Congress could not even assemble "as was intended in this case, by the rebellion."[144]

Lincoln passed off to his Attorney General the difficult responsibility of justifying the legality of his disregard of judicial orders. Bates's explanation falls pretty short.[145] Bates argued at length that the President's power necessarily included detaining people in times of insurrection. But what about a judicial order to produce someone so detained? Bates claimed that the writ of habeas corpus cannot run against the President or his subordinates, something that would surprise history before and since. After all, as Bates acknowledged, the framers "knew that the English government had, more than once, assumed the power to imprison whom it would, and hold them, for an indefinite time" and "desired, no doubt, to interpose a guard against the like abuses in this country." Obviously at a loss, Bates then simply waved his hand—"Besides, the whole subject-matter is political and not judicial"—before saying of the Constitution's Suspension Clause, "I am by no means confident that I fully understand it myself."[146] Conceding judicial precedent to the contrary, Bates boldly asserted the President had the power to suspend the writ. The one thing Bates never really got around to explaining satisfactorily was the precise question put: Can the President simply ignore a writ issued to him? Yes, was Bates's answer, but the stew of his reasoning did not quite add up to supper.

Lincoln's most persuasive explanation for the suspension may well have been one that failed to justify his action in the legal sense but was compelling nonetheless. Coming to the crux of the matter, Lincoln put the telling question to Congress: "[A]re all the laws, *but one*, to go unexecuted, and the government itself go to pieces, lest that one be violated?"[147] Lincoln quickly denied that "this question was presented" and went on to offer his more legalistic arguments, such as that suspension of the writ was in his hands at a time when Congress could not assemble. But one suspects his deepest sentiment lay where he began: "[W]ould not the official oath be broken, if the government should be overthrown, when it was believed that disregarding the single law, would tend to preserve it?"[148]

It also was the case that in his conflict with Taney, as with most like wartime measures, Lincoln had public opinion heavily on his side. People were focused on winning the war, not on the cost in terms of liberty lost. Commenting on congressional legislation, *Harper's Weekly* said: "The President of the United States has, in effect, been created Dictator. . . . And this is well."[149] Some northern Democrats sought to embarrass the administration on issues of civil liberties.[150] But these were the clear minority. In response to Taney's order, *The North American Review* opined that ordinarily "whatever addresses itself to the popular mind as a vindication of the right of personal freedom against oppression in any of its forms must meet a ready and hearty approval." Here, however, "the Chief Justice . . . failed to secure the support of the people . . . because there were circumstances of no ordinary character involved in the case."[151] *The New York Times* was more direct, accusing the Chief Justice of treason: "Too feeble to wield the sword against the Constitution, too old and palsied and weak to march in the ranks of rebellion and fight against the Union, he uses the powers of his office to serve the cause of the traitors."[152]

Plainly, defiance of court orders had not died a complete death. On the other hand, if there ever were extraordinary circumstances, these were. Even so, with public opinion firmly behind him, Lincoln nonetheless struggled to reconcile what must be done with what the judges declared. The positions taken may have been disingenuous or evasive, but in the very nature of those positions it again becomes clear that unvarnished defiance had melted away as a legitimate response to the Court.

RECONSTRUCTION AND LEGISLATIVE SUPREMACY

"Congress . . . is wisely made the chief and superior branch"

What, then, was to be done about the Court in times of tension? This issue would move to the fore as Congress sought to reconstruct the South. At the close of the war, the country faced two interrelated sets of questions. First, on what terms would the southern states and their citizens be readmitted to full participation in the political life of the nation? Second, what was to be done with the former slaves? What rights and protections would they have? Congress made clear it would brook no opposition from the other branches as it moved to resolve these questions.

Andrew Johnson, who succeeded to the presidency after Lincoln's assassination, took an approach to Reconstruction that was unpalatable to Congress in the face of continued southern intransigence. Although the Thirteenth Amendment brought a formal end to slavery, the South continued to subjugate blacks. Southern states adopted Black Codes that imposed disabilities on such central aspects of life and citizenship as labor, freedom of movement, and testifying in court.[153] Then, in 1865, the South sent numerous former high-ranking Confederates, including Vice President Alexander Stephens, and a number of generals, colonels, and members of the Confederate Congress, to the Thirty-ninth national Congress. A displeased Congress declined to seat the representatives from the southern states. The clerk of the House of Representatives offered to explain the reasons to a dismayed Tennessee loyalist who had remained in Congress throughout the war.[154] "It is not necessary," interjected Thaddeus Stevens, the Republican majority leader from Pennsylvania. "We know all."[155]

The recalcitrant conduct of the South, explained *The Nation* (an aptly named antislavery journal founded in 1865), "forced upon the early attention of Congress the question of how the liberties of the black race were to be made secure."[156] To deal with matters, Congress created the Joint Committee on Reconstruction early in 1866. Congressional legislation proposed to extend the Freedmen's Bureau, charged with the enormous tasks of aiding former slaves and with managing all lands confiscated during the war. Congress also enacted its 1866 civil rights legislation.[157]

During the remainder of 1866, the relationship between Congress and the President disintegrated. Johnson vetoed the Freedmen's Bureau bill and the Civil Rights Act of 1866. Congress overrode the latter, the first override of a veto of major legislation in the country's history. In June, Congress sent the Fourteenth Amendment to the states for ratification. Johnson opposed the amendment, on the ground (among others) that it was invalid because it was passed by a Congress that excluded southerners.[158] In July, Congress overrode Johnson's veto of yet another Freedmen's Bureau bill. Johnson went on his "Swing Around the Circle" speaking tour against congressional Reconstruction, which proved disastrous for him and his policies.

Congressional elections in the fall of 1866 served as a ringing endorsement of the Fourteenth Amendment and Congress's approach to Reconstruction. Enough Republicans were elected to override any presidential veto easily. *The Nation* called it "the most decisive and emphatic victory ever seen in American politics."[159] Nonetheless, between October 1866 and January 1, 1867, all ten southern states rejected the Fourteenth Amendment, with only a grand total of thirty-three legislators voting for it in all those states.[160]

In this fraught environment, the Supreme Court handed down two major decisions, both of which suggested that Congress might have a problem with the judiciary as well. Congressional Republicans had hoped they could count on the Supreme Court. Five of the nine justices were Lincoln appointees, including Chief Justice Salmon P. Chase (who had also been Lincoln's Secretary of the Treasury). When the Court appeared as though it might be unreliable to northern and Republican interests, the press was almost hysterical. The *Newark Evening Courier* said that "the Judiciary has swung from its Union moorings and gone over" to the President's side, while *The Cincinnati Daily Gazette* saw judges "whose political sympathies were kept quiet . . . warmed into reptile life again by treachery in the Executive."[161]

Ex parte Milligan involved the question of the constitutionality of military tribunals, on which the legality of congressional Reconstruction turned.[162] Lambdin Milligan was sentenced to death during the war by a military tribunal for treason. He was accused of conspiring to release and arm prisoners in order to foment uprisings.[163] Milligan was tried and convicted in a northern state, Indiana, in which a loyal civilian government, with ordinary criminal courts, was operating. The importance of *Milligan* lay in the fact that at the time, the entire South was under military control; the military supervised the vital tasks of governance and order or selected civilian authorities to do so. All this was backed up by the military's system of justice.[164] "Congress has reconstituted the army and conferred upon its officers absolute, despotic powers of government over the people of the States in question," allowed one angry commentary on the Reconstruction measures.[165] But was this system legitimate? A congressional opponent, arguing no, explained that Congress had "abolished all law over nine million people and substituted in its place the arbitrary, unrestrained will of a colonel of infantry or cavalry. . . ."[166]

Although the justices were unanimous in reversing Milligan's conviction and sentence, it was the rationale of the majority opinion that was ominous for continued military rule of the South. Four of the justices, in a concurrence written by Chief Justice Chase, would have held simply that Milligan's conviction had to be overturned because Congress had not authorized the use of military tribunal in cases like his. The Chief Justice's opinion was emphatic in reassuring the nation that Congress could have employed military tribunals had it wished to do so.[167] The five-justice majority went further, however, and held the use of military tribunals unconstitutional in any state that acknowledged the authority of the national government and in which civilian courts were functioning.

Depending on the perspective of the one reading the ruling, the majority opinion in *Milligan* either hinted that military rule of the South was unconstitutional as well or provided a basis for distinguishing Milligan's case.[168] In the heated cauldron into which the *Milligan* decision fell, few were willing to assume the best. The decision was denounced in the Republican press as "Dred Scott Number Two."[169] *Harper's Weekly* reported that "rebels have already possession of two of the three branches of the Government—the Executive and the Judiciary—leaving the Legislative only to the Union men of the country."[170] The *Chicago Tribune* observed that the Supreme Court "seems to have joined hands with a corrupt and treacherous Executive, to give victory to the rebellion."[171]

The Court aggravated matters further when it invalidated the use of certain loyalty oaths. To modern ears such oaths may seem a meaningless formality, but during Reconstruction the oath was crucial. It set the terms upon which southerners and their sympathizers would regain the right to participate in the Union's affairs.[172] Johnson would have required only that the affiant promise future loyalty to the Union. Disagreeing, members of Congress insisted that "[t]he people of the North are not such fools as to fight through such a war as this . . . and then turn around and say to the traitors, 'All you have to do is . . . take an oath that henceforth you will be true.'"[173] Congress's Ironclad Oath, one of those invalidated, included swearing that one had never voluntarily rendered assistance to the Confederacy, disabling many from future participation.[174] The Supreme Court ruled that the Ironclad Oath violated the constitution by imposing retroactive punishment.[175] "Dred Scott Number Three has just been enacted in the Supreme Court of the United States" was the lead in the Senate Republicans' organ, the *Daily Morning Chronicle*.[176] The fact that the split on the Court was again 5–4 did not help matters.[177]

These decisions—*Milligan* in particular—threw Congress into high gear on plans for Reconstruction. Just days after the *Milligan* decision, Thaddeus Stevens, the leader of the Radical Republicans, who were then firmly in control of Congress, took to the floor of the House. "[T]he late decision of the Supreme Court of the United States has rendered immediate action by Congress upon the question of the establishment of governments in the rebel States absolutely indispensable." *Milligan* might appear "not as infamous as the *Dred Scott* decision," Stevens instructed his colleagues and the nation, but in truth it was "far more dangerous" by reason of its "operation upon the lives and the liberties of . . . every loyal man, black or white, who resides [in the South]."[178]

Although the Court appeared to pose a threat to congressional plans, little doubt was allowed about which branch would hold the upper hand. "No other branch of the Government, no other Department, no other officer of the Government," Stevens insisted, "possesses one single particle of the sovereignty of the people." *Harper's Weekly* concurred: "The President, by the Constitution, is made a co-ordinate but not a co-equal branch of the Government. So, also, is the Supreme Court. But Congress . . . is wisely made the chief and superior branch."[179]

All that disempowered congressional opponents could do was mock the principle of legislative sovereignty. "When this modest Congress has swallowed all the other co-ordinate branches of this Government," asked the

Cairo Democrat, "will it then have the great kindness to swallow itself?" Johnson's paper, the *Daily National Intelligencer*, chose facetiousness: "It is truly lamentable that both the Executive and the judiciary stand in the way of the almighty legislative department of the Government."[180] Even *The Nation* asked: As "the majority of Congress is sure not to do wrong, why have a Constitution at all? Why restrain this body of sages by any restrictions whatsoever?"[181]

Congress exercised its power with a close eye on the American people, who by all appearances were following events extraordinarily closely.[182] "In this country," Thaddeus Stevens explained, "the whole sovereignty rests with the people; and is exercised through their Representatives in Congress assembled."[183] Members regularly claimed to act in the name of the people.[184] Voter turnout in the elections of 1864 and 1868 exceeded 80 percent of the eligible electorate.[185] Shifting electoral results often had an important influence on congressional policy, and elections were hotly contested.[186] Newspapers kept readers remarkably informed; they contained detailed, blow-by-blow descriptions and verbatim accounts of proceedings in Congress and in the Supreme Court.[187]

Members of Congress and the popular press made perfectly clear that the Court would not be permitted to stand in the way of congressional plans. Senator Frederick Frelinghuysen, a New Jersey Republican and strong proponent of congressional Reconstruction, remarked, "It would be a strange thing if this nation, after all the wars we have had, after living for ninety years thinking we lived under Republican democracy," should find that "our Government was an aristocracy, and that one or five members of the Supreme Court could regulate the political interests and relations of the country."[188] *The Philadelphia Inquirer*, deeply loyal to the Union throughout the war (and distributed to many of the troops), agreed that "the whole theory of our institutions would be destroyed" if the Court "not chosen by the people" were to become "superior to Congress."[189]

The stakes were simply too high to brook judicial interference. A ruling by the Court invalidating military rule in the South prior to readmission of the rebel states on Congress's terms would have been wholly unacceptable. Even the relatively moderate *New York Times* said the "people will not believe that the hands of their representatives are tied in the presence of conspirators, or that the Government is constitutionally helpless in the presence of rebellion."[190] *The Nation*, which more than any other Republican publication tended to defend judicial independence, was on this point intractable: "[I]f there is any lesson which history teaches clearly, it is that there never has existed, and there never is likely to exist, a nation which will allow constitutions or any forms of any kind on paper to stand between it and such a change in policy as it deems necessary to its safety." According to *The Nation*, the "question of reconstruction" was simply "too momentous . . . to allow of its being submitted to any court of law or decided upon any technical rules of interpretation."[191]

STRIPPING JURISDICTION

"[T]his court cannot proceed to pronounce judgment in this case"

Facing interference from the other branches, Congress ultimately was driven to take action that matched the heated rhetoric of legislative sovereignty. Andrew Johnson's meddling brought the first impeachment of an American President. When the Supreme Court seemed poised to rule on the constitutionality of military rule of the South, Congress considered several measures to tame the Court. It settled on stripping the Court's jurisdiction to hear the case.

On March 2, 1867, in the waning moments of the Thirty-ninth Congress, the nation's representatives adopted crucial Reconstruction legislation mandating that in order to reenter the Union, the rebel states must hold a convention—with blacks and whites voting—and ratify the Fourteenth Amendment.[192] The Fourteenth Amendment was central to congressional plans. It overruled *Dred Scott*'s citizenship holding by providing that "all persons born or naturalized in the United States" are citizens of the United States and the states in which they reside. States were required to respect the rights of these citizens, and Congress was given the authority to enforce the amendment "by appropriate legislation."[193] A veto by the President was overturned. Supplementary legislation was passed by the Fortieth Congress immediately thereafter.[194] These laws provided for military rule until all this was accomplished. They also set the stage for a collision between Congress and the Supreme Court.

Key southerners adopted the strategy of having Congress's Reconstruction plan declared unconstitutional before enough states ratified the Fourteenth Amendment to make it part of the Constitution.[195] The terms of the congressional plan, as well as the electoral calendar and shifting political party strength, all made for a footrace. The Democratic Party made a surprisingly strong showing in state elections in the North in 1867, suggesting some discontent with the terms being imposed on the South. Congressional leaders believed it essential that southern ratification of the Fourteenth Amendment occur before the 1868 elections.[196]

Nothing came of the South's first attempts to obtain adjudication of the constitutionality of the congressional plan.[197] In November 1867, however, the military handed the southerners a lawsuit that met their purposes. William H. McCardle was a Vicksburg, Mississippi, newspaper editor with a poisonous pen. A rabid foe of congressional Reconstruction, McCardle urged "every honorable gentleman of the Caucasian race" not to vote in the ratification elections and offered "to pay a dollar for the name of each voter" so that he could publish the names.[198] The military arrested McCardle for disturbing the peace and inciting insurrection. McCardle applied for a writ of habeas corpus, which was denied, remanding him to military custody. Released on bail pending appeal, in December 1867 McCardle brought his case, *Ex parte McCardle*, to the Supreme Court claiming that military rule of the South was unconstitutional.

There was great irony in McCardle's suit.[199] As part of Reconstruction, Congress had enlarged the jurisdiction of the federal courts, giving them wide power to grant writs of habeas corpus to "prisoners in custody of state officials" for the first time.[200] The reason for the expansion of jurisdiction was somewhat unclear, but most likely it was prompted by the state courts' treatment of emancipated slaves under the Black Codes.[201] When Congress expanded the jurisdiction of the federal courts, it provided a statutory route to the Supreme Court to review habeas decisions.[202] So a law designed to assist federal officials and southern blacks was first being utilized in defense of an unreconstructed southern racist.

The initial proceedings in the *McCardle* case suggested to some in Congress that the Court might actually decide on the constitutionality of military rule prior to the 1868 elections. McCardle's appeal was filed in the Supreme Court on December 23, 1867.[203] The Court's term was to end in May 1868, and the South needed resolution prior to the autumn 1868 elections. McCardle's counsel asked the Court to advance the case on the docket, a move that was protested by the government's lawyer, Lyman Trumbull. (Trumbull was also a senator from Illinois and chair of the Senate Judiciary Committee.) Given that McCardle was already free on bail, Trumbull "could not imagine any reason" for advancing the case.[204] Over Trumbull's objection, and rejecting his motion to dismiss for lack of jurisdiction, the Court set argument for the first Monday in March. In recognition of the weighty issues posed by the suit, each side was given three times the usual allotment of time for the argument.[205] Oral argument took place against the backdrop of Andrew Johnson's impeachment trial in the Senate, at which the Chief Justice was presiding.[206]

The Court's attention to the *McCardle* case spurred Congress to quick action. A bill was passed in the House requiring a two-thirds vote of the Supreme Court to strike any congressional enactment as unconstitutional.[207] Objecting, Representative Frederick Stone of Maryland, a Democrat, said: "Two hours only were deemed sufficient to destroy what it took the Convention of 1789 months of anxious deliberation to perfect—the judiciary of the United States."[208] A yet stronger version that would have required a unanimous vote was offered.[209] In the Senate, Trumbull introduced a measure that would have declared the Reconstruction Acts inherently "political" and therefore not suitable for judicial action.[210] Although the unanimity and political question bills failed, the two-thirds majority provision did pass in the House of Representatives before being defeated in the Senate.[211]

While Congress debated what precise action to take, the Radical Republican press egged it on, and moderate voices fretted. "There is a danger of an adverse decision from the Supreme Court," declared *The Independent*. "Let the bill pass. . . ." *Harper's Weekly* agreed: "[I]t is wholly unsafe to leave these questions to the decision of a bare majority of the Judges." The *Chicago Tribune* was blunt: "[T]he same power which has endowed this Court with such dangerous authority, can strip it of its ability to do mischief. . . . One Dred Scott decision in a century must suffice." Still, the *Chicago Republican* worried over what was happening. It could not "sit by quietly and see a hand lifted against the Court or the Constitution, whether by our National Congress or the Southern traitors."[212]

In the face of the press furor, Congress ultimately settled on a bill that stripped the Court's statutory jurisdiction to hear *McCardle*. Initially the jurisdiction stripper was slipped through Congress with barely a notice, as a rider to a noncontroversial bill.[213] When opposition members discovered what had happened, they were furious. Senator Charles Buckalew of Pennsylvania, a Democrat who had succeeded to David Wilmot's seat, complained that a "bill . . . was gotten through the Senate . . . without an opportunity to debate the measure not explained."[214] Johnson promptly vetoed the bill, despite his pending impeachment trial. The provision, he protested, "takes away the right of appeal to that court in cases which involve the life and liberty of the citizen, and leaves them exposed to the judgment of numerous inferior tribunals."[215]

The attention of the country was galvanized. Every move in Congress and every action by the Court (and sometimes simply rumors of the same) were recorded in the press.[216] Some papers urged the Court to act despite

Congress. The Washington correspondent to the *Boston Post* suggested the Court would step in "in defense of its own dignity, and to show that the Court cannot be trifled with by reckless partisans who flippantly speak of 'clipping the wings of the Court.'" The moderate *Springfield Republican* was grateful that the Court "bows down to the will of Congress, and has postponed the *McCardle Case* till Congress has more definitely settled the Reconstruction question."[217] Senator Reverdy Johnson confirmed the latter course, informing Congress "that the Supreme Court has come to that determination, as long as this bill is pending it is not their purpose to dispose of a case which has already been argued. . . ."[218]

Following a debate notable for its lack of forthrightness on the part of the Radicals, Congress overrode the President's veto, and the bill became law, on March 27, 1868.[219] Opponents echoed Johnson's claim that passage of the act "will be justly held by a large portion of the people as an admission of the unconstitutionality of the act on which [the Court's] judgment may be forbidden or forestalled."[220] Despite all the hot talk of congressional authority over the Court on prior occasions, only one of the Republicans defended the measure as a permissible means of controlling the Court.[221] Instead, in a stunning display of disingenuousness, Senator Trumbull—counsel for the government in *McCardle*, after all—denied that there was any case pending to which the repealer applied.[222] It remained for the opposition to call him on this, stating, "We all know, the whole world knows, that this case of McCardle is pending in the Supreme Court . . . [I]t is important because it involves the constitutionality of the reconstruction acts . . . it is because men know that these acts will be decided to be unconstitutional."[223]

Though the Radicals feigned ignorance, the press was quite clear on what had happened. *The Independent* called "that little bill which put a knife to the throat of the *McCardle Case*" a "splendid performance." "This Congress will not brook opposition from the Court in political matters," it added accurately. Agreed the *Springfield Republican*: "Congress does not intend to permit the Supreme Court to overthrow it or revive rebellion, if it can help it."[224]

All eyes turned to the Court to see how it would respond. When counsel for McCardle asked about a rumor that the Court had decided to delay resolution of the case while Congress debated the jurisdiction-stripping measure, Justice Samuel Nelson, presiding while Chief Justice Chase was at the impeachment trial, inquired whether counsel cared to argue the point. The government objected on the ground that no motion was pending.[225] Tempers flared. An emotional Justice Robert Cooper Grier intervened, expressing regret for the opprobrium the Court had brought on itself and wanting to vindicate himself in the face of expected criticism.[226] He subsequently issued a formal "protest" that Justice Stephen Field (a pro-Union Democrat appointed by Lincoln) joined. "This case," Grier wrote, "involves the liberty and rights not only of the appellant, but of millions of our fellow-citizens. . . . By the postponement of the case we shall subject ourselves, whether justly or unjustly, to the imputation that we have evaded the performance of a duty imposed on us by the Constitution. . . ."[227]

Ultimately, the Court capitulated and the South's position was lost. The last day of the Court's term was April 30. Chase had suggested sitting in June "but met no support."[228] On the last day of the term, the *McCardle* case was held over, along with *Georgia v. Grant*, to the next term.[229] On July 9, 1868, the Fourteenth Amendment was ratified.[230]

The next term, after the contest was over, the Court released its opinion in *McCardle*, holding that it lacked jurisdiction to hear the case. "We are not at liberty to inquire into the motives of the Legislature," wrote the Chief Justice for the Court. "We can only examine into its power under the Constitution; and the power to make exceptions to the appellate jurisdiction of this Court is given by express words." "It is quite clear," Chase's opinion said, that "this court cannot proceed to pronounce judgment in this case."[231] There was a wink at the end of the opinion, a hint from the Court that there were other jurisdictional routes available to reach it. By then, though, it was too late. "Congress," wrote former justice Benjamin Curtis, "with the acquiescence of the country, has subdued the Supreme Court."[232] Counsel for the South's litigation campaign, Jeremiah Black, put it in coarser terms: "The court stood still to be ravished and did not even hallo while the thing was getting done."[233]

A HUMBLED COURT; A RELUCTANT PUBLIC

"[I]t will not be . . . easy to restore the public respect and reverence for the tribunal"

The McCardle incident was not the only instance during the Civil War and Reconstruction in which Congress bent the Supreme Court to its will. No fewer than three times, Congress altered the size of the Court to ensure a sound majority in important cases. There was no small irony in this sort of manipulation: Congress simultaneously was learning of the importance of the federal courts to help keep order in the nation and the damage a hostile Supreme Court could do. The consequence was that a Supreme Court unable to comprehend the limits of its own authority repeatedly found itself humbled and made the subject of derision.

In modern parlance, "packing" the Supreme Court refers to manipulating the size of the Court, to ensure favorable outcomes in cases. In the language of the times, "packing" referred more broadly to the simple practice of appointing justices who would decide cases the right way.[234] As Lincoln explained, given the inability to "ask a man what he will do," it was necessary that "we must take a man whose opinions are known."[235]

During the Civil War and Reconstruction, Congress engaged in both forms of Court packing when necessity demanded it. The size of the Supreme Court was increased to ten members in 1863, in the midst of the Civil War, in an effort to ensure a pro-Union Court.[236] *The New York Times* observed that passage of the bill would "speedily remove the control of the Supreme Court from the Taney School."[237] Then Congress reduced the size of the Court from ten to seven, to be accomplished through attrition, in order to deprive Andrew Johnson of appointments.[238] In a revealing instance of doublespeak, *The American Law Review* said this was "in no sense a political measure, however much political feelings may have aided its passage."[239] Edward Bates, Lincoln's Attorney General, was more candid, lamenting that "[t]he *Supreme Court* is to be a mere party machine; to be manipulated, built up and pulled down as party exigencies require."[240] Finally, on the eve of Johnson's departure from office, with the reliable Republican general Ulysses S. Grant headed to the White House, Congress restored the size of the Court again to nine.[241]

In each of these instances an apolitical rationale was offered for manipulating the size of the Court. At the time, the justices were still assigned circuit-riding duties, with the consequence that they were almost always chosen from their home circuits.[242] Especially after Andrew Jackson's circuit court reorganization, the South constantly held a majority of seats on the Court, despite its constituting a minority of the country's population.[243] At the least, much of the "reform" was an attempt to address sectional imbalance on the Court, which was intimately tied in the minds of the public to the outcome of cases.[244]

Nonetheless, it was hardly a secret what motivated Congress to take these steps when it did. Court packing often was discussed in the press as the appropriate way for Congress to control the Court. "The Constitution, in giving Congress power to remove the President by impeachment, and to reorganize the Supreme Court by increasing the number of judges, establishes the necessary final supremacy of the Legislature," explained *Harper's Weekly*.[245] Following *Milligan*, *The New York Herald* said that "reconstruction of the Supreme Court . . . looms up into bold relief. . . . [B]y increasing or diminishing the number of the judges, the Court may be reconstructed in conformity with the supreme decisions of the war."[246] During the debate over the *McCardle* jurisdiction stripping, Pennsylvania's Senator Charles Buckalew referred directly to prior instances of Court packing by asking: "Have we not sought to mold and to conform it, to some extent at least, to our own will?"[247]

Despite the brazen manipulation of the Court during the Civil War and Reconstruction, there was a palpable discomfort in Congress and the country about doing so. Nowhere was such discomfort more evident than during the controversy over the Legal Tender Cases, which played out in the public eye between 1869 and 1871.[248] In the first legal tender case, *Hepburn v. Griswold*, decided in 1869, the Court invalidated Congress's mandate that paper money be used to pay debts incurred preceding passage of the act, citing fears of steep depreciation of bills after the war and a horror of federal interference in private contracts.[249] The decision caused a tempest because Chief Justice Chase's majority opinion implied Congress might lack the power to issue paper money altogether. The storm around *Hepburn* was exacerbated because the decision was by a 4–3 vote, on a Court that was shy two of its authorized members.[250] The *Daily Morning Chronicle* remarked that "few of the public journals seem disposed to accept the legitimate results of the recent decision of the Chief Justice in the legal-tender case."[251] Following *Hepburn*, President Grant filled the Court's two vacancies. Shortly thereafter, in *Knox v. Lee*, *Hepburn* was reversed by a 5–4 vote.[252]

The reversal of *Hepburn* in *Knox v. Lee* provoked revulsion on both sides of the political aisle. After *Hepburn*, the assumption had been that Grant would fill the empty seats with justices who would reverse that decision. Many urged him to do so.[253] But after the deed was done, the press called the decision a "judicial comedy," "humiliating," "contempt"-provoking, and "a terrible blow at the independence and dignity of the profession."[254] The *New York Tribune* concluded that "it will not be as easy to restore the public respect and reverence for the tribunal which this decision has sacrificed."[255] "[P]opular reverence for, or confidence in, the Court," said *The Nation*, "cannot possibly survive the addition, subtraction, multiplication, and division which it has been undergoing during the last five or six years."[256]

The tension the Congress faced was that as much as it was unwilling to tolerate a truly independent Supreme Court, it simultaneously was experiencing a growing appreciation of the role the Court could play. During the debate *McCardle* sparked, over the measure to require a two-thirds majority of the Court before a law was invalidated, even Bingham deemed *Marbury v. Madison* a "sound decision" and called John Marshall "peerless."[257] Moderate Republicans joined with Democrats to defend the Court when, following *McCardle*, additional anti-Court measures were proposed. Speaking in defense of the Court, a Vermont Republican conceded that the Court some-times interfered in political matters, but the "greatest safeguard of liberty and of private rights, . . . is found, not in the legislative branch of a government, not in the executive branch of a government, but in its fundamental law that secures those private rights, administered by an independent and fearless judiciary."[258]

Congress and Union supporters were coming to realize how much they needed the federal judiciary.[259] The decision of the Constitutional Convention to use judicial review to ensure state fidelity to national authority continued to resonate. Recognizing they were essential to make national authority felt in the South without the military, Congress was especially anxious to create lower federal courts.[260] This period saw the greatest enlargement of federal jurisdiction ever.[261] The option to remove cases from state to federal court was extended to many more cases and parties, habeas corpus jurisdiction was expanded, and for the first time ever Congress opened the federal courts' doors for adjudication of all federal questions so long as the controversy involved a specified jurisdictional amount.[262] But one page of debate after Bingham had threatened to annihilate an unruly Supreme Court, he said, speaking of a measure to protect southerners loyal to the Union, "I would give remedy by law in United States courts in all cases if these State governments are not sufficient for the efficient protection of life and property therein."[263] In fact, the very bill stripping the Court's jurisdiction in *McCardle* expanded the jurisdiction of the Supreme Court in revenue collection cases.[264]

Still, the Supreme Court was constantly in jeopardy during this period, apparently because the justices were unable to read the public mood or unwilling to temper their actions in the face of it. In *Milligan*, the five justices who insisted on reaching the constitutional question explained that "[d]uring the late wicked Rebellion, the temper of the times did not allow that calmness in deliberation and discussion so necessary to a correct conclusion of a purely judicial question. . . . *Now* that the public safety is assured," the Court continued, clearly misreading its milieu, "this question, as well as all others, can be discussed and decided without passion. . . ."[265] Obviously that proved a serious misjudgment, akin to that in moving the *McCardle* litigation ahead on the docket and then having to back down when jurisdiction was stripped, or to deciding *Hepburn* with two decisive vacancies on the Court. From *Dred Scott* through the end of Reconstruction, Congress exercised control over the Court when the justices proved unable to understand what they could and could not safely accomplish. The Supreme Court's conduct, and congressional supervision of it, brought the derision of the country upon the justices.

5

CONSTITUENCY

*"[C]orporations are desirous of having all their causes
removed to the Federal courts"*

T he Supreme Court experienced a remarkable rise in respect and importance during the generation following the Civil War. In 1885, the
lawyer and historian William Montgomery Meigs described with wonder the prevailing understanding of the Supreme Court's power, how its "judgment in a suit between A. and B." was taken as "finally and forever settling
as to everybody and all departments of government the great questions of constitutional law." Meigs believed the idea "almost an absurdity" but acknowledged that the view was so "ordinarily accepted" that "an argument on the
other side runs a very good chance of not even being listened to."[1]

Though observers then and now attributed the rise of the Court's authority to unthinking acquiescence on the part of the public, it is better understood in terms of constituency.[2] The Court found its way to the center of
the American stage by rendering decisions that catered to the needs of
those who had power over it. Melville Fuller, the Chief Justice at the time
Meigs wrote, nodded to this fact when he said of the Court: "Of course its
decisions on what may be termed political questions have been in accordance with the general views previously entertained by the majority."[3]
(Fuller's conception of who constituted "the majority" was somewhat narrower than would obtain today.)

The renaissance of the Court occurred in two steps, each of which can be
tied, ironically, to two pieces of legislation enacted by the lame-duck Republican Congress in 1875. The first, the Civil Rights Act of 1875, granted black

citizens equal access to public accommodations, such as transportation, theaters, and hotels.[4] The second, the Judiciary and Removal Act of 1875, dramatically expanded the jurisdiction of the federal trial courts.[5]

While the act expanding federal court jurisdiction might have been thought to serve the purposes of the civil rights law by opening the doors of the federal courts still wider to blacks seeking to enforce their rights, history had it otherwise. The new jurisdiction was invoked first and foremost by corporations, while the Supreme Court slammed the courthouse door in blacks' faces. In the *Civil Rights Cases* of 1883, the Court declared the Civil Rights Act of 1875 unconstitutional, one of a series of major decisions undoing Congress's efforts to grant rights to blacks that they could enforce in federal court.[6] But even as it was casting out the freedmen, the Supreme Court took corporate America under its wing, offering interstate businesses a refuge from the hostile actions of state governments and state courts.

By abandoning blacks and embracing corporations, the Court rose to the pinnacle of power. For its work dismantling Reconstruction, the Court received widespread plaudits from an American populace fatigued by the effort to guarantee African-Americans their security, political rights, and some measure of equality. And while many grumbled about the Court's pro-corporate decisions, they amply served the purposes of the dominant Republican Party and its chief patrons, the tycoons of America's flourishing big businesses.

The Supreme Court apparently now understood the value of having a constituency, i.e., those with the political power to protect it. Giving up on Reconstruction was easy enough; bowing to public sentiments may well have accorded with the proclivities of a majority of the justices. The decisions in favor of business and property rights, on the other hand, were the product of a deliberate effort by the country's rulers to pander to the captains of industry. With much riding on the willingness of the federal judiciary to protect corporate interests from state interference, the tycoons demanded, and obtained, judicial appointees sympathetic to their cause. These federal judges then acted as anticipated, favoring business and property in their decisions well into the twentieth century. Once again, the Court's authority was bolstered by national interests that needed it to protect them from state action.

THE PROGRAM OF CONGRESSIONAL RECONSTRUCTION

"[T]he law which operates upon one man shall operate equally upon all"

The Reconstruction Congress labored from the end of the Civil War until its last act in 1875 to specify and protect the rights of newly emancipated blacks. This process yielded three constitutional amendments and many major congressional enactments. While struggling with the theoretical question of how precisely to define equality, Congress was forced to deal with the very practical problem of continuing southern recalcitrance. Looking back, James Blaine of Maine, congressional leader and failed Republican presidential candidate, observed that southerners seemed to view readmission to the Union "only as the beginning of the era in which they would more freely wage conflict against that which was distasteful and, as they claimed, oppressive."[7]

Following the war, Congress quickly took steps to ensure black equality. The Thirteenth Amendment, which banned "slavery" and "involuntary servitude," was ratified in 1865. Congress was given power to enforce the amendment "by appropriate legislation."[8] Then the Civil Rights Act of 1866 granted blacks the right to contract and own property and to participate as suitor and witness in court proceedings, on equal terms with whites.[9]

There were two difficulties with these measures that led to further constitutional amendments. First, freeing the slaves served ironically to increase the political strength of the rebel states. The Constitution allocated congressional seats on the basis of each state's population. Slaves, who were not entitled to vote, still counted as "three-fifths" of their personhood for the purposes of determining a state's representation in Congress. Once the slaves were emancipated, the southern states actually gained increased congressional seats from the increase in "population." Although emancipation enhanced southern political power, the laws in those states still did not extend the franchise to blacks. This meant, as a practical matter, that all of the South's new congressional seats were likely to go to opposition Democrats. Second, there was the question, even among its supporters, of whether the Civil Rights Act of 1866 qualified as "appropriate legislation" authorized by the Thirteenth Amendment to eliminate "slavery."[10]

The Fourteenth Amendment solved one of these problems and dealt with the other in part. Making up for any shortcoming of the Thirteenth Amendment, the first section of the Fourteenth Amendment protected rights and equality directly. Section 5 of the Fourteenth Amendment then gave Congress the power to enact enforcing legislation.[11] Describing this combination, Thaddeus Stevens, one of the amendment's drafters, said it "allows Congress to correct the unjust legislation of the States, so far that the law which operates upon one man shall operate equally upon all."[12] Together these clauses plainly provided Congress with authority for the 1866 Civil Rights Act, which was repassed as a precaution in 1870.[13] Section 2 of the Fourteenth Amendment solved the voting problem. It held that to the extent a state failed to permit voting by any "male inhabitants" (other than for "participation in rebellion, or other crime"), representation was reduced accordingly.[14] Section 2 did nothing to assure Republican control of the southern states, but it did guarantee that those states did not gain political power from emancipation.

The final constitutional amendment gave black men the vote, felicitously conferring an electoral advantage on Republicans. The *National Anti-Slavery Standard* explained that "evenly as parties are now divided in the North, it [the Republican Party] needs but the final ratification of the pending Fifteenth Amendment, to assure . . . the balance of power in national affairs."[15] Ratified in 1870, the Fifteenth Amendment provided that the vote could not be "denied or abridged . . . on account of race, color, or previous condition of servitude." It too granted power for congressional enforcement.[16] In the South, enfranchising blacks aided the Republican Party immeasurably. Observing these political benefits, Radical congressman William D. Kelley said, "[P]arty expediency and exact justice coincide for once."[17]

Three constitutional amendments, however, were hardly enough to deter southerners determined to subjugate blacks and overturn rule by Reconstruction authorities. The Ku Klux Klan, and later other organizations, engaged in terrorist activities to recover southern white rule. Federal judge Hugh L. Bond, who traveled to North Carolina to deal with Klan violence, wrote his wife: "I never believed such a state of things existed in the United States." Fearing to put on paper what he had heard and seen, he would say only: "I do not believe any province in China has less to do with Christian civilization."[18] Election-related violence was the worst. A federal marshal on the ground in Gibson County, Tennessee, reported "a mob at every poll" and "a perfect reign of terror. Intimidation, violence . . . and preventing of the colored citizens from voting was the order of the day."[19]

Doing its "utmost to strengthen the hands of the president in a contest with these desperate elements," Congress passed Enforcement Acts in 1870 and 1871. These measures were aimed primarily at protecting black suffrage and eliminating Klan violence.[20] One act, for example, made it illegal for "two or more persons" to "conspire or go in disguise on the highway or on the premises of another, for the purpose of depriving" anyone of "equal protection under the laws."[21]

The final Reconstruction measure was the Civil Rights Act of 1875, which guaranteed blacks equal access to certain public accommodations, such as hotels, transportation, and public entertainment. "The effects of the late civil strife," noted Ulysses S. Grant in his Second Inaugural Address in 1873, asking Congress for more legislation, "have been to free the slave and make him a citizen. Yet he is not possessed of the civil rights which citizenship should carry with it."[22] Opponents objected to the civil rights bill's intrusion into many areas of traditional state responsibility. "[T]here is not one single act or omission in this bill which is not already punishable in Louisiana under her State statute," protested Allen G. Thurman, a Democratic senator from Ohio.[23] They also complained about the direct regulation by Congress of private activity. Thurman pointed out that the Fourteenth Amendment said "no state shall," yet the proposed legislation was "aimed against the acts of individuals."[24] But supporters insisted on the need to go after private violators directly: "We desire to protect the right by punishing the wrongdoer," to ensure no state law "shall protect the criminal from punishment."[25]

THE SUPREME COURT RAVAGES RECONSTRUCTION

"[K]eeping a promise to the colored man's ear and breaking it to his hope"

Even before the enactment of the Civil Rights Act of 1875, the Supreme Court was limiting severely the reach of Congress's ambitious Reconstruction measures. Engaging in typical understatement, Senator Blaine would look back and say that "[b]y decisions of the Supreme Court, the Fourteenth Amendment has been deprived in part of the power which Congress no doubt intended to impart to it."[26] Within a decade the Court had undone much that Congress had sought to do legislatively. In 1888, George Holt published a comprehensive treatise on the jurisdiction of the state and federal courts. The section entitled "Civil Rights Suits" was a short one indeed. Though it went on just a few lines longer, the first sentence held all the punch: "The legislation of Congress for the protection of civil rights has been held by the United States Supreme Court to be, in its principal general provisions, unconstitutional."[27]

The Supreme Court first construed the reach of the Fourteenth Amendment in the 1873 *Slaughterhouse Cases.* Given that the central impetus for that amendment was to ensure the rights and equality of the freedmen, it undoubtedly influenced the Court's interpretation that this first case under the amendment was brought by white butchers challenging a monopoly established by the city of New Orleans.[28] *The Nation* called it a "curious case," reminding its readers that "at the time of the passage of the Fourteenth Amendment some politicians objected . . . on the ground that, though only intended to establish the civil rights of negroes, its terms were so far-reaching that it might possibly be construed by the courts into something much more dangerous."[29]

The *Slaughterhouse Cases* involved a law enacted by Louisiana following the Civil War, which required that all butchering in the city of New Orleans be done at the facilities of the Crescent City Live Stock Landing and Slaughterhouse Company.[30] The ostensible and salutary purpose of the law was that consolidating butchering in one locale would ensure the sanitary conditions essential to the elimination of yellow fever.[31] Still, the butchers (any of whom could do his own butchering at Crescent City so long as a fee was paid) bristled. It was common knowledge, and subsequently adjudicated, that Crescent City was a "wholesale bribery concern" that had paid legislators handily to obtain its monopoly.[32] The butchers claimed the law violated the Fourteenth Amendment.

The opinion for the majority in the *Slaughterhouse Cases* gutted one of the Fourteenth Amendment's chief provisions, the Privileges or Immunities Clause. The amendment begins by making all persons "born or naturalized in the United States . . . citizens of the United States and of the State wherein they reside." It goes on to provide that no state "shall abridge the privileges or immunities of citizens of the United States." Though historians debate to this day precisely what the privileges or immunities formulation was meant to accomplish, the weight of authority is that the Reconstruction Congress intended to put under federal protection all the basic rights of citizenship, such as many core guarantees of the Bill of Rights.[33] Given the free labor ideology of the time, the right to ply one's own trade asserted by the butchers at least arguably fell within such privileges and immunities.[34] Nonetheless, the majority of the *Slaughterhouse* justices, loath to see the Supreme Court placed in the role of "perpetual censor" over state laws, would not take this step.[35] The opinion for the Court by Justice Samuel Freeman Miller, a Kentucky Republican appointed by Lincoln, first drew a distinction between "citizenship of the United States, and citizenship of a State." It was only the "former which are placed by this clause under the protection of the Federal Constitution."[36] Second, Miller took an extraordinarily narrow view of what constituted the rights of national citizenship, limiting it to such rarely contested matters as "to come to the seat of government to assert any claim he [the citizen] may have" and "to demand the care and protection of the Federal government over his life, liberty, and property when on the high seas or within the jurisdiction of a foreign government."[37] In this way the clause was deprived of almost any meaning.

The four dissenters on the *Slaughterhouse* Court were beside themselves (all wrote but Chief Justice Chase, who was not to live out the year).[38] Justice Noah Swayne said the Court had turned "what was meant for bread into a stone."[39] His colleague Justice Stephen Field noted wryly that under the majority's decision, the Fourteenth Amendment "was a vain and idle enact-ment, which accomplished nothing, and most unnecessarily excited Con-gress and the people on its passage."[40]

Underlying the denial of the butchers' claims was the *Slaughterhouse* majority's desire to limit the extent to which the Civil War and Reconstruc-tion altered antebellum understandings of the relationship between the states and the national government. Conceding that the war demonstrated that the states presented a "true danger to the perpetuity of the Union," Justice Miller still did not "see in those amendments any purpose to destroy the main fea-tures of the general system."[41] To rule as the butchers wished would "fetter and degrade the State governments by subjecting them to the control of Con-gress, in the exercise of powers heretofore universally conceded to them." The Court simply would not buy a view of the Fourteenth Amendment that "radically changes the whole theory of the relations of the State and Federal governments to each other and of both those governments to the people."[42]

This rationale for the *Slaughterhouse* ruling contradicted what many in the Reconstruction Congress envisioned as the result of the war. True enough, the Fourteenth Amendment's supporters had denied any intent to achieve "consolidated Government."[43] Still, they were quite clear that the war had changed things. "I had in the simplicity of my heart, supposed that 'State rights' being the issue of the war, had been decided," declared Radical Rich-ard Yates of Illinois.[44] Another Radical colleague agreed: "Hitherto we have taken the Constitution in a solution of the spirit of State rights. Let us now take it as it is sublimed and crystallized in the flames of the most gigantic war in history."[45] On the *Slaughterhouse* Court, Justice Joseph Bradley, who himself eventually came to play a leading role in dismantling Reconstruction, was dismayed. "The amendment was an attempt to give voice to the strong National yearning for that time and that condition of things," he wrote. "In my judgment, it was the intention of the people of this country in adopting that amendment to provide National security against violation by the States of the fundamental rights of the citizen."[46]

Even after *Slaughterhouse*, the carnage ultimately made of congressional Reconstruction legislation was not a foregone conclusion. The Civil Rights Act of 1875 was passed following the *Slaughterhouse* decision. Senator Charles Sumner was quick to make the point that the Supreme Court's ruling did not disturb the impending civil rights legislation "by a hair's breadth."[47] Given the *Slaughterhouse* decision, proponents of the civil rights measure simply switched their basis for the civil rights law from the Privileges or Immunities Clause to the provision of the Fourteenth Amendment prohibiting any state from denying "to any person within its jurisdiction the equal protection of the laws."[48] After all, the *Slaughterhouse* majority itself, in denying the butchers' claims under this provision, had stressed that the "one pervading purpose" of the Fourteenth Amendment was "the freedom of the slave race."[49]

By the time the Court was through with Reconstruction legislation, however, Congress might have saved its energies throughout the 1870s. *United States v. Cruikshank* and *United States v. Reese* both involved criminal prosecutions under the Enforcement Act of 1870 for gross violations of the freedmen's rights. *Reese* arose out of a naked scheme to deny the vote to blacks in Lexington, Kentucky, by refusing them the right to pay poll taxes.[50] The Court in *Reese* proclaimed that the Fifteenth Amendment did not protect the right to vote, which remained primarily under the auspices of the states, but only the right to be free from racial discrimination while voting. Because the Enforcement Act punished all interferences with the right to vote, not just those motivated by race, it exceeded Congress's power under the Fifteenth Amendment.[51]

In *Cruikshank* the Court similarly limited Congress's powers. The case arose out of the mass slaughter of almost three hundred blacks in the struggle for political control of Louisiana.[52] With the election results of 1872 still in doubt, on Easter Day in 1873 a mob of Democrats seized the Colfax, Louisiana, parish seat by force, killing many defenders after they had surrendered or were in custody. The Justice Department obtained convictions of several of those responsible.[53] Reversing the convictions, the justices adopted an extremely technical reading of the indictment, which plainly talked of racial slaughter, holding that it nonetheless was insufficient because it did not specifically state that the right to vote was impeded on the basis of race.[54] The opinion might have stopped there, but it did not. The Court went on to reiterate the narrow view of the Fifteenth Amendment that it had expressed in *Reese* and to announce a similarly narrow interpretation of the Fourteenth Amendment.[55] The duty of protecting "the equality of rights," the Court held, "was originally assumed by the States; and it still remains there. The only obligation resting upon the United States is to see that the States do not deny the right. This the Amendment guarantees, but no more."[56] One southern lawyer described the reaction in Louisiana to the *Cruikshank* decision as "the utmost joy . . . and with it a return of confidence which gave best hopes for the future."[57] A Radical Republican paper commented that as construed, the act was "only a pretense, keeping a promise to the colored man's ear and breaking it to his hope."[58]

In 1883, the Court struck down the Civil Rights Act of 1875. Ruling in the

Civil Rights Cases, the Court held that the Fourteenth Amendment did "not invest Congress with power to legislate upon subjects which are within the domain of State legislation," nor did it "authorize Congress to create a code of municipal law for the regulation of private rights."[59] Put simply, Congress lacked the power under the Fourteenth Amendment to reach the acts of private individuals. This time it was Justice Bradley, who had been a *Slaughterhouse* dissenter, writing for the majority, and his tone displayed an unmistakable change of heart.[60] Referring to the freedmen with evident impatience, he said: "[T]here must be some stage in the progress of his elevation when he takes the rank of a mere citizen and ceases to be the special favorite of the laws. . . . There were thousands of free colored people in this country before the abolition of slavery," Bradley observed, yet "no one at that time thought that it was any invasion of his personal status as a freeman because he was not admitted to all the privileges enjoyed by white citizens."[61]

Ultimately, the Supreme Court's decisions left vulnerable the emancipated slaves' most basic rights of citizenship, so long as the states engaged in subterfuge when denying them. While explicit discrimination by law was forbidden, it took only a little artifice on the part of states to accomplish the same goals in effect. Even the rights to serve on juries and to vote were subsequently curtailed by state governments, with the Court unwilling or unable to intervene.[62] The *Chicago Tribune* explained in 1890 that to avoid federal interference, "the Southern States all have constitutional provisions and election laws which apparently guarantee the Negroes the right to vote," but nonetheless "[u]nder this cover election cheating has been reduced to a system and the blacks are practically disenfranchised in several Southern States."[63] To cite but one example, plucked from Charleston's *News and Courier*, a leading Democrat in the 1876 gubernatorial election in South Carolina called on each Democrat to "control the vote of one negro by intimidation, purchase, keeping him away or as each individual may determine."[64]

THE COURT APPLAUDED

"[A] general apathy among the people concerning the war and the negro"

Had the Court unraveled this much of Congress's handiwork at any other time in history, it would have evoked an angry response. In this case, undoing Reconstruction served only to enhance the Court's reputation, for by the time it acted the bulk of the American people—North and South, Republican and Democrat alike—had tired of the entire endeavor.[65] There were dissenting voices, of course—notably blacks and their dwindling supporters—but the Court's decisions dismantling Reconstruction were met to a remarkable degree by the widespread plaudits of the popular press.

When Reconstruction began, there was a buoyant optimism about the ability of the freedmen to serve as free laborers and citizens. "When the war was over the question, 'What shall we do with the blacks?' agitated the whole country," noted a correspondent to the relatively moderate *New York Times* in 1867. But "to the joy of his friends and the discomfiture of his enemies, the negro became an industrious worker." At the same time, "[t]o justify the faith reposed in him, the colored man began eagerly to fit himself by education for citizenship." The widely popular *Harpers' Weekly* stamped this assessment with its seal of approval: "[W]e have not seen an apparently truer picture of the actual conduct and temper of this important class of citizens."[66]

As late as 1872, Reconstruction looked as if it might succeed. The federal government was making progress in suppressing Klan violence and protecting the freedmen's rights. In addition to the Enforcement Acts of 1870 and 1871, Congress also had created the Department of Justice, centralizing the Attorney General's functions for the first time.[67] The combination of congressional authorization and aggressive government enforcement had served largely to suppress the Klan, and the country enjoyed its most peaceful Reconstruction election.[68]

Already, though, there were troubling signs that the northern will was cracking. Horace Greeley, editor of the *New York Tribune* and a former abolitionist, ran on the Democratic and Liberal Republican tickets against Grant. Greeley talked of "reconciliation" and advocated "local self-government," a code for abandoning military control in the South. Grant trounced Greeley, but now many people were questioning the continuing reconstruction of the South.[69] The changing national mood can be seen in the shifting positions of Republican representative James A. Garfield of Ohio. In 1866, Garfield said he intended to "see to it that, hereafter, personal rights are placed in the keeping of the nation."[70] In correspondence four years later, however, he wrote: "[I]t is not the theory of government that any able bodied citizen shall be carried." Rather, the right to vote was the panacea that "confers upon the African Race the care of its own destiny."[71] In 1871, Garfield opposed passage of the Ku Klux Klan Act on the ground that the protection of personal rights was the realm of state governments.[72] (A decade later the politically astute Garfield became President.)

The positive reaction to the *Slaughterhouse Cases* in 1873 confirmed that the justices were hardly alone in expressing concern about the effect of the Fourteenth Amendment on the federal-state balance. Given *The New York*

World's Democratic leanings, its applause was expected: the "Court very properly decided that . . . the new Amendments, fairly interpreted, leave all the broader relations between the States and the Federal Government unchanged and untouched."[73] But satisfaction swept across Republican journals as well, many of which were backpedaling on their prior commitments to national enforcement of civil rights.[74] *The Nation* gently commended the Court for showing "a very laudable determination to cling to the old and well-settled maxims of interpretation" (read: states' rights).[75] The *New York Tribune* lauded the case as a "most important decision" because it "set up a barrier against new attempts to take to the National Government the adjustment of questions legitimately belonging to State tribunals and legislators."[76] The *Chicago Tribune*, which had supported abolition during the war, proclaimed: "The decision has long been needed, as a check upon the centralizing tendencies of the Administration to enforce its policy and to maintain its power, even at the expense of the constitutional prerogatives of the States. The Supreme Court has not spoken a moment too soon or any too boldly on this subject."[77]

Democrats swept to power in the midterm elections of 1874, in no small part because of increasing popular opposition to Reconstruction. The Panic of 1873 also aided the Democrats' cause, as people's concerns shifted to the economy.[78] Republicans had sought to play down Reconstruction as an election issue, but the Senate's passage of Sumner's civil rights measure that year brought it front and center.[79] Before the election Democrats were down 110 seats in the House of Representatives; afterward they held a 60-seat majority. Democrats also won many state races.[80] James Garfield saw the election results as reflecting "a general apathy among the people concerning the war and the negro."[81]

Ironically, even the debate surrounding the passage of the Civil Rights Act of 1875 betrayed the growing impatience with the freedmen and the use of national authority to protect them. "Is it not time for the colored race to stop playing baby?" asked the *Chicago Tribune*.[82] "In the interest of the negro, we trust that [the Civil Rights Act] may never reach the Court," opined *The Nation* presciently. "The Reconstruction period is ended, and the negro in the future will occupy such a position as his sobriety and industry entitle him to."[83] Although the Senate passed a version of the bill prior to the Republicans' crushing defeat in the 1874 midterm election, it was unclear whether most Republicans supported the measure. As it died in the House, Democrat Charles A. Eldredge told Republicans: "[I]t is the deadest corpse you ever saw and you are all glad of it."[84]

The civil rights bill ultimately was adopted less out of enthusiasm for the cause than as a result of an elaborate game of political chicken. Unexpectedly, a group of Republican representatives revived the measure in the 1874 lame-duck session. Radicals felt a moral obligation to protect blacks. For most Republicans, though, supporting the bill was part of a hair-trigger political calculation. Passage of the bill in 1874 might ensure that blacks would vote in the election of 1876, make the Democrats look racist and unprogressive, and help dispose of the issue before the looming 1876 presidential election. Republicans felt driven to support the bill but feared passage might permanently alienate whites, particularly in the South. Democrats typically opposed the bill but understood that passage might drive a permanent wedge between the Republicans and the white population. One Washingtonian captured the spirit of the conflict, saying: *"As a Democrat, I would manage after a hard fight to be beaten; and as a Republican I would do the same. My opinion is that the side that wins will be beaten before the Country."* [85] The bill passed only after Republicans in the House changed the rules to prohibit a filibuster by opponents. [86] "With the close of this Congress," reported Philadelphia's Republican *American and Gazette*, "the era of reconstruction must be considered closed." [87]

Reconstruction crumbled for many reasons. An attachment to federalism and an unwillingness to turn state functions over to the federal government undoubtedly played a part, though how sincere that attachment was came into question in the next decades. [88] Racism clearly showed its ugly face in the North and South alike. [89] A large part of the explanation was financial. Reconstruction was incredibly costly; one low estimate put it at a quarter of all federal spending. Particularly after the crash of 1873 and the ensuing economic depression, the country lost the will to spend the money necessary to sustain the use of force over the South. [90] Northern capitalists, who had kept the country afloat during the war, envisioned less risky uses of their money. They were instrumental in brokering the resolution of the disputed 1876 Hayes-Tilden election, trading a Republican in the White House for the end of the military presence in the South. [91] All these forces made it difficult for the Republican Party to pursue a steady strategy. [92] A northern perception of widespread corruption in Congress and the Reconstruction governments of the South only made matters worse, especially in hard economic times. [93]

The country tired of the necessity for force and lost faith that legal measures could accomplish what needed to be done. The year the *Slaughterhouse Cases* were decided, *The New York Times* declared: "Law has done all that it can for the negroes, and the sooner they set about securing their future for themselves the better it will be for them and their descendants." [94] Radical Joseph R. Hawley of Connecticut, in debate over civil rights measures, said: "There is a social, and educational, and moral reconstruction of the South needed that will never come from any legislative halls, State or national."[95] Enacting grand principles had proven one thing; subduing the South, another. There was simply no will to get the job done. "We have tried . . . constant partisan intermeddling from Washington and bayonets *ad lib*. The malady," sighed the *Springfield Republican*, "does not yield to the treatment. Let us now try . . . a little vigorous letting alone."[96]

Given these sentiments, it is easy enough to see why the Supreme Court abandoned Reconstruction. Though these same justices might have supported congressional efforts if national opinion had been resolute, with that consensus collapsing the course of least resistance was plainly an attractive one. Some of them, no doubt, disfavored the use of aggressive federal authority to protect the rights of newly emancipated slaves.[97] Even justices who had initially supported a broad interpretation of congressional power, however, gave up the ghost as the national will crumbled. Justice Bradley was the prime case in point.[98] His opinion invalidating the Civil Rights Act of 1875 eliminated a law no one seemed to want. Though the law was "practically a dead letter" for the eight years before the Court ruled, still, said *The New York Times*, "it has been of great influence, and that mischievous. It has kept alive a prejudice against the negroes and against the Republican Party in the South."[99] Rutherford Hayes, who had prevailed in the brokered deal to gain the presidency in 1876 in large part on the basis of his promise to end military rule in the South, wrote the Chief Justice in July 1882 to stress the importance of Republicans' maintaining the friendship of southerners. "With that sentiment right, our cause will advance, with that sentiment wrong, all our efforts will fail." Waite responded two days later, "I agree with you entirely as to the necessity of keeping public sentiment at the south in our favor."[100]

The major press of the nation, though partisan, almost uniformly cheered the Court's decision to eliminate the last major piece of Reconstruction legislation. *The New York Times*, *The Nation*, and *Harper's Weekly* all joined in applauding the Court.[101] *The Nation* lauded the Court for settling "the point forever, that the Fourteenth Amendment merely adds new limitations upon State action . . . and does not change in any way the fundamental structure of the Government."[102] Philadelphia's Republican *North American* supposed that "not many intelligent and thoughtful people will be surprised by the judgment. . . . Sounder and more sensible ideas now prevail" than when the Civil Rights Act was passed.[103] *The New York Times* declared it a fitting burial of Reconstruction: "The judgment of the court is but a final chapter in a history full of wretched blunders, made possible by the sincerest and noblest sentiment of humanity."[104]

THE STATES INHIBIT INDUSTRIAL GROWTH

"[M]uch legislation hostile to corporations"

Just as support for Reconstruction was crumbling, America's economy was nationalizing at a rapid pace. This revolutionary economic change dislocated people and altered ways of living. Popular discontent rose, and protest movements formed. In response, the states adopted a variety of measures to protect the interests of their citizens. These state laws erected barriers to the free flow of capital and interstate trade, posing a challenge to businesses operating in the newly invigorated commercial environment. At the same time, state courts demonstrated a notable bias in favor of the local citizenry in suits involving out-of-state interests. Corporations and those with wealth began to look to the federal courts for relief.

The railroads formed the tip of the industrial spear. Roughly 9,000 miles of track in 1850 had grown to 200,000 miles by century's end. The federal government encouraged growth, granting the railroads more than 158 million acres of land. By 1891 the Pennsylvania Railroad was employing three times the number of men in all branches of America's armed services. In 1895 some eight hundred thousand men worked for the railways, roughly 3 percent of the nation's workforce. Communication followed the rails. Telegraph and then telephone traveled alongside the railcars, the mails inside them.[105]

The growth of the railroads fueled greater industrialization. The gross national product grew almost 15 percent per year from 1870 to 1900. Steel came to replace iron and wood in the building of machinery. The railroads encouraged economic specialization, as goods for production could be transported easily from source to factory. Montgomery Ward opened its doors in 1872; it was the first major trader to operate solely on a mail-order basis.[106]

The agrarian economy gave way to an urban and industrial one. The last census to show a majority of Americans engaged in agriculture was that of 1870. In that year, the average firm consisted of eight people, often family members; by 1900 more than fifteen hundred firms were employing more than five hundred people each. Four million immigrants came to America in each decade between 1870 to 1900.[107] Millions moved from the farms and foreign shores to urban centers of production. Agrarian "island communities" came apart as the people flocked to the cities.[108]

As firms consolidated and the population became centralized, the very nature of doing business changed. In a disparate and agrarian economy, goods were provided by local purveyors of general merchandise. Centralization required a means to get the goods to market, and economies of scale fostered specialization. The general merchant gave way to the middleman and then to the corporate form.[109] By 1900, some 70 percent of those working in industry were employed by corporations.[110] Firms integrated vertically and grew to unfathomable size. "The day of combination is here to stay," declared John D. Rockefeller famously. "Individualism has gone, never to return."[111]

The industrial boom fed both easy credit and speculation. In the aftermath of the Civil War, credit began to move from the financiers of the East to the farmers and businesspeople of the South and West.[112] "The West, as a new country, destitute of capital, has looked to the East for assistance" and been led "to agree to terms rather hard."[113] Looking only to mortgages, one economist estimated that "Indiana must make to non-resident capitalists an annual payment greater than the entire tax levy of the state."[114] Cities and towns in the West sold their souls in the form of municipal bonds to attract the railroads. The debt was incurred, explained a New York advocate for railroad regulation, "by the influences of the railway corporations . . . and a great part of it was doubtless fraudulently contracted through the bribing of local officers."[115] Railroad investment, cried *The Nation*, was "a simple craze . . . madness has ruled the hour."[116]

So much rapid change gave rise to inevitable discontent, which in turn fueled nascent social movements and third parties. Labor unionism was in its infancy, including formation of the National Labor Union in 1866. At its height the union drew sixty thousand attendees to its annual congress.[117] Though the National Labor Union dissolved six short years later, its place rapidly was taken by the Knights of Labor, a secret fraternal society that eventually went public and participated actively in politics.[118] Farmers in the West organized under the auspices of the National Grange of the Patrons of Husbandry (or simply the Grange), formed in 1867.[119] Reform and Anti-Monopoly parties sprang up in the states.[120]

Then the crash. In September 1873, the financial empire of the country's leading investment banker, Jay Cooke, collapsed when it proved impossible to sell further bonds to finance the Northern Pacific Railroad.[121] The country entered a severe economic downturn, which until 1929 was called *the* Great Depression.[122] The "mania of railroad investment" that had "swept through the country like a first-class epidemic," explained *The Nation*, came to a halt "occasioning not less quiet suffering."[123] A year later Grant reported in his annual message to Congress: "Since the convening of Congress one year ago the nation has undergone a prostration in business and industries such as it has not been witnessed with us for many years."[124]

The ugly side of the times became apparent in the great railway strike of 1877. Triggered by the Baltimore & Ohio Railroad's July decision to roll back wages, riots broke out all along the line, from Baltimore to Chicago. Stations were looted, and railroad cars burned. Order was restored only when Grant's successor, President Hayes, called out federal troops, leaving many workers dead.[125] Grant immediately noted the irony in using troops to suppress workers when the nation had refused to do so "to protect the lives of negroes." When he had used troops, "the sound of indignation belched forth," but now "there is no hesitation about exhausting the whole power of the government to suppress a strike on the slightest intimation that danger threatens."[126]

In response to protests from angry citizens and burgeoning popular movements, the states adopted a series of measures to protect local wealth against foreign investors and local businesses from outside competition.[127] This continued throughout the remainder of the century. The result was, as the then federal circuit judge (and later President and Chief Justice) William Howard Taft explained it, "much legislation hostile to corporations. . . . It takes the form of discriminating taxation, of the regulation of rates to be charged . . . and sometimes of the direct deprivation of vested rights."[128]

States regularly repudiated their debts. In the South, it was antebellum debt and bills rung up by Reconstruction governments. "The whole country is in disgrace by reason of this horrid spectacle," said *The Independent*, commenting on southern repudiation.[129] In the West, it was railroad obligations.[130] During the boom the laws had served as little obstacle to taking on new debt; now legal irregularities loomed large as a basis for defaulting. Western issuers of municipal debt sought to repudiate in light of "errors and irregularities in the manner in which such bonds have been issued."[131] As *The Nation* (which had taken an aggressively pro-business turn) put it, "They have got their railroads, but, as a general thing, they now refuse to pay the bonds."[132]

States sought to protect citizens who faced mortgage foreclosures. "[C]onsidering the total volume of foreclosure, where the mortgagees are nonresidents," wrote an economist, "it is apparent that the money brought in by loans has in some way disappeared, and that the financial parasite which before sucked the blood is now swallowing the flesh."[133] Landowners were forced to pay mortgages on land, the value of which had dropped enormously. As an example, Indiana, annoyed at mortgage companies hauling citizens to the Indianapolis federal court for foreclosures, passed a law requiring foreclosure "in the counties where the mortgaged land was located, on penalty of forfeiting the right to transact business in the state."[134]

Insurance companies came in for special ire. Looking for new investments, life insurance companies had become huge mortgage holders.[135] When some states began to tax the insurance companies, home states retaliated, showing (as two legal scholars put it) "that the old Hellenic appetite, which found its satisfaction in the commercial chaos of the Confederation, has been neither extinguished nor slaked." [136] One lawyer asked: Is "retaliation,—in other words, is redress or revenge, partiality or hate, toward a sister State,—a proper factor in State legislation?" [137]

Traveling salespeople and interstate transactions also became targets of state legislation. Where once goods were sold to the hometown merchant who resold them to the locals, national firms began to send agents, derogatorily called drummers, to sell directly to consumers.[138] Local merchants complained. "I know that some of my neighbor merchants in Milwaukee feel that it is a matter of some importance to them that the Philadelphia merchant should be prohibited, to some extent, from coming into Wisconsin, and from selling his goods, through an agent," explained one delegate to a National Board of Trade meeting.[139] States responded by enacting antidrummer laws, which imposed often exorbitant business taxes on the salespeople.[140] Such laws were deemed necessary because without them, as W. S. Hastie of the Charleston Board of Trade argued, "New York, Boston and Philadelphia will absorb the whole business of the country." [141]

Business and propertied interests came to complain volubly about hostile state measures. Legislation regulating rates and repudiating debt was said to be taking on a "socialistic" or "communistic" cast.[142] Even if any particular state's law was acceptable, the divergence among them was problematic. Before the Civil War, there was concern about the "discordance in the fundamental laws of the several states, by which the rights and obligations of the citizens of a commercial country are defined." [143] Now the idea became a drumbeat in corporate circles. "We are growing so rapidly and our business is developing to such great proportions," lamented *The Railway and Corporation Law Journal*, "that it would seem to be impossible to regulate the larger organizations of business by the methods which were devised by our forefathers." Allowing each state to pass its own commercial laws was fine and well in "the eighteenth century," when "there was no commerce between the States which would seem worthy of the name." "But how different now!" We have, the *Journal* argued, "outgrown this state of affairs," and it was time to look to some national authority for relief.[144]

Nothing exemplified the ongoing war between state legislation and corporate interests as much as the fight over Granger legislation of the early 1870s. With farmers' prices dropping in a postwar market, the Grangers turned their anger on the railroads, grain warehouses, and other middlemen. An 1869 call for a farmers' convention in Illinois complained: "During the war but little attention was given to the great increase in the price of freights, as the price of produce was proportionately high," but in the present climate "we are obliged to accept less than half the former prices for much that we raise."[145] Now, explained Charles Francis Adams (son and grandson of Presidents and an accomplished writer, lawyer, diplomat, and politician), "the railroads were no longer the pioneers of dawning civilization or the harbingers of an increased prosperity, they were the mere tools of extortion in the hands of capitalists—the money-changers of the East,—marauders, banditti, usurers, public enemies."[146]

Exercising political muscle, the Grangers got laws passed that regulated the rates charged by railroads and grain elevators.[147] These laws (in Adams's words) "make those who were to use the railroads . . . the final arbiters as to what it was reasonable they should pay for such use."[148] "The outraged popular feeling" at "the unquestionable extortions of the railways," the *Chicago Tribune* told its readers (as though they did not know), took political action "in the way of public meetings, conventions, and organizations, which in due time resulted in legislative enactments."[149] For example, Illinois's Constitutional Convention of 1870, at which farmers were heavily represented, adopted articles governing railroads and corporations. As one delegate explained, "The people expect that this Convention will inaugurate by this article a contest between the people and the railroads." These new provisions of the Illinois Constitution were ratified by overwhelming margins.[150]

In seeking relief from Granger and other legislation, business was particularly skeptical of the state judiciaries. Largely elected to their offices, the state judges could be counted on to favor local interests.[151] State juries were perceived as even worse. "The prejudice of juries against corporations and the difficulty with which the latter can obtain what is their due, even when justice is on their side, is often commented upon."[152] The vulnerability of the state judiciary to popular opinion was evident in an Illinois election contest that drew huge national attention. Pursuant to the mandate of its Constitutional Convention, the Illinois legislature passed laws regulating the rates of warehouses and railroads. In January 1873, the Illinois Supreme Court struck down the railroad legislation. In the next election, Illinois's highly regarded chief justice, C. B. Lawrence, was thrown out of office. The farmers were gleeful. The *Prairie Weekly* chortled: "We had brought public opinion to bear upon legislators and governors in the passage of laws . . . but we had never tried our strength at the polls."[153] Even the *Chicago Tribune*, sympathetic to the Granger movement, was foaming, calling it "the most brutal outrage ever perpetrated in the State of Illinois under the auspices of universal suffrage."[154] Charles Francis Adams wrote of the terrible impression Lawrence's defeat had back east, tossing a judge out "for having presumed to decide a constitutional issue which arose before him as a judge, on principles of law rather than in obedience to a popular demand."[155] After the Illinois incident, *The Nation* urged that "all investors at home or abroad will do well to keep out of Illinois till the State chooses to set up an independent judiciary."[156]

Business and property interests turned increasingly to the federal courts, where the judges possessed a greater degree of autonomy from an angry public.[157] This held true whether corporations were seeking review in the Supreme Court for state court decisions or trying to flee the state courts in the first instance.[158] "That corporations are desirous of having all their causes removed to the Federal courts is a fact so well established that one would have great temerity to deny it," observed *The Central Law Journal*.[159] William Howard Taft observed that out-of-state companies "all carry their litigation into the Federal courts . . . and, in view of the deep-seated prejudice entertained against them by the local population, it is not surprising that they do."[160]

BUSINESS PACKS THE COURT

"The real anxiety of these people is with reference to the Supreme Court"

The Supreme Court's 1877 decision in *Munn v. Illinois*, upholding Granger legislation, caused business and property interests to doubt whether the federal courts would be the dependable allies they needed to deal with hostile state laws and state courts. Fortunately for these business interests, the Republican Party desperately needed corporate wealth to win close elections. By now it was perfectly evident that one way to control the Supreme Court was through favorable appointments. In exchange for campaign support, the country's new tycoons sought Supreme Court justices (and other federal judges) sensitive to their concerns. They got their wish.

The *Munn* decision, rendered the very day before Congress confirmed Hayes as the winner of the 1876 presidential contest and about eight months before the railroad strike of 1877, signaled the Supreme Court's first important foray into the new economic waters.[161] At issue in *Munn* was Illinois's warehouse law, which had been passed in tandem with the railroad law struck down by the Illinois Supreme Court. Given that Chief Justice Lawrence had been removed following invalidation of the railroad law, it perhaps was little wonder that the Illinois high court subsequently upheld the law setting maximum warehouse rates.[162] This set the stage for the Supreme Court of the United States to tackle the constitutionality of the Granger laws. Decision was eagerly awaited. Said *The Nation*: "The whole question of the validity of the laws passed by Wisconsin and other States is now before the

Supreme Court, and will soon be decided by that tribunal finally and without appeal." [163]

As a matter of jurisprudence, *Munn* was a transitional decision. The operators of an Illinois grain elevator argued that the state regulation of elevator
rates was unconstitutional under the Fourteenth Amendment's Due Process
Clause. [164] In light of the outcome in *Slaughterhouse*, one might wonder precisely how the corporate plaintiffs could possibly have thought they had a
chance. The butchers in *Slaughterhouse* had raised a due process claim as
well; reflecting its disdain for hearing challenges to state economic regulation, the Court brushed it away, saying simply: "Under no construction of
that provision that we have ever seen can the restraint imposed by the State
of Louisiana upon the exercise of their trade by the butchers of New Orleans
be held" a constitutional violation. [165]

Although the *Munn* Court also took a very deferential stance toward state
laws, and the business plaintiffs in fact lost, the Supreme Court nonetheless
indicated that it would now scrutinize some state economic measures under
the Fourteenth Amendment. Dissenting in the earlier *Slaughterhouse Cases*,
Justice Field had suggested that the correct question under the Fourteenth
Amendment was whether a given law was a proper exercise of the state's
police power—"regulations affecting the health, good order, morals, peace,
and safety of society." Field explained that "under the pretence of prescribing
a police regulation, the State cannot be permitted to encroach upon any of
the just rights of the citizen, which the Constitution intended to secure
against abridgement." [166] Meeting Field halfway, the *Munn* Court agreed
that such "police" measures were subject to judicial review but also indicated that the states' lawful regulatory powers were much greater with regard to any business that affected the "public interest": "When . . . one
devotes his property to a use in which the public has an interest, he, in effect, grants to the public an interest in that use, and must submit to be controlled by the public for the common good." [167] Such public uses included
grain warehouses, said the Court. Field dissented in *Munn* because he
thought the Court's approach under its "public interest" test was far too lenient toward state laws regulating business: "[T]here is hardly an enterprise or
business engaging the attention and labor of any considerable portion of the
community, in which the public has not an interest in the sense in which
that term is used by the court in its opinion." [168]

The anti-business result in *Munn* undoubtedly satisfied that part of the
American public deeply troubled by corporate power in hard economic times.
The *Chicago Tribune* exulted that "[t]he Granger business was a result and
not a cause. The railroads had become oppressors." [169] James Bryce, a British

diplomat and a savvy chronicler of American politics and culture, observed that public opinion "is stronger in America than anywhere else in the world, and judges are only men." The *Granger* decisions, he wrote, were a "remarkable example." Noting how the decisions "represent a different view of the sacredness of private rights and of the powers of a legislature from that entertained by Chief-Justice Marshall and his contemporaries," Lord Bryce fingered the reason: "They reveal that current of opinion which now runs strongly in America against what are called monopolies and the powers of incorporated companies."[170]

Indeed, it is difficult to read the *Munn* opinion and miss the Court's sensitivity to the political climate that had stirred the Granger measures. Chief Justice Waite's opinion began by announcing that "courts ought not to declare" a law "unconstitutional, unless it is clearly so. If there is any doubt, the expressed will of the legislature should be sustained." Discussing the Illinois Constitutional Convention that provided the impetus for the law before the Court, Waite's opinion recognized that "something had occurred which led the whole body of the people to suppose that remedies such as are usually employed to prevent abuses by virtual monopolies might not be inappropriate here." While reserving its authority to strike down laws enacted without any lawful basis, the Court said that generally speaking, the legislature was the "exclusive judge" of the "propriety of legislative interference within the scope of legislative powers." In a powerful sentence that soon proved ironic, the Court concluded: "For protection against abuses by legislatures the people must resort to the polls, not to the courts."[171]

The reaction to *Munn* among the business class was an angry one. *Dred Scott* was once again a point of comparison. "Years ago, the Court introduced the Slavery struggle with the Dred Scott decision," wrote an author in *The American Law Review*. "Today, it may be that it has introduced the property struggle with the decision of Munn v. Illinois."[172] John Pomeroy, a noted professor of law and the spokesperson for corporate interests on matters of constitutional law, also compared *Munn* with *Dred Scott*: the latter "indirectly struck at the stability of our political fabric; the Elevator Case directly strikes at the stability of private property." The *Munn* doctrine, he said, "involves the *very essence* of the destructive theories maintained by the socialists and communists of France and Germany."[173] Following *Munn*, *The New York Times* was left bitterly to call it "poetic justice" that the immediate impact of the decision "will fall most heavily" upon the westerners. "They can hope for no more money . . . until the investor is protected from the results of their vexatious legislation."[174]

Fortunately for business, it had a weapon to wield in response to *Munn*:

its money. Partisan politics of the Gilded Age lived on a razor edge: the margins of victory were often extremely close.[175] For the most part, America had been a two-party country since the Jacksonian age.[176] Occasional third-party movements like the Grange, or the Reform or Anti-Monopoly parties, while typically small, served only to tighten margins between the major parties even more. Between 1876 and 1890, the average vote differential between the parties was 1.4 percent. Democrats lost two presidential elections in the electoral college for which they had won the popular vote, and in a third race they fell only two thousand votes short out of nine million votes cast.[177] Winning races in this tight electoral environment took money, and one group that had it to spare was America's new class of corporate tycoons.[178]

Although for the most part moneyed interests had supported the Republican Party since the Civil War, the Republicans' problem was that business-people could be extremely fickle in their politics.[179] Outcomes favorable to business mattered far more than the party that delivered them. For example, when Republican officials seemed unwilling or unable to do anything about bond repudiations by southern states, Professor Pomeroy declared: "There are tens and hundreds of thousands of the most intelligent Republican voters, who would rather intrust the public administration to the Democrats, than see it still controlled by a party which is practically abandoning the high principle of nationality that first gave it political life."[180] Pomeroy might have been a bit wide of the mark regarding the electorate as a whole, but he understood business precisely.

What moneyed interests cared about was a good environment for doing business, and this necessarily included courts that would favor them reliably. America during the Gilded Age had little in the way of a bureaucracy to regulate the markets.[181] Courts were available to fill the void, and given their relative unaccountability to public opinion, they were perfect for the job.[182]

Sound courts were particularly useful to tycoons and Republican leaders both. When it came to invalidating popular state measures, it was far better that insulated judges do the job than national politicians who had to stand for election. During the Gilded Age, industrialists joined in a motley alliance with war veterans and farmers to keep the Republican Party in power.[183] Monetary policy and the tariff were the large issues of the day, and on these issues the Republicans managed to keep their coalition members in the fold. A political drawing from the era shows a woman warrior with "Republican Party" emblazoned on her shield, holding aloft a flag favoring the protective tariff, being carried on a litter by figures labeled "Capital," "Labor," "GAR" (war veterans), "Farmer," and "Manufacturer."[184] Obviously, on other issues the interests of these groups were often in tension. Politicians could

avoid political fallout by leaving it to judges to strike laws that business opposed but farmers and others favored.[185]

The priority of business thus became to ensure a federal bench, and particularly a Supreme Court, that was "sound" on the issues that mattered.[186]
Charles Elliott Perkins, head of the Burlington Railroad, wrote to his brother-
in-law J. M. Forbes as late as 1894: "There are so many jack-asses about
nowadays who think property has no rights, that the filling of the Supreme
Court vacancies is the most important function of the Presidential office."[187]
The Central Law Journal aptly noted the "indisputable fact, that the corporations look with displeasure upon any incumbent of the Federal bench, whose
feelings are with the people."[188]

Following *Munn*, moneyed interests withheld contributions to the Republican Party desperately needed to ensure Garfield's victory in the 1880
election until they were assured Garfield would put the right sort of men on
the Court.[189] Whitelaw Reid, the managing editor of the *New York Tribune*,
wrote Garfield: "The real anxiety of these people is with reference to the
Supreme Court. All monied men, and especially all corporations, regarded
the course of the Supreme Court in the Granger cases . . . as bad law and bad
faith. . . . These people hesitate because they say they are unwilling to elect
a President unless they are sure that he disapproves what they call the revolutionary course of the majority of the court." Garfield danced around the
issue, but he effectively yielded a veto on Court appointments. He bridled
at letting donors actually name Court appointees, as this would "appear to
be a delegation of the power vested in the Chief Executive." Yet he promised to appoint justices "entirely sound on these questions" on the basis of
"evidence . . . satisfactory to you as well as me."[190]

Garfield's sole appointment to the Supreme Court, Justice Stanley Matthews, surely fitted business's bill. Matthews had been nominated by Rutherford Hayes but had been rejected by the Senate because of his close ties to
the railroad industry.[191] Renominated by Garfield, Matthews again ran into
fierce opposition. He made it through the Senate by just one vote. The Anti-
Monopoly League denounced Matthews's nomination "as proof of a purpose
to pack the Supreme Court with judges who will reverse decisions in granger
cases." Opponents uniformly saw corporate hands behind the nomination.
James Weaver, who served six years representing Iowa in the House of Representatives and ran for President as the Populist Party candidate in 1892,
concurred. "It is clear that there is some power in this country which is
above the Government and more authoritative than public opinion. . . . A
child can tell you what that power is. It is the omnipresent, omnipotent
corporation." The New York Board of Trade and Transportation (the same sort

of folks responsible for protectionist antidrummer laws) complained that "the great railroad corporations of the country are endeavoring to obtain control of this court of last resort, which has heretofore been the most important bulwark in defending the public interests against corporations."[192]

For the balance of the century, business got the judges it wished.[193] Republicans held the Senate throughout, and the White House was in Republican hands twelve of twenty years. "The Republican party's long lease of power has resulted in making the Federal judiciary almost entirely Republican in political faith," observed *The Nation* in 1885.[194] Pomeroy in 1884 had noted regarding the Court that "all its members, with the single exception of Mr. Justice Field, are now, and for some time have been, Republicans."[195] Field, the dissenter in *Slaughterhouse* and *Munn*, was of course staunchly against regulations that interfered with business. The only Democratic President of the era, Grover Cleveland, proved equally dependable to business, appointing to the Supreme Court some of the most conservative justices who ever sat there.[196] The net result was a bench that safely could be relied upon to protect property rights and corporate interests. "[T]here is a well founded suspicion that men have been elevated to the supreme judicial tribunal in the land," opined *The Central Law Journal* as early as 1884, "if not at the behest of corporate interests, certainly with notice that their prejudices were naturally with those interests, and that they might be expected to care for their protection."[197]

THE FEDERAL JUDICIARY SUPPORTS BUSINESS AND PROPERTY RIGHTS

"[E]minently a question for judicial investigation"

For all of the Supreme Court's Reconstruction Era rhetoric about the importance of preserving the federal-state balance, in the years following Garfield's ascension to the presidency the justices went on a binge of striking down state laws to protect corporate interests and property rights.[198] The Court also developed jurisdictional doctrines that brought corporations flocking into the protective arms of the federal courts. Enhanced judicial authority was needed, it seemed, not to safeguard the rights of emancipated African-Americans but to protect big business and individual wealth from state meddling.[199] Congressional Democrats, especially from the South and West, repeatedly sought to limit federal court jurisdiction. Not only did the Republicans and easterners defeat any such effort, but they favored adding to federal court capacity. Ultimately the latter prevailed, permitting the federal courts to grow and offer security to their corporate constituency.

An article in the 1890 *Political Science Quarterly*, entitled "Recent Centralizing Tendencies of the Supreme Court," described the many cases in which the justices overruled prior precedents to favor corporate interests. "[E]ight years after the court held that the state of Tennessee *could* tax a drummer from Connecticut," the author offered as an example, "it held the same state could *not* tax a drummer from Ohio."[200] Many doctrines of federal law were enlisted to trump state rules that interfered with the ability of corporations to do business on a national scale.[201] There was a sharp increase, for example, in the number of cases that alleged a conflict between the state's police powers and the Constitution's Commerce Clause, which granted the national government authority to "regulate Commerce among the . . . several states." The growth in such cases led two enterprising lawyers to publish an entire treatise on the subject. The surge in such litigation, they hypothesized, was because "in no other branch of constitutional law are there so many conflicting interests arrayed against each other": "the struggle between classes and sections represented in resistance to Granger litigation, and the struggle between capital and labor represented in the protection of carriers against violent interference with their operation."[202]

The "anti-Granger" cases stand as a monument to the Supreme Court's shift in perspective. In 1886, just ten years after the ruling in *Munn*, the Court decided in the *Wabash* case that it ran afoul of the Commerce Clause for states to regulate railroad rates for carriage that crossed state lines, even when the state intended only to regulate the part of the trip within the state.[203] The *Wabash* decision, scoffed *The Nation*, "utterly demolishes the pretension of State Legislatures and railroad commissions."[204] Then, in 1890, the Court held in *Chicago, Milwaukee & St. Paul Railway Company v. Minnesota* that the question of railroad rates "is eminently a question for judicial investigation, requiring due process of law for its determination."[205] In other words, contra *Munn*, courts now were in the business of reviewing railroad rates. Dissenting, Justice Bradley said the decision "practically overrules *Munn v. Illinois*."[206] "We were in imminent danger of permitting our great carrying interests to be irrevocably embarrassed by Socialistic legislation," observed *The Commercial and Financial Chronicle*, breathing a sigh of relief. "The findings of our highest court are such as to put to rest these issues."[207]

The justices encouraged the lower federal courts to develop a uniform federal common law (i.e., a body of judge-made law) that would prevail no matter what the existing law in the states, making the federal courts the preferred venue for corporate interests. Forging federal common law had been the practice since the 1842 decision in *Swift v. Tyson*, the idea being that the state courts ultimately would come to agree with the federal common law rules, thereby facilitating commerce by creating one uniform law all over the United States.[208] As it happened, though, the state courts did not fall into line, preferring their own rules to those written by federal judges. The outcome of a case thus came to depend on nothing other than whether it was tried in state or federal court. "If I can take one side of a given case and succeed in it by going into the United States courts," one critic wrote, "or take the other and succeed in the State court, it is too clear for argument that there is something wrong."[209]

In its zeal to protect property rights, the Supreme Court even started to ignore state high court rulings on what *state* law said. If anything had been sacrosanct up to this point, it had been reverence for a state court's ruling on its own law.[210] But long-established doctrines were disregarded when the justices perceived state court chicanery assisting in the repudiation of debt obligations. In *Gelpcke v. City of Dubuque*, the Court thrust aside a decision of the Iowa Supreme Court in a case involving Dubuque's repudiation of bonds issued to secure railroad construction. "We shall never immolate truth, justice, and the law," the Court proclaimed from its high horse.[211] Constitutional historian William Montgomery Meigs deemed the decision "a most radical departure from precedent and principle."[212]

In addition to its constitutional rulings, the Supreme Court handed down important jurisdictional decisions that threw wide open the doors of federal courts to corporations. "Let it be remembered," said former justice Benjamin Curtis on the occasion of Chief Justice Taney's death in 1864, "for just now we may be in some danger of forgetting it, that questions of jurisdiction were questions of power as between the United States and the several States."[213] Marking the growing importance of federal court jurisdiction, Harvard invited Curtis in the early 1870s to give a series of lectures to its students on the subject.[214] In his 1888 volume devoted solely to the "concurrent jurisdiction" of the state and federal courts, George Holt explained that "[a] party to a legal controversy has frequently an election to resort to one of several tribunals." Then, engaging in remarkable understatement, he continued: "The exercise of such election will, in many cases, exert an important influence upon the progress or result of the litigation."[215] Corporations typically made the choice in favor of the federal courts.

The same Congress that enacted the Civil Rights Act of 1875 passed the Judiciary and Removal Act of 1875, which dramatically expanded federal court jurisdiction in a way that proved useful to the Gilded Age Supreme

Court. Some critics at the time believed the jurisdictional act was designed to benefit blacks seeking to vindicate rights and attacked it as such. Former Attorney General Ebenezer Hoar, serving one term in the House of Representatives, said: "I cannot be in favor of extending all over this country a system which takes from State tribunals and from State domination what properly belongs to it, for the purpose of remedying what I hope is to be a temporary evil."[216] But there is evidence that the jurisdictional act was all along intended as a vehicle for increasing corporate access to the federal courts.[217] In the House the measure was introduced by Representative Luke P. Poland, who referred to "difficulties in the state courts in 'other portions' of the country," possibly a reference to the Granger legislation sweeping the West at the time.[218] Though the House passed only a narrow removal bill, the Senate significantly broadened it, and the Senate's version became the law.[219] Senator Matthew Hale Carpenter, chair of the Judiciary Committee, brought the measure to the floor. He later changed his allegiance, but Carpenter was then and had been a railroad man.[220] Carpenter stated during the debates that the bill was necessary because "[t]he whole circumstances of the people, the necessities of business, our situation, have totally and entirely changed."[221]

Whatever Congress's original intent regarding the act of 1875, the Supreme Court soon enough turned the federal question jurisdiction statute into a great vehicle for corporate access to the federal courts. In the 1886 case of *Santa Clara County v. Southern Pacific Railway Company*, the Supreme Court held that a corporation was a "person" within the meaning of the Fourteenth Amendment and could sue to protect rights of due process and equal protection.[222] Remarkably, this conclusion was reached by the Court without any argument. The Chief Justice waved off counsel, telling them the justices were already decided on the issue. "The court does not wish to hear argument on the question" of whether the Fourteenth Amendment covers corporations, he said. "We are all of opinion that it does."[223] In addition to granting corporations access to the federal courts, this decision opened up a vast body of constitutional rights to the corporations.[224]

Moreover, the Supreme Court built upon its earlier decisions to open the federal court doors to corporations on the basis of their state of residence. The Court's long-standing rule had been that to exercise jurisdiction on the basis of citizenship, there must be "complete diversity," meaning that all parties on one side of a case must be from states different from those of all parties on the other side.[225] But with regard to corporations, the Supreme Court had adopted a "fiction" that all the shareholders were citizens of the state in which the corporation had its home.[226] In his lectures to the Harvard students, Curtis explained the use of such a fiction with reference to Roman practice, a reference that proved allegorical. Under Roman law, "it was necessary, in order to give their important courts jurisdiction, to allege that the plaintiff was a Roman citizen." This became a problem as "the commerce of the city and the empire so extended" and "a number of foreigners had important rights and interests to be vindicated in the courts." The Romans then invented a "fiction" that anyone with an otherwise proper legal complaint "might allege that he was a Roman citizen, and that allegation should not be denied."[227] So it was, said the United States Supreme Court, with corporations: "[A] suit by or against a corporation in its corporate name *may be presumed* to be a suit by or against citizens of the State which created the corporate body, and *no averment* or denial to the contrary is admissible."[228] The Supreme Court relied upon the corporate citizenship decisions to grant corporations broad authority to "remove" cases from state courts.[229] So potent a weapon was this for corporations that a treatise entitled *The Law of Insurance* actually listed removal as among the "remedies" insurance companies had against policyholders.[230]

Responding to these favorable decisions, corporations seeking relief from state laws and courts flooded into the federal judiciary, quickly overwhelming federal dockets. "[T]he small tide of litigation that formerly flowed in Federal channels has swollen into a mighty stream," declared John Dillon, former judge, corporate attorney, and well-recognized legal scholar.[231] The situation was intolerable. Between 1873 and 1890, the caseloads of the lower federal courts jumped from just below thirty thousand to more than fifty thousand cases, and this after much of the bankruptcy litigation had been eliminated. In roughly the same period, the Supreme Court's docket at the beginning of the term tripled from some six hundred cases in 1870 to more than eighteen hundred in 1890.[232] "The present condition of business in the Supreme Court of the United States demands the serious and immediate consideration of Congress," urged *The Washington Post*.[233] Words like "unmanageable" and "evil" were the fodder of articles about the federal court caseloads.[234] *The American Law Review* documented the "constantly repeated complaints" about the Supreme Court's docket and how "the arrears . . . are now so great that two years at least will be required to hear the cases already on its list."[235]

Though relief plainly was needed, Congress was deadlocked. House Democrats, led for most of the period by Texas representative David Culberson, favored sharply curtailing the jurisdiction of the federal courts. Republicans would not agree to this. Four times the House of Representatives considered a bill proposed by Culberson that would have severely limited jurisdiction by raising jurisdictional amounts, treating corporations as citizens of the states in which they did business, and eliminating the right of removal. Each time, the bill was blocked by the Judiciary Committee of the Republican Senate.[236]

One of the commonly offered arguments in favor of Culberson's bill was state prerogatives. Most Democrats in the House represented southern and western constituents who abhorred the transfer of business from state tribunals.[237] *The Washington Post* favored Culberson's measure, in part on the ground that "statutes authorizing the removal of cases from State Courts, are an encroachment upon the domain of State sovereignty."[238] One feels "his State pride offended" at the flow of business to the federal courts, opined *The Central Law Journal*; "[t]he State courts and the jurisprudence of the State have ample power and justice to mete to every one his dues and be governed by no sinister motive or prejudice."[239] Because of the increase in federal jurisdiction, the state courts had become "mere skeletons of what they were."[240]

Related was the argument that corporations should not be able to flee the courts of a state in which they were doing business. Corporations "come into a State for the purpose of making money," insisted Representative James Weaver of Iowa. "[W]hy should they not be compelled to go into the State courts?" Democratic representative James Waddill of Missouri said it was altogether fair to "[r]emit them to their remedy and their defense in the forum erected where they transact their business." (Of course, he recognized that forum choice might have an impact on corporate behavior as well: "[T]hey will soon conform their acts and policy to the situation, so as to have friends among the people in whose midst they prosecute their labors.")[241]

The most persistent complaint, though, was that corporations used their ability to remove cases to federal court to harass individuals and small businesses that sued them. Memorializing the U.S. Senate in 1884, the General Assembly of Iowa complained that removing cases to federal court caused "great inconvenience, unreasonable delay, and unnecessary expense," all resulting in many cases in "a denial of justice."[242] Why should persons who are poor, asked Culberson, "be compelled to litigate a cause of action with a national corporation in a Federal court, often hundreds of miles away from his residence?"[243] "Dragged" was a favorite word, used repeatedly to emphasize the injustice of corporate access to federal court.[244] Examples were given of ordinary people forced to forgo or settle claims because they could not afford the time and money to litigate in federal court.[245] Other litigants lowered their claims for damages to just below the federal threshold jurisdictional amount to avoid removal.[246] "A wealthy corporation or wealthy litigant under the present law, can so harass a poor competitor residing at a remote point from the Federal Courts, as to compel him to abandon a just and meritorious claim."[247]

The most Culberson could get past congressional Republicans was a diluted version of his bill, in 1887, which raised the jurisdictional amount from five hundred to two thousand dollars and curtailed removal somewhat.[248] Senator George F. Edmunds of Vermont told the Senate, "The bill as it came from the House of Representatives was altogether extreme," and so it had been whittled down. "[T]he general benefit of the bill," as he described it, "will be greatly to the interests of the people who have merely local controversies with corporations, and so on, that ought fairly to be tried in the local tribunals."[249] Even so, *The Railway and Corporation Law Journal* reported that the business of lending "small sums" to the West had "sensibly diminished," given that the creditor "has no recourse, as he used to have, to the United States court, where the procedure is regular, businesslike, and easy."[250]

When serious caseload relief finally came, it was in a form much more to the Republicans' liking, and strongly supportive of the federal courts. In 1891, in a measure ever after called the Evarts Bill, Congress restructured the federal judiciary.[251] The lower courts were expanded by creating federal courts of appeals. The Supreme Court's docket was eased by making these new appellate courts the court of last resort in many cases. [252] Review by the Supreme Court would now be discretionary; in cases coming from the federal courts, at least, the Court could pick and choose what it ought to hear.[253] The Supreme Court's backlog dropped quickly, and corporations retained their access to the federal courts.[254]

The federal courts now reigned supreme. They achieved this position because the Supreme Court had rendered decisions that met the needs of those political constituencies most able to sustain federal judicial power. In the instance of dismantling Reconstruction, the Court played to the broad public. Its corporate decisions were a different matter. They furthered the interests of a much narrower, albeit powerful, constituency. It is difficult to say whether the pro-corporate decisions were opposed by, or even salient to, a majority of the populace. Many of the controversial uses of federal judicial power came in suits against individuals rather than in the form of striking down laws popular with the masses. This, however, was about to change. The judiciary was about to be drawn fully into the fast-growing struggle between capital and labor.

6

LAW v. WILL

"[A] government by Judges"

The very height of judicial supremacy coincided, predictably, with the nation's most sustained period of popular clamor about judicial review. Fixing their attention on the major social reform movements whose efforts the courts so often stymied, historians call the decades bracketing the turn of the twentieth century the Populist-Progressive Era. Lawyers say simply "*Lochner*," invoking the name of the most notorious of the period's many controversial court decisions. Among lawyers, *Lochner* stands as the foremost symbol, even more than *Dred Scott*, of judges inappropriately imposing their own views of the Constitution's meaning.[1]

Theodore Roosevelt was one of many who stepped up to lead the fight against the courts. Having already served almost two terms in the White House, Roosevelt ran once again for the presidency in 1912, this time as the candidate of the Progressive (Bull Moose) Party. He spoke out against corporate corruption of politics and the social injustices that were a product of America's industrial revolution. A central target was the judges, who repeatedly struck down progressive legislation intended to better the lives of the lower and working classes.[2] Roosevelt criticized many of these decisions, including *Lochner*—the "Bakeshop Case"—in which the Supreme Court "by a bare majority of one upset a law regulating the hours of labor under unhygienic conditions . . . in the name of liberty of contract."[3] Roosevelt decried "a power which may give one man or three men or five men the right to nullify the wishes of the enormous majority of their ninety million fellow-citizens."[4] He warned that if reform were not forthcoming, the result would be the people "totally taking away this power from the judges."[5] He proposed that the people, under limited circumstances, be permitted to "recall" disfavored judicial decisions.[6]

And he lost. Like so many of the era's notable adversaries of the judiciary, Roosevelt fell while the courts carried on. Commenting on the turmoil surrounding the Supreme Court, *The New York Times* observed: "The old chorus rises, as it is rising now. It will die into silence, as it has died before. . . . Congresses have their little hour of strut and rave. The court stays."[7] The reasons for the repeated failure to adopt judicial "reform" were complex. The result was not: despite the constant outcry, judges continued to strike social legislation that had broad support.

The failure to contain the courts had serious consequences. Given that opinion polling still barely existed, it is impossible to state with certainty whether the contested *Lochner*-era decisions did in fact trump the will of the majority. What is unequivocal is that extremely large numbers of people were frustrated deeply by their inability to control or overturn what the courts did. The American Federation of Labor's Executive Council, in language typical of the times, accused the judiciary of "*destroying government by law* and substituting therefore a government by Judges."[8] Roosevelt put it only slightly more gently: "[T]here has often been much ingenious twisting of the Constitution, doubtless entirely unconscious, in order to justify judges to their own conscience in deciding against a given law."[9]

The result was a colossal loss of faith in the efficacy of law itself. Then, as now, *Lochner*-era judges had their defenders, those who insisted that judicial decisions were grounded in existing jurisprudence.[10] The judges, they said (and some still say), were simply applying the law as it stood. The fact that judges could cite precedents for their decisions, however, placated very few critics, who viewed case outcomes as inexplicably inconsistent and accused the judges of class bias. To persuade people of the legitimacy of the law, it became clear, judicial decisions required more than a basis in precedent. They also had to comport with the "felt necessities of the times."[11]

ENACTING SOCIAL LEGISLATION

"[E]fforts of the masses to break the grip which organized wealth has upon our government"

As the nation's rapid industrialization continued into the twentieth century, it left in its wake extraordinary social dislocation. Workers continued to flood from farm to city, and waves of immigrants arrived on American shores, all in search of economic opportunity. Often they found long hours of labor, an astonishing incidence of workplace accidents, overcrowded and fetid tenement housing, and low wages.[12]

Great disparities of wealth inflamed rising social discontent. Even before the depression of 1893, Populist presidential candidate James Weaver, in his *Call to Action*, pointed to the "millions of people homeless and out of employment; millions more in danger of losing their homes, and still more millions working for wages scarcely sufficient to sustain life and respectability and so meager as to shut out hope for the future."[13] Simultaneously, he conjured images of parties thrown by the rich, including "[g]olden cages filled with sweet singing birds" and "[a]ll the dishes which ingenuity could invent."[14] When the Supreme Court finally upheld a ten-hour workday law for women in the 1908 case of *Muller v. Oregon*, the decision did not make the front page of *The New York Times*.[15] What did was that as entertainment at one of Mrs. Waldorf Astor's fetes, a socialite wore a boa constrictor around her shoulders.[16]

Powerful new social movements formed around and took up the cause of the working poor and bereft. The remnants of the Grange and various Farmers' Alliances flowed into the populist movement.[17] The Knights of Labor, which sought "the complete emancipation and enfranchisement of all those who labor," was succeeded by the American Federation of Labor, the largest of labor's organizations.[18]

The dominant reformers of the era were the populists and the progressives. Formed in Omaha in 1892 by an alliance of labor and farm organizations, the Populist Party had its greatest moment in the early 1890s, including Weaver's run for the presidency in 1892, then dissolved after it joined hands with the Democrats for William Jennings Bryan's campaign of 1896.[19] Populists understood themselves as participating in a class war that had "but two sides": "the allied hosts of monopolies, the money power, great trusts and railroad corporations," on the one hand, and "farmers, laborers, merchants, and all other people who produce wealth and bear the burdens of taxation," on the other.[20]

Progressives were distinctly more forward-looking and upwardly mobile than their populist cousins. Born out of the middle-class mugwump tradition's disgust with corruption in politics, progressives came from every walk of life, including the well-to-do, and appealed to a much wider audience.[21] Given their social status, progressives were of two minds about many problems. They were distressed by labor's woes, but more supportive of legislative solutions than collective action. They voiced support for direct democracy but were suspicious of immigrants and distinctively elitist.[22] By the time Roosevelt ran for President under the Progressive Party banner in 1912, progressivism as a social phenomenon encompassed so many ideas and people that its goals were unavoidably diluted.

Joining hands with these broad social movements was a plethora of voluntary organizations. They ran from the National Child Labor Committee to the Pure Food Association, from the settlement house movement to the Woman's Christian Temperance Union. William F. Willoughby, president of the American Association for Labor Legislation, set out his organization's agenda by saying, "[W]e join forces . . . with other individuals and organizations which, like us, are fighting the battle of social improvement."[23]

Many of the changes demanded by these movements were electoral. In the face of what was widely perceived as the corrupt union of big business and machine politics, the solution was to sidestep established parties and take politics directly to the people. The country moved to direct primaries and the Australian, or secret, ballot. Some states adopted provisions for popular referenda and initiatives. The Seventeenth Amendment, ratified in 1913, provided for the selection of United States senators by direct election rather than by state legislatures.[24] Speaking derisively of these "democratic" reforms, Columbia University president Nicholas Murray Butler wrote, "We are now told that representative government has failed. . . . The remedy is said to be to appeal over the heads of the people's chosen representatives to the people themselves."[25]

Insofar as the judiciary was concerned, however, the battleground was to become "social legislation." The theory of such legislation, explained the great politician, statesman, and administrator Elihu Root, was that in the face of the "great aggregations of capital in enormous industrial establishments," any given worker "is quite helpless by himself."[26] In response, the progressives and their allies helped enact some of the great social measures of the day. The 1894 income tax was a populist triumph.[27] Gilbert Roe, the law partner of senator and Progressive Party leader Robert La Follette, listed "[t]he Anti-Trust law, the laws regulating public service corporations, and shortening the hours of labor, workmen's compensation laws, and many similar measures" as "the efforts of the masses to break the grip which organized wealth has upon our government."[28] Roosevelt repeated a similar litany, adding particular emphasis on laws "for children and for women, to provide for their safety while at work, and to prevent overwork or work under unhygienic or unsafe conditions."[29] The Illinois Women's Alliance joined with labor to obtain hour and workplace inspection laws.[30] The settlement movement lobbied for tenement reforms.[31] The National Child Labor Committee got numerous states to pass laws on child labor and obtained national legislation banning its fruits from commerce.[32]

CONSERVATIVES SEEK REFUGE IN THE CONSTITUTION

"[T]o deny to popular legislation the binding force of law"

Conservatives, often of the moneyed classes, viewed the rise of social movements, labor unrest, and the resultant legislation as a direct threat. Property was under attack. To their cause they mustered an individualistic laissez-faire mentality that, while having long roots in American thought, nonetheless conflicted fundamentally with the popular impetus for state-driven solutions. To hold back the tide, conservatives turned to the Constitution—as they understood it.

Like Weaver, conservatives saw in their world a war among the classes. To the modern sensibility the pronouncements of these conservative figures will seem jarringly candid. Supreme Court justice Henry B. Brown, speaking in Milwaukee to the American Bar Association's 1893 annual meeting, said, "The history of civilized society is largely a story of strife between those who have and those who have not." Undoubtedly (one hopes) grasping at humor, he recounted the story of the Israelites in Egypt as though it were an ordinary labor dispute, "a national protest against the oppression of capital" possessing "the substantial characteristics of a modern strike." But Brown's version of the story had an unusual twist: "How far this revolt was due to the order of Pharaoh that the Israelites should provide their own straw to make bricks, and how far to the hereditary aversion of the Jewish race to manual labor, we shall never know, at least until we hear the Egyptian side of the story."[33]

Observers like Brown could be astonishingly oblivious to the plight of the American worker. William Howard Taft, still a circuit judge, questioned the complaints of laborers, given that "statistics show that the purchasing power of [the laborer's] wages is decidedly greater than in former years."[34] For his listeners in Milwaukee, Justice Brown painted a portrait of the workers' life so idyllic that one wonders if he and his contemporaries inhabited the same universe. The worker, Brown asserted, "not only practically dictates his own hours of labor, but in large manufacturing centers he is provided with model lodging houses for his family, with libraries, parks, clubs, and lectures for his entertainment and instruction [and] with cheap excursion trains for his amusement on Sundays and holidays."[35] Brown may have had in mind Pullman, Illinois, which railroad magnate George M. Pullman had created for his workers. The year after Brown spoke, the Pullman workers engaged in a great strike when the Pullman company curtailed wages by 25 percent but refused to reduce rents on company-owned homes.[36]

Communism and socialism were on the rise, conservatives believed, and needed to be halted. "This assault upon society as now organized," offered John F. Dillon, the railroad lawyer, judge, and sometime professor who had descended from the bench to continue working for the corporations, "is made by bodies of men who call themselves, and are variously called, communists, socialists, anarchists."[37] Columbia president Butler condemned the "definite and determined movement to change our representative republic into a socialistic democracy."[38] Years later, at the end of the era, Taft wrote his brother explaining that "I must stay on the court in order to prevent the Bolsheviki from getting control."[39]

To these conservatives, popular democracy itself posed a threat. Yet another Supreme Court justice, David Brewer, cautioned in an 1898 speech at a private Chicago club that "[a]n unrestricted and absolute legislative freedom would certainly sweep on to despotism of the mob, whose despotism is always followed by the man on horseback."[40] Utah senator and later Supreme Court justice George Sutherland agreed. "A foolish law does not become a wise law because it is approved by a great many people," he declared in 1917.[41] Occasionally conservatives would concede that tensions were heightened by the nation's enormous disparities of wealth. Dillon feared that the wrong policies would produce "an overcrowded population pressing with augmenting force upon the means of subsistence" and "the hopeless separation of the rich and the poor into distinct, hostile and incommunicable classes" resulting in "convulsions of violence."[42] Justice Stephen J. Field, speaking at the celebration of the Supreme Court's centennial in 1890, observed, albeit in passing, that the "inequalities in the conditions of men become more and more marked and disturbing" and that "the enormous aggregation of wealth possessed by some corporations excites uneasiness."[43]

Still, conservatives simply could not comprehend the notion that the state could step in and afford the relief demanded.[44] "The curious notion seems wide-spread," commented Columbia's Butler, "that there exists somewhere and somehow an all-wise and beneficent State or People" that could "take care of us better than we can care for ourselves. . . . That this is crude nonsense," he concluded, "does not prevent its present popularity."[45] Christopher Tiedeman, author of a prominent constitutional law treatise, explained that the laissez-faire ideology had been long dominant but that now "the political pendulum is again swinging in the opposite direction. . . . Governmental interference is proclaimed and demanded everywhere as a sufficient panacea for every social evil which threaten[s] the prosperity of society."[46] Conservatives understood America as a land of rugged individualism in which success was the just result of devoted effort. "Education may do something to equalize men," offered Justice Brown, "but inherent defects can never be wholly remedied, nor inherent virtues wholly suppressed. . . . 'Blood will tell.'"[47]

To stem the rising tide, conservatives and the well-to-do turned to the courts. Judicial review was, according to Dillon, "the only breakwater against the haste and the passions of the people—against the tumultuous ocean of democracy."[48] In the face of "uneasiness," Justice Field noted, "it becomes more and more the imperative duty of the court to enforce with a firm hand every guarantee of the Constitution."[49] The judiciary served conservative interests well because it was insulated from the popular clamor. "In times of political upheaval, of sectional animosity, of Communistic uprising," wrote one commentator, "the nine quiet men . . . spend their lives away from the political field, free from the necessity of demagoguery."[50] Sutherland instructed courts to "set their faces steadily and unswervingly . . . no matter how overwhelming . . . may be the popular sentiment."[51] The life tenure of the justices, commended Tiedeman, "serves to withdraw them from all fear of popular disapproval."[52]

The instrument of the judges was the Constitution, sturdy in its protection of the rights of property. "The written constitution," Sutherland reassured, "is the shelter and the bulwark of what might otherwise be a helpless minority."[53] The *New York Tribune*, perhaps the leading Republican paper of the time, similarly applauded "the Constitution of [the] founders" as "a bulwark of the rights of States and of individual citizens."[54] The "only value" of the written constitution, Tiedeman explained in 1890, is that it "enables [judges to] deny to popular legislation the binding force of law, whenever such legislation infringes a constitutional provision."[55]

THE JUDGES REPEATEDLY STRIKE PROGRESSIVE MEASURES

"[A] conflict of power between the lawmaker and the courts"

Time and again over the course of some thirty years, the courts used the Constitution as a basis for invalidating laws enacted by popular legislative bodies. Unlike most other periods of controversy over the judiciary, when one or a handful of cases provoked heated debate, this period involved hundreds and hundreds of adjudicated disputes in the state and federal courts. George

Alger, a lawyer for labor whose commentary of the era littered the pages of popular journals, informed his readers that fundamentally this was "a conflict of power between the lawmaker and the courts."[56]

When reviewing these decisions, one walks on contested turf. Today, as then, there is sharp disagreement about what the Progressive Era judges were doing when they invalidated laws. Were they merely adhering to settled rules that prevented the use of government power to prefer one group over another? Or were they actually favoring their own social class and its ideals in striking progressive measures? Did the judgments of unconstitutionality dominate the judicial agenda, or were they infrequent drops in a bucket of judicial permissiveness? As the varying reactions to the decisions make clear, progressives at the time told it one way; conservatives, another. Here, first, are the decisions themselves and the conservatives' exultant reaction.

The New York Court of Appeals began the era when, in its 1885 *Jacobs* decision, it struck down New York's prohibition on cigar manufacturing in tenements.[57] "Good men and women who went around alleviating suffering and distress in poor tenements of the overcrowded districts of this city," explained New York mayor William Gaynor, had found cigarmaking establishments in which many (including children) lived and worked in unwholesome conditions. "They applied to the legislature, and had a law passed. . . . The court held that it was 'unconstitutional.'"[58] The law was invalid, the court decided, because it deprived a tenement home owner or lessee "of his property and of some portion of his personal liberty. . . . It cannot be perceived," elaborated the judges, "how the cigarmaker is to be improved in his health or his morals by forcing him from his home and its hallowed associations and beneficent influences, to ply his trade elsewhere."[59]

A year later the Pennsylvania Supreme Court invalidated a law requiring payment of workers at regular intervals in "lawful money" rather than scrip. Laws such as Pennsylvania's, explained one legal commentator, were a response to the practice of "[m]any mining and manufacturing companies," which "forced their employés to receive their wages in goods, and have sold the goods to them at enormous profits, in many cases at double their actual cost."[60] The Pennsylvania court, in *Godcharles v. Wigeman*, held this law violated the employee's right to enter into contracts freely. The court deemed the law "an insulting attempt to put the laborer under a legislative tutelage, which is not only degrading to his manhood, but subversive of his rights as a citizen of the United States. He may sell his labor for what he thinks best, whether money or goods, just as his employer may sell his iron or coal."[61]

Three notable Supreme Court decisions made 1895 a banner year. *Pollock v. Farmers' Loan and Trust* invalidated the income tax.[62] *In re Debs* sustained broad powers in federal judges to issue injunctions to quell labor actions.[63] And *United States v. E. C. Knight* sharply limited the application of the new antitrust law.[64]

Of these cases, *Pollock* was unquestionably the most significant. The tax imposed was 2 percent on incomes over four thousand dollars, probably the top 1 or 2 percent of all incomes at the time.[65] The case was understood as a major battle in the class war. Defending the tax before the Court, James C. Carter warned: "When the opposing forces of sixty millions of people have become arrayed in hostile political ranks upon a question which all men feel is not a question of law, but of legislation, the only path of safety is to accept the voice of the majority as final."[66] Joseph Choate, a leading corporate lawyer, argued in response that the law was "defended here upon principles as communistic, socialistic—what shall I call them—populistic as ever have been addressed to any political assembly in the world."[67] To Carter's warning about popular dissatisfaction, Choate responded stridently that "it is the more vital to the future welfare of this country that this court again resolutely and courageously declare, as Marshall did, that it *has* the power to set aside an act of Congress . . . and that it will not hesitate in executing that power, no matter what the threatened consequences of popular or populistic wrath may be."[68] The majority found the tax a violation of the Constitution's requirement that direct taxes be apportioned evenly throughout the country, even though it had upheld a wartime income tax, and in prior decisions the only direct taxes had been held to be capitation and land taxes.[69] Concurring in the decision, Justice Field warned that "the present assault upon capital is but the beginning. It will be the stepping-stone to others, larger and more sweeping, till our political contests will become a war of the poor against the rich."[70]

The response to *Pollock* in the conservative and business world was jubilation. *The Washington Post* cried: "The income tax is dead. It is a case of Hallelujah!"[71] *The New York Times* found it "further gratifying" to learn that the Court "is capable of resisting the influence of popular clamor," while the *New York Tribune* thanked the Court that "our Government is not to be dragged into communistic warfare against rights of property."[72] "The heat with which Justice Harlan [dissenting] expounded the Marx gospel from the bench showed the brake was applied none too soon," remarked *The Nation*.[73] New York's Senator David B. Hill said the Court was owed the "thanks of the country" for eliminating a tax "clamored for only by Populists, cranks and demagogues."[74]

The case that gave the era its name was decided on April 17, 1905.[75] *Lochner* involved a challenge to a New York law that, among other things, limited bakers to a ten-hour day. The law was said to exceed the police power of the state and to violate the liberty of contract.[76] The genesis of the law may have been an attempt to protect unionized shops from competition by small bakeries where employee hours were not limited.[77] Nonetheless, the law had wide public support as a health measure. The public had been mobilized by muckraking journalism, including a story in the *New York Press* describing the conditions under which bakers worked (often living in the same space) entitled "Bread and Filth Cooked Together."[78] The law received the unanimous assent of the New York legislature.[79] The New York Court of Appeals had upheld the law. One judge concurred in the decision, noting the bakers' "tendency to consumption" (i.e., tuberculosis) and observing that "[v]ital statistics show that those vocations which require persons to remain for long periods in confined and heated atmosphere filled with some foreign substance, which is inhaled into the lungs, are injurious to health, and tend to shorten life."[80]

The Supreme Court struck the law down. CONTRACTS INVIOLABLE, read the headline in the *New York Tribune*.[81] The mainstream press of the day, which was heavily pro-business, again expressed delight. *The Nation* applauded an opinion that "sounds for all the world like Adam Smith in 'The Wealth of Nations'" and that "checks the insidious advance of union tyranny."[82] *The New York Times* crowed how "gratifying" it was that the liberty of contracts did not extend to those "between the demagogues in the Legislature and the ignoramuses among the labor leaders."[83] "The Supreme Court drew the line sharply between sanitation and socialism" was the lead in the *New York Tribune*, which allowed that the decision was "a heavy blow to all varieties of socialists."[84] "If, as a pure labor regulation, the State can forbid a man to work more than ten hours a day," added the *Tribune*, "it is hard to see why it may not go on for the general health to prescribe for him a salutary diet."[85]

Following *Lochner*, the stream of judicial invalidations continued. When the Supreme Court struck down laws prohibiting employment discrimination against labor union members, so-called yellow-dog contracts, *The New York Times* predicted that "[l]abor leaders will regard to-day's court decision as the most disastrous of the series of setbacks they have received from the courts within the last few weeks."[86] Some commentators noted a slowing of judicial invalidations during the war, but "even in these days of grave international concern," the Supreme Court struck down the federal Child Labor Act.[87] The decision "caused the utmost surprise."[88]

The postwar "return to normalcy" once again brought a deluge of court decisions contrary to labor and social welfare legislation.[89] Two were particularly noteworthy. In *Bailey v. Drexel Furniture*, in 1922, the Court overturned

Congress's second attempt at a child labor law, this one based on the taxing power. Then, in 1923, the Court nullified the District of Columbia's minimum wage law for women in *Adkins v. Children's Hospital* on the ground that like the law in *Lochner*, it violated the liberty of contract.[90] In light of prior decisions upholding protective labor laws for women, this decision provoked widespread commentary throughout the country.[91] "The element of the people that favors social reform, even by stretching the Constitution," observed *The Washington Post*, true to its conservative perspective, "will be bitterly disappointed."[92]

THE CLAMOR ABOUT THE COURTS

"[I]t is the supreme issue"

As the courts assaulted popular legislation, figures from politics, social movements, the legal academy, and even the bench struck back. The central complaint in this era of direct democracy, naturally, was that judges were interfering impermissibly with the will of the people. The criticism found widespread popular support, emitting a full-throated roar against judicial power. Some argued the judges were not striking down that many laws, but even if true, it was not the numbers that mattered. In the history of attacks on the judiciary, the sustained attacks of this period stand out as remarkable. Judicial review was a major issue in three presidential campaigns.

The contest with the courts began in earnest at the close of the nineteenth century: the triumvirate of 1895 decisions was met with a storm of disapproval. The income tax ruling, the *St. Louis Post-Dispatch* said in condemnation, "shows that the corporations and plutocrats are as securely intrenched [*sic*] in the Supreme Court as in the lower courts."[93] In response to *In re Debs*, Illinois governor John Altgeld coined a phrase that stuck, referring to "government by injunction."[94] North Carolina Supreme Court justice Walter Clark began his long career attacking the federal courts. As Clark repeatedly explained, "[T]he most dangerous, the most undemocratic and unrepublican feature of the constitution, and the one most subject to abuse, is the mode of selecting the Federal judges."[95] Clark's talk created such a stir that the periodical *Current Literature* ran a follow-up article, "The Nine Arbiters of American Destiny."[96]

As a result of the 1895 cases, the Court became an issue in the presidential election of 1896. William Jennings Bryan was the standard-bearer of the Democratic Party. The Democratic platform said: "[I]t is the duty of Congress" to use all power left after the income tax decision "or which may come from its reversal by the court" to achieve equal taxation.[97] The platform also demanded an end to labor injunctions.[98] The Republicans seized on the issue, trying to paint Bryan as crazy on the issue of the courts, an attack that had him on the defensive.[99] Former President Benjamin Harrison said he could not "exaggerate the gravity and the importance and the danger of this assault upon our constitutional form of government."[100] (Bryan lost to the Republican William McKinley, after many Democrats deserted the party over its economic policies.)[101]

In the aftermath of *Lochner*, prominent lawyers began to attack not just judicial decisions but the institution of judicial review itself. Lawyer and historian William Meigs deemed these views "so radical that a listener fairly catches his breath, no matter who is the spokesman."[102] Justice Clark gave a talk at the University of Pennsylvania that attracted wide notice, claiming the power "to declare acts of Congress unconstitutional is without a line in the Constitution to authorize it."[103] "If five lawyers can negative the will of one hundred million intelligent people," he said, "then the art of government in this country is reduced to the selection of those five lawyers."[104] A month later Dean William Trickett of the Dickinson School of Law published a like attack on judicial review, also pointing out the lack of explicit textual support in the Constitution. The framers could have made it clear "with a line," he said, and then asked: *"Why did they not write that line?"*[105] Learned Hand, a leading progressive figure and eventually America's most prominent and beloved judge, wrote a scathing article in the *Harvard Law Review*: "[W]e should not have the inconsistent spectacle of a government, in theory representative[,] . . . put its faith in a body which was, and ought to be, the least representative of popular feeling."[106]

Public discontent was widespread throughout this ten-year period. William Howard Taft's talk to the American Bar Association in 1895 was entitled "Criticisms of the Federal Judiciary," and it was to popular criticisms that he was responding.[107] In 1906, Roscoe Pound, then dean of the Nebraska Law School but soon to be dean at Harvard, gave one of history's most famous bar addresses to the American Bar Association. It was entitled "Causes of Popular Dissatisfaction with the Administration of Justice." If anything, Pound, well aware of his audience's proclivities, soft-pedaled the issue. (A motion to do nothing more than print and distribute Pound's address was hotly debated by bar members and defeated.)[108] Still, his point was unmistakable: the public was losing faith in the judiciary. "At the very time the courts have appeared powerless themselves to give relief, they have seemed to obstruct public efforts to get relief by legislation."[109] In his 1908 annual message to Congress, Roosevelt agreed, saying that by denying "relief to men of small means or wageworkers who are crushed down by these modern industrial conditions," the judges had hurt public confidence in the judiciary.[110] That same year the party platforms of all parties expressed concern about the judiciary, particularly with regard to labor injunctions.[111]

The fires of public discontent were fanned by strong dissents in controversial cases. The Great Dissenter, John Marshall Harlan, earned many of his stripes during this period. Responding to the blow to the antitrust law in *E. C. Knight*, Harlan fumed that "the general government is not placed by the constitution in such a condition of helplessness that it must fold its arms and remain inactive while capital combines . . . to destroy competition."[112] Oliver Wendell Holmes, Jr.'s dissent in the *Lochner* case quickly became a progressive rallying cry; today it is legendary.

Scholars produced elaborate works about the history of judicial review. Louis Boudin authored an article, "Government by Judiciary," which was to explode into an oft-cited multivolume work.[113] Charles Grove Haines published a magisterial treatise, *The American Doctrine of Judicial Supremacy*.[114] Charles Beard brought into print his controversial history suggesting the Constitution was written by, and to protect, the moneyed classes.[115]

The judicial issue played center stage again in a presidential election in 1912. Incensed by New York decisions like *Jacobs* and *Ives* (striking down a workers' compensation law on federal constitutional grounds), Roosevelt made his Bull Moose run at the presidency. He emphasized that "[i]t is the people, and not the judges, who are entitled to say what their constitution means, for the constitution is theirs."[116] The debate was fierce. Taft, running for reelection against his former mentor Roosevelt, responded strongly to proposals "to take away all those safeguards for maintaining the independence of the judiciary" and declared: "It is said this is not an issue in the campaign. It seems to me it is the supreme issue."[117] "[P]opular magazines," George Alger informed his readers, no doubt telling them what they already knew, "are full of articles upon judicial aggression [and] judicial oligarchies," and lay readers, "unconstrained by any embarrassment through knowledge of law[,] . . . cheerfully lay at the doors of the courts all the ills of our body politic."[118]

Following the election, in which Taft was trounced and the Democrat Woodrow Wilson elected, turmoil surrounding the courts quieted down for a while. Louis Brandeis, a progressive lawyer who soon had his own place on the Court, saw the reason in the election results. Joining the election of a Democratic President was the Sixteenth Amendment, which overturned

Pollock by making express Congress's power to adopt an income tax; the Seventeenth Amendment, providing for direct election of senators; and enactment of the Clayton Antitrust Act.[119] Change was under way on the Court as well: most of the justices in the *Lochner* majority had left the bench.[120] Then World War I gave the country something other than the judiciary on which to focus.

As the world war came to a close and the Court began its next aggressive push, however, the floodgates of criticism opened once again. The 1918 decision in *Hammer v. Dagenhart*, which struck the child labor law, rekindled all the quiescent feelings.[121] Commentary began to focus on the Court's sharply divided decisions. "A nation that will give its blood and money on the battlefield for the freedom of mankind throughout the world," editorialized *The New York Evening Mail*, "will surely find a way, despite five to four decisions, to release from slavery the children of its own hearthstone."[122] Conservative President Warren G. Harding made four appointments to the Court; among them was William Howard Taft, now serving in the position he had dreamed of all his life, Chief Justice. Viewing the Court's labor cases, *The New Republic* concluded that "Taft has justified the worst fears about him more quickly than the sturdiest sceptic was entitled to fear."[123]

The 1923 decision in *Adkins v. Children's Hospital*, striking the District of Columbia's minimum wage law for women, "evoked a more nearly unanimous chorus of disapproval than any other decision in years."[124] The decision, reported the *Chicago Daily Tribune*, "has served to increase the agitation for limiting the power of the court."[125] The *Forum* asked: "Shall We Curb the Supreme Court?," and *Survey* ran a long feature on *Adkins*, which it deemed "the most severe blow which progressive American labor legislation has yet received at the hands of the Supreme Court."[126] *The Christian Science Monitor*, which had started publishing in 1908 and quickly gained a reputation for its careful news analysis, summed up the decision in a poignant headline: THE "INALIENABLE RIGHT" TO STARVE.[127]

When Robert La Follette ran as the Progressive Party candidate in 1924, the courts became an issue in a presidential election for the third time of the era. Fourteen thousand people packed Madison Square Garden to cheer La Follette as he insisted: "Either the court must be the final arbiter of what the law is, or else some means must be found to correct its decisions."[128] *Current Opinion* reported that La Follette's attack on the Court "has drawn more fire from his opponents than any other issue in the Presidential campaign."[129] Sensing an advantage, the Republicans, led by Calvin Coolidge, who went on to win the election, sought to keep the story in the news. "The time to stop those who would loosen and weaken the fabric of our government is before they begin," Coolidge said.[130] La Follette responded: "Always these decisions of the Court are on the side of the wealthy and powerful and against the poor and weak."[131]

Conservatives then (as now) tried to minimize the howl over the courts by arguing that the absolute number of laws struck down by judges was small in comparison with the many laws that were upheld.[132] At the height of hysteria about the courts, in 1913, Charles Warren, an eminent historian and apologist for the Supreme Court whose 1922 multivolume *The Supreme Court in United States History* remains unparalleled today as a compendium of commentary on the Court's work, pointed out that very few congressional laws were invalidated at all.[133] Even with regard to state laws, Warren argued, there still had been relatively few struck down. By Warren's count, of some 560 cases decided between 1887 and 1911 under the Fourteenth Amendment, the Supreme Court took off the books only 3 state laws related to "social justice," including in *Lochner* itself.[134] Modern-day revisionists join Warren in quoting the numbers and asking, "What was all the uproar about?"[135]

A partial answer is that Warren's accounting preceded the binge of decisions in the period after World War I. In the heart of that period, Ray A. Brown's numbers indicated that whereas the Court had nullified only 13 laws in almost 200 cases in the first part of the *Lochner* era, in the years between 1921 and 1927 it had struck down 15 state and federal laws in just over 50 cases.[136] He noted that "in the six years since 1920 the Supreme Court has declared social and economic legislation unconstitutional . . . in more cases than in the entire fifty-two previous years."[137] Felix Frankfurter, a Harvard law professor and later Supreme Court justice, compiled a list that indicated more than 220 state laws struck down between 1897 and 1938. A modern recount confirms this.[138]

Even if Warren and the revisionists were correct about the relatively low numbers, though, the tempest against the courts made plain the error of focusing on numbers alone. Given the relatively slow pace of judicial review prior to this time, the new rate of judicial action seemed a torrent. Then there was the ripple effect of the decisions. *Lochner*, as the conservative *New York Tribune* explained to its readers, "disposes for once and for all of the constitutionality of the labor laws throughout the United States."[139] Speaking of the *Jacobs* decision, a particular bugaboo of his, Roosevelt said it had "retarded by at least twenty years the work of tenement-house reform, and was directly responsible for causing hundreds of thousands of American citizens now alive to be brought up under conditions of reeking filth and squalor, which immeasurably decreased their chance of turning out to be good citizens."[140] Or, as Frankfurter later remarked, "a single decision may decide the fate of

many measures."[141] "Wide and serious resistance to an institution in a popular government does not arise from slight and trivial pretexts," admonished
The Saturday Evening Post, in words that would seem to address today's revisionists as much as its contemporary readers.[142]

PURSUING JUDICIAL REFORM

"[A]n even greater evil"

With criticism of courts so abundant, reformers eagerly searched for a solution to the judicial veto, proposing a smorgasbord of ideas to bring the judiciary into line. *The Saturday Evening Post* sought to educate its readers about
the "serious consideration" given to "such remedies as the recall of judges
and what is named the recall of judicial decisions."[143] Some of these measures
found their way into law in a few states, and moderate reforms were taken
at the national level as well. Still, it is noteworthy that nothing was adopted
at the national level to quiet the widespread discontent over judicial review.
Though the reasons for this were complex, and bear consideration, the result was unequivocal: the power of the judiciary remained unchecked.

The first of the era's proposals was the election of federal judges. As early
as 1890, *The American Law Review* reported that "the people are already beginning seriously to consider the question whether this is a government of the
people, or whether it is a government by nine lawyers holding their offices for
life and responsible to no one." As such, the remedy seemed apparent: "[T]he
agitation for the election of senators by a popular vote will be followed by an
agitation, and a successful one, for the election of Federal judges by a popular vote."[144] Following *Pollock*, Washington, D.C.'s *Evening Star* ran a column
with the bold headline BY THE PEOPLE, suggesting that the Court's decision
would mobilize forces to push for the election of federal judges.[145] Sure
enough, by 1896 James Weaver was suggesting just this.[146] Similarly, granting that judicial review, "however illegally grasped," was unlikely to be eliminated, Walter Clark concluded that "the only remedy which can be applied
is to make the judges elective."[147]

Despite the insistence of figures such as Weaver and Clark, there never
was any serious movement to elect federal judges, largely because progressives were troubled by the notion of electing judges at all. One of the great
reform efforts of the Progressive Era, which remains an issue still, was attempting to end partisanship in the selection of judges. Partisan elections
of judges reeked of machine politics: "[T]he use of the Republican or Democratic insignia in city elections served as a sort of 'smoke-screen,' behind

which municipal spoilsmen and office-brokers could hide in safety."[148] After studying the matter, the National Economic League concluded that "where today we have appointive courts these courts in conservative communities have been liberal in questions of constitutional law where elective judges, holding for short terms, have been strict and reactionary."[149]

Rather than elect judges, some suggested "recalling" them if their performance was unsatisfactory. The recall of officials was another common Progressive Era reform. In 1911, Senator Robert Owen of Oklahoma proposed extending the recall to federal judges, arguing that "[t]he mere fact that the people do not like a judge and do not desire him to serve them justifies recall."[150] As La Follette's law partner, Gilbert Roe, explained, the "recall of Judges merely means that where a Judge has shown, from any cause, that he is not discharging the functions of the judicial office in fundamental and important matters, as the people desire, he will be discharged and a new judge . . . selected in his place."[151]

Owen's idea gained no traction at the federal level. "Are not the judges the servants of the people?" asked Nicholas Murray Butler rhetorically, answering emphatically: "No! . . . The judges are primarily the servants not of the people, but of the law."[152] Opponents believed the recall violated the judges' "most solemn of covenants to consider nothing but the law and the facts and to obey no voice save the compelling voice of his own instructed conscience."[153] In one of the era's more fraught battles, Taft, as President, vetoed Arizona's admission to the Union because its constitution provided for the recall of judges. Taft, an ardent opponent of the judicial recall, said the provision was "so pernicious in its effect, so destructive of independence in the judiciary . . . that I must disapprove a Constitution containing it."[154]

Roosevelt had his own unique solution to the problem. He advocated the recall not of judges but of judicial decisions. He intended his idea to apply to only state, not federal, decisions. With cases like *Jacobs* and *Ives* in mind, Roosevelt recommended that if courts struck a law as unconstitutional, the people should have the right of reconsideration. Roosevelt and others viewed this proposal as more moderate than the recall of judges because it would avoid having the judges' fate tied to the popular hand on the election lever.[155] The proposal was a detailed and thoughtful one: "[A]fter a period of due deliberation, a period which could not be less than two years after the election of the legislature which passed the original law," the people should have a right to decide whether the law was constitutional.[156] Others disagreed, believing the "wholly untrained layman" incompetent to perform "the highly specialized and technical work of a judge."[157]

The run of judicial overrulings, beginning with the first child labor decision and continuing into the 1920s, gave rise to even more novel—and some
thought radical—proposals for reform. The prize undoubtedly went to Robert
La Follette's suggestion that lower federal courts be barred from striking congressional enactments altogether and that Congress have the power to overrule any Supreme Court invalidation of its laws.[158] *The Nation* (now squarely
in the liberal camp) favored the idea, editorializing that it would be used
rarely but "that the possession of such powers in Congress would do much
toward leading the Supreme Court toward more progressive views."[159] Undoubtedly it would, but many thought it would also give Congress too much
power.[160] Senator George Wharton Pepper of Pennsylvania, debating the
measure on the pages of the *Forum* magazine, said it "would mean that Senators and Congressmen would become the sole interpreters of the Constitution."[161] "It may well be that every player on both of two contending baseball
teams is as intelligent as the umpire," he analogized, "but the rules of the
game are more likely to be kept intact if he and not the players" gets to enforce them.[162] Even La Follette never formally introduced his suggestion as
a proposed constitutional amendment.

A somewhat milder approach was Senator William Borah's proposal to require seven votes—a supermajority of the Court—to strike down a statute.[163]
The impetus of the idea was clear enough: "During the last thirty years
there have been some forty-odd exceedingly important cases determined in
the Supreme Court by decisions of five to four." The decisions "have given
rise to more criticism of the court than any other one thing which I am able
to recall," wrote Borah.[164] The primary line of attack on Borah's idea was
that it would create rule by the Court's minority. "Either the Supreme Court
has the power of veto or it has not," insisted the *New York Evening Post*. "[I]f
it has, then it should be allowed to exercise that power by a majority vote,
no matter how narrow."[165]

Why nothing came of these proposals is one of the puzzles of the Progressive Era.[166] After all, this was the time when other great popular measures,
such as the initiative, the referendum, the recall of officials, the direct election of senators, and women's suffrage, were adopted. The outcry against the
judges and judicial review was severe. If ever there was a moment when one
would have expected action against the judges to succeed, this was it. Why
did it not?

A partial explanation is that the progressives in particular were deeply
split about the desirability of effecting judicial change. Lawyers were prominent in the progressive movement, and they were often quite conservative
in their views toward courts.[167] Most of them believed in judicial review. One

of Roosevelt's arguments in favor of some limited reform was that the alternative "may result in even greater evil," that being "such a revulsion in the minds of the people at large as to result in totally taking away this power from the judges—action which I should deplore."[168] William L. Ransom, a New York lawyer writing in support of Roosevelt's recall proposal, conceded that "[i]f there is any branch of the government about which the American people have been genuinely 'conservative,' it has been the judiciary."[169]

Even if they could agree on the need for action against the courts, progressives could not agree on what that action was.[170] To cite one example, strong concern about Roosevelt's proposal was expressed by activist lawyer Gilbert Roe, who favored the recall of judges. Roosevelt, on the other hand, did not "believe in the recall" of federal judges. "I do not wish to see steps taken which would hurt the usefulness and dignity of our fine National judiciary."[171] The socialists could not bring themselves to support La Follette's idea: "Congress is reactionary enough; this would make it still more so," opined the socialist *New York Call*.[172]

In addition, the proposals offered up in this era were both difficult to adopt and not necessarily efficacious. Most, if not all, of the measures would have required a constitutional amendment, never an easy task to accomplish. None would have addressed the federal and state judiciaries alike.

Still, it would be wrong to think the judiciary escaped the period unscathed. Less drastic, but nonetheless significant, reforms were adopted at the national level. In *Ex parte Young*, the Supreme Court upheld the contempt citation of Minnesota's attorney general, for enforcing that law's railroad rate legislation in the face of a federal injunction.[173] The ruling came in 1895, the same year the Court struck down the income tax. Federal injunctions were already a matter of great controversy. The *Ex parte Young* decision touched a nerve; people were furious about "one little judge stand[ing] against the whole State." Lee Slater Overman, North Carolina's first senator to be elected by popular vote, insisted emphatically: "[Y]ou find the people of the State rising up in rebellion."[174] After *Ex parte Young*, some in Congress wanted to prohibit such injunctions altogether; as a compromise Congress passed a milder measure requiring a court composed of three federal judges before an injunction of a state law could issue.[175]

Further reform was forthcoming when, in the 1911 *Ives v. South Buffalo Railway Company* decision, the New York Court of Appeals struck down that state's workers' compensation scheme as a "deprivation of liberty and property under the federal and state Constitutions."[176] The decision caused a furor.[177] Because of a quirk in the Supreme Court's jurisdiction, however, it was unable to review the decision. The drafters of the Judiciary Act of 1789, apparently not anticipating any difficulty if a state's high court struck down state laws based on the federal Constitution, provided no Supreme Court review in such cases. In the face of intense controversy, progressives and conservatives united to expand the Supreme Court's jurisdiction to solve the problem.[178]

Congress even abolished one unpopular court entirely, evoking images of the repeal of the Circuit Judges Act during Jefferson's presidency. In 1887, after extended turmoil over railroad rates, Congress created the Interstate Commerce Commission to regulate the railroads. In order to centralize review of the commission's rulings, in 1910 Congress established the Court of Commerce. The Commerce Court quickly made itself unpopular by reversing orders of the ICC. It proved a short-lived enterprise, despite Taft's efforts to save it. The railroads were no happier with the new court than the public; without powerful supporters, the court was doomed.[179] After Democrats took over the government in the 1912 election, Congress successfully did away with the disliked court. Overruling the preferences of the House, however, the Senate refused to eliminate the judges' positions (as had been done in 1801), moving them instead to the circuit court.[180]

Some of the more dramatic reforms that failed nationally were actually adopted in a few of the states.[181] Borah's supermajority idea had enough appeal that three states adopted some version of it, and two retain it in full force today.[182] Colorado was the only state ever to adopt the recall of decisions, and the issue died with Roosevelt's defeat.[183] Still, seven states adopted the recall of their judges.[184] Taft vetoed Arizona's constitution when it was seeking admission to the Union, because it contained a judicial recall; once admitted, Arizona reinstated the recall anyway.[185] Eleven states moved to nonpartisan judicial elections for at least some of their judges.[186]

In fact, when one compares the states where the more dramatic reforms were adopted with those where they were not, it emerges that the judiciary may have avoided further interference only because of certain electoral dysfunctions that served to restrain the popular will from having its way. There is a high congruence between states that adopted various progressive measures—such as workplace regulations, the referendum, and the initiative—and those that adopted reforms of the judiciary.[187] States that adopted neither judicial reforms nor progressive measures often suffered from a suppression of the vote, sometimes as the result of conscious effort, sometimes as the unintended effect of progressive reforms.[188] Following labor strife and Bryan's near miss at the presidency at the end of the nineteenth century, southern conservatives consciously disenfranchised large portions of the population, including blacks and the lower classes. In the North, voter participation dropped precipitously from the highs of the late nineteenth century, apparently at the same time that many Progressive Era electoral reforms were being adopted.[189] It is at least open to question whether a broader extension and exercise of the franchise may have spelled yet greater difficulty for the independence of the judiciary.

LOSING FAITH IN LAW

"[A] growing distrust of the integrity of the courts"

Pressure built up as judges continued to strike laws enacted by democratically elected bodies and legislative proposals to control their veto failed. Many people—progressives, academics, workers—came to believe that unconsciously or not, the judges' biases were deciding cases—usually in favor of corporations and the well-to-do. When defenders maintained that the judges were simply adhering faithfully to the law, the result was a loss of faith in law itself. Critics charged that the law lacked any meaningful content and so was easily turned to the predispositions of the judges.

The complaint came early and often that the judges, unconsciously or not, reflected the biases of those who put them on the bench. "The bench, both State and National," the populist James Weaver explained, "must be supplied from eminent members of the bar, and practically all the so-called distinguished members of the profession are in the service of the corporations."[190] *The Arena*, a progressive era monthly with a circulation of some thirty thousand, endorsed "frank, free [and] honest criticism" of "decisions that are rendered by men who have been elevated to the bench through the influence of privileged interests and who, though perhaps thoroughly honest in their intentions, are also thoroughly biased."[191] In 1912, *Everybody's Magazine* ran a muckraking series entitled "Big Business and the Bench," setting out in elaborate detail how corporate lawyers moved onto the bench and, once there, favored corporations. The last issue included a cartoon poem:

> *This is the People, bound and sold*
> *By the crafty Boss all brazen and bold,*
> *That joins with Business, out for gold,*
> *To send the lawyer in to mold*
> *The mind of the judge all proud and cold.*[192]

Those biases, it was widely claimed, made judges stooges for members of their own class and slavish sycophants of the corporations they had once served. In 1891, George E. McNeil, of the Knights of Labor, explained anti-labor decisions as "new revelations of an old fact, that the interpretation of the law rests largely upon the public sentiment of the wealthy part of the community."[193] The view persisted. "The charge against the courts is that their judges habitually think in the terms of the rich and powerful," Gilbert Roe explained.[194] "I should not suppose," wrote the historian Brooks Adams in 1913, "that any man could calmly turn over the pages of the recent volumes of the reports of the Supreme Court of the United States and not rise from the perusal convinced that the rich and the poor, the strong and the weak, do not receive a common measure of justice before that judgment seat."[195]

Simply put, the "layman" was coming to believe that judging was all about favoring the ruling class.[196] So said public figures with good reason to know. Jane Addams was a leader in the settlement house movement. "From my own experience, I should say perhaps that the one symptom among working-men . . . is a growing distrust of the integrity of the courts, the belief that the present judge has been a corporation attorney, that his sympathies and experience and his whole view of life is on the corporation side."[197] Illinois governor Altgeld was hilariously sarcastic. Judges, he noted, wear black robes "to impress the people with their infallibility." The problem, he observed, was that of late the people had seen through them, questioning unpatriotically "the justice of having to bear the burdens of government while the rich escape." Perhaps, he wondered, "would it not be well to have each judge wear two gowns for a while, until the storm blows over?"[198]

Progressive judges and lawyers, some of whom later became giants of the bench and the bar, said much the same. Louis Brandeis complained that "scientific half-truths like 'The survival of the fittest,'" had been written "by judicial sanction into a moral law."[199] In 1921, Benjamin Cardozo, a judge on New York's highest court, delivered a set of lectures entitled *The Nature of the Judicial Process* that mesmerized his audience and became a classic once in print. He explained: "Deep below consciousness are other forces, the likes and dislikes, the predilections and the prejudices, the complex of instincts and emotions and habits and convictions, which make the man, whether he be litigant or judge."[200]

Judicial defenders responded then, as revisionist scholars do today, that the judges were simply applying long-established doctrines to the cases coming before them. Modern-day revisionists have done a great service in correcting the sometime impression that judges during the *Lochner* era were simply making the law up as they went along. Rather, there were established legal principles, like the prohibition on "class legislation," upon which judges relied when invalidating progressive measures. John Dillon stated the class legislation principle clearly: "Discriminating legislation for the benefit of the rich against the poor, or in favor of the poor against the rich, is equally wrong and dangerous. Class legislation of all and every kind is anti-republican and must be repressed."[201] The most famous legal treatise of the time explained: "Equality of rights, privileges, and capacities unquestionably should be the aim of the law. . . . The State, it is to be presumed, has no favors to bestow, and designs to inflict no arbitrary deprivation of rights."[202]

The difficulty with the revisionist defense of judicial decisions during the *Lochner* era, however, is that critics at the time were well aware of the doctrines the judges ostensibly were applying, but still, they found the law itself to be wanting. It was simply too imprecise and flexible to provide certain outcomes. In the face of law's malleability, the judges' biases necessarily decided cases. This was true, for example, of the class legislation principle itself. "The corporations and special interests of every class created during the past twenty-five years by various species of class legislation and favoritism, have grown rich and powerful," scoffed James Weaver. "They are now pleading to be let alone."[203] One of the lawyers defending the income tax noted the same phenomenon. "It is said that there are no classes in this country, and that class distinctions should never be alluded to," but that notion ran against the fact that "there is a distinction between rich and poor which cannot be wiped out under our present civilization."[204] Why was it, one commentator wondered, that the doctrine seemed to have bite in "labor decisions, but in none others?"[205] "The same Constitution which is unable to protect the life or liberty of innocent persons, is quick and powerful to guard the property of public service corporations," pointed out another commentator. "Were the Constitution and its amendments written this way? Or has some one inserted a 'joker' clause which favors privilege?"[206]

With regard to liberty of contract, one of the most important doctrines of the era, influential figures were glad to say that judges had made the whole thing up. As early as 1890, a student at Harvard Law School won a writing prize for a paper in which he concluded that including "the right to follow any lawful calling" in the term "liberty" "seems, upon examination, to have little real foundation either in history or principle."[207] Learned Hand insisted: "[T]o construe the term 'liberty'" as containing a right to contract "is entirely to disregard the whole juristic history of the word."[208] Thomas Reed Powell, a sharp-tongued professor at Harvard Law School, stated flatly: "No such doctrine is stated in the Constitution."[209]

Even if the judges' decisions had a firm foundation in prior jurisprudence, observers believed that those jurisprudential rules were simply too malleable to keep bias from creeping in. "The tests of constitutionality are not sufficiently objective to warrant the denunciation of laws as void," insisted Dickinson Law School dean William Trickett early on.[210] *The New York Times* complained about the outcry over the income tax decision: That "men of equal intelligence, candor, and caution" could reach "widely different conclusions" on a legal issue "does not justify and does not even excuse the intemperance with which the decision . . . is condemned."[211] But this was precisely the point: If people "of equal intelligence" could decide the case either way, why was the Supreme Court interfering with the decisions of elected officials? "A vote of the court necessarily depends not upon any fixed rules of law," stated Learned Hand matter-of-factly, "but upon the individual opinions upon political or economic questions of the persons who compose it."[212]

Charles Warren's argument that the courts were in fact striking down relatively few laws served only to exacerbate the criticism. It seemed difficult to justify those decisions that did invalidate legislation. "The courts do not agree with each other; they do not agree with themselves," observed a legal commentator as early as 1898, putting his finger on precisely the problem.[213] Commentators delighted in juxtaposing irreconcilable results. "To forbid barbers to work on Sunday is reasonable. To forbid women to work at night is unreasonable."[214] The Supreme Court upheld a maximum hour law for miners in *Holden v. Hardy* and then struck down the same for bakers in *Lochner*.[215] Given the "striking parallelism of the two cases," wrote respected University of Chicago law professor Ernst Freund, "our confidence in the value of precedents must be seriously shaken."[216]

Nothing inflamed passions like shifting decisions resulting from close votes of judges.[217] It was apparent to all that the income tax was struck down only because one justice switched his vote between argument and reargument. "What makes a tax unconstitutional is the Supreme Court's decision, interpreting the written Constitution." Yet this constitutional decision was the product "of the one judge who changed his mind," complained the *Outlook*.[218] *The Washington Post*, scolding continuing criticism of the Court several months following the *Lochner* decision, observed that "there were two opinions in the legislature and in each of the courts that had to do with the act. It happened in the court of last resort that the majority agreed with the minority in the inferior courts."[219] But such seeming happenstance was exactly what led to the complaint about malleability. Following *Adkins*, many again reacted strongly to the split Court. Thomas Reed Powell parodied the outcome. Looking to all the decisions leading up to that of the Supreme Court, he wrote, "[W]e have a total of thirty-two judges voting in favor of the constitutionality of minimum-wage legislation and nine judges voting against it." Somehow the nine prevailed. Not only that, but the vote against depended on the fortuity of who happened to be on the Supreme Court when the case was heard. Thus "the unconstitutionality of minimum-wage legislation has been dictated by the calendar rather than by the Constitution."[220]

Split judicial decisions undercut any pretense that in close cases, judges were adhering to a well-established rule known as clear mistake. During this period, Harvard law professor James Bradley Thayer published a paper that became an instant classic. In it he documented with meticulous citation to numerous cases the appropriate rule governing judicial review. The court "can only disregard" a law "when those who have the right to make laws have not merely made a mistake, but have made a very clear one,—so clear that it is not open to rational question." The reason for this was obvious: "The courts are revising the work of a co-ordinate department, and must not, even negatively, undertake to legislate."[221] But there was a sharp divergence between judicial word and deed. Political scientist Blaine Moore conducted a study of judicial adherence to the Thayerian principle, concluding that as early as 1898 "the court seems to have quite reversed its ancient attitude in approaching this question."[222] Judges knew what they were supposed to do; they just didn't do it. Like a child caught with its hand in the cookie jar, Justice Rufus Peckham, author of the *Lochner* decision, protested a bit too much: "This is not a question of substituting the judgment of the court for that of the legislature."[223] As Beulah Ratliff explained, writing in the pages of *The Nation*, "The rule that the Supreme Court has always professed to follow . . . is that where reasonable doubt exists the statute shall stand. . . . [W]here four of the learned judges disagree with the other five, everybody except possibly lawyers and judges can see only ground for scoffing at the conflict between the court's profession and practice."[224]

THE BIRTH OF REALISM

"The fiction that the judge does not make law"

Not everyone was willing to attribute so quickly the cause of the problem to the inherent shortcoming of the law or the bias of judges. Others, particularly in the legal world, believed the problem was that judges tackled the fate of social legislation on the basis of abstract concepts and categories when they should have paid closer attention to the hard, cold facts on the ground. The solution proposed was for judges to shift their attention to social realities. Legal realism, one of the most influential jurisprudential movements of the twentieth century, was born.

At the turn of the twentieth century, many judges and some prominent academics took a "formalist" approach to legal interpretation, in which answers to legal questions could be derived as a doctrinal matter purely from the cases themselves."[225] Harvard's legendary dean Christopher Langdell deemed law a science, the study of which could be mastered by discerning the governing rules from a set of cases. From that followed, some believed, "the fiction that the judge does not make law; that he simply declares what was the pre-existing law."[226] Morris Cohen referred to this as the "phonograph theory of the judicial function," by which the judge "merely repeats the words which the law has spoken to him."[227] Constitutional law professor Robert E. Cushman expanded on Cohen's understanding, explaining that many saw the judge as a "vocal medium" for "preëxisting legal principles" that are "absolute and immutable" and for which "the judge has no responsibility."[228]

Progressive lawyers and judges scoffed at this sort of legal formalism. "The certainty" from relying on formal tests, pronounced Oliver Wendell Holmes, speaking what many believed, "is only an illusion, nevertheless."[229] Holmes speculated that judges avoided discussing policy because "the moment you leave the path of merely logical deduction you lose the illusion of certainty which makes legal reasoning seem like mathematics."[230]

When judges decided cases in decisions that relied primarily on formal legal tests, they often were taken to task for ignoring social realities. New York City's Mayor Gaynor found it "almost inconceivable" that the New York Court of Appeals would strike down a "humane and benevolent" hours law as "an infringement of the 'liberty' of women, guaranteed as they said by the constitution, to work in factories all night and as many hours as they saw fit."[231] Criticizing the *Adkins* decision, *The Christian Science Monitor* said that apparently "the inalienable right to life, liberty, and the pursuit of happiness includes the right of a woman to see her labor for less than the cost of subsistence, and the right of an employer to enforce not merely a starvation wage, but any conditions of employment which may contribute to his profit."[232] Chastising one of the Court's important labor decisions, *The New Republic* complained: "For all the regard that the Chief Justice [Taft] of the United States pays to the facts of industrial life, he might as well have written this opinion as Chief Justice of the Fiji Islands."[233] Similarly, Roosevelt said of *Jacobs* that it "was rendered by well-meaning men who knew law, but who did not know life."[234]

Judges were criticized for failing to defer to legislative judgments precisely because many of the cases were understood to turn on facts about which the judiciary possessed no special expertise. Writing in *The Atlantic*

Monthly, George Alger said, "The essential conflicts between the courts and the legislatures on these subjects are over questions of fact."[235] Mayor Gaynor was expansive on the subject, condemning the decision in *Jacobs* striking the tenement law. "The claim that the manufacture of tobacco in such places was detrimental to health, especially the health of children, and might therefore be prohibited by the legislature, received short shrift from the venerable and learned judges."[236] The views on *Lochner* were similar. The *Outlook* said that "it does not give the legislative branch of the Government even the benefit of a doubt."[237] "The legal weakness of this reasoning," explained the British *Law Quarterly Review*, "if we may say so, is that no credit seems to be given to the State legislature for knowing its own business."[238] Criticizing the Court for the *Adkins* ruling, *The Nation* accused it of having "substituted its judgment of economic wisdom," and "as a result the people of the United States are without power, unless they amend the Constitution."[239]

No one contributed so much to the critique of the era's "abstract mechanical jurisprudence" as Harvard dean Roscoe Pound. Pound published article after article decrying "this sort of legality."[240] "[T]he application of law is not and ought not to be a purely mechanical process," he insisted.[241] "[Law] must not become so completely artificial that the public is led to regard it as wholly arbitrary."[242]

Pound urged "a pragmatic, a sociological legal science."[243] Central to his "sociological jurisprudence" was a better understanding of the facts upon which legislation rested. Holmes saw the need for this early on, predicting in his famous essay "The Path of the Law" that "the black-letter man may be the man of the present, but the man of the future is the man of statistics and the master of economics."[244] Roosevelt made Pound's point to Congress in 1908: "The rapid changes in our social and industrial life . . . have made it necessary that, in applying to concrete cases the great rule of right laid down in our Constitution, there should be a full understanding and appreciation of the new conditions to which the rules are to be applied."[245] Harvard professor Felix Frankfurter wished for "the invention of some machinery by which knowledge of the facts . . . may be at the service of the courts as a regular form of the judicial process."[246]

Louis Brandeis and his associate Josephine Goldmark were two pioneers who answered Frankfurter's call. Their brief in *Muller v. Oregon* was loaded with facts about the condition of working women and only two pages of legal argument.[247] Today's eyes would see more than a hint of sexism in Brandeis's approach in *Muller*—the brief stressed the impact of long working hours on women, in order to justify upholding the legal limit on the hours they were permitted to labor—but it succeeded, leading Frankfurter to call the approach "epoch making." [248] Soon it was common parlance to label such fact-laden briefs "Brandeis briefs."

The two prevailing critiques of Progressive Era judicial decision making—that legal doctrine was indeterminate, on the one hand, and that it failed to take account of social reality, on the other—gave birth to the most prominent jurisprudential school of the twentieth century, legal realism.[249] Realists made a sport of pointing out the malleability of law and insisted on an honest understanding of how cases were decided. If one could see that judges' biases infected legal outcomes, perhaps doctrines and devices could be found to purge them. The use of the word "realism" may have originated with Frankfurter, who in 1916 published an important article addressing the failure of judges to take account of social reality entitled "Hours of Labor and Realism in Constitutional Law." [250] At its core, realists agreed, "the law had come to be out of touch with reality." [251] "Ferment is abroad in the law," Columbia law professor Karl Llewellyn breathlessly proclaimed in a realist manifesto.[252] Eventually legal realism grew beyond being a jurisprudential "school" to a "movement" and ultimately even a "mood." [253]

The impact of the Progressive Era attacks on judges was enduring. Ironically, the fact that no significant controls over judges were adopted during the *Lochner* era served only to undermine faith in law itself. For generations after, lawyers worried that legal principles were too indeterminate to provide the "most essential element of a fundamental law, certainty of meaning," and that legal outcomes depended much too much on the accident of who happened to be on the bench.[254]

7

ACCEPTANCE

"[T]he Constitution . . . is a living thing"

The crash of 1929 put an end to the Republican Party's long-standing claims of being the "party of prosperity."[1] After nearly four hapless years, during which the Hoover administration attempted to deal with the Great Depression, in 1932 the country overwhelmingly elected Theodore Roosevelt's Democratic cousin Franklin to govern it. Central to the second Roosevelt's agenda was the expansion of governmental authority—particularly that of the federal government—to address the nation's social and economic problems.

Time and again, Roosevelt found his program stymied by a Supreme Court refusing to interpret the Constitution to cede broad control over the economy either to the federal government or to the states. Judicial decisions invalidated key New Deal measures and threatened to overturn others. Here is how FDR explained the situation to his fellow citizens in one of his fireside chats in March 1937:

> The American people have learned from the depression. For in the last three national elections an overwhelming number of them voted a mandate that the Congress and the President begin the task of providing that protection—not after long years of debate, but now.
>
> The Courts, however, have cast doubts on the ability of the elected Congress to protect us against catastrophe by meeting squarely our modern social and economic conditions.[2]

A man of action as well as words, Roosevelt launched a dramatic attack on the Supreme Court in January 1937. In common parlance, Roosevelt proposed packing the Court with as many as six additional justices. The debate over Roosevelt's plan riveted the nation for five months.

The Court-packing plan presented the American people with a stark choice. Roosevelt urged the public to support him, even at the cost of subjugating the Court's will, to ensure that the government had the tools to deal with the Depression. Roosevelt's opponents raised the specter of dictatorial government, stressing the need for an independent judiciary to protect individual rights.

What ultimately happened in the spring of 1937 has become constitutional law's great whodunit. In the heat of battle over the Court-packing plan, the justices appeared to do an about-face. Through a series of headline-grabbing decisions and one timely retirement, the justices indicated they no longer would stand in the way of government asserting the power it needed to manage the economy. After the Court's apparent capitulation, Roosevelt's plan went down in defeat. Ever since, the question has been whether the Court's change in direction was the result of "law" or "politics." Did the Court cave in the face of Roosevelt's threat, or was this the justices' independent interpretation of the Constitution? Had the nation's most fundamental law been altered as a result of naked political pressure? The papers of the swing justices have been combed to answer the unanswerable: What precisely were they thinking?

The true significance of 1937 requires no hidden clues; it was plain for all to see. The American people signaled their acceptance of judicial review as the proper way to alter the meaning of the Constitution, but only so long as the justices' decisions remained within the mainstream of popular understanding. Even those who deny that the Supreme Court shifted direction suddenly in the spring of 1937 concede nonetheless that fundamental constitutional change occurred over the next few years, as Franklin Roosevelt ultimately filled seven of the Supreme Court's nine seats.[3] The new justices, all agree, wrote a new Constitution. And unlike the fight over the propriety of packing the Court, this method of constitutional change was widely hailed as the proper one.

ROOSEVELT'S MANDATE

"The Nation asks for action, and action now"

It is difficult to overstate the depth of misery of the Great Depression. Between the crash of the stock market in 1929 and the 1932 election, unemployment in the United States rose to fully 25 percent, while industrial output and prices both dropped by roughly a third.[4] Steel mills were running at 12 percent of capacity.[5] The mortgage default rate among urbanites was about 20 percent, though that number doubled in some cities; by 1933, fully 40 percent of farm owners had lost their land.[6] The economic downturn spared few. The nation's poorest were forced to live in shantytowns—dubbed Hoovervilles—and ferret through trash dumps seeking subsistence.[7] Running for the Republican nomination in 1936, Idaho's progressive senator William E. Borah said that Americans "have seen hunger and nakedness and millions of children undernourished. . . . They have been made to know what it is to approach dependent old age. They have lost their homes, millions of them, and seen their savings swept away."[8]

In the face of widespread suffering, the country found President Herbert Hoover's response remarkably impoverished. Hoover was hardly hardhearted. As Secretary of Commerce during the Harding administration, he had worried over the problem of unemployment during times of depression and he had advocated the use of public works programs to combat it.[9] But Hoover believed primary responsibility rested with state and local governments. The states, though, were under tremendous economic pressure and either would not or could not do nearly enough.[10] Hoover's remark in 1931 that he would jump-start the federal effort "if the time should ever come that the voluntary agencies of the country together with the local and State governments are unable to find resources with which to prevent hunger and suffering in my country" must have seemed oblivious of the reality that millions of Americans faced.[11]

Franklin Roosevelt and the Democrats challenged Hoover's approach, demanding "drastic change in economic governmental policies."[12] The Democrats' program was vague and conservative in its own right—the platform called for balancing the federal budget and for a drastic cut in expenditures—but still it stood in contrast with Republican insistence that "[t]he people themselves, by their own courage, their own patient and resolute effort in the readjustment of their affairs, can and will work the cure."[13] Two critical speeches of FDR's touched the national nerve. In his famous "forgotten man" radio address of April 7, 1932, he stated baldly, "[W]e are in the midst of an emergency at least equal to that of war," and insisted the government "provide at least as much assistance to the little fellow as it is now giving to the large banks and corporations." Then, at Oglethorpe University the next month, Roosevelt delivered what became his mantra: "The country needs and, unless I mistake its temper, the country demands bold, persistent experimentation."[14]

The Democrats swept into power with wide support. The electoral college margin was 472–59, with FDR taking seven million more votes than Hoover out of some thirty-eight million cast.[15] Many Republican progressives—the "insurgents"—came to his support.[16] Roosevelt's victory was aided by business owners and people of all economic classes.[17]

As Roosevelt was sworn into office, the country faced collapse. Banks in thirty-eight states had closed their doors, and major stock and commodities exchanges had ceased trading.[18] "The Nation asks for action, and action now," Roosevelt said in his inaugural address, and he promised to deliver it.[19]

THE SUPREME COURT'S VETO

"A State cannot do it, and the Federal Government cannot do it"

Roosevelt's stumbling block, as the country was to learn soon enough, was the Supreme Court. The key question, in case after case, was whether the federal or state governments had sufficient power under the Constitution to address what Roosevelt had called "modern social and economic conditions."[20] In several critical decisions, the justices' narrow interpretations of government power appeared to threaten New Deal legislation intended to address the economic challenges of the Depression. More important than the individual decisions were their implications for the future of FDR's recovery plan.

From the beginning it was clear that the fate of the New Deal rested not with the Congress or the voters, but with the justices. That the Court Roosevelt inherited posed a potential threat was something he understood well. In a campaign speech in 1932, Roosevelt incurred criticism for stating that as of March 1929, "the Republican Party was in complete control of all branches of the federal government," suggesting the Court was but a political arm of the Republican Party.[21]

The composition of the Court made it anyone's guess (and guessers were busy guessing) what would happen when the justices encountered New Deal legislation. There were three identifiable "camps." The conservative justices were McReynolds, Butler, Sutherland, and Van Devanter. From these four, exclaimed FDR's Attorney General Homer Cummings, the administration could not expect a favorable vote "if the Angel Gabriel made the argument."[22] The four conservative justices were often referred to by New Deal sympathizers as the Four Horsemen of the Apocalypse or simply the Four Horsemen.[23] Poised against them were three "liberals"—Brandeis, Cardozo, and Stone.[24]

In the middle, holding the balance of power, were two of Herbert Hoover's appointees: Chief Justice Charles Evans Hughes and Justice Owen Roberts.[25]

Early decisions suggested that in light of dire economic straits, the justices would allow government the necessary power to pass economic measures, but only under a temporary "emergency" rationale. In early 1934, the Court resolved the *Blaisdell* case, upholding a Minnesota mortgage moratorium law enacted when the state's farmers were near revolt.[26] Under the law, mortgage holders could not force defaulting property owners into foreclosure proceedings so long as the owners paid a reasonable rent. The Chief Justice's opinion upheld the law, stating: "While emergency does not create power, emergency may furnish the occasion for the exercise of power."[27] The difficulty with this argument, explained Justice Sutherland, authoring a dissent for the Four Horsemen, was that the Constitution itself had been drafted when the economic situation was desperate, and the framers had apparently intended its provisions to bar precisely such measures.[28] "The present exigency is nothing new," Sutherland insisted. The Constitution "does not mean one thing at one time and an entirely different thing at another time."[29] Justice Brandeis, who joined Hughes's majority, penned a personal note to "My dear Sutherland": "This is one of the great opinions in American constitutional law. Regretfully, I adhere to my error."[30]

Three months later the Court's decision in *Nebbia v. New York* made it appear as though the justices were prepared to interpret the Constitution more generally to allow state governments to adopt measures regulating the economy. The *Nebbia* case involved a challenge to New York's minimum price law for milk, an effort to support prices as production exceeded demand. Justice McReynolds, citing the controversial but nonetheless enduring *Lochner*-era decision against a minimum wage law in *Adkins*, recalled that "[t]his Court has . . . emphatically declared that a State lacks power to fix prices in similar private businesses."[31] But McReynolds was in dissent. Writing for the five-person majority, Justice Roberts put government authority over minimum prices on a solid constitutional footing. "So far as the requirement of due process is concerned, . . ." he wrote, "a state is free to adopt whatever economic policy may reasonably be deemed to promote public welfare." And what of the *Lochner*-era precedents that seemed to protect the sellers' right to set the price? "[N]either property rights nor contract rights are absolute. . . . The due process clause makes no mention of sales or of prices any more than it speaks of business or contracts."[32] Lawyer, statesman, and later reform politician Dean Alfange described *Nebbia* as a case in which the Court "proceeded calmly to tear down the limitations upon price-fixing which it had set up during the past few decades; and so naively as almost to give the impression that such limitations had never existed."[33]

Nebbia and *Blaisdell* involved state laws, but the federal government won an important victory as well in early 1935, when the Court upheld the decision to take the nation off the gold standard.[34] So huge was the interest in the cases that the Court took the unprecedented step of announcing at the end of each week that a decision was not coming down the next Monday.[35] In the event of a loss, Roosevelt, who had no love of judicial authority, had a speech ready to give defying the Court and quoting Lincoln at his first inaugural.[36] But in a 5–4 decision, the Court effectively sanctioned the act of going off the gold standard by holding no party liable for any loss incurred in paying debts in other legal tender.[37] Alfange pointed to "[t]he Gold Clause decisions" as yet "another striking example of the Court's willingness and ability to adjust constitutional law to dominant political and economic realities."[38] Dissenting angrily, Justice McReynolds declared from the bench (in words that do not appear in the published dissent): "[A]s for the Constitution, it does not seem too much to say that it is gone. Shame and humiliation are upon us now."[39]

Roosevelt's honeymoon with the Court came to an abrupt halt in the winter and spring of 1935. In the first constitutional decision ever holding that Congress had delegated authority too broadly to the executive, the Court struck down an industrial code adopted as part of the National Industrial Recovery Act.[40] The NIRA attempted to deal with the problem of economic collapse by permitting businesses in different economic sectors to enter into cooperative codes of fair competition, which also were to include provisions for collective bargaining and wages and hours.[41] Then the Court invalidated Congress's retirement plan for railroad workers, a move Justice Stone, referring to *Lochner*, feared "will plague us as long as the famous Bake Shop Case did."[42] Finally, on May 27, 1935, a day commentators dubbed "Black Monday," the Court handed down three decisions against the administration, the leading one being its wholesale voiding of the NIRA in the *Schechter Poultry* case.[43] The latter decision came as a particular shock because the Court was unanimous in its conclusion to strike down the major New Deal program.[44] Even as far away as Great Britain, *Schechter* was "the thunderbolt judgment of the Supreme Court of the United States, which has struck down a vast scheme of remedial legislation in that country."[45] At the end of 1935, newspaper editors voted "United States Supreme Court rulings affecting the New Deal" the leading story of the year.[46]

Schechter called into question the extent to which the Supreme Court was prepared to permit Congress, acting pursuant to its constitutional power

to regulate "Commerce among the several States," to enact legislation regulating the national economy. At issue in *Schechter* was the application of a
NIRA Live Poultry Code to a slaughterhouse in Brooklyn. The defendants,
citing prior Supreme Court precedents, argued that the NIRA exceeded congressional power under the Commerce Clause because by the time the chickens arrived at the defendants' business all interstate commerce had ceased;
any further transactions were solely intrastate. "Production, whether by way
of manufacture, mining, farming or any other activity, is not commerce and
is not subject to regulation under the commerce clause." To hold otherwise
"would be destructive of our dual system of government and extend to the
Federal Government the power to nationalize industry."[47] The government
defended the law on the ground that wages and hours, even at a local business, affected the interstate market. In addition to trying to halt a "sharp decline in wages, prices and employment," argued the brief for the United States,
the wage and hour provisions "are reasonable means for the prevention of labor disputes . . . and so are adapted to protecting interstate commerce from
the burdens caused by labor disturbances."[48]

The Supreme Court unanimously rejected the government's arguments,
in an opinion that limited Congress's authority under the Constitution to
adopt economic legislation. "Extraordinary conditions do not create or enlarge
constitutional power," announced the Court at the outset, limiting the utility
of *Blaisdell's* emergency rationale.[49] Then the Court explained that the Constitution did not allow Congress to reach its regulatory fingers into the states
in this way. "So far as the poultry here in question is concerned, the flow in
interstate commerce had ceased." Any impact of the wage and hour provisions on interstate commerce, the Court said, was purely "indirect." "If the
commerce clause were construed to reach all enterprises and transactions
which could be said to have an indirect effect upon interstate commerce,"
the upshot would be "virtually no limit to the federal power and for all practical purposes we should have a completely centralized government."[50]

The problem with the *Schechter* decision was not the invalidation of the
NIRA so much as its import for future congressional legislation. By the time
of *Schechter*, the NIRA was just months away from expiration anyway and
was perceived as widely unpopular.[51] (History's quick condemnation of the
NIRA may be a bit hasty yet; polls showed that in later years a majority of
Americans believed the law should be revived.)[52] But the Court's opinion
clearly called into question the constitutionality of other pending legislation,
most notably the National Labor Relations (or Wagner) Act, which provided
federal protection to collective bargaining union activity. WHOLE OF NEW
DEAL PROGRAM IN CONFUSION, headlined *The New York Times*, while labor

was described as "dazed" by the decision, "fearing that its program of labor legislation" was imperiled.[53]

Following the *Schechter* decision, Roosevelt gave a lengthy and thought-ful press conference in which he raised profound questions about the Su-preme Court's understanding of how the Constitution applied to America's modern economy. "Does this decision mean that the United States Govern-ment has no control over any national economic problem?" Explaining that the integrated economy of the 1930s differed a great deal from that at the time the Constitution was adopted, Roosevelt worried aloud: "We have been rele-gated to the horse-and-buggy definition of interstate commerce."[54]

Negative public reaction to his "horse-and-buggy" comment persuaded FDR that "the occasion and tone of his remarks constituted a blunder," and from here on out he was much more circumspect in responding to unfavor-able decisions.[55] All FDR had suggested was that if the Court adhered to its views, amendment of the Constitution might be necessary.[56] Roosevelt's com-ments about the *Schechter* decision, however, were interpreted as an attack on the Court, which "still was one of the most revered institutions in the land."[57] Roosevelt was accused of making statements that were "dangerous and inflammatory."[58] Even some liberals criticized the speech. George Fort Milton, editor of *The Tennessean*, expressed concern that the tenor of the Pres-ident's remarks would damage the case for reform, because there would not be popular support for "a program bottomed on a criticism of the Court itself."[59]

FDR's chastening may have been the Court's emboldening. Constitu-tional historians have wondered why the Court, after its early decisions favor-ing the New Deal, took a sharp turn to the negative. The matter was far less perplexing to leading journalists Joseph Alsop and Turner Catledge, who wrote *The 168 Days*, following the defeat of FDR's Court plan: "Surely the howls of the editorial pages, the bellows of the politicians and the milder evidences of popular displeasure suggested to Roberts and the Tory justices that the performance of the NRA decision might be repeated with impunity."[60]

Next to go was the Agricultural Adjustment Act, FDR's elaborate plan to bolster farm prices. "From 1929 to 1932 available cash income from farming operations . . . dropped from five billion to barely one and a half billion dol-lars" with "devastating" effect on "rural life." The AAA sought to "restore the relative level of farm income" basically by paying farmers not to grow over-abundant crops. The fees were paid from a tax imposed on processors of farm products.[61]

Once again, the Court interpreted the Constitution to limit the scope of congressional power over the economy, in order to preserve state authority.

The question in the AAA case was the extent to which Congress could use its power to tax and spend for the "general welfare" as a means of addressing national economic conditions. Writing for a six-person majority that included the Four Horsemen and the Chief Justice, Justice Roberts was willing to concede a certain breadth to Congress's spending power. In Roberts's view, though, the AAA was not so much a spending program as "a scheme for purchasing with federal funds submission to federal regulation of a subject reserved to the states."[62] In other words, the AAA was a regulatory law in the guise of a spending provision. The act's "purpose is the control of agricultural production, a purely local activity." As such, it "invades the reserved rights of the states." "It hardly seems necessary to reiterate," Roberts wrote, "that ours is a dual form of government."[63]

The AAA decision set off a firestorm. The program itself was of dubious popularity.[64] After all, its effect was to raise farm prices, and by paying farmers not to produce, no less.[65] Still, observed Robert Carr, a government professor at Dartmouth, "very few people, New Dealers, students of constitutional law, and Republicans, alike, were prepared for the Court's sweeping condemnation of the Administration's agricultural policy."[66] *The New York Times*'s savvy correspondent Arthur Krock observed that after this decision even the most steadfast defenders of judicial review "must be aware . . . that a great national debate of the issue, with possible action by the people, is drawing near."[67] The six justices in the majority were hanged in effigy in Iowa, and calls for constitutional amendments now were heard with some regularity.[68] The cruel irony of the Court's opinion, one commentator pointed out, was "the fact that no state has ever undertaken any serious exercise of such power, and . . . could not possibly make any such regulation effective."[69]

This time critics of the Court's decision were aided by blunt words from the Court's dissenters. "As the present depressed state of agriculture is nation wide in its extent and effects," wrote Justice Stone, for himself and Justices Brandeis and Cardozo, "there is no basis for saying that the expenditure of public money in aid of farmers is not" for the "general welfare."[70] Stone had harsher words yet for his colleagues. Courts, he reminded them, "are concerned only with the power to enact statutes, not with their wisdom." Hinting in a barely veiled way that the majority had "abused" its authority, he concluded: "[C]ourts are not the only agency of government that must be assumed to have the capacity to govern."[71]

Then, in its *Carter Coal* decision of May 1936, the Court "shot the Guffey Coal Control Act all to pieces."[72] So said *The Wall Street Journal*, which explained that the law was intended to ensure labor peace in "the country's most important 'sick industry.'"[73] Excess production had led to "cutthroat competition" over both prices and wages, and labor strife in the coalfields had occasioned frequent use of federal troops.[74] The act allowed for wage and hour agreements and "confer[red] the power to fix the minimum price of coal at each and every coal mine in the United States."[75] FDR had urged Congress to pass the statute even though after *Schechter* "no one is in a position to give assurance that the proposed act will withstand constitutional tests." "Admitting that mining coal, considered separate and apart from its distribution in the flow of interstate commerce, is an intrastate transaction," the President explained, "the constitutionality . . . depends upon the final conclusion as to whether production conditions directly affect, promote, or obstruct interstate commerce in the commodity." Still, FDR counseled, "I hope your committee will not permit doubts as to constitutionality, however reasonable, to block the suggested legislation."[76]

The five-justice majority opinion in *Carter Coal* followed *Schechter* in barring Congress from regulating economic activity occurring solely in one state, even if the effect of that activity reverberated throughout the national economy. Whereas in *Schechter*, the Court explained, "the federal power was asserted with respect to commodities which had come to rest after their interstate transportation," the Guffey Act "deals with commodities at rest before interstate commerce has begun." This, however, was a "difference without significance."[77] The dissenters thought the reasoning specious: "Mining and agriculture and manufacture are not interstate commerce considered by themselves, yet their relation to that commerce may be such that for the protection of the one there is need to regulate the other."[78]

Carter Coal appeared a definitive blow to Congress's ability to use its constitutional commerce power to regulate the national economy. "If the federal authority cannot be extended over coal production it is hard to imagine how it could be spread over other industries," concluded *The Wall Street Journal*.[79] Pointing to "menace to the public, deeply concerned in a steady and uniform supply of a fuel so vital to the national economy," Justice Cardozo insisted in dissent that "Congress was not condemned to inaction in the face of price wars and wage wars so pregnant with disaster."[80] The Court was unmoved. The five-person majority (Justice Roberts and the Four Horsemen) took care to reject the "proposition, often advanced and as often discredited, that the power of the federal government inherently extends to purposes affecting the nation as a whole with which the states severally cannot deal or cannot adequately deal."[81] The Chief Justice, who joined in striking down the wage and hour provisions (though he would have withheld judgment on the price setting), said the only recourse was constitutional amendment. "If the people desire to give Congress the power to regulate industries within the State, and the relations of employers and employees in those industries, they are at liberty to declare their will in the appropriate manner, but it is not for the Court to amend the Constitution by judicial decision."[82]

Then, on June 1, the same five-justice majority struck down New York's minimum wage law for women in a case called *Tipaldo*.[83] The decision was met with "[a]stonishment, indignation and disappointment" from all quarters, especially because the 1934 *Nebbia* case had seemed to signal that such laws would have been upheld. *Commonweal* deemed the decision "a blunder of magnitude."[84]

Tipaldo interpreted the Constitution in a way that looked to place the nation in a regulatory void when it came to addressing economic conditions. *Carter Coal* had limited federal authority over wages because "the evils are all local evils over which the federal government has no legislative control."[85] Yet in *Tipaldo* the Court was denying local authorities this very same authority, relying upon the Due Process Clause. Prior to *Tipaldo*, one interpretation of the New Deal decisions was that the state governments had authority over the economy even if Congress did not. Now the Court was saying that neither did. FDR captured the sentiments of many when he said the decision created a "no-man's land where no Government—State or Federal—can function. . . . A State cannot do it, and the Federal Government cannot do it."[86] Even the Republican platform that year insisted laws like that struck down in *Tipaldo* were "within the Constitution as it now stands."[87] According to Merlo Pusey, Chief Justice Hughes's biographer, "[a] rumble of discontent swept through the land."[88]

EVOLVING POPULAR UNDERSTANDINGS

"[W]e want the government to assume social responsibility"

The Supreme Court's decisions challenged the legislative program of a popular President. But they did more than that. They also ran up against the American people's evolving judgment of what the Constitution meant. As the Court repeatedly interpreted the Constitution to deny government the authority to deal with changing economic and social conditions, the people were coming to quite the opposite conclusion: that existing constitutional power was adequate to the task. Disagreement on this fundamental issue set the stage for the conflict that was about to unfold.

"[T]oday there is a real question," wrote W. Y. Elliott, the chair of Harvard's government department in 1936, "whether the organization of our government, either in its federal or its functional aspects, can meet the needs of the times and the national will of a country grown out of the changes and the consolidations of a century and a half." [89] This was a question being asked by many. In 1934, John Parker, a respected federal appellate judge whose recent nomination to the Supreme Court had failed by one vote in the face of the concerns of blacks and labor, spoke to lawyers about "The Federal Constitution in a Period of Change." "The greatest problem of statesmanship at the present time," explained Judge Parker, "is to preserve the fundamental rights of the individual . . . without impairing the power of the government to undertake measures essential to the general welfare." [90] The "simple but vital question," echoed Donald Richberg, who had run the NIRA before the Supreme Court deep-sixed it, was "whether the National Government now possesses or should be given ample power to protect the freedom and the security of all the American people." By way of emphasis he added that this question could not be "settled finally by the opinions of the Supreme Court," but only "by the people." [91]

The American people were closely focused on this question of whether the Constitution granted government sufficient power to deal with modern economic conditions. Closing a debate over New Deal policies in New York, a speaker said, "Now, everybody talks the Constitution. All are 'Constitution Conscious.'" [92] The American Academy of Political and Social Science (serving "thoughtful business and professional people") gave over the entire May 1936 issue of its *Annals* to the topic "The Constitution in the Twentieth Century." Such was the interest in the subject that summary versions of the papers were read on the National Broadcasting Company's radio network. [93]

The scope of federal power over the economy had been an issue since the late nineteenth century. [94] Even before Teddy Roosevelt ascended to the presidency, the federal government had put in place the means of administering a vast pension system for veterans and performing elementary supervision of interstate railway transportation. Roosevelt had been the first of a string of Presidents—Taft, Wilson, and Hoover as well—who believed in sound administration and the use of governmental power for the good of the commonweal. [95] Felix Frankfurter, a Harvard law professor who was one of FDR's chief advisers, observed quite properly that "one may mark McKinley's administration as the end of a period of *laissez faire*." Frankfurter rattled off a list of new national measures that included "[t]he Safety Appliance Act, the Hours of Service Law, an invigorated Interstate Commerce Act, the Pure Food and Drugs Act, the Meat Inspection Law." With the New Deal still on the horizon, Frankfurter had already found "something touching about the

Congressman who only the other day introduced a joint resolution for a Commission on Centralization" to report on what needed to be done to "restore the government to its original purposes."[96]

It was hardly the case, though, that the public had expressed avid support for the growth of federal authority in the period between Theodore's and Franklin's administrations. In 1914, after all Teddy Roosevelt had done, the president of the American Association for Labor Legislation conceded that "we have never converted the people whole-heartedly to the principle that the determination of the fundamental conditions under which industry should be carried on, and labor performed, is, or should be, a prime function of the state."[97] World War I did see a terrific increase in federal economic authority, but Warren Harding's election after the war on a promise of a return to "normalcy" meant, in part, dismantling federal administrative machinery.[98]

Strong resistance to the role of the federal government in economic matters was the apparent philosophy of Herbert Hoover and many others during the Depression. Well into the crisis, Hoover was saying, "The moment [that] responsibilities of any community, particularly in economic and social questions, are shifted from any part of the nation to Washington, then that community has subjected itself to a remote bureaucracy."[99] In 1931, nationally prominent University of Chicago political scientist and Chicago politician Charles Merriam gave a series of public lectures on "The Written Constitution and the Unwritten Attitude." "There was probably never a period in history," he told his audience, "when social change was as rapid as at present and when the need for adjustment and adaptation was as great." Yet the American people resisted it. "The real difficulty lies in the unwillingness of many Americans to face in government what they meet in industry, the constant need for readjustment and reorganization."[100] As late as 1933, the American Bar Association was still opposing the Child Labor Amendment as "an unwarranted invasion by the Federal Government of a field in which the rights of the individual states and of the family are and should remain paramount."[101] "Perhaps the dominant feeling about government today is distrust," Frankfurter said in 1930. "I do not refer merely to the current skepticism about democracy, but to the widely entertained feeling of the incapacity of government, generally, to satisfy the needs of modern society."[102]

It was FDR's leadership, combined with the exigencies of the moment, that led people to see the necessity of broad national authority over the economy. "[A]fter a short period of very painful popular education," explained Richberg to the *Annals* audience, "we find that millions of citizens are demanding that the Government . . . shall reorganize or regulate the economic system so that it can be relied upon to provide a decent and assured living for all people."[103] Roosevelt realized early on that "[i]f forty states go along with adequate legislation and eight do not . . . we get nowhere."[104] He in turn (in the words of reporters Alsop and Catledge) "educated the people; under his tutelage they learned to expect the federal government to see to their private welfare as well as to the public safety and convenience."[105]

Roosevelt's initial New Deal measures were justified by the emergency, and they found broad bipartisan support. "The House is burning down, and the President of the United States says this is the way to put out the fire," said House Minority Leader Bertrand Hollis Snell, as the House passed FDR's banking bill (by acclamation) after thirty-eight minutes of debate.[106] Judge Parker explained to the American Bar Association in 1933 that "in recent months the country has been confronted with an unprecedented situation in that regulations of commerce have been rendered necessary and relief measures have become imperative which in normal times would not be thought of at all."[107]

Soon, though, it became commonplace to explain what was happening as a response not to an emergency but to changed social and economic conditions that likely would persist. A district court upholding the Guffey Act (prior to its ultimate demise in *Carter Coal*) pointed to numerous factors such as "[m]odern technology" and "a rapid system of transportation and communication" to conclude that "[i]f commerce is to be regulated . . . it must be by the national government, because the states lack the power to make effective their own regulations."[108] Stanley Reed, as Solicitor General, the government's lawyer in the Supreme Court, said the same in an eloquent talk to the Virginia Bar entitled "The Constitution and the Problems of Today." "America is a single community . . . engaged in an unbelievably intricate system of production, distribution and consumption," he insisted, pointing to the fact that "[o]ur clothing, our car, or our house, is composed of the products of many States, may be the result of the labors of American citizens scattered from coast to coast."[109] In response to the AAA decision, *The* (London) *Times* observed incredulously: "The Constitution was written in 1787. Since then modern methods of production, trade, transport and communications have largely obliterated State boundaries in matters of business and economic development."[110]

The results of the 1934 election reaffirmed Roosevelt's pursuit of federal economic legislation. The initial spirit of cooperation had begun to cool; Roosevelt increasingly faced opposition among the upper-class and business interests, often framed in constitutional terms.[111] In the summer of 1934, the ostensibly bipartisan American Liberty League formed to oppose New Deal policies, leading *Newsweek* to observe that the "Tories have come out of ambush."[112] The Chamber of Commerce was soon to repudiate the New Deal, and Herbert Hoover wrote *The Challenge to Liberty*, in which he likened Roosevelt's program, which he called "National Regimentation," to "Fascism, Socialism, Communism, or what not."[113] Still, in the midterm elections of 1934, Roosevelt's party scored a stunning victory. Reversing the usual terms of a midterm election, the opposition Republicans actually lost 13 seats in the House.[114] Senator William Borah explained why: "They [the people] are offered the Constitution—but the people can't eat the Constitution."[115] Democrats now held 322 of the House's seats and more than two-thirds of the Senate.[116] *The New York Times* called it the "most overwhelming victory in the history of American politics."[117]

The New Deal gradually won over many doubters—if not with regard to specific programs and their details, then to the idea of deep federal government involvement in economic affairs. Instructive was the testimony of the president of a southern coal company before a hearing on the Guffey bill. "[U]p to the time the National Recovery Act was passed" he and other operators had "zealously opposed any form of Federal legislation." But now he had become "thoroughly convinced" that his "previous attitude" was "unsound" and "that the only chance to keep the coal industry from getting back to its former deplorable condition is the enactment of some form of Federal legislation."[118] By 1935, governors who complained that "[n]o possible emergency can justify . . . scrapping the states and filling the land with federal agents" were a distinct minority. Wilbur Cross, the governor of Connecticut, said: "In the emergency I am ready to lay aside the unsubstantial ghost of state sovereignty."[119] Seven states filed amicus briefs in the Supreme Court in favor of federal power in *Carter Coal* (none filed against it).[120]

Changing views toward federal support for the needy—be it relief, public works, or Social Security—were emblematic of the shift in thinking about government's involvement in economic and social conditions.[121] The author of the 1935 monograph *Government in Business* wrote: "That which was anathema in 1931 is now universally admitted to be urgent public business." "The New Deal has repudiated the idea," he continued, "that the misery of the unemployed is due to their own improvidence. This, for America, is a genuinely revolutionary conception."[122] That same year only one out of thirty-seven governors polled thought relief was the responsibility of state governments.[123] Overwhelming passage of the Social Security law—it had a 3–1 margin among Republicans—led Roosevelt's Secretary of Labor Frances Perkins to note the "progress which the American people have made in thought in the social field."[124]

There were dissenters, of course (even here cracks were showing). An *Annals* speaker acknowledged this was an issue that split the country into "two schools of thought." While one school saw government "as a means of correcting those economic maladjustments which have nation-wide causes and effects," the other school viewed "thoroughgoing control over the economy" as "dangerous political power."[125] Even among the antis, though, there were those who conceded that some problems of regulation "have now become national, and with the changes in industrial organization and in the means of transportation and communication, the National Government has of necessity increasingly come to exercise" its power.[126] While opposing the New Deal as excessive federal intervention, some conservative business groups came to see the need for greater regulation "as society grows more complex."[127]

Polls, particularly Gallup's, confirmed the tide of public sentiment shifting toward greater government and national authority. Though respondents were deeply conflicted in late 1935 about the AAA (Democrats wildly favored; Republicans opposed even more strongly), there was broad and uniform support for the federal government's providing old-age pensions. A poll taken in April 1936 showed that more than 60 percent of the country favored a constitutional amendment providing Congress the power to regulate and ban child labor.[128] More than 67 percent of the country favored a minimum wage regulation.[129] A solid majority favored amending the Constitution to give the Congress greater authority over industry and agriculture.[130] When asked whether respondents favored "concentration of power in the Federal Government, or concentration of power in the state governments," a solid majority chose the former. A 1937 poll showed a large majority favored the federal government's setting maximum hours. (There also was consistent support for a revival of the NIRA.)[131] The support for government relief for the needy was overwhelming.[132]

The election of 1936 put squarely to the voters the question of whether government in general, and the federal government in particular, should have broad economic authority. The Democratic platform was unequivocal, declaring it a "truth . . . self-evident" that "government in a modern civilization has certain inescapable obligations to its citizens. . . . The Republican platform proposes to meet many pressing national problems solely by action of the separate States," the Democrats chided. Yet "[t]ransactions and activities which inevitably overflow State boundaries call for both State and Federal Treatment." These included "minimum wages, maximum hours, child labor, and working conditions in industry, monopolistic and unfair business practices."[133] FDR's final address at Madison Square Garden was a forceful statement of where he stood. "The Nation looked to Government," he said, referring to the twelve years before his own, "but the Government looked away." His administration, on the other hand, "instead of twirling its thumbs has rolled up its sleeves" and had worked and would continue to work "to reduce hours over-long, to increase wages that spell starvation, to end the labor of children." [134]

Indicative of the general shift in opinion, Roosevelt's opponent, the progressive governor of Kansas Alf Landon—supported much of the New Deal agenda as well. [135] The conservative *Baltimore Sun* refused to endorse either candidate, believing both to be "heavily tarred with the same stick of authoritarian government." [136] The Republican platform also pledged "old age security," "the right of labor to organize and to bargain collectively," to "abolish sweatshops and child labor, and to protect women and children with respect to maximum hours, minimum wages and working conditions." Republicans even believed "this can be done within the Constitution as it now stands." [137]

Nonetheless, there was an important difference in emphasis for the Republicans. Their platform promised to "maintain the American system of Constitutional and local self government." Rather than pledge the national government to these tasks, Republicans looked "to the energy, self-reliance and character of our people, and to our system of free enterprise." [138] Hoover gave a hugely well-received address to the Republican National Convention in 1936. "Either we shall have a society based on . . . the initiative of the individual or we shall have a planned society that means dictation no matter what you call it or who does it." [139]

Newspapers highlighted *"America's Choice."* "[A] basic issue in the coming national election will be that of concentration of powers in the national government." "It is a choice between . . . the representative democracy which American has always been and a centralized dictatorship. It is a choice between free enterprise and autocracy, between the sovereignty of the Constitution and the sovereignty of collectivism." [140] "The people are to choose . . . between an administration that is moving toward regimentation of the people and all business and industry under control of the government . . . and one that would preserve the Jeffersonian ideal of free industry, free enterprise and free society." [141]

Given that choice, the voters handed Roosevelt one of history's greatest electoral victories. [142] A remarkable new coalition of urbanites, blacks, labor, northern liberals, reliefers, Jews, and Catholics flocked to the Democratic Party banner, transforming American politics for decades to come. [143] Taking all the states but Maine and Vermont, Roosevelt beat Landon by eleven million votes out of more than forty-five million cast, with more than 60 percent of the total.[144] Democrats captured 334 of the House's 435 seats and held three-quarters of the Senate.[145]

It is never an easy task to read a mandate, but this one was no mystery to most of those watching. The liberal representative Maury Maverick, writing in *The New Republic*'s series on "The Next Four Years," summed up the results as most saw them, saying, "Keep up the New Deal, we want the government to assume social responsibility."[146] Some conservatives were more grudging, saying the landslide represented nothing other than support for FDR himself or, if not his policies, then their results.[147] But William Allen White, a personal friend of Landon's, spelled it out pretty clearly. "It was not a Roosevelt victory and not a Landon defeat," he said. Rather, "it was a revelation of a changed attitude toward government."[148]

THE CONSTITUTIONAL LOGIC OF ROOSEVELT'S SOLUTION

*"[O]ur Constitution ought to be construed in the light
of the present-day civilization"*

In light of the election returns and public sentiments about government power over the economy, it was plain that something had to be done to prevent the constant unraveling of the New Deal legislative agenda by the Supreme Court. Congress was awash in proposals to amend the Constitution. "For weeks," reported Roosevelt confidant George Creel in *Collier's* magazine, "the loudest noise in the land has been the scratching of pens as senators and representatives framed amendments designed to meet every known and anticipated need."[149] Some of these were directed to finding constitutional language that would plainly empower Congress to pass New Deal economic measures. Others were aimed at restricting the power of the justices to invalidate those laws—for example, by requiring a supermajority of the Court to hold a law unconstitutional or by stripping the power of judicial review over particular laws altogether. Another idea still was to allow the Congress to overrule the Court in certain circumstances.[150] Yet Roosevelt eschewed the amendment route for a different alternative entirely. He joined many Americans in believing the Constitution to be a "living" document that already provided ample authority to government if only it were interpreted correctly. Out of this belief came his plan for the Supreme Court.

The election had only exacerbated Roosevelt's Court problem. "Mr. Roosevelt had promised more than he could deliver," wrote Merlo Pusey. "The voters had instructed him . . . to go ahead with his plans," but he could not do that without "breaking through what appeared to be a blockade of judicial

decisions."[151] Much of Roosevelt's existing legislative agenda was already under assault: there were judicial challenges pending to such key legislation as
Social Security and the National Labor Relations Act.[152] "Two obstacles still
interpose," the conservative *Herald Tribune* reassured its readers after the
election. "They are the Constitution and the Supreme Court."[153]

Roosevelt highlighted the problem in his January 1937 State of the Union
Address. "The statute of N.R.A. has been outlawed. The problems have not.
They are still with us." So too, he said, were the problems faced by labor
and agriculture, which could not be solved "through parallel and simultaneous action by forty-eight States." "Means must be found," FDR insisted, "to
adapt our legal forms and our judicial interpretation to the actual present
national needs of the largest progressive democracy in the modern world."
Roosevelt made it clear the judges were the problem, saying he did "not ask
the Courts to call non-existent powers into being," but there was a "right to
expect that conceded powers or those legitimately implied shall be made effective instruments for the common good."[154] Every line in Roosevelt's speech
that could be interpreted as an attack on the Court was delivered to loud
applause.[155]

Roosevelt believed that the constitutional amendment route, which many
continued to advocate in the coming months, had a very practical shortcoming. He was seeking swift and certain action.[156] Roosevelt certainly was not
heartened by the fate of the Child Labor Amendment; thirteen years after
Congress had proposed it with large popular support, it still had not been ratified.[157] It would be difficult to get all the parties to agree on one amendment
among the swirling alternatives and to draft language that would achieve its
goals precisely. Even if key players agreed on an amendment, getting it passed
would be an enormous challenge. "About 37 state legislatures will meet in
January, 1937, not assembling again until 1939," explained *Collier's* Creel,
channeling FDR's thoughts.[158] Then there were still the justices. "Judges who
resort to a tortured construction of the Constitution may torture an amendment," Robert Jackson explained to the Senate once hearings on Roosevelt's
plan had begun.[159]

More fundamentally, Roosevelt did not believe that the Constitution
needed amending. He had addressed the point in his 1933 Inaugural Address,
saying, "Our Constitution is so simple and practical that it is possible always
to meet extraordinary needs by changes in emphasis and arrangement without loss of essential form."[160] Speaking through *Collier's* Creel, FDR set out
the view that the framers had "racked their brains to set down every national need" and then, "out of the consciousness that other needs were
bound to arise," added additional general authorization.[161] After the inaugu-

ration, Roosevelt told a colleague that when he faced Chief Justice Hughes, repeating the oath to "protect and defend the Constitution of the United States," he wanted to cry out, "Yes, but it is the Constitution as *I understand it*, flexible enough to meet any new problem of democracy—not the kind of Constitution *your Court* has raised up as a barrier to progress and recovery."[162]

In holding to this view, Roosevelt was connecting with evolving public sentiments about the nature of the Constitution and the role of judicial review in altering it. The period from the *Lochner* era to the Court-packing plan often is read as of one sustained struggle over judicial authority.[163] In truth, there were important discontinuities. Much changed as the debate progressed. In the 1890s, the Constitution was understood as fixed; the judges were thought unfaithful or heretical when they molded it to their views, which is what the *Lochner*-era judges were accused of doing. By the time the conflict over the New Deal Court erupted, the Constitution was widely understood as greatly flexible; the error of judges was now seen to be failing to construe it as the public believed it should be construed, to keep pace with the changing times.[164] During the *Lochner* era, the Court was criticized for interfering with democratic will; by the time of Roosevelt's attack, the dominant criticism was of the justices' ages and their being out of step with the times.[165]

The country had traveled a long way to this pervasive realism about the Constitution and judging. Recall James Weaver, the People's Party candidate in 1892, who so vigorously attacked the Supreme Court in the 1890s. In *A Call to Arms*, Weaver expressed disgust with one justice who, when narrowing a prior precedent, gave as a reason that the membership of the Court had changed in the interim. "What had that fact to do with the Constitution?" Weaver asked. "Are we to have a new interpretation of that instrument every time we have a change of judges?"[166] Similarly, North Carolina Supreme Court justice Walter Clark, another *Lochner*-era antagonist of judicial review, found frustrating the naive view of "the masses . . . that *law* is the one stationary, unmoving, and immovable thing in all creation, and that precedents bind judges and lawyers to the past, hand and foot."[167]

By the time of the New Deal, views had changed; it was widely understood that judges' philosophies influenced constitutional decisions. In a 1931 article, *The New York Times* said, "Theoretically . . . no Supreme Court Justice is either liberal or conservative, since the court's duty is to interpret the law, not to decide public policy." Then it tore down the gauze: "Actually most important cases do come before the court in such a form that a judge's philosophy of law, of government and of human relations must enter into his construction of the Constitution and the statutes."[168] An article in *The*

Yale Law Journal explained that "[c]riticisms of the Court are centered not on the fact of flexibility of construction and interpretation, which is inescapable and indeed desirable." Rather, the issue is "whether the Court correctly reflects the prevailing *mores*."[169] In Charles Merriam's 1931 lectures on the Constitution, he pointed out that "all words may be interpreted" and predicted that should the views of the people regarding constitutional meaning "change radically, the whole attitude of the court would change."[170] A *New York Times Magazine* feature in March 1936 ran the headline NINE JUDGES — AND NINE MEN, TOO. When a judge takes the bench, "he does not cease to be a man with opinions, convictions, prejudices and a definite political philosophy."[171]

When the Court claimed otherwise, it was subject to ridicule. In *Butler*, Justice Roberts asserted that the Court's sole task was "to lay the article of the Constitution which is invoked beside the statute which is challenged and to decide whether the latter squares with the former."[172] *The New York Times*'s Arthur Krock was blunt. "Who can doubt," he asked, that if three Roosevelt appointees "had been on the bench in Hoosac Mills instead of Justices Sutherland, Van Devanter and McReynolds, the decision would have been the other way?"[173]

The notion that the Constitution was inherently flexible enough to meet current needs became prevalent. The common trope was "the living Constitution."[174] Roosevelt's point to Creel was that fidelity to the framers' intentions denied the need for any amendment. Writers and speakers frequently credited the framers, as well as Chief Justice John Marshall, for having written and interpreted the Constitution in a manner capable of ensuring that it functioned in changing times.[175] (Recall Marshall's famous words in *McCulloch v. Maryland* that the Constitution was "intended to endure for ages to come" and must be "adapted to the various *crises* of human affairs.")[176] In 1934, the president of the Federal Bar Association gave a radio address entitled "John Marshall and the New Deal," with this same theme.[177] His key point was that the Constitution's broad language allowed for modern interpretations to meet the needs of the times. Charles Beard, perhaps then America's most famous constitutional historian, explained: "Since most of the words and phrases dealing with the powers and the limits of government are vague and must in practice be interpreted by human beings, it follows that the Constitution as practice is a living thing."[178]

It therefore was the job of the judges to ensure that the Constitution was kept current with the times. Nebraska's progressive senator George Norris declared on the floor of the Senate: "Our Constitution ought to be construed in the light of the present-day civilization instead of being put in a straightjacket made more than a century ago."[179] FDR sounded a similar note in his State of the Union Address: "The vital need is not an alteration of our fundamental law, but an increasingly enlightened view with reference to it." [180] Although the Senate Judiciary Committee was to disagree with Roosevelt on the means of changing the Constitution, the senators conceded that "[t]rue it is, that courts like Congresses, should take account of the advancing strides of civilization. True it is, that the law, being a progressive science, must be pronounced progressively and liberally." [181]

In light of these understandings, it makes sense that by 1937 there was a pervasive sentiment that the real problem lay not with the Constitution but with the justices—"nine old men" who could not understand that times had changed. FDR struck the nerve of the country's reverence for the Court when he complained of a horse-and-buggy interpretation of the Constitution, but he also was tapping into what people were increasingly thinking and saying. After *Butler* the President received a huge volume of mail; many letters focused on the ages of the justices. One person wrote FDR: "That they are behind the times is very plain—all you have to do is look at Charles Hughes' whiskers." [182] In October 1936, Washington pundits Drew Pearson and Robert Allen published their bestseller, serialized in many newspapers, with a telling title, *The Nine Old Men*. [183] "Probably the faults of the system could be reduced if there were an age limit for justices," suggested *New York Times* correspondent and dean of the Washington press corps Arthur Krock, quoting back at Chief Justice Hughes an earlier suggestion he had made to this effect. [184] The public agreed. Throughout the next year, polls showed that whatever Americans thought about other methods of court reform, they supported a mandatory retirement age by huge margins. [185]

For some time FDR and Attorney General Homer Cummings had begun looking for a solution to the Court problem. Writing to an Assistant Attorney General in 1934, Cummings asked: "Has any study been made in this office of the question of the right of the Congress, by legislation, to limit the terms and conditions upon which the Supreme Court can pass on constitutional questions?" [186] In 1936, after the AAA had been felled, Roosevelt asked Cummings (referring to the Reconstruction Era case in which the Court had acceded to the stripping of its jurisdiction): "What was the McArdle case . . . ? I am told that the Congress withdrew some act from the jurisdiction of the Supreme Court?" [187]

As a potential solution, Court packing seemed to have a pedigree. On occasion Roosevelt would mention the British example of packing the House of Lords to gain acquiescence to shifting power to the Commons. [188] More to the point, though, were the changes in the size of the Supreme Court throughout history, particularly during Reconstruction. [189] Still, Roosevelt and his advisers were concerned that the country would consider packing the Supreme Court a "distasteful idea," that it was "taboo."[190]

Eventually all the pieces fell into place in a way that made the plan palatable and plausible to FDR. Edward Corwin, a political scientist and constitutional scholar at Princeton and a public intellectual who also was a sometime adviser to the administration, published an article in a Philadelphia paper suggesting a limitation on judges holding office after the age of seventy. This occasioned a letter from a colleague at Harvard suggesting something akin to what FDR ultimately proposed: that the President be permitted to appoint a new judge any time a sitting judge reached seventy without retiring. Corwin passed the suggestion on to Cummings, who liked it.[191] At about this time, Cummings stumbled into an ironic "precedent" for the idea: while Attorney General during Woodrow Wilson's presidency, Justice McReynolds had proposed precisely the same thing for lower-court judges.[192] Cummings suggested wrapping the matter up in a veil of broader court reform, and FDR decided to go ahead.[193]

THE CASE AGAINST COURT PACKING

"PROPOSAL WILL LEAD TO A DEPRIVATION OF CIVIL LIBERTIES"

On February 5, 1937, in an elaborately orchestrated cabinet meeting and press conference, Roosevelt announced his plan for the "reorganization" of the federal judiciary. "The simple fact is that today a new need for legislative action arises," Roosevelt informed Congress, "because the personnel of the Federal Judiciary is insufficient to meet the business before them."[194] Though the plan had several elements, aimed at what Roosevelt framed as the inability of the federal judiciary to keep up with its work, its crux was this: for any judge who did not retire upon reaching the age of seventy, the President was empowered (within limits) to appoint additional judges.[195] Given the current composition of the Supreme Court, FDR would get six new appointments, barring retirements.[196] The plan was widely attacked as disingenuous. It soon, however, encountered a far more serious challenge: that an independent judiciary was essential to the protection of civil liberties.

The reaction to FDR's proposal was profound, more than he could possibly have imagined. "To listen to the clamor," wrote Harold Ickes, Roosevelt's Secretary of the Interior, "one would think that Moses from Mt. Sinai had declared that God himself had decreed that if and when there should be a Supreme Court of the United States, the number Nine was to be sacred."[197] Although the plan was presented as "a routine and moderate effort to speed up justice and improve the whole Federal bench," reported New York's *Herald Tribune*, "beneath this veneer of politeness, the brutal fact is that President Roosevelt would pack the Supreme Court with six new justices of his own choosing."[198] Roosevelt also was criticized because he had not signaled at any time during the recent electoral contest that the Court was on the table. "There is nothing in the Democratic platform about the proposed rape of the Supreme Court," Representative Hamilton Fish objected volubly.[199]

Roosevelt's initial message on the plan was not nearly as disingenuous as critics complained. True, he had camouflaged the attempt to pack the Court in a broader, legitimate plan for judicial reform. Still, Roosevelt's argument about the plan was entirely consistent with the dominant criticism that the justices were not keeping the Constitution in line with the times. "Modern complexities call also for a constant infusion of new blood in the courts," Roosevelt told Congress. "A lowered mental or physical vigor leads men to avoid an examination of complicated and changed conditions." Roosevelt was quite clear that the problem was of "old glasses fitted . . . for the needs of another generation" and "older men, assuming that the scene is the same as it was in the past."[200]

In Roosevelt's defense, voters knew perfectly well the Court was an issue. Roosevelt had chosen not to run against the Court and was careful about what he said, but his supporters were not as restrained. At the Democratic National Convention, Senator Alben Barkley of Kentucky went after the justices tooth and tong, to roars from the crowd. "Is the Court beyond criticism?" he asked. "May it be regarded as too sacred to be disagreed with?"[201] The media repeatedly identified the Court as an issue. New York's *Daily News* said the question might be "dodged" by the candidates, but "it is the next fundamental issue for the American people" whether "old judicial gentlemen . . . can forever be permitted to override the will of the people."[202] Republicans repeatedly claimed Roosevelt was after the Court. A keynote speaker at a Republican Party conference declared, "The preservation of the basic principles of the Constitution: This is the supreme issue of the hour."[203] The party platform said Roosevelt had "flouted" the "integrity and authority of the Supreme Court" and promised "to resist all attempts to impair the authority of the Supreme Court of the United States."[204] In his closing speech of the campaign, at Madison Square Garden, Landon said of Roosevelt: he "has been responsible for nine acts declared unconstitutional. . . . He has publicly belittled the Supreme Court of the United States."[205]

The chief argument against the plan, though, was none of this. Rather, it stressed the danger of dictatorship, and it invoked the need for an independent judiciary to preserve individual liberty. While the country saw the need to grant broad powers to the government, it was deeply conflicted about the implications of doing so.[206] Roosevelt's plan fell upon the country at a time when the fear of "totalitarianism" had become widespread.[207] Roosevelt failed to anticipate the depth of this opposition to his plan, in part because his own resentment of judicial authority blinded him to mounting support for an independent judiciary among the public.[208] Announcement of the Court plan came at a time of growing unease about the expansion of executive and administrative power. The burgeoning administrative state—and particularly the "headless 'fourth branch'" of independent agencies—still had not found a comfortable place within America's traditional tripartite system of separated powers.[209] As one New Deal measure followed another, old-time progressives, who were otherwise New Deal supporters, developed an allergy to FDR's consolidation of power.[210] Just prior to the announcement of the Court plan, FDR had also proposed a broad reorganization of the executive department; taken together, the two proposals struck observers as too bold a move for overwhelming executive authority.[211]

Thus the immediate response to the Court plan was to suggest that FDR was seeking dictatorial powers or to draw a comparison with totalitarian regimes. One Texas state senator claimed that plan would "establish a dictatorship equal to that of Hitler or Mussolini."[212] The *Des Moines Register* opined: "The historic truth is that . . . executive aggrandizement is not safe for democracy."[213] A former head of the American Bar Association instantly attacked the plan "as a short cut to dictatorship."[214] The nationally prominent columnist H. L. Mencken, who often faced off against Roosevelt, proposed a new draft constitution: "Section One: All governmental power of whatever sort shall be vested in the President of a United States."[215] Dorothy Thompson, the grand dame of editorial opinion, also was scathing:

> No people ever recognize their Dictator in advance. He never stands for election on the platform of dictatorship. . . . Since the great American tradition is freedom and democracy you can bet that our dictator, God help us! will be a great democrat, through whose leadership alone democracy can be realized. And nobody will ever say "Heil" to him or "*Ave Caesar*" nor will they call him "Führer" or "Duce." But they will greet him with one great big, universal, democratic sheeplike blat of "O.K. Chief!" Fix it like you wanna, Chief! Oh Kaaay![216]

An independent judiciary was now vaunted as the antidote to accumulating governmental power. "The national sentiment which favors separation of powers and an independent judiciary may be divinely inspired or it may be just so much . . . rubbish," said a skeptical administration insider after the plan's defeat, ". . . but there it is."[217] The Senate Judiciary Committee did not think it rubbish at all: "The condition of the world abroad must of necessity cause us to hesitate at this time and to refuse to enact any law that would impair the independence of or destroy the people's confidence in an independent judicial branch of our Government."[218] In Senate debate, North Carolina senator Josiah Bailey made the most effective speech against the plan. *The New York Times*'s Alsop and Catledge described how the "Senators listened with complete attention" as he "shouted his warnings of what would come if the independence of the judiciary were impaired."[219] A cartoon in the *Chicago News* showed "The People" standing quaking shipboard behind Captain Roosevelt, who is looking at "Life Preservers—Power of the Supreme Court—For the Protection of the People" and saying, "Now to get rid of these old things." It was captioned "But Captain!"[220]

In light of the Court's behavior during the *Lochner* era, it is remarkable that pleas to support the judiciary as the bulwark of liberty had any traction with the public. For some, particularly those who had cut their political chops during the Progressive Era, it did not. Provocative journalist Isidor Feinstein, later known as I. F. Stone, said the story was "persuasive, until one begins to fill in the details."[221] Two things accounted for the skepticism: judges had "failed to apply the constitutional provisions for the protection of civil rights of individuals and minority groups," and they had applied those provisions "so as to deprive large masses of workers and non-conforming minorities of their constitutional privileges."[222] Maury Maverick, the member of Congress who was to rush down the aisle to sponsor FDR's Court plan in the House of Representatives, wrote just before it was introduced: "If you look at the cases on sedition, espionage and the rest . . . the courts declared pretty nearly every silly law constitutional during and following the World War. There was not much protection of civil liberties in this country."[223] In 1936, Roger Baldwin, the founder and head of the American Civil Liberties Union, wrote: "In a dozen ways the Bill of Rights has been emasculated by the Supreme Court. In a few unimportant ways, its provisions have been sustained."[224]

In the past, when arguments favoring the Court as the protector of liberties had been advanced, liberals and progressives scoffed. In the 1924 campaign, for example, both Coolidge and John W. Davis had defended the Court from its attackers, saying it was necessary to protect citizens' rights.[225] La Follette responded, "[S]how me one case in which the courts have protected human rights and I will show you twenty in which they have disregarded human rights to protect private property."[226] In an unsigned editorial in *The New Republic*, Frankfurter chastised both candidates, especially Davis, who "by grave omissions in his treatment of the courts and the Constitution . . . conveyed a mutilated and, therefore, untrue picture."[227] Indeed, in 1923 H. L. Mencken said of the Court: "As things stand today, the rights of the citizen are nearly gone, but his property, if he has any, remains safe."[228]

Slowly, though, the Court had begun to address issues of race and civil liberties, the sorts of things progressives cared about. After years of doing little to protect dissenting speech, the Court began to change its views.[229] In a 1925 case upholding a prosecution for speech, the Court nonetheless announced that "we may and do assume that freedom of speech and of the press—which are protected by the First Amendment from abridgement by Congress—are among the fundamental personal rights and 'liberties' protected by the due process clause of the Fourteenth Amendment from impairment by the States."[230] Then, in 1931, the Court invalidated both a California law making it illegal to display a "red flag" and a local ordinance that permitted courts to enjoin the publication of certain newspapers as a nuisance.[231] The decisions created a sensation. The *Literary Digest* called it "[j]ust about the biggest Washington news of the decade," and *Current History* headlined the story THE SUPREME COURT IN A NEW PHASE.[232] Chief Justice Hughes was hailed as a liberal hero.[233] In 1936 the Court was at it again, striking down an ordinance that megalomaniac Louisiana governor Huey Long had used to attack the local press.[234]

Two mid-twenties individual rights cases also caught the country's attention. In 1923, in *Meyer v. Nebraska*, the Court struck down a law prohibiting teaching students in any language but English.[235] Then, two years later, in *Pierce v. Society of Sisters*, the Court overturned an Oregon law prohibiting all private and parochial school education.[236] The law had been passed under Ku Klux Klan influence as a means of shutting down Catholic schools.[237] During the 1924 election controversy over the judiciary, Chief Justice Taft, acting behind the scenes, was promoting *Meyer* as a response to La Follette's attacks on the Court.[238] The popular press noticed. In an election article entitled "The Oregon and Election Acts," the *Chicago Tribune* pointed to the two cases as examples "not merely of what may happen, but of what most certainly will happen, if there is no independent and judicially trained agency to insist upon constitutional rights."[239]

Prior to the 1930s, the Court had done little to protect racial minorities either. There were a few decisions in which racially discriminatory laws were held unconstitutional; among them were one involving residential real estate and another the Texas Democratic primary election.[240] Also, in 1923, the Court had overturned an Arkansas state court verdict in which blacks were sentenced to death by an all-white jury in a case overshadowed by the threat of mob violence.[241]

Then the decisions involving the "Scottsboro boys" became an international sensation. Alabama had charged nine young blacks with raping two white women on a freight train. All but one of the defendants were sentenced to death in sham trials conducted under the threat of mob violence. Serious doubt existed about the defendants' guilt.[242] In the 1932 decision in *Powell v. Alabama*, the Court invalidated the convictions on the ground that the trial court's appointment of "all the members of the Bar" as the defendants' lawyers was a meaningless gesture tantamount to denial of the right to counsel. "Public opinion doubtless will approve of the decision," said *The Washington Post*.[243] Three years later the Supreme Court overturned Alabama's second try for reasons of jury discrimination.[244] (In 1936, in *Brown v. Mississippi*, the Supreme Court also condemned torture tactics Mississippi law enforcement officials had used to extract "confessions" from blacks.)[245]

Throughout the Court fight, opponents pointed to this collection of decisions in defense of the Court's important role in protecting civil liberties.[246] It was not a lot, but it was enough to make the argument plausible. In a nationwide broadcast, publisher Frank Gannett told the story of how his Jewish barber said, "I am deeply interested in preserving the Supreme Court" because "I am a Jew, and therefore one of a minority." Gannett observed that members of the "colored race must feel the same" way, given that the Court had "again and again" protected them. His examples were *Pierce* and Scottsboro.[247] The Senate Judiciary Committee went on at great length on this point, mentioning or discussing Scottsboro, *Pierce*, and other civil liberties cases. The "only place the citizen has been able to go in any of these instances for protection against the abridgement of his rights," said the Judiciary Committee, "has been to an independent and uncontrolled and incorruptible judiciary."[248]

This evolving image of the Court as protector of civil liberties posed a serious challenge to Roosevelt's plan, and his administration struggled to deal with the issue. A presidential adviser prepared a memo dated March 3, an "ANSWER TO THE ARGUMENT THAT THE PROPOSAL WILL LEAD TO A DEPRIVATION OF CIVIL LIBERTIES." His best response was that the same justices who voted in favor of expansive government powers also voted to protect civil liberties.[249] On March 9, in his fireside chat, the President addressed the matter directly. "This proposal of mine will not infringe in the slightest upon the civil or religious liberties so dear to every American."[250] He offered up his record as evidence he would not abuse his power. Others, however, pointed out that a later President might not be so judicious.[251]

THE FIGHT IS CLOSE

"[T]he political drama of a generation"

The fight over the plan, wrote Alsop and Catledge, was "the political drama of a generation. Suddenly, the shabby comedy of national politics, with its all-pervading motive, self interest, its dreary dialogue of public oratory and its depressing scenery of patronage and projects, was elevated to a grand, even a tragic plane."[252] Merlo Pusey put it more simply: "Politics had been set aside for a good, old-fashioned constitutional scrap."[253] *The New York Times* reported that in Congress "all matters except" the Court plan "paled into insignificance," the rest of business being "transacted in desultory fashion."[254]

Signs of trouble appeared at once. Departing from the meeting with the President when the plan was announced, Hatton Sumners of Texas, the chair of the House Judiciary Committee, told his colleagues, "Boys, here's where I cash in my chips."[255] When the bill was read in the Senate, FDR's Vice President, John Nance Garner, held his nose and made the thumbs-down sign.[256] Letters opposing the plan, often by a margin of nine to one, poured in to representatives and senators and numerous newspapers came out against it.[257] Frank Gannett's National Committee to Uphold Constitutional Government was only the most prominent of numerous groups that went into action against the plan.[258] Many of the more conservative southern Democrats in Congress failed to support it, in part because of the plan and in part because of disagreement with Roosevelt over other matters.[259] Labor backed FDR formally but failed to really put its muscle behind the plan. Farm interests proved remarkably resistant.[260]

Given this dissent, the Republicans quickly decided their best strategy was to sit back and let the New Deal's own supporters take the lead in attacking the plan.[261] In this way the challenge to FDR would avoid a "partisan tinge."[262] Particularly problematic for Roosevelt was "a wide-open split" among the progressive Republican senators he usually counted on for support.[263] Senator Burton Wheeler of Montana, a Democrat who also had been La Follette's running mate in 1924, quickly stepped up to head the opposition.[264]

To put the opposition in context, some of the senators who fought Roosevelt favored a course of action more radical than the President's. Wheeler, for example, preferred an amendment to permit Congress to override Supreme Court decisions. "I am against the President's proposal," he explained, "because it . . . doesn't accomplish one of the things that the liberals of America have been fighting for. It merely places upon the Supreme Court six political hacks."[265] It was possible to chalk such disagreement up to principle, but some thought it was a matter of political prerogative as well. The position of the progressive Republicans, Arthur Krock observed snidely, "is against extensions of Presidential power over the courts and for Congressional extensions."[266] Supporters of the plan chastised these deserters for not "moving along the only line which is immediately practicable, to wit, the President's program."[267]

Legislators sought a way out. Many supported constitutional amendments that either would clarify Congress's substantive powers or limit those of the Court. Seeking to forestall trouble, Representative Hatton Sumners saw to it that the House quickly passed and Roosevelt signed a measure ensuring that Supreme Court justices could retire at full pay; the sense was that some justices had delayed retirement because they were concerned about what it would mean financially.[268] A number of legislators threatened to back a less dramatic alternative to FDR's plan, but only if there were retirements from the Court.[269]

Despite fierce controversy, the betting remained with FDR. After announcing his opposition, Democratic senator Carter Glass of Virginia conceded: "I don't imagine for a minute it'll do any good. . . . If the President asked Congress to commit suicide tomorrow they'd do it."[270] Early negative returns likely represented the views of many of Roosevelt's traditional opponents. On February 13, *Newsweek* said the "[w]eekend conclusion of most analysts" was that "the House would pass the bill in short order; the Senate . . . probably would pass it after prolonged debate."[271]

Roosevelt stepped up to defend the plan and answer initial charges of disingenuousness. He gave a fiery talk at the Democratic Victory Dinner on March 4, exhorting his followers: "Here is one-third of a Nation ill-nourished, ill-clad, ill-housed—NOW!" Alluding to the Court, he said, "I cannot tell you with complete candor that in these past few years democracy in the United States has fully succeeded."[272] Five days later he delivered a fireside chat to the nation chastising the judiciary directly: "The courts . . . have cast doubts on the ability of the elected Congress to protect us against catastrophe by meeting squarely our modern social and economic conditions."[273]

Hearings on the measure began in the Senate. Roosevelt's team had hoped it would be considered first in the House. Several factors, including Hatton Sumners's implacable opposition, persuaded them this was not a winning strategy.[274] Wanting the bill to move quickly, the administration put on a short case, but Judiciary Committee chair Senator Henry Ashurst was not a man to be pushed, and the hearings ran until April 23.[275]

The real fight took place outside Washington, among the American people. The matter was topic A in civic clubs, in newspapers, and even in movie newsreels.[276] Authors rushed books into print explaining the controversy to "non-specialists," "non-lawyers," and "nonprofessional readers"—in short, to "laymen."[277] A cartoon in the *Richmond Times-Dispatch* captioned "Wherever two or three gather" showed Mr. Pro ("Roosevelt is right! The Supreme Court needs new blood!") having it out with Mr. Con ("Roosevelt is wrong! The country needs no dictators!")[278]

The wait was on to see where public opinion would settle.[279] Legislators who announced early often did so at their peril. The Texas legislature quickly censured the plan, and then the Texas House of Representatives did an about-face. "I went home over the week end," one representative explained. "The rank and file, I found, are just as loyally supporting the President as they did on election day."[280] Raymond Moley, Roosevelt's former adviser turned pundit, authored a fictional dialogue in which a senator "elected to support the President" explained to another liberal senator influenced by all the mail against the plan that though the initial returns arrived "in embossed stationery," or with other signs that it came from the well-to-do, soon Congress would hear "the authentic voice of the people."[281] Sure enough, the mail "gradually swung the other way" with *Newsweek* reporting the "little fellow" now would be heard from.[282] The *New York Post* cautioned Congress not to "be misled by [hostile] reaction." It reminded readers that "with 80 per cent of the editors of the nation shouting 'Villain!' at the top of their lungs—the American people chose to return Mr. Roosevelt to office" by an enormous margin.[283]

Six weeks into the fight, the Gallup Poll showed support for the plan narrowly outpacing opposition, with many uncertain voters.[284] It is quite probable, in addition, that Gallup was not capturing some portion of the President's support.[285] FDR's new coalition of 1936 held a strong component of those least likely to show up on pollsters' radar.[286] Democrats strongly favored the plan, and Gallup, which had underestimated FDR's margin of victory the past November by almost 7 percent (though it had worked to improve in the interim), may not have had a balanced sample.[287] The one certain thing was that as the end of March approached, it was very, very close.

"THE SWITCH IN TIME THAT SAVED NINE"

"Why shoot the bridegroom after a shot gun wedding?"

And then, in the heat of battle, the Court seemed to switch directions, handing down several dramatic decisions that upheld state and federal economic measures. On March 29, the *Los Angeles Times* ran a cartoon about the debate over the Court plan titled "Humpty Dumpty's 1937 Dilemma." The fabled egg (labeled "Supreme Court Packing") was pictured sweating it out on a wall ("Public Opinion"), all of FDR's men watching anxiously below.[288] That same day the Court itself helped Humpty decide which way to fall. These pro–New Deal Court decisions and one critical retirement from the bench substantially undercut any justification for packing the Court.

FDR's lieutenant Robert Jackson dubbed March 29 "White Monday," the day the Court handed down *West Coast Hotel v. Parrish*.[289] The issue before the Court was the constitutionality of Washington State's minimum wage law for women. Given the Court's prior decisions in *Adkins* and *Tipaldo*, one would have thought the justices would strike down the measure. Yet by a 5–4 vote the justices upheld the law, overruling *Adkins* in the process. *Tipaldo*, which had caused such a stir, was explained away on a technicality.[290] Then, two weeks later, on April 12, the Court seemed to reverse itself again, this time in the Wagner Act cases.[291] The Wagner Act put the government's stamp of approval on union activity and mandated collective bargaining in any business in interstate commerce. The National Labor Relations Board was applying the law to many industries whose operations might have been thought beyond the power of the federal government under cases like *Schechter*, *Carter Coal*, or *Jones & Laughlin Steel*. The Court nonetheless upheld the act (and its application to specific businesses by the NLRB) in five cases resolved on the same day—four by a 5–4 vote and one (involving an interstate bus line) unanimously.[292]

The opinion in the lead Wagner Act case, *Jones & Laughlin Steel*, was remarkable. It was authored by the Chief Justice, who only a year earlier in *Carter Coal* had said that "production—in this case mining—which precedes commerce is not itself commerce" and who had added for good measure that if the public did not like that result, it should amend the Constitution.[293] Now his tune sounded quite different. After describing the interstate activities of the J&L Steel Corporation, Hughes said: "In view of respondent's far-flung activities, it is idle to say that the effect [of labor strife] would be indirect or remote. It is obvious that it would be immediate and might be catastrophic." "[C]ommerce," he added, "must be appraised by a judgment that does not ignore actual experience." *Carter Coal* was dispensed with by a wave of Hughes's hand as "not controlling here."[294] Thomas Emerson, one of the New Deal lawyers present when the decision was handed down, marveled at Hughes's "amazing performance." "You would have thought that he was deciding the most run of the mill case, that the law had always been this way, that there had never been any real dispute about it, and that he was just applying hundreds of years of decisions to a slightly new kind of situation."[295]

Although J&L Steel's activities were "far-flung," the Court upheld application of the Wagner Act to businesses that were quite local in nature. The case that looked to be the greatest departure from prior decisions was that involving the Friedman–Harry Marks Clothing Company. As the dissenting justices explained, Friedman–Harry Marks was "a typical small manufacturing concern which produces less than one-half of one per cent. of the men's clothing produced in the United States," employing only eight hundred people, with no evidence in the record of any labor strife. "If [it were] closed today, the ultimate effect on commerce in clothing obviously would be negligible."[296] The Court majority nonetheless upheld application of the Wagner Act to the clothing company in a short opinion that did nothing but state the facts and then point to *Jones & Laughlin Steel* for its conclusion.[297]

The Court's apparent change of direction was a major turning point for the plan, and everyone knew it. Alsop and Catledge reported that on learning of the decisions, Roosevelt threw a fit.[298] *The Atlanta Constitution* subhead was "Expected to Sway Bench Bill Fight," and separate coverage reported the sentiment on the issue.[299]

Now was the time to talk compromise. Publicly, Roosevelt enthusiast Senator James Byrnes of South Carolina put on a brave face. When asked about the impact of the Wagner Act cases, he told *The New York Times* that "he did not know what effect the decision would have on the plan but he had an idea that the plan had had quite an effect on the decisions."[300] Privately, he asked: "Why run for a train after you've caught it?"[301] Similarly, Senate Majority Leader Joseph T. Robinson insisted publicly that FDR would move forward, as the effort cannot "be suspended by the variableness of the opinion of a single justice."[302] Yet he called in a presidential aide and said: "The thing to do . . . is to settle this thing right now. . . . [I]f the President wants to compromise I can get him a couple of extra justices tomorrow."[303]

Then Justice Willis Van Devanter announced his retirement, the only "other step . . . needed to complete the liquidation of the court-packing scheme."[304] Van Devanter had been thinking of retiring for some time, and Hatton Sumners's bill guaranteeing judicial pensions eliminated the financial worry attached to it. Senator Borah urged his friend Van Devanter to step down, realizing what a service it would do in defeating the plan. On May 18, Van Devanter sent FDR his retirement letter, effective at the end of the Court's term.[305] (A week later the Court handed down yet another thunderbolt, upholding the Social Security Act. Once again the vote was 5–4, with the Four Horsemen dissenting.)[306]

Van Devanter's retirement took the remaining wind out of the plan's sails and increased pressure on FDR to seek a compromise. *Time* reported a Washington wag's asking, "Why shoot the bridegroom after a shot gun wedding?"[307] In his tract against the plan written in the heat of battle, Merlo Pusey put it more formally: "[T]he resignation of Justice Van Devanter, suggesting the natural shifts in the Court's membership which take place in virtually every administration, further emphasizes the lack of any warrant for the fight which the President continues to wage."[308] The Gallup Poll registered a large drop in support for the plan upon Van Devanter's retirement.[309]

Things now went from bad to worse for Roosevelt. In mid-June, the Senate Judiciary Committee released its negative report on the plan. The vote, which took place and was announced publicly on the same day Van Devanter retired, was 10–8. Joining three Republicans were seven members of Roosevelt's own party.[310] The report was biting, accusing the administration of being disingenuous and applying "force to the judiciary." A paean to judicial independence, it recommended the plan be "so emphatically rejected that its parallel will never again be presented to the free representatives of the free people of America."[311]

Van Devanter's retirement posed another thorny problem for FDR, causing him to delay for two critical weeks before authorizing talk of a compromise. Under the leading compromise proposals, FDR would likely get three justices almost immediately.[312] The problem was that he long ago had promised a slot to Robinson himself, whose lifelong ambition was a seat on the Court. Yet FDR feared that Robinson, basically conservative, might not in fact do much to alter the Court's balance.[313] While the senators anointed Robinson informally, FDR stewed. Finally, he bowed to the inevitable and gave Robinson the go-ahead.[314] An alternative measure was proposed that would give Roosevelt Van Devanter's seat plus two others to fill.[315] On June 16, FDR held a huge picnic for Democratic representatives to rally support for the plan.[316]

Then fate intervened, and any hope of selling the plan collapsed. Though pundits still supposed FDR would prevail on the compromise, it was not going to be an easy sell.[317] Robinson seemed to believe he had only forty-four or forty-five sure votes, while the opposition claimed forty-two. Worse yet, the threat of a filibuster loomed.[318] When debate began in July, no one was certain of the outcome. The debate was fierce, and Washington's hot weather only made conditions worse. Robinson was clearly under tremendous pressure. On July 13 he left the Senate floor complaining of pain in his chest. The next day he was found dead in his room, next to a copy of the *Congressional Record*.[319] "Had it not been for the Court plan he would have been alive today," cried Burton Wheeler, the leader of opposition to the plan. "I beseech the President to drop the fight lest he appear to fight against God."[320] The Senate voted to recommit the plan to committee by a 70–20 vote.[321]

LAW OR POLITICS?

"Did they adjust their convictions in the hope of saving the Court?"

For all practical purposes this was the end of the story, but controversy has raged about what happened ever since. To this day, scholars continue to fight over whether the Court "switched" under pressure. "Were they intimidated by the Administration's assault upon the Court?" asked Merlo Pusey at the time. "Did they adjust their convictions in the hope of saving the Court from the ignominy of being packed?"[322] More than a half century later, scholars still are arguing over the answer. The 1990s alone saw four major books that have at their heart a position on whether the Court changed direction that spring.[323] A conference discussing the implications of the New Deal Court plan took place at Yale Law School in 1998, with numerous articles discussing the issue.[324]

Much is thought to turn on this question of whether the justices switched. If the Court changed direction with a political gun to its head, it speaks volumes to the independence of the judiciary and the insulation of law from politics. It also has troubling implications for the process of constitutional change. How is it, many ask, that the Constitution's meaning can be altered so dramatically simply because the judges change their minds—and without resorting to the formal amendment process? Judicial alteration of constitutional meaning is thought to be all the greater a problem if the judges are susceptible to political pressure, because then the Constitution threatens to become nothing more than a way of ratifying the passions of the majority, rather than serving as a bulwark against them.[325]

Concerns about the independence of the Supreme Court from politics, and about the proper process of constitutional change, *are* deeply important, but the obsessive focus on whether the justices switched—i.e., whether they changed their position on crucial constitutional questions because of the threat to the Court—is a bit misplaced. For one thing, the question may be unanswerable: search though they have for years, historians have failed to produce the crucial evidence as to precisely what the justices in the middle of the Court were thinking when they voted on key New Deal measures in the spring of 1937. For another, even if the evidence existed, it still would not tell us what we most need to know: about the extent of public support for judicial review and an independent judiciary.

To be sure, despite vehement protestations that the justices did not switch under pressure, there is certainly evidence that they felt the pressure acutely and took some peculiar, if not outright illegitimate, steps in response to it. Take Justice Roberts, the man in the middle of the Court. Troubled by lingering allegations of a switch in response to events, and contrary to the justices' usual discretion, Roberts actually provided Frankfurter with a memorandum (which Frankfurter made public after Roberts's death) explaining Roberts's seeming flip between *Tipaldo* and *West Coast Hotel*.[326] That explanation did little to settle doubts, not altogether a surprise given that in later years Roberts wrote that "it is difficult to see how the Court could have resisted the popular urge" for change in the Court's doctrine.[327] But Roberts's odd apologia was nothing compared with the steps taken by the Chief Justice. Hughes, a consummate politician, former governor of New York, and close contender for the presidency in 1916, acted in ways that were positively Machiavellian. He endeavored to time the release of the Court's blockbuster decisions in the spring of 1937 in order to influence public reaction to the Court-packing plan.[328] He also engineered the most damning moment in the case against the plan, providing the Senate opposition with a letter he authored denying Roosevelt's charges that the Court was behind on its work and needed help. The letter implied much else, including that the Court disapproved of the plan.[329] The justices typically lie low during political brawls involving the Court, but as Robert Allen explained in a late May 1937 article in *The Nation* entitled "Hughes Checkmates the President," "Few realize how important a part Mr. Hughes has played in the fight against the court bill."[330] Finally, there was Van Devanter's crucial retirement, which Alsop and Catledge wrote had been "planned in the utmost detail" and in particular was timed to hit the President's desk the very same day the Judiciary Committee voted down the plan, thereby maximizing publicity against it.[331] If the justices were willing to take these extraordinary actions, why is it so implausible that they would have voted in pending cases to save the court, especially given the fact that had FDR's plan succeeded, constitutional law was bound to change in the direction of the switch anyway?

The proper question, however, is not what individual justices perceived or did in response to the attack on the Court, but how much pressure the American people were willing to see put on the Court when they disagreed with its decisions and what this indicates that we as a nation believe is the appropriate relationship between constitutional law and politics. Even if the justices wish to stand their ground, an aroused public opinion still could insist on measures that would tame the Court. The answer to this critical question rests not in the private papers of the justices but in the readily available record of public events.

In assessing the Court's vulnerability to public pressure, what matters is not so much whether the justices consciously changed the direction of constitutional law under pressure as whether the public believed they had. If the public rejected the plan, as it ultimately clearly did, without perceiving that the Court had changed direction, this suggests a certain invincibility on the part of the Court. On the other hand, if public sentiment turned definitively against the Court only once the public saw what it believed was a flip, this suggests that the plan might well have succeeded if the justices had not persuaded the public they were switching. Public events in the spring of 1937 strongly suggest that had the Court not indicated its capitulation when it voted to uphold government economic measures and had Van Devanter not retired, the Court would likely have been disciplined.

On the question of whether the public believed the Court had switched direction, there is no mystery whatsoever. To all eyes, *West Coast Hotel* was a complete flip, and Roberts was the reason for it. MINIMUM WAGE LAW CONSTITUTIONAL: THE SUPREME COURT SWITCH DUE TO ROBERTS, shouted *The New York Times*.[332] *The Hartford Courant* headlined ROBERTS GOES OVER TO SIDE OF LIBERALS.[333] *Time* magazine could only say, "It was incredible that he should reverse himself on so similar a case. Yet he did."[334] Another correspondent commented: "Didn't the Welshman on the Supreme Court do a pretty good job of amending the Constitution yesterday?"[335] Frankfurter (who later labored to restore Roberts's and the Court's integrity) wrote Justice Stone that what Roberts "now subscribes to he rejected not only on June first last, but as late as October twelfth."[336] Senate Majority Leader Joe Robinson took the Senate floor to announce: "Today the Supreme Court has completely reversed itself and directly and explicitly overruled . . . the Adkins case."[337]

Such was the case too with *Jones & Laughlin Steel*: the words and actions of people before and after the decision make clear they believed something significant had changed. The betting before the case was that the Court would strike down the Wagner Act, at least with regard to its application to some local manufacturing concerns. Alsop and Catledge tell us that "the great majority believed with the President and his general staff that the Washington law decision was no more than a tactful preface to the Wagner act's destruction."[338] Harvard law professor Thomas Reed Powell was the consummate Court watcher. In January 1937, before the plan was announced, he predicted that in light of *Carter Coal* it is "almost certain that the Wagner

Labor Act will be denied application to manufacturing concerns by six votes and possibly by nine." [339] Immediately after the Wagner Act was passed, lawyers were advising clients and businesses not to comply with it on the ground it was unconstitutional. Admittedly these were lawyers with a bias, but in the Wagner Act cases that made it to the Supreme Court, the overwhelming majority of court of appeals judges had also found the arguments against the constitutionality of the NLRA persuasive. [340]

That is why when *Jones & Laughlin Steel* was handed down, the public reaction was one of profound surprise. *The Atlanta Constitution* ran a screaming banner headline announcing SUPREME COURT UPHOLDS WAGNER LABOR ACT IN SERIES OF 5 DECISIONS, 4 OF THEM 5 TO 4. Immediately below, it said (accurately): "Officials Startled by Ruling Validating Federal Power." [341] The next day, *The New York Times*'s Arthur Krock wrote a column entitled "Why the Manufacturing Decisions Were Unexpected." "[T]he court's opinion in the Carter Coal Company case appeared to doom the Wagner act," he explained. [342] *Time* magazine said: "Last week nearly every lawyer agreed that one afternoon in the Supreme Court Chamber, the interstate commerce clause of the U.S. Constitution had been rewritten and enlarged to include many things which for 149 years past it has never held within its few brief elastic words." [343] Thurman Arnold, on loan to the Justice Department from Yale Law School, noted: "Roosevelt has already accomplished his objectives and we are rewriting all our briefs in the Department of Justice in terms of the new definition of the commerce power." [344]

The question then becomes: If the public had not observed the Court switch direction, would the plan (or something like it) have passed anyway? Although this is a counterfactual, the consensus at the time was yes. Commentators believed the Court was acting in response to politics and that by switching, the justices had avoided discipline. That is precisely why pundits at the time described the events in the spring of 1937 as "the switch in time that saved the nine." [345]

The overwhelming view of those watching was that the Court had heard the loud voice of the people and was acquiescing. Commenting on the switch in the Wagner Act cases, Raymond Moley, formerly an FDR adviser and now a columnist for *Newsweek*, was sure that this was what had just happened: "[T]he Court did yield to the pressure of public opinion as to changing conditions." [346] Charles Wyzanski, himself later a judge, delivered one of the key arguments on the government's behalf in *Jones & Laughlin Steel*. His opponent, John W. Davis, delivered high praise, saying, "In my palmiest days, I could not have touched that argument." [347] But Wyzanski did not believe he and his colleagues had turned the tide: "[T]he cases were won not by Mr. Wyzanski but either by Mr. Roosevelt or, if you prefer, by Mr. Zeitgeist."[348] Historian and public intellectual Henry Steele Commager wrote that "we may suspect that recent decisions on New Deal legislation were not announced in a judicial void, nor uninfluenced by the threat of judicial reform."[349] Scoffing at those who denied the Court's susceptibility to political pressure, Howard Brubaker wrote facetiously in *The New Yorker*, "We are told that the Supreme Court's about-face was not due to outside clamor. It seems that the new building has a sound-proof room, to which justices may retire to change their minds."[350]

Even more to the point, the common wisdom also was that had the decisions gone the other way, Roosevelt would have been in the driver's seat. *Time*'s reporting on the *Jones & Laughlin* argument noted the excitement because "[i]f these decisions went against the Wagner Labor Act the political hue and cry against the Court would be raised once more."[351] The *New York Herald Tribune*, a consistent foe of the plan, was practically winking at the Court with its headline SHELVING OF COURT PLAN CONSIDERED IF NEW DEAL WINS WAGNER ACT CASES.[352] The *New York Evening Journal* applauded the administration's cleverness for bringing the Court plan while the Wagner Act cases were pending, "put[ting] the New Deal in a win-win position whichever way the Supreme Court votes." If the Court ruled against the law, "invalidation would cause such popular resentment that Congress would have to act. . . . [T]he howl will be so loud that the nine justices will find things happening fast in their marble palace."[353]

Polling evidence verifies the significance of the perceived switch to the fate of the plan, the fortunes of which clearly rose and fell in reaction to the major events described here. After *West Coast Hotel*, support for the plan began to decline. Then, after Van Devanter's retirement, support plunged yet again.[354] The only irony is that following the Wagner Act cases, support for the plan actually moved up a bit.[355] Apparently the transparent nature of the switch in the Wagner Act cases lent itself to such cynicism about the justices' responsiveness to politics that support for packing the Court actually ticked up a notch. After all, if one vote could flip the Court so quickly, could not that single vote change again down the road?[356]

All told, contemporary evidence suggests powerfully that had the Court not switched, the public would have supported disciplining it. "On the Court's decisions on these two laws hung the whole future of the court fight," concluded Alsop and Catledge afterward.[357] Reflecting on the events of the past spring, Robert Allen concluded: "Had the court invalidated one

Administration measure last term, nothing could have prevented the President from winning."[358] For all of history's frequent talk about the independence of the judiciary, that independence exists only at public sufferance.

THE LEGITIMATE PROCESS OF CONSTITUTIONAL AMENDMENT

"[O]rderly but inevitable change"

There is an incredible irony, and an essential lesson, in what happened and did not happen next. In the years immediately following 1937, the substance of constitutional law changed in fundamental ways. Ultimately, the Court did what it had not in *Jones & Laughlin Steel*: it flat out overturned the doctrines that it previously had used to strike down New Deal legislation, abdicating virtually all responsibility to patrol economic legislation for its consistency with the Constitution. No one disputes this, just as no one doubts the reason why. The Constitution changed dramatically on the question of government control over the economy not because the country ratified a constitutional amendment but because after 1937 Roosevelt obtained enough appointments to transform the Court entirely and the new justices changed the Constitution through interpretation. Yet there was absolutely no furor about this method of constitutional change at the time. This change too was plainly "political," but it apparently was the sort of constitutional change with which the country was comfortable. What the aftermath of the New Deal fight reveals is that although changing the Constitution through the exercise of naked political power was of dubious acceptability, changing it through political appointments was just fine.

Between 1937 and 1943, Roosevelt captured the Court. By 1943 he had appointed seven of the justices: only Roberts and Stone remained.[359] When Hughes resigned as Chief Justice in 1941, Roosevelt named Justice Harlan Fiske Stone to replace him (and filled Stone's old seat with his able lieutenant Robert Jackson). Of Roosevelt's appointees, the only remotely controversial one was that of Senator Hugo Black of Alabama, who had to live down former ties to the Ku Klux Klan.[360] Otherwise, Roosevelt's loyal supporters took their seats with little opposition.

Constitutional law began to change in ways some found dizzying. Frank Hogan, the president of the American Bar Association in 1939, gave an angry address. "Those who think lightly of shifts in constitutional doctrines must think lightly also of the importance of knowing what the law is."[361] But in 1939, when Hogan wrote, the Court had barely gotten started. Five years later an article in the *American Bar Association Journal* was entitled "The New Guesspotism."[362] An unhappy Owen Roberts quipped that precedents were falling "into the same class as a restricted railroad ticket, good for this day and train only."[363] Thomas Reed Powell would joke that when teaching constitutional law on days the Supreme Court was sitting, he had to check the clock to know what to tell his students the law was.[364]

In a sharp contrast with the decisions of 1935 and 1936, the Roosevelt Court determined to uphold virtually all state and federal legislative judgments on economic legislation.[365] With regard to congressional legislation adopted pursuant to its authority under the Commerce Clause, the Court abandoned any pretense of supervision altogether, a decision it was to adhere to for decades to come. In 1941, in *United States v. Darby*, the Court overruled its prior precedent holding that Congress lacked the power to prohibit child labor. Even more dramatic was the 1942 decision in *Wickard v. Filburn*. At issue in *Wickard* was a penalty imposed upon a farmer for violating a provision of the AAA, which had been reenacted in 1938, essentially for using for personal consumption some excess wheat he had grown. By almost any standard preexisting 1937, this would have seemed entirely local conduct immune from regulation under the Commerce Clause. Now, though, the Court simply said it would defer to Congress. "Congress may properly have considered that wheat consumed on the farm where grown if wholly outside the scheme of regulation would have a substantial effect in defeating . . . its purpose to stimulate trade therein at increased prices."[366]

The papers of Justice Robert Jackson reveal just how deliberate the decision was to change the meaning of the Constitution.[367] When Jackson suggested the test of basically absolute deference to Congress for resolving the *Wickard* case, his clerk wrote back asking: Are "*all* the old formulae and tests junked? . . . Is the Court never to seek to preserve 'our dual system of government' by denying that the Commerce Power can reach" such indirect effects?[368] Jackson conceded to his clerk that "[i]f we sustain the present Act, I don't see how we can ever sustain states' rights again as against a Congressional exercise of the commerce power."[369]

Remarkably, given the fight over the Court in 1937, this profound change in the meaning of the Constitution occasioned almost no dissent. Apparently, acceptable constitutional change—even fundamental change—required only "patience" while the membership of the Court rotated. Even before Roosevelt proposed his plan, *The New York Times* urged that "[t]he impatient amenders at Washington would do well to stand aside for a while and observe how nature and time will do the work which they would only bungle if they set their hands to it."[370] The Senate Judiciary Committee felt the same way about Roosevelt's plan. "Even if every charge brought against the so-called 'reactionary' members of this Court be true, it is far better to await orderly but inevitable change of personnel than that we impatiently overwhelm them with new members."[371] After Justice Sutherland left the Court, the *Times* picked back up the theme, reminding "impatient souls that by the natural process of time new blood has flowed again and again into the Supreme Court."[372] The *Times* returned once more—angrily this time—when Roosevelt boasted that "the 'objectives' of his 1937 proposal for enlarging the Supreme Court have been realized." "If the complexion of the Supreme Court had been changed, not in the peaceful course of affairs, but by the drastic method [of the plan,] . . . [t]he whole nature of our Government would have undergone a sinister change."[373]

The Constitution changed dramatically between 1936 and 1943. Where once the Supreme Court interpreted the Constitution to limit governmental authority over the Constitution, after 1943 the Court abdicated such authority altogether, allowing the federal and state governments to pass what economic legislation they might. Roosevelt's threat to pack the Court to achieve this end ran into trouble; Americans saw the Supreme Court as a protector of individual liberty and were reluctant to see its independence tampered with by politics. Even so, had the Court not capitulated in 1937, Americans might well have approved Roosevelt's plan. The 1937 fight over the Court ushered in the modern era of judicial review and American constitutionalism: judicial review now was widely valued, but only so long as important judicial decisions did not wander far from the mainstream of American belief about the meaning of the Constitution.

8

LIMITATIONS

"Implementation of decisions can rest on reaction of public"

T o those who lived through it, as well as to those who looked back on it, the work of the Supreme Court during Earl Warren's tenure as Chief Justice was breathtaking. "For the sheer breadth and depth of its impact on the life of the nation, its work is unprecedented," gushed *Newsweek* in 1964, allowing comparison only with the work of the Court headed by John Marshall.[1] That same year University of Chicago law professor Philip Kurland also invoked the great Chief, saying of the modern Court, "[T]he Justices have wrought more fundamental changes in the political and legal structure of the United States than during any similar span of time since the Marshall Court."[2] Ever since, commentators, whether they applauded the Warren Court or deplored it, have looked to this period as the epitome of what a determined Supreme Court could accomplish.[3]

Though critics complained constantly that the Warren Court was running ahead of the crowd, at least one perceptive observer understood that the Court did what it did because the public supported these outcomes and no other organ of government would provide them.[4] That was Anthony Lewis, who won a Pulitzer Prize for his work covering the Supreme Court for *The New York Times*. In a probing 1962 feature story, Lewis explained that the Supreme Court's rapid development of the law in the areas of race relations, legislative apportionment, and the rights of criminal suspects reflected "a demand of the national conscience."[5] The Court stepped into these areas because powerless groups could obtain from the judiciary what they could not in the political process, and the broader public approved of the outcomes. Lewis also explained that the Warren Court wielded the authority it did because it served to ensure that "the national ideal is prevailing over state orientation."[6]

Lewis's optimistic account of the Warren Court's achievements was tempered by his recognition that without public backing, implementation of the Court's decrees would fail. With regard to school desegregation, he acknowledged that "[i]t is only in the last few years, as public opinion in the rest of the country solidified behind the Court's moral condemnation of segregation, that the school decision has been enforced in the Deep South." Similarly, without support in the area of school prayer, "prayers will simply go on in the thousands of schools." Lewis's article was headlined PUBLIC MOOD PLAYS BIG ROLE IN COURT DECISIONS, and it was framed by two telling subheadlines, "Decisions Running Counter to the Broad Consensus Do Not Last" and "Implementation of Decisions Can Rest on Reaction of Public."[7]

Despite the breathless way people spoke, and still speak, about the Warren Court, the deeper lesson of that time was not about the judiciary's ability to effect revolutionary change but about the inherent limitations that the Supreme Court faces when it attempts to do so. In pursuing its liberal agenda, the Warren Court tapped into a reservoir of support for civil liberties that had been long neglected by the political branches. But factors beyond the Court's control—the Cold War and its Red scare, naked racism, and spiraling crime rates—served as counterweights to dampen the public's appetite for sweeping judicial reforms. When the Court got too far ahead of the national majority, its agenda faltered; even with popular support, ensuring compliance among determined dissenters could be a problem. Violent opposition at times caused the Court to stall or backtrack, evasion of unpopular rulings was frequent, and when the national majority abandoned it—on the issue of crime—the Warren Court itself was lost.

THE COURT ON THE BRINK

"The very purpose of a Bill of Rights"

In the wake of the New Deal Court-packing fight, the justices shifted their attention from issues of economic liberty, such as the right of employers to pay employees what they wished, to what we today think of as individual rights. The shift was gradual. Having just eschewed such intervention in the economic realm, the justices struggled to come up with a legal theory that would justify their intervening to protect civil liberties. Conceptually, the problems with developing such a theory were vast. The Court's transition was further hampered by World War II, the emerging Cold War, and then the conflict on the Korean peninsula. Times of war do not typically prove the most auspicious for the aggressive protection of civil liberties.

When Roosevelt's new justices took up an agenda of civil rights and civil liberties in the 1940s, they quickly encountered what became known as the problem of the double standard.[8] Scholars engaged in a heated debate on the subject, much of which bespoke of great internal hand-wringing. Looking back on the era, Columbia Law School professor Herbert Wechsler lucidly explained the problem that weighed so heavily on his contemporaries' minds: "How can we defend a judicial veto in areas where we thought it helpful in American life—civil liberties area, personal freedom, First Amendment— and at the same time condemn it in the areas where we considered it un-helpful?"[9] Historian and leading public intellectual Henry Steele Commager put it this way: "Is it possible to make a distinction between judicial review of legislative acts having to do with ordinary administrative or economic matters and those having to do with what we call 'civil liberties'?"[10]

The problem of the double standard caused consensus on the Court to shatter. The noted liberal historian Arthur Schlesinger, Jr., observed in the pages of *Fortune* magazine that "[t]he problem of the constitutionality of New Deal legislation would not flutter a hair" in the Court's Saturday conferences. But emerging civil liberties issues were another matter altogether, as the subhead of Schlesinger's *Fortune* piece explained: "The Justices are not di-vided on political issues but on the understanding of their function."[11] All the new justices were assumed to be political liberals, but they adopted dra-matically different stances on the extent to which they believed the Court could legitimately use judicial power in pursuit of that liberalism.

For some of the justices, consistency required judicial "restraint" across the board. If one believed that the judiciary should keep its hands off eco-nomic legislation, then one should do the same when civil liberties were at stake. Chief among those who held this view was Justice Felix Frankfurter. Frankfurter was given to pointing out that the Constitution's Due Process Clause protected "life, liberty and property." How is it, he asked, that the Court could simply abandon property and then take up the cause for lib-erty?[12] "Our power does not vary according to the particular provision of the Bill of Rights which is invoked."[13] Especially given that Frankfurter had spent his life criticizing judicial activism—first during the *Lochner* era, then during the New Deal—the idea of now engaging in such activism (albeit on behalf of liberal causes he purported to support) was particularly hard to swallow.

So Frankfurter urged judicial restraint across the boards. In almost all cases, he believed, the Court should defer to the decisions of democratically elected branches.

The difficulty with Frankfurter's "restraintist" philosophy, as Yale Law School dean Eugene Rostow explained, was that it informs "when it may be wise for the Court not to act" but tells us "next to nothing about when the Court should act or what it should do when it does."[14] Even Frankfurter had trouble holding the line himself; on those occasions in which he voted to strike down laws, he found it difficult to offer a persuasive explanation as to why.[15]

Among those justices willing to take a more aggressive, or activist, stance in striking down laws, the challenge lay in coming up with a theory to justify judicial intervention. Such theories were abundant, but the "most articulate" one was offered by Justice (later Chief Justice) Harlan Fiske Stone in the famous Footnote Four of his *Carolene Products* opinion.[16] Although the main message of the *Carolene Products* decision was that the justices would no longer engage in careful review of economic legislation, Stone's provocative footnote suggested those instances in which more rigorous judicial scrutiny of governmental action might now be warranted. Two in particular foreshadowed the work of the Warren Court. First, the justices would pay special attention to ensuring that democracy itself was functioning properly, so that those oppressed by existing laws could work to change them. They would turn a skeptical eye toward "legislation which restricts those political processes which can ordinarily be expected to bring about repeal of undesirable legislation." Second, the Court would look out for the rights of groups that could not operate as successfully in the political process because of discrimination, scrutinizing with care statutes that were the product of "prejudice against discrete and insular minorities."[17]

The contending judicial philosophies of activism and restraint were on full display in the flag salute cases of the early 1940s, in which the Court dramatically reversed itself within the space of three years. Jehovah's Witness children refused to salute the flag, believing it forbidden by scripture. For failing to do so, the young children were expelled from public school. In the 1940 decision in *Minersville School District v. Gobitis*, the Court upheld mandatory flag salutes.[18] The Court was 8–1 with Frankfurter writing for the majority and only Stone in dissent. But in 1943, in *West Virginia State Board of Education v. Barnette*, the Court flipped, leaving Frankfurter to respond angrily.[19]

Many were wont to explain the Court's change of direction as a reaction to events and public opinion. The decision in *Gobitis* was issued during the

German invasion of France and the Netherlands.[20] "The consequent up-surge of national feeling and the intensification of patriotic fervor had its effect even on the Supreme Court," observed Court-watching political scientist C. Herman Pritchett.[21] Nevertheless, the Court's decision was a major disappointment for editorialists. More than 150 periodicals chastised the Court.[22] *The New Republic* complained bitterly: "[W]e are in great danger of adopting Hitler's philosophy in the effort to oppose Hitler's legions."[23] When the Court reversed position in *Barnette* following this barrage of criticism, critics charged that the Court had changed direction in "recognition of the unpopularity of the *Gobitis* decision."[24]

The opinions in the flag cases provided a forum for the justices to battle it out publicly over their competing notions of the judicial function. Noting that as a Jew he was a member of "the most vilified and persecuted minority in history," Frankfurter said in *Barnette* that the case was not about his "personal attitude."[25] Although he acknowledged that requiring a flag salute may be a "foolish" way to instill good citizenship in children, he simply deemed it "beyond my constitutional power to assert my view of the wisdom of this law against the view of the State of West Virginia."[26] "As a member of this Court I am not justified in writing my private notions of policy into the Constitution."[27] Justice Robert Jackson (FDR's former Attorney General), writing for the *Barnette* majority, directly took on Frankfurter's theory of restraint by focusing on the judiciary's role in protecting fundamental rights against the excesses of democracy. "The very purpose of a Bill of Rights," he explained, "was to withdraw certain subjects from the vicissitudes of political controversy, to place them beyond the reach of majorities and officials and to establish them as legal principles to be applied by the courts."[28] In a memorable and oft-quoted flourish to his opinion, Jackson concluded: "If there is any fixed star in our constitutional constellation, it is that no official, high or petty, can prescribe what shall be orthodox in politics, nationalism, religion, or other matters of opinion."[29]

Despite the pyrotechnics, *Barnette* hardly signaled a new burst of judicial activity in defense of civil liberties. "The affirmative influence of the Court and the Constitution on American life since 1946 has been very little," wrote John Frank in the *Vanderbilt Law Review*'s 1951 symposium on "Current Constitutional Problems." His article was entitled "Court and Constitution: The Passive Period."[30] Although Frank's characterization was something of an exaggeration, undoubtedly reflecting the regret of a liberal hungry for greater judicial activism, many attributed the Court's relative quiescence to Truman's appointees. Truman, who made a habit of appointing cronies, put four justices on the Court, including Chief Justice Fred Vinson.[31] But these judges may simply have been reflecting the national mood. The Cold War had broken out, and the country was in the grip of a Red scare yet again.[32] "For the most part," sighed a disappointed John Frank, "the Court has demonstrated the aphorism that 'courts love liberty most when it is under pressure least.'"[33]

The Court seemed so quiet that a prominent member of the Association of the Bar of the City of New York suggested it was an opportune time to secure the justices' independence. Still troubled by FDR's proposed packing of the Court, he authored a report recommending that the association take advantage of the calm by pushing for the enactment of a constitutional amendment protecting the Court from, among other things, any future attempt to pack it or strip it of its jurisdiction.[34] The report was titled, ironically, "In Time of Peace Prepare for War."[35] On May 11, 1954, the Senate approved a constitutional amendment that would do just that. The Senate sponsor was John Marshall Butler, a name that bears remembering.[36] In the House, conservatives generally favored the amendment; liberals largely opposed it.[37] All this was to change within the week.

BROWN V. BOARD OF EDUCATION

"The South will not abide by nor obey this . . . decision"

On May 17, 1954, the Supreme Court decided *Brown v. Board of Education.*[38] *Brown*, which held public schools segregated pursuant to state law a violation of the Constitution, was both the first and perhaps the most important work of the Warren Court. For years *Brown* has stood as a symbol of the Court's role as brave defender of minority rights against the majority, of what the justices' moral clarity could bring to an issue and what their decisions could achieve.[39] From the outset, though, the justices worried about public reaction to their decision and their ability to ensure their orders were followed. History proved their worries justified.

The Path to *Brown*

Racially segregated schools were part of the Jim Crow laws that flourished in the South after Reconstruction. School segregation was justified with reference to the Court's "separate but equal" doctrine of *Plessy v. Ferguson.*[40] *Plessy* involved a challenge to Louisiana's law that railroads provide segregated (but ostensibly equal) accommodations for whites and nonwhites. Plessy was, in the racial terminology of his day, an octoroon; only one-eighth of his ancestry was African-American. Louisiana enforced its law against him, and the Supreme Court upheld this. Drawing a distinction between "political equality" and "social equality," the Court stated that the Fourteenth Amendment was not meant to abolish all social distinctions maintained by law. The Louisiana statute was reasonable, the Court held, because it merely enacted "established usages, customs, and traditions of the people, and with a view to the promotion of their comfort, and the preservation of the public peace and good order."[41] *Plessy* was understood to mean that the Fourteenth Amendment's equal protection guarantee was not violated by separate but equal facilities.[42]

By the late 1940s segregated education was under attack, largely as a result of the efforts of the National Association for the Advancement of Colored People. Created in 1909 to deal with a rash of racial violence, the NAACP soon turned its attention to inequality in education.[43] Initially the NAACP had pursued a strategy of seeing that separate schools were funded equally, but in 1950, it decided to forgo a policy of seeking true school "equalization" in favor of ending segregation in education.[44] The NAACP's lead litigator in this effort was Thurgood Marshall, who would one day sit on the Supreme Court himself.

Racial attitudes in the nation were undergoing a substantial transformation by the 1940s.[45] Much of this had to do with the Second World War. The nation's revulsion at the racist practices of Hitler's Germany sat uneasily alongside segregation in the South.[46] In addition, as a federal district court judge in Los Angeles explained in striking down racially restrictive housing covenants, "Certainly there was no discrimination against the Negro race when it came to calling upon its members to die on the battlefields in defense of this country."[47] Negro servicemen often encountered violence when they returned home, a fact many Americans found disturbing. The blinding of black veteran Isaac Woodard by a southern sheriff was a catalytic event.[48] Other forces included the success of black athletes like Jesse Owens, Joe Louis, and Jackie Robinson.[49] In 1944, Gunnar Myrdal published his gripping report *An American Dilemma*: "When we say there is a Negro *problem* in America, what we mean is that the Americans are worried about it. It is on their minds and on their consciences."[50]

Politics also was changing in a way that favored blacks' rights. The country had seen the Great Migration of African-Americans from the rural South to the northern cities in search of jobs. There they voted, becoming part of the Democrats' New Deal coalition.[51] Recognizing the need for this black support, both parties began bidding for it. For this reason, and in the face of incidents like that involving Isaac Woodard, Truman created a commission to study civil rights.[52] He also took some decisive steps in favor of racial equality, none more so than ordering desegregation of the military.[53] Truman was left to act on his own, however, as southern members of Congress inevitably filibustered any civil rights legislation.[54] This was precisely the sort of legislative logjam that often was pointed to in justifying the Warren Court's endeavors.

In 1950, in an environment in which racial attitudes were improving, the Supreme Court invalidated two states' "separate but equal" programs in higher education. Still, a Court unanimous in its result could not see clear to overruling *Plessy*. Rather, the justices found a denial of equality by focusing on the intangible disadvantages of a segregated education.[55] In *Sweatt v. Painter*, for example, the Court held that Texas's efforts to launch a separate black law school were not enough. The white school "possesses to a far greater degree those qualities which are incapable of objective measurement but which make for greatness in a law school."[56] *New York Times* correspondent Arthur Krock noted that the Court had put such a steep "price-tag" on segregation in higher education that many communities were likely to abandon such segregation altogether. Krock also presciently observed that ending segregation in primary and secondary education, where the "social bases of segregation are much broader and deeper," was likely to be far more difficult. "If and when the Supreme Court applies today's formula and solution to these, where it finds segregated facilities 'unequal,' the real test of community acceptance will come."[57]

Receiving the *Brown* Decision

When *Brown* was handed down in 1954, the biggest surprise was that the decision was unanimous.[58] Only later did it become clear how hard the justices, deeply concerned about the public reaction to a divided decision on such a controversial topic, labored to make this so. After three days of oral argument in the fall of 1952, the justices decided, contrary to usual practice, not to vote immediately, but only to share their views with one another.[59] The Court was closely split, and it was uncertain whether there would be five votes to ban school segregation.[60] To buy more time, the Court set the case for reargument the following year. Just prior to reargument, Chief Justice Vinson, who appeared to be against overruling *Plessy*, died.[61] Fulfilling a campaign promise, President Eisenhower appointed California governor Earl Warren to head the Court. Warren provided the clear fifth vote to order school desegregation. From that point on, the Court worked to achieve unanimity.[62]

The public mood had come far in helping the Court to this result. The Cold War's global competition between democracy and communism played a large role in affecting attitudes toward racial segregation.[63] The United States was taking a drubbing in world opinion over its mistreatment of blacks.[64] As early as 1946, Truman's Undersecretary of State (later Secretary) Dean Acheson had written the Fair Employment Practices Committee to say that "the existence of discrimination against minority groups in this country has an adverse effect upon our relations with other countries."[65] This was a vast understatement by the time of *Brown*.[66] In 1947, the NAACP had captured worldwide attention by filing "An Appeal to the World" with the United Nations, saying, "It is not Russia that threatens the United States so much as Mississippi."[67] Russia drove home the point by pushing the UN to establish a Subcommission on the Prevention of Discrimination and Protection of Minorities.[68] The Truman administration's court brief in *Brown* made much of the international environment: "It is in the context of the present world struggle between freedom and tyranny that the problem of racial discrimination must be viewed."[69]

Polls over the summer showed that slightly more than half the country agreed with the *Brown* decision, and from that point on and for some time to come there was a "steady increase in the percentage of the total population approving of the Court's action."[70] Praise flowed in from religious organizations, civic groups, academics, editorial boards, and ordinary people.[71] World opinion was also strongly supportive.[72] There were two defining themes in the favorable reaction. People believed that the decision was morally correct. A columnist for *The* (Nashville) *Tennessean* called the decision "historic" because "it marks a long-sought perfecting of American democracy."[73] And the worldwide struggle between communism and democracy commanded it. "Nothing has so weakened the efforts of this nation to commend to others its conception of democracy . . . as our ambiguous record on the race issue," commented the *Christian Century*.[74] *Time* magazine called *Brown* the most important Supreme Court decision of all time, save *Dred Scott* itself. Referring to the "many countries . . . where U.S. prestige and leadership have been damaged by the fact of U.S. segregation," *Time* said the decision "will come as a timely reassertion of the basic American principle that 'all men are created equal.'"[75]

In the South, of course, *Brown* was greeted with less joy.[76] Some officials were immediately defiant. "The South will not abide by nor obey this legislative decision by a political court," thundered Mississippi's reactionary senator James O. Eastland.[77] Yet the initial reaction in much of the South was more temperate.[78] The Jackson, Mississippi *Clarion-Ledger*, while calling it a "black day of tragedy for the South," still insisted *Brown* should not cause "any violent emotional reactions."[79] Some in the South even praised the decision.[80]

Massive Resistance

The South's initial reaction was milder than it might have been in part because the Court's first decision in *Brown* did not actually order anything to be done. While holding that "separate but equal" in public schools was dead, the Court rescheduled the case for yet another argument, this one on the question of how to go about eliminating school segregation. In its second *Brown* decision, the Court finally ordered desegregation, but its time frame was vague: "all deliberate speed."[81]

The Court's "all deliberate speed" standard ultimately provided cover for desegregation's glacial pace, something the records of the justices' deliberations make clear was intentional. They acted thus out of concern that the Court not be made to appear powerless. Justice Black, who had opposed the original reargument, welcomed it the second time. "Let it simmer," he said. "Let it take time. It can't take too long."[82] Black believed "nothing could injure the court more than to issue orders that cannot be enforced."[83] Justice Minton did not want the court to "reveal its own weakness" by handing down a "futile" decree.[84] This had been Frankfurter's fear all along: "Nothing could be worse from my point of view than for this Court to make an abstract declaration that segregation is bad and then have it evaded by tricks."[85]

The Court certainly had reason to be on its guard. Even before the first ruling, two governors had pledged defiance. Georgia's Herman Talmadge said flatly, "As long as I am governor, Negroes will not be admitted to white schools." South Carolina's James F. (Jimmy) Byrnes, who had served a brief stint himself on the Supreme Court as a Roosevelt appointee before becoming bored with the job, said, "South Carolina will not, now nor for some years to come, mix white and colored children in our schools."[86] In order to forestall desegregation, Byrnes had the state dedicate an enormous sum to making the Negro schools actually equal. South Carolinians already had voted to amend their constitution to allow school closings in the event they were ordered to integrate.[87] During an astonishing moment in the oral argument, S. Emory Rogers, the lead lawyer for the South, basically told the Chief Justice he could not promise compliance with the Court's orders:

ROGERS: Mr. Chief Justice, to say we will conform depends on the decree handed down. I am frank to tell you, right now in our district I do not think that we will send—the white people of the district will send their children to the Negro schools. It would be unfair to tell the Court that we are going to do that. I do not think it is. But I do think that something can be worked out. We hope so.

CJ: But you are not willing to say here that there would be an honest attempt to conform to this decree; if we did leave it to the district court?

ROGERS: No, I am not. Let us get the word "honest" out of there.

CJ: No, leave it in.

ROGERS: No, because I would have to tell you that right now we would not conform—we would not send our white children to the Negro schools."[88]

Frankfurter's worst fear—evasion—came true almost immediately after the second *Brown* decision. If reaction to the decree was initially "temperate," it was only because no one thought anything would happen anytime soon.[89] As *The Tennessean* put it, the decree "was widely interpreted in the South yesterday to mean considerable delay in school desegregation."[90] For years to come, southern school boards engaged in a variety of tactics—from slow-walking "pupil placement" laws to the actual closing of all public schools—to avoid integration.[91] As of 1963, almost a full decade after the initial *Brown* decision, there were no desegregated schools in Alabama, and only 1 percent of all African-American students in the South attended a school with whites.[92]

Events quickly conspired to turn a moderate initial reaction into "massive resistance."[93] Intellectual firepower was provided by a series of articles in the *Richmond News Leader* written by columnist James J. Kilpatrick. Kilpatrick advocated interposition, a call not heard since Calhoun and the Civil War. In the first half of 1956, five southern states adopted pro-segregation laws, asserting the right to interpose state legislative authority over the decision of the Supreme Court.[94] Then 101 of the 128 southerners in Congress signed the Southern Manifesto, vowing support for "those states which have declared the intention to resist forced integration by any lawful means."[95] Byrnes authored an article in *U.S. News & World Report*, "The Supreme Court Must Be Curbed," in which he insisted "approximately 40 million white Southerners will do everything that lawfully can be done to prevent the mixing of races in the schools."[96]

Resistance was so intense that in 1957 Eisenhower finally was forced—very much against his inclinations—to send federal troops into Little Rock, Arkansas, to restore order. Though Eisenhower had signed off on the government's brief calling for school desegregation, he personally believed the Court was making a mistake.[97] The summer before Little Rock, he said, "I can't imagine any set of circumstances that would ever induce me to send federal troops . . . into any area to enforce the orders of a federal court."[98]

Eisenhower's hand was forced by the grandstanding tactics of Arkansas's governor, Orval Faubus. As Little Rock's Central High poised to open that fall, Faubus stirred the populace until a mob threatened to prevent the nine black children trying to enter.[99] When violence broke out, the children were hustled away, and the mayor of Little Rock sent a telegram to Eisenhower, pleading with him to send in troops.[100] Pointing to the "tremendous disservice" that was being done the nation "in the eyes of the world," Eisenhower announced his firm resolve to see that court orders would be enforced.[101]

In the wake of the Little Rock controversy, the Supreme Court issued what is arguably its strongest statement of judicial supremacy in all of American history.[102] Of course this was only after the President had already sent in the troops to support it. When the Little Rock federal district court granted a lengthy delay of desegregation to accommodate for the chaos, the Court had had enough. In a remarkable order signed individually by all nine justices, the Court referred to *Marbury v. Madison* and reasserted the "basic principle that the federal judiciary is supreme in the exposition of the law of the Constitution. . . . No state legislator or executive or judicial officer can war against the Constitution without violating his undertaking to support it."[103] The Court was the Constitution, and the Constitution was the supreme law—at least so long as there was force backing it up.

The Civil Rights Act and Enforcement

Southern schools were not desegregated until the country demanded it in the mid-1960s. By then it was crystal clear that the Congress stood behind the Court, not just on the principle of enforcing court orders but on the merits of ending Jim Crow. The catalyst for congressional action was the civil rights movement, and it is difficult to know precisely what role the Court's decisions played.[104]

The civil rights movement took off when four college students staged a quiet sit-in at the lunch counter of the Greensboro, North Carolina, Woolworth's. Many more joined in, to be met with violent counterprotests and jailings.[105] As the movement captured national attention, both political parties adopted "outspoken anti-segregation planks."[106] In the spring of 1961, Freedom Riders traveled south to enforce the Supreme Court's ban on segregated bus station terminals, only to be met with yet more violence.[107] In September 1962, still more violence erupted on the campus of the University of Mississippi at Oxford when James Meredith tried to register. President John F. Kennedy was forced to call in the troops this time.[108] If any moment was galvanizing, it was when the Reverend Martin Luther King, Jr., brought his movement to Birmingham in 1963. Seeking to integrate the downtown shopping district, King's followers and the African-American community were met with fire hoses and police dogs. Shortly afterward a black church in Birmingham was bombed, killing four young teenagers. The photographs from Birmingham were nauseating.[109] The country had had enough.

President Kennedy had addressed the country a few months before Birmingham, saying in June 1963: "We are confronted primarily with a moral issue. It is as old as the scriptures and is as clear as the American Constitution. . . . It is time to act. . . ."[110] He sent a strong Civil Rights Act to Congress.[111] In August of that year, the country watched an integrated crowd of a quarter million people march peacefully on Washington and heard the Reverend King tell the nation, "I have a dream" of black and white equality.[112] When Kennedy was killed in Dallas by an assassin's bullets in November, Lyndon Johnson told a bereaved nation, "[N]o memorial oration or eulogy could more eloquently honor President Kennedy's memory than the earliest possible passage of the civil rights bill for which he fought so long."[113]

Over the longest filibuster in Senate history, almost three months, Congress adopted the Civil Rights Act of 1964. In addition to aiding the desegregation of schools, it provided for an end to discrimination in all public accommodations.[114] The Court now had Congress's support. It also had that of the Department of Justice, which was authorized for the first time to enforce desegregation decrees in court.[115] In an extraordinarily rapid six months after passage, the Court declared the provisions of the Civil Rights Act constitutional.[116]

From here on out, desegregation moved much more swiftly, as the justices issued orders of increasing clarity and force.[117] Rather than integrate, Prince Edward County, in Virginia, had shut its public schools for five years. Now the Court effectively ordered them reopened. "The time for mere 'deliberate speed' has run out."[118] In 1968 the Court was even more direct. It insisted that integration in New Kent County, Virginia, begin in the middle of a school year, telling the school board "to come forward with a plan that promises realistically to work, and promises realistically to work *now*."[119]

Finally, the Court mustered the wherewithal to face the one racial issue it had feared to confront amid all the controversy, laws banning interracial marriage. Although *Brown* dealt only with segregated education, in a number of subsequent unsigned summary orders the Court invalidated state-supported segregation of virtually any sort. The issue of mixed marriages came to the Court immediately after *Brown*, in a case called *Naim v. Naim*.[120] Mixed marriage was a sensitive issue throughout the country.[121] The case was within the Court's mandatory jurisdiction, yet as one of the justices' clerks said in a memo, "In view of the difficulties engendered by the segregation cases it would be wise judicial policy to duck this question for a time."[122] The problem was how to avoid the issue and "be honest."[123] Frankfurter simply advocated doing so disingenuously to avoid "thwarting or seriously handicapping the enforcement" of *Brown*, and his colleagues apparently agreed.[124] That is what the Court did. It was only in 1967, some thirteen years after *Brown* and well after passage of the Civil Rights Act, that the Court finally struck down such laws as unconstitutional, in the aptly named case *Loving v. Virginia*.[125]

THE DOMESTIC SECURITY CASES

"[T]he Kremlin is composed of 11 men and the Supreme Court only 9"

If the issue of school desegregation made clear how much the Supreme Court depended on the support of the public and the federal branches to see its orders enforced, the "Communist" cases demonstrated that the Court was still vulnerable to frontal assault when it misjudged that support. Throughout the 1950s, the Court's decisions in domestic security cases seesawed between backing the government and protecting civil liberties, as public sentiment (responding to world events) moved to and fro on these issues itself. It appeared many of the justices did not like what was being done on the national security front, but they were loath to intervene so long as public opinion favored stringent government measures. Then, in what only could have been a miscalculation of public sentiments, during the 1956 term the Court handed down twelve decisions in domestic security cases, every single one of which defended the rights of suspected Communists and fellow travelers. "Not since the Nine Old Men shot down Franklin Roosevelt's [NRA] in 1935 has the Supreme Court been the center of such general commotion in newspapers and in the bar," allowed *Time*, putting the brouhaha on its cover.[126] Congress sought to strip the Court's jurisdiction in retaliation, and the Court once again appeared to switch. Although there are ambiguities regarding precisely what happened in 1957 (as was true in 1937), it is still unequivocal that these controversial decisions sparked an effort to discipline the Court that came within a hairbreadth of succeeding.

On the basis of the Supreme Court's major domestic security decision early in the decade, one would hardly have expected it to be under attack for protecting civil liberties too vigorously. In 1951, in *Dennis v. United States*, a major test of the government's power to go after Reds, the Court considered the constitutionality of the Smith Act. The question was whether the act, which made it a crime to advocate in speech or print the overthrow of the United States government, violated the First Amendment.[127] As Justice Black noted, the defendants were not charged with "overt acts of any kind designed to overthrow the Government"; rather, they were accused only of agreeing "to use speech or newspapers and other publications in the future to teach and advocate the forcible overthrow of the Government." [128] It was a stretch for the Court to uphold the Smith Act convictions, but stretch it did. Only Justices Douglas and Black dissented. [129]

Perhaps it would have been surprising to find the Court ruling differently in *Dennis*, given world events and the reaction to them at home. [130] In a 1946 talk at Westminster College in Missouri, with President Truman at his side, Winston Churchill announced the onset of the Cold War: "[A]n iron curtain has descended across the Continent." [131] Soon Truman was telling a joint session of Congress, "At the present moment in world history nearly every nation must choose between alternative ways of life." [132] By decade's end, the country had witnessed the Berlin airlift to save a city under siege, watched China fall to communism, and learned that Russia had the Bomb, and in 1950 it sent its troops to the "police action" on the Korean peninsula. [133] Alger Hiss was convicted of perjury in January 1950 for lying to Congress about spying for the Soviets; on February 4, Klaus Fuchs admitted to having leaked nuclear secrets to the USSR. [134] Five days later, Senator Joseph McCarthy got his big start Red hunting, claiming to "have in my hand 57 cases of individuals who would appear to be either card carrying members or certainly loyal to the Communist Party, but who nevertheless are still helping to shape our foreign policy." [135] By the late summer, a full-scale Red scare was under way. [136]

Justice Black hit the nail on the head in his *Dennis* dissent when he predicted, "Public opinion being what it now is, few will protest the conviction of these Communist petitioners." [137] In response to *Dennis*, the *Los Angeles Times* editorialized, "A time may come again when a Communist will be a harmless member of a political splinter party. . . . But that time is not now or in the foreseeable future." *The New York Times* chimed in that "liberty shall not be abused to its own destruction." [138] The country was hardly open to anyone's bucking the anti-Red tide. Democrats who aroused McCarthy's opposition were roundly defeated in the 1950 midterm elections. [139]

Within five years, though, there was a dramatic turnaround in world events, and public opinion shifted in response to them. In *Dennis*, Justice Black had expressed the hope that "in calmer times, when present pressures, passions and fears subside," the Court would repent. [140] By 1957 there was plenty of evidence that such "calmer times" had arrived. Stalin died in 1953, and the Korean conflict ended. The Army-McCarthy hearings burst McCarthy's bubble in 1954, and he was censured later that year, only to die of complications from alcoholism three years later. In the midterm elections of 1954, Democrats regained the Senate and began investigating the loyalty investigations.[141] In 1955, two notables met with the Russians. William R. Hearst, Jr., the conservative heir of the publishing magnate, traveled to Russia only to report that "the Soviet leaders are quite sincere about co-existence and improvement of relations with the United States." He and his staff won a Pulitzer for their reporting.[142] Then Ike himself traveled to Geneva to meet with the Soviets to discuss reducing tensions.[143] Both trips would have been unthinkable a short time earlier.

The Supreme Court's decisions in 1956 and 1957 reflected this changing climate.[144] Earl Warren signaled the shift in an article in *Fortune*'s November 1955 issue, declaring forthrightly that "our Bill of Rights is under subtle and pervasive attack . . . not only from without, but from our own indifference." Warren pointed a finger directly at the government's "security procedures" and urged resisting adoption of "totalitarian security methods."[145] In that very term the Court handed down two decisions limiting state antisubversive efforts.[146]

The Court's following term was a blockbuster by any account. It decided no fewer than twelve cases involving Communist activities and investigations, and the government lost in every one.[147] Democratic representative Howard Smith of Virginia, a ringleader of the coming fight and the namesake of the Smith Act, said, "I do not recall any case decided by the present Court which the Communists have lost."[148] On one day alone, June 17, 1957—quickly dubbed "Red Monday"—the Court decided four such cases.[149] As a government lawyer said following the 1956 term, "Never but never has the government taken so many shellackings from the Supreme Court in one period."[150] FBI director J. Edgar Hoover was beside himself.[151]

There had been changes in the membership of the Court since *Dennis*, but they did not seem to account fully for the Court's sudden change of heart.[152] The pro–civil liberties majorities in the 1956 and 1957 cases were not narrow and included some justices who had voted with the government in *Dennis*.[153] And two of the majority justices in 1957, Frankfurter and Harlan, were soon to desert the liberal camp.

Pundits believed that the justices had sensed a change in the public mood and felt free to respond by curtailing the excesses of the McCarthy era. The dean of columnists, Walter Lippmann, noted that the Court "has waited a long time—some ten years—before it has intervened." The Court was not essentially more liberal than it had been before, he thought. Rather, "the times have changed."[154] *Time* wrote: "Mr. Dooley was just being Mr. Dooley when he said that the court follows the election returns, but in a far broader sense the court does change with the political climate."[155] The mainstream press applauded the justices. *The New York Times*, which had sympathized with the

Dennis decision, now announced that "the Supreme Court has shown itself by far the most courageous of our three branches of Government in standing up for basic principles."[156] *The Washington Post* commended the Court for re-asserting "its guardianship of individual liberty [which was] long overdue."[157] *The Atlanta Constitution* agreed the Court was clearing away "the murk in which Joe McCarthy and his like left basic American rights and liberties."[158]

But the Court had climbed out of its foxhole before the danger had truly passed. Although public sentiment on the immediacy of the threat posed by the Cold War had shifted, there were still plenty of people sufficiently worried about communism that they were reluctant to protect the liberties of those accused. In addition, the Court's national security decisions provided an opportunity to segregationists still stewing over *Brown*, who joined with anti-Communists in an all-out attack on the Court.[159] After Red Monday, *The* (Columbia, South Carolina) *State* compared the Court with the Kremlin in "the exercise of dictatorial powers"; the only difference was that "the Kremlin is composed of 11 men and the Supreme Court only 9."[160] "The boys in the Kremlin may wonder why they need a fifth column in the United States," the *Chicago Tribune* observed sarcastically.[161] *The* (Cleveland) *Plain Dealer* wryly told Communists, "Well, Comrades, you've finally got what you wanted. The Supreme Court has handed it to you on a platter."[162] Edward Corwin, the respected Princeton constitutional authority, suggested the Court needed to have its "nose well tweaked."[163]

A full-scale attack on the Court was launched in Congress. The House Minority Leader claimed on ABC's *College Press Conference* that the Court had "crippled the investigating committees," and Senator William Ezra Jenner of Indiana announced his intention of curbing it.[164] By August 1958, the House of Representatives had considered no fewer than five bills that would limit the Court's authority to decide or reverse its decisions in cases involving national security.[165]

The heart of the anti-Court attack involved two pieces of legislation. The first, which originated in the Senate, was the Jenner-Butler bill. The cosponsor of the bill was none other than John Marshall Butler, who, immediately prior to the ruling in *Brown*, had supported measures to protect the Court's independence. As originally proposed in 1957, the bill stripped the Supreme Court of jurisdiction in five subject areas that were the basis for major rulings in the national security cases. When it went to the floor in 1958, the Jenner-Butler bill had been toned down by compromise. The modified version deprived the Supreme Court of jurisdiction in only one area—cases involving admission of lawyers to the state bar—but reversed the substance of other Court rulings.[166] The other major piece of anti-Court legislation before the

Congress was H.R. 3, a House measure designed to overrule the Supreme Court's 1956 decision in *Pennsylvania v. Nelson*, in which the justices interpreted federal law to preempt the states from pursuing domestic security prosecutions within the ambit of the federal government.[167] H.R. 3 would allow states to pursue their own subversion prosecutions alongside the feds.[168] Both Jenner-Butler and H.R. 3 were seen as plain slaps at the Supreme Court.[169]

In the Senate, the votes were much tighter than anyone, especially Senate Majority Leader Lyndon Baines Johnson, anticipated. Understanding full well that the votes would split his party and also fearing that it would hurt his presidential hopes for a Democratic Senate to enact anti-Court legislation, LBJ had done everything he could to keep the bills from coming to a vote on the Senate floor.[170] When his hand was forced, Johnson chose to bring the Jenner-Butler bill up ahead of H.R. 3, thinking the jurisdiction-stripping measure was certain to go down in defeat.[171] It was tabled as expected, but the vote was surprisingly tight, 49–41.[172] H.R. 3 proved an even closer call. When LBJ called it up, the liberals held their tongues, opting for a quick vote. They were certain, and had been assured, that this bill too was going down. When the motion to table actually failed, by a 39–46 vote, LBJ hastily adjourned the Senate.[173] That night and the next day, fierce lobbying went on among senators to muster votes. When the roll call vote came, it looked as if it were going to be a tie. This would have forced Vice President Richard Nixon to cast the deciding vote, something he preferred not to do, in light of his own presidential aspirations. (Apparently he would have voted against.) A final senator came out of the coatroom and—contrary to his own inclinations, but believing it was necessary to help Nixon—voted no.[174] In this way the congressional vote to "reverse the Court" failed by the slimmest of margins.[175]

WHY THE COURT MIGHT HAVE SWITCHED

"[T]he most meaningful criticism yet of the highest federal court"

After the close call in Congress, observers accused the Court of doing again what it had done in 1937—i.e., of switching. In the next few years, committee investigations and Smith Act prosecutions that many believed to have been ruled out entirely after the 1957 decisions once again received the Court's approval.[176] The seeming change of direction gave rise to charges, as it had in 1937, that the justices were reversing course in response to public discontent and threats of political reprisal. This is difficult to prove. Not only are the motives of the switching justices unclear, but there are legal arguments that the decisions before and after the congressional proceedings can be reconciled with one another. Still, the evidence certainly suggests that a switch occurred, not only in response to public pressure but also in the face of severe criticism from some of the justices' chief constituencies in the legal community.[177]

It took only two votes to swing the Court from its votes in favor of civil liberties in 1956 and 1957 to its more pro-government posture after the fight. Justices Frankfurter and Harlan were the ones who looked to have gotten the message. From the time of the congressional fight on, Frankfurter voted with the government in virtually all domestic security cases, even while protesting to Justice Brennan that "there isn't a man on the Court who personally disapproves more than I do of the un-American Committees, of all the Smith prosecutions, of the Attorney General's list, etc. etc."[178] If not for concern about the Court's reputation, it is difficult to see why else Frankfurter, who professed to dislike it all, suddenly retreated to his former position of restraint. Chief Justice Warren reportedly said, "Felix changed on Communist cases because he couldn't take criticism."[179] Harlan, for his part, had claimed to find anti-Communist legislation "dumb" and "McCarthyite garbage."[180] His actions in 1955–1957 certainly were consistent with this view: he authored some of the key decisions in 1956 and 1957 in favor of civil liberties. Yet after the storm, he too did an about-face, voting regularly for the government.[181]

The mainstream media certainly believed a switch had occurred. After one pro-government decision, *The New York Times* wryly commented, "What Senator Jenner was unable to achieve the Supreme Court has now virtually accomplished on its own."[182] After another, *The Washington Post and Times-Herald* asked bluntly, "What has happened to the Supreme Court?" It cautioned that court watchers should not jump to conclusions, but acknowledged that "now many are saying that [the Court] has taken a conservative turn or a series of backward steps," an opinion echoed in *The Wall Street Journal*.[183] A 1959 editorial in the *Chicago Tribune* claimed that "the court has, in effect reversed positions adopted in 1956 and 1957. . . ."[184]

The mystery deepens, however, because in 1957, unlike 1937, the Court seemed to seek cover after the storm had already passed.[185] (The attack came too quickly to allow much opportunity beforehand.[186]) Though historians have recognized that the Court changed directions in response to the 1958 congressional attack, one might wonder why.[187] The Democrats did well in the November 1958 elections. Several of the most virulent anti-Court members either retired or lost their seats.[188] Although the House continued to pass anti-Court bills in 1959, these measures remained hopelessly bottled up in Senate committees and thus posed little threat to the Court.[189] Hence it is fair to ask: Was it really necessary for the justices to back down?

If Justices Frankfurter and Harlan did in fact switch their positions, it may well have been in reaction not only to Congress but to what was a remarkably high-profile series of attacks from the Court's most important observers, the legal community. Immediately on the heels of the 1958 Senate votes (and in the middle of the Little Rock crisis), the legal establishment weighed in loudly against the Court. The chief justices of the states' highest courts issued an unprecedented report on the Supreme Court, urging it "respectfully" to "exercise to the full its power of judicial self-restraint . . . by eschewing . . . the exercise of essentially legislative powers."[190] (The chief justices' complaints primarily involved decisions forcing reforms on state criminal justice systems.) The report was anything but respectful. The justices were accused of trampling on the prerogatives of the states and taken to task for assuming the "function of policy maker" rather than a court.[191] *Time* called it "the most meaningful criticism yet of the highest federal court."[192]

The American Bar Association also spoke up, passing a series of resolutions critical of the Court's domestic security decisions. The ABA had been on the Court's case since the summer of 1957, when Earl Warren was embarrassed at a meeting in London by the harshly critical tone taken by an ABA committee and the outgoing President. (Warren resigned his membership in the organization immediately afterward.)[193] The February 1959 resolutions, though, were the first official statements of disapproval by the organization. The ABA said that "decisions of the United States Supreme Court have created problems of safeguarding national and state security and have been severely criticized as unsound by many responsible authorities."[194] After praising the relevant congressional committees, the ABA called for legislation overturning troublesome Court decisions.[195]

Even the legal academy jumped into the fray. Though many had been howling at the Court since *Brown*, law professors had remained mum until they could contain themselves no longer. "With such a hue and cry being raised, one should be very careful that he does not join it," explained Erwin Griswold, dean of the Harvard Law School.[196] The reason, as another Harvard professor, Paul Freund, explained, was that "all criticism of the Court runs the risk of fanning the fires of lawlessness and cynicism that have been ignited in the wake of the school desegregation cases."[197]

The dam of academic criticism burst open in 1958, when, on the heels of the ABA resolutions, Judge Learned Hand took the podium of the Harvard

Law School to give the Oliver Wendell Holmes Lectures. The talks were given to overflowing crowds; it was like "the entrance to a big theatre where a hit was playing."[198] Hand, a figure of the progressive movement in his youth, had served for years on the federal trial and appellate bench. He was widely revered for his keen mind, his erudition, his wit and his prose, which while captivating could also be difficult to follow.[199] Everyone had always believed that Hand might be granted a place on the Supreme Court, but he never made it there.[200] Adding to this poignancy, Hand was eighty-six at the time he spoke; this was to be his valedictory.

Hand's talk was a paean to judicial restraint and a thinly veiled criticism of the Warren Court. Grudgingly conceding the necessity of judicial review, Hand still insisted that judges should use their power sparingly, always asking how "importunately the occasion demands an answer."[201] He emphasized the impropriety of the Court's acting as a "third legislative chamber," particularly when the meaning of the Constitution was not fixed or certain.[202] After making clear his skepticism about *Brown*, Hand concluded: "For myself it would be most irksome to be ruled by a bevy of Platonic Guardians, even if I knew how to choose them, which I assuredly do not."[203]

The next year, Columbia law professor Herbert Wechsler followed Hand to the podium at Harvard and chastised the Warren Court once again, particularly for its decision in *Brown v. Board of Education*. Though Wechsler was more committed to judicial review than Hand, his concern was that judicial decisions rest upon a "neutral principle." Cases could not be deemed right or wrong on the basis of the winner's race or social status. Wechsler saw *Brown* as a case involving freedom of association—the Constitution protects to some extent the liberty of people to associate with whom they choose—and asserted the decision could not be justified in that light. How could the Court decide, he challenged, between the black children who wanted to go to the integrated schools and whites who did not want them there?[204]

Once the floodgates were open, it became a blood sport to take the Warren Court to task. Anthony Lewis expressed wonder at what he called the "new academic criticism" of the Court.[205] When they were polite, critics faulted the justices' opinions for lacking "workmanship," being "result-oriented," and displaying "intellectual incoherence."[206] (In private the derision ran much deeper. Hand referred to Warren as "that Dumb Swede" while Frankfurter called his colleague Hugo Black, who grew up in rural Alabama, "Hillbilly Hugo."[207] Among themselves, the critics scoffed at Earl Warren's habit of leaning over the bench to ask whether what had happened was "fair" or "just."[208]) The University of Chicago's Philip Kurland published an astonishingly tart article in which he likened the Court to a saloon musician for whom the sign DON'T SHOOT THE PIANO PLAYER. HE'S DOING HIS BEST applied. "It is still possible, however," Kurland continued, "to wish that he would stick to the piano and not try to be a one-man band. It is not too much to ask that he take piano lessons."[209]

Though the academics claimed to be trying to save the Court, their efforts served only to undermine the justices in the public eye. Yale Law School's Alexander Bickel, perhaps the most prominent law professor of his generation, expressed the desire to distinguish the tradition of "critical professional re-examination [of] the nature of the Court's function" from the "deafening, interminable" shouting of the "segregationists and security-mongers," but the mainstream media inevitably conflated the two.[210] U.S. News & World Report informed its readers of "criticism of the Court from a new and powerful source—recognized authorities in jurisprudence."[211] Newsweek linked the "know-nothings of the extreme right to the savants of the law schools."[212] Hand's lectures were music in the ears of the Court-bashing members of Congress; he was cited so much in debate over the Jenner-Butler bill that he ultimately had to write Congress and express his disapproval of the jurisdiction-stripping measures.[213]

Certainly the chief lesson, which could not have escaped the justices in 1957, is that running afoul of public opinion, including that of the legal community itself, would mean harsh criticism and the very real possibility of reprisal. As in 1937, it is impossible to know for sure whether Frankfurter and Harlan switched under pressure. But there is a strong basis for believing that they did.

CHANGING VIEWS OF DEMOCRACY

"[T]he process is neither minority rule nor majority rule"

Given profound criticisms of its national security and desegregation decisions, what motivated the Warren Court to continue its activism into the 1960s? The law professors' post-1957 attacks on the Court had a common and telling theme. Echoing Frankfurter's own philosophy of judicial restraint, these academic critics cautioned the justices not to outrun their proper role in a democracy. But this criticism, which had resonated so strongly during the *Lochner* era, sounded hollow by the late 1950s and early 1960s. The world had changed, or at least the public's perception of it had, in ways that suggested an important role for an invigorated judiciary. It was this new sort of thinking that figured heavily in the Warren Court's dramatic endeavors soon to come.

The constant theme of the Court's prominent critics in the legal academy after 1957 was that majority will is frustrated when unelected and unaccountable judges strike down legislative and executive acts. The Court's academic critics happily allied themselves with critics in the Progressive Era, when concerns about the judiciary interfering with the popular will also were prevalent. Like the progressives, the Warren Court's academic antagonists regarded judicial restraint as their byword.[214]

The stunning exemplar of the legal academics' critique of the Supreme Court was Alexander Bickel's *The Least Dangerous Branch*. Bickel was a star student at Harvard Law School who went on to clerk for Felix Frankfurter. Ultimately, he settled into teaching at Yale Law School. Bickel quickly became one of the nation's leading constitutional authorities; from his Yale perch he regularly contributed to high-profile periodicals such as *The New Republic* and *The New York Times*.[215] In 1962, Bickel published the book that was destined to become one of the great classics of constitutional thought. Although *The Least Dangerous Branch* actually was a defense of judicial review, a deeply thoughtful and nuanced one, its greatest influence may have followed from the attack Bickel leveled on the practice in the early pages of the book.

"The root difficulty," Bickel declared in *The Least Dangerous Branch*, in language destined to become famous, "is that judicial review is a counter-majoritarian force in our system." By this he meant that "when the Supreme Court declares unconstitutional a legislative act or the action of an elected executive, it thwarts the will of representatives of the actual people of the here and now; it exercises control, not in behalf of the prevailing majority, but against it." Bickel conceded that his depiction of American democracy was in many ways "highly simplistic"—he acknowledged that political scientists would describe the process in more complex ways—but he insisted that "nothing in these complexities can alter the essential reality that judicial review is a deviant institution in the American democracy."[216] American government was supposed to be democratic; courts were not; ergo the problem.

In at least three important ways, however, this familiar criticism of judicial review—so prominent in the Progressive Era, was not nearly as apt as it once had been. Times had changed. To begin with, legal academics imagined a polity in which legislative action represented "majority will." Judicial decisions striking down statutes purportedly interfered with that majority will. But political scientists who studied how American democracy was actually operating had been busy for some time debunking the notion that (as leading Harvard political scientist and voting expert V. O. Key explained), "the government is identical with the mass of the population and that by some mysterious process the 'will of the people' is translated into governmental decision and thereby the people 'rule themselves.'" [217] Rather, society was comprised of groups, and as many political scientists of the day would agree, politics "is the process of group or interest conflict." [218] This "pluralist" conception of society clearly did a better job of describing political outcomes since the turn of the century than did the facile idea of majoritarian democracy. As Robert Dahl, Bickel's equally well-respected political science colleague across the Yale campus, explained, "[P]olicy at the national level is the outcome of conflict, bargaining, and agreement among minorities; the process is neither minority rule nor majority rule but what might better be called *minorities* rule, where one aggregation of minorities achieves policies opposed by another aggregation." [219] Thus the entire description of courts as trumping "majority rule" may have been grossly inapt.

Second, courts were understood to play an essential role patrolling the functioning of the political process. As a general rule, interest groups could be counted on to bargain to an acceptable accommodation in the legislative bazaar. Yet certain dysfunctions infected the democratic and legislative process in ways that required judicial intervention. This was the central point of Justice Stone's Footnote Four in *Carolene Products*: courts must at least step in to make sure the processes of democracy are open to all. [220] In the national Congress, the filibuster allowed southern senators to block majority efforts for civil rights. [221] The federal system presented another problem. Outlier states could defeat or simply ignore an emerging national consensus, as was clearly the case with race. [222] Michigan governor George Romney, a devotee of "decentralization," nonetheless complained that the states' rights advocates "want to make the states into a road block to progress." His comments were run in a *Newsweek* article that opened by declaring, "States' rights are becoming the last refuge of reactionaries." [223] Worse yet, within the states the political process could break down entirely. [224]

These dysfunctions created stalemates in the rest of government that sometimes made courts a last, and necessary, resort. A 1966 cartoon in the *Washington Star* showed a figure labeled "Congress" entering an airplane and saying over its shoulder to a departing "Supreme Court": "Well, don't do anything I wouldn't do." [225] The message was plain: Congress wasn't doing anything. Justice Jackson, himself no flaming liberal, said of *Brown v. Board of Education*, "I suppose that realistically the reason this case is here is that action couldn't be obtained from Congress." [226] An article by constitutional scholar Alpheus Thomas Mason in 1964 commented that the Warren Court "has repeatedly stepped into a vacuum created by the failure of Congress, the President (though less flagrantly), and the states to discharge their responsibility for a more equitable functioning of democracy."[227]

Even when legislatures acted, judicial review might be necessary to remedy what a growing number of critics saw as the failings of interest group pluralism. Theodore Lowi's influential book *The End of Liberalism* made the case that pluralism benefited only powerful organized interests.[228] As the political scientist E. E. Schattschneider put it, "The flaw in the pluralist heaven is that the heavenly chorus sings with a strong upper-class accent."[229] Consumer activists such as Ralph Nader released stinging reports drawing the attention of the media and government officials to previously ignored groups and perspectives.[230] Little surprise it was, then, that public interest attorneys increasingly turned to the courts as a vehicle for reform.[231] These attorneys imitated the litigation strategies established in earlier decades by the NAACP and the ACLU, but the range of causes they tackled was much broader than their predecessors'.[232] By the late 1960s, legal organizations dedicated to the rights of consumers, employees, and the mentally ill were receiving generous funding from the Ford Foundation, as were environmental groups like the National Resources Defense Council.[233] These attorneys found an ally in the Warren Court, which plainly sympathized with the notion that interest group pluralism was not protecting everyone's rights effectively.[234]

Finally, there was the problem that left to its own devices, "[the] dominant majority may behave toward those who are not of the majority in such a manner as to undercut the moral basis of democracy itself." This was how another Yale law professor, Charles Black (who had been involved with the NAACP in the school desegregation effort), put it, stating what had to be obvious to anyone who looked around America in the late 1950s.[235] One prominent political science text included case studies of litigation campaigns, such as that run by the NAACP to achieve racial equality, which were believed to indicate the essential role the judiciary played in American democracy.[236]

This new understanding of democracy and its needs is what motivated the justices of the Warren Court in the early 1960s. Though they may have retreated in the domestic security cases, these were but one small part of a larger, still-developing agenda. Just a few years later the justices were at it again, banning officially sponsored prayer in schools and ordering the reapportionment of America's legislative districts. Some attribute the Court's new energy to membership changes, but the membership had not yet changed enough to explain the difference satisfactorily.[237] Popular understandings of the Court's role had. No matter what its view of particular decisions, the public in the 1960s saw the Court as playing a vital role in protecting the proper workings of American democracy and conquering the stasis of the other branches.

BANNING PRAYER IN SCHOOLS

"Let's see what the Supreme Court will do about that"

In 1962, the Supreme Court banned officially sponsored prayer in public schools. The decision was met with huge protest, but it quieted down surprisingly quickly. A respect for religious pluralism undoubtedly played a role. Yet it also was the case—and this may have been the most important factor—that many who disagreed simply continued to pray. Judicial decrees prove particularly difficult to enforce when they are as diffuse as the school prayer ban, requiring many people in many places to do something (or abstain from doing something) when they would prefer otherwise.

By the time of the school prayer decisions, America's devotion to religion was running high. Church membership was at almost 70 percent in 1960.[238] Eisenhower, who doubted "the American people are going to follow anybody who's not a member of a church," was baptized as a Presbyterian after taking office.[239] Ike's cabinet shared a prayer at all meetings, and one day while Ike was in church, the pastor suggested that to the Pledge of Allegiance be added the words "one nation under God." Eisenhower signed the law on Flag Day of that year.[240]

This religious revival may have been related to world events.[241] Fordham University's president said in 1942: "We are beginning to recognize as a nation that the real enemy of democracy is atheism, whether it be adorned with a black swastika, a red star or a Ph.D."[242] The evangelist Billy Graham, who was to counsel many Presidents, sparked his tent crusades preaching, "The world is divided into two camps!" Communism, he told the faithful, had "declared war against God, against Christ, against the Bible, and against all religion!"[243]

The Supreme Court's first attempt to separate religion from public education was no more than that, an attempt. In the 1947 *Everson* case, the Court scrutinized a New Jersey township law providing funds for bus fare to parents who sent their children to parochial schools. (Free bus transportation was available to the public schools.) Justice Black's lengthy majority opinion wrote into the case law Jefferson's metaphor of a "wall between church and state." This wall, Black insisted, "must be kept high and impregnable."[244] Then, over the votes of four dissenters, he upheld the law nonetheless, leading Justice Jackson to say that the "case which irresistibly comes to mind as the most fitting precedent is that of Julia who, according to Byron's reports, 'whispering "I will ne'er consent,"—consented.'"[245] Apparently the majority was unwilling to go where its own logic led.

Next came a judicial flip-flop that some of the justices angrily attributed to their colleagues' caving in the face of hostile public reaction. In a 1948 Illinois case, *McCollum*, the Court struck down a state release time law that allowed public school children time off for religious training on the premises. There was but one dissent on the Court.[246] Four years later, in *Zorach v. Clauson*, the Court upheld New York's release time law. In seeking to distinguish the cases, the majority justices in *Zorach* pointed to the fact that unlike in Illinois, the students in New York attended religious classes off-site.[247] This, the three angry *Zorach* dissenters argued, was a distinction that had no basis in *McCollum* itself; Justice Jackson called the distinction "trivial, almost to the point of cynicism."[248] Dissenting, Justice Black clearly implied that public hostility caused several justices in the *McCollum* majority to rethink their views, noting that "few opinions from this Court in recent years have attracted more attention or stirred wider debate" than *McCollum*.[249] "Today's judgment," wrote Justice Jackson derisively in his own dissenting opinion, "will be more interesting to students of psychology and of the judicial processes than to students of constitutional law."[250]

In the interim between *McCollum* and *Zorach*, New York's Board of Regents adopted a plan to begin each school day with a short, nondenominational prayer the regents drafted. The plan had widespread support from major public figures, including Governor Thomas Dewey and the Reverend Dr. Norman Vincent Peale.[251] The Catholic Archdiocese of New York said it would be "unreasonable and undemocratic to insist that the nihilism of the unbeliever overrule the will of most American parents that their children acknowledge the existence of a personal God and their duty to obey His moral law."[252] There were dissenters, of course; the president of the United Parents Association protested that "religious feelings should be developed not by 'mere verbalization' but must 'come from the family.'"[253]

In 1962, in *Engel v. Vitale*, the Court struck down the Regents' prayer.[254] While disclaiming any "hostility toward religion," the Court held that "by using its public school system to encourage recitation" of the religious prayer, the regents breached the wall of separation.[255] "[I]t is no part of the business of government to compose official prayers for any group of the American people to recite as a part of a religious program carried on by government."[256] Justice Potter Stewart was the sole dissenter. He could not "see how an 'official religion' is established by letting those who want to say a prayer say it."[257]

The decision ran into a gale of disagreement. By now anything the Court did was certain to run into problems with the segregationists, who certainly could turn a phrase. A representative from Alabama said, "They put the Negroes in the schools and now they've driven God out."[258] At his annual picnic, Senator Harry F. Byrd of Virginia led his thirty-five hundred guests in reciting the banned prayer. "The Warren court [sic] was not satisfied with rewriting the Constitution," he said; "now it appears it wants to rewrite the Bible."[259] But the southerners were hardly alone. "For several days," reported Anthony Lewis, "all the serious business of the Congress of the United States was put aside while members spent their time denouncing the Supreme Court."[260] Constitutional amendments to revise the decision were introduced in both houses.[261]

The country's reaction to *Engel*, though mixed, also tended to be very negative. "The divines were . . . divided, in part along denominational lines," quipped Kurland. Jews tended to approve, Catholics disapproved, and Protestants were split.[262] *Newsweek* reported that a "thunderclap of outrage and shock cracked across the land," and *Time* said that newspapers, "snowed under by the wrathful letters from readers, erupted in editorial anger."[263] A Gallup Poll taken a month after the decision showed that nearly 80 percent of respondents approved of religious observances in public schools.[264] Another taken a year later showed that 70 percent disapproved of the Court's decision itself.[265] The Court received five thousand pieces of mail on the subject in 1962, and the Government Printing Office sold some thirteen thousand copies of the decision, "the largest public demand for any one opinion that anyone can remember."[266] One letter to the editor of *Newsweek* observed, "Sometimes a nation abolishes God, but fortunately God is more tolerant."[267] Meanwhile, "Los Angeles Municipal Judge Ida May Adams . . . concluded her usual court-opening prayers with a new plea: 'God bless the Supreme Court and in Your wisdom let it be shown the error of its ways.'"[268]

Why did the Supreme Court step out on this precarious limb? Given the religious sentiments of Americans, the hostile reaction to the *Engel* decision ought not to have been impossible to predict. Obviously, some of the justices simply felt strongly that this was the correct interpretation of the Constitution.[269] Yet it also is possible that the justices obtained a skewed picture of the public's likely reaction or were more likely to misjudge in this instance. Opposition to school prayer tends to be highest among the better educated and more well-to-do in society.[270] Mainstream Protestant denominations were more apt to support the justices on this issue than their evangelical and fundamentalist cousins, though the membership in mainstream denominations may have been less supportive than their leadership.[271] Moreover, in an era in which anti-Catholic prejudice was still intellectually respectable, some of the Court's members may have been willing to ignore the strength of Catholic opposition to the decision.[272]

The justices' surprise at the public backlash suggests that they had miscalculated public opinion on the issue and had underestimated how effective their critics would be in spinning their decision as antireligious. Justice Black, who authored the decision, "departed from his normal practice of not replying to critics and answered some of the letters that came to his chambers."[273] Justice Clark went further still, taking the highly unusual step of publicly defending the Court's decision. "[T]he news media announcements," he complained, "were not complete, most of them merely reciting the content of this twenty-two-word prayer and the fact that the Court had held it unconstitutional for a teacher to have her pupils recite it."[274] Chief Justice Warren's son, Earl Junior, felt compelled to speak up in his father's defense: "My father is the most religious man I ever knew. And here he was being attacked as being against God."[275]

Remarkably, despite the Court's holding the next year that reading of Bible verses and the recitation of the Lord's Prayer in public schools also was invalid, the tempest surrounding the school prayer issue quelled rather quickly.[276] Less than two months after *Engel*, Raymond Moley reported in his *Newsweek* column: "The protests over the Supreme Court's ruling against the New York Regents' prayer have died down."[277] Similarly, *Washington Post* writer James Clayton observed that during the summer of 1962 the "avalanche of letters" to the Court, initially negative, "began to include many from Americans who thought the Court was right."[278] Writing a year later, *The New York Times* said the "angry public reaction" to *Engel* "had simmered down to a great extent." Though the Lord's Prayer decision also was not met happily, especially in Congress, Anthony Lewis reported that "the reaction was certainly much more accepting of the court's doctrine."[279]

A variety of factors may account for the leveling off of anger at the Court. There is evidence that people initially misunderstood the scope of the Court's ruling.[280] It did not hurt that President Kennedy spoke up right away on the Court's behalf. While recognizing that "a good many people obviously will disagree with it," he said, in this case there was "a very easy remedy, and that is to pray ourselves." "I would hope," the President continued, "that as a result of this decision that all American parents will intensify their efforts at home, and the rest of us will support the Constitution and the responsibility of the Supreme Court in interpreting it."[281] The mainstream Protestant churches also backed the Court. Not only had "various major church groups" endorsed *Engel*, explained Anthony Lewis, but they had "prepar[ed] their flocks for the same result in the Lord's prayer and Bible-reading cases."[282] Even while the decisions were being announced, the United Presbyterian Church issued a statement saying, "Now that the Court has spoken, responsible Americans will abide by its decisions in good grace."[283]

Pluralist understandings of democracy plainly benefited the Court as well. Much of the discussion about the decisions was directed to the question of the appropriate place of school prayer in American society. *The New York Times* editorialized that "those who oppose school prayers are a minority. But the Constitution was designed precisely to protect minorities."[284] A professor of education at Pittsburgh Theological Seminary called on Protestants to apply the same standards to themselves that they would to "our Roman brothers. We can do that now by accepting openly and gladly the fact that this is a pluralistic country."[285] *Commonweal* magazine ran a long editorial on the Court's decisions, explaining that the "violent reaction" to *Engel* shows the "nation as a whole is thoroughly muddled about the meaning of pluralism in our contemporary society."

The difficulties of sanctioning school prayer in a pluralist nation soon became clear to Congress. It was one thing for legislators to make speeches in favor of school prayer. As the noted political scientist Robert McCloskey explained, "Congressmen feel that defending prayer is like defending motherhood: it wins them some votes and costs them almost none."[286] Taking the dramatic step of amending the Constitution to permit prayer was another thing entirely, and all efforts to draft a "nonsectarian" prayer ended in rampant disagreement. When Congress finally held hearings in 1964, key religious leaders opposed any amendment. As *Time* magazine reported, "Almost every Protestant denomination—ranging from the Seventh-day Adventists to the Episcopal National Council—has gone on record endorsing the [Supreme Court's] decisions." Early mail to Congress favoring amendment by margins of as high as twenty to one began to run just as high against.[287]

What may really have silenced critics, though, was the perverse fact that the Court simply could not enforce its decree in every public school classroom in the country. As the prayer decisions made clear, the Court was on weak footing when it handed down unpopular decisions that required many different people to conform. Immediately after *Engel*, a trustee of a Long Island school board said if Congress did not establish an official prayer, it would prepare its own. "Let's see what the Supreme Court will do about that."[288]

While the school prayer decisions changed conduct in many places, equally clearly the change was not universal.[289] Political scientists Kenneth Dolbeare and Philip Hammond set out to examine why some communities complied with the Court's ruling and others did not, but when they followed up their initial questionnaires with fieldwork, they realized they had not been told the truth. Even in supposedly compliant communities, violation of the Court's rules was widespread. The authors were reluctant to call it defiance, though; people just seemed to interpret the Court's mandates in accordance with their own preferences.[290] As Dolbeare and Hammond rightly noted, "Enforcement is rendered even more difficult by the fact that actual implementation is in the hands of a large number of people—the classroom teachers of the nation, subject, we may assume, to the close and sometimes emotional attention of some parents."[291] Obviously, the diffuse nature of school prayer enforcement would not have mattered if the Supreme Court's decision had had strong support in local communities, but it did not.

REAPPORTIONING THE LEGISLATURES

"[N]o decision . . . ever has achieved so much so soon"

At the same time as it was banning school-sponsored prayer, the Supreme Court was also ordering widespread reapportionment of the nation's legislative assemblies. If the school prayer decisions underscored the Court's weakness in enforcing its decrees without public support, the reapportionment decisions highlighted all that it could accomplish with popular support on its side.

The Constitution of the United States, as well as state constitutions, provide for the periodic redrawing of the lines of legislative districts, to ensure that each member of a popular assembly represents roughly the same number of constituents. But such reapportionment is unlikely to be in incumbents' self-interest, as it could mean voting oneself out of a job. Despite constitutional commands, state legislators systematically refused to redraw legislative districts. The Vermont legislature had not been reapportioned since 1793, and Mississippi's since 1890.[292] The Supreme Court initially refused to have anything to do with requiring reapportionment, deeming it a "political question." In *Colegrove v. Green*, a 1946 decision, Justice Frankfurter put it succinctly: "Courts ought not to enter this political thicket."[293]

In its 1962 decision in *Baker v. Carr*, the Supreme Court gave the go-ahead to judicial supervision of reapportionment. The Court's opinion was dry and technical; it said only that as a formal legal matter, nothing barred reapportionment suits, which were amenable to judicial resolution.[294] Notably, the Court was completely silent about the standards the lower courts were to apply in such cases; it said nothing about how much voting disparity would justify ordering reapportionment or by what standard district lines had to be drawn.[295] Justice Frankfurter wrote a most passionate dissent, condemning the "massive repudiation" of the past. "[A]ppeal for relief does not belong here," he insisted. Rather, it "must be to an informed, civically militant electorate." By now Frankfurter's message was a familiar one, even if it was falling on deaf ears. "In a democratic society like ours, relief must come through an aroused popular conscience that sears the conscience of the people's representatives." Frankfurter castigated the "futility of judicial intervention in the essentially political conflict" and warned that the decision would hurt the Court, whose authority "ultimately rests on sustained public confidence in its moral sanction."[296] (Apparently the struggle over the outcome exhausted the eighty-year-old Frankfurter, who suffered the first of several strokes immediately afterward and soon retired.)[297]

Subsequent Supreme Court decisions established the famous one person, one vote rule. Each legislative district must contain roughly the same number of voters as every other within the state, at least "as nearly as is practicable."[298] Opponents of the rule often argued that there was nothing improper in having at least one of the state's legislative houses apportioned by some standard other than the number of voters in each district, such as each county's having one vote. After all, they pointed out, each state held two votes in the United States Senate, no matter what the state's population size.[299] In 1948, while governor of California and a candidate for Vice President, Earl Warren had himself embraced such arguments, stating that he opposed "restricting the representation in the [state] senate to a strictly population basis" because "[m]any California counties are far more important in the life of the State than their population bears to the entire population of the State."[300] However, Warren's Court rejected these arguments. "Legislators represent people, not trees or acres," Warren explained for the Court in 1964 in *Reynolds v. Sims*. They are "elected by voters, not farms or cities or economic interests." Accordingly, "[w]eighting the votes of citizens differently, by any method or means, merely because of where they happen to reside, hardly seems justifiable."[301] In *Wesberry v. Sanders*, also in 1964, the Court applied the one person, one vote rule to congressional districts.[302]

The reaction of officials to the reapportionment decisions was precisely what Frankfurter predicted and much along the lines about which he complained. Once again, Congress shoved aside all business to deal with the Supreme Court's ruling.[303] South Carolina senator Strom Thurmond fumed that "these decisions could ultimately destroy the existing political structure of at least 44 of the 50 States."[304] Senate Minority Leader Everett Dirksen published a lengthy piece in *The Saturday Evening Post* complaining that "six members of the United States Supreme Court took what may prove to be the longest step toward creating a judicial dictatorship in this country."[305] The House of Representatives passed a jurisdiction-stripping bill. (All the Senate managed was a bill to delay enforcement.)[306] In a fit of pique, Congress also trimmed the pay raise of Supreme Court justices, below that of what "all other top judges, members of Congress and executive officers" were getting.[307] The Assembly of the States, a group that grew out of the Council of State Governments, proposed three constitutional amendments to deal with reapportionment and the Court more generally.[308] "Apparently," complained Raymond Moley in *Newsweek*, "the only kind of democracy that is to be tolerated in the present dispensation is Supreme Court democracy."[309]

The hunch among the cognoscenti was that enforcement of the decisions "will be a slow process . . . probably as slow as the school desegregation process."[310] Columbia Law School's Herbert Wechsler said one might have predicted "this egalitarian démarche would have produced disaster, with defiance of the Court throughout the land."[311] Yale's Alexander Bickel doubted *Wesberry* would move past "the litigation stage during the next four, six, or even eight years."[312] One member of Congress, when asked how long before *Baker* might take effect, asked in return, "What is the timetable for a glacier?"[313]

As it happened, though, progress was remarkably quick. The speed of compliance with *Reynolds* defied prognostication, Wechsler conceded: "[N]o decision in the history of the judicial process ever has achieved so much so soon."[314] Almost immediately after *Baker*, state courts began imposing reapportionment decrees. In just the "few months since the decision was handed down," there was "action by the lower courts swifter and more far-reaching than" anything in seven years of desegregation efforts.[315]

The reason for the prompt action and the defeat of all attempts to forestall it was obvious: the public loved these decisions.[316] While expressing their doubt and disapproval, legal academics were nonetheless forced to admit that *Baker* was "peculiarly popular" and "that it has not impaired, indeed that it has enhanced, the prestige of the Court."[317] Said Bickel: "The court's rulings on apportionment have been popular. They favor majority control, and there is hardly a strain of opinion in American political life which does not think that it represents or can represent a majority."[318]

Academics could whine about the decisions, and legislators could grumble as they were reapportioned out of a job, but the Supreme Court had read its public well: frustration over the issue had been building in the body politic for a long time. The years leading up to the decisions were filled with stories about the inequities of malapportioned legislatures. These articles featured stark statistics as well as folksy complaints, such as that of Nashville mayor Ben West: "The pigs and chickens in our smaller counties have better representation in the Tennessee legislature than the people of Nashville!"[319] Journalistic bombardment made clear the costs of a failure to reapportion: overly reactionary legislatures ignoring problems vital to the cities.[320] A few months before the first round of oral arguments in *Baker v. Carr*, CBS ran a special on dysfunctions in democracy such as malapportionment (also included were gerrymandering and the electoral college).[321] The Court was not the only body to take notice of this barrage: the Kennedy administration supported the *Baker* plaintiffs, filing an amicus brief that argued that Tennessee's legislative apportionment was "so grossly discriminatory as to violate the Fourteenth Amendment."[322] And immediately following the Court's announcement of its decision in *Baker*, John F. Kennedy said, "The right to fair representation and to have each vote counted equally is, it seems to me, basic to the successful operation of a democracy."[323]

The public invited the Court in because relief was not forthcoming elsewhere. It was just plain silly for Frankfurter to talk about seeking redress through political action. The generally conservative Justice Clark put it in precisely these terms in joining the *Baker* majority: "Although I find the Tennessee apportionment statute offends the Equal Protection Clause, I would not consider intervention by this Court into so delicate a field if there were any other relief available to the people of Tennessee."[324] *The Christian Science Monitor* asked in 1959, "[I]f the very ones who want redress are the ones who are underrepresented, what do they do?"[325] This question was a widespread one in the run-up to *Baker*, and the Court provided an apparently felicitous answer when it said, "The judiciary."

THE CRIMINAL PROCEDURE REVOLUTION

"Let's Have Justice for Non-Criminals, Too!"

It was the Warren Court's last great push that was its undoing: the effort to reform the law governing the conduct of criminal investigations and trials. Even in this area, which proved to be quite charged, most of the Court's major decisions were met initially with public acceptance, if not outright applause. Things changed quickly after the Court decided *Miranda v. Arizona*. In part, the Court grew a little too sure of itself. Equally, though, it was the victim of bad timing. *Miranda* was handed down just as lawlessness spiked and public concern about crime rose precipitously. The Court tried to retreat a bit, but it was too late. In the 1968 election, Richard Nixon ran against crime, and the Court, and won.

By the 1930s, high-profile cases had made clear the necessity for some form of national intervention to regulate the criminal process. Traditionally, the states had been left to conduct criminal investigations and prosecutions as they saw fit. The railroading of the "Scottsboro boys" and the brutal tactics condemned in *Brown v. Mississippi* left little room for doubt that the status quo could not be tolerated.[326] Police activities often occurred outside public view, making adequate supervision difficult. Race was frequently a factor in the pattern of police misconduct. As Truman's Civil Rights Commission reported, "[T]he incidence of police brutality against Negroes is disturbingly high."[327]

The Supreme Court brought national uniformity to the laws governing the treatment of criminal suspects by gradually applying the Bill of Rights to the states. This was done though a process of "incorporating" the Bill of Rights into the Fourteenth Amendment's definition of "due process." In 1833, in *Barron v. Baltimore*, the Court had made clear that the provisions of the Bill of Rights applied only against the federal government.[328] In the 1947 case of *Adamson v. California*, Justice Black offered historical argument that the Fourteenth Amendment was intended to apply the entire Bill of Rights to the states. He got three other justices to agree with him, but this was the closest that the total incorporation theory ever came to succeeding.[329] Nonetheless, through a long process of "selective incorporation," of working clause by clause through each of the Constitution's first amendments, the Court found that most of the Bill of Rights was a part of the "due process" that bound state governments.

As for why the Supreme Court was doing this at all, the answer was by now familiar: no one else would. "[I]t seems to me quite clear," said Erwin Griswold, responding to the state chief justices' criticisms of the Warren Court, "that if the state courts had done a better job of being scrupulous in their regard for the basic elements of fair trial . . . it would have been far less necessary for the Supreme Court to step into this area."[330] "[I]t is naïve or disingenuous to expect the Court to hold its hand when its hand is the only one raised or raisable," said Herbert Packer, a pathbreaking criminal law scholar.[331] *The Self-Inflicted Wound* was a powerful book about the *Miranda* decision and the Warren Court's criminal revolution written by Fred Graham, Anthony Lewis's replacement as the *New York Times* Supreme Court correspondent. It described how even as late as 1961, "defendants who could not afford counsel were still floundering . . . against seasoned prosecutors," "[p]o-lice were still flouting laws against illegal searches, [and] '[d]ragnet' arrests were used to round up possible offenders, in hopes that interrogation would show who, if any, were guilty."[332] Against these unrestrained abuses, the Court clearly felt compelled to act.

The first really big decision was in 1961, when, in *Mapp v. Ohio*, the Court prohibited the admission in state court proceedings of evidence seized by police in violation of the Fourth Amendment's prohibition on illegal searches and seizures.[333] This "exclusionary rule" had been, and remains, a heated topic. Dueling quotations by famous judges frame the issue. In a case involving whether evidence from an illegal wiretap could be admitted in court, Justice Brandeis said, "If the Government becomes a lawbreaker, it breeds con-tempt for law."[334] The idea was that courts tainted their hands by permitting the introduction of evidence that police had seized in violation of the Fourth (or any other) Amendment. On the other hand, Benjamin Cardozo (while serving on New York's highest court prior to his appointment to the Supreme Court) lamented a rule by which "[t]he criminal is to go free because the con-stable has blundered."[335] Why should society lose a conviction of a guilty per-son because of police misconduct?

The justices' ruling in *Mapp* should have come as little surprise.[336] The Court had mandated the exclusionary rule in federal trials in 1914.[337] As late as 1949, the justices declined to impose the rule on the states, but their ap-parent hope was for the states to get the hint themselves and do something about police violating the Fourth Amendment's prohibition on "unreasonable searches and seizures."[338] Although more and more states were moving slowly in this direction, by 1961 a majority of the Court had reached the limit of its patience. Without the exclusionary rule, it stated, the Fourth Amendment would be "a form of words."[339]

To listen to the reaction of the police to the ruling in *Mapp*, explained Yale Kamisar, a University of Michigan law professor and an expert on criminal justice, "[y]ou would have thought we had just passed the Fourth Amend-ment at a constitutional convention." Kamisar quoted New York City's deputy police commissioner, who said the case "was a shock to us. We had to reor-ganize our thinking, frankly. Before this, nobody bothered to take out search warrants."[340] This of course only underscored the Court's point that a judi-cially enforceable safeguard was needed to ensure protection of constitu-tional rights. Although police complained, the decision appears to have been in line with popular opinion, at least to the extent the public was paying at-tention. As Anthony Lewis wrote in *The New York Times*, the Court's decision reflected "a national moral sentiment" that refused "to tolerate police misbehavior in any state." "If the Court has changed," he concluded, "it is because we have changed."[341]

Mapp was followed by the Warren Court's most popular criminal decision, *Gideon v. Wainwright,* which granted lawyers to all felony defendants who could not afford to pay for them.[342] The road to *Gideon* was by now a familiar one. In 1932, the Supreme Court required states to provide counsel for all indigent defendants in capital cases.[343] In 1942, in a case called *Betts v. Brady,* the Court put the burden on state court judges to decide on a case-by-case basis if "special circumstances" required the appointment of counsel in state noncapital felony trials.[344] By the time of *Gideon,* forty-five states were requiring that all indigents accused of felonies be provided counsel.[345] Because the five remaining states, all in the South, often simply ignored *Betts,* Warren had his clerks on the lookout for a case in which to overrule it and impose a general federal rule.[346]

For many, *Gideon* crystallized all that was good in the Warren Court's activism: equal justice for all; the furthering of national values against foot-dragging states; the Court acting because others would not. As Clarence Earl Gideon's pencil-written papers in the Supreme Court read, "The question is very simple: I requested the court to appoint me attorney and the court refused."[347] In an ironic twist, the Court appointed one of Washington, D.C.'s topflight lawyers and later a Supreme Court justice, Abe Fortas, to represent Gideon in the High Court.[348] Florida sought the support of other states on its behalf; as it happened, more than twenty of them actually filed on Gideon's side.[349] Minnesota's attorney general (and later Vice President of the United States), Walter Mondale, responded to Florida's request: "I believe in federalism and states' rights too. But I also believe in the Bill of Rights."[350] The *Gideon* decision itself was an eloquent tribute to a simple truth: "In our adversary system of criminal justice, any person haled into court, who is too poor to hire a lawyer, cannot be assured a fair trial unless counsel is provided for him."[351] "Without the Supreme Court," said Gideon, "it might have happened sometime, but it wouldn't have happened in this state soon."[352]

The reaction to *Gideon* was "almost entirely favorable."[353] Several Supreme Court justices hit the hustings to lobby for defender systems, and large grants were made to defender programs by foundations, particularly the Ford Foundation.[354] The chair of the Mississippi Bar Association's criminal law committee called the decision "far-sighted": "Our penitentiary is loaded with inmates who are there because of no representation or improper representation."[355] The chief justice of Arkansas told the Conference of Chief Justices he had "no fault to find" with the decision.[356] Even the governor of Florida conceded the point, asking the legislature to enact a defender law: "In this era of social consciousness, it is unthinkable that an innocent man may be condemned to penal servitude because he is . . . unable to provide counsel for his defense."[357] Gideon had a lawyer on his retrial and was acquitted.[358]

It was police interrogation of suspects that posed the really thorny problem, the one that ultimately did the Court in. The Fifth Amendment provides that no person can be "compelled" to be "a witness against himself," what often is referred to as "self-incrimination." Several high-profile cases had made it clear that police frequently placed a fair amount of pressure on suspects they were interrogating—sometimes physical, sometimes psychological.[359] The difficulty was that police questioning took place away from the public eye, making it hard to know precisely what occurred or to patrol it. "[T]he third degree," observed Illinois Supreme Court justice Walter Schaefer in 1956, "has aroused more concern than any other aspect of criminal procedure."[360] There was a tension here as well. As the chief judge of the Second Circuit explained in 1963, "Our instincts and our reason all revolt at the idea of permitting the police to use their custody of a person for the purpose of coercing a confession." This was the case whether the confession is "truthful or not." On the other hand, "reason and experience tell us that in the vast majority of cases where people are asked about a crime and where they know something about it, they are willing to and they do tell the police what they know."[361]

The Court had struggled to find a solution, but prior efforts had fallen short. In a feature article entitled "Concern About Confessions," *Time* magazine explained to the public the problem of policing secret interrogations.[362] The common law rule asked whether any statement given to police was "voluntary," requiring police candor about exactly what went on when they obtained the confession. Trial courts had to be tough about finding the facts and reporting them. The voluntariness of confessions was assessed under a "totality of the circumstances" approach, which required analysis of each case on its own unique facts. The justices were finding it difficult to provide general guidance that would stanch the flow of cases coming to them.[363]

In its 1966 *Miranda* decision, the Supreme Court put in place a procedure it believed would safeguard constitutional rights in the interrogation room, eliminating the need for case-by-case determinations of voluntariness. Police officers taking a suspect into custody were required to read a set of warnings, informing the suspect of the right to remain silent and to counsel, including that a lawyer would be provided to anyone who could not afford one. Any confession obtained without following the Court's procedures could not be used as evidence in court. The decision was 5–4.[364]

What followed was a crescendo of disagreement. The heated *Miranda* dissents led the way; Justice Clark went so far as to say he was "proud" of the police agencies, whose efforts were not "fairly characterized by the Court's opinion."[365] *The New York Times* described the immediate reaction to *Miranda* as "mild," but that changed rather quickly.[366] The *Times*'s own editorial page, while it approved the principle animating the decision, regretted that the Court had made "so deep an excursion into lawmaking."[367] Police officers around the country were apoplectic.[368] Soon *Time* was fanning the flames, describing how the Court had released "Kidnaper-Rapist Ernesto Miranda, Mugger Roy Stewart, Stickup Man Michael Vignera and Bank Robber Carl Westover."[369] A *Reader's Digest* article implored the Court, "Let's Have Justice for Non-Criminals, Too!"[370] Political cartoonists had a field day: one showed the hand of a justice extending outside the Supreme Court building to dump a SUPPORT YOUR LOCAL POLICE sign into the trash; another had Earl Warren saying to a man standing over a murdered woman's body, "Mum's the word, bub"; yet another showed Warren carrying a bad-looking type in his arms and saying, "Is Daddy's Itsy-Bitsy Boy Comfy?"[371]

Many believed the Court had rushed too far ahead of—if not dampened—other reform efforts. While the Court was considering *Miranda*, the American Law Institute was drafting a Model Code that would have governed interrogation, and both the American Bar Association and the National Crime Commission had agreed to back it.[372] The only real difference between the ALI proposal and the Court's decision was the requirement to offer counsel, something few suspects requested anyway.[373] In *Miranda* itself, twenty-seven states (plus Puerto Rico and the Virgin Islands) had filed a friend of the court brief urging the Court to stay its hand, in order to let the ALI reach a conclusion.[374]

Under ordinary circumstances, the controversy surrounding *Miranda* might have passed quickly. Suddenly, though, for reasons having little or nothing to do with the Court, came the tempest. Race riots broke out across the country. The first of these was in 1964 in Harlem; then another in Watts in 1965. Riots after *Miranda* the following summer "made it appear that domestic turmoil had become part of the American scene."[375] That same year Huey P. Newton and Bobby Seale formed the militant Black Panthers.[376] Then came the "long hot summer" of 1967; Newark, New Jersey, alone saw twenty-three deaths and more than ten million dollars' worth of damage.[377] Detroit was worse.[378] House Minority Leader Gerald Ford asked, "How long are we going to abdicate law and order . . . in favor of a soft social theory that the man who heaves a brick through your window or tosses a firebomb into your car is simply the misunderstood and underprivileged product of a broken home?" Support for civil rights was slipping.[379]

Simultaneously, crime rates were rising, dramatically by media accounts.

Scholars had long debated whether the FBI's crime indexes were correct, but by the mid-1960s a consensus was forming that crime was definitely on its way up.[380] In 1965, the president of the American Bar Association (and later Supreme Court justice) Lewis Powell pointed to the "alarming increase of crime" and wondered about an "apathetic" public.[381] He did not have to wonder long, as—in the words of Fred Graham—"crime replaced communism as the hobgoblin of American politics."[382] In 1967, a court of appeals judge named Warren Burger earned the respect of Richard Nixon with an address at Ripon College—reprinted in *U.S. News & World Report*—in which he argued pointedly that while "[n]o nation on earth goes to such lengths or takes such pains to provide safeguards [to accused persons] as we do," the chief duty of government was rather "to foster the rights and interests of its citizens— to protect their homes and property, their persons and their lives."[383]

"Fear" was again the watchword of society. Crime had simply replaced communism. Studies showed that many Americans were afraid to go out at night or talk to strangers.[384] "Fear haunts . . . too many American communities," said President Lyndon B. Johnson. "It assails us all, no matter where we live, no matter how little we own. . . . America cannot tolerate enduringly this climate of fear."[385] Edward Kennedy told *The Saturday Evening Post* that "fear is a part of the daily lives of many Americans—whether they are walking alone on a dark street, or working in a shop, or driving a cab, or even sitting in their own homes."[386]

This time there was a culprit close at hand, the courts. *Senior Scholastic*, a magazine for high school students (and their teachers), debated whether police were failing at their job, then turned to the alternative: whether the "crime problem lies not so much in any police ineptness as in legal shackles that often prevent the police from acting as effectively as they might."[387] Between 1965 and 1968, polls showed a jump from 48 percent to 63 percent of Americans who thought the courts were too lenient with criminal defendants. Some two-thirds thought *Miranda* was wrong, and if the polls themselves misrepresented what the decision actually said, the verdict was still in.[388]

It was in precisely this climate that Richard Nixon ran against the Court on crime. Crime and the Vietnam War were two of the most important issues in the 1968 presidential contest.[389] Nixon played to the public's fears: "A cab driver has been brutally murdered and the man that confessed the crime was let off because of a Supreme Court decision." His central argument was that "some of our courts and their decisions . . . have gone too far in weakening the peace forces as against the criminal forces in this country."[390] Politically, Nixon was sandwiched between Hubert Humphrey, who called for order but said the "answer does not lie in an attack on our courts," and the segregationist former governor of Alabama George Wallace, who was busy one-upping Nixon: "If you walk out of this hotel tonight and someone knocks you on the head, he'll be out of jail before you're out of the hospital, and on Monday morning, they'll try the policeman instead of the criminal."[391]

In the spring of 1968, Congress went after the Court again, ultimately passing a bill that purportedly repealed *Miranda* in federal trials (but not in the states). Given that *Miranda* was a constitutional decision, it was unclear that Congress had this authority. The House bill would have done much more, including stripping the Court's jurisdiction over cases in which a state supreme court found a criminal defendant's confession voluntary.[392] The mood of the Senate Judiciary Committee was captured by a federal judge who testified that under the Court's decisions, "[s]ometimes I feel . . . as though I am in a topsy-turvy world—I am not trying the accused, I am trying the policeman."[393] During debate, one senator propped up a graph of the FBI's crime index; at the points where the rates spiked were indicated major Supreme Court decisions.[394]

There is some evidence that the Warren Court saw the trouble it was in and tried to switch directions. *Terry v. Ohio* was the headliner in 1968 for a collection of cases asking extremely important and provocative questions about police interactions with citizens on the street. Though the Court referred to the practice by its colloquial "stop and frisk" or the yet blander "field interrogation practices," the looming issue was police encounters with urban blacks.[395] The police viewed their tactics as essential for law enforcement; the subjects of the searches experienced them as unjustified harassment.[396] In *Terry* the Court okayed the frisks, departing from its prior relatively stringent adherence to the requirements of probable cause and a warrant.[397] "These decisions," suggested one pundit, "could be read as pristine examples of the Court's tendency to follow (or perhaps forecast) the election returns."[398]

"REQUIEM FOR THE WARREN COURT"

"Statesmen, including judges, must do as well as they can with what they see"

Nixon won. Soon thereafter, events conspired to allow him to begin to remake the Court. Warren resigned to allow a lame-duck Lyndon Johnson to appoint a new Chief Justice. Johnson nominated associate justice Abe Fortas. Congress was not in the mood to put a Warren Court liberal in the center chair, let alone one who had served as a close LBJ adviser even while on the Court. The nomination had to be withdrawn. Shortly afterward, Fortas's financial dealings raised questions that caused him to resign the bench.[399] *U.S. News*

& *World Report* reported that after Fortas's resignation, "President Richard Nixon now has the opportunity to change the complexion of the Supreme Court—a Court that under Chief Justice Earl Warren has been involved in controversy since 1954." [400] The judge who gave the anticrime address at Ripon College, Warren Burger, got the Chief's job. The Warren Court was to become the Burger Court. Fortas's job went to Harry Blackmun, Burger's childhood friend and "Minnesota twin." [401]

The Warren Court had shown both what a Court could do and what it could not. And though history has frequently emphasized the former, the latter was most instructive regarding the ultimate power of the Supreme Court. The very nature of Warren Court activism—that the Court's decisions required so much social reform—helped spur the growth of a new field of political science, impact studies. [402] Political scientists would look at what the Court ordered and try to measure how much society changed as a result. Ultimately, the political scientists confirmed what Alexander Hamilton suggested long ago: possessing neither sword nor purse, the judiciary necessarily depends on public support to accomplish its aims. [403]

Legal scholars summing up Warren's tenure made much the same point, though their disappointment was palpable. On Earl Warren's last day on the bench, University of Texas School of Law professor Vincent Blasi walked directly from his lecture to his desk and penned a poignant "Requiem for the Warren Court." He conceded that though the "Warren Court directly changed the American scene," it was "not nearly as much as the popular folklore would have it." Blasi ran down a laundry list of things that had not really changed, among them: "Segregation is *de facto* instead of *de jure*. God is alive and well in the public schools." Seeking solace, Blasi concluded it was "unfair . . . to judge a court in terms of its immediate results. That is not the way judicial reform works. The process is subtle. It entails . . . gently nudging and tugging the nation, laying the doctrinal foundations for future change, taking the long view." [404] "The Court backed off, as must an institution without a base of power, but only after the enemy had been exposed." [405]

Of like mind was the most famous of all the Warren Court commentators, Alexander Bickel. The title of his book *The Least Dangerous Branch* had been intended as an ironic reference to Alexander Hamilton's comment in "Federalist No. 78" that the judiciary, lacking the "purse" and the "sword," would be the least threatening or powerful of the federal branches of government. Bickel looked around him in the early 1960s and saw, to the contrary, that the Court was ordering sweeping change. Although Bickel understood from the start that there was only so far the Court could get ahead of the crowd, still he expressed the belief that the Court could act as a "republican schoolmaster," leading the nation to its better self.

By the end of the Warren Court, though, Bickel was fatalistic about what the Supreme Court could hope to accomplish. He delivered his dirge in the 1969 Holmes Lectures. Bickel expressed skepticism; he looked around him and did not believe desegregation, criminal justice reform, or reapportionment were working out.[406] The man who once expressed hope about the Court as schoolmaster was now deeply disillusioned.

Ultimately, it was Anthony Lewis who proved the Court's most perceptive spectator. Covering Bickel's address, Lewis wrote that he "suffers from the same idealism that he lays to judges. He holds the Supreme Court to standards infinitely higher than any other political institution; he wants its vision to be perfect or its hand to be stayed." This is not how it is in politics, explained Lewis. "[L]ife is not perfect. Statesmen, including judges, must do as well as they can with what they see."[407] This, he thought, the Warren Court had done, even if it could do no more. The coming years were to demonstrate that the Warren Court had changed the idea of constitutional judging forever, even if it could not alter the reality of the constraints the Court faced.

9

INTERPRETATION

"The public cares about results and has little patience for reasons"

In the summer of 1987, Ronald Reagan nominated Robert Bork to be an associate justice of the Supreme Court. Bork's nomination was the crowning moment of a generation of efforts to influence the direction of constitutional law by appointing justices who would adhere to a particular method of interpreting the Constitution. Richard Nixon began the process, vowing to nominate only "strict constructionists."[1] Many, including Nixon, believed Warren Court activism had been the product of justices who were too quick to read their own beliefs into the Constitution's text. The antidote was to insist on a method of interpretation that would limit the justices' discretion. Announcing Bork's nomination, Ronald Reagan said, "[H]e shares my view that judges' personal preferences and values should not be part of their constitutional interpretations."[2]

Ironically, Robert Bork had been profoundly skeptical of Nixon's strict constructionist line. In an article in *Fortune* magazine written after the 1968 election, Bork, then a professor at Yale Law School, declared that "it is naïve to suppose that the Court's present difficulties could be cured by appointing Justices determined to give the Constitution its 'true meaning.'" Bork's own approach to constitutional interpretation was fuzzy, but he was unequivocal about what would *not* work. The "text of the Constitution" was simply too imprecise. "History can be of considerable help," Bork acknowledged, but still, it "tells us much too little about the specific intentions of the men who framed, adopted, and ratified the great clauses."[3]

By the time Reagan nominated him to the Supreme Court, Bork had changed his tune entirely. He had become the nation's leading apostle of "originalism," the idea that the Constitution must be interpreted according to the intentions of those who authored it. Bork's remarkable turnaround was in response to what he perceived as the Supreme Court's unabated activism. Although Nixon ultimately got to appoint four justices in his effort to remake the Court, between 1970 and 1975 the justices nevertheless overturned the capital punishment statutes of every state, bestowed constitutional equality on women, and legalized abortion. Conservatives, including Bork, were apoplectic. Their response was to insist on a rigid methodology for interpreting the Constitution. As Bork now explained, "[N]o philosophy of judging that is not based on original intent can confer legitimate power upon the judiciary."[4]

Conservatives were not the only ones who appeared to be tailoring their interpretive methodology to meet ideological preferences. Seeking to defend the Court's decisions, liberals turned to the metaphor of "the living Constitution" and urged judges to infuse constitutional interpretation with nakedly moral judgments. Ronald Dworkin, the nation's preeminent legal philosopher, was a case in point. In 1977, as the Court continued to deliver liberal decisions, he embraced "activism," telling judges they should rely on the "so-called vague constitutional provisions" to "work out principles of legality, equality, and the rest . . . and judge the acts of Congress, the states, and the President accordingly."[5] Ten years later, as judges appointed by conservative Republican Presidents flooded the federal bench, Dworkin condemned activism and insisted that the "justices enforce the Constitution through interpretation, not fiat, meaning that their decisions must fit [existing] constitutional practice, not ignore it."[6] In other words, preserve the status quo.

Reagan's nomination of Bork to the swing seat on the Court roused a storm of opposition, largely because Bork had condemned so many of the Supreme Court's decisions on the basis of his originalist philosophy. In a sense, the country was given a choice between the Supreme Court's prior decisions and a justice whose method of interpreting the Constitution might require overturning them. Following a confirmation process that looked more like a "national plebiscite," Bork went down in defeat.[7] Senator George Mitchell summed up why: "The American people agree with the Supreme Court. They don't agree with Judge Bork."[8]

In the years following the Warren Court, both liberal and conservative thinkers tried to control the direction of constitutional law by defining how justices should interpret the Constitution. But the justices went their own way, and for the most part the American people seemed to approve. As the noted legal historian Leonard Levy put it early in the tenure of Chief Justice

Warren Burger, "The public cares about results and has little patience for reasons."[9]

NIXON'S "STRICT CONSTRUCTIONISTS"

"[A]n instrumentalist tactic for reaching desired results
under a judicial guise of objectivity"

On June 23, 1969, Richard Nixon came to the Supreme Court for the swearing in of Warren Burger. Appearing as a member of the bar, Nixon offered the country's appreciation to Earl Warren and spoke of the "transition which will shortly take place." He took as his theme "[c]hange with continuity." "For all the world," remarked Alex Bickel, writing in the pages of *The New Republic*, "it looked like a transfer of power, witnessed by the broker who engineered it."[10]

Nixon was explicit about what he wanted from his nominees, and he got a remarkable four seats early in his presidency.[11] Repeatedly he insisted that what he sought were "strict constructionists."[12] "I am not concerned about whether the man is a liberal or conservative in his economic or social philosophy," Nixon would say. "My interest is how does he regard his role with regard to the Constitution."[13]

Observers expressed skepticism that the idea of strict constructionism held any meaning other than as a code phrase for justices who would decide cases as Nixon wished. Leonard Levy was insistent that strict constructionism was only "an instrumentalist tactic for reaching desired results under a judicial guise of objectivity."[14] Philip Kurland wrote facetiously that "there are only as many such living 'strict constructionists' as there are living dodo birds."[15] Even Nixon's appointees dismissed the "strict constructionist" term. Warren Burger told *Reader's Digest* that "[l]abels are generally sophomoric oversimplifications. All judges are 'strict constructionists' on some portions of the Constitution, 'activists' on others."[16]

Context did not help Nixon's credibility. The strict constructionist pledge was first made during a televised election address to southern audiences, as part of his "Southern Strategy."[17] Nixon offered southerners one of their own on the Court and administration assistance on the school busing issue.[18] *The Chicago Defender*, the nation's leading African-American newspaper, considered the "furtive label" "strict constructionism" a "convenient euphemism for a reactionary school of thought committed against the progressive forces that have ushered in a new era in the American social order."[19] Nixon's nominees left little room for reassurance. When Justice Fortas resigned, Nixon's first two choices to replace him were condemned as hostile to civil rights. One, G. Harrold Carswell, actually had run for office as a segregationist.[20]

Most agreed that if strict constructionism had any value, it was as a call for judges to eschew the activism of prior years for "judicial restraint." As they testified before the Senate, Nixon's nominees pledged such restraint. "I personally feel that the Constitution is a document of specified words and construction," said Harry Blackmun. "I would do my best not to have my decision affected by my personal ideals and philosophy, but would attempt to construe that document in the light of what I feel is its definite and determined meaning."[21] Lewis F. Powell, Jr., who was nominated to fill Hugo Black's seat, told the Senate Judiciary Committee, "I believe in the importance of judicial restraint. . . . [T]he judge must make a conscious and determined effort to put aside his own political and economic views and his own predilections."[22]

THE BURGER COURT

"The Counter-Revolution That Wasn't"

Despite the uncertainty regarding the precise nature of Nixon's judicial philosophy, no one doubted the Supreme Court was in for a change in direction. Realists conceded that "the near-revolutionary changes in 16 years in civil rights, criminal procedure, and reapportionment can hardly be reversed."[23] Even James J. Kilpatrick, writing in the *National Review*, admitted that decisions like *Brown*, *Baker v. Carr*, *Gideon*, and *Miranda* "will have a lasting impact on the law." Still, Kilpatrick expected that "a reconstituted court under Burger will clip the wings of some of these spread-eagled doctrines."[24]

In the area of criminal procedure, the Burger Court largely met expectations of being tough on criminals. After Burger was nominated, a Washington, D.C., restaurant, well aware of the portents, put a "Warrenburger" on its menu: three cents for a slice of bread and a glass of water on the side.[25] Legal scholars were to observe that though by the end of the era most of the Warren Court landmarks remained standing, there was little forward progress and much backtracking.[26] This, Leonard Levy pointed out, should come as "no surprise. Burger, Blackmun, Powell and [William] Rehnquist [who was appointed after Justice Harlan resigned] got their seats on the bench because of their supposed or known lack of sympathy for the rights of the criminally accused."[27]

Beyond the criminal cases, though, early news reports quickly switched from self-fulfilling prophecy to confusion and then to outright reversal. "Some

Nixon appointees are turning out not as conservative as expected," *U.S. News & World Report* told its readers in 1975, engaging in what by then already was vast understatement, given the Court's decisions on issues such as the death penalty, abortion, and women's equality.[28] In 1980, *The Economist* concluded that the Burger Court was "far more 'liberal'... than most Supreme Courts through most of American history."[29] An academic study of the Burger Court published that same year was aptly subtitled "The Counter-Revolution That Wasn't."[30]

Legal scholars and close Court watchers cautioned that conservative change was in fact afoot, but it was stealthy—a "covert counterrevolution."[31] Writing in *Harper's Magazine*, one professor said that though "it might seem that the Court Mr. Nixon has created has proved far more 'liberal' than the one he envisioned," still, "far more is going on than meets the eye." He described "The Techniques of Subtle Erosion"—the distinguishing of prior cases or refusal to extend them, the "small verbal changes" that have "enormous potential impact."[32] In the little-watched area of judicial procedure in particular, the justices were slowly closing off the access of many civil rights plaintiffs to the federal courts.[33]

What the public saw, though, were the blockbusters—anything but a timid bench. In 1971, newspapers began publishing the Department of Defense's secret history of the Vietnam War, dubbed "The Pentagon Papers." The administration rushed to enjoin publication, but in an unusual expedited proceeding the Court, "while we were at war, withstood all the pressures of patriotism and of Government" and permitted publication to continue.[34] The Court expedited review again when Richard Nixon, embroiled in the Watergate scandal, refused to turn over secret tape recordings of Oval Office conversations to the special prosecutor. Nixon's Court ruled against him— unanimously (though Justice Rehnquist removed himself)—"a bold and stunningly successful instance of judicial activism" that ultimately drove Nixon from office.[35] In *Buckley v. Valeo*, the Court struck down major portions of Congress's new campaign finance law.[36] When the Court held Congress's "legislative veto" of executive branch decisions unconstitutional in 1983, estimates were that from 60 to 200 laws were invalidated.[37] *The Economist* declared: "[O]ne fact is clear. In America, the Supreme Court is supreme."[38] The numbers were impressive. By the count of one Supreme Court historian, the Burger Court struck down 31 federal laws (counting the legislative veto as just one) and almost 300 state ones, compared with the Warren Court's 21 federal and 150 state laws.[39] Summing up the Burger Court's work, *The New York Times*'s Anthony Lewis proclaimed, "We are all activists now."[40]

It was the Burger Court's social reforms, though, that stirred the debate about how the Constitution should be interpreted. Some observers viewed the Burger Court's dramatic pronouncements on capital punishment, abortion, and women's equality as unexpected, but they were perfectly explicable in light of trends in social thought. The decisions were highly controversial, nonetheless, because as the social revolution begun in the 1960s continued apace, the Constitution spoke less and less obviously to present-day problems. The inevitable judicial creativity required to get the old constitutional blanket to cover each new situation, coupled with strong public disagreement with some of the decisions, made the method by which the Constitution was interpreted a matter of broad public concern.

INVALIDATING THE DEATH PENALTY, THEN BACKTRACKING

"[A] large proportion of American society continues to regard it as . . . appropriate"

In light of Nixon's anticrime stance, the last thing one might have expected was for the Supreme Court to strike down the death penalty statutes of every state that had one. Yet that is what it did, in *Furman v. Georgia*. In fairness, each of Nixon's four justices was in dissent; it required the agreement of the other five to reach this conclusion.[41]

The immediate reaction to *Furman* was shock. *The New Republic* called *Furman* "one of the biggest surprises" in the Court's history. Even at the NAACP's Legal Defense Fund, the lawyers representing the death-sentenced inmates, the reaction was "[g]eneral disbelief. Numbness. Tears in people's eyes. . . . 'This place looks like we just landed a man on the moon.'"[42] At the time *Furman* was argued, the justices themselves did not anticipate the conclusion they ultimately reached. Justice Douglas remarked: "For the life of me I do not see from listening to any member of the Court, how anyone would entertain the thought that as a matter of constitutional law the death penalty was prohibited."[43]

Of course, *Furman* was precisely the sort of departure from existing constitutional law that provoked calls for "strict construction." Dissenting, Justice Powell emphasized that to reach the conclusion it did, the majority had to reject "the clearest evidence that the Framers of the Constitution" did not believe the death penalty unconstitutional. Among other things, the Constitution specifically refers to use of the practice. As Powell also pointed out, the Court had brushed "aside an unbroken line of precedent reaffirming the heretofore virtually unquestioned constitutionality of capital punishment."[44] Indeed, just one year earlier, in *McGautha v. California*, the Court had flatly dismissed the claim that the trial procedures commonly used for death penalty cases were unconstitutional.[45]

In light of social trends, though, the *Furman* decision was hardly surprising. If there ever was a moment in American history when social indicators suggested that abolition of the death penalty was possible, this was it.[46] Imposition of the penalty had been dropping for years. A peak occurred in 1935 with just under two hundred executions. By 1965 the number had dropped to seven.[47] There was a flood of evidence that public sentiments were tipping against capital punishment. As late as 1953, the Gallup Poll showed support for capital punishment at a high of 68 percent. From there it fell steadily to an all-time low of 41 percent in 1966. In that year the number of opponents topped supporters, even in the South.[48] Abolition was occurring in many other countries in the 1950s and 1960s, including Canada, Great Britain, New Zealand, and Australia. The territories of Alaska and Hawaii abolished the death penalty in 1957, followed by the states of Delaware, Oregon, New York, Iowa, Vermont, and West Virginia. Other states cast close votes; some governors instituted a moratorium. Politicians and leading religious organizations came out against the death penalty in the 1960s. In 1968, the first year of no executions, Attorney General Ramsey Clark asked Congress to abolish the penalty for federal offenses.[49]

With sentiment close on the death penalty in general, public concerns about discriminatory enforcement could easily tip the balance. As was the case with Warren Court reforms, the South was again an outlier. By 1950, more than half the national executions were coming from southern states. The vast majority of states with a death penalty for crimes other than murder were below the Mason-Dixon line. Worries about racial disparity were rampant.[50] Several of the *Furman* justices—in the majority and in dissent— alluded to this issue.[51] Of the 771 people executed for rape between 1870 and 1950, more than 700 were black.[52] Johnson's Attorney General, Nicholas deB. Katzenbach, chaired the Commission on Law Enforcement and the Administration of Justice. He said that though commission members (like the country at large) differed on capital punishment, they agreed "unanimously that it is handled in this country, for the most part, very badly—in a very dilatory, very discriminatory way." He pointed to the fact that poverty was a big factor in who was sentenced to death and said the commission believed that "if it is not applied justly, it should be abolished."[53]

It was the arbitrary enforcement of the death penalty that ultimately swayed the deciding votes on the Court. The Eighth Amendment bans "cruel and unusual" punishments. Justices White and Stewart, whose views later proved most important, interpreted "unusual" to mean a sentence that was rarely invoked and even more rarely carried out. Justice White believed the death penalty unconstitutional because its rarity meant it could not serve the deterrent or retributive purposes of punishment.[54] Justice Stewart captured the essence of the problem in one crisp sentence: "These death sentences are cruel and unusual in the same way that being struck by lightning is cruel and unusual."[55]

Public reaction to *Furman* was immediate, negative, and harsh. Though support for capital punishment seemed to be falling prior to *Furman*, when confronted by the Court with the possibility of abolition, the country clearly made up its mind in the opposite direction. As death row inmates "cheered and whooped," Alabama lieutenant governor Jere Beasley suggested that a majority of this nation's highest court "had lost contact with the real world."[56]

Furman left the door open a crack on future death penalty laws, and the country was quick to run through it. California was the first. That state's high court had struck down the death penalty several months before *Furman*, but by overwhelming margins in a state referendum the voters insisted on reinstatement in November 1972.[57] Nixon called upon Congress to reenact a new law.[58] Opinion polls showed skyrocketing support for the penalty—more than 60 percent by 1975—and states were quick to meet voter demand. In January 1973, the ACLU reported that the "move to reinstate the death penalty is bigger and faster than we had expected."[59] Almost half the states had new death penalty laws within a year of *Furman*. In 1974, just under 150 inmates were sentenced to death.[60] The *Chicago Tribune* was moderate of tone but firm: "Those who say that the Supreme Court has ruled out the death penalty are wrong in fact; it will be a shame if they turn out to be right in effect."[61]

By the time the Supreme Court revisited the issue in the mid-1970s, thirty-five states and the federal government had passed new death laws, and the justices were under great pressure to uphold them. The Court took a variety of cases representing "nearly all the ways that have been devised to date in efforts to draft a capital punishment law that would meet the standards set in the 1971 ruling."[62] Richard Nixon's new Solicitor General, Robert Bork, entered the cases aggressively in favor of the death penalty. It "may have been possible, it was possible, to think differently about moral standards" at the time of *Furman*, Bork conceded graciously, but "once we have thirty-five [state legislatures and] the Congress of the United States adopting a penalty, it is impossible to say that it is in conflict with current morality."[63]

The Supreme Court quickly moved into line with public opinion. Justices White and Stewart switched sides, joining the original four *Furman* dissent-

ers as well as John Paul Stevens, whom President Ford had nominated to replace the ailing Justice Douglas. *Furman*'s 5–4 vote against the death penalty
had become 7–2 in favor. The Court struck down the somewhat rare mandatory death penalties, as well as the imposition of death for rape.[64] However, it upheld state laws that adopted variants of a model statute approved
by the American Law Institute. These statutes "bifurcated" the sentencing
proceeding from the determination of guilt, allowing the defendant to exercise his Fifth Amendment right to remain mum at the "guilt phase" but to
plead for mercy (or offer any other germane facts) at sentencing. The statutes also attempted to cabin jury discretion, and thus solve the problem of
freakish imposition, by requiring a finding of specified "aggravating circumstances" that warranted death, which jurors would then weigh under some
formula against "mitigating circumstances."[65]

Justices Stewart and White had plainly bowed to intervening events. It
was simply implausible that the concerns about arbitrary and discriminatory
enforcement standing behind their votes in *Furman* were now eliminated.
Stewart's lead opinion said his worries in *Furman* about jury discretion were
"met by a carefully drafted statute that ensures that the sentencing authority
is given adequate information and guidance."[66] Yet he acknowledged what
was undoubtedly a large factor in his decision, the many new death penalty
statutes making it "now evident that a large proportion of American society
continues to regard it as . . . appropriate."[67] In voting to uphold the new statutes, Justices White and Stewart simply brushed aside counsel's strenuous
argument on behalf of the condemned inmates that the entire process of
capital punishment still was shot through with discretion of the sort *Furman*
seemed to condemn. "Mistakes will be made and discriminations will occur
which will be difficult to explain," Justice White conceded. But the arguments offered by counsel for the NAACP Legal Defense Fund about widespread discretion still present in the system of death were "in final analysis
an indictment of our entire system of justice."[68] The Court was not going to
travel this hazardous road.

The Christian Science Monitor cast a skeptical eye on the Court's justification. "[L]egal scholars," it reported, believed the "practical effect" of the
rulings "will be to leave things essentially as they had been" prior to *Furman*.
"Prosecutors, judges, juries, appellate courts, and governors continue to en-
joy broad discretion," and death row populations "continue to include disproportionate numbers of blacks, poor people, and the young." The *Monitor*
attributed the original *Furman* decision to an error "more political than legal":
the *Furman* justices had engaged in the "unwarranted assumption" that the
country was ready to do without the death penalty.[69]

THE COURT AND THE EQUAL RIGHTS AMENDMENT

"[W]e ought to support laws that provide equal opportunity to women"

A short time later, *The Christian Science Monitor* was reporting on yet another judicial effort at transformative social change. This time it was one that stuck. "[T]his court, under conservative Chief Justice Warren E. Burger," the *Monitor* told its readers, "has broken more ground in sex discrimination cases than any Supreme Court in history."[70] That was putting it mildly. Not only did the Court's decisions buck existing legal understandings of the Constitution, but they advanced women's constitutional equality in the face of the nation's refusal to ratify the Equal Rights Amendment. In other words, just as the country was balking at adopting new constitutional language to protect women's equality, the justices were doing it anyway by interpreting existing language.[71]

The Supreme Court took its first step toward gender equality in 1971. The case, *Reed v. Reed*, involved a statute that preferenced men over women in the administration of estates. Under the Equal Protection Clause, the Court had heretofore adopted two tests. Most laws that treated one group differently from another got "rational basis" scrutiny. In order for the Court to find a law unconstitutional, the justices basically had to conclude that the lines it drew among groups or individuals were irrational, which almost never happened. For certain "suspect" classifications, though—most notably those based on racial differences—the Court's scrutiny was "strict." These laws were almost always struck down.[72] The Chief Justice's opinion in *Reed* broke this pattern, striking the discriminatory law at issue under rational basis review as "arbitrary."[73] Plainly, the Court had not wanted to deem gender classifications "suspect," like those based on race. Still, constitutional scholar Gerald Gunther concluded, "it is difficult to understand [the *Reed*] result without an assumption that some special sensitivity to sex as a classifying factor entered into the analysis."[74]

As modest a move toward gender equality as *Reed* was, it nonetheless collided with the original understanding of the Equal Protection Clause's meaning.[75] Ruth Bader Ginsburg, who was the litigator responsible for bringing the Burger Court around in *Reed* (as well as most of its other major gender decisions), felt going into the case that "the possibility of getting a favorable decision seemed nil."[76] "It was very clear that the framers of the 14th Amendment did not have women in mind," she told a Ford Foundation audience in the early 1970s.[77] An unbroken line of Supreme Court precedents reinforced this. "The natural and proper timidity and delicacy" of women made them unfit "for many of the occupations of civil life," Justice Bradley explained as the Court denied women the right to practice law in 1873.[78] When, in 1948, women challenged a law barring them from serving as bartenders (unless related to the owners), Felix Frankfurter turned them away, saying the question "need not detain us long."[79] Exemptions of women from jury service were acceptable as of 1961, the Court held in *Hoyt v. Florida*, because "woman is still regarded as the center of home and family life."[80]

By the 1960s, though, the Court's decisions were running up against reality. Women flooded into the workplace, only to encounter great discrimination once there. Between 1940 and 1960, the number of women working outside the home doubled. As of 1970, 43 percent of women held jobs; they included many more young women than previously.[81] A Columbia economics professor deemed this transformation "the single most outstanding phenomenon of our century."[82] Yet most women continued to work in "pink collar" positions specially slotted for them. To underscore the point, newspaper want ads segregated positions by sex.[83] In the mid-sixties, women worked for about 60 percent of what men were paid and constituted a tiny portion of the professions.[84]

Discrimination continued as the women's movement coalesced in the 1960s. Betty Friedan's *The Feminine Mystique* provided the spark. In it she described the deep unease of "[m]illions of women . . . kissing their husbands goodbye . . . depositing their stationwagonsful of children at school, and smiling as they ran the new electric waxer over the spotless kitchen floor."[85] Friedan urged women to "do the work that you are capable of doing."[86] Women's workplace equality made unexpected legal headway when Title VII of the Civil Rights Act of 1964 was amended to prohibit employment discrimination based on "sex."[87] The amendment was offered as part of a strategy to derail the bill, but once it was proposed women flocked to support the measure.[88] Then the Equal Employment Opportunity Commission refused to enforce Title VII. One EEOC director called it "a fluke . . . conceived out of wedlock," and even *The New Republic* asked, "Why should a mischievous joke perpetrated on the floor of the House of Representatives be treated by a responsible administration body with this kind of seriousness?"[89] Infuriated women mobilized, forming the National Organization for Women in 1966.[90] By 1974, NOW had grown to forty thousand members under Friedan's leadership. Women also gathered in countless small groups, organizing from the bottom up.[91]

The movement for women's equality burst into the public eye in 1970, a year that, like the decision in *Reed* that followed on its heels, demonstrated how far women had come and how far they had yet to go.[92] The major media began to do pieces on "women's liberation," many as cover stories. The title of the "Mushroom Effect," a directory of the hundreds of extant women's groups, captured the growing phenomenon.[93] The catalyzing event was the women's strike, which Friedan conceived to mark the fiftieth anniversary of the Nineteenth (women's suffrage) Amendment.[94] "Don't iron while the strike is hot" was the slogan for a day of numerous demonstrations conducted in a carnival atmosphere to bring attention to the push for equality.[95] Supporters marching up New York's Fifth Avenue overwhelmed police, who expected far fewer participants.[96] Even Madison Avenue reached out to the new woman with a new cigarette, Virginia Slims, whose slogan was "You've Come a Long Way, Baby."[97] Still, the dismissive commentary of male reporters demonstrated the attitude that women faced. *Time* said the strike provided "not only protest but some of the best sidewalk ogling in years."[98] At ABC, Howard K. Smith began his report with this observation: "[T]hree things have been difficult to tame. The ocean, fools, and women." (He was hopeful progress would be made soon on the ocean.)[99]

The Supreme Court continued to support women's equality in its next big decision, in 1973, but this time the justices fragmented on the standard of scrutiny applicable to gender cases. The issue in *Frontiero v. Richardson* was whether the military could allow automatic dependency benefits to servicemen with spouses, yet require servicewomen to prove the dependency of their partners. The Court said no by a vote of 8–1. Writing for himself and three others, Justice William Brennan concluded that "classifications based upon sex," like those based on race, "are inherently suspect, and must therefore be subjected to strict judicial scrutiny."[100] The other justices thought Brennan was going too far.[101]

The division on the *Frontiero* Court reflected a question with which women had struggled for some time: Ought an amendment to the Constitution be secured to ensure gender equality, or was the existing Equal Protection Clause flexible enough to allow for all that was needed? The two approaches were in some tension, for the Constitution could not already grant women equality and still be in need of amending.[102] There had been a push among women since they gained suffrage to add an equality provision to the Constitution, but it was opposed by many who worried that such a provision would threaten labor legislation that protected the interests of women and that had been won at hard cost.[103] President Kennedy's Commission on the Status of Women concluded that the "principle of equality" was already "embodied in the Fifth and Fourteenth Amendments." Instead of an ERA, "judicial clarification is imperative in order that remaining ambiguities with respect to the constitutional protection of women's rights be eliminated."[104]

Ironically, it was only in 1969, when the EEOC ruled that Title VII prohibited labor legislation singling out women for protection, that women themselves could unite on a dual strategy of pursuing an ERA and at the same time seeking favorable interpretation of the existing Equal Protection Clause.[105] Civil rights activist Pauli Murray was instrumental. In the early 1960s, working as a staffer for Kennedy's commission, Murray urged women to "build up the Fourteenth Amendment . . . without sacrificing the principle of the [Equal Rights] Amendment" so that women could "escape from our dilemma."[106] In 1970, Murray, disenchanted with the Supreme Court, urged the American Civil Liberties Union not to testify against the ERA, pointing to the fact that the protective legislation issue was gone.[107] As Mary Eastwood, a Department of Justice attorney active with NOW (and Murray's sometime coauthor), put it, "[E]ven if the ERA fails to pass, vigorously pushing for it will show women are demanding equal rights and responsibilities under the law."[108]

The ERA launched like a rocket out of Congress in 1972, helped along by the tireless efforts of Martha Griffiths, the Democratic representative from Michigan. It seemed destined for quick success. Both houses had passed the legislation by huge margins, sending it to the states for ratification. Within a month, fourteen states had signed on, often with wide support and little debate. In three months there were twenty states, and thirty within the year.[109] A Ford Foundation report said that "supporters feel ratification is likely . . . in the first half of 1973."[110]

By the time the justices were considering how to resolve *Frontiero*, though, the drive to ratify the ERA had already stalled. Phyllis Schlafly, a longtime conservative Republican activist, dedicated herself to halting the groundswell in favor of the ERA.[111] In her February 1972 report "What's Wrong with 'Equal Rights' for Women," Schlafly issued an obvious and direct challenge to Betty Friedan. Family, wrote Schlafly, "the basic unit of society, which is ingrained in the laws and customs of our Judeo-Christian civilization," is "the greatest single achievement in the history of women's rights," assuring women "the most precious and important right of all—the right to keep her own baby and to be supported and protected in the enjoyment of watching her baby grow and develop."[112] Adopting the slogan "You can't fool Mother Nature," Schlafly's group—Stop ERA—set out to do just that.[113]

Brennan's colleagues disagreed with his adoption of the strict scrutiny test precisely because it appeared to defer too little to the debate over ratification of the ERA. As the legal publication *United States Law Week* remarked later, the justices "came within a vote of rendering state ratification of the Equal Rights Amendment superfluous."[114] "By acting prematurely and unnecessarily," wrote Justice Powell, "the Court has assumed a decisional responsibility at the very time when state legislatures, functioning within the traditional democratic process, are debating the proposed Amendment."[115]

Justice Brennan's decision to apply strict scrutiny despite the brawl over the ERA was no accident; he could count. His early draft avoided the more demanding standard, but once Justices White, Douglas, and Marshall indicated they wanted to go all the way, he happily obliged. When Justices Powell and Blackmun wrote to complain about leapfrogging the national debate, Brennan wrote back, saying: "Since rejection in 13 states is sufficient to kill the Amendment it looks like a lost cause. . . . I therefore don't see that we gain anything by awaiting what is at best an uncertain outcome."[116]

Although it was a bit of a trick pulling strict scrutiny of gender classifications out of the Constitution, especially with the ERA facing rejection, Brennan understood he had a tailwind of popular support behind him. As he noted in internal Court memos, not only had both houses of Congress recently favored the measure by overwhelming margins, but "the legislatures of more than half the States have already determined that classifications based upon sex are inherently suspect."[117] Polls also showed overwhelming support for the amendment.[118] (Some of those polls would prove suspect in the face of later state losses, but no one quite understood that yet.)[119] Whereas the parties had no particular agenda for women's equality in the late 1960s, both 1972 party platforms had substantial women's rights planks, including support for the ERA.[120] Women also played large roles in the major party conventions for the first time that year.[121] Richard Nixon issued a proclamation on the fifty-second anniversary of the suffrage amendment saying: "As significant as the ratification of the Nineteenth Amendment was, it was not the cause for ending women's efforts to achieve their full rights in our society. Rather, it brought an increased awareness of other rights not yet realized."[122] And as in past matters, those states refusing to ratify the ERA were overwhelmingly southern.[123] The Court once again looked to be moving to bring errant states in line with national opinion, in this case counteracting the anti-majoritarian tendencies of the amendment process.

Brennan and the other three justices who joined him also may have been sensitive to the pounding the Court had taken for not moving sooner. Martha Griffiths had told Congress: "There never was a time when decisions of the Supreme Court could not have done everything we ask today."[124] When it passed the ERA, the Senate report agreed: "The Supreme Court has been slow to move."[125] Brennan's *Frontiero* opinion cited a wealth of political and intellectual materials supporting the movement for women's equality, including a *Harvard Law Review* note attributing the ERA campaign to the "Court's failure to eliminate legal sex discrimination."[126]

By 1976, most of the justices were willing to go along with Brennan—if not quite the whole distance, then for at least a good part of the way. The case, *Craig v. Boren*, was an odd one in that it involved discrimination against young men in the purchase of alcoholic beverages.[127] Writing for the Court, Justice Brennan held the law unconstitutional, adopting a new and "intermediate" level of scrutiny. "[C]lassifications by gender must serve important governmental objectives and must be substantially related to achievement of those objectives."[128] This time Brennan got six clear votes and a grudging sort of support from another two. The test would stick. The very year the ratification campaign ran out of time and steam, the Supreme Court applied this scrutiny to invalidate a ban on men attending Mississippi's all-women university. The Court's first woman justice, Sandra Day O'Connor, wrote the opinion, stating that gender-based discrimination would be upheld only upon "exceedingly persuasive justification."[129]

If the turnabout of the justices seemed to make little sense in light of the ERA's downfall, the ongoing march toward gender equality could explain things. The year *Craig* was decided, *Time* named twelve women its "Man of the Year," saying that "the women's drive penetrated every layer of society, matured beyond ideology to a new status of general—and sometimes unconscious—acceptance."[130] (That very same year Dr. Benjamin Spock revised his legendary manual on child rearing, taking account of the fact of working mothers and offering a substantial role for fathers to play.)[131] The Harris Poll was finding a steady rise in support for "most of the efforts to strengthen and change the status of women in society."[132]

By the time of *Craig*, the Court's clear adherence to principles of gender equality was nothing more than what ERA *opponents* themselves were claiming.[133] ERA opponents emphasized their basic commitment to women's equality even as they worried over how far it could reach. The fight over the ERA touched on a host of issues, from the relatively improbable to the heartfelt. Stop ERA's letters to the Alabama legislature fretted about how the Supreme Court would decide to apply the ERA to "conscription, combat duty, alimony, child support, wife support, divorce, homosexuality, public restrooms, separate gym classes and athletic teams, single sex education, sexual crimes, and prostitution."[134] But in their fight to win the minds of the American people, those opponents were ready to acknowledge the importance of women's equality.[135] ERA supporters consoled themselves with this knowledge after the fight was over, noting "the ideological concessions made to sexual equality by conservatives in a decade of debate."[136] Senator Sam Ervin, the leading opponent to the ERA behind Phyllis Schlafly, a man enjoying national status for his role in having led the Senate's Watergate investigation, argued from the start that no amendment was necessary because the Constitution already protected equality for women. "I am convinced, and my conviction is shared by some of the greatest legal scholars of this country, that all unfair or unreasonable or arbitrary discriminations made by law against women in our country are unconstitutional" under the Fifth and Fourteenth Amendments.[137] A widely circulated opposition pamphlet, *A Christian View of the Equal Rights Amendment*, stated forthrightly (before explaining why it was against the ERA), "As Christians, we ought to support laws that provide equal opportunity for women."[138]

As if to underscore its marriage to public opinion, in the years after *Craig* the Court was to use the flexibility of the intermediate scrutiny test to uphold precisely those discriminatory laws that had mattered so to ERA opponents. For example, no single issue had stirred the debate as concern about women serving in the military and in combat.[139] In *Rostker v. Goldberg*, the Court easily upheld Congress's decision to reject President Jimmy Carter's plea for universal registration and sign up only men.[140] Similarly, a concern about weakening sex crimes was mentioned by many ERA opponents.[141] In *Michael M. v. Superior Court of Sonoma County*, the Court upheld a statutory rape law that applied only to men.[142] The Court's new test for gender discrimination allowed for the flexibility that most people at the time believed was essential in the area. "It was not the sort of declaration that is carved on public buildings," wrote *The Washington Post*. "It was murky and subjective. It said there were times governments could single out women for different treatment and times they couldn't."[143]

CONSTITUTIONALIZING ABORTION

"[T]he most emotional issue of politics and morality"

In the midst of the controversy over the ERA, the Supreme Court decided *Roe v. Wade*, recognizing a woman's right to obtain an abortion.[144] As with the death penalty and sex discrimination, *Roe* was a response to evolving social views. There was a difference, though. The Court misjudged public opinion on the death penalty by a long shot, but it had left itself room to backtrack and did. The gender cases worked a middle ground where ERA opponents and proponents could largely agree with each other, and the Court's decisions reflected that area of agreement.[145] When it came to abortion, however, the country was hopelessly split on an issue that seemed to present a stark choice.[146] The reaction to *Roe* was tidal, but the Court stuck to its guns. *Roe* was to join *Brown v. Board of Education* as a decision that defined the Supreme Court in the latter half of the twentieth century, but in a much more controversial way.

"A right to abortion," wrote *The New York Times*'s cub reporter (and later Supreme Court correspondent) Linda Greenhouse in 1970, the wonder evident in her words. "Such a notion, at first hearing, sounds fantastic, illusory. . . ."[147] The very fact that Greenhouse was talking about abortion in a major news publication was itself a recent phenomenon. Lawrence Lader, one of the founders of the National Association for the Repeal of Abortion Laws, wrote in his 1966 book *Abortion* that it "is the dread secret of our society . . . relegated for so long to the darkest corners of fear and mythology that an unwritten compact virtually requires that it remain untouched and undiscussed."[148] "In my day at the bar," agreed retired Supreme Court justice Tom Clark, "all discussion of abortion was taboo."[149]

Like everything else about abortion, its history is deeply contested.[150] The common law rule, in place at the country's founding, was that abortion was a crime only after the fetus was "quick"—i.e., fetal movement could be discerned.[151] Abortion was plainly available in the antebellum era; advertisements in newspapers attest to this.[152] By the late nineteenth century, though, almost every state in the country had passed criminal abortion statutes.[153] Many women who wanted abortions still obtained them, but often with the terrible dangers attendant to an illegal and unregulated practice.[154]

The legalization of abortion thrust itself into the public eye in the 1960s for many reasons. It was in part a function of the women's movement and the sexual revolution taking place in America. In addition to the increase of women in the workplace, many more women were going to college.[155] Fertility rates dropped dramatically from the 1960s to the mid-'70s.[156] Overpopulation was a genuine concern, so much so that former Presidents Truman and Eisenhower became Planned Parenthood cochairs.[157]

Two public health crises served as galvanizing events. Sherri Finkbine, a television personality, learned she had taken the tranquilizer thalidomide in 1962; when news of her pending abortion became public, it was refused her, and she was forced to fly to Sweden for the procedure. Finkbine's situation became a media cause célèbre. Gallup reported huge margins of approval of her obtaining an abortion. Then, in the mid-1960s, a German measles epidemic swept the country. More than eighty thousand pregnant women caught it. Many sought and could not obtain abortions. As many as fifteen thousand deformed children were born.[158]

In response to these public events and professional concern about the consequences of illegal abortions, states began to reform their criminal abortion laws along the lines recommended by the American Law Institute.[159]

The ALI's draft law was similar to what the American Medical Association had recommended in the mid-1960s. It allowed for noncriminal abortion if two doctors certified "substantial risk that continuance of the pregnancy would gravely impair the physical or mental health of the mother," if the child would be born with "grave physical or mental defect," or if the pregnancy resulted from rape or incest.[160] These new laws, however, did not begin to meet the demand for legal abortions. By the early 1970s, only four states—Hawaii, Alaska, Washington (by referendum), and New York—had placed the decision to have an abortion between the woman and her physician, and attempts at further liberalization seem to have stalled.[161]

Meanwhile, public anxiety was growing over who managed to receive lawful abortions and who was forced into the back-alley practice. Former justice Clark attributed public attention on the abortion issue to the "growing antagonism toward the double standard which permits those with social status and financial ability to obtain abortions, while those in the lower social and economic classes are denied this opportunity."[162] "There is no facet of medical care in which social position and dollars play so ugly a role, as the acquirement of legal abortion," declared Alan Guttmacher, Mount Sinai Hospital's head of obstetrics and gynecology who became a leading abortion proponent.[163] Lader was scathing, describing how minority groups in particular were "forced into the underworld of abortion, into the grasp of hacks and butchers. The result has been an abnormally high percentage of abortion deaths."[164] In Southern California, a twenty-four-hour Clergymen's Counseling Service began referring needy women to safe providers.[165]

The Supreme Court's decision in Roe v. Wade in 1973 often is described as every bit as surprising as Furman, yet it once again followed social trends. Polls suggested strong support for leaving the decision to women and their doctors. "Majority, in Shift, Now Favors Liberalized Laws," reported The New York Times about a 1972 Gallup Poll showing a majority of the country, including a majority of Roman Catholics, favored letting the woman and her doctor decide.[166] The files of Justice Blackmun, the author of Roe v. Wade, contained a clipping from The Washington Post reporting the same poll, showing a "record high" of 64 percent in support of "full liberalization."[167] The initial mainstream media reaction to Roe was overwhelmingly positive.[168]

Medical and legal professional organizations had also come to the conclusion that the abortion decision was better left to women and health care providers. By 1970, the American Medical Association opted to support the view that abortion was properly resolved as a medical matter based on "sound clinical judgment" and "informed patient consent."[169] The American Public Health Association issued standards for abortion that year that plainly made it a matter of choice by women, in consultation with doctors and trained counselors.[170] The American Bar Association agreed on a law that would also have left it a physician-woman decision in the first twenty weeks of pregnancy (and turned to the familiar limitations after that).[171]

There were some troubling signs on the horizon, but it is difficult to know if the justices missed them or simply chose to ignore them. Some focused polls suggested overwhelming support for abortion in the case of birth defects, rape, incest, or threats to a woman's health, but diminishing support for reasons relating more to economics or personal choices.[172] A 1972 referendum in Michigan failed in the face of a strong effort by pro-life activists, and New York's liberal law would have been repealed but for the veto of Governor Nelson Rockefeller.[173]

What was plainly noteworthy about the decision in *Roe* was its breadth and sweep—altogether reminiscent of *Miranda*. Justice Harry Blackmun's opinion for the Court established the now-familiar trimester framework. Through the first trimester, the decision about abortion was to be left to the woman and her physician, with little state interference. During the second trimester, the state was accorded increasing latitude to regulate for reasons of maternal health. Not until roughly the third trimester, at viability, could the state largely ban abortion "in promoting its interest in the potentiality of human life."[174] The Court's decision, called by the media "legislative" and an "unusually detailed timetable for the relative legal rights of pregnant women and the states that would control their acts," had been the product of extensive internal court negotiation.[175]

Almost instantly the Court faced intense pressures to back away from *Roe*. Pro-life advocates, caught off guard, began quickly to organize. (On the other hand, the pro-choice forces were lulled into quiescence.)[176] Although some of the post-*Roe* legislation certainly tried to comply with the Court's ruling, frequently legislatures pushed against the ruling. Over the intervening years, states sought to regulate where abortions were performed, how they were performed, when they were performed, what women were told before they obtained abortions, how long women had to wait to get them, and who in addition to the woman had to consent.[177]

The only major concession the Court made to abortion opponents was when the states and the federal government curtailed publicly funded abortions. "Taxpayers should not have to pay for something they regard as a crime," insisted Republican senator Jake Garn of Utah, just one of many like voices.[178] Absent private funding, of course, the effect was a restoration of precisely that state of affairs that had troubled so many before *Roe*. A cartoon in *Newsweek* showed an old man labeled "Supreme Court" opening the door of an abortion clinic and saying to the young African-American woman standing there: "If you have to ask how much, you can't afford one." [179] The Court also showed some leeway in laws requiring the notification or consent of parents, so long as an adequate judicial bypass mechanism was in place. [180]

While public opinion continued to harden over the abortion issue, waves stirred by *Roe* radiated out in two very different directions. In the world of law and legal interpretation, ongoing discussions about how the Constitution was to be interpreted quickly moved to a fever pitch. In the world of politics, activists mobilized to fight the issue in the forum of public opinion. A 1981 *Time* magazine cover story stated, "Abortion. It is, without question, the most emotional issue of politics and morality that faces the nation today." [181] Soon enough these waves were to collide in the great struggle over Robert Bork's nomination to the Supreme Court. When they did, the issue of abortion would be lurking quietly underneath.

A MATTER OF INTERPRETATION

"[I]t is not constitutional law"

Justice Blackmun's opinion in *Roe* instantly came under blistering attack, not only for what it established but for how it established it. Spilling well beyond the bounds of the abortion issue, the decision in *Roe v. Wade* provoked a sustained intellectual debate over a fundamental question: How should the Constitution be interpreted? The debate was fueled by the anxiety of legal professionals, as the Court's decisions seemed to move into areas well beyond anything anticipated or addressed by the Constitution's framers. Expressions of concern about the Court's decisions were every bit as intense from some of the Court's ostensible allies as from its detractors. As liberals sought to justify the Court's work, conservatives expressed skepticism that the liberals' methods of interpretation represented constitutional law at all.

At the heart of the intellectual challenge to *Roe* was disbelief that the Constitution protected the right to abortion. As *The New York Times*'s Linda Greenhouse explained, "The Constitution is searched in vain for any mention of it." [182] Sarah Weddington, the lawyer representing Jane Roe, appeared to concede the point the second time the case was argued: "Certainly we cannot say that there is in the Constitution—so stated—the right to an abortion." When she was pressed on the issue, Weddington's answer only highlighted the problem: "We had originally brought this suit alleging both the due process clause, equal protection clause, the Ninth Amendment, and a variety of others." At that point a member of the Court dryly interjected: "And anything else that might obtain."[183]

Like much in the Constitution, the right to abortion is a matter of interpretation. As always, it is a question of how one construes the text, the intentions of its authors, and existing precedents to resolve the question before the Court. Weddington's concession had an edge to it, for as she went on to point out, abortion and privacy are hardly alone in finding no specific constitutional mention. "Neither is there stated the right to travel, or some of the other very basic rights that this Court has held are under the United States Constitution."[184]

There certainly were cases that provided judicial precedent for the sort of right at stake in *Roe*. In *Skinner v. Oklahoma*, the Court had invalidated a state law providing for sterilization of certain criminals. The Court said it was dealing with "one of the basic civil rights of man. Marriage and procreation are fundamental to the very existence and survival of the race."[185] In the case of *Griswold v. Connecticut*, the Court relied upon the "right to privacy" in striking down a law barring the use of contraceptives by (or the provision of them to) married couples.[186] *Eisenstadt v. Baird* extended that holding to single people. "If the right of privacy means anything," wrote Justice Brennan in words pregnant with possibility for *Roe*, which was pending at the time, "it is the right of the *individual*, married or single, to be free from unwarranted governmental intrusion into matters so fundamentally affecting a person as the decision whether to bear or beget a child."[187]

The prime difficulty was that *Griswold* avoided stating exactly where in the Constitution this right to privacy resided.[188] Justice Blackmun's opinion for the Court in *Roe* also evaded this critical question. He began a touch too candidly perhaps: "The Constitution does not explicitly mention any right of privacy." After exploring the possible locations of the right in various clauses of the Constitution, he then concluded with what many thought was a wave of the hand: "This right of privacy, whether it be founded in the Fourteenth Amendment's concept of personal liberty and restrictions upon state action, as we feel it is," or in the Ninth Amendment (which states that the "enumeration, in the Constitution, of certain rights, shall not be construed to deny or disparage others"), "is broad enough to encompass a woman's decision whether or not to terminate her pregnancy."[189]

There was a reason for all this elusiveness: the ghost of *Lochner*. In *Griswold*, Justice Harlan identified what he believed to be a perfectly good location for the right to privacy, the Due Process Clause of the Fourteenth Amendment.[190] Most of his colleagues would not go along with that. They recalled what had happened to the Court the last time it embarked on the endeavor of giving substantive content to the Fourteenth Amendment, in the early-nineteenth-century cases involving the right of contract. "Overtones of some arguments suggest that *Lochner* . . . should be our guide," wrote Douglas in *Griswold*, but "we decline that invitation."[191]

Criticism of the *Roe* opinion was to be expected from opponents; what really set the abortion debate on fire in legal circles was what some of the Court's friends had to say about it.[192] No one turned a sharper pen to *Roe* than the brilliant young law professor John Hart Ely. Ely had clerked for Warren and taught at Yale, then Harvard. (He eventually became Stanford's dean.) In an article entitled "The Wages of Crying Wolf," rushed into print after *Roe*, Ely professed deep sympathy for the woman seeking an abortion. "Let us not underestimate what is at stake: Having an unwanted child can go a long way toward ruining a woman's life." Still, he considered the question impossibly difficult. "Abortion is too much like infanticide on the one hand, and too much like contraception on the other, to leave one comfortable with any answer; and the moral issue it poses is as fiendish as any philosopher's hypothetical." Ely believed judges should not touch the question, because the Constitution "simply says nothing, clear or fuzzy, about abortion." He insisted this was "a charge that can responsibly be leveled at no other decision of the past twenty years" and offered a scathing indictment about *Roe*: "[I]t is *not* constitutional law and gives almost no sense of an obligation to try to be."[193]

After Ely, the dam broke open, revealing a problem running deeper than *Roe* itself: how to defend the sort of constitutional interpretation that had basically been going on since liberals took over the Court after the New Deal fight. This was a debate with real consequences, as intellectuals on both the left and the right were quick to point out. "This debate is not an abstract conversation in academic political theory," law professor Michael Perry told an audience that had convened at a conservative think tank, the American Enterprise Institute, to discuss the problem. "The future of our constitutional rights and liberties—and of the courts' role in protecting them—is at stake."[194] Gary McDowell, a conservative thinker who soon played an important behind-the-scenes role at the Justice Department, concurred, calling it "a political battle of the first order . . . nothing less than a fierce fight over what theory of constitutionalism will guide this nation into the twenty-first century."[195]

In seeking to justify the Court's decisions, some liberals adopted what Stanford law professor Thomas Grey referred to as "[o]ur characteristic contemporary metaphor . . . 'the living Constitution.'"[196] The dean of Michigan

Law School, Terrance Sandalow, explained the concept: "The meaning of the Constitution is never fixed; rather, it changes over time to accommodate altered circumstances and evolving values."[197]

The chief difficulty with living constitutionalism was that it permitted judges a fair amount of leeway in interpretation. Scholars with political views as divergent as those of Ely and Bork would share this concern. It was particularly infuriating to those on the right, however, as judicial discretion seemed invariably to lead courts to what McDowell called the "liberal promised land."[198] J. Clifford Wallace, a conservative judge who went on to have a widely respected career on the federal bench, accused the left of favoring the "'living Constitution' school" because it allowed the judiciary to act "as a social instrument to effectuate change." Wallace was blunt: "[A]ctivism loses much of its appeal if one considers the possibility of a court composed of judges whose activism favored social positions diametrically opposed to one's own philosophy."[199]

Despite difficulty, the living Constitution metaphor had a lot going for it. For one thing, it had a pedigree: it was precisely the notion used to criticize the Supreme Court as it struck down legislation during the New Deal. For another, it had curb appeal. In 1976, Justice Rehnquist gave a talk condemning judicial activism. "At first blush it seems certain that a *living* Constitution is better than what must be its counterpart, a *dead* Constitution," he said facetiously. Then, in words that were to prove prophetic, he suggested that if a poll were taken on whether the Constitution should be living or dead, "the overwhelming majority of the responses doubtless would favor a *living* Constitution."[200] Living constitutionalism seemed to capture the necessities of constitutional law in a changing world. Explaining why sex discrimination should be outlawed under the Equal Protection Clause, Pauli Murray and Mary Eastwood argued that "[t]he genius of the American Constitution is its capacity, through judicial interpretation, for growth and adaptation to changing conditions and human values."[201] When Justice Powell retired, he pointed out: "I have been alive eighty of the two hundred years of our Constitution. This country is very young. How can you say the Constitution should be frozen in time, that it is not a living document that must be interpreted?"[202]

It was here, though, at the crucible, that liberal legal academics took an ill-fated interpretive turn, arguing that judges should let go of the notion that they had to be tethered to the Constitution at all. The starting point was fair enough; indeed, it was irrefutable. They argued that traditional sources of constitutional interpretation simply could not justify large bodies of existing constitutional law. Two articles, by Stanford law professors Thomas Grey and Paul Brest, made the point emphatically. In his 1975 work "Do We Have an Unwritten Constitution?" Grey's answer was unequivocally yes.[203] *Brown v. Board of Education, Baker v. Carr,* and *Furman* and *Roe* were just some of the cases that would tumble otherwise.[204] In a 1980 piece, "The Misconceived Quest for the Original Understanding," Brest argued that "[s]trict originalism cannot accommodate most modern decisions under the Bill of Rights and the fourteenth amendment, or the virtually plenary scope of congressional power under the commerce clause."[205]

From this starting ground, liberal academics basically came to insist that judges should be moral philosophers. Grey at least advanced the claim, later fleshed out by Professor Suzanna Sherry, that the framers themselves believed there were natural rights unbounded by the Constitution.[206] Brest simply asserted judges should ask "How well, compared to possible alternatives, does the practice contribute to the well-being of our society—or, more narrowly, to the ends of constitutional government?"[207] Ronald Dworkin without question became the leading spokesperson for this sort of judging.[208] Referring to "the so-called vague constitutional provisions," he said a court "that undertakes the burden of applying these clauses fully as law must be an activist court, in the sense that it must be prepared to frame and answer questions of political morality."[209]

Though these liberal theories undoubtedly had their own tight internal logic, conservatives were quick to make the obvious point: this did not look like constitutional *law* at all. Speaking at the American Enterprise Institute forum, Gary McDowell parodied the liberals' turn, saying: "The question today is not so much how to read the Constitution as *whether* to read the Constitution."[210] One member of the bar with scholarly inclinations wrote an article entitled "Abandoning the Constitution: The New Wave in Constitutional Theory."[211] Reliance on Grey's label of traditional constitutional reading as "interpretivism"—and his discussion of going "beyond interpretivism"—made it commonplace to refer to the liberals' alternative infelicitously as "non-interpretivism."[212] This led Reagan's first Attorney General, Edwin Meese, in an all-out attack on liberal methodology, to say there were those for whom "constitutional adjudication . . . is not primarily a matter of construction at all. They appear to view the United States Constitution as a document virtually without legally significant, discernible meaning."[213] "The professors' constitutionalism, if that term is even appropriate," Robert Bork archly observed, "effectively ignores and bypasses the actual Constitution."[214]

THE RISE OF THE RIGHT

"[A] far-reaching 'social agenda'"

While liberals struggled to justify the Supreme Court's work, conservatives mobilized against it. In 1980, Ronald Reagan was elected President, and the Republicans gained control of the Senate. This was seen as a tremendous victory for the New Right, a growing grassroots coalition concerned with "family" issues, such as school prayer, gay rights, the ERA, and—most notably—abortion.[215] Given the President's profession of faith, conservatives expected progress on their agenda. By the end of his first term in office, however, conservatives were deeply disappointed. It turned out to be surprisingly difficult for the political branches of government to undo what the courts had done.[216]

Social issues galvanized the political right in the 1970s. The ERA fight made activists of a lot of people, particularly women, who were troubled by the perceived licentiousness of 1960s social movements. Opponents such as Phyllis Schlafly saw "an attack on marriage, the family, the homemaker, the role of motherhood, the whole concept of different roles for men and women." They capitalized on this. "What we did was take these cultural issues and bring into the conservative movement people who had been stuck in the pews. We taught 'em politics."[217] Though by the end of the fight Schlafly's Eagle Forum had only sixty thousand members to NOW's more than two hundred thousand, commitment counted.[218] The 1977 International Year of the Woman Conference provided a window on the gulf that separated the two sides. Ten thousand proud women converged in Houston to celebrate the suffragettes and to rally for the ERA. Three First Ladies presided over the opening ceremonies.[219] To many, though, the lingering conference image involved passage of the gay rights plank, complete with delegates hoisting provocative signs, such as one saying (in clear response to Schlafly), MOTHER NATURE IS A LESBIAN.[220] Across town, Schlafly collected her supporters to applaud the family and motherhood. (She began her talk, as she often did, by thanking her husband for allowing her to attend.) Attendance at Schlafly's counter-rally was double that at the main event.[221]

The Supreme Court's decision in *Roe v. Wade* provided an enormous impetus to grassroots social conservatives. The fight against *Roe* was led initially by the Catholic Church, which provided seed money to pro-life groups and in 1975 took "The Big Plunge" by adopting a tough pastoral plan for political action.[222] Not unlike the women's movement, however, much of the pro-life organization was built from the bottom up by people isolated from the reality of abortion—precisely those for whom the decision in *Roe* was a "bolt out of the blue."[223] The largest contingent of pro-lifers after *Roe* were homemakers.[224]

These social issues, many of which involved policies set by the courts (including the Warren Court's ban on school prayer), stirred a sleeping behemoth, what became known as the Religious Right.[225] In 1978, an evangelical Christian minister named Jerry Falwell organized conservatives for political action as the Moral Majority. "The only hope for America is to awaken the religious people."[226] "Televangelists" like Falwell and Pat Robertson garnered millions who tuned in to religion and got a good side helping of politics to go with it. Leaders sought self-consciously to form an alliance of not only Protestant evangelicals but conservative Roman Catholics, Mormons, and even Orthodox Jews.[227] In 1980, Dallas hosted the "National Affairs Briefing," a political revival attracting thousands. The theme was "It's time for Christians to crawl out from under the pews."[228] *The Christian's Political Action Manual*, published that same year, complained, "For too long Christians have voluntarily removed themselves from the political arena" and "America has suffered the consequences."[229] The "growing acceptance of abortion," said a book entitled *Bayonets and Roses: Comprehensive Pro-Life Political Action Guide*, "can be explained primarily by confusion in the Christian community toward corporate social action."[230]

By the midterm elections of 1978, the coalition of social conservatives was beginning to show its strength, calling itself the New Right, and the election of 1980 represented the New Right's ascendance to power. For the first time since 1940, the Republican platform opposed the ERA and supported a constitutional amendment to ban abortion.[231] In 1977, Reagan laid out his political strategy in a speech to the American Conservative Union. The "so-called social issues—law and order, abortion, busing, quota systems—are usually associated with the blue collar, ethnic, and religious groups who are traditionally associated with the Democratic Party." The time had come, Reagan said, to see if these could be united with the traditional Republican concerns for "inflation, deficit spending, and big government."[232] Though Reagan's campaign focused on the economy and foreign affairs, he appointed a Family Policy Advisory Committee to keep touch with his conservative base.[233] Polls showed that Reagan won because of the sluggish economy and unhappiness with Jimmy Carter's administration, but the New Right justifiably claimed its share of the credit.[234] In most southern states, Reagan's edge over incumbent Carter, himself a born-again Christian, was little more than 1 percent of the vote. Feeling betrayed by Carter on social issues, conservative Christians had turned out for Reagan in force.[235] Not only did the Senate change hands, but many conservative Republicans took many progressive Democratic seats. Democrats barely held the House.[236]

New Right conservatives came to Washington with an ambitious social agenda, much of it aimed at undoing the work of the Supreme Court. Jesse Helms, the darling of the New Right, was one of several conservatives who sponsored constitutional amendments and legislation designed to control the Court and see *Roe* overturned. A year after the election, *Time*'s cover story was on Helms and the influence of the New Right.[237] Similarly, *Newsweek* reported that "[t]he anti-abortion bill is just part of a far-reaching 'social agenda' that conservatives are slowly beginning to press on Capitol Hill—from permitting prayer in public schools to eliminating all busing for school desegregation."[238]

What the New Right learned soon enough was that moving its social agenda forward was going to take more than ordinary electoral politics. True, Reagan sought to put the New Right's agenda on the back burner during his first term, concerned, as *Newsweek* explained, "that battles over social issues will endanger its [the administration's] top priority: the economic package of budget and tax cuts."[239] But changes the New Right wanted—in particular the overruling of *Roe v. Wade*—were embedded in constitutional law. Change here would require extraordinary effort, and it was not forthcoming. Proposals to amend the Constitution fell far short of the required two-thirds congressional vote.[240] James McClellan was the opinionated cofounder, along with Gary McDowell, of the Center for Judicial Studies and the editor of its pithy journal *Benchmark*. In its first issue, in 1984, he wrote that it "is a melancholy fact that, in spite of the campaign rhetoric and the Republican Party Platform of 1980, which held out hope of judicial reform, nearly all of the Supreme Court doctrines and decisions which brought us to our present state of affairs remain securely intact."[241]

THE ORIGINAL UNDERSTANDING

"[T]o institutionalize the Reagan revolution"

Conservatives came to understand that in order to overturn decisions they disfavored, they had to rewrite constitutional law itself.[242] Bruce Fein, a constitutional lawyer who left the Heritage Foundation to work at the Reagan Department of Justice, and who acknowledged the failures of political activism to achieve the New Right's agenda, said matter-of-factly, "The President has to do it by changing the jurisprudence."[243] The conservatives' response was "originalism," a jurisprudential theory that adopted founding-era under-

standings of constitutional meaning and was an obvious counter to the liberals' "living constitutionalism." Although judges had always looked to the
framers' intentions about the meaning of the Constitution as one part of
constitutional interpretation, conservatives turned it into a fetish: no other
method of interpretation was legitimate, they insisted. They also tailored the
approach to serve their ideological ends.

The 1983 decision in *City of Akron v. Akron Center for Reproductive
Health* highlighted the difficulty conservatives faced, an established body of
constitutional precedent they found distasteful. Akron's law required a
woman to receive counseling that "the unborn child is a human life from
the moment of conception" and then to wait twenty-four hours after the
counseling before the abortion could be obtained.[244] Despite the pleas of
conservatives that he ask the Court to overrule *Roe v. Wade* flat out, Reagan's
first Solicitor General, Rex Lee, argued instead that the Court could approve
Akron's law while remaining faithful to *Roe*.[245] Lee's position was that under *Roe*, the Court should strike only those abortion regulations that "unduly
burden" the woman's exercise of the right to choose.[246] Justice Sandra Day
O'Connor, Reagan's sole appointment to the Supreme Court thus far, wrote
a decision adopting Lee's "undue burden" standard.[247] In draft language she
did not publish, she went further, however, calling *Roe* "completely unprincipled."[248] O'Connor's opinion drew but two other votes; the majority struck
down Akron's law as inconsistent with *Roe*.

Rex Lee's approach to the *Akron* case reflected the doctrine of stare decisis, the belief that judges should adhere to prior precedents, overruling
them as rarely as possible. As Justice Powell explained for the six-person
majority in *City of Akron*, "[T]he Court repeatedly and consistently has accepted and applied the basic principle" of *Roe*, and thus the doctrine "demands respect in a society governed by the rule of law."[249] Stare decisis is said
to have less force with constitutional decisions because the only other way
around them is by constitutional amendment. Still, Supreme Court justices
traditionally have been reluctant to reverse established precedent. This had
been the difficulty for conservatives from the beginning of the Burger Court.
Explaining why the Nixon justices did not rapidly overturn Warren Court
decisions, Anthony Lewis said that "irony must be part of the answer. Conservative judges—meaning by that term those who are more cautious in
lawmaking—are naturally committed to the doctrine of *stare decisis*."[250]

Conservatives on the New Right were different; stare decisis held little
appeal when it came to their effort to reshape constitutional law. Indeed,
Rex Lee earned their undying enmity for failing to urge that *Roe* be overturned. Writing in *Benchmark*, McClellan fairly scalded Lee for his "slavish

submission to prior rulings," calling him a "judicial supremacist."[251] Judge
J. Clifford Wallace rued how judicial restraint gives "activist judges . . . a
certain advantage, because judges who deplore their innovations will nonetheless often retain, though rarely extend, them."[252] Charles Fried was chosen to succeed Rex Lee as Solicitor General. As *The Wall Street Journal*'s
Stephen Wermiel told it, Fried remained "acting" in the job until after he
filed a brief explicitly asking the Supreme Court to go all the way and overrule *Roe*.[253]

Conservative theorizing about how to change the nature of constitutional law took place in many venues, but one of the most significant was
the Federalist Society. Early in Reagan's term, young conservatives at Yale
Law School, looking for kindred spirits in a lonely environment, began an
organization whose influence was to spread deep into the administration
and well beyond.[254] Their accomplishment was of the first order. Soon the
Federalist Society had numerous law school and lawyer chapters throughout the country. The society served as a forum for conservative debate, an
employment network for conservative law students, and a gathering place
for conservative lawyers. At the University of Chicago Law School, its first
faculty adviser was Reagan's next appointee to the Supreme Court, professor (and later judge) Antonin Scalia.[255] By the beginning of Reagan's second
term, Federalist Society conservatives were firmly in control of new Attorney
General Edwin Meese's Department of Justice.[256] Steven Calabresi, one of
the Federalist Society founders, who went on to Justice after clerking for
Judge Robert Bork, bragged to *The New York Times* when Scalia was nominated to the Court: "more than half of the 153 Reagan-appointed Justice Department employees and all 12 assistant attorneys general are members of
or have spoken at Federalist Society events."[257]

At the July 1985 meeting of the American Bar Association, Attorney
General Ed Meese announced the conservatives' answer to the problem of
stare decisis: "a *jurisprudence of original intention*." Meese was critical of the
Court's existing jurisprudence, which he saw as unbounded and incoherent.
"Those who framed the Constitution chose their words carefully," Meese
said, and "[i]t is incumbent upon the Court to determine what that meaning was."[258] Meese sought to return to "first principles," explained one of his
deputies. Originalism was the antidote to the "almost exclusive attention to
the decisions of the Court, itself, as the meaning of the Constitution."[259]

The Attorney General's remarks set off a firestorm of public and scholarly protest, including some from the justices themselves.[260] Meese was
claiming more than that the framers' intentions should be one piece of evidence open to courts. He was saying that those intentions should be deter-

minative. Two justices, Brennan and Stevens, gave public speeches explicitly deriding Meese's proposal. Justice Brennan was brutally direct, calling the theory "arrogance cloaked as humility." It was "arrogant to pretend that from our vantage we can gauge accurately the intent of the framers on application of principle to specific, contemporary questions." The pleas for resort to original intentions, he chided, "must inevitably come from persons who have no familiarity with the historical record."[261] On the bench, Justice White, a persistent opponent of *Roe*, said much the same. "[T]his Court does not subscribe to the simplistic view that constitutional interpretation can possibly be limited to the 'plain meaning' of the Constitution's text or the subjective intention of the Framers."[262]

Now it was the left's turn to go after its counterparts on the right; in the academy, scholars churned out stacks of articles attacking the plausibility of applying a jurisprudence of original intention.[263] Who were the framers, precisely? Those who attended the Constitutional Convention expressed very clear views, but on a limited number of matters. The proceedings of the convention were secret, so the voters at state ratifying conventions were not privy to those intentions. The ratifiers were themselves a vast and motley bunch. How could one aggregate their many disparate intentions into any coherent whole? Worse yet, most of the ratifiers did not reveal their intentions on any question at all, let alone the questions of a contemporary society. The framers' world was vastly different from our own, so any attempt to speak for them on today's problems was dismissed as the wildest speculation. Scholars on the left even pointed out that it was not the framers' intention that we should rely on their intentions.[264]

All this was interesting (even if not entirely new), but most of it failed to engage with the real motivations behind Meese's challenge: to change fundamentally the country's understanding of what the Constitution meant.[265] In his speech, Meese made what might seem like a surprising statement: "The Court is what it was understood to be when the Constitution was framed—a political body. The judicial process is, at its most fundamental level, a *political* process." What he meant was that it provided the locus "wherein public deliberations occur over what constitutes the common good under the terms of a written constitution."[266] That was precisely the goal: to influence the public perception of the "common good" under the Constitution. Meese's spokesperson, Terry Eastland, told the press with pride, "No Administration has thought longer and more deeply about law since that of F.D.R., and we have thought more deeply than that Administration."[267] That made sense. Roosevelt's administration had fostered a revolution in constitutional law, and Ronald Reagan sought to do the same. Meese candidly explained that his goal was "to institutionalize the Reagan revolution so it can't be set aside no matter what happens in future presidential elections."[268] (Note the frequent usage of the word "revolution" among Reagan-era conservatives.)

Although conservative thinkers in and outside the Department of Justice obviously did not conjure up the idea of originalism out of thin air, the brand of originalism they promoted plainly was a doctrine of their own creation. For much of American history, courts had looked to both the Constitution's text and framing-era assumptions. Still, it was just one of many interpretive strategies they used, including also stare decisis and the idea of the evolutionary Constitution.[269]

Conservative thinkers shaped the concept of originalism to suit their particular purposes. For example, when critics pointed out the implausibility of ever discerning the original "intentions" of the framers, Meese's theory quickly morphed into that of original "meaning" or "understanding." The difference between the two incarnations of originalism was that whereas the first focused on the elusive specific intentions of the drafters of the Constitution itself, original meaning looked instead to the general views of the entire ratifying generation. These latter views were obviously far more malleable and amorphous than those expressed at the Constitutional Convention or held by those who attended it.[270]

Conservatives claimed that the jurisprudence of original understandings represented history's one true method of constitutional interpretation, but this claim ran into some difficulty, given the obvious participation of Federalist Society members in shaping the doctrine. The Justice Department's Office of Legal Policy prepared a "sourcebook" on originalism. It claimed that "during most of our nation's history" courts had utilized the technique. This historical pedigree was important to conservatives, because it gave credence to originalism. Even so, Federalist Society members could not resist taking credit for shaping the idea. Stephen Markman, who headed up judicial selection efforts in Reagan's second term and who had begun the Washington, D.C., lawyers' chapter of the Federalist Society, explained how the chapter helped "refine" Meese's original "nomenclature" "in a very useful way to original meaning jurisprudence."[271] Similarly, the society's executive director, Eugene Meyer, detailed how "these discussions and debates led not all but most conservatives to abandon original intent and adopt original meaning."[272] Ed Meese himself described a moment when Judge Antonin Scalia, participating in a seminar at the Department of Justice, "clarified the meaning of originalism."[273] There was no small tension between the claim that originalism had a long history and the gushing excitement

Federalist Society leaders expressed about their "refinement" of the doctrine: long-established and well-accepted methods of interpreting the Constitution do not need to be hashed out in skull sessions.[274]

Because this was a revolution, not an academic exercise, most originalists also refused to commit suicide by taking their theory to its logical conclusions. The growth of the federal government during and after the New Deal was hardly what the framers had in mind. Although some hard-core conservatives looked to roll back the New Deal decisions, even Bork simply conceded that was too far gone a point to bother fighting.[275] Similarly, most conservatives agreed that the Fourth Amendment's prohibition on searches and seizures would apply to electronic surveillance.[276] As the OLP sourcebook explained in something akin to Orwellian doublespeak, while the Constitution's "provisions may be applied to new circumstances as our society changes, its meaning remains fixed and timeless."[277]

No case illustrated the tensions within conservative originalism better than *Brown v. Board of Education*.[278] It was hard to argue that the framers of the Fourteenth Amendment had any intention to mandate school desegregation. Recall, for example, that the provision for desegregated schools had had to be removed from the Civil Rights Act of 1875, given broad opposition. Raoul Berger was the patron saint of originalism. He had begun skewering conservative causes with his Nixon-era books *Impeachment* and *Executive Privilege* and then turned his pen on liberal interpretations of the Fourteenth Amendment. During the Reagan years, he was the darling of conservatives.[279] But unlike those who had to make their theories palatable to the public, Berger could afford to take the logic of originalism where it led, to the unquestionable conclusion that *Brown* could not be justified on the basis of originalism.[280] Movement conservatives could not say this in public and hope to be taken seriously. Liberals bridled at what they viewed as blatant hypocrisy when it came to *Brown*: originalism somehow magically invalidated decisions conservatives wanted to eliminate, but not those they felt the need to keep. "[I]f the Court's ruling in *Roe* were illegitimate" on the basis of original intention, insisted Michael Perry, "the Court's ruling in *Brown* would have to be deemed illegitimate too."[281]

As one solution to the problem, conservatives seized on the idea of identifying the relevant level of "generality" at which to analyze the framing generation's understandings. This was a move that afforded considerable interpretive latitude.[282] Typically, conservatives argued that one should adopt the most specific level of generality. For example, while the framers might have expected a certain amount of liberty in general from government intrusion regarding intensely personal decisions, the correct question was whether they intended specifically to create a right to obtain an abortion. Thus the woman's right to choose was not protected.[283] But sometimes a broader level of generality was helpful and would be adopted. Robert Bork's reasoning about *Brown* was instructive. Bork conceded that the framers did not intend to bar segregated schools. But, he explained, they did want some measure of racial equality. The difficulty was that both elements of the framers' reasoning "could not be honored." "The Court's realistic choice, therefore, was either to abandon the quest for equality by allowing segregation or to forbid segregation in order to achieve equality." For Bork it was "obvious the Court must choose equality and prohibit state-imposed segregation."[284] Fine, replied Paul Brest. If the framers' general concern for equality trumps specific intentions, why not gender equality too—or protection for gays, for that matter?[285] No, answered Bork, because the framers were talking about race. "[E]quality on matters such as sexual orientation was not under discussion."[286] Critics claimed originalism suffered the same ill that conservatives accused living constitutionalism of: it allowed judges interpretive leeway to reach results they found felicitous.[287]

Still, for some originalists at least, the new originalism solved the problem of stare decisis by providing a justification for a jurist committed to "judicial restraint" to engage nonetheless in aggressive overruling.[288] Bork announced: "An originalist judge would have no problem whatever in overruling a nonoriginalist precedent because that precedent, by the very basis of his judicial philosophy, has no legitimacy."[289] Judge J. Clifford Wallace explained that constitutional decisions with "important effects" can be overruled if they "are clearly wrong." Decisions will "tend to be clearly wrong, for example, when judges, influenced by 'living Constitution' jurisprudence, spin twentieth-century sociology out of eighteenth- or nineteenth-century language."[290]

One final virtue of originalism was that it served to marry conservative constitutional theory with popular democratic governance. "The only way the inherently undemocratic power of judicial review can be reconciled with our republican form of government is by keeping it tied to the written Constitution," insisted Gary McDowell.[291] The idea was that judges should disturb democratic decisions as little as possible. The only permissible time was when the people who wrote the Constitution intended the democratic will to be trumped. In an unintentionally revealing comment, Robert Bork said that if originalism did not exist, "we would have to invent" it, because there was no other way to "confine courts to a defined sphere of authority."[292] If it was odd to hear conservatives advocating a brand of constitutionalism that required deferring to the popular will, electoral reality made sense of the move: Republicans were winning elections.

None of this is to say that conservative thinkers were being purely in-strumental. Ideas take hold and flower when they make sense of the world in which they are planted. Just as discussion of the living Constitution flowed logically from the pens of liberals in the 1970s, originalism fitted con-servative intuitions about the Constitution in the 1980s. As Stephen Mark-man pointed out, "The fact that it does happen to be consistent with our policy goals, that's great . . . but how does that gainsay the validity of the legal theory?"[293]

SELECTING JUDGES

"[P]eople of a certain judicial philosophy"

In addition to an interpretive theory, conservatives sought judges who would further their revolution on the bench. Few administrations have made as vigorous an effort as Ronald Reagan's to influence the courts through care-ful judicial selection.[294] This too ultimately proved insufficient to achieve conservative ends. By the middle of Reagan's presidency, the Supreme Court still was adhering (albeit narrowly) to the precedents conservatives wanted overturned.[295]

Conservatives believed that prior Republican administrations had not focused single-mindedly enough on getting judges on the bench who would further conservative values.[296] For this very reason, Reagan created the Of-fice of Legal Policy in the Department of Justice and charged it with vetting judicial candidates carefully.[297] Stephen Markman, who took over the OLP during Reagan's second term, bragged that the administration had "in place what is probably the most thorough and comprehensive system for recruiting and screening federal judicial candidates of any Administration ever."[298]

Soon enough, the administration was up to its ears in controversy over its "litmus test" for judicial nominees. Reports escaped from vetting sessions of judicial candidates being asked their views on matters like abortion and school prayer.[299] Groups such as the newly formed Center for Judicial Stud-ies, the Washington Legal Foundation, and Paul Weyrich's Free Congress Foundation claimed they were able to kill potential nominees whose views were not true enough.[300] A National Public Radio story on the issue carried a state court judge saying, "I guess most of us have accepted that we're not going to get these judgeships unless we're willing to commit to a particular position which we think would be improper."[301] The administration quickly denied the reports, maintaining that it was talking to the candidates only about their approach to law. Still, presidential counselor Fred Fielding did say the administration was looking for "people of a certain judicial philosophy."[302]

Judicial selection became even more of a priority during Reagan's second term. By 1984, the Republican platform had dropped all pretenses about the kind of judges Republicans wanted. After applauding "President Reagan's fine record of judicial appointments," the party offered its support "for the appointment of judges at all levels of the judiciary who respect traditional family values and the sanctity of innocent human life."[303] In 1986, the President hit the hustings for Republican Senate candidates, emphasizing the importance of the issue. "In many areas—abortion, crime, pornography, and others—progress will take place when the federal judiciary is made up of judges who believe in law and order and a strict interpretation of the Constitution."[304]

In the lower courts, the administration made great headway. By the end of Reagan's time in office, he had appointed roughly half the federal judiciary, an accomplishment not matched since Franklin Roosevelt.[305] Numerous conservatives moved from the academy to the court of appeals, including now-prominent judges such as Richard Posner, Frank Easterbook, Alex Kozinski, and J. Harvie Wilkinson. The oldest of these judges was Posner, at forty-two.[306] The court of appeals positions proved useful for vetting possible Supreme Court candidates.

By 1987, Reagan also had made two appointments to the Supreme Court, as well as replaced the Chief Justice. Sandra Day O'Connor had been an Arizona legislator and state court judge. She was "the most conservative woman we could find," said one Justice Department official (though some on the right worried that was not conservative enough).[307] Then Chief Justice Burger stepped down. In a clever move, Reagan appointed sitting associate justice William Rehnquist to succeed him and Judge Antonin Scalia to fill Rehnquist's slot. Though Scalia was a deeply conservative jurist, it was Rehnquist's appointment that drew the fire.[308] His jurisprudence was questioned, but a major issue was whether Rehnquist had been candid with the Senate when he was first put on the bench. A memorandum that Rehnquist authored while a clerk to Justice Robert Jackson had surfaced. It strongly urged against ordering school desegregation in *Brown v. Board of Education*. Rehnquist claimed at the time that he was summarizing Jackson's views at the justice's request, something that was subsequently called into question.[309] After what Utah Republican senator Orrin Hatch, himself a hero of the right, referred to as a "Rehnquisition," the Senate confirmed the new Chief Justice by a 65–33 vote. Scalia sailed through 98–0.[310]

Still, the law did not change to suit social conservatives. In addition to the familiar issues such as abortion and school prayer, affirmative action (or reverse discrimination; terminology enforced the divide) provided a new source of anger at the justices. *U.S. News & World Report* said, "What conservatives had been hoping would be a year of triumph at the Supreme Court turned out to be a time of frustration."[311] In March 1987, *The New York Times* reported that in all the big cases of the term, "William H. Rehnquist . . . has been in dissent" and that "William J. Brennan Jr., the Court's senior liberal," has been "in charge."[312] As late as September 1987, *Time* reported that "for all the talk of a Reagan Revolution . . . the social agenda of the New Right has remained largely unfulfilled."[313]

THE BORK FIGHT

"The constitutional referendum of 1987"

Justice Powell stepped down in June 1987, and Ronald Reagan nominated Robert Bork to be an associate justice of the Supreme Court. "All at once," wrote *Time* magazine, "the political passions of three decades seemed to converge on a single empty chair."[314] This was the moment conservatives had been dreaming about and liberals had been dreading.[315]

Powell's decision to resign was momentous; in many of the areas that concerned social conservatives, including the death penalty, the Supreme Court was split 5–4, and Powell frequently had been the deciding vote.[316] In at least two of the recent affirmative action cases, Powell's vote had also decided which way the case came out (layoffs were not acceptable under affirmative action plans; promotions were).[317] In *Thornburgh v. American College of Obstetricians and Gynecologists*, Charles Fried had done as conservatives hoped and asked the Court to overrule *Roe*. He had been turned aside, but this time Chief Justice Burger defected; the Court was now 5–4.[318] Unless Justice Scalia shocked everyone by voting in favor of *Roe*, Powell was the fifth vote on abortion too. The *Thornburgh* decision, Republican senator Gordon Humphrey said, "demonstrates once again how much is riding on the next appointment to the Supreme Court."[319]

The nomination of Robert Bork gave the country a stark choice. Introducing him to the nation, Ronald Reagan said Judge Bork was "widely regarded as the most prominent and intellectually powerful advocate of judicial restraint."[320] Democratic senator Edward Kennedy of Massachusetts had quite a different view. He immediately took to the floor to denounce the nomination. "Robert Bork's America," Kennedy declared, "is a land in which women would be forced into back-alley abortions, blacks would sit at segregated lunch counters, rogue police could break down citizens' doors in midnight raids," and so on. Later Kennedy explained this was part of a "freeze" strategy: "The statement had to be stark and direct so as to sound the alarm and hold people in their places until we could get material together." [321]

James Reston of *The New York Times* urged Democrats not to follow Kennedy down this "stormy path." It was too late. Liberal civil rights groups had been preparing for the day for some time. After all, as Reston conceded, if Bork were confirmed, he "might well cast the decisive vote against abortion, affirmative action and church-state issues." [322]

Conservatives, on the other hand, were exultant. Jerry Falwell declared, "We are standing on the edge of history." [323] Dan Popeo, the head of the Washington Legal Foundation, said there was the "opportunity now to roll back thirty years of social and political activism by the Supreme Court." [324] "The nomination," declared Patrick McGuigan of Weyrich's Free Congress Foundation, "has the potential not to institutionalize Reaganism, but to institutionalize the shift in political gravity—to the right." [325]

The White House moved quickly to put a damper on this sort of talk. Its strategy was to stress Bork's qualifications for the job and to play down his ideology. The White House sought to portray Bork as a moderate. It prepared a briefing book explaining that "Judge Bork's appointment would not change the balance of the Court." One conservative staffer working on the nomination exploded, "If he wouldn't change the balance of the Court, why the hell are we nominating him?" [326] Bruce Fein, echoing conservative discontent, said the strategy was "counterproductive": "[I]n the long run jurisprudence won't change unless the President says . . . we wanted to change the Supreme Court, and Bork represents the kind of judge who will correct the errors the court has made in the past." [327] Conservatives were also angry that the White House seemed to take the summer off on the nomination, not gearing up for a fight until the fall. [328]

On the liberal side, a battle plan had been in place long before the nomination occurred. Liberals formed a huge coalition of opposition groups, operating closely under a joint umbrella. Their effort, organization, and discipline were extraordinary. They ran focus groups and conducted a poll to see which issues resonated with the public. [329] Senator Joseph Biden of Delaware was the chair of the Judiciary Committee. (He was also a presidential candidate, though he withdrew during the hearings when it emerged that he was borrowing some of his speech material without attribution.) The year before, he had said that if Bork were nominated, "I'd have to vote for him, and if the groups tear me apart, that's the medicine I'll have to take." [330] Instead, he joined Senator Kennedy in leading the Senate fight against the nomination.

It was clear early on that the battle would be over Bork's "philosophy." A *Wall Street Journal* editorial began: "Judge Robert Bork is *the* most qualified American alive to serve on the Supreme Court."[331] The left did not demur. No "smoking guns or skeletons" would play a role. "It's going to come down to philosophy," said Nan Aron, of the Alliance for Justice, one of the leading opposition organizations. Senator Gordon Humphrey agreed that it would be "all about philosophy, and everyone knows it."[332]

The issue that played a surprisingly little public role, though, was abortion. Everyone was well aware of what was at stake. Much of the early coverage emphasized the point, and Bork said senators told him the issue was at the forefront.[333] But each side's strategy mandated that talk of abortion remain in the background—the White House's because it was staying away from ideology, and its opponents' because focus groups told them it was chancy ground.[334]

The main issues for the opposition were thus Bork's views on civil rights and "privacy." The latter was a reference to the Supreme Court's decision in *Griswold*, the Connecticut contraception case from which the right to abortion and much else followed.[335] Bork had challenged *Griswold* vigorously, yet opposition polling suggested high support for the notion that the Constitution embodied a right to privacy.[336] Although there was no mention of personal animosity on issues of race—if anything, quite the contrary—Bork's past positions on civil rights provided fertile ammunition.[337] In the 1960s, Bork had opposed imposing nondiscrimination rules on private businesses. (He had done so on libertarian grounds, as had the 1964 Republican nominee, Barry Goldwater.[338]) He had argued that *Bolling v. Sharpe*—the companion case to *Brown v. Board of Education* regarding the federal government as opposed to the states—could not be justified.[339] There was some logic to the position: the Equal Protection Clause applies to the states, not the federal government. Still, as a matter of practical appeal the argument was a complete nonstarter. Bork also attacked the reasoning of the case in which the Court struck down poll taxes.[340] Bork did not believe the Equal Protection Clause provided special scrutiny for gender classifications.[341] Coming out against the nominee, Biden said, "Everybody—the left, the right, and the middle, senators and press alike—say this has the potential of turning the clock back 30 years."[342]

Polls going into the hearings showed that those who were paying attention in the country at large (and many were not yet) were evenly divided.[343] Liberal groups decided they would not testify in person, so as to keep the focus on Bork's philosophy and off their (perhaps too liberal) agendas.[344] Suzanne Garment, an accomplished conservative author and spouse of Leonard

Garment, who had been Nixon's Special Counsel and who fought tirelessly for Bork, explained that this "self-effacing tactic left Bork as the undisputed center of the hearings."[345] For five grueling days Bork sat in front of the television cameras and answered at long length questions concerning his views regarding the Constitution and constitutional law.

During the course of the proceedings, it appeared to many that Bork experienced a "confirmation conversion." Senator Patrick Leahy of Vermont coined the phrase to refer to Bork's seeming willingness to back away from past positions to a more moderate stance.[346] Although there is considerable ambiguity in his words, Bork indicated, for example, that he would find greater protection for women under the Equal Protection Clause and support broader First Amendment rights than prior writings suggested.[347] He also promised senators he would adhere on the Court to what he told them in the hearings.[348] Liberals portrayed the changes as flip-flops and said he could not be trusted, while the apparent moderation of his views disgusted conservatives.[349]

By the end of the hearings Bork was finished, though he chose to fight the matter to a final Senate vote. Polls had turned against him in response to his testimony, media coverage, and the enormous campaign against him.[350] The decisive moment was the "earthquake of southern Democratic opposition" that emerged late on the Judiciary Committee and in the Senate.[351] The committee vote was 9–5 against.[352] The President made a last-minute forceful personal push for his candidate, but it could not turn the tide. Bork stayed in to make the case that the "process of confirming justices for our nation's highest court has been transformed in a way that should not and indeed must not be permitted to occur again."[353] The Senate vote was 58–42 against, a landmark of a negative vote.[354]

All sides agreed that the nomination had captivated the nation and engaged it in "perhaps the deepest exploration of fundamental constitutional issues ever to capture the public limelight."[355] Harvard law professor Laurence Tribe, who played a key role in opposition, called it "the constitutional referendum of 1987."[356] *The Wall Street Journal* rubbed its editorial hands together in anticipation at the outset: "We've been looking forward to a great constitutional debate."[357] Supporting his nominee in a weekly radio address, the President said, "During his confirmation hearings, Judge Bork had given us all a national lesson in our legal tradition and the importance of judicial restraint."[358] Many, such as Suzanne Garment, decried that "judges are not supposed to be chosen by popular election," serving only to underscore how public and engaging the proceedings had been.[359] "Wherever you go," observed Senator Robert Dole of Kansas, "and some of us go a lot of places, this is generally question number one or number two in any town meeting in America." [360]

After it was over, conservatives were eager to argue that the defeat was the result of a smear campaign with no broader meaning about the Constitution or the Supreme Court's jurisprudence. It is true that the fight against Robert Bork had not been pretty. At the start, *The Washington Post* labeled "wrong, wrong, *wrong*" liberal organizations' calls for "a mass mobilization": "This isn't a mud-pie contest." [361] By the end, the *Post*, which finally came down against Bork, said the campaign "did not resemble an argument so much as a lynching." [362] It goes to show, claimed *The Wall Street Journal*, that "a group of intellectual charlatans can win by peddling mendacity and deceit on a massive scale." [363]

On the other hand, many members of the media believed the fight had elicited the informed sentiments of the American people. National Public Radio's Nina Totenberg concluded that "the public seemed to support most of the Court's decisions in the areas of race and sex discrimination, free speech, privacy, and even abortion. [364] Ethan Bronner of *The Boston Globe* watched it all and afterward wrote a book that was extremely sensitive to Bork's ordeal. Nonetheless, he was unequivocal. When Bork argued that the Court had over the last generation "stretched the national charter beyond its capacities, stitching together new rights with random bits of constitutional cloth . . . the results of his nomination indicated that most Americans disagreed." [365] Linda Greenhouse said the nomination provided competing "visions of the Constitution" as part of a "national lesson on the Constitution in its bicentennial year." Her roundup focused on an answer Bork gave when asked if he agreed that when "a court adds to one person's constitutional rights, it subtracts from the rights of others." Bork said yes, "I think it's a matter of plain arithmetic." This "zero-sum" vision of the Constitution, Greenhouse concluded, was "sharply at variance with the vision put forward by Judge Bork's opponents." They "spoke of the Constitution in organic rather than arithmetical terms, as a system elastic enough so that adding to the rights of some did not necessarily diminish the rights of others." [366]

Given the extreme polarization of the Bork nomination, it might seem easy to write these conclusions off as the thoughts of the liberal media, but that would be a mistake. There was plenty of evidence that these reports captured the views of the broad electorate. [367] Polls conducted toward the end of the hearings showed a public unwilling to vote for a candidate who had criticized civil rights or the right to privacy. Conservative law professor Stephen Carter was to write critically about what confirmation hearings had become. Still, he believed, "the fundamental charge against Judge Bork—that the results that a Justice Bork might reach would not match the results that the American people would prefer—was true."[368]

The conservative South was key to the fate of the nomination, and here too Bork lost on his vision of the Constitution. Southern votes against Bork in the Senate had a lot to do with pleasing African-American constituencies, to be sure. As Louisiana Democrat J. Bennett Johnston explained to fellow Democrat and Alabama senator Richard Shelby, "[Y]ou're not going to turn your back on 91 percent of the black voters in Alabama who got you here." Still, "the expected groundswell of support from southern conservatives wasn't taking shape."[369] To the contrary, an *Atlanta Journal* and *Constitution* poll showed the South firmly against Bork.[370] Lloyd Bentsen, a Democratic senator from Texas, worried aloud "that you could turn back the clock on civil rights. We've already fought those fights, and we're happy with the outcome."[371]

Leading conservatives agreed fundamentally with liberals that Bork lost because his arguments of legal theory failed to calm concerns about what his decisions would look like for the American people. "Bork" became a verb, as in to "be borked." Terry Eastland defined the phrase in the *Legal Times*: "Your opponents attack you on a matter involving law and criticize you in terms of policy outcomes. You defend yourself by discussing the issue in legal jargon." Eastland concluded that when it came to civil rights, "he [Bork] was never able to overcome what had been stated in laymen's language."[372] This was precisely the reason *The Washington Post* ultimately came down against him: because of his perceived detachment from the costs legal decisions can impose on real people. In a remarkable moment in the hearings, Bork was thrown the softball question why he wanted a seat on the Court. He replied, "I think it would be an intellectual feast just to be there."[373] But being a justice involved more than resolving legal questions in theoretical terms, the *Post* argued. He never showed that "he had a feeling for justice, not just for the law. They are not always the same."[374]

Though conservatives were deeply troubled about the campaign against their man, some conceded that their opponents understood exactly what was at stake. Patrick McGuigan, a conservative Christian journalist–cum–political operative, was deeply committed to Bork and devoted countless hours of his time to the struggle. Afterward he cowrote a passionate account of the fight. Although Bork opponents "frequently lied in their advertising," he said, they "largely understood exactly what his nomination meant for the liberal jurisprudence and politics which dominated America."[375] Bork was "borked" in advertisements, he said, "not because he was misperceived by his opponents, but because he was *correctly* perceived."[376]

THE NEXT JUSTICE

"I am searching . . . for the correct balance"

It took the administration two more tries, but it ultimately filled Justice Powell's seat. Justice Blackmun, who had been Nixon's third try for the Fortas seat, sent the nominee a note welcoming the newest member of the "old number three" club.[377] It was clear from the confirmation hearings that the country could count on Anthony Kennedy to be a very different sort of judge from Robert Bork.

After Bork's nomination failed, the administration was considering Kennedy and Douglas Ginsburg. Both were judges on the federal court of appeals. Conservatives were nervous about Kennedy, especially on the issue of gay rights. Ginsburg got the nod. Shortly thereafter, information came out about Ginsburg that made conservatives nervous about whether their choice was sufficiently firmly behind the cause. When it also emerged through the reporting of National Public Radio's Nina Totenberg that Ginsburg had used marijuana as a law professor, the nomination was yanked.[378]

Given his shot in the nominee's chair, Anthony Kennedy quickly established that he had an approach to judging quite distinct from Bork's. A judge should act "within the context of settled legal principles," he said. Still, "[c]ompassion, warmth, sensitivity, and an unyielding insistence on justice are the attributes of every good judge."[379] As for how he would interpret the Constitution, Kennedy said he did not have "an over-arching theory, a unitary theory of interpretation." Like "many judges are," he said, "I am searching . . . for the correct balance."[380] Questioned about his past membership in exclusive clubs, Kennedy replied, "Over the years, I have tried to become more sensitive to the existence of subtle barriers to the advancement of women, and of minorities, in society. And this was an issue on which I was continuing to educate myself."[381]

Kennedy's ideas about the framers' intent, while not unique, stood in stark contrast with Bork's originalism. Kennedy thought the framing intentions should be a "starting point," a "guide."[382] "The doctrine of original intent does not tell us how to decide a case."[383] He believed that as time went on, those intentions became "more pure, more clarified."[384] "I think 200 years of history gives us a magnificent perspective on what the framers did intend."[385] In other words, judges should understand the framers through present-day eyes, rather than vice versa.

Calming liberal concerns, Kennedy said his idea of liberty was "spacious." Immediately he was asked about the idea of unenumerated rights, the very sort of thing Bork so stridently criticized. Kennedy declared it is "central to our American tradition" that "there is a zone of liberty, a zone of protection, a line that is drawn where the individual can tell the Government: Beyond this line you may not go."[386]

Kennedy's apparent moderation was quickly deemed acceptable. JUDGE KENNEDY: TILTING RIGHT BUT NOT FAR, headlined *The New York Times*.[387] "Nominee Kennedy is a Conservative, but Not like Bork," concluded *The Wall Street Journal*.[388] Perhaps it was just fatigue. But Kennedy's search for "balance" seemed to be what the country wanted in a replacement for its swing justice, Lewis Powell. The Senate quickly confirmed him by a vote of 97–0.[389]

The failure of the Bork nomination presented a stark question, one that had been brewing ever since the New Deal: What exactly did it mean to live under the Constitution?

In retrospect, it is difficult to read the 1937 Court fight and its aftermath as anything but public approval of the Supreme Court's role in interpreting the Constitution. Yet the word "interpreting" hardly begins to capture the extent to which the Court appeared to be changing the Constitution's meaning during the 1970s and 1980s, often in fundamental ways. In the decades since 1937, the Court had dramatically expanded constitutional liberties, to a degree that even the citizens of 1937, who supported the Court largely on an argument about the importance of this role, would have viewed with wonder. The struggle over methods of interpretation that culminated in the Bork confirmation hearings was surely a function of intense ideological disagreement. But it also reflected understandable anxiety over how constitutional meaning could change so much and still be regarded as an "interpretation" of *the Constitution*.

Still, if anything was true, it was that the Court's interpretations of constitutional meaning swam comfortably in the channels of changing social mores and met with broad approval from the American people. When they did not, the Court backtracked or adjusted. Intellectuals struggled mightily over how to justify this process of constitutional change, to square it up with the common understanding of the Constitution as a foundational document. But the American people did not.

IO

ACTIVISM

"[T]he court reflects what people are thinking"

The Supreme Court that Chief Justice William Hubbs Rehnquist presided over between 1986 and 2005 regularly was described by its critics as one of the most "activist" in history, even if they could not quite agree on what the word meant. Reviving notions of constitutional federalism, Rehnquist's Court struck down an unprecedented number of congressional laws. It denied, and then recognized, the fundamental rights of homosexuals.[1] It dramatically altered the scope of a woman's right to choose to have an abortion.[2] After a long silence, it sanctioned affirmative action in university admissions.[3] And in a move without parallel in the Court's long history, the justices effectively awarded the presidency to Republican George W. Bush, resolving the contested election of 2000.[4] Much of this occurred by votes of 5–4.[5]

For the first time ever, the Supreme Court became the target of sustained criticism from the political left and right simultaneously. Critics on both sides of the ideological divide challenged the justices' assertiveness and decried "judicial supremacy." In 2005, conservative pundit Mark Levin made it to the bestseller list with his polemic *Men in Black*. His first chapter was entitled "Radicals in Robes," the very same title chosen by the left's Cass Sunstein for his attack on the conservative direction of the Court.[6] Two other authors—one on the left and one on the right—published savage treatments of the Court identically named *Courting Disaster*.[7] Interest groups on both the left and the right mobilized over the Court, their primary mission being to spring into action the instant any vacancy was announced. The Chief Justice

observed in his 2004 report on the state of the judiciary that "[a]lthough arguments over the federal Judiciary have always been with us, criticism of judges,
including charges of activism, have in the eyes of some taken on a new turn
in recent years." Rehnquist was referring to congressional attempts to direct
the Court's jurisdiction, to appoint monitors of the judiciary, and threats even
to impeach justices.[8]

Yet what truly distinguished this period of attacks on the Supreme Court
from all others was neither the vehemence nor the unanimity of critics: it was
the equanimity of the public at large. As detractors hurled epithets at the justices and panted over the next open seat on the Court, the American people
yawned. The Supreme Court's approval rating was typically high, regularly
topping that of the other institutions of government. How to explain this dis-
juncture between the Court's harsh critics and the public at large?

American politics at the turn of the twenty-first century had been hi-
jacked by intense partisans, whose attacks on the justices revealed the
Court as centrist and its antagonists as the real activists. Polls showed that
the issues that stirred criticism of the Court ranked low on the list of what
mattered most to the American people. Supreme Court decisions with which
activists disagreed, using them as wedge issues or to motivate their partisan
bases, consistently found majority support. Quite naturally, some portion of
the public disliked any individual decision. Still, the people at large regularly
signaled their broad approval of what the Court was doing. Partisan campaigns against the Court excited the American people no more than most of
the political maneuvering of the period.

The Rehnquist era ended on an ironic note, as frustrated critics began to
express anger with the justices precisely because they were deciding cases in
a way that mirrored public opinion. This was said to deprive the people of the
opportunity to settle their disagreements on their own. The story of judicial
review had come full circle. Apparently, now the Supreme Court was usurping
democracy not by defying the people but by giving them what they wanted.

THE FIRST REHNQUIST COURT: PULLING BACK FROM THE BRINK

"[A] moment of great institutional danger"

Over its roughly twenty-year history, the Rehnquist Court revealed three distinct personalities. The first Rehnquist Court ran from the appointment of
the Chief Justice until roughly the end of the Court's 1992 term.[9] Membership
on the Court changed dramatically during these early years, as four new justices took the bench.[10] Its docket reflected a preoccupation with "social issues,

such as abortion (and in particular whether *Roe v. Wade* would be overruled) . . . affirmative action, and government speech on religious topics (such as school prayer and crèches in city hall)."[11] Despite intense pressure from activists on the right, on all these issues the first Rehnquist Court showed a surprising moderation. Centrist justices cared more about protecting the integrity of the institution than giving in to the wishes of political operatives.[12]

Republican presidents having made a crucial number of appointments, people expected conservatives to prevail on a broad range of social issues. George H. W. Bush, caught between pressure from his right wing and a Democratic Senate, chose David Souter for the Court when William Brennan retired. Little was known about Souter, a former New Hampshire attorney general and a justice of that state's high court. The media christened him the "stealth" nominee.[13] Then Bush replaced Thurgood Marshall with Clarence Thomas, the conservative former head of the Equal Opportunity Employment Commission and a federal court judge.[14] The assumption was that Souter and Thomas would join the Chief Justice and Justices Scalia, O'Connor, and Kennedy to form a solid conservative majority.[15] *Los Angeles Times* Supreme Court correspondent David Savage published *Turning Right*, an account that reflected widespread perceptions of the Court's movement during this early period.[16]

Yet it was James F. Simon's 1995 chronicle *The Center Holds* that captured what actually came to pass. "This is the story of a conservative judicial revolution that failed," Simon wrote.[17] As he explained, "[T]he center held largely because liberal justices were able to attract support from their more moderate brethren who refused to join the ideologically committed conservatives on the right wing of the Court."[18] Repeatedly, centrist justices stepped back from the brink, at least in part out of concern for the Court's own reputation and authority.[19]

The first Rehnquist Court sat during a time of great political volatility. Bill Clinton won the White House in 1992, defeating an incumbent Republican who had enjoyed astonishing approval ratings only a year earlier.[20] Then, in 1994, the Republicans made a midterm showing of strength that was nothing short of remarkable. Running on representative (and soon to be House Speaker) Newt Gingrich's "Contract with America," Republicans swept control of the Congress for the first time in forty years.[21] Facing some of the country's most contentious issues, the justices in the middle of the Court proved to be remarkably politically astute, as they consistently refused to reach the outcomes urged on them by extremists.

The Court moved to the right on affirmative action, but it did so in a cautious and equivocating way, rejecting calls to eliminate the practice entirely.

Under the Supreme Court's tiered analysis for equal protection cases, laws that discriminate against racial minorities are held to a "strict scrutiny" standard, which invariably leads to their demise. However, the Court had wavered over whether to subject affirmative action's "benign" discrimination to such a stringent test. In its 1995 decision in *Adarand v. Pena*, the Court held that congressional laws adopting affirmative action programs would indeed receive strict scrutiny.[22] Still, Justice O'Connor, who wrote for the majority, took pains to "dispel the notion that strict scrutiny is 'strict in theory but fatal in fact,'" stating: "When race-based action is necessary to further a compelling interest, such action is within constitutional constraints. . . ."[23] In other words, some affirmative action might survive. The far right of the Court—Justices Thomas and Scalia—made a point of saying that government classifications based on race are never permissible.[24]

Adarand tossed the problem of affirmative action right back in politicians' laps. Reporting on the decision, *The New York Times*'s Linda Greenhouse noted: "The Court could have made politicians' lives easier by adopting" the hard-line approach of Scalia and Thomas, and "simply barring racial preferences as unconstitutional." "But," she observed, "the decision . . . did not offer that kind of political cover."[25]

Political turmoil in the aftermath of *Adarand* revealed the justices' wisdom in not unequivocally resolving such a hot potato of an issue. In the years leading up to the decision, race-baiting and playing to white anger had been a successful Republican wedge strategy, peeling lower- and middle-class voters from their traditional Democratic home.[26] Bill Clinton tried to meet the issue head-on, with limited success. Running for President in 1992, he accused Republicans of the "old scam" of scaring the "living daylights" out of lower-class voters, so they will stop asking, "Why have you let all of our incomes go down for the last 10 years?"[27] Following the 1994 midterm elections, neoconservative commentator and strategist William Kristol crowed that affirmative action is "a winner for us any way you look at it."[28] Reeling from the Democrats' loss in that election, even Clinton appeared to back down, setting up a task force to examine the government's affirmative action policies. "We shouldn't be defending things we can't defend."[29]

Yet *Adarand* left the Republican Party in complete disarray on an issue that had become radioactive. The rapid immigration of minority groups whose partisan leanings were uncertain—particularly Latinos—complicated the political calculation. Following *Adarand*, Republican presidential candidate and senator Phil Gramm introduced a bill ending affirmative action in certain contracting programs. In the interim Bill Clinton, with the work of his task force in hand, proposed that the nation reaffirm its commitment to affirmative action programs. He adopted the slogan "Mend it, but don't end it."[30] In a sharp rebuff to the Gramm bill, the Republican Senate voted 84–13 for a Democratic alternative that reflected the Clinton administration's more liberal interpretation of *Adarand*.[31] *The Washington Post* reported that Republicans "have found that the issue is more divisive within their party than some had initially believed."[32] In 1996, the party's nominee for the presidency, Bob Dole, introduced a measure to end all federal government affirmative action. As the bill stalled in Congress, Dole's cosponsor expressed frustration that the Republican leadership "has been spinning around like a weather vane in a hurricane on this issue."[33] *The Atlanta Journal* and *Constitution* published a story entitled "Divided They Stand . . . GOP Pulls Back on Delicate Issue," and the *Los Angeles Times* quoted an unnamed civil rights lobbyist attributing Republican hesitation to "election-year jitters and the support moderate Republicans have voiced for affirmative action."[34] Republican House Speaker Newt Gingrich vacillated repeatedly on the issue, at one moment promising "an all out effort to end affirmative racism" in America and at another insisting the party should hold off till it had something to offer in its place.[35]

Another issue on which the justices resisted pressure from the far right was religion. In particular, despite urgent pleas to bend on the issue, the Court continued to hold the line against prayer in schools. *Lee v. Weisman* asked the Court to approve a prayer at graduation exercises.[36] Justice Kennedy had voted with his conservative colleagues in cases involving religious displays on public grounds, but he balked when faced with the ever-contentious issue of school prayer.[37] In *Lee*, Kennedy joined liberals in refusing to uphold the practice, authoring the 5–4 decision himself. His opinion relied heavily on the "coercion" felt by students who could not easily skip the event.[38]

Kennedy's position on school prayer proved politically prudent. Since the Court's 1960s ban on the practice, polls had showed consistent support for school prayer and even for a constitutional amendment permitting it.[39] Yet appearances were a little deceiving. Religious denominations regularly split on the issue in their briefs before the Court.[40] The leaders of mainstream denominations, not always representing the views of their constituents, typically urged the Congress to maintain the separation between church and state when it came to school prayer.[41] The public rated school prayer low on the scale of things it cared about. Polls in recent years had strongly favored a moment of silence over uttered prayer of any sort.[42]

Ultimately, as with affirmative action, Republican politicians backed away on the issue of school prayer. When Speaker Gingrich suggested raising a school prayer amendment shortly after the 1994 elections, Republican governors went bananas. "If we don't deal with economic issues," replied Michigan's

Republican governor John Engler, "we'll need more than prayer to solve our problems."[43] New Jersey's Christine Todd Whitman echoed Engler, lecturing that "what got everyone elected this year was fiscal issues."[44] On the merits, Massachusetts's William Weld put it bluntly: "A moment of silence, fine. Mandatory prayer, no."[45] Gingrich quickly recanted: "I am opposed to any organized school prayer. I am opposed to the teacher having a prayer. I am opposed to an official prayer."[46]

Nothing, though, demonstrated the middle justices' political sensitivity quite so well as the common ground they forged on the issue of abortion. In 1989, a Republican administration once again asked the Court to overrule *Roe v. Wade*. The case was *Webster v. Reproductive Health Services*.[47] The fight over the Bork nomination had demonstrated the perils of attacking the "right to privacy." Thus the *Webster* oral argument offered the amusing spectacle of Charles Fried, who was no longer Solicitor General but who had been called back into service by the first Bush administration to argue this one case, trying hard to defend the Court's sexual privacy decisions while urging the Court to overturn those dealing with abortion. "[W]e are not asking the Court to unravel the fabric of unenumerated and privacy rights which this court has woven in cases like . . . *Griswold*. Rather," said Fried, "we are asking the Court to pull this one thread. . . . [A]bortion is different." (Opposing counsel quickly disagreed: "I think the Solicitor General's submission is somewhat disingenuous when he suggests to this court that he does not seek to unravel the whole cloth of procreational rights, but merely to pull a thread. It has always been my personal experience that when I pull a thread, my sleeve falls off.")[48]

The Bush administration fell short in its attempt to overrule *Roe*, but only narrowly. The Chief Justice, joined by Justices White, Scalia, and now Kennedy, deemed *Roe* "unsound in principle and unworkable in practice."[49] This time Sandra Day O'Connor stopped short of the brink. She adhered to the view that *Roe* should be watered down, that only those laws that posed an "undue burden" to the abortion choice should be struck down. But overturn outright she would not.[50]

The close call in *Webster* quickly educated the country about the political perils of threatening *Roe v. Wade*. *Time* magazine recounted the Chief Justice's reading of his *Webster* dissent. "Before he was through, it was clear that the country was about to be plunged into the most corrosive political struggle it has experienced since the debate over the Viet Nam war."[51] Even before *Webster*, abortion rights groups had begun organizing. On the eve of the case, they staged a huge march on Washington, D.C., involving hundreds of thousands.[52] Following the decision, which emphasized how narrow support on the Court was for retaining *Roe*, those groups mobilized rapidly. While pro-lifers sought ever more restrictive laws, pro-choice organizations like the National Organization for Women, Planned Parenthood, and the National Abortion Rights Action League saw their memberships skyrocket and their incomes increase two- or threefold.[53] The backlash against *Webster* was so intense that for the first time since 1980 the House of Representatives actually rejected a limit on abortion funding.[54] Then came the political repercussions: in two big governors' races in 1989—in Virginia and New Jersey—abortion was a decisive issue in the election victories of pro-choice candidates.[55]

It quickly became clear that like affirmative action, abortion was an issue for Republicans to avoid like the plague. Following the 1990 elections, founding neoconservative Irving Kristol (father of William Kristol) predicted that come the 1992 elections, "one [would] find very few Republicans who will have so firmly a negative posture toward abortion."[56] Lee Atwater, the cunning strategist and chair of the Republican National Committee, whose expertise had been manipulating wedge issues to elect Republican candidates, all of a sudden described the party as a "big tent," capable of accommodating diverse views, particularly on the issue of abortion.[57] During Justice Souter's confirmation hearings in August 1990, a *Time* poll showed that 59 percent of the country would oppose a justice who would overturn *Roe* while only 29 percent supported such a move.[58]

It was just at this moment that pro-choice advocates decided to force the conservative justices' hands. "In a calculated move to intensify the political debate on abortion," wrote one *New York Times* national political correspondent, pro-choice activists "made clear they were looking beyond the Supreme Court and trying to make the abortion policies of the Bush Administration an issue in the 1992 election."[59] They challenged a Pennsylvania law that imposed a variety of regulations on women seeking abortions, including a twenty-four-hour waiting period, forced counseling about the abortion choice, and a requirement to seek a spouse's consent.[60] All these would seem to have been impermissible under *Roe*.[61] The Planned Parenthood brief posed the stark question: "Has the Supreme Court overruled Roe v. Wade, holding that a woman's right to choose abortion is a fundamental right protected by the United States Constitution?"[62]

In *Planned Parenthood v. Casey*, the three justices in the center of the Court found a middle way. Four of their colleagues—the Chief Justice, Justice Scalia, Justice Thomas, and Justice White—made clear their readiness to overturn *Roe*.[63] The other two, Stevens and Blackmun, said they would preserve it.[64] But Justices Kennedy, O'Connor, and Souter coauthored an unusual joint opinion that split the difference, ostensibly reaffirming *Roe* yet modifying it substantially. Now only regulations that posed an "undue burden"—placed a "substantial obstacle" in the way of the abortion choice—would be invalidated.[65] Applying this test, the justices upheld most of the Pennsylvania law. Only the spousal notification provision fell.[66]

There was nothing subtle in the joint opinion's explanation of why it had taken the course that it had; the motivating force was the "legitimacy" of the Court. In a section of the joint opinion apparently written by Justice Souter, the plurality said that even if *Roe* had been erroneously decided (a point the opinion hardly conceded), it could be overruled only "at the cost of both profound and unnecessary damage to the Court's legitimacy, and to the Nation's commitment to the rule of law. It is therefore imperative to adhere to the essence of *Roe*. . . ."[67] *The New York Times* commented: "The message of the opinion was . . . straightforward: the pressure to overturn *Roe v. Wade* has brought the Court to a moment of great institutional danger."[68]

THE SECOND REHNQUIST COURT: CONSERVATIVE FEDERALISM REVOLUTION

"[A] band of radical judicial activists"

Shortly after the *Casey* decision, the Rehnquist Court took an apparent sharp turn to the right. The justices, by what quickly became a predictable 5–4 vote, launched a federalism "revolution," overturning laws enacted by a Democratic Congress with a frequency remarkable by any historical standard.[69] With judicial power moving in a bold new conservative direction for the first time since the Warren Court, liberals were quick to make accusations of activism.

The Supreme Court's 1995 decision in *United States v. Lopez*, overturning a federal law that imposed criminal penalties on anyone possessing a firearm in a school zone, signaled the start of the federalism revolution.[70] Although rulings as early as 1992 had given hints that a states' rights turn might be brewing, the 1995 *Lopez* decision was the first time since the New Deal "switch in time" that the justices had invalidated a law on the ground that Congress lacked power to adopt it.[71] The Court held that the challenged federal law was "a criminal statute that by its terms has nothing to do with 'commerce' or any sort of economic enterprise, however broadly one might define those terms."[72] The dissenting justices echoed the federal government in maintaining that the pervasive presence of guns in schools plainly diminished the ability to provide a sound educational environment, which would "substantially affect[]" interstate and foreign commerce in the long run.[73]

Justice Breyer attached a thirteen-page list of literature that supported this conclusion.[74] The Chief Justice, however, was unimpressed. If gun possession in schools could be defined as interstate commerce, anything could.[75]

The *Lopez* decision, said National Public Radio's Supreme Court correspondent Nina Totenberg on *All Things Considered*, "sent shock waves through the body politic and the legal community." "While some of this may sound like dry constitutional theory," she explained, "it has enormous real-life consequences, and in the halls of the nation's leading law schools, the constitutional law professors were literally screaming out lines from the opinion in amazement."[76]

Over the next six years, the Court extended the tentacles of its federalism jurisprudence in three distinct directions—immunizing states from lawsuits seeking money, holding that states need not assist federal enforcement efforts, and further limiting the commerce power—typically in 5–4 decisions.[77] Perhaps the most noteworthy of these decisions was *United States v. Morrison*, which struck down a provision of the Violence Against Women Act that permitted a federal lawsuit by any woman who was the victim of gender-motivated violence.[78]

For liberals, who had listened to conservatives preach the evils of judicial activism since the Warren Court, it was payback time. Never in the country's history had federal laws toppled more quickly at the Court's hands. *The Economist* told its readers that "a determined band of conservative justices has cast aside its cherished doctrine of judicial restraint in pursuit of another conservative treasure: states' rights."[79] Anthony Lewis deemed the Court "a band of radical judicial activists determined to impose on the Constitution their notion of a proper system of government." After recent decisions, he concluded, "we should hear no more conservative talk about original intent, strict construction or judicial restraint."[80]

Now, all of a sudden, editorial pages and law journals rang with accusations of judicial activism. The *Colorado Law Review* held a symposium on "Conservative Judicial Activism."[81] Cass Sunstein said it was "a remarkable period of right-wing judicial activism."[82] Linda Greenhouse found it difficult to reconcile "the majority's current activism" and "its frequently professed commitment to judicial restraint."[83] Two law professors penned an article poignantly titled in the vernacular, "Dissing Congress."[84]

To hear reaction from the left on the federalism decisions, one would have thought the sky was falling. The *Los Angeles Times*'s editorial page carried an opinion piece by a liberal law professor calling *Morrison* "another salvo" in the Supreme Court's "jihad against the federal government."[85] The *Los Angeles Times* quoted another law professor, Erwin Chemerinsky, who said of the sovereign immunity cases: "This is a radical change in American government."[86] *The New York Times*, critical of the Court from the start of the federalism push, claimed it "ignored decades of understanding" on Congress's power and fostered a "profound and divisive debate."[87]

CALLING THE 2000 PRESIDENTIAL ELECTION

"[B]etrayed the nation's trust in the rule of law"

Then, in the midst of its controversial federalism initiative, the Supreme Court did something that was by any measure extraordinary. In what will surely always stand as one of the most controversial episodes in its history, the Court stepped in and resolved the hotly contested presidential election of 2000, awarding the prize to the Republican George W. Bush.[88] Liberal discontent with the Court turned to frenzy. Leading constitutional scholars accused the justices of partisanship and questioned the Court's legitimacy in ways that under almost any other circumstances would have been deemed heretical.

The presidential election of 2000 was so close that the television networks reversed themselves not once but twice.[89] The outcome turned on who had won Florida's twenty-five electoral votes. Bush, the governor of Texas, appeared to have taken Florida, but by just under two thousand votes out of six million cast.[90] It was common to point out that the "margin of victory . . . was less than the margin of error."[91] Vice President Al Gore, Bush's challenger, telephoned his opponent and conceded the presidential election, only to call again and retract the concession. An annoyed George Bush told the Vice President that Jeb Bush (his younger brother and the governor of Florida) had assured him Bush had won the state. Gore reportedly replied, "Your younger brother is not the ultimate authority on this."[92] At that point, no one would have ventured to suggest that the Supreme Court of the United States was.

Though the election in Florida was subject to challenge for a variety of reasons, Gore decided to focus his efforts primarily on one, the "undercount" in some counties.[93] These were ballots on which no presidential vote was recorded. Several counties in Florida used a punch card voting system in which a stylus was used to displace a "chad," signaling for whom the vote was cast. Difficulties with the use of the stylus could cause a voter to displace the chad partially rather than knock it out entirely, leading the vote count machinery to fail to record any vote at all.[94]

Gore faced a race against the clock. Florida law divides election controversies into two stages, a "protest" stage that precedes the certification of final results and a "contest" stage that follows afterward.[95] Manual recounts in some counties showed Gore gaining on Bush, but those counts could not be completed by Florida's statutory November 14 date for certification.[96]

Gore went to court to obtain an extension of the certification period, which was denied by the lower courts. The Supreme Court of Florida, however, delayed certification until November 26, giving Gore more time. Bush appealed to the Supreme Court, which took the case and vacated the Florida court's decision on the ground that the justification for the extension was unclear. On remand, the Florida Supreme Court, this time giving more reasons, reaffirmed its extension to November 26.[97]

Because this was a presidential election, however, Gore faced pressure on the other side of the time line. Under federal law, any state with preset rules that certified its presidential electors by December 12 fell within a "safe harbor," so that Congress could under no circumstances reject those votes.[98] Then federal electors cast their votes on December 18, and Congress was to count the electoral votes on January 6. By extending the protest phase, Gore shortened the time for the contest proceedings, a fact that ultimately decided his case, and the election with it.[99]

After Bush had been certified the winner of the election on November 26, now by fewer than six hundred votes, Gore filed his contest. Florida's secretary of state, Katherine Harris, who by law was responsible for certifying the election results, had been the cochair of Bush's Florida campaign, and her actions were seen as highly partisan. In certifying the result, she declined to accept partial recounts from several counties that had not yet completed their manual recount. These votes would have narrowed Bush's lead even further.[100] A Florida state court judge rejected Gore's contest of the election results and his request that hand counts in certain counties be completed.[101]

The Florida Supreme Court, on December 8, issued a sweeping (but split) decision favoring Gore. Florida's high court ordered a manual count of all undervotes in the state. It also ordered the ballots in partial recounts to be added to Gore's total.[102] With Gore breathing down Bush's neck, manual recounting began across the state on Saturday, December 9. Then, in a dramatic move that paused the counting but not the ticking clock, the Supreme Court of the United States issued a stay and ordered oral arguments in the litigation for Monday, December 11.[103]

On Tuesday, December 12, the Supreme Court halted Florida's counting of the ballots and effectively named George Bush the President of the

United States. In a per curiam (unsigned) decision, the Court held that Florida's recount violated the Equal Protection Clause of the United States Constitution because there was no uniform standard on how undercount ballots were to be evaluated. The Florida Supreme Court had erred, the justices said, when it left each county free to count the various partially displaced or "dimpled" chads as it saw fit.[104] Although seven justices joined in this reasoning, two of those justices, Breyer and Souter, believed the Florida Supreme Court should have been permitted to identify the appropriate standard for determining the voter's intent and then let the recount proceed.[105] However, the "Federalism Five" voted over the sharp dissent of the other four justices that the recount must cease immediately.[106] Gore conceded the next day. "[W]hile I strongly disagree with the court's decision," he said, "I accept the finality of this outcome."[107]

To place the left's extraordinary reaction to the *Bush v. Gore* decision in context, almost no one in the entire legal academy, on either end of the political spectrum, was prepared to defend the Court's actual reasoning. With regard to the outcome mandated by the decision, "[w]ith a few notable exceptions, political orientation tended to be a very reliable predictor of whether one supported or opposed" the Court.[108] But how the Court justified its result—and, more important, whether there were *legal* grounds for the decision—was the subject of extensive commentary, almost uniformly negative.[109] Law professor Nelson Lund, who vigorously supported the Court in his article "The Unbearable Rightness of *Bush v. Gore*," conceded that "[t]he Court's legal analysis has hardly a friend in the world."[110]

It is unclear whether the Constitution and federal law anticipated any role for the Supreme Court in resolving a contest for President. The Constitution provides for the appointment of each state's presidential electors "in such Manner as the Legislature thereof may direct."[111] When the election of 1876 ended in remarkably similar confusion to that of 2000, Congress appointed an electoral commission to resolve contested issues, then voted on that resolution itself.[112] In the aftermath of the 1876 election, Congress enacted the Electoral Count Act—the legislation that allowed the "safe harbor" for a state to choose its electors—to address similar problems should they arise again.[113] The Electoral Count Act provides that any dispute over a state's electors is to be resolved by a vote of the House of Representatives and the Senate.[114] The two houses might differ over the proper outcome, of course. Indeed, this was a high probability in 2000, given the rest of the national election results.[115] If so, the tiebreaker set out in federal law would be which slate was certified by Florida's governor.[116] This too could have been messy had the Florida Supreme Court gotten into a tangle with the governor of Florida, Jeb Bush, about which results to certify.[117] Nonetheless, the electoral count legislation clearly relied on Congress and state officials to resolve contested presidential elections and eschewed any role for the Supreme Court. Indeed, its sponsor specifically noted that some had proposed the Supreme Court as a tiebreaker should the two houses of Congress disagree, "[b]ut there [is] a feeling in this country that we ought not to mingle our great judicial tribunal with political questions, and therefore this proposition has not met with much favor."[118]

The Supreme Court's equal protection ruling was certainly problematic.[119] The Court held that "[h]aving once granted the right to vote on equal terms, the State may not, by later arbitrary and disparate treatment, value one person's vote over that of another."[120] This holding was, at best, deeply ironic, given that the very need for the manual recount in Florida resulted from the counties' use of differing technologies for registering votes. Must states now use one single voting method, so that no disparities result from technological differences? As if to acknowledge the shaky ground of its ruling, the Court took the highly unusual step of essentially limiting the holding to the case before it: "Our consideration is limited to the present circumstances, for the problem of equal protection in election processes generally presents many complexities."[121]

Even if the Court's equal protection argument worked, it still seemed grossly inappropriate for the Supreme Court to end the recount rather than simply require a uniform vote count standard and remand to the Florida Supreme Court. According to the five justices in the majority, the December 12 safe harbor date had come, and the Florida Supreme Court previously had indicated the state's desire to fall within the safe harbor. Thus the recount simply should be ended.[122] The problem with this reasoning was that it was a question of state law over which the Florida Supreme Court ought to have had the last word. True, the Florida justices had previously identified the state's intention to fall within the safe harbor. But faced with choosing between finishing by December 12 and counting all the votes, the Florida court might well have chosen the latter. Though counting the undervotes manually by the necessary time would have been extremely difficult, it was not entirely impossible.[123] Michael McConnell, then a conservative law professor and soon thereafter a federal court judge, penned an opinion piece in *The Wall Street Journal* generally approving of the decision, but disagreeing with the remedy. The Court should not have ended the controversy, he said, but sent it back to the Florida state court to decide what to do.[124]

Most of those who defended the result in *Bush v. Gore*, primarily (but not exclusively) conservatives, did so not because the law supported the outcome but because of the perceived need to resolve the contested election quickly.[125] "Amid the chaos," wrote Charles Krauthammer in *Time*, "somebody had to play Daddy."[126] Or as the well-respected and conservative judge Richard Posner put it, "I do not see what the point would have been of risking precipitating a political and constitutional crisis merely in order to fuss with a statistical tie that—given the inherent subjectivity involved in hand counting spoiled ballots—can never be untied."[127] Needless to say, most on the left contested the idea that there was any crisis that needed resolving: constitutional mechanisms existed to resolve a contested election, and they were political, not judicial.[128]

The outrage that followed *Bush v. Gore* was unlike anything that had met the Court, since at least *Dred Scott*.[129] *USA Today*'s Joan Biskupic reported that the Court was receiving "thousands of letters from angry Americans," not a few of whom were sending in their voter registration cards, "suggesting that going to the polls in November was a waste of time." One letter said simply: "For shame!"[130] The Court was widely condemned for naked partisanship.[131] "[W]hen the U.S. Supreme Court entered the fray," wrote the editor in chief of *U.S. News & World Report* and self-proclaimed conservative Mortimer Zuckerman, "the expectation was that it would resolve the matter based on legal principles, not political partisanship. That, clearly, is not what happened."[132] Maureen Dowd parodied the Chief Justice, saying that "we still need to anoint Bush president" but "[w]e'll just have to work harder to hide the truth: that we are driven by all the same petty human emotions as everybody else in this town—ambition, partisanship, political debts and revenge."[133] Even conservative activist Michael Greve conceded that "[i]t would be silly to deny that partisan considerations in *Bush v. Gore* influenced . . . the justices' rulings."[134]

Worse yet (if worse were possible), some claimed that the justices had made their choice in order to assure the continued conservative ideology of the Supreme Court.[135] "[T]he court did more than choose a new president," continued *U.S. News*'s Zuckerman. "It gave a powerful push to perpetuate itself."[136] "The Supreme Court cannot be permitted to arrange for its own succession," lectured Yale law professor Bruce Ackerman, insisting that Congress filibuster any future Bush nominations to the Court.[137]

To the left, the justices had besmirched their very legitimacy. The usual disagreement over how cases were decided was nothing new. Even in their disagreement, the Court's critics were typically also its greatest supporters. This was something different entirely. Yale's Bruce Ackerman, an acclaimed scholar of the Court, was plaintiff. Having spent his "entire academic career" defending against the "slogan that law is just politics," he had to conclude that

Bush v. Gore was nothing but a partisan act.[138] The Court had "betrayed the nation's trust in the rule of law."[139] Supreme Court journalist and law professor Jeffrey Rosen published a scorching screed entitled "Disgrace: The Supreme Court Commits Suicide." The Court had "made it impossible for citizens of the United States to sustain any kind of faith in the rule of law. . . ."[140] At least 585 law professors signed an ad published in *The New York Times* on January 13, 2001, denying that the decision was law by any standard.[141] The widespread betting, said Cass Sunstein, was that the "Court will not have the same kind of national respect it had before."[142] Gary Kamiya, self-proclaimed liberal and executive editor of the online magazine *Salon*, penned a piece entitled "Supreme Court to Democracy: Drop Dead," in which he argued the Court had "squandered its most precious possession: its reputation."[143]

Claims of judicial activism now rained down on the Court like confetti at a ticker tape parade. Jeffrey Rosen observed that conservatives "have lectured us for more than 30 years about the activism of the Warren and Burger Courts. Those tinny and hypocritical lectures are now, thankfully, over."[144] The day after the *Bush v. Gore* decision, New York University law professor (and later Stanford dean) Larry Kramer's op-ed in *The New York Times* was titled "No Surprise, It's an Activist Court." Kramer argued that no one should have been caught off guard by the Court's action because "conservative judicial activism is the order of the day."[145] *Nation* columnist Calvin Trillin resorted to verse:

> *Though "activist" is what they've railed against*
> *These five Supremes said, "Just this once, let's try it.*
> *We know which candidate we want to win*
> *We'll simply find a way to justify it."*[146]

THE THIRD REHNQUIST COURT: THE COURT TURNS LEFT

"[A] shockingly progressive set of decisions from a supposedly conservative court"

With the second Rehnquist Court clearly favoring the right's agenda, liberals and conservatives settled comfortably once more into their roles of, respectively, challengers and defenders of the Court. No sooner had they done so than the Court appeared to drift back to the left.[147] The federalism revolution sputtered as challenges to federal legislation on states' rights grounds began to fail once again. Supposedly conservative justices took the extraordinary step of overturning some elements of the Republican President's war on terror.[148] Since the Warren Court, the one area in which the Supreme

Court had been reliably conservative was in cases involving criminal defendants, but even in these cases the Court provided surprisingly liberal rulings. To top it off, during the 2002 term, the Court handed down decisions favoring gay rights and affirmative action.[149] As the Court recessed in the summer of 2003, conservative activist Michael Greve authored an online critique in which he dubbed 2002 "The Term the Constitution Died."[150]

The right, apoplectic, had an explanation. The Court, it insisted, had been captured by "elite intellectual opinion."[151] Some conservatives called it the Greenhouse effect, suggesting the justices were overly sensitive to the media, in particular to *The New York Times'* prominent and left-leaning Supreme Court correspondent Linda Greenhouse.[152] Culprits were everywhere; in addition to the media, elite opinion was fostered in the law schools and especially by the ACLU.[153] Justices on the far right of the Court echoed the idea. Justice Thomas referred to affirmative action's supporters as the "cognoscenti."[154] Justice Scalia, dissenting and furious in the gay rights case *Lawrence v. Texas*, said the decision was "the product of a Court, which is the product of a law-profession culture, that has largely signed on to the so-called homosexual agenda."[155]

Certainly the headliner among right-wing critics was the Court's support for gay rights. From the perspective of conservatives, especially those on the religious right, the Supreme Court got the issue of gay rights correct in its 1986 decision in *Bowers v. Hardwick*. The case involved a couple of gay men caught in flagrante delicto by Georgia police. They were cited for violating a Georgia statute that made sodomy a crime, but the authorities declined to prosecute.[156] The men nonetheless challenged the law and their arrest as a violation of their constitutional rights. In *Bowers* the Court, by a 5–4 vote, held that there was no constitutional right to engage in "homosexual sodomy." Justice White conceded that the Constitution contained "unenumerated" rights but said any claim that the right to engage in "such conduct" is "'deeply rooted in this Nation's history and tradition' . . . is, at best, facetious."[157]

The *Bowers* decision came under harsh criticism from the left and the mainstream press. Justice Blackmun authored a passionate dissent in which he pointed out that the statute at issue criminalized sodomy for everyone. Why, then, the Court's "obsessive focus on homosexual activity?"[158] More important, the focus on sex rather than intimacy in the underlying relationship caused the Court to misunderstand the right at issue.[159] The media noted the particularly nasty and dismissive tone of Justice White's opinion, calling it "sarcastic" and "cold, almost mocking." The novelist John Rechy, a frequent contributor to the *Los Angeles Times* opinion section, observed: "Not since the Supreme Court declared in the Dred Scott case that slavery was legal and blacks were not citizens has there been a high court ruling as seeped in prejudice as this one."[160] The Court, said *The Christian Science Monitor*, "seemed to be making a *moral* judgment as much as a *legal* one."[161] Conservatives, though, felt vindicated. The Reverend Jerry Falwell applauded the decision for two reasons: for recognizing "the right of a state to determine its own moral guidelines" and for issuing "a clear statement that perverted moral behavior is not accepted practice in this country."[162]

Imagine conservative dismay when, seventeen years after *Bowers*, the Court reversed itself in *Lawrence v. Texas*.[163] Unlike the Georgia law, Texas's antisodomy law was aimed only at homosexuals. Justice Kennedy, whom conservatives had worried about at the time of his nomination as not being reliable enough on the gay rights issue, wrote for the majority. He told Justice Marshall's wife that the proper result was so obvious to him that he wrote the opinion over the weekend.[164] Not only was *Bowers* overruled, but Kennedy said it had been wrong "when it was decided."[165] "To say that the issue in *Bowers* was simply the right to engage in certain sexual conduct demeans the claim the individual put forward, just as it would demean a married couple were it to be said that marriage is just about the right to have sexual intercourse."[166] The only justice who switched a vote between the two decisions, Sandra Day O'Connor, wrote separately. She too thought the law unconstitutional, but on the ground of equality, not fundamental rights.[167]

Conservative reaction was strong and angry. The Reverend Pat Robertson, head of the Christian Coalition and 1992 presidential candidate, launched a twenty-one-day "prayer offensive." Pointing to the health conditions of some of the liberal justices, he asked his television audience to "pray for the retirement" of certain justices "so they can be replaced by conservatives."[168] Richard Lessner, senior analyst for the Family Research Council, lamented that "bigamy, incest, polygamy, bestiality, prostitution and anything else you can think of" would now be protected.[169] The president of the Christian Coalition of Alabama asked God to "have mercy on America," and a pro-family lobbyist in Sacramento described the decision as "an error of biblical proportions."[170]

The Court's affirmative action decisions, which came down the same week as *Lawrence*, further inflamed conservatives. "What an astounding week!" exclaimed Supreme Court journalist Dahlia Lithwick in *Slate*, commenting on what she called "a shockingly progressive set of decisions from a supposedly conservative court."[171] The Supreme Court had before it not one but two challenges to the affirmative action policies of the University of Michigan. One challenge was to a system used by the College of Literature, Science, and the Arts that awarded automatic points to applicants simply on the basis of race, ensuring the admission of some of these students who would not have been admitted without the points.[172] The other was an attack on the law school's policy of taking race into account as one factor in admissions decisions. Under this policy, no student was admitted who was not qualified, but qualifications based on exam scores and Law School Admission Test scores would not guarantee admission. Rather, the law school used a variety of "soft variables" to assure a diverse class.[173] One clear goal was to enroll enough minority students so as to ensure that there was a "critical mass" in each entering class. The questions in the cases were whether diversity was a sufficiently "compelling interest" to justify government support for affirmative action, and whether each school's program was "narrowly tailored" to achieve this end without violating the Constitution.

Justice O'Connor was the primary architect of a split decision in the affirmative action cases. The Court held that there was a "compelling interest in attaining a diverse student body."[174] The undergraduate program's point system was invalid because it automatically gave points for race and "does not provide for" "individualized consideration."[175] On the other hand, the law school's program was acceptable because it did not take race into account so mechanically, although it was undeniably a factor.[176] Only two justices, Clarence Thomas and Antonin Scalia, explicitly disapproved of ever using race as a factor.[177] The Chief Justice ducked the issue, and Justice Kennedy simply indicated his dislike of Michigan's particular system.[178]

The Court's decisions were open to interpretation, but no one doubted some measure of affirmative action had been approved. *The Washington Post* called it "a qualified but resounding endorsement of affirmative action in higher education," saying that the use of race was permissible as a "plus factor" so long as school officials were careful to evaluate applicants individually on the basis of their "ability to contribute to a diverse student body."[179] One academic expert concluded that the Supreme Court "gave a blinking yellow light to affirmative action programs in higher education."[180] Calling the decisions "a bit of legal fudge," *The Economist* said: "[A]ffirmative action will [now] go underground. It will be like one of those old clubs that had no rules banning Jews; they just didn't seem to have any."[181]

Conservatives were furious. "The real losers from this week's decisions," allowed *The Economist*, "have been those conservatives who had hoped that Mr. Bush would persuade the court to eliminate all racial preferences, not only in university admissions, but in every area of American life."[182] In *The Weekly Standard*, Peter Berkowitz wrote that the "diversity rationale for affirmative action—which traffics in stereotypes, rewards hypocrisy, and cultivates intellectual conformity—is difficult to swallow."[183] An op-ed piece in the *Los Angeles Times* condemned equating "one's 'culture' with one's skin color" and pointed out that in a recent California referendum barring affirmative action, 26 percent of blacks had opposed the practice.[184] The conservative pundit Michelle Malkin characterized what the Court said as "Go ahead and trample the 14th Amendment's equal protection clause. Just don't make it so damn obvious."[185]

It was not just the social issues on which the Court looked to be turning left; the federalism revolution was running out of steam as well. Despite prior rulings limiting Congress's ability to hold states liable for money damages in Fourteenth Amendment cases, the Supreme Court affirmed provisions of the Family and Medical Leave Act and the Americans with Disabilities Act that did just that. Chief Justice Rehnquist and Justice O'Connor broke ranks from their conservative colleagues in the first case, O'Connor alone in the second.[186] *The Christian Science Monitor* commented that the "federalism revolution . . . appears to have hit a speed bump named Sandra Day O'Connor."[187] Michael Greve was fatalistic, claiming that "among all the strands of federalism jurisprudence . . . it's hard to see that any of them have any bite any longer."[188] Then, in 2005, the Supreme Court in *Gonzales v. Raich* upheld the federal government's right to criminalize possession of a small amount of marijuana for medical purposes.[189] California, by referendum, had voted to legalize the use of "medical marijuana." Legal drugs versus federalism posed a tough choice for conservatives. In an amusing article entitled "Dude, Where's My Integrity?," *Slate*'s Dahlia Lithwick predicted the case would test the Court's "true love of federalism," and she was right: the decision seemed hard to square with the 1995 ruling regarding guns near schools.[190] Justices Scalia and Kennedy, both of whom had joined the majority in striking down the gun law in *Lopez*, jumped ship this time.[191] *The Wall Street Journal* said: "*Raich* would appear to end the *Lopez* line of reasoning, since the two decisions don't seem reconcilable."[192] UP IN SMOKE; STATES' RIGHTS was *The Economist's* headline retort.[193]

Then, remarkably, the Court, including many of its conservative members, began to call into question the executive branch's right to handle military matters as it wished. On September 11, 2001, Islamist terrorists flew airplanes into the Pentagon and the World Trade Center; it seemed as if the world had changed following that day. With what was, at least initially, overwhelming national support, the Bush administration launched a war on terror, complete with a conventional invasion of Afghanistan and far less conventional military and intelligence actions elsewhere.[194] (The administration's subsequent decision to unseat Iraq's ruler, Saddam Hussein, proved far more controversial.) As part of the war on terror, the government set up a supersecret detention facility at the naval base on Guantánamo Bay and held prisoners there and elsewhere, often incommunicado.[195] In 2004 and again in 2006, the Court heard high-profile cases involving U.S. citizens held by the federal government and detainees held in custody at Guantánamo Bay. Defying the adage that during times of war the courts are reluctant to challenge the executive branch, the justices ruled that the Constitution required far more judicial process than the Bush administration had been willing to give.[196] Pundits and politicians on the far right were furious that the Court had intruded into the clear domain of executive conduct of war and foreign relations. "Courts now second-guess the commander in chief in time of war and confer due process rights on foreign enemy combatants," complained Mark Levin.[197]

The Court even overcame its allergy to protecting the rights of criminal defendants and death row inmates. In 2000 the Court declined, in *Dickerson v. United States*, a clear chance to overrule *Miranda*.[198] The decision was a bit of a shock, not the least because Chief Justice Rehnquist, an unyielding opponent of the *Miranda* ruling, authored the opinion for the Court.[199] In two closely watched cases, the Court then invalidated state laws that imposed the death penalty on minors and the mentally retarded.[200] Conservative jurist (and failed Supreme Court nominee) Douglas Ginsburg was scathing with regard to the decision on executing the mentally retarded, calling it "as frankly a legislative decision as the Court has ever rendered" and concluding it "has nothing to do with the constitutionality of capital punishment and everything to do with the Justices' personal senses of decency."[201] Conservatives were particularly up in arms that in the death penalty cases, the justices relied on foreign precedents to support their interpretation of the Constitution— something they also had done in *Lawrence*.[202] Ronald Reagan's former Attorney General Ed Meese spoke up to say that "[p]erhaps nothing troubles [him] more than justices who invoke international law and the decisions of international tribunals in interpreting the Constitution. . . . [These] are not legitimate guideposts for interpreting the Constitution."[203]

Conservatives, who had been notably silent about judicial activism during the intervening years, now rose up once again to condemn it—volubly. Any sense of restraint was gone. James Dobson, founder of Focus on the Family, compared "men in white robes, the Ku Klux Klan" to the "black-robed men" of the Supreme Court. Mark Levin's *Men in Black* had a long laundry list condemning what "activist judges" had done, including permitting "racial discrimination in law school admissions" and holding that "morality alone is insufficient justification for legislation."[204] Phyllis Schlafly published a book-length rant at "activist judges" who "have been legislating a liberal agenda."[205] Pat Robertson's *Courting Disaster* raged about "a five-member majority of the nine judges" who "thumb their noses at tens of millions of American citizens and their elected representatives."[206] Conservative Republican representative James Sensenbrenner suggested appointing a federal inspector general "to field complaints and conduct investigations" into the judiciary.[207] The rhetoric coming from Republicans on Capitol Hill grew so heated that Justice O'Connor felt the need to invite some of them to lunch to discuss matters and try to cool tempers.[208]

THE EMPTY CONTENT OF JUDICIAL ACTIVISM

"[T]hey like judicial activism just fine when it advances their own agendas"

Criticizing the justices grew ever more complicated as the Supreme Court's rulings seemed to swing to and fro. Although the most frequent criticism heard during the Rehnquist Court was that of judicial activism, critics on the left and right could not agree on what the term even meant.[209] Each side believed that it hewed to a principled definition, and each accused the other of simply complaining about decisions it did not like. Shifting rulings caused much reshuffling of critics' positions. Claims of hypocrisy became the order of the day, as critics turned their attention from the Court and took to calling one another names.

For a time conservatives and liberals seemed to concur that judicial activism was "a relative willingness to exercise judicial power . . . in the form of striking down state or federal statutes as unconstitutional."[210] So they could agree that a more activist court was one striking down more laws. Lino Graglia, longtime conservative critic of the Court who was rejected for the federal court of appeals because of his extreme views, said: "By judicial activism I mean, quite simply and specifically, the practice by judges of disallowing policy choices by other governmental officials or institutions that the Constitution does not clearly prohibit."[211] Cass Sunstein, on the left, likewise identified a "purely descriptive" measure: "how often a court strikes down the actions of other parts of government, especially those of Congress."[212]

The Rehnquist Court's spate of federalism decisions striking down congressional laws in the name of state authority complicated the lives of conservatives who had complained about judicial activism in these terms. After all, they had been preaching "restraint" for the last forty years. Yet if activism was striking down laws, then the federalism revolution was activism on a grand scale. "[T]hey like judicial activism just fine when it advances their own agendas," Adam Cohen wrote in *The New York Times*, commenting on the federalism decisions.[213] Thomas Keck published a scholarly study entitled *The Most*

Activist Supreme Court in History. "[T]here is no realistic sense in which this Court can be described as a tribunal committed to restraint," he concluded.[214]

Looking the problem squarely in the face, a surprising number of conservatives suggested that giving up on the idea of restraint altogether might be best for the cause. In his 2003 *National Review* article "A Conservative View of the Court: Getting Beyond 'Activism' and 'Restraint,'" Michael Greve said that in their continued adherence to the language of restraint, conservatives had demonstrated "a dismaying lack of intellectual mobility. . . . Thanks perhaps to its past preoccupation with judicial 'restraint' and style, the GOP lacks the capacity to engage in any direct debate about constitutional issues."[215] Not only had the federalism cases demonstrated how activism could advance the conservative agenda, but decisions like *Lawrence* indicated it might be necessary to fight activist fire with activist fire. In an interview with Jeffrey Rosen, the journalist and law professor whose work on the Supreme Court and constitutional law frequently graced the pages of *The New Republic, The New Yorker,* and *The New York Times Magazine,* Greve was even more direct. "Judicial activism will have to be deployed. It's plain that the idea of judicial deference was a dead end for conservatives from the get-go."[216] Conservative public interest litigation groups sprang up with the precise purpose of urging a conservative brand of judicial activism. In 1989, Greve joined others in forming the Center for Individual Rights, whose goal was to "reimpose constitutional limits on a meddlesome, interest-group-infested government."[217] CIR, which had handpicked the Michigan affirmative action case plaintiffs, had the motto "Bringing lawsuits for a better America."[218] Clint Bolick and William "Chip" Mellor started the Institute for Justice in 1991. "We litigate to secure economic liberty, school choice, private property rights, freedom of speech, and other vital individual liberties, and to restore constitutional limits on the power of government."[219] A CIR funder called groups like these "'do-tanks,' rather than a think tank."[220]

Other conservatives simply adopted a new definition of judicial activism. Instead of measuring how many laws were struck down, what mattered was how the Court ruled: "[T]he Court should be considered activist only when it is striking down democratically enacted statutes *without a firm constitutional basis for doing so.*"[221] In other words, it wasn't activism if one was striking down the right laws. Reflecting the change in conservative perspective, Justice Scalia announced, "I am not a strict constructionist, and no one ought to be. . . ."[222] Angry that Vermont judges had required that state to recognize some version of gay partnership, conservative Asa Hutchinson complained on CNN's *Crossfire* about the "activist judiciary." He was then asked about one of the federalism decisions. "[J]ust because a court strikes down a law of Congress," he responded, "does not make it inherently bad. . . . It doesn't mean it's activist if they're interpreting the Constitution."[223]

The problem with this definition of judicial activism was that it was entirely contingent on one's point of view. What was true of conservatives was true of liberals as well, suggested Benjamin Wittes in *The Washington Post*. "There simply is no difference for them between their policy preferences and the requirements of the Constitution."[224] NPR's Nina Totenberg hit the nail precisely on the head following the Court's 2002 term, when she said, "[O]ne person's judicial activist is another person's faithful interpreter."[225] *The Daily Show*'s Jon Stewart, in his parody of politics entitled *America (the Book)*, explained that "the interpretation of the word 'interpretation' has itself evolved over the years, and now means 'the political beliefs of whoever appointed you.'"[226]

In the face of the Supreme Court's turn to the right, Jeffrey Rosen explained, those on the left had become "the partisans of judicial restraint."[227] Take Cass Sunstein, whose early work explained how judges could act to correct dysfunctions in the legislative process.[228] By 1996 he was urging "minimalism" upon the justices, a point he made repeatedly in his books *One Case at a Time* and *Radicals in Robes*.[229] Caution was needed because "[u]nelected judges . . . lack a strong democratic pedigree; they do not stand for reelection."[230] Liberal academic Mark Tushnet had always been wary of judicial power. Still, in 1999 he published *Taking the Constitution Away from the Courts*, urging the abandonment of judicial review altogether.[231] These were extreme examples, but the liberal community, long bullish on judicial review, now was spending a lot of time attacking the practice.[232] Greve was thickly sarcastic about how "the Rehnquist Court's federalism decisions led to the Left's startling discovery of judicial activism."[233]

The simple fact was that with the Supreme Court tacking left and right, it was difficult for either side to take a position on judicial activism and stick to it. In 2006, the Supreme Court came out of its federalism hibernation to strike another blow for states' rights, this time to invalidate the federal government's attempt to undermine Oregon's referendum-adopted law permitting assisted suicide.[234] Attorney General John Ashcroft had threatened to yank doctors' medical licenses for using federally controlled drugs in the procedure. *The Wall Street Journal* wryly noted how the Court's "liberal wing" had "suddenly discovered the Constitutional virtues of federalism." Still, the *Journal* was critical of the Bush administration for "abandoning for political purposes what ought to be its own federalism principles. . . . Results-oriented jurisprudence isn't any more admirable from the right than it is from the left."[235] "Federalism and the commerce clause bring out the hypocrite in all of us," the *Los Angeles Times* had observed in the medical marijuana case.[236] The same might have been said of judicial review altogether.

THE STRUGGLE OVER JUDICIAL APPOINTMENTS

"[T]he highest prize"

As if in tacit recognition that it was difficult to identify (and impossible to enforce) a principled position on judicial review, interest groups on the left and right decided simply to duke it out over who got a seat on the Court. In the face of his failed nomination to the Supreme Court, Robert Bork had predicted a struggle over "the courts and the Constitution." The Constitution, he said, is "the highest prize, and control of the selection of judges is the last step on the path to that prize."[237]

Unfortunately for the highly mobilized groups on the left and right, the appointments to the Court between 1987 and 1994 afforded little opportunity to make a difference. Describing stealth nominee David Souter, constitutional scholar Bruce Fein said, "The president has sacrificed philosophical purity and certitude for foreclosing any hostile opposition from special interest lobbying groups or the Senate Judiciary Committee."[238] President Clinton's nominations of Justices Ruth Bader Ginsburg and Stephen Breyer turned into lovefests, in large part because both were seen as moderate. Leading Republican Senate Judiciary Committee member Orrin Hatch joined Senator Edward Kennedy in pushing Breyer on the White House.[239] Only Clarence Thomas's nomination had the potential to be polarizing, and George H. W. Bush cleverly defeated that by playing the race card. While many on the left opposed Thomas, some African-Americans offered support. Having split interest groups on the left, Thomas was on his way to confirmation before it was almost derailed by allegations of sexual harassment.[240] While Thomas was confirmed by the lowest recorded vote ever, 52–48, the left ultimately failed to win the one fight that might have mattered.[241]

Appointments became an issue of singular focus for the left and right alike. Liberals came to believe, as Cass Sunstein said, that the battle for the Court was "one-sided" because the Democrats were not ideological enough about appointments. Clinton had nominated good judges, but "centrists" nonetheless.[242] In 2001, with the Bush administration in place, New York's Democratic senator Charles Schumer generated a lot of attention with an op-ed piece insisting that "[i]f the president uses ideology in deciding whom to nominate to the bench, the Senate . . . should do the same in deciding whom to confirm."[243] The right was similarly obsessed with ideological appointments. Warning that the left was but one vote short of "imposing a social revolution on America," Pat Buchanan said, "In court-nomination battles, Republicans have proven to be diffident warriors. Democrats are not."[244]

Over the intervening years, ideological interest groups multiplied, their purpose to spring into action the moment a Supreme Court vacancy was announced. These interest groups put elaborate quick reaction systems in place to influence the confirmation process. They built "war rooms" filled with computers and phones. Volunteers were ready to report at a moment's notice to begin sending out e-mail alerts and making phone calls. Money filled coffers in anticipation of media ad campaigns.[245]

When—remarkably—no vacancy occurred for more than ten years, mounting tensions over judicial appointments erupted in the great filibuster battle of 2004. The filibuster was a great weapon to wield in the Senate, which prided itself on open debate. In order to defeat a measure—any measure, including the appointment of judges—opposition senators could simply talk it to death until the other side conceded defeat.[246] Faced with the prospect of Republican domination of all branches of government, liberals had urged senators to use the filibuster to challenge the most extreme of the Bush appointees.[247] Ralph Neas, the head of People for the American Way, put it this way: "We have only three checks and balances—the filibuster, Sandra Day O'Connor and Anthony Kennedy."[248] Republicans, in turn, grew increasingly angry as Democrats used the filibuster to block some of Bush's nominees. Senate Majority Leader Bill Frist called the filibustering of judicial nominees "nothing less than a formula for tyranny by the minority."[249] In truth, both sides had been playing games with the lower courts for some time, at least on a limited basis. Frist's counterpart, Senate Minority Leader Harry Reid, shot back defensively: "Two hundred and three federal judges were approved—203. Ten were turned down."[250] Trent Lott, the former Majority Leader of the Senate, and John McCain conceded of Clinton's nominees: "We bottled them up in the Judiciary Committee, which was the functional equivalent of a filibuster."[251]

The struggle over the filibuster became a major media event, as Republicans threatened to exercise what came to be known as the nuclear option.[252] According to the Senate's usual practice, it took sixty votes to "invoke cloture" and overcome a filibuster. This the GOP could not muster. Instead, Republicans engineered the idea of a rule change in which the filibuster would be ruled out of order with regard to judicial nominees. This rule change could be accomplished by a simple majority of the Senate—likely with Vice President Dick Cheney casting the deciding vote.[253] The procedure was called the nuclear option because the proposed rule change was, as a *New York*

Times correspondent explained, "so explosive that Democrats have threatened to shut down Senate business if Republicans invoke it."[254]

As the day of reckoning approached, the entire fight began to look like a parody of interest group politics. Organizations on the left and right went head to head, spending millions of dollars on national advertising.[255] MoveOn.org ran one commercial showing Frist as the villain Darth Vader from the *Star Wars* epic and another with "a herd of Republican elephants trampling Congress."[256] The Alliance for Justice ran its own spot, with the character Phil A. Buster asking Americans to "save checks and balances."[257] War rooms and phone banks whirred into action. On the right, Christian groups organized a nationwide telecast from a megachurch featuring leading politicians like Frist and many evangelical leaders. The program was entitled "Justice Sunday: Stopping the Filibuster Against the People of Faith."[258]

It all ended when a centrist "Gang of 14" reached a compromise. Moderates had begun to worry about just what the nuclear option would mean for the Senate and for their own political futures. "You want to think down the road. The Senate's going to change. It's not always going to be Republican," cautioned a retired Bob Dole.[259] The deal involved Democrats' letting three of Bush's controversial nominees go through, without commitment on two others. The signers agreed to henceforth "exercise their responsibilities under the advice and consent clause of the United States Constitution in good faith." Only "under extraordinary circumstances" would signatories filibuster in the future. In exchange, Republicans would "commit to oppose the rules changes."[260]

On both the left and right, the deal became the target of great scorn and frustration. *The Washington Post* called it the "perfect storm for the blogosphere, an issue on which both right-wingers and left-wingers could rise up in rare unison and smite the craven offenders."[261] James Dobson and the Alliance for Justice's Nan Aron both expressed "disappointment."[262] *The Wall Street Journal* dubbed it a "charade," and *The Washington Times* asked: "What shall we call these 14 Senators? Trustees, Regents, Governing Board Members, Blessed Ones, Lord Protectors, Proconsuls, Oligarchs, Cabalists, Conspirators, Usurpers?"[263]

AT A LOSS ABOUT JUDICIAL SUPREMACY

"[B]lack-robed tyrants"

The left and right now agreed: the problem of the Supreme Court transcended mere judicial activism and had become one of judicial supremacy

ACTIVISM ∞ 349

or even "exclusivity." The justices wanted sole control over the meaning of the Constitution. A cry rose up from both sides of the ideological divide.

As liberals saw it, the Court was seeking a new form of power. Over time, Americans had become accustomed to judicial "finality," the idea that once the judiciary had spoken about the meaning of the Constitution, all officials must comply. Now, however, as law professor Larry Kramer emphasized, the Court did not want just the last word; it wanted "the *only* word."[264] The Court's decisions showed it was dismissive of what others, including co-equal branches of government, thought the Constitution meant or should mean. "More Supreme than Court" was one academic's account of how the Court had forgotten its place.[265] Liberals launched a movement to counteract judicial supremacy, which they dubbed "popular constitutionalism."[266] The idea was to recapture the Constitution from the Supreme Court. As Kramer explained, "[O]ur theory and our practice have always reserved substantial space for the people to have a say in interpreting their Constitution. . . ."[267] Many joined Kramer in calling on Congress and the people to reassert themselves against a renegade Court.[268]

As it happened, critics on the right were expressing precisely the same concerns. Kramer's book criticizing the justices' aggressive approach to judicial review, *The People Themselves*, got an extremely favorable review from none other than Newt Gingrich.[269] Mark Levin accused the justices of the Supreme Court of "abusing and subverting its constitutional role. It has chosen to become the unelected, unassailable social engineer of American society."[270] Phyllis Schlafly's attack on judicial activism was entitled, appropriately, *The Supremacists*.[271] The Court, Pat Buchanan insisted, had perverted democracy by "dictating all-or-nothing solutions, against which a majority had no recourse," thereby "ignit[ing] America's culture wars as surely as General Beauregard ignited our Civil War when he ordered the Confederate guns to fire on Fort Sumter."[272] Pat Robertson accused the Court of being "black-robed tyrants."[273]

The question was what could be done. Authors practically wrung their hands in despair as they recalled all the old favorites, jurisdiction stripping, impeachment, Court packing.[274] None of this appeared likely to happen. Discussion of the difficulty of controlling the judiciary was so pervasive that after criticizing all the talk of impeachment and jurisdiction stripping, even the Chief Justice conceded a relevant question was: "[H]ow can we be certain that the Judicial Branch is subject to the popular will?" His answer was: "the gradual process of changing the federal Judiciary through the appointments process."[275] But many were losing faith. "For a time," Pat Robertson said, "some people believed that if Republican presidents could simply appoint enough conservative justices to the bench, there might be a chance of restoring balance in the Court. It is apparent now that was a mistake."[276]

The cry went up across the land to do something—*anything*—to put the Court in its place. On this score, ideological lines had collapsed entirely. *The Wall Street Journal* said, "We've long thought—and still do—that Congress ought to pass a constitutional amendment to make it clear that in our system of government the people are sovereign." As for precisely what, the editors were agnostic: "Just about any amendment would do."[277] The year *Bush v. Gore* was decided, Kramer put the challenge contentiously: "The Supreme Court has made its grab for power. The question is: will we let them get away with it?"[278]

ACTIVISTS, POLARIZATION, AND BASE POLITICS

"[M]ost Americans have somewhat ambivalent, generally moderate attitudes"

And yet a strange and inexplicable silence. Despite anxious pleas from the left and the right, nothing happened. There were occasional threats of reprisal against the justices and the Court, but they went nowhere. It was gradually becoming clear why. Politics in fin de siècle America had been taken over by partisan extremists. These extremists screamed at one another across the great divide, but they no longer represented the views of the American people. While most Americans agreed on controversial issues or sought compromise, activists dueled it out from the fringes. In this environment, the Supreme Court's decisions provided particularly good fodder to mobilize one's base or seek to drive a wedge into the other side's voters. Yet the attacks on the Supreme Court left most voters cold.

The media and pundits loved to say the United States was split right down the middle, politically and ideologically. *The Economist* called the United States a "50-50 nation."[279] Election results would seem to confirm it. The country had been divided into "red" and "blue" states, representing whether the people of the state were likely to go Republican or Democrat in the electoral college.[280] The split was understood to occur mostly over social issues. "Nothing short of a great Civil War of Values rages today throughout North America," wrote James Dobson and Gary Bauer, two leading lights of the religious right.[281] "You've got 80 percent to 90 percent of the country that look at each other like they are on separate planets," agreed Matthew Dowd, one of George W. Bush's leading pollsters and political strategists.[282] In *Courting Disaster*, Pat Robertson presented a picture of "two Americas" that most would see as a parody, one side favoring "abortion-on-demand, radical feminism, intrusive central government, homosexual rights (including ho-mosexual marriage), pornography and sexual license, weakened military de-fense, an ever-increasing role of nonelected judges, and the removal of our historic affirmation of faith from the public arena." (The other side was of course a paragon of virtue.)[283]

In truth, though, this familiar caricature was also wrong. Most Americans at the turn of the twenty-first century sat near the middle, professing mod-erate views and seeking compromise, not divide. Asked to place themselves ideologically, about a third of Americans tended to choose four on a seven-point scale, and most clustered around that point.[284] This held true in red and blue states alike. On the contentious issues, voters regularly indicated moderation and compromise. "Despite the polarized nature of the rhetoric on cultural issues," reported one political scientist, "most Americans have somewhat ambivalent, generally moderate attitudes toward them."[285]

What had become polarized were the political parties. "[R]ecent American politics have seen virtually unprecedented levels of ideological polarization between the Republican and Democratic parties," reported the Annenberg Foundation in a recent study on American democracy.[286] One could cut the country along all sorts of lines—religious, education, gender—and find little polarization. Yet, in the 2003–2004 House of Representatives, "every Repub-lican was more conservative than any Democrat; every Democrat, more liberal than any Republican."[287] While Americans put themselves in the middle of the seven-point scale, their perceptions of the parties differed sharply. They placed the Republican and Democratic parties at two and six, respectively.[288]

Party polarization was the result of both parties' having been taken over by activists.[289] In the old days, parties had patronage to hand out and attracted people from all walks of life.[290] Now, however, the main ticket to party power was a willingness to invest time and energy, less for patronage than for ideo-logical outcomes. This is what defined an activist: ideological commitment. Bobbie Killberg was a George H. W. Bush White House official who ran for the nomination for lieutenant governor of Virginia and lost to a candidate from the religious right. Explaining the result, she insisted that "the majority of Republican voters are in the center of the party" but are an unorganized, hence ineffective voting bloc. Moderates are "into too many other things with their lives. But people who are ideological and who believe they are directed by God to do something have an enormous force and enormous energy."[291] Of course, there were activists on the left with similarly strong motivations. "[B]y the 1990s," reported Morris Fiorina, the Stanford political scientist who most vigorously disputed the notion of a national culture war, "the activist tail had come to wag the party dog."[292] A study of convention delegates in 1992 showed them much more divided ideologically than the public at large.[293]

Polarization—or its appearance—was exacerbated by the two-tiered structure of party elections. In the primary system, those candidates who play well to the extremes fare better. Inevitably, then, Americans are treated to candidates whose views are more extreme than their own come the national election.[294] Partisan gerrymandering of voting districts made matters only worse. Aided by computers, experts now could do a remarkably good job of creating voting districts that heavily favored the candidates of one party over another. The upshot was that in most elections the primary became everything, driving candidates (and ultimately elected officials) farther to the extremes.[295] Arlen Specter, the Republican senator from Pennsylvania and former chair of the Senate Judiciary Committee, lamented that when he came to Congress in 1981, some twenty-two senators had attended the moderates' weekly lunch. By 2005 this number was down to two.[296]

All this explains why America looked to be so divided politically, even if it was not. Imagine the voting public clumped at the center. Now, give those voters just two choices in an election, one at each extreme. Each will have to choose an extreme or not vote at all. The result: the appearance, but not the reality, of a fifty-fifty nation. As Fiorina summed it up, "We divide evenly in elections or sit them out entirely because we instinctively seek the center while the parties and candidates hang out on the extremes."[297] The same dynamic was true of the substantive issues. Tom Smith, of the National Opinion Research Center at the University of Chicago, concluded in 1989 that Americans "are neither prolife nor prochoice" and "don't want to take sides," but "if you try to force them into one camp or another, you can get different majorities."[298] The Third Way report The Politics of Polarization concluded that "most people still fall into the big mushy middle on the abortion debate."[299]

Social issues proved to be useful in American politics at the turn of the twenty-first century. They could be used as a wedge to dislodge voters who, on economic or foreign policy matters, might have gone with the other party.[300] Politicians had also come to realize that with the electorate's choosing one party or the other by narrow margins, elections could be won simply by "mobilizing the base"—i.e., by providing incentives to turn out the votes of those closer to the fringes. "[Y]ou can lose the swing voters and still win the election," pollster Dowd's memo to the Bush camp reported, "if you make sure your base is bigger than theirs."[301] Social issues—especially hot topics like abortion and gay rights—could be used effectively here too, because they were salient for voters at the extremes.[302]

This dynamic brought the Supreme Court to the center of American politics, but not in the most desirable of ways. The Court had become a political foil. The justices decided social issues, and social issues were what motivated the base and served as a wedge. So it was that the Court was under constant fire. In days past, when the Court angered some group, individuals spontaneously organized to respond. Now organized groups regularly played the Court to their political advantage. Activists could complain about the Supreme Court, but in some perverse way disfavored decisions actually were more useful politically than preferred ones. It was difficult to mobilize the base over something the base agreed with.

The strategy of playing the Court for political advantage was evident in the response to the 1992 *Casey* abortion decision, in which each side insisted, oddly enough, that the other had won.[303] Ted Koppel spelled out the logic on the news program *Nightline*. The "true believers on both sides," he elaborated, would claim dissatisfaction in order to "reclaim[] the issue from the court system" so that they could "fight the issue out in the political arenas."[304] "In an apparent effort to galvanize their supporters," explained *The Wall Street Journal*, "combatants on both sides declared that they had lost."[305]

Still, the evidence suggested that activists' battles over the courts left the public cold. Writing in *Newsweek*, Eleanor Clift described the enormity of the filibuster conflict. "[B]oth sides are suiting up for a huge conflagration of their party bases with liberal activists, feminists and environmentalists on one side and conservative groups arrayed with corporate interests on the other." Yet, she observed, "[m]illions will be spent in a show of muscle that for most Americans will pass unnoticed."[306] While social issues were the things activists fought over, "polls consistently show[ed] that a substantial majority of citizens find other types of political concerns to be more pressing."[307] Fiorina put it this way: "Most citizens want a secure country, a healthy economy, safe neighborhoods, good schools, affordable heath care, and good roads, parks, and other infrastructure." What seemed to get discussed ad nauseam, though, were "issues like abortion, gun control, the pledge of allegiance . . . and other narrow issues that simply do not motivate the great bulk of the American people."[308]

THE SUPREME COURT AND POPULAR OPINION

"[R]eflecting cultural shifts"

Activist yapping about the Supreme Court fell on deaf ears because despite all the hype, it turned out the public agreed with the justices' decisions. Or perhaps it is more accurate to say that the justices were following social trends and by doing so were often deciding cases consistent with public opinion. As Mark Tushnet explained in his book *A Court Divided*, "[T]he patterns discernible in the Rehnquist Court's decisions reproduced the patterns occurring in American politics generally."[309] From the first Rehnquist Court right down to the third, most, if not all, of the major decisions could be seen as keeping within the mainstream of popular opinion. Even if the Court occasionally missed the mark, the public was forgiving. When asked, the people approved of the justices' role in American life. Compared with the other branches of American government, the Court enjoyed stunning support.

Take the first Rehnquist Court. The hot issues were social ones. In these cases, commentators came to understand, the middle justices were "splitting the difference." When common ground could be found, the justices found it; when it could not, they seesawed back and forth. Justice O'Connor's equivocation on many issues over many years proved very much to be a mirror of American public opinion.

Abortion, which was the most fraught issue the justices faced in this period, provides a case in point. The vast marches in Washington by pro-life and pro-choice forces and the constant drumbeat of the issue in partisan politics created the image that the country was split sharply on the issue. Not true. The vast majority of Americans supported a woman's right to obtain an abortion in some circumstances. Well into the 1990s, more than 50 percent of the country agreed that abortion should be available for a wide range of reasons.[310] By the same token, there was equally great agreement about the propriety of restrictions on the availability of abortion.[311]

In *Planned Parenthood v. Casey*, a decision attacked volubly by activists on both sides, the justices who authored the joint opinion nonetheless hit the bull's-eye of public sentiment.[312] *USA Today* proclaimed: "Activists on both sides of the abortion debate have loudly berated the Supreme Court justices for being out of touch with the American people. But in the Pennsylvania abortion case, it seems the justices have issued a ruling in touch with many people—and out of touch with activists."[313] Gallup did extensive polling just after the decision (as did others). The overwhelming conclusion was that the majority of the people supported both abortion rights and the various restrictions Pennsylvania had placed on them.[314]

In the media's eyes, the Court and country were united on the issue of abortion. In the aftermath of the decision, "mirror" was a favored word. *The Washington Post*'s headline was JUSTICES' ABORTION RULING MIRRORS PUBLIC OPINION.[315] *The Wall Street Journal* essentially agreed.[316] "Judging from the hubbub outside the Supreme Court last week, you might have thought the High Nine had staged a coup d'état," wrote Eleanor Clift in *Newsweek*. "But," she summed up, "the court came down just where most people are—in the middle." [317]

Revisiting the Federalism Revolution

Contrary to the views of commentators, the Supreme Court's federalism decisions, while frequently attacked as "activist," hardly came out of thin air either. In addition to keeping within the mainstream of public opinion, those decisions also reflected broader developments in American politics. [318]

Ever since Richard Nixon's run for the presidency, there had been a visible strain of discontent with the New Deal expansion and bureaucracy of the federal government. One of Nixon's prominent agenda items was a "New Federalism." "The time has come now in America," he said in his 1971 State of the Union Address, "to reverse the flow of power and resources from the States and communities to Washington, and start power and resources flowing back from Washington to the States and communities and, more important, to the people all across America." [319] Nixon's instinct was to divide power functionally, with the federal government doing what it was best suited for, and likewise the states. [320] In 1976, the Supreme Court decided *National League of Cities v. Usery*, an early (post–New Deal) states' rights case. [321] Though widely challenged at the time as unprecedented, both the decision and the justices who rendered it were very much the product of Nixon's philosophy of federalism. [322]

Then, in 1980, Ronald Reagan made federalism a centerpiece of his presidency, or at least he attempted to do so. Unlike Nixon's functional brand of federalism, which often involved giving the states money with strings attached, Reagan wanted "to curb the size and influence of the federal establishment and to demand recognition of the distinction between the powers granted to the federal government and those reserved to the states or to the people." [323] When Reagan succeeded in cutting taxes and slashing the federal budget, columnist Russell Baker wrote: "In the end even the Democrats were agreeable to the death of the New Deal, which took place this week at the Capitol." [324] However, Reagan's ambitious program of block grants ultimately faced insurmountable opposition from Congress and from state and local officials, who feared they were getting more responsibility with less money. [325] As Senate Finance Committee chair Bob Dole explained, in a reference to turning the food stamp program over to the states, "It sounds good at first blush. But I'm not so certain a program that vast could be administered 50 different ways." [326] The 1985 reversal of *National League of Cities* in *Garcia v. San Antonio Transit Authority* came after Reagan's block grant program foundered.[327] The wind appeared to have gone out of the federalism sails.[328]

By 1995, however, when the "Federalism Five" decided *Lopez*, federalism was once more the hot ticket. An article in the *National Journal* reported: "New Federalism is back. Again. But this time—the third try—may be the charm."[329] Though the Contract with America did not mention federalism per se, at its heart was an agenda to move power from the federal government to the states. A Heritage Foundation report explained: "Central government attempts to solve many problems have only made them worse; thus, the Contract with America represents specific practical steps that can be taken in a wide range of government activities to roll them back."[330] Gingrich himself told *The Washington Times* on the first day of his Congress, "What I can do between now and Easter is break up the Washington logjam, shift power back to the fifty states. . . ."[331] Following the 1994 election, the idea of returning power from Washington to the states—what was now called devolution— was on everyone's lips.[332]

Republicans were hardly alone in the federalism crusade. "This time around," reported the *National Journal*, "New Federalism isn't only a Republican thing; it's also a central feature of the New Democrat theology."[333] Running for President in 1992, Clinton had said he would "end welfare as we know it," and in 1993 he told the National Governors Association he was an "ardent devolutionist."[334] That same year, even before the 1994 Republican surge, Clinton, responding to persistent complaints of state and local officials about federal regulatory burdens, signed an executive order entitled "Enhancing the Intergovernmental Partnership" and eased the waiver process for state experimentation with federal programs.[335] In his 1996 State of the Union Address, Clinton announced, "The era of big Government is over."[336]

In light of all this, the Court's federalism decisions could hardly have come as a surprise. Several of the cases tracked legislative developments or apparent popular preferences. The subtheme of both *Lopez* and *Morrison* was leaving crime control to the states. At the time these cases were decided, many were decrying the "federalization" of criminal laws.[337] Following one of the most visible sovereign immunity decisions, *The New York Times* quoted a member of the conservative Cato Institute, explaining, "What's happening in the Supreme Court dovetails nicely with what's happening in the 104th Congress."[338] *The Washington Post* agreed: "The pattern at the Court matches the trend in the Republican-majority Congress to move away from national social policies in favor of state-by-state control, no matter how policies and services differ."[339]

Nor were the federalism decisions nearly as dramatic as critics made them out to be.[340] True, they carried the potential to disrupt the federal government substantially, but those with perspective were keeping their powder dry until this potential turned to practice. While Clinton made political hay of *Lopez*, polishing his tough-on-crime image, his Assistant Attorney General, Walter Dellinger, called it a "relatively narrow decision."[341] The *Chicago Tribune*, in an article headed "A Shot Across Congress' Bow," said: "Despite the cries of some commentators that the sky is falling, this is a healthy decision, a needed reminder to Congress that its powers are not unlimited."[342] One would have thought the *Morrison* decision (striking the civil remedy provision of the Violence Against Women Act) would come in for particularly harsh media attack, given the sensitivity of the women's issues involved, but reality was quite to the contrary, even among the liberal press. Acknowledging that the Court might take its decisions too far, *The Washington Post* editorialized that "in this one, the Court got it right. If Congress could federalize rape and assault, it's hard to think of anything it couldn't."[343] Stanford Law School dean Kathleen Sullivan published an op-ed in *The New York Times* labeling the reactions of her colleagues in the academy to the federalism decisions "hyperbolic.[344]

Even if some of the specific federalism decisions were hard to follow and others barely registered, the American public was by all accounts well behind the idea of devolving power to the states. They were motivated by the same disgust with business as usual in Washington that had propelled the Republicans to power. In 1964, some 76 percent of Americans said they could "trust the government in Washington to do what is about right." By 1994, that number had plummeted to 21 percent.[345] At the same time, 77 percent reported they would be "very or somewhat confident" about transferring power to the states.[346] Another poll reported that 61 percent of Americans trusted the states more than the federal government to "do a better job of running things."[347] As former Tennessee governor and then senator Lamar Alexander said of the 1994 election, "What happened on November 8 was just a huge scream from the gut about the arrogance of Washington, D.C. It's moved from the head to the stomach, and therefore is something that can't be ignored."[348] Polls in 1995 not only showed huge support for states running things like education, crime fighting, and job training but also showed the public's ability to distinguish functions that were better suited to the federal government, such as the environment, civil rights, and the economy.[349] In 1998, political scientist Keith Whittington concluded: "It is no longer clear whether the American political system is committed to centralization."[350]

Accepting *Bush v. Gore*

Even the judicial thunderbolt of *Bush v. Gore* was met with equanimity, if not outright welcome, by much of the American public. It may be difficult in retrospect to see the country as willing to accept such easy resolution of a presidential election, but as Professor Sanford Levinson explained, "[I]n those halcyon days of Autumn 2000"—a year before the terrorist attacks on New York's World Trade Center and the beginning of the war on terror—the differences between the candidates were seen as slight.[351] Extensive polling was done during the election crisis and in the immediate- and longer-term aftermath of the decision itself. Gallup concluded that "Americans . . . felt that the Supreme Court was the best institution to make a final decision to resolve the controversy in Florida—much more so than the Florida Supreme Court, the Florida legislature, or even the U.S. Congress."[352] The numbers were overwhelming. The Court garnered 61 percent support as the appropriate body to resolve the controversy; its nearest competitor, Congress, came in at 17 percent.[353] Larry Kramer fumed that this view would have been unfathomable during the contested Hayes-Tilden election of 1876.[354] He was right, yet the level of confidence in the Court suffered barely a shudder after *Bush v. Gore*. For a short period polls showed that Democrats lost faith in the Court, but that was more than made up for by Republican gains. One year later even Democrats were expressing confidence in the Court at rates that exceeded pre–*Bush v. Gore* levels.[355]

It is difficult to know why Americans so willingly accepted the Supreme Court's resolution of the election. After all, a plurality of the country's voters had preferred Al Gore in the election itself.[356] A majority of those asked believed the justices were influenced by their "personal feelings" in deciding the presidential election, and only a bare majority thought the decision "fair."[357] Some political scientists posit that the Court enjoys what they call "diffuse support," which is to say that the Court has so much political capital that the public will accept a few decisions (apparently even major ones) with which it disagrees.[358] The Court may simply have drawn down some of its capital in deciding the case. On the other hand, given that 61 percent of those polled thought the Supreme Court was the institution most appropriate to resolve the dispute, it is equally possible the Court was doing the job Americans wanted it to do.

The Moderate Third Rehnquist Court

Although conservatives insisted that the high-profile decisions of the third Rehnquist Court were driven by elite opinion, not the will of the public, evidence suggests otherwise. There were undoubtedly some instances in which the Court, happily supported by the media, may have given in to a certain set of values distinct from those held by the majority of the American people. With regard to the big-ticket issues about which conservatives complained the most, however, the Court seemed to be following cultural trends with remarkable steadfastness. That was true of gay rights and affirmative action, to be sure. Even on issues like the war on terror, the Court looked to be tracking public reaction to rapidly developing events. The decisions against the government came some time after the 9/11 attacks and after the increasingly unpopular war in Iraq. They were handed down in the face of widespread public revulsion at the mistreatment of prisoners at the American-run prisons at Abu Ghraib and after it had become clear the executive branch was lying to the American public about torturing detainees.[359] As the public became skeptical about what its government was doing, the Court reined the executive in. Even then, the decisions were extremely narrow and tentative in scope.

Gay rights, which raised so much ire among some conservatives (particularly the religious right) was a screamingly evident case of the Court's running right along the tracks of popular opinion.[360] It was also a good example of the difference mobilization against Supreme Court decisions could make. Prior to *Bowers v. Hardwick*, the 1986 decision denying gay claims, gay organizations had been making headway against societal discrimination.[361] Then, amid the general conservativism of Ronald Reagan's 1980s, gay activism engendered its own backlash. Anita Bryant, previously famous as the advertising personality for the orange juice industry, launched the first successful repeal of a gay rights ordinance, saying, "Tonight the laws of God and the cultural values of man have been vindicated."[362] *Bowers* also was decided at the height of public hysteria about the AIDS epidemic. While polls from 1977 to 2003 showed a steady increase in public willingness to accept the decriminalization of sodomy, data collected right around the time that *Bowers* was decided revealed a sharp reversal in this trend, with only 33 percent of the country supporting legalization.[363] All too typical of commentary at the time was the sort of bile spewed by Pat Buchanan. Gays, he said, "have declared war upon nature, and now nature is exacting an awful retribution."[364] Large numbers of Americans, almost a majority, supported quarantining AIDS victims.[365]

Bowers joined the AIDS epidemic in radicalizing the gay community. Soon enough, *The Washington Post* observed, "the decision they considered a major setback might actually further their cause."[366] "National Coming Out Day" signaled the gays' resolve to raise their profile and use their resources to become a political and social force. Hundreds of thousands marched in gay rights parades the year after *Bowers*.[367]

By the late 1990s, the transformation in public debate and opinion was remarkable. *The Washington Post's* Pulitzer Prize–winning book critic Jonathan Yardley published a heartfelt essay entitled "The March of Time," explaining the transformation of his own views. "Like innumerable others of similar background and upbringing, I have come a long way in a few short years." Events had served "to make tolerable what once seemed abhorrent."[368] Gay culture by now was prominent in the media. Corporate America, anxious to retain a talented part of its workforce, had begun offering domestic partnership benefits to gay couples. Six in ten Americans thought sodomy laws should be overturned.[369]

The antidiscrimination argument for gay rights resonated particularly strongly. Public opinion polls showed 77 percent of Americans disfavored employment discrimination on the basis of sexual orientation.[370] President Clinton, who raised a furor early in his first term by trying to welcome gays into the military—he had to settle for the peculiar Don't Ask, Don't Tell policy— became the first President to address a gay group. Discussing antidiscrimination laws, he said, "Being gay, the last time I thought about it, seemed to have nothing to do with the ability to read a balance book, fix a broken bone, or change a spark plug."[371] When the Supreme Court struck down a Colorado referendum that forbade gay rights and antidiscrimination ordinances, *The Wall Street Journal* urged, "Calm down, everybody," and noted how this decision and *Adarand* seemed poised to "make colorblindness a reality."[372]

When the Supreme Court overruled *Bowers* in 2003 in *Lawrence v. Texas*, numerous commentators reflected on just how in line with popular opinion the decision was. *The Wall Street Journal* referred to the "mainstreaming of gay culture" and acknowledged that "an increasing number of Americans" share the Court's view.[373] Justice Kennedy noted that in the interim since *Bowers*, "[t]he 25 States with laws prohibiting the relevant conduct . . . are reduced now to 13, of which 4 enforce their laws only against homosexual conduct."[374] A surprising number of conservatives spoke up on the air accepting the decision.[375] William Kristol, in response to comments that the judiciary had usurped the role of legislator in deciding the case, suggested that most Americans would simply think that "maybe the court exceeded doing what courts normally should but . . . maybe it'll work, that we basically are going to cease to distinguish in our public life, in our public law, between heterosexuality and homosexuality in any way."[376] On CNN's *Late Edition with Wolf Blitzer*, former Clinton prosecutor Kenneth Starr explained that the Court was "reflecting cultural shifts."[377] President George W. Bush went after "[a]ctivist judges" who "have begun redefining marriage by court order, without regard for the will of the people and their elected representatives," but never once did he suggest that *Lawrence* was wrong.[378]

The Supreme Court's decisions on affirmative action that same year like-wise mirrored public sentiments; an equivocating Court matched a confused public somewhere in the middle on the issue. There was plentiful evidence that the public held two possibly contradictory positions simultaneously: support for affirmative action and opposition to racial preferences. Polls regularly evidenced both these positions, and slight changes of wording easily affected results.

There had been three contested referenda on ending affirmative action. The states of California and Washington passed theirs; the city of Houston's failed. California's and Washington's referenda talked of ending "preferences"; Houston's of "affirmative action."[379] Just the week before the Michigan decisions were handed down, polls showed that some 61 percent of Americans polled favored "merit" admissions even if this meant only relatively few minority students would be admitted.[380] Yet a 2003 CBS–*New York Times* poll showed that a whopping 79 percent believed it "important for a college to have a racially diverse student body."[381] The Pew Research Center released a poll taken on the verge of the Michigan decisions that showed a strong shift in attitudes from the time of the 1995 *Adarand* decision. Support for affirmative action had jumped, with support outpolling opposition 63–29 percent (as opposed to 58–36 in 1995). Underscoring the importance of the language of particular polls, there was even strong support for "special preferences"—albeit to "*qualified* blacks, women and other minorities." Compared with an even split of 46–46 percent in 1995, now the numbers showed support topping opposition 57–35 percent.[382]

Following the turmoil over *Adarand*, George and Jeb Bush pioneered the Republican Party's new posture on affirmative action. Serving as governors of two of the nation's largest states, they toned down the rhetoric on immigration, recognizing their political dependency on racial and ethnic minorities, especially Latinos.[383] When affirmative action activist Ward Connerly brought his anti–affirmative action referendum campaign to Florida, Jeb Bush quickly produced an alternative, realizing the political jeopardy Connerly's campaign put him in.[384] After a federal court of appeals struck down Texas's affirmative action program for its university system, George Bush advanced the "10 percent" plan, under which the top 10 percent of all high school graduates were automatically admitted to the university. This was said to assure a diverse university population (though others argued it worked only if the public schools were racially imbalanced).[385] George Bush's cabinet picks as President plainly evidenced the value he placed on diversity in his own administration.[386]

The briefs in the Michigan cases clearly indicated to the Court that there would be broad support for their ultimate rulings. Of the fifty-eight amici, representing groups and organizations of many kinds, the vast majority favored the University of Michigan.[387] One of the most powerful briefs was filed by sixty-five Fortune 500 companies.[388] America's CEOs told the Court that affirmative action had worked for them and was requisite to retain global competitiveness.[389] Another brief was authored by extremely prominent retired military commanders. These military officers argued that affirmative action admission policies were essential to the military academies for maintaining a qualified yet diverse officer corps.[390] The Bush administration filed a brief in opposition to the Michigan plans but touting the 10 percent alternative.[391] Upon filing, Bush said, "I strongly support diversity of all kinds, including racial diversity in higher education."[392]

Media response to the Michigan decisions overwhelmingly indicated the Court had ruled where the American people stood: "ambivalent." "Split Decision," trumpeted *U.S. News & World Report*.[393] Referring to the Michigan decisions, *The Washington Post* said Justice O'Connor "has a knack for landing pretty near the spot where the public uneasily settles. Pure conservatives have sometimes complained that she is a reed in the wind, but . . . her decisions might strike average Americans as common sense."[394] Ken Starr, again on CNN, said that "the court, as we saw, is very deeply ambivalent about affirmative action, just as the country as a whole is."[395] COURT MIRRORS PUBLIC OPINION was the *Washington Post* headline. The paper said: "[P]olls make clear that affirmative action is an idea most Americans approve of in theory but are wary of in practice." It reported that the director of the Pew Research Center marveled at "how closely the court resembled public sentiment."[396]

Public Support

Most of the Rehnquist Court decisions discussed here were still controversial, of course. The Court cannot bring peace to troubled waters, despite its stated wish (in cases such as *Dred Scott* and *Casey*) to do so.[397] One of the greatest engines of constitutional change has been mobilization against Supreme Court decisions by those unhappy with the results. Sometimes that mobilization requires many years to come to fruition. Sometimes it never does, if the center of public opinion remains with the Court.

But to judge by opinion polls, the Rehnquist Court was an extremely popular institution of government, and the public seemed well content with the role it was playing. Marveling over *Bush v. Gore*, journalist Tom Wicker said the Court had reached a position that, "if not untouchable, is at least as authoritative and accepted as that of any institution in the nation."[398] At the end of the term that included the gay rights and affirmative action decisions, a Fox News poll showed a majority agreed that the Court "is in touch with what is going on in the country."[399]

When asked about their confidence in institutions of American government, the public persistently put the Court high on the list. A 1994 Gallup Poll showed those who express at least "some" support for the court at more than 80 percent, roughly the same number it got six months after *Bush v. Gore*.[400] When asked what institutions they trust, the Supreme Court typically came in as much as 20 percent above such other governmental entities as Congress.[401] Despite years of activist pummeling, poll numbers just after the Rehnquist era ended confirmed the Court's staying power. Amid lobbying scandals and discontent over the Iraq War, trust in Congress and the President fell to below 50 percent.[402] A 2006 Gallup Poll showed Congress's approval rating at 29 percent, the President's at 39 percent, and the Court's at 60 percent.[403] Since 2001, the Court's approval has always exceeded that of Congress.[404]

If anything displayed the public support for the Supreme Court's role, and, in particular, its exercise of judicial review, it was the ironic response to one of its most unpopular decisions. In a case called *Kelo v. City of New London*, the Court declined to strike down the actions of local Connecticut authorities who had condemned private property for purposes of development.[405] When the Court upheld the Connecticut officials' authority, the ruling "set off a political earthquake."[406] In other words, contrary to all the criticism of judicial activism, the Court got into some of its most serious trouble of the era when it *refused* to be activist, upholding government action despite what many apparently saw as a constitutional violation. This could be confusing to those used to playing the Court for profit. Tom DeLay, the House Majority Leader, declared, "This Congress is just not going to sit by and let an unaccountable judiciary make these kinds of decisions," seemingly oblivious to the fact that the Court had *upheld* the power of elected officials and that all the legislation proposing to deal with the problem stripped governments, not the Court, of power.[407] As one commentator explained, "[T]he reflexive denunciation of *Kelo* as judicial activism" was "extraordinary" because the decision "defers to a local policymaking body" and is "not activist in any reasonable sense of the word."[408] David Savage made just the same point. Often the Court was criticized for "'judicial activism' for . . . for strik[ing] down the laws or decisions of state or local officials," but here the justices "were sharply criticized for doing the reverse."[409] It was now clear the public warmly embraced judicial review, and displayed great unhappiness when the Court failed to do what was expected of it.[410]

THE COURT COMES FULL CIRCLE

*"[T]oo-quick, or at least too-complete, judicial acquiescence
in the democratic process"*

By the end of the Rehnquist Court, it was a widely acknowledged fact that
the Court was mirroring public opinion. All the pundits and Court watchers
seemed to be saying so. In the ultimate irony, however, critics began to challenge the Court, not because it was defeating the popular will but because
it was fulfilling it.

Sometime around the end of the first Rehnquist Court, a small band of
political scientists and law professors questioned the common assumption
that judicial review ran contrary to the popular will. As a simple matter of
power politics, they asked, how could the Court hope to sustain itself in the
face of popular opposition? Their answer: it didn't. Rather, the Court ran in
the range of popular opinion, sometimes ahead, sometimes behind, but never
far from the mainstream. When the Court deviated substantially, it was
quickly brought into line.[411] Though the point seemed obvious to these scholars, this view for the most part remained buried in the academy—hardly
prominent even there.

By the end of the Rehnquist Court, though, the idea had become common in public discourse. Following the *Lopez* decision, Cokie Roberts, the
National Public Radio congressional correspondent, appeared on *This Week
with David Brinkley.* She explained the decision, saying that "we are in an era
where people are moving back to states' rights" and that "the court reflects
what people are thinking and, in fact, when it gets out of synch with where
people are, it switches."[412] After *Lawrence* something similar happened. The
conservative editor of *The Weekly Standard*, Fred Barnes, and the more liberal
Morton Kondracke, editor of *Roll Call*, appeared together on a Fox News
show. Barnes was distressed that the Constitution seemed to have changed
over seventeen years, without anything to explain it. "Well, what has changed?
I mean, the Constitution hasn't changed," he insisted. "The only thing that
changed is. . . ." As he trailed off, Kondracke finished his thought: "Public
attitude."[413] At the end of the Rehnquist Court, CNN's Jeffrey Toobin wrote
a bestselling book on the Court entitled *The Nine.* His conclusion: "[T]he
Court is a product of a democracy and represents, sometimes with chilling
precision, the best and worst of the people."[414]

On the left and right, it was dawning on judicial critics that the Court
was in line with America. Jeffrey Rosen likely was the first to label the
Court's (and particularly Justice O'Connor's) decisions "split-the-difference"

jurisprudence. Faced with a contentious issue, O'Connor often found a middle ground between the contending sides. The result, Rosen explained, was that the Court frequently followed public opinion. He wrote a book about the Supreme Court, which he called provocatively *The Most Democratic Branch*.[415] In a retrospective on the Rehnquist Court, the prominent conservative judge (and former law professor) J. Harvie Wilkinson, picked up Rosen's theme with a vengeance, referring to the "jurisprudential threading the needle" in "controversial areas."[416] Wilkinson conceded that "in splitting the difference on contentious social issues," the Court was "in sync with the views of most Americans" and "in the place that most Americans preferred."[417]

Yet Rosen (on the ideological left) and Wilkinson (on the right) were troubled by this split-the-difference jurisprudence. Rosen complained that "the last thing the country needs is another O'Connor to short-circuit all of our most contested political debates. By splitting every difference, she aggrandized her own power at the expense of Congress and the states."[418] Wilkinson agreed, complaining that "[s]plitting the difference ought not to be confused with judicial restraint."[419]

Rosen and Wilkinson were hardly alone. Law professor David Strauss worried over the Court's engaging in a "too-quick, or at least too-complete, judicial acquiescence in the democratic process."[420] Larry Kramer, on the other hand, chastised the American people for being overly acquiescent in the Court's exercise of power, even as he nodded to the literature suggesting that the Court was likely not to wander far from public sentiments without being punished. Wilkinson and Kramer fretted from opposite sides of the ideological divide that given the Supreme Court's active exercise of its powers, "the ideal of . . . democracy as a robust arbiter of differences . . . began to slip slowly from America."[421]

This sort of critique represented a big shift from the tune that had been fiddled against the Court for so many years. For two centuries the dominant understanding of the Supreme Court had been that it frustrated public opinion, often on the most important and central issues the polity faced. The justices were berated, chastised, vilified, hated, defied, and, occasionally, deified on these very grounds. Now the justices were under attack yet again. This time, though, it was for giving the people what they wanted.

CONCLUSION: WHAT HISTORY TEACHES

"[A] dialogue . . . with the people"

As the baton of one Chief Justice passed to another, it became clear that while the story of judicial review is constantly evolving, it retains an eerie familiarity. The same arguments for and against the practice are offered time and again. There is a reason for this, an important one: these arguments reflect the intractable tension between majority rule and constitutionalism that is innate to the American system of government. Despite the persistent claims of critics, judicial review has never been the source of the problem. It merely reflects (and perhaps exacerbates) it. In a constitutional democracy, minority rights are going to come into collision with majority rule, whether there are judges to say so or not.[1]

Judicial review did evolve, though, and what most have failed to see is that in its evolution, judicial review actually has become the American way of mitigating the tension between government by the people, and government under a Constitution. Our Constitution is almost a quarter of a millennium old. It is unavoidable, and plainly apparent to all but those willfully blind to the fact, that what the Constitution is understood to encompass has changed over time in ways that are dramatic, sweeping, and often permanent.[2] Although these changes are reflected in judicial decisions, they are rarely initiated there and in any event never would endure without the blessing of the American people. Ultimately, it is the people (and the people alone) who must decide what the Constitution means. Judicial review provides a catalyst and method for them to do so. Over time, through a dialogue with the justices, the Constitution comes to reflect the considered judgment of the American people regarding their most fundamental values. It frequently is the case that when judges rely on the Constitution to invalidate the actions of the other branches of government, they are enforcing the will of the American people.

THE ONCE AND FUTURE COURT

The long-awaited change in the membership of the Supreme Court finally came in the summer of 2005. Sandra Day O'Connor retired from the Court.[3] President George W. Bush nominated John Roberts to fill O'Connor's spot. Roberts was a District of Columbia Court of Appeals judge who had served in both the White House Counsel's and Solicitor General's offices. Deeply conservative, he was widely admired, even among liberals, for his intellect and ability. Before Roberts's confirmation hearings commenced, the Chief Justice died of the cancer he had battled for some time. Bush promoted Roberts, picking him to fill Rehnquist's center chair.[4]

Roberts's confirmation hearings as Chief Justice were a cakewalk. Though some viewed this as a "defeat for liberal advocacy groups," it was not clear their hearts were really in it.[5] Roberts, who had clerked for Chief Justice Rehnquist, was generally seen as an ideological swap. "It's hard to imagine a choice more similar to Chief Justice Rehnquist than John Roberts," observed former Solicitor General Walter Dellinger.[6] Add to that the fact that Roberts's performance during the hearings was "almost flawless," leaving everyone wowed.[7] No sense going to war over Superman, especially if it might not matter to the long-term direction of the Court. The Senate approved Roberts 78–22.[8]

"The pivotal appointment is the next one," declared Democratic senator Dianne Feinstein.[9] This nominee would replace Sandra Day O'Connor, who had been the heart of the Court for more than a decade. "We are all living now in Sandra Day O'Connor's America," Jeffrey Rosen wrote in his 2001 article "A Majority of One." "Take almost any of the most divisive questions of American life, and Justice O'Connor either has decided it or is about to decide it on our behalf."[10] The person who filled this seat, many believed, could decide the future of the Court for a long time to come. The moment was compared with Justice Powell's retirement in 1987, which had led to the contentious fight over Robert Bork.[11]

George Bush's first nominee to the position to fill O'Connor's seat, his counsel Harriet Miers, was savaged—by conservatives in his own party no less.[12] "The decisive element," wrote Norman Dorsen, New York University School of Law professor and old school liberal, ". . . was the opposition of right-wing Republicans who concluded that she would not be reliable on the 'social' issues—including abortion, gay marriage and voluntary end of life."[13] So Bush traded "a fight with his conservative base for a war with liberals," nominating a fan of the right, Judge Samuel Alito.[14] In Alito, wrote law professor Andrew Siegel on the pages of *The New Republic*, liberals "may have met their worst nightmare."[15] Once again, the airwaves and webwaves were filled with hysteria. The left, for example, attacked an Alito decision in which he voted to uphold the strip search of a ten-year-old girl on the scene of a drug bust; the right responded with a commercial saying the "'left-wing extremists" opposing Alito's nomination "may have found new allies, drug dealers who hide their drugs on children."[16] It was business as usual in the confirmation wars.

Despite the intensity of the fight among activists, most of the country snored its way to Alito's confirmation. Polls showed a clear majority in favor of putting him on the bench. Many Democrats voted against him, recognizing the importance of the seat and under pressure from left-wing interest groups. Still, Alito was confirmed 58–42, largely along party lines.[17] Having "squandered" the filibuster "on a series of ultimately insignificant lower court appointments," opined *The San Diego Union-Tribune*, the Democrats had given us "a nominee who, though modest and affable, is a literal avatar of right-wing jurisprudence."[18]

As they had been at other times in the past, prognosticators were again certain that there was a working conservative majority on the Court. *The New York Times* reported gloomily that adding Alito to the bench was "expected to tilt the balance of the court to the right on matters like abortion, affirmative action, and the death penalty, and partisans on each side said the outcome would echo through American politics for decades."[19] A former Reagan Justice Department official and conservative law professor crowed: "It is a Reagan personnel officer's dream come true. It is graduation. These individuals have been in study and preparation for these robes all their professional lives."[20]

Time will tell how well this latest round of predictions about a conservative Court proves out. The pundits' take on the Roberts Court seems to change after every term.[21] But the long-run fate of the Roberts Court is not seriously in doubt; its decisions will fall tolerably within the mainstream of public opinion, or the Court will be yanked back into line. Whether or not this is a good thing—the question typically is obscured in passionate debates over the proper role of judges in a democracy—is far more difficult to say.

THE WILL OF THE PEOPLE

Throughout history, contending forces have had basically two opposing things to say about the Supreme Court. Those unhappy with the justices have accused them of interfering with the will of the majority.[22] Call this the *threat* of judicial review. Those supportive have emphasized the need for judicial review to protect constitutional rights.[23] Call this the *hope*.

It is about the threat of judicial review that we have heard the most over the years. In his classic *The Least Dangerous Branch*, Alexander Bickel gave this problem a descriptive but ungainly name, the "counter-majoritarian difficulty."[24] In theory, majority will is supposed to govern, yet judicial review runs against that principle. Thus it is "counter-majoritarian." (The "difficulty" represents the problem Bickel and other intellectuals have seen in trying to justify judicial review given its anti-majoritarian tendencies.)[25] Bickel's concern about judicial power has echoed throughout American history whenever the Supreme Court has seemed to be exercising great authority.

Ironically, though, the expressions of both the hope and the threat of judicial review rest on a common supposition: that the judiciary even has the *capacity* of running contrary to the will of the majority. Those who express fear of judicial review, who worry that judicial decisions trump majority will, presume the judges could do so with regularity if they wished.[26] Those who hope that the judges will stand up against the majority, however, need to make precisely the same assumption.[27]

As must certainly be clear by now, this underlying assumption, central to both perspectives on judicial review, is deeply problematic. The people and their elected representatives have had the ability all along to assert pressure on the judges, and they have done so on numerous occasions. The accountability of the justices (and thus the Constitution) to the popular will has been established time and time again. To the extent that the judges have had freedom to act, it has been because the American people have given it to them. Judicial power exists at popular dispensation.

Shrewd witnesses to Roosevelt's fight with the Court understood this relationship between judicial review and public opinion quite well. "No appointive body of nine men can fly in the face of public opinion for too long without provoking an answering attack," explained the journalists Alsop and Catledge.[28] Of similar view was Dean Alfange, whose book *The Supreme Court and the National Will* was one of several written to assist "nonprofessional readers" in an "understanding of the relation of judicial review to the processes of democratic government." "No institution," Alfange wrote, "can survive the loss of public confidence, particularly when the people's faith is its only support." For this reason, the Court has, "with but few exceptions, adjusted itself in the long run to the dominant currents of public sentiment."[29]

Those who doubt the accountability of the Supreme Court to the popular will point to the recent assertiveness of the justices. They fret that the Court has gone well beyond the accepted practice of judicial review and insisted upon final, if not exclusive, authority over the meaning of the Constitution.[30] There certainly are hints of this in some of the Rehnquist Court's decisions. In one instance, the late Chief Justice stated unequivocally, as have his colleagues in other instances, that the Congress and President can have their views about the Constitution, but the Supreme Court is the "ultimate expositor of the constitutional text."[31] It is these sorts of assertions that have led to broad attacks from the left and the right.

In off-the-bench remarks, however, several of the justices have been quite candid in acknowledging the Court's dependence on popular support. In his own early days on the Supreme Court, Justice Rehnquist was asked whether the justices are able "to isolate themselves from the pressure of public opinion." His response was that "we are not able to do so and it would probably be unwise to try."[32] For many years Justice Sandra Day O'Connor sat in the middle of the Court. Hers were the votes that led the Court to the center of public opinion on such controversial issues as abortion and affirmative action. Justice O'Connor was quite frank in explaining that "[w]e don't have standing armies to enforce opinions." Instead, "we rely on the confidence of the public in the correctness of those decisions. That's why we have to be aware of public opinions and of attitudes toward our system of justice, and it is why we must try to keep and build that trust."[33]

Not only have the justices acknowledged the importance of public opinion, but, as we have seen time and time again, their decisions plainly reflect the tug of public views. Some express concern about judicial hegemony nonetheless, arguing that of late the people have become complacent.[34] This is a dubious claim. Anti-Court activism has been rampant to such a degree in recent years that the justices and others have gone on the stump to protect judicial independence in the face of particularly strident criticisms and legislative measures they view as a threat.[35] The legal academy likewise responded: in 2005, 75 percent of the nation's law school deans signed a letter opposing congressional calls for judicial impeachment of activist judges.[36] Yet none of the attacks on judges has gotten very far, and it is unlikely that complacency is the reason. The weight of the evidence seems to support a quite different reading, that by and large, for now, the people are simply content with the system of judicial review. Perhaps more than ever before, Supreme Court decisions run in the mainstream of public opinion. If the people were unhappy with the courts, they could, as they have in the past, signal that discontent.

Yet polling data indicate widespread satisfaction with the judiciary, in sharp contrast with other branches of government.[37]

THE POLITICAL COURT

While the close relationship between popular opinion and judicial review goes a long way toward addressing Bickel's "counter-majoritarian difficulty," it actually raises a question that is far more profound and tends to receive far too little attention. If any worry seems legitimate, it is that the "hope" of judicial review too often proves effervescent, that the justices kowtow to public opinion and pay insufficient heed to the traditional role of judicial review in protecting minority rights.[38] Even conceding for the moment the very odd fact that the Court of late seems to be doing a better job than the Congress in meeting public expectations, it is still difficult to argue that such a state of affairs justifies judicial review. Is it really the role of the Supreme Court only to rubber-stamp public opinion?

Just as the Court has been criticized for interfering with the popular will, so it has been condemned equally strongly throughout history for failing to stand up for the Constitution when necessity demanded it. Take, for example, what might be the Court's greatest single failure (at least from this perspective) in all its history, the decisions in the Japanese internment cases. During World War II, more than one hundred thousand American citizens of Japanese descent (along with many other noncitizen Japanese) were herded from their homes on the West Coast and locked in detention camps in the middle of the country.[39] There was virtually no evidence of a security risk; the stark racism behind the internment later became clear.[40] The question of the internment's constitutionality came to the Supreme Court in the later days of the war, when its needlessness was already somewhat apparent, and in any event its constitutional difficulties should have been. Nonetheless, the justices upheld the acts of the President and military officials in decisions that are hard to justify intellectually or accept emotionally.[41] In time, the country rightly tripped over itself apologizing. Many today would pick *Dred Scott* as the Court's greatest gaffe, but at least in that case the justices thought they were standing up for minority rights, albeit the property rights of slaveholders.[42] It is difficult to understand *Korematsu*, the most prominent of the internment cases, as anything but stark capitulation to the decisions made by military and political authorities.[43]

Although no work of scholarship has really attempted to come to grips with what motivated the justices to decide *Korematsu* as they did, the currents of public opinion against the interned Japanese came to be very strong.[44]

Gallup did remarkably little polling on the question, which is itself telling of how little most people really seemed to care what was going on.[45] But the answers Gallup did elicit are a little chilling. In 1942, Gallup asked whether those interned inland should be allowed to return at the end of hostilities. By a 48–34 percent margin, the answer was no (the rest had "no opinion"). In a follow-up of "no" voters on what should happen, the most popular responses advocated throwing them out of the country or sending them back to Japan, and 3.8 percent indicated that they should just be killed.[46] The *Los Angeles Times* issued an editorial praising *Hirabayashi*, a predecessor to the *Korematsu* decision, stating that the decision would help stymie "[a]gitation for the return of Japs to the Pacific Coast."[47] It is not very encouraging to think the Supreme Court might be responsive to this sort of public opinion.

What we ought to care deeply about, what we ought to be asking, is how much capacity the justices have to act independently of the public's views, how likely they are to do so, and in what situations. Is the Court even capable of standing up for constitutional rights when they are jeopardized by the majority? Imagine the Court as tethered to public opinion by a bungee cord. The justices plainly have a certain freedom of movement. But what determines how far the Court can move away from the public before it is snapped back into line?

These are questions for which our understanding is remarkably impoverished, an embarrassing fact, given that we are more than two hundred years into our national experiment with judicial review and democracy. Far too much time has been spent and ink spilled debating *whether* the judiciary is beholden to or independent of majority will (even among those who should know better). Surprisingly little is devoted to analyzing where between these two poles the answer rests and how the system of judicial review actually works.

The failure to devote adequate attention to these important questions traces back to a long-standing disagreement between political scientists and legal scholars over whether law or politics motivates the Supreme Court's decisions, one dating back to the aftermath of Roosevelt's Court-packing plan.[48] In recent years, fortunately, scholars in both law and politics have begun to move past this silliness. Plainly what the justices do is law, and it does not detract from this point to acknowledge that they have a certain amount of discretion, even a large amount of it. But politics plainly influences the Court as well, in numerous ways ranging from the appointments process to responsiveness to public sentiments. Recent scholarship endeavors to say something tangible about the Supreme Court's responsiveness to (and independence from) popular politics, about what decides cases, and how all this works.[49] What we know is tentative; it may amount to little other than an agenda for further research. But if we can at long last move past the question of *whether* the justices are influenced by popular opinion, a question whose only conceivable answer is yes, we can at least start to tackle the really meaningful question of when and how the justices are free to stand up to the popular will in the name of the Constitution.

THE ALIGNMENT OF THE JUSTICES WITH POPULAR OPINION

Understanding how much freedom of movement the Supreme Court enjoys requires answering a prior question: Why might the justices' decisions come into line with public opinion in the first place? Only by examining what motivates the justices to listen to the siren call of public opinion can we assess how beholden to it that they are likely to be.[50]

Undoubtedly, the fact that Presidents select Supreme Court justices and the Senate confirms them plays some role in ensuring that the Court heeds the cry of public opinion.[51] But it probably does not explain nearly as much as one would think. Contrary to folk wisdom, Presidents can usually get the sort of justice they want; however, they rarely are driven to appoint justices who capture the mainstream of popular thought.[52] Only recently have Presidents become so single-mindedly focused on the ideology of their appointees, and in doing so they often have proven beholden to extremists in their own party.[53] Even if a justice is appointed as a perfect proxy for public opinion, things may not remain that way for long. Historically, a justice has retired about every two and a half years, putting each of them on the Court on average for more than a generation, though that period of service is going up as justices are appointed younger and live longer.[54] In the years between appointment and present decisions, justices may experience "ideological drift," which is to say their views may move right or left. Even if they stick to their guns—and evidence suggests most of them do drift by the tenth year on the bench—the nature of the issues coming to them may make their views outmoded.[55] The appointments process, standing alone, cannot guarantee responsiveness to public opinion.

On the other hand, the fact that the justices are only human may say a lot for why responsiveness to public opinion occurs. The justices are no less vain than the rest of us, and it is human nature to like to be liked or even applauded and admired. Part of being a judge means getting used to the fact that you always are disappointing one of the parties before you. The Supreme Court is a bit different, though: it decides issues as much as individual controversies, and the justices' decisions regularly are front-page news and the subject of numerous editorials. Some justices appear to play to immediate public opinion. Chief Justice Chase desperately wanted to be President. William O. Douglas liked the image of populist champion.[56] Many others are undoubtedly affected by what is said about them.

Aligning the Court with public opinion does not require many justices on the Court at any time to be sensitive to public opinion. The Court will always have its extremists. But the justices make decisions by majority vote, giving the "median" justice, the justice in the middle of the Court, enormous power. Recent studies suggest that when it actually comes to drafting opinions, as opposed to deciding the outcome of cases, the authority of the median may not be all it appears. Still, it is a rare (and likely far from significant) case in which the extreme justices are going to be calling the shots.[57]

The most telling reason why the justices might care about public opinion, though, is simply that they do not have much of a choice. At least, that is, if they care about preserving the Court's institutional power, about having their decisions enforced, about not being disciplined by politics. Americans have abolished courts, impeached one justice, regularly defied Court orders, packed the Court, and stripped its jurisdiction. If the preceding history shows anything, it is that when judicial decisions wander far from what the public will tolerate, bad things happen to the Court and the justices.

One might wonder why given the nature of the sticks used to beat up on the Court for its decisions, the opinion of the *public* matters, as opposed to, say, that of the President or the Congress. Political scientists in particular tend to focus on the institutions of government, rather than the people at large.[58] But the United States is a democracy, and the will of the people still prevails, at least on the big issues. Of course, the justices have to pay attention to what the Congress and the President are saying.[59] But they must do more. Typically, there is some slack between what the governed want and what the governors provide, but that slack closes up when issues rise to the top of the public's consciousness.[60] When the public has a view, its elected officials tend to heed it. The Court has to be attuned to aroused public opinion because it is the public that can save a Court in trouble with political leaders and likewise can motivate political leaders against it.

Astute outside observers of the American system have long noted the influence of public opinion on the Supreme Court. In *Democracy in America*, the French intellectual Alexis de Tocqueville described the Supreme Court's power as "immense, but it is the power springing from opinion." It is no wonder that having made his tour of the United States in 1831, as the Cherokee conflict raged and defiance of the Court's decisions was the constant talk of politics, Tocqueville qualified his remarks by saying the justices retain their authority "so long as the people consent to obey the law; they can do nothing when they scorn it."[61] James Bryce was a British diplomat and scholar who spent considerable time here and wrote a multivolume work on the United States. Like Tocqueville, he concluded: "The Supreme Court feels the touch of public opinion." Bryce was observing the Court's response to Granger legislation firsthand, which is what led him to recognize that "[o]pinion is stronger in America than anywhere else in the world, and the judges are only men." If not entirely comfortable with the arrangement, Lord Bryce did not see that the judiciary had any choice. "To yield a little may be prudent, for the tree that cannot bend to the blast may be broken."[62]

Skeptics might point out—in fact some do—that it has been a long time since the justices were disciplined in any significant way.[63] Court packing disappeared in 1937; impeaching the justices never really got off the ground. The Jenner-Butler jurisdiction-stripping measure in 1957 failed. True, Congress recently stripped the Court of jurisdiction to hear the claims of Guantánamo detainees, but it was a naked political ploy that the justices (those appointed by Republicans and Democrats alike) swatted away like a gnat.[64] Indeed, if anything seems paradoxical, it is that in recent years, as these weapons to control the justices look to have been ruled off the table or lost their force, the Court has come most directly into line with public opinion.

The explanation for this paradox is that it has taken the Court and the public some time to learn how their relationship might work; now that it is understood, violent upheaval is no longer necessary.[65] What would transpire over the course of two hundred–plus years was hardly obvious at the outset to either the justices or those who would control them. To the contrary, history has been full of misjudgments and corrections.[66] It took the Court quite a while to understand the limitations that motivated public opinion imposed on its freedom of movement. By the same token, it took the public several iterations to assess how it felt about disciplining the Court, and in what ways. The relationship between the people and the justices developed slowly over time, as in any other marriage. As in any other marriage too, a few serious dustups were to be expected at first, until the rules got ironed out.

Now that the justices and the public understand how things work, the system tends to rest in a relatively quiet equilibrium.[67] Political scientists call this anticipated reaction.[68] The justices don't actually have to get into trouble before retribution occurs; they can sense trouble and avoid it. The people do not actually have to discipline the justices; if they simply raise a finger, the Court seems to get the message. If one wants the relationship to continue, and there is every indication the American people and the justices want this one to, then meeting expectations becomes the norm, and it does not take as much as it used to in the way of repercussions.

THE INDEPENDENCE OF THE JUSTICES

None of this is to say the Court will always be in line with public opinion. The justices neither need to, nor necessarily do, respond to what the public wants. To name a couple of relatively recent examples, the Court's school prayer and flag burning decisions have been wildly unpopular.[69] If anything, public opposition has seemed to make the justices only more resolute on these issues. There are a variety of factors that protect the justices' independence and allow them to deviate from popular opinion. Even these suggest, however, that over the long term on the important issues the people are going to have their way.

One obvious candidate as a safeguard for the Supreme Court's independence is the sheer difficulty of enacting a law to punish the justices. The American separation of powers system is designed to make it difficult to pass legislation, requiring majorities in two houses of Congress and the President's signature on the bill. But it is not just the President who has a "veto"; so too do the relevant congressional committee chairs, who can stall hearings or avoid them altogether. (Emanuel Celler, a New York representative who served in the House for half a century, stalled consideration of any response to the school prayer decisions for two years.)[70] There is a certain range—what political scientists describe as the gridlock interval—in which it is hard to overturn any policy because of the difficulty in mustering legislative support.[71]

Still, as we have already seen, and as political scientists seem to acknowledge, the force of mobilized public opinion can be a great way of overcoming congressional gridlock.[72] (Political pressure ultimately forced Celler to hold hearings on the school prayer amendment.)[73] Besides, it does not require enacting legislation to exercise one of the biggest sticks against the Court: defiance. The states—or the people of the states—have done quite well on their own. Witness here the widespread defiance of the 1820s to which Tocqueville plainly was alluding, the "massive resistance" in response to *Brown v. Board of Education*, and the low-grade evasion that has afflicted the school prayer rulings. If the Court engenders widespread resistance, it threatens its legitimacy; even lower levels of defiance eat away at its credibility. No judge wants to be defied, and the threat of a harsh counterreaction has certainly given some pause. The justices tempered the remedy in the school desegregation cases precisely because they feared defiance.

The Court also has a better chance of going its own way in cases that are of low public salience. The Court decides lots of cases, and only so many of them can make it to the public consciousness. In others, the Court can fly under the radar, unnoticed. The Roberts Court has decided a large number of "pro-business" cases, often decided by large margins, if not unanimously.[74] Though this has gotten some attention in the press, for the most part the media's focus has been on certain high-profile cases like those involving abortion, pupil assignment to schools, gun control, and the like.[75]

Yet, again, the justices need be mindful that any decision or string of decisions could suddenly become an issue of great moment. The Supreme Court decides few enough cases, and the decisions are of sufficient import, that interested eyes always are watching the docket. Lest they forget this, there are periodically painful reminders, such as the enormous negative (and likely unanticipated) public reaction to the *Kelo* case regarding government taking of private property for ostensible public uses.[76] To the extent the pro-business decisions start to step on enough toes, there will be coverage.

It also is sometimes the case that the justices listen to elite voices, rather than that of the average person. This is a frequent complaint against the Court, and it may well explain the school prayer and flag burning decisions. To say that the justices like to be popular is to fail to ask, "With whom?" If a justice is in tune with his peer group, and his peers have elite views not shared by most of the country, the justice will seem to be going his own way.[77] Thus even those justices who appear not to care a farthing for what the public thinks may actually just have a particular public they play to. Antonin Scalia delights in being controversial; as a matter of constitutional theory and of personality, winning plaudits in the daily press plainly is not what he thinks he is supposed to be doing.[78] But Scalia is plenty popular with his colleagues in the Federalist Society.[79] One infers that satisfying this particular "base" sustains him well enough.

The cases in which the Supreme Court seems to deviate from public opinion most often are those involving the First Amendment, which could be explained because the First Amendment has its own special constituency, the press. Journalists love the First Amendment for obvious reasons (it protects freedom of the press).[80] The justices are more likely to be attacked in print (or praised) for their decisions in First Amendment cases than almost any other.[81] But journalists also may provide the justices with a distorted view of public opinion. The fondness of the media may explain the Court's particular willingness to stand tough on certain First Amendment rights—such as for pornography and against school prayer—even when the country generally expresses contrary views.

Sometimes the justices look to be independent when they are simply poorly informed about popular preferences. While elite views provide one example of this, another important one is provided by the novel case.[82] When the justices approach a matter for the first time, they have a decent chance of misreading public opinion even if they seek to be attuned to it. The public may not have considered a matter fully, public opinion may not have jelled, or the justices may simply lack good information. And the justices are most likely to get in trouble with the public when a case presents itself only once, or in one short period of time, so that they lack the opportunity to ensure that their decisions converge with public views. *Dred Scott* and *Korematsu* both might present examples of the problem the justices face with one-off issues.[83]

Ultimately, though, the best explanation for the justices' independence may simply be that the public decides to grant it to them. Although the public seems to insist on the Court's being relatively in line on most issues, "relatively" and "most" are the key words here. When it comes to public support for institutions like the Supreme Court, political scientists distinguish two types, "diffuse" and "specific" support.[84] Specific support is the obvious one; people stand behind the Court (or other institutions) when they like its specific decisions and desert it otherwise.[85] "Diffuse" support, on the other hand, refers to the idea that there is enough institutional support for the Court that people will tolerate a certain amount of deviation, a number of decisions they dislike.[86] In short, diffuse support is the measure of the slack the Court has to go its own way on some issues.

It is not entirely clear why diffuse support would exist. Perhaps the Court has simply been around a long time, and people resist change to long-standing institutions even if they are angry with them. At least one study shows that the longer a country has a high court, the more diffuse support it enjoys.[87] Perhaps nobody really wants a Supreme Court that simply panders to majority opinion. Maybe people figure that although they do not agree with particular decisions, down the road they may want the majority to refrain from attacking the Court when it sides with their unpopular cause.[88] Some people may welcome the Court's unique perspective. Theories abound; all have some supporting evidence, and none is conclusive.

History provides "anecdotal" evidence that diffuse support exists. Take *Bush v. Gore* as an example. Many people loathed that decision and thought it was infected by partisan bias, but polls showed that support for the Court quickly returned to where it had been.[89] Yet it turns out to be extremely difficult to measure the extent of diffuse support. This is too bad. Ultimately, diffuse support may be the measure of the length of the Court's leash. Studies regularly show the existence of diffuse support, but the tests used by those studies are problematic. Surveys ask people whether they would support responses such as packing the Court or stripping its jurisdiction if the justices issued unpopular decisions.[90] It's the "if" that is tricky here; the volatility in polling measures during the Court-packing fight of 1937 suggests it is difficult for people to reach a firm conclusion on disciplining the Court even when the chips are down. When they are not, it is all a bit too hypothetical to trust what people say.[91] The bottom line is that to the extent the Court can and does deviate from public opinion, it may be for no other reason than that the public allows it to, but we do not know nearly enough about popular preferences in this regard.

The Supreme Court's ultimate reliance on public dispensation calls into question the much-vaunted separation between "law" and "politics." When people speak of holding the two apart, what they typically mean is that judicial decisions ought not to be influenced by political considerations. In particular as it matters to this discussion, judges should not simply give in to the will of the mob.[92]

One can see the concern over the demarcation between law and politics in the justices' reaction to the annual pilgrimages to the Supreme Court in support or protest of the 1973 abortion rights decision in *Roe v. Wade*. Some years these marches have reached into the tens and even hundreds of thousands.[93] The justices' anxiety about the crowds outside their windows burst into public view in the 1992 decision in *Planned Parenthood v. Casey*. Justices O'Connor, Kennedy, and Souter's plurality opinion said that in light of the "sustained and widespread debate *Roe* has provoked," it was all the more important that the Court's decisions be seen "as grounded truly in principle, not as compromises with social and political pressures."[94] Though Justice Scalia dissented on the merits in *Casey*—he favored overruling *Roe*—he too agreed on the need to separate judicial decision making from political pressure. "How upsetting it is," he wrote, "that so many of our citizens . . . think that Justices should properly take into account their views, as though we were engaged not in ascertaining objective law but in determining some kind of social consensus."[95]

In theory, this desire to separate law and politics is an admirable one. Certainly we do not want trial judges who are deciding the fate of individual cases to be swayed by aroused community sentiments.[96] Studies showing that the chance that a death sentence will be upheld increases as state high court judges come closer to their elections are simply nauseating.[97] There has to be some room for law to decide which way the chips fall without the immediate pressure of public opinion.

Yet the instinct to keep politics entirely separate from decisions about constitutional law is plainly impossible with regard to the Supreme Court. It simply is the case that the judiciary's capacity to give the Constitution meaning, to protect minority rights, always has been limited by popular support for those decisions. The *Dred Scott* justices believed they were protecting constitutional rights; ultimately that judgment fell to contrary popular opinion and America's bloodiest war. Consensus was a long time developing, but when it did, the justices' interpretation of the Constitution gave way to the popular will. The justices in *Brown v. Board of Education* argued they were protecting constitutional rights, but once again it was evolving national views that supported the Court's judgment and enabled its enforcement. The decisions of the justices on the meaning of the Constitution must be ratified by the American people. That's just the way it is.

THE DEMOCRATIC CONSTITUTION

This brings us back to the extraordinarily important question with which we began: If the Supreme Court ultimately is accountable and responsive to the will of the people, doesn't that threaten the whole idea of constitutionalism? If the judiciary always, or even often, trumped the popular will, we would have a crisis of democracy. But if the facts tend to the opposite, what is there to preserve the Constitution against the majority?

On "I Am an American Day" in 1944, Judge Learned Hand gave an address in Central Park that became an instant classic. His words were eloquent, his topic "The Spirit of Liberty." In his address, Hand wondered whether "we do not rest our hopes too much upon constitutions, upon laws, and upon courts" to preserve the spirit of liberty. Calling these "false hopes," Hand insisted that "[l]iberty lies in the hearts of men and women; when it dies there, no constitution, no laws, no courts can even do much to help it." But "[w]hile it lies there it needs no constitution, no law, no court to save it."[98]

Hand's words, though heartfelt and gripping, seem oddly out of place for a man who served so long on the federal bench. Courts and the Constitution have *nothing* to add? Hand was an old-line progressive who saw courts at what he believed was their worst, and he never got over it. But was he right to be so pessimistic?

Hand's error, like that of many others, was in focusing solely, or even primarily, on the role *courts* play in the process of judicial review and constitutional interpretation. Courts say they are the last word, and many believe them. The fight becomes whether courts should have this power or not.

What matters most about judicial review, however, is not the Supreme Court's role in the process, but how *the public reacts* to those decisions. This is the most important lesson that history teaches. Almost everything consequential about judicial review occurs after the judges rule, not when they do. Judges do not decide finally on the meaning of the Constitution. Rather, it is through the dialogic process of "judicial decision—popular response—judicial re-decision" that the Constitution takes on the meaning it has.

To say that the Supreme Court follows popular opinion, or even that it should, is hardly to say that the Court ought to be responsive to every passing fancy, to the immediate demands or wishes of the American people.[99] Even those leading Americans who have called on the Supreme Court to be responsive to the people have distinguished between the passions of the moment and some deeper sense of the popular will. "What we should ask of our judges," wrote Woodrow Wilson several years before becoming President, "is that they prove themselves such men as can discriminate between the opinion of the moment and the opinion of the age." Theodore Roosevelt, who spent much of his career arguing that judges should not interfere with the people's will, said much the same. He distinguished between the "permanent popular will," which he said judges should follow, and "popular opinion at the moment," which a "good judge" should not.[100]

The problem is that there is something romantic, and plainly unrealistic, about asking judges to distinguish on their own between the "permanent" will of the people and the "opinion of the moment." Judicial robes are worn by ordinary mortals, typically political appointees. It is asking a lot of them to imagine they are any better than the rest of us in evading the pressures of the moment in favor of some deeper, more enduring set of values. The fact that Supreme Court justices have lifetime appointments provides some insulation, but history suggests that it often is not enough. Decisions like *Korematsu* indicate the difficulty with putting one's faith in the notion that judges will be able to perceive the difference between what is momentarily popular and what is ultimately right, let alone that those judges will be able to hold the line against an aroused citizenry.

The magic of the dialogic system of determining constitutional meaning, however, is that it works whether the judges rule properly or not—precisely because everything important happens after they render their decision.[101] What history shows is assuredly not that Supreme Court decisions always are in line with popular opinion, but rather that they come into line with one another *over time*. There was a very good argument that the Supreme Court's decision in *Roe v. Wade* was consistent with social trends, but still, it attracted only plurality support in polls, and there was profound disagreement with the Court's conclusion that had not received an extended public hearing. By the time the Court handed down its decision in *Planned Parenthood v. Casey*, however, which watered down *Roe* in important ways and which—all polls and pundits agreed—was remarkably in line with popular opinion, a generation of vibrant public debate had occurred.

When it comes to alignment with popular opinion, the justices will often seem to blow it badly the first time out on an issue, precisely because the public has not yet really made up its mind. The death penalty decision in *Furman v. Georgia* makes this clear. The same phenomenon was apparent during the New Deal. Although the early decisions striking down New Deal measures were met with some dismay, the President's criticism of the Court apparently angered the citizenry more. Public opinion was unsettled. It clarified quickly, though, and when it did, the Court had little choice but to come into line. In fact, if there is any worry about the New Deal, it is that with a big gun pointed at their head, the justices came into line too quickly. (If there is any reassurance, it is that the New Deal "settlement" was tested time and time again thereafter and endured by and large in the public mind.)[102]

It is through the process of judicial responsiveness to public opinion that the meaning of the Constitution takes shape. The Court rules. The public responds. Over time, sometimes a long period, public opinion jells, and the Court comes into line with the considered views of the American public.

Indeed, it turns out that one of the most important features of Supreme Court decisions interpreting the Constitution is that they are "sticky," which is to say that they are difficult to change or get around. Either the people must amend the Constitution, or they must persuade the justices to change their minds. This is what bothers critics of judicial review, what accounts for the concern about the "counter-majoritarian" nature of the practice.[103] But it turns out there is a certain virtue in this stickiness; it plays an essential role in separating out the considered "constitutional" views of the American people from passing fancy. Precisely because it is difficult to get around constitutional decisions, the debate that surrounds them proceeds differently from our other political debates. If judges interpret a statute in an unpopular way, Congress can change it. When a decision is put on constitutional grounds, it takes greater mobilization, and often more time, to develop the political will to change it.[104]

One of the most valuable things that occurs in response to a Supreme Court decision is backlash. People who disagree with the decision tend to react more strongly than those who agree, and they dissent in any variety of ways. If over time those dissenters muster strong support, then, and only then, the Court tends to fall into line with the dissenting opinion. For this reason, social movements play an enormous role in shaping public constitutional understandings.[105]

It is apparent time and again that what the Supreme Court responds to most often is the sustained voice of the people as expressed through the long process of contesting constitutional decisions. This is what Woodrow

Wilson and Theodore Roosevelt were calling for when they insisted that the Court should follow the "permanent popular will," when they asked the Court to distinguish the "opinion of the moment" from the "opinion of the age." The system works not because the justices are solons with a special capacity for distinguishing between the two but because separation occurs through the regular process of decision, response, and redecision, as it plays out over time.

This give-and-take between the courts and the people is of the utmost consequence, for through it the substance of constitutional law itself is forged. Supreme Court justice Ruth Bader Ginsburg noted this phenomenon, explaining that judges "do not alone shape legal doctrine." Rather, she observed from experience, "they participate in a dialogue with other organs of government, and with the people as well."[106] Justice O'Connor made much this same point: "[R]eal change, when it comes," she said, "stems principally from attitudinal shifts in the population at large. Rare indeed is the legal victory—in court or legislature—that is not a careful by-product of an emerging social consensus."[107] As we have seen, Owen Roberts, the swing vote on the Court Franklin Roosevelt attacked, conceded years later, once he was off the bench, that "it is difficult to see how the Court could have resisted the popular urge" for change in the Court's doctrine.[108] As judicial rulings respond to social forces, and vice versa, constitutional law is made.

The making and enforcing of constitutional meaning thus are the result of an extended dialogue between and among the courts and the American people. Learned Hand had it right, and wrong, at the same time. Unless the people possess the spirit of liberty, constitutions are parchment barriers and courts are false hopes. But perhaps the central function of judicial review today is to serve as the catalyst for the people to take their Constitution seriously, to develop their constitutional sensibilities, in the hope that they will adhere to those sensibilities when the chips are down. When Hand spoke, he was echoing in some fashion the words and worries of a famous mentor of his, James Bradley Thayer. At the World's Fair in Chicago in 1893, Thayer gave an address that became a classic, one of the most famous constitutional tracts of all time. In it, Thayer worried about the power of judicial review. His concern was that if judges took on this task too aggressively, the people (or at least their representatives) would abandon it to them and thus lose their own constitutional sensibility. The people, he feared, "not being thrown back on themselves, on the responsible exercise of their own prudence, moral sense, and honor, lose much of what is best in the political experience of any nation."[109]

American politics has been a constant, unrelenting process of constitutional contestation and dispute. Though Hand's and Thayer's worry is a reasonable one, it has also proven to be false. It is difficult to know what our society would be like without judicial review, as we have rarely lived without it. But it is impossible to spend any time looking at the television, the Internet, or a newspaper and miss the fact that we live in a *constitutional* democracy, that the terms of our Constitution are constantly being debated and discussed. The Constitution is central to American political discourse.

Ultimately, Thayer's and Hand's instinct is correct: we have nothing but ourselves to fall back upon. But it is wrong to claim, as many have, that the judges have stolen the Constitution from us. Judicial review is our invention; we created it and have chosen to retain it. Judicial review has served as a means of forcing us to think about, and interpret, our Constitution ourselves. In the final analysis, when it comes to the Constitution, we are the highest court in the land.

NOTES

Introduction

1. William Allen White, "White Calls Vote a 40-Year Flood," *N.Y. Times*, Nov. 8, 1936, at N3.
2. "John Doe Also Speaks Mind on President's Proposal," *Newsweek*, Feb. 20, 1937, at 17. Merlo J. Pusey, *The Supreme Court Crisis* (1937), 1.
3. "Another 5–4 Conservative Decision," *N.Y. Daily News*, June 2, 1936, quoted in Marian C. McKenna, *Franklin Roosevelt and the Great Constitutional War* (2002), 214.
4. "Court Plan Backed by Clothing Union," *N.Y. Times*, Feb. 20, 1937, at 4.
5. The events summarized here are described in Chapter 1, infra. For an outstanding discussion of the precursors of judicial review, see Philip Hamburger, *Law and Judicial Duty* (2008); Philip Hamburger, "Law and Judicial Duty," *Geo. Wash. L. Rev.* 72 (2003): 1–44. Hamburger demonstrates that as part of their "judicial duty" to decide in accordance with "the law of the land," English judges long exercised something akin to what we today call the power of judicial review. He also describes how this power extended not only to royal (or executive) acts, but to legislative ones as well, though his examples of the latter are quite meager. (Hamburger acknowledges that the acts of Parliament itself were exempt from judicial review; see Chapter 1, infra.) Still, Hamburger himself concedes that the early English practice was more constrained and humble than what we today think of as American-style judicial review. Indeed, Hamburger points out that (somewhat ironically), the early practice was "both more authoritative and less dangerous than that which prevails today." Hamburger, *Law and Judicial Duty*, supra, at 627. Even at its inception, however, the practice of judicial review that grew up in the United States, one founded uniquely on written constitutions and popular sovereignty, feels somewhat distinct from the English practice Hamburger details. Certainly it evolved into something far grander. Chapter 1, infra, describes the similarities identified by Hamburger that unquestionably made the practice seem sound when introduced in the new United States. The fol-

lowing chapters tell of the slow evolution into the practice of judicial review so familiar today.

6. This power extended, Brutus said, even "to determine what is the extent of the powers of the Congress." Brutus, "Essay No. XV," March 28, 1788, in *The Complete Anti-Federalist*, ed. Herbert J. Storing (1981), 2:438.

7. Brutus, "Essay No. XV," in id. at 2:437–39 (emphasis added). Brutus is believed to have been Robert Yates, of New York. Storing, "Essays of Brutus," id. at 2:358. His essays, while not widely read, prompted Hamilton's famous reply in "Federalist No. 78." See Larry Kramer, *The People Themselves: Popular Constitutionalism and Judicial Review* (2004), 79–81.

8. Franklin D. Roosevelt, "A 'Fireside Chat' Discussing the Plan for Reorganization of the Judiciary," March 9, 1937, in *The Public Papers and Addresses of Franklin D. Roosevelt*, vol. 6: *The Constitution Prevails, 1937*, ed. Samuel I. Rosenman (1941), 123–24.

9. For an account of the relationship between presidential leadership and Supreme Court authority, see Keith E. Whittington, *Political Foundations of Judicial Supremacy: The Presidency, the Supreme Court, and Constitutional Leadership in U.S. History* (2007).

10. Quoted in *Thomas Jefferson, Political Writings*, ed. Joyce Oldham Appleby and Terence Ball (1999), 357.

11. Abraham Lincoln, "First Inaugural Address," March 4, 1861, reprinted in *The Collected Works of Abraham Lincoln*, ed. Roy Basler (1953), 4:268.

12. "Roosevelt's Own Creed Set Forth," *N.Y. Times*, Aug. 7, 1912, at 8.

13. Accord Charles Gardner Geyh, *When Courts and Congress Collide: The Struggle for Control of America's Judicial System* (2006). See generally Chapter 10, infra.

14. United States v. Butler, 297 U.S. 1, 62–63 (1936).

15. West Virginia State Bd. of Educ. v. Barnette, 319 U.S. 624, 638 (1943).

16. Quoted in *The Supreme Court Issue and the Constitution: Comments Pro and Con by Distinguished Men*, ed. William R. Barnes and A. W. Littlefield (1937), 36. Gannett letter transcript available at: http://www.archives.gov/education/lessons/separation-powers/gannett-statement.html.

17. March 8, 1937, broadcast over Mutual Broadcasting, reprinted in James Truslow Adams, "What the Supreme Court Does for Us," *Vital Speeches of the Day*, March 15, 1937, 3:322. Broadcast transcript available at: http://newdeal.feri.org/court/adams.htm.

18. Franklin D. Roosevelt, "A 'Fireside Chat' Discussing the Plan for Reorganization of the Judiciary," March 9, 1937, in Rosenman, *Public Papers of FDR*, vol. 6, supra note 8, at 124, 126.

19. See L. A. Powe, Jr., "Are 'The People' Missing in Action (and Should Anyone Care)?," *Tex. L. Rev.* 83 (2005): 864 ("[I]f someone as astute as James Madison could change his views on the role of the judiciary, then a natural question arises: Why can't the people themselves change with experience too?"). Charles Geyh provides a lively account of the way in which informal norms and customary practice serve to curtail Congress's means of disciplining the judiciary and how those norms evolved over time. See Geyh, *When Courts and Congress Collide*, supra note 13.

20. Alexander Hamilton, "The Federalist No. 78," in *The Federalist Papers*, ed. Clinton Rossiter (1961), 465.

21. Cong. Globe, 39th Cong., 2d Sess. 501–02 (1867), quoted in Bruce A. Ackerman, *We the People*, vol. 2: *Transformations* (1998), 196.

22. See Chapter 4, infra, for a discussion of these events.

23. See generally Chapter 3, infra.

24. Robert G. McCloskey, *The American Supreme Court* (1960), 225.

25. A similar evolution in thinking, but with regard to the state judiciary rather than the federal, can be seen in Jed Shugerman's dissertation "The People's Courts: The Rise

of Judicial Elections and Judicial Power in America" (2008, unpublished manuscript, on file with author).

26. See Chapter 2, infra.
27. See Chapter 3, infra.
28. See Chapter 3, infra.
29. See Chapter 4, infra.
30. See Chapter 5, infra.
31. See Chapter 6, infra.
32. Accord David S. Law, "A Theory of Judicial Power and Judicial Review," *Geo. L. J.* 97 (2009): 730 ("The relationship between judicial power and popular rule is not antagonistic, but symbiotic").
33. Neal Devins, "The Majoritarian Rehnquist Court," *L. & Contemp. Probs.* 67 (2004): 76; James L. Gibson, Gregory A. Caldeira, and Lester Kenyatta Spence, "The Supreme Court and the US Presidential Election of 2000: Wounds, Self-Inflicted or Otherwise?," *British J. Pol. Sci.* 33 (2003): 538.
34. See Jeffrey Rosen, *The Most Democratic Branch: How the Courts Serve America* (2006), 3 ("[T]he Supreme Court in recent years has become increasingly adept at representing the views of the center of American politics:"); see also the Conclusion, infra.
35. Alexis de Tocqueville, *Democracy in America*, tr. George Lawrence (2000), 150 (describing the power of the Supreme Court as "springing from opinion"); James Bryce, *The American Commonwealth* (1888; repr. 1995), 1:242 ("The Supreme Court feels the touch of public opinion").
36. See Irving Crespi, *Public Opinion, Polls, and Democracy* (1989), 131; V. O. Key, Jr., *Public Opinion and American Democracy* (1961), 91–92; Walter Lippmann, *Public Opinion* (1922), 204–07. This begins to change in the era of opinion polling. For an examination of the impact of polling, see Sarah E. Igo, *The Averaged American: Surveys, Citizens, and the Making of a Mass Public* (2007).
37. See Jürgen Habermas, *The Structural Transformation of the Public Sphere: An Inquiry into a Category of Bourgeois Society*, tr. Thomas Burger (1989), 246–47 (identifying "quasi-public opinion" as those "opinions that circulate in a relatively narrow circle—skipping the mass of the population").
38. This was in part the result of Progressive Era "reforms" that disenfranchised the poor or African-Americans. See Eileen L. McDonagh, "Race, Class, and Gender in the Progressive Era: Restructuring State and Society," in *Progressivism and the New Democracy*, ed. Sidney M. Milkis and Jerome M. Mileur (1999), 157.
39. For an engaging account of the development of American democracy, see Alexander Keyssar, *The Right to Vote: The Contested History of Democracy in the United States* (2001). For a similar account of antebellum democracy, see Sean Wilentz, *The Rise of American Democracy: Jefferson to Lincoln* (2005).
40. See Key, *Public Opinion and American Democracy*, supra note 36, at 7 ("Not all these policy innovations have been willed by a power elite of 100 or 200 persons; nor have they been entirely unconnected with mass sentiment"); id. at 443 (describing the function of political parties as both leading and being driven by popular opinion).
41. See Ackerman, *We the People*, vol. 2: supra note 21, at 384–86 (describing the "transformative moments" of Reconstruction and the New Deal fight as including the participation of the elected branches, the Court, and the public); see also Walter Lippmann, *The Phantom Public* (1930), 66–67 (claiming that generally only in times of crisis does public opinion become aroused until "a workable adjustment that overcomes the crisis has been made").
42. For a sampler of information on important Supreme Court decisions, see *The Public Debate over Controversial Supreme Court Decisions*, ed. Melvin I. Urofsky (2006).

Chapter 1: Conception

1. U.S. Const. art. II, § 2, cl. 2.

2. Accord Annals of Cong. (D.C.: Gales and Seaton, 1834): 1:591 (statement of Rep. Vining); id. at 533 (statement of Rep. White).

3. Id. at 599. The vote was actually the reverse, 20–34, as the proposal voted down was to strike the words "to be removable by the President" from the bill. Id. at 576. On the removal debate, see David P. Currie, *The Constitution in Congress: The Federalist Period, 1789–1801* (1997), 36–41; Edward S. Corwin, "Tenure of Office and the Removal Power Under the Constitution," *Colum. L. Rev.* 27 (1927): 360–69. The question arose in the context of a proposed bill to establish the Department of Foreign Affairs. See Annals of Cong., supra note 2, at 1:473.

4. Annals of Cong., supra note 2, at 1:485 (statement of Rep. White); accord id. at 491–92 (statement of Rep. Gerry).

5. Id. at 582. For further examples of those in favor of the presidential removal power and supporting judicial review, see id. at 585 (statement of Rep. Sylvester) ("It is certain that the Judiciary will be better able to decide the question of Constitutionality. . . . If we are wrong, they can correct our error"); id. at 505 (statement of Rep. Lawrence) ("If the laws shall be in violation of any part of the Constitution, the judges will not hesitate to decide against them"); id. at 496 (statement of Rep. Ames) ("[I]f we declare improperly, the judiciary will revise our decision; so that at all events, I think we ought to make the declaration"). Only Madison stood clearly outside the fold on this point. He acknowledged, "in the ordinary course of Government, that the exposition of the laws and Constitution devolves upon the Judiciary" but wondered "upon what principle it can be contended, that any one department draws from the Constitution greater powers than another, in marking out the limits of the powers of the several departments?" Id. at 520. Madison's theory later became known as departmentalism or co-ordinate construction; its claim is that all branches share equally in interpretive authority over the Constitution. As the quotation itself suggests, however, it was unclear whether Madison's departmental view extended at that time to anything beyond questions of the "constitutional boundary" of the departments. Madison's views on the scope of judicial review were to change over time. See Larry D. Kramer, *The People Themselves: Popular Constitutionalism and Judicial Review* (2004), 145–47; Jack N. Rakove, "Judicial Power in the Constitutional Theory of James Madison," *Wm. & Mary L. Rev.* 43 (2002): 1513–47.

6. See Gordon S. Wood, "The Origins of Judicial Review Revisited, or How the Marshall Court Made More out of Less," *Wash. & Lee L. Rev.* 56 (1999): 792–93 (referring to the "remarkable transformation" that had occurred: "From minor magistrates identified with the colonial executives, the courts became an equal and independent part of a modern tripartite government"); see also Gordon S. Wood, *The Creation of the American Republic, 1776–1787* (1969), 453–63.

7. Alexander C. Hanson, "Political Schemes and Calculations, Addressed to the Citizens of Maryland," Annapolis, 1784, quoted in Wood, *Creation of the American Republic*, supra note 6, at 406.

8. William Blackstone, *Commentaries*, 1:*156. On the British rejection of judicial review at the time of Blackstone, see Daniel J. Hulsebosch, *Constituting Empire: New York and the Transformation of Constitutionalism in the Atlantic World, 1664–1830* (2005), 39–40; William Michael Treanor, "Judicial Review Before *Marbury*," *Stan. L. Rev.* 58 (2005): 468–70 & n48.

9. Dr. Bonham's Case, 77 Eng. Rep. 646 (C.P. 1610). See generally Hulsebosch, *Constituting Empire*, supra note 8, at 30–31; Kramer, *People Themselves*, supra note 5, at 19–20.

10. *Dr. Bonham's Case*, 77 Eng. Rep. at 652. For discussions of subsequent interpretations of *Bonham's Case* as supporting judicial review, see Raoul Berger, *Congress v. The Supreme Court* (1969), 23–28, 349–68, and Kramer, *People Themselves*, supra note 5, at 19–23.

11. Blackstone, *Commentaries*, supra note 8, at 1:*91. Blackstone does not mention Lord Coke explicitly in connection with his discussion of parliamentary omnipotence, though his use of precisely the same example is telling. For a discussion of Blackstone and *Bonham's Case*, see Hulsebosch, *Constituting Empire*, supra note 8, at 39–40. An extensive discussion of what was going on in *Bonham's Case* can be found in Philip Hamburger, *Law and Judicial Duty* (2008), 622–30.

12. For an outstanding depiction of the customary constitution as fundamental law, see Kramer, *People Themselves*, supra note 5, at 9–34.

13. John Phillip Reid, *Constitutional History of the American Revolution* (abr. ed. 1995), 3, 7.

14. Kramer, *People Themselves*, supra note 5, at 14–16.

15. Richard B. Morris, *The Forging of the Union, 1781–1789* (1987), 113. Philip Hamburger concurs, and argues Parliament was supreme as well because it was England's highest court. Hamburger, *Law and Judicial Duty*, supra note 11, at 237–47.

16. Blackstone, *Commentaries*, supra note 8, at 1:*156; see Reid, *Constitutional History*, supra note 13, at 22–25 (explaining how by the eighteenth century the original constitution of rights had become subordinated to one of parliamentary sovereignty). But see Philip A. Hamburger, "Revolution and Judicial Review: Chief Justice Holt's Opinion in City of *London v. Wood*," *Colum. L. Rev.* 94 (1994): 2111, 2152 (explaining that the people possessed the "extrajudicial" remedy of dissolving Parliament if an act was unlawful); see also Hamburger, *Law and Judicial Duty*, supra note 11, at 247–54 (discussing debate over whether Parliament was above the law). Coke came ultimately to concede that "the power and jurisdiction of the Parliament, for making of laws in proceeding by Bill, it is so transcendent and absolute, as it cannot be confined either for causes or persons within any bounds." Edward Coke, *The Fourth Part of the Institutes of the Lawes of England* (1669), 36; see Philip Hamburger, "Law and Judicial Duty," *Geo. Wash. L. Rev.* 72 (2003): 14. Coke's change in views may well have been the result of a change of position: he wrote the Fourth Institute while a member of the House of Commons. See Hulsebosch, *Constituting Empire*, supra note 8, at 32.

17. See Bernard Bailyn, *The Ideological Origins of the American Revolution* (enlarged ed. 1992), 170–75; Jack N. Rakove, *Original Meanings: Politics and Ideas in the Making of the Constitution* (1996), 105–07; Wood, *Creation of the American Republic*, supra note 6, at 362–63.

18. Va. Const. of 1776, § 2 (Bill of Rights), in *The Federal and State Constitutions, Colonial Charters, and Other Organic Laws of the States, Territories, and Colonies Now or Heretofore Forming the United States of America*, ed. Francis Newton Thorpe (1909), 7:3813.

19. N.C. Const. of 1776, § 1 (Declaration of Rights), in Thorpe, *Federal and State Constitutions*, supra note 18, at 5:2787; Md. Const. of 1776, § 1 (Declaration of Rights), in id. at 3:1686.

20. See Hulsebosch, *Constituting Empire*, supra note 8, at 47; Wood, *Creation of the American Republic*, supra note 6, at 135–39, 274; William Clarence Webster, "Comparative Study of the State Constitutions of the American Revolution," *Annals Am. Acad. Pol. & Soc. Sci.* 9 (1897): 82–85; John Phillip Reid, "Legislating the Courts: Judicial Dependence During the Era of the Early Republic" (unpublished manuscript, July 2005), 6 (noting that in effect all government powers were located in the legislature).

21. On the struggle for independence of colonial judges from the crown, see Bailyn, *Ideological Origins*, supra note 17, at 105–09.
22. On crown appointment, see William C. Morey, "The First State Constitutions," *Annals Am. Acad. Pol. & Soc. Sci.* 4 (1893): 229, and Reid, "Legislating the Courts," supra note 20, at 6 (noting that the "judiciary was perceived as a subordinate function of the executive"). On reliance on the lower houses, see William E. Nelson, *Americanization of the Common Law: The Impact of Legal Change on Massachusetts Society, 1760–1830* (1975; repr. 1994), 32.
23. See Christine A. Desan, "The Constitutional Commitment to Legislative Adjudication in the Early American Tradition," *Harv. L. Rev.* 111 (1998): 1383.
24. Nelson, *Americanization of the Common Law*, supra note 22, at 20–21, 32–35.
25. Donald S. Lutz, *Popular Consent and Popular Control: Whig Political Theory in the Early State Constitutions* (1980), 96–97; Morey, "The First State Constitutions," supra note 22, at 229; Reid, "Legislating the Courts," supra note 20, at 10, 14–22 (chronicling the travails of New Hampshire's early judiciary).
26. James Madison, "Vices of the Political System of the United States," in *Letters and Other Writings of James Madison, Fourth President of the United States* (J. B. Lippincott & Co., 1867).
27. Giles Hickory, "Government," *The American Magazine, Containing a Miscellaneous Collection of Original and Other Valuable Essays in Prose and Verse, and Calculated for Instruction and Amusement* (1788), 1: 206; see Wood, *Creation of the American Republic*, supra note 6, at 411.
28. See G. Alan Tarr, *Understanding State Constitutions* (1998), 73, 75–81. On the tradition of popular enforcement of constitutional norms, see Kramer, *People Themselves*, supra note 5, at 27–28; John Phillip Reid, "In a Defensive Rage: The Uses of the Mob, the Justification in Law, and the Coming of the American Revolution," *N.Y.U. L. Rev.* 49 (1974): 1043–91.
29. Charles Grove Haines, *The American Doctrine of Judicial Supremacy* (1914), 124–38; Lutz, *Popular Consent*, supra note 25, at 94–99; Tarr, *Understanding State Constitutions*, supra note 28, at 87–88; Wood, *Creation of the American Republic*, supra note 6, at 432–39, 453–56.
30. Pa. Const. of 1776, § 47, in Thorpe, *Federal and State Constitutions*, supra note 18, at 5:3091.
31. Lutz, *Popular Consent*, supra note 25, at 132, 147; Morris, *Forging of the Union*, supra note 15, at 124.
32. Haines, *American Doctrine*, supra note 29, at 137.
33. James Madison, "The Federalist No. 48," in *The Federalist Papers*, ed. Clinton Rossiter (1961), 308.
34. *The Debates in the Several State Conventions on the Adoption of the Federal Constitution as Recommended by the General Convention at Philadelphia, in 1787*, ed. Jonathan Elliot (1891), 3:450 (statement of George Nicholas). Jesse Turner writes that Nicholas was alluding to the case of the outlaw Josiah Philips, who allegedly was executed pursuant to a legislative attainder. Jesse Turner, "A Phantom Precedent," *Am. L. Rev.* 48 (1914): 322–23, 328. William Crosskey argues that Edmund Randolph purposefully misattributed the concept of judicial review to this case during the Virginia ratifying debates; although the legislature passed such an attainder, Philips was apprehended before it went into effect, and so his trial (with Randolph, as attorney general, prosecuting) and execution were pursuant to proper indictment. The attainder does remain an example of the Virginia legislature's disregard for Virginia's Bill of Rights. William Winslow Crosskey, *Politics and the Constitution in the History of the United States* (1953), 944–48; see also William Michael Treanor, "The

Case of the Prisoners and the Origins of Judicial Review," *U. Pa. L. Rev.* 143 (1994): 491n1, 538n212.

35. On this disgust, see Edmund S. Morgan, *Inventing the People: The Rise of Popular Sovereignty in England and America* (1988), 252–54; Wood, *Creation of the American Republic*, supra note 6, at 403–09, 430–38.

36. Willis P. Wichard, *Justice James Iredell* (2000), xiv–xv, 29, 90.

37. Letter from James Iredell to Hannah Iredell, May 18, 1780, in *Life and Correspondence of James Iredell*, ed. Griffith J. McRee (1857), 1:446.

38. Letter from William Plumer to Daniel Tilton, Dec. 16, 1787, quoted in Timothy A. Lawrie, "Interpretation and Authority: Separation of Powers and the Judiciary's Battle for Independence in New Hampshire, 1786–1818," *Am. J. Legal Hist.* 39 (1995): 318. On Plumer, see William Plumer, Jr., *Life of William Plumer* (1857), passim; John Phillip Reid, *Controlling the Law: Legal Politics in Early National New Hampshire* (2004), 90, 114, 126.

39. Wood, *Creation of the American Republic*, supra note 6, at 405–06. For a discussion of how Madison's argument in "Vices" fitted into his larger theory of government, see Larry D. Kramer, "Madison's Audience," *Harv. L. Rev.* 112 (1999): 629.

40. James Madison, "Vices of the Political System of the United States," in *Letters and Other Writings*, supra note 26, at 1:325; see also Jack N. Rakove, "The Origins of Judicial Review: A Plea for New Contexts," *Stan. L. Rev.* 49 (1997): 1056.

41. Letter from James Iredell to Richard Spaight, Aug. 26, 1787, in McRee, *Correspondence of James Iredell*, supra note 37, at 2:173.

42. *The Records of the Federal Convention of 1787*, ed. Max Farrand (rev. ed. 1966), 1:26–27 (statement of Edmund Randolph).

43. Several commentators have made the argument that all the early judicial review cases involved judges' striking down laws that implicated the judiciary. This argument is advanced, by some at least, as a ground for so limiting judicial power in the present. See, e.g., Robert Lowry Clinton, Marbury v. Madison *and Judicial Review* (1989), 1–2. Clinton finds "cases of a judiciary nature" to be those "which involve constitutional provisions directly addressed to the courts," and it is only in those cases "that the Supreme Court's refusal to apply a relevant law is *necessarily* final." Id. at 29. But see Dean Alfange, Jr., "*Marbury v. Madison* and Original Understandings of Judicial Review: In Defense of Traditional Wisdom," *Sup. Ct. Rev.*, 1993: 388n275 (critiquing Clinton's understanding of "judiciary nature"). A variation on the argument is that as an empirical matter, judges were more apt to find laws that implicated judicial prerogatives to be unconstitutional. See Treanor, "Judicial Review Before *Marbury*," supra note 8, at 497 (describing early cases as involving "judicial matters" or "the right to a jury trial").

This claim about the narrow scope of judicial review seems untenable. First, commentators simply commit a category error when they lump the jury trial right among judicial matters. At the time, juries were used as a limit on the authority of judges, so judges were not necessarily protecting their prerogative when insisting on juries. See Nelson, *Americanization of the Common Law*, supra note 22, at 20–21. Second, it is difficult to see why a claim that a law was "ex post facto" is a "judicial matter" unless every claim of right was. See Treanor, "Judicial Review Before *Marbury*," supra note 8, at 509 (discussing *Taylor v. Reading*, summarized in *State v. Parkhurst*, N.J.L. 9 (1802), 444). Similarly, it is equally difficult to see how striking down state laws as inconsistent with treaty obligations constitutes a "judicial matter." See Treanor, "Judicial Review Before *Marbury*," supra note 8, at 520–21 (discussing Hamilton v. Eaton, 11 F. Cas. 336 (C.C.D.N.C. 1792)).

44. The first case in which the issue was raised may have been the 1782 Virginia case called the *Case of the Prisoners*, or *Commonwealth v. Caton*. Commonwealth v. Caton, 8 Va. (4 Call.) 5 (1782). The case involved a pardon by one house of the Virginia legislature of individuals who had been convicted of treason and sentenced to death. Virginia's attorney general Edmund Randolph claimed the pardon invalid, as it was contrary to a Virginia statute that required both houses of the Virginia legislature to concur. The prisoners then made their own point: the statute seemed to violate the Virginia constitution, which permitted a one-house pardon. Newspapers dubbed the possibility that the judges actually might strike down the statute as "this great Constitutional Question." The novelty of the problem of judicial review led the Court to seek the views of leading figures of the bar, many of whom appeared and argued in favor of the power of judicial review. Even Randolph eventually agreed the Court ought to strike down the law if it was found to be unconstitutional. Having come to this conclusion with some reluctance, he opted for candor with the Court. Despite all the attention to the matter, the Court ultimately held the statute constitutional, and thus the judges were able to avoid coming to any firm conclusion regarding whether the opposite course was open to them. Treanor, "Case of the Prisoners," supra note 34, at 495–96, 500–05, 512, 529–32; see also Pendleton's "Account of the *Case of the Prisoners*," in *The Letters and Papers of Edmund Pendleton, 1734–1803*, ed. David John Mays (1967), 2:416–27.

45. Vanhorne's Lessee v. Dorrance, 2 U.S. (2 Dall.) 304, 314 (C.C.D. Pa. 1795). Paterson, as a federal judge, also had the advantage of not being accountable to the Pennsylvania legislature.

46. Philip Hamburger's truly excellent article on the historical precursors of judicial review makes this point vividly. Hamburger, "Law and Judicial Duty," supra note 16, at 1, 9–12. Hamburger extends his argument in Hamburger, *Law and Judicial Duty*, supra note 11, explaining there that judicial review reflected long-established judicial duty to apply the "law of the land."

47. Blackstone, *Commentaries*, supra note 8, at 1:*59, *87, *89.

48. The Privy Council had authority to review colonial laws to determine whether they were inconsistent with English law and colonial charters and therefore null and void. Hamburger, "Law and Judicial Duty," supra note 16, at 17. The Privy Council alternated between upholding English law and deferring to colonial practice. Mary Sarah Bilder, *The Transatlantic Constitution: Colonial Legal Culture and the Empire* (2004), 4; see also Hulsebosch, *Constituting Empire*, supra note 8, at 238; James B. Thayer, "The Origin and Scope of the American Doctrine of Constitutional Law," *Harv. L. Rev.* 7 (1893): 130–31.

49. William M. Meigs, *The Relation of the Judiciary to the Constitution* (1919), 103; see also Hulsebosch, *Constituting Empire*, supra note 8, at 248.

50. R.I. Charter of 1663, in Thorpe, *Federal and State Constitutions*, supra note 18, at 6:3215. Bilder concludes that review under the repugnancy clauses ultimately formed the basis for judicial review. Bilder, *Transatlantic Constitution*, supra note 48, at 195–96; see also Mary Sarah Bilder, "The Corporate Origins of Judicial Review," *Yale L. J.* 116 (2006): 502–66. The primary authority on the subject of Privy Council review is Joseph Smith. See Joseph Henry Smith, *Appeals to the Privy Council from the American Plantations* (1950), passim; Joseph Henry Smith, "Administrative Control of the Courts of the American Plantations," *Colum. L. Rev.* 61 (1961): 1210–53.

51. Hulsebosch, *Constituting Empire*, supra note 8, at 44.

52. On Rhode Island, see Bilder, *Transatlantic Constitution*, supra note 50, at 84–90; on Pennsylvania, see Smith, "Administrative Control," supra note 50, at 1217–22.

53. See Frank E. Melvin, "The Judicial Bulwark of the Constitution," *Am. Pol. Sci. Rev.* 8 (1914): 173–74.
54. *Journals of the Continental Congress, 1774–1789*, ed. Roscoe R. Hill (1936), 32:176–84; see also Melvin, "Judicial Bulwark," supra note 53, at 173–74.
55. Hill, *Journals of the Continental Congress*, supra note 54, at 32:183. Years later, in trying to solve a mystery about a supposed Massachusetts case of judicial review, A. C. Goodell, Jr., the editor of the *Acts and Resolves of the Province of Massachusetts Bay*, wrote a letter, published in the *Harvard Law Review*, explaining: "There was . . . another application of the word 'Constitution' then much in vogue, and particularly in reference to the subject of legislation covered by these Resolves. This was the treaty obligations entered into with Great Britain, by the General Congress." A. C. Goodell, Jr., "An Early Constitutional Case in Massachusetts," *Harv. L. Rev.* 7 (1894): 417.
56. An account of the case was printed in 1784 in pamphlet form, and in 1866 it was reprinted with a historical introduction, in Henry B. Dawson, *The Case of Elizabeth Rutgers versus Joshua Waddington, Determined in the Mayor's Court, in the City of New York, August 7, 1786* (1866). Dawson gives a detailed account of the facts of the case in his introduction.
57. "Brief of Alexander Hamilton No. 6, Rutgers v. Waddington," in *The Law Practice of Alexander Hamilton*, ed. Julius Goebel (1964), 1:389; see Meigs, *Relation of the Judiciary*, supra note 49, at 83.
58. Goebel, *Law Practice of Alexander Hamilton*, supra note 57, at 1:298–300, 304–06.
59. Brinton Coxe, *An Essay on Judicial Power and Unconstitutional Legislation, Being a Commentary on Parts of the Constitution of the United States* (1893), 230; Kramer, *People Themselves*, supra note 5, at 262n68.
60. James Duane, decision in *Rutgers v. Waddington*, reprinted in Meigs, *Relation of the Judiciary*, supra note 49, at 88; see also Goebel, *Law Practice of Alexander Hamilton*, supra note 57, at 1:309.
61. Dawson, *Case of Elizabeth Rutgers Versus Joshua Waddington*, supra note 56, at 29.
62. This is a central claim of John Phillip Reid's magisterial *Constitutional History of the American Revolution*. See Reid, *Constitutional History*, supra note 13, passim. Philip Hamburger documents the prevalence of this sort of thinking in resolutions, lower-court decisions, and decisions striking executive and judicial acts. Hamburger, *Law and Judicial Duty*, supra note 11, at 359–94.
63. Kramer, *People Themselves*, supra note 5, at 20–21.
64. John Adams, "Contemporaneous Notes of the Writs of Assistance Hearing in February 1761," reprinted in M. H. Smith, *The Writs of Assistance Case* (1978), 544. Larry Kramer suggests Otis's comment may have been nothing more than "statutory interpretation." Kramer, *People Themselves*, supra note 5, at 21–23. Others have argued that to the contrary, Otis was referring to judicial review. Hamburger, "Law and Judicial Duty," supra note 16, at 5–6. Indeed, historians disagree over the extent to which Coke's opinion in *Bonham's Case* played a predominant role in revolutionary thought. Compare Edward S. Corwin, "The Establishment of Judicial Review," *Mich. L. Rev.* 9 (1910): 107 with Kramer, *People Themselves*, supra note 5, at 19–23. Coke undeniably is cited in some of the early briefs in judicial review cases, such as *Trevett v. Weeden*, and played an important role in the arguments against the Stamp Act. See Hamburger, "Law and Judicial Duty," supra note 16, at 6 (confirming this point but explaining that eventually, in light of Blackstone's *Commentaries*, reliance on *Bonham's Case* came into "disrepute").
65. Massachusetts House of Representatives, quoted in Edmund S. Morgan and Helen M. Morgan, *The Stamp Act Crisis: Prologue to Revolution* (1953), 101–02.

66. Thomas Hutchinson, quoted in Meigs, *Relation of the Judiciary*, supra note 49, at 55.
67. Bayard v. Singleton, 1 N.C. (Mart.) 5 (Super. L. & Eq. 1787); see Kramer, *People Themselves*, supra note 5, at 67; Meigs, *Relation of the Judiciary*, supra note 49, at 108–09. Iredell's role in the case is a bit obscure. His notes suggest he was retained as counsel for Singleton, even though his public writings suggest he would have been more sympathetic to the plaintiff and the official report of the case lists him as counsel for the plaintiff. It is possible that the case report is indicating he participated in the proceedings on the constitutionality of the statute as amicus curiae, or friend of the court. Wichard, *Justice James Iredell*, supra note 36, at 10–12. Philip Hamburger suggests that Iredell was retained in a related case to keep him from acting in accord with his sympathies. This is why he spoke out anonymously. See Hamburger, *Law and Judicial Duty*, supra note 11, at 463.
68. *Bayard*, 1 N.C. (Mart.) at 5.
69. James Iredell, "To the Public," 1786, reprinted in McRee, *Correspondence of James Iredell*, supra note 37, at 2:145–49; Letter from James Iredell to Richard Spaight, Aug. 26, 1787, in McRee, *Correspondence of James Iredell*, supra note 37, at 2:172–76; see also Wichard, *Justice James Iredell*, supra note 36, at 12–14.
70. James Iredell, "To the Public," 1786, reprinted in McRee, *Correspondence of James Iredell*, supra note 37, at 2:146; see also Stanley N. Katz, "The American Constitution: A Revolutionary Interpretation," in *Beyond Confederation: Origins of the Constitution and American National Identity*, ed. Richard Beeman et al. (1987), 35.
71. See Bailyn, *Ideological Origins*, supra note 17, at 176–84; Hamburger, "Law and Judicial Duty," supra note 16, at 21.
72. James Iredell, "To the Public," 1786, reprinted in McRee, *Correspondence of James Iredell*, supra note 37, at 2:146; see also Vanhorne's Lessee v. Dorrance, 2 U.S. (2 Dall.) 304, 308 (C.C.D. Pa. 1795) ("What are Legislatures? Creatures of the Constitution; they owe their existence to the Constitution: they derive their powers from the Constitution: It is their commission; and, therefore, all their acts must be conformable to it, or else they will be void").
73. There is no official report. For an account, see James M. Varnum, *The Case, Trevett against Weeden* (1787).
74. Coxe, *An Essay on Judicial Power*, supra note 59, at 234–35.
75. For reports of the case, see "Newport, October 2," *Providence Gazette & Country J.*, Oct. 7, 1786, at 2; "Providence, Sept 30," *Conn. Gazette & the Universal Intelligencer*, Oct. 6, 1786, at 3; "Extract of a Letter from a Gentleman in Newport, to His Friend in Providence, Dated Sept 26," *Boston Gazette & the Country J.*, Oct. 2, 1786, at 3.
76. Varnum, *Trevett against Weeden*, supra note 73, at 3. Despite the claim, his was likely not the first lawyer to ask a court to refuse effect to an unconstitutional statute. See Austin Scott, "*Holmes v. Walton*: The New Jersey Precedent," *Am. Hist. Rev.* 4 (1899): 457–58 (describing the arguments of the plaintiff's attorney in *Holmes v. Walton* (1780), including the claim that a six-person jury violated the "Laws of the Land").
77. Varnum, *Trevett against Weeden*, supra note 73.
78. Bilder, *Transatlantic Constitution*, supra note 50, at 5. Most states adopted their first constitutions by legislative action, and a couple, such as Rhode Island, determined simply to rely on colonial charters. Pennsylvania's use of a Council of Censors in 1776 was the first instance of power being delegated to a nonlegislative body to amend a colony's constitution. This provision was used by Vermont when it amended its written constitution by a special constitutional convention in 1786. When the people of New Hampshire in 1778 and of Massachusetts in 1779 demanded a special state convention to form new constitutions, the trend began to shift to using conventions of the people, something that became an essential part of

American constitutionalism. Wood, *Creation of the American Republic*, supra note 6, at 132–33, 273–76, 307, 339–43. Wood writes that "[b]y the 1780's [the convention process] had become such a firmly established way of creating or changing a constitution that governments formed by other means actually seemed to have no constitution at all." Id. at 342.

79. Varnum, *Trevett against Weeden*, supra note 73, at 25. See Kramer, *People Themselves*, supra note 5, at 40–41 (explaining why Varnum's argument worked as a matter of customary constitutional law, despite Rhode Island's failure to adopt a constitution by popular consent).

80. Kamper v. Hawkins, 3 Va. 20 (Gen. Ct. 1793); see Margaret V. Nelson, "The Cases of the Judges: Fact or Fiction?," *Va. L. Rev.* 31 (1944): 249–50.

81. *Kamper*, 3 Va. at 78.

82. Letter from James Iredell to Richard Spaight, Aug. 26, 1787, in McRee, *Correspondence of James Iredell*, supra note 37, at 2:172. On the importance of a written constitution, see Kramer, *People Themselves*, supra note 5, at 50–52; Suzanna Sherry, "The Founders' Unwritten Constitution," *U. Chi. L. Rev.* 54 (1987): 1127–77; Wood, "Origins of Judicial Review," supra note 6, at 794–96.

83. Varnum, *Trevett against Weeden*, supra note 73, at 26–27.

84. *Bayard*, 1 N.C. (Mart.) at 7.

85. *Kamper*, 3 Va. at 81.

86. *Kamper*, 3 Va. at 82–83. For a discussion of fundamental law, see Wood, "Origins of Judicial Review," supra note 6, at 794–95.

87. *Kamper*, 3 Va. at 36, 40.

88. Letter from James Iredell to Richard Spaight, Aug. 26, 1787, in McRee, *Correspondence of James Iredell*, supra note 37, at 2:173.

89. *Bayard*, 1 N.C. (Mart.) at 7.

90. Daniel Hulsebosch argues that early judicial review cases overwhelmingly protected loyalist rights, and that courts did so, and exercised judicial review generally, in part to increase the stature of the young country as a trading partner and political equal of European nations. Daniel J. Hulsebosch, "A Discrete and Cosmopolitan Minority: The Loyalists, the Atlantic World, and the Origins of Judicial Review," *Chi.-Kent L. Rev.* 81 (2006): 826–27.

91. See Kramer, *People Themselves*, supra note 5, at 65–68.

92. Scott, "*Holmes v. Walton*," supra note 76, at 457–62.

93. *Votes and Proceedings of the General Assembly of the State of New Jersey*, Dec. 8, 1780 (1841), 52.

94. Scott, "*Holmes v. Walton*," supra note 76, at 460–61.

95. Id. at 463.

96. *State v. Parkhurst*, N.J.L. 9 (1802), 444. Accord Hamburger, *Law and Judicial Duty*, supra note 11, at 544. Hamburger agrees that acquiescence ultimately was the norm in these early instances of striking statutes. Id. at 544–46.

97. Melancton Smith et al., "To the People of the State of New York," *N.Y. Packet & the Am. Advertiser*, Nov. 4, 1784, at 1.

98. John C. Hamilton, *History of the Republic of the United States of America, as Traced in the Writings of Alexander Hamilton and of His Contemporaries* (1859), 3:21.

99. "New York, Nov. 16," *Pa. Packet & Daily Advertiser*, Nov. 20, 1784, at 3.

100. "Eighth Assembly, First Meeting," *N.Y. Assembly J.*, Oct. 4–Nov. 29, 1784, quoted in Goebel, *Law Practice of Alexander Hamilton*, supra note 57, at 1:313.

101. "Extract of a Letter from a Gentleman in Newport, to His Friend in Providence, Dated Sept 26," *Boston Gazette & the Country J.*, Oct. 2, 1786, at 3; see also "Newport, October 2," *Providence Gazette & Country J.*, Oct. 7, 1786, at 2. Some argue that the

decision was not strictly judicial review, but that the court simply dismissed the case for want of jurisdiction. See Patrick T. Conley, "Bicentennial Law Day Address: The Constitutional Significance of *Trevett v. Weeden*," May 3, 1976, reprinted in *R.I. Bar J.*, May 1976, at 2:24; Hamburger, "Law and Judicial Duty," supra note 16, at 12n37. The confusion is understandable. The judges handed down no written opinion, and when called before the legislature, one of the judges pointed out that technically all they had done was dismiss for lack of jurisdiction. Varnum, *Trevett against Weeden*, supra note 73, at 38. However, contemporaneous newspaper accounts reported that the judges stated their opinions from the bench. Unless the newspapers were incorrect, four of the five judges were against the act, and at least two clearly indicated the statute was unconstitutional. Judge Howell declared the law to be "repugnant and unconstitutional," and Judge Tillinghast "took notice of the striking repugnancy . . . of the act" and "gave his judgment the same way." The Chief Justice was silent, though being "a good whig, a friend to trial by jury," he was presumed to have agreed with his colleagues' ruling. "Newport, October 2," *Providence Gazette & Country J.*, Oct. 7, 1786, at 2; see also "Extract of a Letter from a Gentleman in Newport, to His Friend in Providence, Dated Sept 26," *Boston Gazette & the Country J.*, Oct. 2, 1786, at 3; "Providence, Sept 30," *Conn. Gazette & the Universal Intelligencer*, Oct. 6, 1786, at 3. In addition, in the assembly proceedings to censure the judges, the attorney general indicated that the decision was "conformable to the principles of constitutional law." Varnum, *Trevett against Weeden*, supra note 73, at 51.

102. Varnum, *Trevett against Weeden*, supra note 73, at 38. Judge Howell, who had most unequivocally declared the law to be unconstitutional (see note above), spoke for six hours in defense of the court's decision. John Winslow, *The Trial of the Rhode Island Judges: An Episode Touching Currency and Constitutional Law* (1887), 1.

103. Varnum, *Trevett against Weeden*, supra note 73, at 44, 51, 53; see also Conley, "Constitutional Significance of *Trevett v. Weeden*," supra note 101, passim.

104. Conley, "Constitutional Significance of *Trevett v. Weeden*," supra note 101, passim.

105. Farrand, *Records of the Federal Convention*, supra note 42, at 2:28 (statement of James Madison).

106. Bilder, *Transatlantic Constitution*, supra note 48, at 191.

107. For mention of the sanction, see Haines, *American Doctrine*, supra note 29, at 204–06; Kramer, *People Themselves*, supra note 5, at 68.

108. See Kramer, *People Themselves*, supra note 5, at 73 ("[T]he Framers clearly opted for judicial review as a device to control state law"); Rakove, "Origins of Judicial Review," supra note 40, at 1036, 1047 ("What is the Supremacy Clause about if it is not about something we would readily recognize as judicial review?"). Bradford Clark argues that the language of the Supremacy Clause makes judicial review of federal statutes equally clear. See Bradford R. Clark, "The Supremacy Clause as a Constraint on Federal Power," *Geo. Wash. L. Rev.* 71 (2003): 99–105; Bradford R. Clark, "Unitary Judicial Review," *Geo. Wash. L. Rev.* 72 (2003): 323–24.

109. Farrand, *Records of the Federal Convention*, supra note 42, at 1:97 (statement of Elbridge Gerry) ("In some States the Judges had [actually] set aside laws as being agst. the Constitution. This was done too with general approbation"); id. at 2:28 (statement of James Madison) (Madison appears to refer to *Trevett*).

110. Saikrishna B. Prakash and John C. Yoo, "The Origins of Judicial Review," *U. Chi. L. Rev.* 70 (2003): 939 & n207; Treanor, "Case of the Prisoners," supra note 34, at 496. Charles Warren also lists Richard Spaight, Iredell's friend, as counsel in *Bayard*, relying on newspaper reports at the time. Charles Warren, *Congress, the Constitution and the Supreme Court* (1930), 46. For a description of the *Caton* case, see supra note 44.

111. Number one was the "[f]ailure of the States to comply with the Constitutional requisition." James Madison, "Vices of the Political System of the United States," in *Letters and Other Writings*, supra note 26, at 1:320. See generally Jenna Bednar, *The Robust Federation: Principles of Design* (2008), 66–73 (discussing problem of opportunism on parts of subnational governments).

112. Farrand, *Records of the Federal Convention*, supra note 42, at 1:26 (statement of Edmund Randolph). For more on the problem of union under the Confederation, see Jack N. Rakove, *The Beginnings of National Politics: An Interpretative History of the Continental Congress* (1979), 333–59; Rakove, "Origins of Judicial Review," supra note 40, at 1043–46.

113. Farrand, *Records of the Federal Convention*, supra note 42, at 1:21 (statement of Edmund Randolph). Edmund Randolph presented this idea and the rest of the Virginia Plan, but its chief architect was James Madison. Kramer, "Madison's Audience," supra note 39, at 640. On Madison's arsenal of tools to control the states, see James S. Liebman and William F. Ryan, "'Some Effectual Power': The Quantity and Quality of Decisionmaking Required of Article III Courts," *Colum. L. Rev.* 98 (1998): 710–11. For a full discussion of the theory of government that Madison proposed at the convention, see Kramer, "Madison's Audience," supra note 39, passim.

114. See Kramer, "Madison's Audience," supra note 39, at 649–53, for a compelling argument that the delegates at Philadelphia largely misunderstood Madison's broader argument for the congressional negative.

115. Farrand, *Records of the Federal Convention*, supra note 42, at 2:28 (statement of Gouverneur Morris).

116. Letter from Thomas Jefferson to James Madison, June 20, 1787, in *The Writings of Thomas Jefferson*, ed. Paul Leicester Ford (1892), 4:390.

117. Farrand, *Records of the Federal Convention*, supra note 42, at 2:27 (statement of Roger Sherman).

118. Id. at 2:28 (statement of James Madison).

119. Letter from James Madison to Thomas Jefferson, Oct. 24, 1787, in *Letters and Other Writings*, supra note 26, at 1:349.

120. U.S. Const. art. VI, § 1, cl. 2; see Prakash and Yoo, "Origins of Judicial Review," supra note 110, at 945–46. For a discussion of the emergence of the Supremacy Clause in the convention, see Kramer, *People Themselves*, supra note 5, at 73–78, and Liebman and Ryan, "Some Effectual Power," supra note 113, at 705–73.

121. Farrand, *Records of the Federal Convention*, supra note 42, at 1:124 (statement of John Rutledge).

122. U.S. Const. art. III, § 1; see Richard H. Fallon, Jr., et al., *Hart and Wechsler's The Federal Courts and the Federal System*, 5th ed. (2003), 7–9; Michael G. Collins, "Article III Cases, State Court Duties, and the Madisonian Compromise," *Wis. L. Rev.*, 1995:39; Martin H. Redish and Curtis E. Woods, "Congressional Power to Control the Jurisdiction of Lower Federal Courts: A Critical Review and a New Synthesis," *U. Pa. L. Rev.* 124 (1975): 52–55.

123. But see Clark, "Unitary Judicial Review," supra note 108, at 325–33; see also Meigs, *Relation of the Judiciary*, supra note 49, at 151–60.

124. Farrand, *Records of the Federal Convention*, supra note 42, at 1:21 (statement of Edmund Randolph).

125. Id. at 2:73 (statement of James Wilson).

126. Id. at 1:97 (statement of Elbridge Gerry).

127. Id. at 1:109 (statement of Rufus King).

128. Id. at 2:73 (statement of James Wilson).

129. Id. at 2:298 (statement of John Mercer). The Virginia case was *Commonwealth v. Caton*. See supra note 44.
130. Farrand, *Records of the Federal Convention*, supra note 42, at 2:299 (statement of John Dickinson). Writing as "Fabius," Dickinson seemed to take a more favorable view during the ratification debates, citing the power of "independent" federal judges to check an overweening federal government by determining the constitutionality of its laws. Fabius, "Observations on the Constitution Proposed by the Federal Convention," *Pa. Mercury & Universal Advertiser*, Apr. 19, 1788, at 2.
131. See Kramer, *People Themselves*, supra note 5, at 78 (explaining that the ratification debates are of greater interest than the convention); see also infra Chapter 9 (discussing modern originalism doctrine that focuses on "original understanding").
132. Saikrishna B. Prakash and John C. Yoo, "The Puzzling Persistence of Process-Based Federalism Theories," *Tex. L. Rev.* 79 (2001): 1510; Prakash and Yoo, "Origins of Judicial Review," supra note 110, at 955 ("The ratification materials provide even more support than the Philadelphia debates for the conclusion that the Founders understood the Constitution to authorize judicial review of federal legislation").
133. See Kramer, *People Themselves*, supra note 5, at 79–83, 91. Because both sides assumed the existence of judicial review, it was not necessary for either side to belabor the point. Berger, *Congress v. The Supreme Court*, supra note 10, at 138.
134. It seems that no one denied the power of judicial review. Prakash and Yoo, "Origins of Judicial Review," supra note 110, at 974. However, the ratification debates are quite vast, and something may have been overlooked. On "ominous meanings," see J. M. Sosin, *The Aristocracy of the Long Robe: The Origins of Judicial Review in America* (1989), 260.
135. Elliot, *Debates in the Several State Conventions*, supra note 34, at 2:196 (statement of Oliver Ellsworth).
136. See Prakash and Yoo, "Origins of Judicial Review," supra note 110, at 956, 960, 964.
137. Elliot, *Debates in the Several State Conventions*, supra note 34, at 3:325 (statement of Patrick Henry).
138. Prakash and Yoo, "Origins of Judicial Review," supra note 110, at 956–57.
139. Id. at 970–71; Prakash and Yoo, "Puzzling Persistence," supra note 132, at 1506–07, 1518–19.
140. Letter from Samuel Osgood to Samuel Adams, Jan. 5, 1788, in *The Documentary History of the Ratification of the Constitution*, ed. John P. Kaminski and Gaspare J. Saladino (1984), 15:265.
141. Brutus, "Essay No. XII," Feb. 14, 1788, in *The Complete Anti-Federalist*, ed. Herbert J. Storing (1981), 2:427. On Brutus's fears, see Edward A. Purcell, Jr., *Originalism, Federalism, and the American Constitutional Enterprise: A Historical Inquiry* (2007), 142.
142. Brutus, "Essay No. XI," Jan. 31, 1788, in Storing, *Complete Anti-Federalist*, supra note 141, at 2:420.
143. Melancton Smith et al., "To the People of the State of New York," *N.Y. Packet & the Am. Advertiser*, Nov. 4, 1784, at 1.
144. Letter from Richard Spaight to James Iredell, Aug. 12, 1787, in McRee, *Correspondence of James Iredell*, supra note 37, at 2:169–70.
145. Hambden's letters ran in every issue of the *Middlesex Gazette* from June 16 to September 8, 1792, but Philopatriae did not begin the debate until mid-July. The debate was prompted by a proposal in the Connecticut legislature to exempt minors from the poll tax, which seems to have ultimately failed. *Middlesex Gazette*, June 2, 1792, at 3; "Middletown, June 9," *Middlesex Gazette*, June 9, 1792, at 3. Hambden argued for the exemption, while Philopatriae argued against it, but the main focus of their de-

bate was on the proper role and powers of the various branches of government. See generally Donald F. Melhorn, Jr., "A Moot Court Exercise: Debating Judicial Review Prior to *Marbury v. Madison,*" *Const. Comment.* 12 (1995): 343 & n95.

146. Melhorn, "A Moot Court Exercise," supra note 145, passim.

147. See Zephaniah Swift, *A System of the Laws of the State of Connecticut* (1795), 1:93–94.

148. Letter from Richard Spaight to James Iredell, Aug. 12, 1787, in McRee, *Correspondence of James Iredell,* supra note 37, at 2:168–69.

149. Philopatriae, "Letter to the Editor," *Middlesex Gazette,* July 14, 1792, at 1.

150. Letter from Richard Spaight to James Iredell, Aug. 12, 1787, in McRee, *Correspondence of James Iredell,* supra note 37, at 2:169.

151. Brutus, "Essay No. XV," Mar. 20, 1788, in Storing, *Complete Anti-Federalist,* supra note 141, at 437–38.

152. Melhorn, "A Moot Court Exercise," supra note 145, at 349, 351.

153. Swift, *A System of the Laws,* supra note 147, at 1:52–53.

154. Smith et al., "To the People of the State of New York," supra note 97, at 1.

155. Letter from Richard Spaight to James Iredell, Aug. 12, 1787, in McRee, *Correspondence of James Iredell,* supra note 37, at 2:169. The advocates at Litchfield argued similarly: "As to the omnipotence of the Legislature they are [sic] for a time omnipotent—they are the representatives of the people, & while they continue so they have all the power of the people in their hands." Melhorn, "A Moot Court Exercise," supra note 145, at 349 ("sic" in original).

156. Philopatriae, letter to the editor, *Middlesex Gazette,* July 21, 1792, at 1.

157. Philopatriae, letter to the editor, *Middlesex Gazette,* July 14, 1792, at 1.

158. Philopatriae, letter to the editor, *Middlesex Gazette,* July 21, 1792, at 1; Letter from Richard Spaight to James Iredell, Aug. 12, 1787, in McRee, *Correspondence of James Iredell,* supra note 37, at 2:169–70.

159. James Iredell, "To the Public," 1786, reprinted in McRee, *Correspondence of James Iredell,* supra note 37, at 2:147. Here Iredell echoed Varnum in *Trevett,* who told the Rhode Island Supreme Court that it ought to decide the case "in discharge of the great trust reposed in them, and to prevent the horrors of a civil war." Varnum, *Trevett against Weeden,* supra note 73, at 26. On the change from petitioning to instructing, see Wood, *Creation of the American Republic,* supra note 6, at 189–90.

160. Letter from James Iredell to Richard Spaight, Aug. 26, 1787, in McRee, *Correspondence of James Iredell,* supra note 37, at 2:175; accord James Madison, "The Federalist No. 50," in *Federalist Papers,* supra note 33, at 317, 319. Even Spaight acknowledged that elections "will in some degree remedy, though [they] cannot prevent, such evils as may arise." Letter from Richard Spaight to James Iredell, Aug. 12, 1787, in McRee, *Correspondence of James Iredell,* supra note 37, at 2:170.

161. Letter from Richard Spaight to James Iredell, Aug. 12, 1787, in McRee, *Correspondence of James Iredell,* supra note 37, at 2:169.

162. Treanor, "Judicial Review Before *Marbury,*" supra note 8, at 497. Treanor deserves great credit for excavating these cases. See also Hamburger, "Law and Judicial Duty," supra note 16, at 27–32 (discussing instances of "nonadjudicatory" judicial review).

163. Charles Warren, *The Supreme Court in United States History* (Boston: Little, Brown and Company, 1922), 1:68–69.

164. The case, *Champion v. Casey,* was decided in June 1792. There is no official report. See Charles Warren, "Earliest Cases of Judicial Review of State Legislation by Federal Court," *Yale L. J.* 32 (1922): 26–28; Julius Goebel, Jr., *The Oliver Wendell Holmes Devise History of the Supreme Court of the United States,* vol. 1, *Antecedents and Beginnings to 1801,* ed. Paul A. Freund (1971), 589.

165. Warren, "Earliest Cases," supra note 164, at 28. For examples of reporting newspapers, see *Columbian Centinel*, June 20, 1792, at 115; and "Providence, June 16," *Providence Gazette & Country J.*, June 16, 1792, at 3.

166. See James Kent, "Introductory Lecture," in *American Political Writing During the Founding Era, 1760–1805*, ed. Charles S. Hyneman and Donald S. Lutz (1983), 2:941–42; St. George Tucker, *Blackstone's Commentaries with Notes of Reference to the Constitution and Laws, of the Federal Government of the United States and of the Commonwealth of Virginia* (1803), 1:353 ("In England the judiciary may be overwhelmed by a combination between the executive and the legislature. In America (according to the true theory of our constitution,) it is rendered absolutely independent of, and superior to the attempts of both, to control, or crush it"); James Wilson, "Comparison of the Constitution of the United States, with That of Great Britain," in *The Works of James Wilson*, ed. Robert Green McCloskey (1967), 1:329–30.

167. Swift, *A System of the Laws*, supra note 147, at 1:51.

168. Currie, *Constitution in Congress*, supra note 3, at 120 ("Repeatedly and without contradiction, members of the First Congress acknowledged that the constitutionality of their actions would be subject to judicial review"); Maeva Marcus, "Judicial Review in the Early Republic," in *Launching the "Extended Republic": The Federalist Era*, ed. Ronald Hoffman and Peter J. Albert (1996), 25–35; Maeva Marcus, "Is the Supreme Court a Political Institution?," *Geo. Wash. L. Rev.* 72 (2003): 98 & n115 ("While Congress never enacted a statute providing for judicial review of executive and legislative actions, it did make public its faith that the judiciary would exercise that power").

169. Annals of Cong., supra note 2, at 1:457 (statement of Rep. Madison).

170. Id., at 2:1979 (statement of Rep. Boudinot).

171. For support for this statement and refutations of the arguments against it, see Berger, *Congress v. The Supreme Court*, supra note 10, at 101, 106–07 & n273, 227n25, 255, 270, 274–77; Prakash and Yoo, "Origins of Judicial Review," supra note 110, at 979–80; see also Clark, "Supremacy Clause as a Constraint," supra note 108, at 103–04; Clark, "Unitary Judicial Review," supra note 108, at 323–34.

172. Jurisdiction existed in the Supreme Court over any case involving "the validity of a treaty or statute of, or an authority exercised under the United States" when the state courts ruled against its validity, as well as any case involving a state statute or authority challenged as "repugnant to the constitution, treaties or laws of the United States, and the decision is in favour of such their validity." *An Act to Establish the Judiciary Courts of the United States* [Judiciary Act of 1789] (Sept. 24, 1789), *Stats at Large of USA* (Boston: Charles C. Little and James Brown, 1845): 1:73.

173. Some later commentators have suggested that this represents congressional "authorization" of the power rather than "recognition" or that the Court could "acquiesce" in the state decision but not decide of its own accord. Edward S. Corwin, *Court over Constitution: A Study of Judicial Review as an Instrument of Popular Government* (1938; repr. 1957), 52–53; Horace A. Davis, *The Judicial Veto* (1914), 120. These strained arguments, too clever by far more than half, emphasize how hard some have struggled to avoid the obvious conclusions about the foundations of judicial review.

174. Rather than strike down the law, judges on the United States Circuit Court for the District of Pennsylvania wrote the President explaining they could not execute the terms of the act. Other judges agreed to hear the claims, but as "commissioners" rather than in their judicial capacity. After the Pennsylvania court refused to hear William Hayburn's claim under the act, he petitioned Congress for relief. See *The Documentary History of the Supreme Court of the United States, 1789–1800*, vol. 6, *Cases: 1790–1795*, ed. Maeva Marcus (1998), 33–36; Max Farrand, "The First Hay-

burn Case, 1792," *Am. Hist. Rev.* 13 (1908): passim; Marcus, "Political Institution," supra note 168, at 102–04; see generally Hayburn's Case, 2 U.S. (Dall. 409) 408 (U.S. Pa. 1792).

175. Letter from Fisher Ames to Thomas Dwight, Apr. 25, 1792, in *Works of Fisher Ames with a Selection from His Speeches and Correspondence*, ed. Seth Ames (1854; repr. 1971), 1:117.

176. Letter from William Vans Murray to John Gwinn, Apr. 15, 1792, in Marcus, *Cases: 1790–1795*, supra note 174, at 50–51.

177. "Communication," *Nat'l Gazette*, Apr. 19, 1792. The same article was also reported in "Philadelphia, April 19," *Salem Gazette*, May 1, 1792, at 3; see also "The Editor of the Gen. Advertiser," *Gen. Advertiser*, Apr. 21, 1792, at 3.

178. Letter from William Vans Murray to John Gwinn, Apr. 15, 1792, in Marcus, *Cases: 1790–1795*, supra note 174, at 50. Congress eventually revised the act to avoid the constitutional difficulties raised by the judges, but this did not resolve questions on the validity of the claims put forth in 1792, prior to the revision. See id. at 39–41. Attorney General William Bradford brought suit to recover payments made to veteran Yale Todd, who had been previously awarded a pension. In *United States v. Yale Todd*, the Supreme Court ruled that Todd had to repay the money, offering no reasoning. But Bradford explained in a private letter that the Court had determined that the adjudications granting Todd's pension under the prior law were "not valid." Id. at 41–44.

179. Annals of Cong., supra note 2, at 3:557 (statement of Rep. Murray).

180. Cooper v. Telfair, 4 U.S. 14, 19 (1800).

2: Independence

1. Richard E. Ellis, *The Jeffersonian Crisis: Courts and Politics in the Young Republic* (1971), 4–5.

2. Annals of Cong. (D.C.: Gales and Seaton, 1851): 11:947.

3. *N.Y. Evening Post*, reprinted in *N.H. Sentinel*, Feb. 4, 1804, at 1.

4. In addition to Jefferson, Edmund Pendleton and John Taylor serve as prime examples. Pendleton, a judge, had been one of the first to support the exercise of judicial review. See Letter from Edmund Pendleton to James Madison, Feb. 15, 1766, in Massachusetts Historical Society, *Proceedings of the Massachusetts Historical Society* (2d Series, 1905), 19:111 (threatening to declare British Parliament's Stamp Act unconstitutional); *Cases of the Judges of the Court of Appeals*, 8 Va. (4 Call.) 135, 1788 WL 56, at *5 (Va. 1788) (describing remonstrance of the Virginia judges signed by Pendleton that stressed "[t]he propriety and necessity of the independence of the judges" given that "they are to decide between government and the people, as well as between contending citizens"); Edmund Pendleton, "Statement," June 12, 1788, in *The Documentary History of the Ratification of the Constitution,* ed. John P. Kaminski and Gaspare J. Saladino (1993), 10:1197 (noting Pendleton's approval that his fellow judges "have prevented the operation of some unconstitutional acts" at Virginia's ratifying convention). Yet in 1801 he authored a political tract, "The Danger Not Over," suggesting that federal judges be removable upon a simple vote of Congress. *Kline's Carlisle Weekly Gazette* (Pa.), Nov. 11, 1801, at 1. John Taylor challenged the constitutionality of a national carriage tax before the federal circuit court, arguing the Constitution "interposes the judiciary between the government and the individual. It provides for its independency upon either. . . ." John Taylor, "Argument on the Carriage Tax," in *The Documentary History of the Supreme Court of the United States, 1789–1800*, vol. 7, *Cases: 1796–1797*, ed. Maeva Marcus (2003), 385. After the 1800 election, however, Taylor crafted the intellectual arguments to support the Republican attack on the judiciary and went on to write lengthy and dense tracts against political power. See John Taylor, *New Views*

of the Constitution of the United States (1823; repr. 1971); John Taylor, *Tyranny Unmasked*, ed. F. Thornton Miller (1822; repr. 1992); John Taylor, *Construction Construed and Constitutions Vindicated* (1820; repr. 1970).

5. Letter from Thomas Jefferson to James Madison, June 20, 1787, in *The Writings of Thomas Jefferson*, ed. Paul Leicester Ford (1899), 4:391.

6. Letter from Thomas Jefferson to James Madison, March 15, 1789, in id. at 5:80–81.

7. See, e.g., Letter from Thomas Jefferson to Thomas Ritchie, Dec. 25, 1820, in id. at 10:170.

8. Annals of Cong., supra note 2, at 11:648 (statement of Rep. Bayard); id. at 823 (statement of Rep. Nicholson).

9. James Madison, "Vices of the Political System," in *James Madison: Writings*, ed. Jack N. Rakove (1999), 76–79; James Madison, "The Federalist No. 10," in *The Federalist Papers*, ed. Clinton Rossiter (1961), 77–84; see also Lance Banning, *The Sacred Fire of Liberty: James Madison and the Founding of the Federal Republic* (1995), 202–14; Larry D. Kramer, "Madison's Audience," *Harv. L. Rev.* 112 (1999): 629–34.

10. Letter from Thomas Jefferson to Francis Hopkinson, March 13, 1789, in Ford, *Writings of Thomas Jefferson*, supra note 5, at 5:76.

11. George Washington, "Farewell Address," Sept. 19, 1796, in *Writings of George Washington*, ed. Lawrence B. Evans (1908), 547. Though Washington's face was straight, the line was written by that great Federalist partisan Alexander Hamilton, possibly to provide the Federalists with an electoral advantage. Bruce A. Ackerman, *The Failure of the Founding Fathers* (2005), 23–24.

12. David Hackett Fischer, *The Revolution of American Conservatism: The Federalist Party in the Era of Jeffersonian Democracy* (1965), 182–87; James Roger Sharp, *American Politics in the Early Republic* (1993), 5; Joanne B. Freeman, "The Election of 1800: A Study in the Logic of Political Change," *Yale L. J.* 108 (1999): 1964–69.

13. See William Nisbet Chambers, *Political Parties in a New Nation: The American Experience, 1776–1809* (1963), 36–39, 53–56; Stanley Elkins and Eric McKitrick, *The Age of Federalism* (1993), 114–23, 258–63.

14. Mark Robert Killenbeck, M'Culloch v. Maryland: *Securing a Nation* (2006), 22–24.

15. See id. at 15, 19–21.

16. Richard E. Ellis, *Aggressive Nationalism*: McCulloch v. Maryland *and the Foundation of Federal Authority in the Young Republic* (2007), 34–36.

17. Letter from Fisher Ames to Thomas Dwight, Jan. 23, 1792, quoted in Killenbeck, M'Culloch v. Maryland, supra note 14, at 31.

18. See Chambers, *Political Parties*, supra note 13, at 42–43; Elkins and McKitrick, *Age of Federalism*, supra note 13, at 303–450; Ellis, *Jeffersonian Crisis*, supra note 1, at 272–73; Sharp, *American Politics*, supra note 12, at 70–74. On party politics at the turn of the century generally, see George Lee Haskins,*The Oliver Wendell Holmes Devise History of the Supreme Court of the United States*, vol. 2, pt. 1, *Foundations of Power: John Marshall, 1801–1815*, ed. Paul A. Freund (1981), 50–73.

19. Sarah J. Purcell, *Sealed with Blood: War, Sacrifice, and Memory in Revolutionary America* (2002), 123; Rosemarie Zagarri, "Women and Party Conflict in the Early Republic," in *Beyond the Founders: New Approaches to the Political History of the Early American Republic*, ed. Jeffrey L. Pasley et al. (2004), 110.

20. See Sharp, *American Politics*, supra note 12, at 167–68; Richard H. Kohn, *Eagle and Sword: The Federalists and the Creation of the Military Establishment in America, 1783–1802* (1975), 208–18; Kathryn Turner, "Federalist Policy and the Judiciary Act of 1801," *Wm. & Mary Q.* 22 (1965): 7. In early 1798, both Adams and the extreme Federalists aligned with Alexander Hamilton, known as High Federalists, considered war with France virtually inevitable. Although the High Federalists pressured Adams

to seek a congressional declaration of war against France, Adams refrained from doing so and focused on strengthening America's naval defenses. The High Federalists went so far as to investigate the possibility of seeking a declaration of war without Adams's support, but the President's desire to follow public opinion by negotiating peace and avoiding full-scale hostilities with France prevailed. Alexander De Conde, *The Quasi-War: The Politics and Diplomacy of the Undeclared War with France, 1797–1801* (1966), 77–78, 89–90, 168, 189.

21. See Chambers, *Political Parties*, supra note 13, at 134; Sharp, *American Politics*, supra note 12, at 171.

22. Adams reported to Congress that dispatches from envoys led him to doubt that accommodation could be reached with France "compatible with the safety, honor, or the essential interests of the nation." John Adams, "Message," March 19, 1798, quoted in Sharp, *American Politics*, supra note 12, at 173. Republicans were not alone in calling for publication of the dispatches; some Federalists did as well. Id. at 174. But the benefit of the release redounded to the Federalists.

23. Chambers, *Political Parties*, supra note 13, at 134–35; Sharp, *American Politics*, supra note 12, at 175.

24. *An Act Concerning Aliens* [Alien Act], (June 25, 1798), *Stats at Large of USA* (Boston: Charles C. Little and James Brown, 1845): 1:570; *An Act Respecting Alien Enemies* [Enemy Alien Act] (July 6, 1798), *Stats at Large of USA*, supra, at 1:577; *An Act in Addition to the Act, Entitled "An Act for the Punishment of Certain Crimes Against the United States"* [Sedition Act] (July 14, 1798), *Stats at Large of USA*, supra, at 1:596.

25. Geoffrey R. Stone, *Perilous Times: Free Speech in Wartime from the Sedition Act of 1798 to the War on Terrorism* (2004), 19 (referring to Sedition Act as "perhaps the most grievous assault on free speech in the history of the United States"). On the progressive nature of the Sedition Act, see John C. Miller, *Crisis in Freedom: The Alien and Sedition Acts* (1951), 70, 82; Stone, *Perilous Times*, supra, at 43–44; Gary D. Rowe, Note, "The Sound of Silence: *United States v. Hudson & Goodwin*, the Jeffersonian Ascendancy, and the Abolition of Federal Common Law Crimes," *Yale L. J.* 101 (1992): 936–38.

26. See Sharp, *American Politics*, supra note 12, at 176–80; Stone, *Perilous Times*, supra note 25, at 67–68.

27. Not entirely. Washington had sent the Supreme Court's first Chief Justice, John Jay, to Britain to negotiate an end to existing disagreements. Jay was an accomplished diplomat, but his appointment was controversial on party terms; the resulting treaty, which bore his name, was wildly unpopular and galvanized Republicans. Chambers, *Political Parties*, supra note 13, at 76–80. Adams sent Chief Justice Oliver Ellsworth on a mission to France. Elkins and McKitrick, *Age of Federalism*, supra note 13, at 619. Jefferson joined others in complaining about these appointments of judges to high diplomatic posts. The executive "has been able to draw into this vortex the Judiciary Branch of the Government . . . to make [it] auxiliary to the Executive in all its views. . . ." See Thomas Jefferson, "Notes on Prof. Ebeling's letter of July 30, 1795," quoted in Charles Warren, *The Supreme Court in United States History* (Boston: Little, Brown and Company, 1922), 1:167.

28. Stone, *Perilous Times*, supra note 25, at 63–64.

29. Elkins and McKitrick, *Age of Federalism*, supra note 13, at 710.

30. Francis Wharton, *State Trials of the United States During the Administrations of Washington and Adams* (1849), 336.

31. Julius Goebel, Jr., *The Oliver Wendell Holmes Devise History of the Supreme Court of the United States*, vol. 1, *Antecedents and Beginnings to 1801*, ed. Paul A. Freund (1971), 592. On the performance of Federalist judges under the Sedition Act, see

Miller, *Crisis in Freedom*, supra note 25, at 136–38; Stone, *Perilous Times*, supra note 25, at 67–69.

32. Elkins and McKitrick, *Age of Federalism*, supra note 13, at 710–11.

33. See Stone, *Perilous Times*, supra note 25, at 71–73.

34. Miller, *Crisis in Freedom*, supra note 25, at 221; Jeffrey L. Pasley, *The Tyranny of Printers: Newspaper Politics in the Early American Republic* (2001), 101, 106.

35. Goebel, *Antecedents and Beginnings*, supra note 31, at 620–23; William H. Rehnquist, *Grand Inquests: The Historic Impeachments of Justice Samuel Chase and President Andrew Johnson* (1992), 95–96; Maeva Marcus, "Is the Supreme Court a Political Institution?," *Geo. Wash. L. Rev.* 72 (2003): 96–97 & n10. For examples of the charges, see *The Documentary History of the Supreme Court of the United States, 1789–1800*, vol. 2, *The Justices on Circuit, 1790–1794*, ed. Maeva Marcus (1988); *The Documentary History of the Supreme Court of the United States, 1789–1800*, vol. 3, *The Justices on Circuit, 1795–1800*, ed. Maeva Marcus (1990).

36. Rehnquist, *Grand Inquests*, supra note 35, at 95; Haskins, *Foundations of Power*, supra note 18, at 222.

37. *United States Oracle of the Day* (Portsmouth, N.H.), May 24, 1800, at 3.

38. *Federal Gazette and Baltimore Daily Advertiser*, Apr. 10, 1799, quoted in Warren, *Supreme Court*, supra note 27, at 1:166.

39. See Jed Handelsman Shugerman, "*Marbury* and Judicial Deference: The Shadow of *Whittington v. Polk* and the Maryland Judicial Battle," *U. Pa. J. Const. L.* 5 (2002): 67 (describing Federalist Jeremiah Townley Chase and Republican Gabriel Duvall running against each other as electors for the 1800 presidential election while sitting on Maryland's General Court). See also Warren, *Supreme Court*, supra note 27, at 1:275–76 and Wharton, *State Trials*, supra note 30, at 46–47 for other examples of judges' partisan political activity.

40. *Aurora*, Aug. 9, 1800, in *The Documentary History of the Supreme Court of the United States, 1789–1800*, vol. 1, bk. 2, *Commentaries on Appointments and Proceedings*, ed. Maeva Marcus and James R. Perry (1986), 895; Pasley, *Tyranny of Printers*, supra note 34, at 79, 96.

41. The Republican victory was known after South Carolina voted for presidential electors on December 12, 1800. James M. O'Fallon, "*Marbury*," *Stan. L. Rev.* 44 (1992): 242; Sharp, *American Politics*, supra note 12, at 246–47. Jefferson did not take office until March 4, 1801. Noble E. Cunningham, Jr., *The Jeffersonian Republicans in Power: Party Operations, 1801–1809* (1963), 3.

42. See Ackerman, *Founding Fathers*, supra note 11, at 122–28; William E. Nelson, Marbury v. Madison: *The Origins of Judicial Review* (2000), 50.

43. Nelson, Marbury v. Madison, supra note 42, at 51–52; Louis H. Pollak, "*Marbury v. Madison*: What did John Marshall Decide and Why?," *Proceedings of Am. Phil. Soc.* 148 (2004): 3.

44. *An Act to Provide for the More Convenient Organization of the Courts of the United States* [Circuit Judges Act] (Feb. 13, 1801), *Stats at Large of USA*, supra note 24, at 2:89.

45. Ackerman, *Founding Fathers*, supra note 11, at 124–25.

46. Ellis, *Jeffersonian Crisis*, supra note 1, at 15.

47. See id. at 15–16; Warren, *Supreme Court*, supra note 27, at 1:185; Turner, "Federalist Policy," supra note 20, at 8–12, 29–32.

48. *Aurora*, March 29, 1800, quoted in Turner, "Federalist Policy," supra note 20, at 13.

49. Chambers, *Political Parties*, supra note 13, at 169.

50. Letter from Gouverneur Morris to Robert R. Livingston, Feb. 20, 1801, quoted in Ellis, *Jeffersonian Crisis*, supra note 1, at 15.

51. Letter from Thomas Jefferson to John Dickinson, Dec. 19, 1801, in *The Writings of Thomas Jefferson*, ed. Andrew A. Lipscomb and Albert Ellery Bergh (1903), 10:301–02. A few years later Jefferson wrote Abigail Adams, describing filling these positions as the "one act of Mr. Adams's life, and one only, [that] ever gave me a moment's personal displeasure. I did consider his last appointments to office as personally unkind." Letter from Thomas Jefferson to Abigail Adams, June 13, 1804, in Ford, *Writings of Thomas Jefferson*, supra note 5, at 8:307.

52. Warren, *Supreme Court*, supra note 27, at 1:195. He declined to do so. Id. at 195–97; see also Pasley, *Tyranny of Printers*, supra note 34, at 208.

53. Quoted in Warren, *Supreme Court*, supra note 27, at 1:197–98 (no citation provided).

54. See Marbury v. Madison, 5 U.S. (1 Cranch) 137, 137–38 (1803); Haskins, *Foundations of Power*, supra note 18, at 183–84; Pollak, "*Marbury v. Madison*," supra note 43, at 3–6; Warren, *Supreme Court*, supra note 27, at 1:204–05. Dennis Ramsay, Robert Townsend Hooe, and William Harper were also plaintiffs in the case. *Marbury*, 5 U.S. (1 Cranch) at 137.

55. *Marbury*, 5 U.S. (1 Cranch) at 153–54; Alfred J. Beveridge, *The Life of John Marshall* (1919), 3:111.

56. See Chambers, *Political Parties*, supra note 13, at 32–33. In Virginia, 25 percent of white males, some 50 percent of the electorate, came to choose electors for the 1800 presidential election, while the gubernatorial election in Pennsylvania saw a turnout twice what it had been before. Richard P. McCormick, *The Presidential Game* (1982), 71.

57. On deferential politics, see generally Chambers, *Political Parties*, supra note 13, at 23–24, 109–10, 125; J. R. Pole, "A Whig World of Politics and Society," in *Politics and Society in Colonial America: Democracy or Deference*, ed. Michael G. Kammen (1967; repr. 1973), 131–32, 135; Andrew W. Robertson, "Voting Rites and Voting Acts: Electioneering Ritual, 1790–1820," in Pasley et al., *Beyond the Founders*, supra note 19, at 58–59; Joel H. Silbey, *The American Political Nation, 1838–1893* (1991), 14–15. The process of transitioning from a deferential to partisan political process described here was a lengthy one and subject to much scholarly disagreement. See, e.g., Kammen, *Politics and Society in Colonial America*, supra. Deference already was giving way by the American Revolution, which sped it along. See Pole, "A Whig World," in Kammen, *Politics and Society in Colonial America*, supra, at 135; Bernard A. Weisberger, *America Afire: Jefferson, Adams, and the Revolutionary Election of 1800* (2000), 39; Chilton Williamson, "Suffrage and the Revolution," in Kammen, *Politics and Society in Colonial America*, supra, at 101 (noting that after 1787, American political leaders faced "a politics that would no longer permit the members of an elite to only talk to each other"); Gordon S. Wood, *The Creation of the American Republic, 1776–1787* (1969), 563. Still, deference persisted in this period—and in the minds of some much beyond it, perhaps until the onset of Jacksonian democracy. See Pole, "A Whig World," in Kammen, *Politics and Society in Colonial America*, supra, at 146; Silbey, *American Political Nation*, supra, at 14. Jeffersonian parties were far more elitist in nature than Jacksonian ones. Chambers, *Political Parties*, supra note 13, at 206–07. The Jacksonian movement represented a far greater leap in democratization. See Chapter 3, infra.

58. James Madison, "Public Opinion," *Nat'l Gazette*, Dec. 19, 1791, at 59.

59. David Copeland, "America: 1750–1820" in *Press and the Public Sphere in Europe and America, 1760–1840*, ed. Hannah Barker and Simon Burrows (2002), 149; Donald H. Stewart, *The Opposition Press of the Federalist Period* (1969), 15.

60. Frank Luther Mott, *American Journalism: A History of Newspapers in the United States Through 250 Years: 1690–1940* (1941), 158–59; Stewart, *Opposition Press*, supra note 59, at 17.

61. See Cunningham, *Party Operations*, supra note 41, at 238; Pasley, *Tyranny of Printers*, supra note 34, at 14, 105.

62. See Noble E. Cunningham, Jr., *The Jeffersonian Republicans: The Formation of Party Organization, 1789–1801* (1957), 31, 52, 67; Cunningham, *Party Operations*, supra note 41, at 103.

63. Alexander Addison, *Liberty of Speech and of the Press* (1799), 12.

64. Miller, *Crisis in Freedom*, supra note 25, at 31–33; Pasley, *Tyranny of Printers*, supra note 34, at 98; Stone, *Perilous Times*, supra note 25, at 33–36.

65. Alexander Addison, "Reports of Cases," quoted in Pasley, *Tyranny of Printers*, supra note 34, at 123.

66. Several sources estimate that Republicans held 66 of the 106 seats in the House following the 1800 election. Chambers, *Political Parties*, supra note 13, at 160–61; Cunningham, *Party Organization*, supra note 62, at 247. However, according to the Office of the Clerk of the United States House of Representatives, there were 68 Republicans in the House after the 1800 election. Clerk of the United States House of Representatives, "Party Divisions of the House of Representatives," http://clerk.house.gov/art_history/house_history/partyDiv.html.

67. Jerrold G. Rusk, *A Statistical History of the American Electorate* (2001), 52. The voter turnout for presidential elections, calculated as the total votes cast for President divided by the number of people eligible by law to vote according to citizenship, race, sex, and age suffrage restrictions was 23.1 percent in 1796 and 29.9 percent in 1800. Id.

68. Cunningham, *Party Organization*, supra note 62, at 239.

69. Letter from Alexander Hamilton to James Bayard, Apr. 1802, quoted in Cunningham, *Party Operations*, supra note 41, at 7.

70. Thomas Jefferson, "First Inaugural Address," March 4, 1801, in Ford, *Writings of Thomas Jefferson*, supra note 5, at 8:3.

71. See Ellis, *Jeffersonian Crisis*, supra note 1, at 32–33.

72. Letter from John Mercer to James Madison, Feb. 8, 1801, quoted in Turner, "Federalist Policy," supra note 20, at 20. Turner also discusses the outrage of Republican newspapers over the passage of the Circuit Judges Act. Id.

73. Ellis, *Jeffersonian Crisis*, supra note 1, at 44.

74. Letter from Stevens Thomas Mason to James Monroe, Dec. 21, 1801, quoted in Ellis, *Jeffersonian Crisis*, supra note 1, at 44. On the constitutional reservations of Republicans expressed after the repeal was effectuated, see Haskins, *Foundations of Power*, supra note 18, at 165.

75. Annals of Cong., supra note 2, at 11:23.

76. Alexander Hamilton raised money to start the *New York Evening Post* but gave the task of editing the paper to attorney William Coleman. Pasley, *Tyranny of Printers*, supra note 34, at 237.

77. N.Y. *Evening Post*, March 1, 1802, at 3; *Nat'l Intelligencer*, Feb. 15, 1802, at 1.

78. See, e.g., Annals of Cong., supra note 2, at 11:510 (statement of Rep. Bayard) ("[P]eople in various quarters of the Union [a]re preparing to tell us what they [think] on the subject"); id. at 512 (statement of Rep. Giles) ("[Public] sentiment is with us"); id. at 515 (statement of Rep. Smilie) ("[P]ublic opinion should be attended to . . ."); id. at 688 (statement of Rep. Huger) ("We are nothing more or less than the mere agents of the people . . .").

79. See, e.g., id. at 152–53, 522, 545, 568.

80. See, e.g., *Columbian Centinel* (Boston), Feb. 6, 1802, at 1; *Gazette of the United States* (Phila.), Feb. 3, 1802, at 2; *Nat'l Intelligencer*, Jan. 20, 1802, at 1, 2.

81. N.Y. *Evening Post*, March 1, 1802, at 3; *Nat'l Intelligencer*, Feb. 3, 1802, at 3; *Gazette of the United States*, reprinted in *Connecticut Courant* (Hartford), Feb. 22, 1802, at 2.

For other accounts of speeches, see, e.g., *Wash. Federalist*, Feb. 6, 1802, at 2 (describing speeches of Federalist senators as "luminous," "uncommonly eloquent," and "unanswerable"); *Nat'l Intelligencer*, March 1, 1802, at 3 (describing Rep. Giles's speech as "a fortress, which neither declamation or sophistry can shake").

82. Thomas Jefferson, "First Annual Message," Dec. 8, 1801, in Ford, *Writings of Thomas Jefferson*, supra note 5, at 8:123. On the inaccuracy of Jefferson's statistics, see Haskins, *Foundations of Power*, supra note 18, at 154–55; Max Farrand, "The Judiciary Act of 1801," *Am. Hist. Rev.* 5 (1900): 685.

83. *Commercial Advertiser*, June 18, 1802, at 2.

84. See, e.g., Annals of Cong., supra note 2, at 11:33 (statement of Sen. Jonathan Mason); id. at 541 (statement of Rep. Hemphill); id. at 576 (statement of Rep. Stanley).

85. On Republicans' concerns over the "good Behaviour" argument, see Ellis, *Jeffersonian Crisis*, supra note 1, at 45–46; Warren, *Supreme Court*, supra note 27, at 1:204. On Republican position that the "good Behaviour" requirement applied only to the executive, see Annals of Cong., supra note 2, at 11:525–27 (statement of Rep. Henderson); Annals of Cong., supra note 2, at 11:577–78 (statement of Rep. Stanley).

86. Annals of Cong., supra note 2, at 11:27–28 (statement of Sen. Breckinridge); see also id. at 35 (statement of Sen. Wright) ("[T]he Constitution meant to guard the officer and not the office").

87. Id. at 548 (statement of Rep. Thompson).

88. Id. at 631 (statement of Rep. Bayard); see also *Connecticut Courant* (Hartford), quoted in *N.Y. Spectator*, Feb. 20, 1802, at 3 (discussing Bayard's point).

89. Annals of Cong., supra note 2, at 11:779 (statement of Rep. Griswold).

90. Id. at 91 (statement of Sen. Morris); id. at 743 (statement of Rep. Rutledge); id. at 144 (statement of Sen. Colhoun).

91. Id. at 518 (statement of Rep. Dana).

92. Id. at 92 (statement of Sen. Breckinridge). The imagery appears in the speeches of Federalist senators Tracy and Colhoun; see id. at 58, 144. Breckinridge appears to have been mocking it.

93. Id. at 851 (statement of Rep. Smith).

94. Id. at 48 (statement of Sen. Jackson); see also id. at 583 (statement of Rep. Giles) ("It is sometime, sir, since we have seen the zealous judge stoop from the bench to look out for more victims for judicial vengeance!"); id. at 652 (statement of Rep. Randolph); id. at 714 (statement of Rep. Macon).

95. Id. at 664 (statement of Rep. Randolph); see also id. at 804 (statement of Rep. Nicholson) (decrying judges who abuse their positions for partisan purposes).

96. Ellis, *Jeffersonian Crisis*, supra note 1, at 50. *Nat'l Intelligencer*, Feb. 5, 1802, at 3.

97. *S.C. State Gazette*, March 20, 1802, at 3; *N.Y. Spectator*, Feb. 10, 1802, at 3.

98. *Boston Indep. Chron.*, March 15, 1802, at 2; see also *N.H. Gazette*, March 16, 1802, at 2 (reprinting from "the Chronicle" the rhetorical query by "Old South": "[I]f in the opinion of the legislature there are no services' for them to do . . . I would enquire . . . whether by the *spirit of the constitution* they are entitled to any compensation?"). On the *Chronicle*, see Pasley, *Tyranny of Printers*, supra note 34, at 92, 141.

99. *Nat'l Intelligencer*, March 5, 1802, at 2.

100. Michael J. Klarman, "How Great Were the 'Great' Marshall Court Decisions?," *Va. L. Rev.* 87 (2001): 1116–17 (arguing that both parties were committed to judicial review by the time of *Marbury*).

101. Annals of Cong., supra note 2, at 11:56 (statement of Sen. Tracy); id. at 842 (statement of Rep. Dennis); id. at 926 (statement of Rep. Dana); id. at 940 (statement of Rep. Tallmadge).

102. Id. at 648 (statement of Rep. Bayard); id. at 529 (statement of Rep. Henderson); see also id. at 33 (statement of Sen. J. Mason); id. at 529 (statement of Rep. Henderson); id. at 783 (statement of Rep. Griswold); id. at 919 (statement of Rep. Dana).

103. Id. at 529 (statement of Rep. Henderson); see also id. at 542 (statement of Rep. Hemphill) (describing the view that "the judges have no right to declare a law to be unconstitutional" as "a doctrine new and dangerous"); id. at 919 (statement of Rep. Dana).

104. Id. at 844 (statement of Rep. Dennis).

105. Id. at 876 (statement of Rep. Gregg). David Currie makes much the same point, finding that the dispute over the legitimacy of judicial review was but a piece of the larger debate over the importance of judicial independence. David P. Currie, "The Constitution in Congress: The Most Endangered Branch, 1801–1805," *Wake Forest L. Rev.* 33 (1998): 230. Currie's article provides one of the best short summaries of the repeal debate. See id. at 222–38.

106. Annals of Cong., supra note 2, at 11:178–79 (statement of Sen. Breckinridge).

107. Id. at 180 (statement of Sen. Morris).

108. *Green Mountain Patriot* (Peacham, Vt.), March 24, 1802, at 3.

109. Annals of Cong., supra note 2, at 11:661 (statement of Rep. Randolph).

110. See, e.g., id. at 698 (statement of Rep. Smith) ("It is true your judges have authority . . . to decide a law void, which directly infringes the Constitution. . . . [B]ut prudent judges will exercise this right with great caution, knowing the Legislature has an equal right to put constructions").

111. Id. at 115 (statement of Sen. Wright).

112. Letter from Jefferson to Abigail Adams, quoted in David N. Mayer, *The Constitutional Thought of Thomas Jefferson* (1994), 269. On Jefferson's view of judicial review generally, see Mayer, supra, at 257–94; see also Larry D. Kramer, *The People Themselves: Popular Constitutionalism and Judicial Review* (2004), 106–08 (arguing that Jefferson "embraced [a departmentalist] theory throughout his political life"). But see Keith E. Whittington, *Political Foundations of Judicial Supremacy: The Presidency, the Supreme Court, and Constitutional Leadership in U.S. History* (2007), 108–10.

113. Annals of Cong., supra note 2, at 11:553 (statement of Rep. Thompson).

114. Id. at 646 (statement of Rep. Bayard).

115. Id.

116. Id. at 879 (statement of Rep. Gregg); see also id. at 59 (statement of Sen. S. T. Mason) ("I agree with gentlemen, that it is important, in a well regulated Government, that the judicial department should be independent. . . . [Y]et I have never believed that they ought to be independent of the nation itself. Much less have I believed it proper, or that our Constitution authorizes our courts of justice to control the other departments of the Government").

117. Id. at 824 (statement of Rep. Nicholson).

118. Id. at 48 (statement of Sen. Jackson).

119. Thomas Jefferson, "Marginal note on draft of address," quoted in Mayer, *Constitutional Thought*, supra note 112, at 269. The full text of the excised paragraph is reprinted in Beveridge, *Life of John Marshall*, supra note 55, at 3:app. A.

120. Annals of Cong., supra note 2, at 11:649 (statement of Rep. Bayard).

121. Id. at 611 (statement of Rep. Bayard).

122. *An Act to Amend the Judicial System of the United States* (Apr. 29, 1802), *Stats at Large of USA*, supra note 24, at 2:156. On passage of the bill, see Ross E. Davies, "A Certain Mongrel Court: Congress's Past Power and Present Potential to Reinforce the Supreme Court," *Minn. L. Rev.* 90 (2006): 692–94.

123. Annals of Cong., supra note 2, at 11:1210 (statement of Rep. Holland).

124. Ackerman, *Founding Fathers*, supra note 11, at 177 (describing the 1802 elections as a "crushing victory" for the Republicans, placing 102 Republicans in the House compared with 39 Federalists and leaving only 9 Federalist senators).

125. The pending *Marbury* litigation was cited repeatedly throughout the repeal debate as evidence of the threat the Republicans faced from Federalist judges overstepping their bounds. See Annals of Cong., supra note 2, at 11:662 (statement of Rep. Randolph); id. at 11:596 (statement of Rep. Giles). The *National Intelligencer* likewise chastised the Supreme Court, which "ought to have refused any instrumentality into this meditated, and[,] we may add, party invasion of Executive functions." *Nat'l Intelligencer*, Feb. 2, 1803, at 3.

126. For an excellent discussion of the background of *Stuart*, see Ackerman, *Founding Fathers*, supra note 11, at 172–81. In August 1802, Delaware circuit judge Richard Basset published a protest in which he urged the Supreme Court to "disobey Congress's command to resume circuit-riding, and . . . strike down the congressional statute that destroyed his court." Id. at 276–97; Ellis, *Jeffersonian Crisis*, supra note 1, at 62. On January 27, 1803, a memorial from eleven circuit judges whose offices had been eliminated by the Repeal Act was presented to the House and Senate. Annals of Cong. (D.C.: Gales and Seaton, 1851): 12:30–31, 427–28; Haskins, *Foundations of Power*, supra note 18, at 178–80. The judges wanted Congress to define their duties, since they argued they were still entitled to judicial positions and compensation regardless of the repeal act. The judges also offered to submit their claim "to judicial examination and decision, in such manner as the wisdom and impartiality of Congress may prescribe." Annals of Cong., supra, at 12:31, 427. The judges' memorial was rejected by a strict party line vote in both the House and the Senate. Ackerman, *Founding Fathers*, supra note 11, at 178. Additionally, one of the judges whose position was destroyed on the third circuit filed a lawsuit challenging the constitutionality of the repeal act in 1803. Warren, *Supreme Court*, supra note 27, at 1:272n1. However, the judge dropped his claim before it reached the Supreme Court. Ackerman, *Founding Fathers*, supra note 11, at 180; see also James M. O'Fallon, "The Case of Benjamin More: A Lost Episode in the Struggle over Repeal of the 1801 Judiciary Act," *Law & Hist. Rev.* 11 (1993): 43–58 (describing a case in which a justice of the peace whose position was created by the Judiciary Act of 1801, and who was charged with illegally taking fees for services rendered as a justice of the peace after the repeal act destroyed his position, defended himself by arguing the repeal act was unconstitutional).

127. See *Stuart v. Laird*, 5 U.S. (1 Cranch) 299, 303, 305 (1803). Lee argued that riding circuit infringed on judicial independence because a Supreme Court justice who hears a case below will feel "committed" to his prior decision and want to see it upheld by the Supreme Court, violating litigants' rights to an "unbiased" court. Lee also argued that legislation requiring circuit riding was an unconstitutional appointment by the legislature of judges to new courts since the President appointed Supreme Court justices only to a court of appellate jurisdiction, whereas Congress required judges to sit on circuit courts of original jurisdiction.

128. See Ellis, *Jeffersonian Crisis*, supra note 1, at 60–61; Haskins, *Foundations of Power*, supra note 18, at 169–78.

129. Letter from John Marshall to William Paterson, Apr. 19, 1802, in *The Papers of John Marshall*, ed. Charles F. Hobson and Fredrika J. Teute (1990), 6:109. Bruce Ackerman suggests that at least Marshall and Chase were in favor of declining their circuit duties. See Ackerman, *Founding Fathers*, supra note 11, at 164–72.

130. See Ackerman, *Founding Fathers*, supra note 11, at 175–76; Ellis, *Jeffersonian Crisis*, supra note 1, at 63. Apparently Marshall's opinion in the lower-court decision has not

survived. Ackerman, *Founding Fathers*, supra note 11, at 175, 345n29. *Stuart* was one of several test cases brought by Federalists challenging the constitutionality of the circuit courts as constituted under the 1802 repeal statute. As with *Stuart*, the others were similarly rebuffed by courts over which Supreme Court justices presided. See Ellis, *Jeffersonian Crisis*, supra note 1, at 62–63; Kramer, *People Themselves*, supra note 112, at 119–20.

131. Ackerman, *Founding Fathers*, supra note 11, at 191–92. Attorney General Levi Lincoln did appear and made arguments regarding the scope of executive privilege. Haskins, *Foundations of Power*, supra note 18, at 191–92.

132. Senator Breckinridge opposed granting Marbury's petition to the Senate for a certified copy of the Senate's debate on the appointments of the justices of the peace for use in his case because this would be to "administer to the means of assailing the Executive Department of the Government." Annals of Cong., supra note 126, at 12:35 (statement of Sen. Breckinridge); accord id., at 37 (statement of Sen. Wright); id., at 39 (statement of Sen. Jackson).

133. Id., at 12:437–38 (statement of Rep. Nicholson).

134. Id. at 12:460.

135. Albert Gallatin, acting for the administration, asked William Plumer, the Federalist senator from New Hampshire, to get Pickering to resign. Plumer refused. Ellis, *Jeffersonian Crisis*, supra note 1, at 70–71. See also Charles Gardner Geyh, *When Courts & Congress Collide: The Struggle for Control of America's Judicial System* (2006), 125–31.

136. Peter Charles Hoffer and N.E.H. Hull, *Impeachment in America, 1635–1805* (1984), 195–205.

137. *Marbury v. Madison*, 5 U.S. (1 Cranch) 137, 167–70 (1803).

138. *Marbury*, 5 U.S. (1 Cranch) at 170.

139. Id. at 166.

140. Id. at 163.

141. Id. at 174. Although this interpretation suited Marshall's needs in the short run, in the long run it put the Court into further jeopardy. The Constitution grants the Supreme Court appellate jurisdiction over most cases, "with such Exceptions, and under such Regulations as the Congress shall make." U.S. Const. art. III, § 2. By prohibiting Congress from moving cases from the appellate to the original jurisdiction, Marshall seemingly authorized Congress to take what cases it wished out of the Court's appellate jurisdiction entirely. This would prove a serious vulnerability of the judiciary. See infra Chapters 4 and 8 for battles over the appellate jurisdiction of the Court. The question of Congress's power to strip the appellate jurisdiction of the Supreme Court has given rise to a vast literature. See, e.g., Akhil Reed Amar, "The Two-Tiered Structure of the Judiciary Act of 1789," *U. Pa. L. Rev.* 138 (1990): 1499–1567; Barry Friedman, "A Different Dialogue: The Supreme Court, Congress and Federal Jurisdiction," *Nw. U. L. Rev.* 85 (1990): 1–61; Henry M. Hart, Jr., "The Power of Congress to Limit the Jurisdiction of Federal Courts: An Exercise in Dialectic," *Harv. L. Rev.* 66 (1953): 1362–1402; Martin H. Redish and Curtis E. Woods, "Congressional Power to Control the Jurisdiction of Lower Federal Courts: A Critical Review and a New Synthesis," *U. Pa. L. Rev.* 124 (1975): 45–109; Lawrence Gene Sager, "The Supreme Court, 1980 Term—Foreword: Constitutional Limitations on Congress' Authority to Regulate the Jurisdiction of the Federal Courts," *Harv. L. Rev.* 95 (1981): 17–89. For an argument that the "Exceptions" clause is not properly interpreted to allow Congress to move cases from the appellate jurisdiction at all, see Robert N. Clinton, "A Mandatory View of Federal Court Jurisdiction: A Guided Quest for the Original Understanding of Article III," *U. Pa. L. Rev.* 132 (1984): 776–80.

142. *Marbury*, 5 U.S. (1 Cranch) at 176.

143. Id.

144. Id. at 177. Marshall's reliance on a written constitution was notable (though not new), given an existing tradition of enforcing unwritten natural law principles. See Suzanna Sherry, "The Founders' Unwritten Constitution," *U. Chi. L. Rev.* 54 (1987): 1127–1177; Arthur E. Wilmarth, Jr., "Elusive Foundation: John Marshall, James Wilson, and the Problem of Reconciling Popular Sovereignty and Natural Law Jurisprudence in the New Federal Republic," *Geo. Wash. L. Rev.* 72 (2003): 137; see also supra Chapter 1 on the significance of a written constitution to judicial review.

145. *Marbury*, 5 U.S. (1 Cranch) at 177–78.

146. Id. at 178.

147. See *Stuart*, 5 U.S. (1 Cranch) at 303–05. The Court held that Congress could establish inferior tribunals and cause cases to be transferred between them and that circuit-riding duties for Supreme Court justices (reestablished by repeal of the Circuit Judges Act) were not unconstitutional. Id. at 309. It is unclear why the Court dealt only with the circuit-riding argument. It may well have been that as a technical legal matter, the litigant in *Stuart* simply had no standing to complain about the dismissal of judges he did not appear before, as opposed to those he did, the Supreme Court justices on circuit. Yet the Court did not say this. Dean Alfange asserts that the Court did not address the constitutionality of removing judges by abolishing their offices out of fear of the "political consequences" of doing so. Dean Alfange, Jr., "*Marbury v. Madison* and Original Understandings of Judicial Review: In Defense of Traditional Wisdom," *Sup. Ct. Rev.*, 1993: 363–64.

148. *Stuart*, 5 U.S. (1 Cranch) at 309. Technically, this undoubtedly was a reference to the fact that the justices had accepted circuit-riding duties in the past, and so the constitutionality of their doing so was settled by past practice. But the opinion had made this point already, and the last sentence really does read as the last word on the whole matter.

149. See, e.g., Robert G. McCloskey, *The American Supreme Court*, 3d ed. (2000), 25–28 ("The danger of a head-on clash with the Jeffersonians was averted by the denial of jurisdiction. . . . But the touch of genius is evident when Marshall, not content with having rescued a bad situation, seizes the occasion to set forth the doctrine of judicial review"). Dean Alfange agrees with McCloskey, finding that Marshall's opinion evinces "extraordinary political acumen." Alfange, "*Marbury v. Madison* and Original Understandings," supra note 147, at 380–83. James O'Fallon also finds Marbury to be an explicitly political decision but, far from being a "masterwork," simply "another iteration of the basic Federalist position." O'Fallon, "*Marbury*," supra note 41, at 219, 249.

150. *Marbury*, 5 U.S. (1 Cranch) at 176–80.

151. Mark A. Graber, "Establishing Judicial Review? *Schooner Peggy* and the Early Marshall Court," *Pol. Res. Q.* 51 (1998): 234–36.

152. See Chapter 1 supra. Sylvia Snowiss nonetheless claims Marshall's reliance on a written constitution and his treatment of it as "ordinary law" are what set his *Marbury* opinion apart from prior decisions. See Sylvia Snowiss, *Judicial Review and the Law of the Constitution* (1990), 3. Although Snowiss's book presents an interesting account of early judicial review, she plainly overstates this, her central point. See generally Gerald Leonard, "Iredell Reclaimed: Farewell to Snowiss's History of Judicial Review," *Chi.-Kent L. Rev.* 81 (2006): 867–82 (refuting Snowiss's argument that Iredell saw judicial review as a political rather than legal act). Marshall bolstered his conclusion with many compelling hypothetical conflicts between the Constitution and a statute, in order to emphasize that a judge must follow the Constitution. But

these were little different from examples given by members of Congress during the repeal debate. See, e.g., Annals of Cong., supra note 2, at 11:646–47 (statement of Rep. Bayard) (Congress passes a bill of attainder, or suspends habeas corpus during peacetime); id., at 841 (statement of Rep. Dennis) (Congress establishes a national church, compelling all to attend or face penalties).

153. This is the case despite the gushing claim of Marshall's biographer Albert Beveridge to the contrary. See Beveridge, *Life of Marshall*, supra note 55, at 3:128 ("The theory of the Chief Justice that Section 13 of the old Judiciary Law was unconstitutional was absolutely new, and it was as daring as it was novel. It was the only original idea that Marshall contributed to the entire controversy. Nobody ever had questioned the validity of that section of the statute which Marshall now challenged"); see also Susan Low Bloch and Maeva Marcus, "John Marshall's Selective Use of History in *Marbury v. Madison*," *Wis. L. Rev.*, 1986: 328–31 (arguing that prior to *Marbury* it was accepted that Congress could move cases from the appellate to the original jurisdiction).

154. Representative Thomas Davis argued that the Judiciary Act of 1801 was unconstitutional because it granted the Supreme Court original jurisdiction in areas not contemplated by the Constitution. See Annals of Cong., supra note 2, at 11:556; see also id., at 903–05 (statement of Rep. Dana) (responding to Davis's claim by arguing that a writ of mandamus is an exercise of appellate, not original, jurisdiction). For discussions of the relationship between Representative Davis's argument and John Marshall's opinion in *Marbury v. Madison*, see David E. Engdahl, "John Marshall's 'Jeffersonian' Concept of Judicial Review," *Duke L. J.* 42 (1992): 329n163; James E. Pfander, "*Marbury*, Original Jurisdiction, and the Supreme Court's Supervisory Powers," *Colum. L. Rev.* 101 (2001): 1583–84; Gordon E. Sherman, "The Case of *John Chandler v. The Secretary of War*," *Yale L. J.* 14 (1905): 435–36.

155. While there is no direct evidence Marshall heard Davis's argument, the debates were attended by many notables, and speeches frequently were published verbatim in the newspapers. See, e.g., *Nat'l Intelligencer*, Feb. 24, 1802, at 4 (reprinting the House debate, including Davis's argument, from February 17, 1802).

156. R. Kent Newmyer, *John Marshall and the Heroic Age of the Supreme Court* (2001), 173; William W. Van Alstyne, "A Critical Guide to *Marbury v. Madison*," *Duke L. J.* 18 (1969): 6–8.

157. He possessed evidence—whether the commissions had been signed and sealed— that the Federalist suitors were having trouble prying from Congress and the executive. Beveridge, *Life of Marshall*, supra note 55, at 3:124–26.

158. Van Alstyne, "A Critical Guide," supra note 156, at 8. Indeed, it was far more clear Marshall should not have participated in *Marbury* than in *Stuart*, where he had been a lower-court judge. Not infrequently in those days, members of the Court sat in cases they had judged below. Bruce Ackerman argues Marshall removed himself from *Stuart* so as not to face the embarrassment of approving congressional action that arguably violated his opinion in *Marbury*. See Ackerman, *Founding Fathers*, supra note 11, at 186–88.

159. Van Alstyne lays out the arguments on this question in his "critical guide" to *Marbury*. See Van Alstyne, "A Critical Guide," supra note 156, at 14–34. On the prior precedents, see Bloch and Marcus, "John Marshall's Selective Use," supra note 153, at 319–32.

160. See Ackerman, *Founding Fathers*, supra note 11, at 8 (*Marbury* was a "strategic retreat"); Kramer, *People Themselves*, supra note 112, at 121–23.

161. Kramer, *People Themselves*, supra note 112, at 123 (endorsing Jefferson's perception of the *Marbury* opinion as "a politically motivated attack on his presidency"); Newmyer, *John Marshall and the Heroic Age*, supra note 156, at 162 (discussing legal and political aspects of *Marbury*).

162. *Wash.* (D.C.) *Federalist*, Feb. 25, 1803, at 2 ("highly important opinion"); *The New Haven Visitor* (Conn.), "Letter from 'A Federalist,'" May 3, 1803, at 213. Federalist newspapers that printed the decision included the *Wash. Federalist*, March 14, 1803, at 3; *Alexandria Advertiser and Commercial Intelligencer* (Va.), March 17, 1803, at 2; and *N.Y. Herald*, March 26, 1803, at 1, 2, 4.

163. *N.Y. Evening Post*, March 23, 1803, at 3.

164. Warren, *Supreme Court*, supra note 27, at 1:272–73; see also Nelson, Marbury v. Madison, supra note 42, at 72 (noting the Republican press gave the *Marbury* decision extensive coverage but "refrained from attacking it").

165. Ellis, *Jeffersonian Crisis*, supra note 1, at 66; Warren, *Supreme Court*, supra note 27, 1:248–53. But Warren notes that several leading Republican papers did not criticize the opinion at all. Warren, *Supreme Court*, supra note 27, at 1:248.

166. From the *Virginia Argus*, reprinted in the *Nat'l Intelligencer*, May 11, 1803, at 1. For reprints of items in the series, see *Aurora*, Apr. 23, 26, 30 and May 2, 5, 1803; *Republican Watch-Tower*, May 21, 25, 28, 1803. Of a similar thrust was the facetious letter from "A Student of Law" to one of the justices in Boston's *Independent Chronicle*. "I take it for granted that the Supreme Court of the nation would not from party motives volunteer an extrajudicial opinion, for the sake of criminating a rival department of government." But then how to explain what purported to be the Court's decision in Marbury? "Is it," Student asked, "a Libel upon the Court, or a true Report of the Case?" *Boston Indep. Chron.*, June 16, 1803, at 2.

167. *Wash. Federalist*, Apr. 20, 22, 27, 1803. According to Warren, the "Unlearned Layman" attacks were practically the only sustained critique of Marshall's assertion that the Court had the power and duty to review the constitutionality of legislation. See Warren, *Supreme Court*, supra note 27, at 1:252. Befitting its status as a party organ, the *Washington Federalist* published a response to the "Unlearned Layman" defending Marshall's opinion on April 29, 1803.

168. Accord McCloskey, *American Supreme Court*, supra note 149, at 28.

169. *Republican Watch-Tower*, May 21, 1803, at 3. See also Mark A. Graber, "Establishing Judicial Review: *Marbury* and the Judicial Act of 1789," *Tulsa L. Rev.* 38 (2003): 627 (stating that *Marbury* was not cited by the Supreme Court until 1887 and by hardly anyone before that).

170. See Forrest McDonald, *States' Rights and the Union: Imperium in Imperio, 1776–1876* (2000), 56–57 (*Marbury* decision prompted the impeachment campaign against Justice Chase).

171. Letter from Thomas Jefferson to Joseph Nicholson, May 13, 1803, in Lipscomb and Bergh, *Writings of Thomas Jefferson*, supra note 51, at 10:390.

172. The motion to remove Chase from office was rejected by a vote of 41–20; the resolution asserting the unconstitutionality of his dual appointments was kept from a vote by a 32–29 margin. Jane Shaffer Elsmere, *Justice Samuel Chase* (1980), 42–51; James Haw, *Stormy Patriot: The Life of Samuel Chase* (1980), 167–74.

173. Warren, *Supreme Court*, supra note 27, at 1:273 ("Of all the Judges, no one was more hated than Chase"); see generally Haw, *Stormy Patriot*, supra note 172.

174. Addison was convicted by the Pennsylvania Senate on January 26, 1803. Hoffer and Hull, *Impeachment in America*, supra note 136, at 198, 204. Jefferson sent the Pickering materials to the House on February 4, 1803. Annals of Cong., supra note 126, at 12:460.

175. Letter from Thomas McKean to Thomas Jefferson, Feb. 7, 1804, cited in Irving Brant, *Impeachment: Trials and Errors* (1973), 60.

176. *City Gazette and Daily Advertiser*, June 16, 1803, at 2.

177. Beveridge, *Life of Marshall*, supra note 55, at 3:173. Delaware representative James Bayard refused to represent Chase, pleading personal difficulties, but it is more

likely that he wanted to distance himself and the Federalist Party from a doomed man. See Haw, *Stormy Patriot*, supra note 172, at 219.

178. Letter from John Quincy Adams to John Adams, March 8, 1805, in *The Writings of John Quincy Adams*, ed. Worthington Chauncey Ford (1914), 3:108.

179. See *Portsmouth Oracle*, Jan. 28, 1804, at 2 (also explaining charges not brought until Republicans had necessary two-thirds majority to convict in Senate).

180. Ackerman, *Founding Fathers*, supra note 11, at 199; Beveridge, *Life of Marshall*, supra note 55, at 3:160; Brant, *Impeachment*, supra note 175, at 84–87.

181. Letter from John Marshall to Samuel Chase, Jan. 23, 1805, in Hobson and Teute, *Papers of John Marshall*, supra note 129, at 6:347.

182. See Beveridge, *Life of Marshall*, supra note 55, at 3:171 (describing Republicans molding public opinion against Chase for months prior to presenting articles of impeachment to the House); Haskins, *Foundations of Power*, supra note 18, at 219–20.

183. Haskins, *Foundations of Power*, supra note 18, at 234, 238–41.

184. Samuel H. Smith and Thomas Lloyd, eds., *Trial of Samuel Chase* (1805), 1:5; see also Hoffer and Hull, *Impeachment in America*, supra note 136, at 184, 229–30.

185. Smith and Lloyd, *Trial*, supra note 184, at 1:5–7. Jefferson provided Callender financial support in the 1790s, when Callender was publishing the attacks on the Federalists that landed him in Chase's courtroom. Disappointed by Jefferson's failure to reward him adequately for his efforts, Callender quickly turned his sights on Jefferson himself. Callender was the source for the original accusation that Jefferson had a relationship with the slave Sally Hemings. See Jerry W. Knudson, *Jefferson and the Press: Crucible of Liberty* (2006), 37–46.

186. Smith and Lloyd, *Trial*, supra note 184, at 1:7–8; see Hoffer and Hull, *Impeachment in America*, supra note 136, at 230–31.

187. Annals of Cong. (D.C.: Gales and Seaton, 1852): 14:674–75.

188. *Nat'l Intelligencer*, May 20, 1803, at 3.

189. Letter from Nathaniel Macon to Joseph Nicholson, July 26, 1803, quoted in Warren, *Supreme Court*, supra note 27, at 1:274.

190. See, e.g. *Wash.* (D.C.) *Federalist*, Jan. 9, 1805, at 3; *Newport Mercury* (R.I.), March 23, 1805, at 2; *Richmond* (Va.) *Enquirer*, March 30, 1805, at 3.

191. *Nat'l Intelligencer*, May 8, 1805, at 2.

192. Letter from Uriah Tracy to James Gould, Feb. 4, 1805, quoted in Ellis, *Jeffersonian Crisis*, supra note 1, at 96; see also Annals of Cong., supra note 187, at 14:100 (describing the decoration of the Senate chamber for Chase's trial).

193. Smith and Lloyd, *Trial*, supra note 184, at 2:365–66.

194. Beveridge, *Life of Marshall*, supra note 55, at 3:171.

195. Richard B. Lillich, "The Chase Impeachment," *Am. J. Legal Hist.* 4 (1960): 62 ("If the general public had been led to believe that impeachment was a purely partisan matter, it had also been conditioned to the idea that Chase, guilty of gross judicial misconduct, would be convicted").

196. Smith and Lloyd, *Trial*, supra note 184, at 1:257, 258; see also Eleanore Bushnell, *Crimes, Follies, and Misfortunes: The Federal Impeachment Trials* (1992), 71–72.

197. *Nat'l Aegis*, Jan. 25, 1804, at 3.

198. Bushnell, *Federal Impeachment Trials*, supra note 196, at 60, 335n14.

199. Lillich, "Chase Impeachment," supra note 195, at 63.

200. Emily Field Van Tassel and Paul Finkelman, *Impeachable Offenses: A Documentary History from 1787 to the Present* (1999), 102. For a full breakdown of each senator's votes on each article, see Smith and Lloyd, *Trial*, supra note 184, at 2:493; *City Gazette and Daily Advertiser*, March 3, 1805, at 2.

201. One theory has some Republicans supporting acquittal out of spite at the leader of
the House managers, John Randolph. Randolph opposed national efforts to compen-
sate victims of the Yazoo land frauds, the product of a corrupt Georgia legislature.
See Ackerman, *Founding Fathers*, supra note 11, at 212–17; Ellis, *Jeffersonian Crisis*,
supra note 1, at 87–90, 93–95, 104–05; Haskins, *Foundations of Power*, supra note 18,
at 245; Haw, *Stormy Patriot*, supra note 172, at 240–41; Rehnquist, *Grand Inquests*,
supra note 35, at 110–13. However, contemporaries dismissed this possibility, with
Federalist senator Timothy Pickering saying that "that will not have the smallest influence on the impeachment" and that "the whole pack united as usual" on other
aspects of impeachment, even after Randolph's conduct. Letter from Timothy Pickering to Rufus King, Feb. 24, 1805, in *The Life and Correspondence of Rufus King*,
ed. Charles R. King (1897), 441. Another explanation is that some Republicans voted
for Chase's acquittal in light of Jefferson's support of Chase's conviction as revenge
for Jefferson's choice of George Clinton from New York as Vice President instead
of Aaron Burr. See Frank Thompson, Jr., and Daniel H. Pollitt, "Impeachment of
Federal Judges: A Historical Overview," *N.C. L. Rev.* 49 (1970): 99n72; see also Raoul
Berger, *Impeachment: The Constitutional Problems* (1973), 96n202 (citing Thompson
and Pollitt). The difficulty with this theory is that Burr himself presided over the
Chase impeachment trial with impeccable decorum and fairness, and Thompson
and Pollitt do not present evidence to establish that the Republican defectors voted
as they did to avenge Burr or that the Republican defectors were in fact Burr supporters. However, we do know that two Republicans who voted to acquit Chase on
all eight articles of impeachment, John Smith of Ohio and Samuel Latham Mitchill
of New York, were Burr associates, the former being forced to resign from the Senate in 1808 because of his involvement in the Burr conspiracy scandal. See generally
Smith and Lloyd, *Trial*, supra note 184, at 2:493; Alan David Aberbach, *In Search of
an American Identity: Samuel Latham Mitchill, Jeffersonian Nationalist* (1988), 28–35;
Robert W. Wilhelmy, "Senator John Smith and the Aaron Burr Conspiracy," *Cincinnati Hist. Soc'y Bull.* 28 (1970): 39–58.
202. Letter from Samuel L. Mitchill to Mrs. Mitchill, March 1, 1805, in Henry Mills Alden, "Dr. Mitchill's Letters from Washington: 1801–1813," *Harper's New Monthly
Magazine* (1879): 740, 749.
203. Ackerman, *Founding Fathers*, supra note 11, at 209.
204. Smith and Lloyd, *Trial*, supra note 184, at 1:181. On prompting, he did agree that
Chase's conduct was calculated to "abash and disconcert [defense] counsel." Id.
205. Quote attributed to Senator Bradley of Vermont, one of the Republican defectors,
in a letter from Timothy Pickering to Richard Peters, Feb. 24, 1805, quoted in Warren,
Supreme Court, supra note 27, at 1:290n2.
206. See, e.g., Annals of Cong., supra note 187, at 14:357 (statement of Sen. Hopkinson)
and id. at 432–33 (statement of Sen. Martin). But see Smith and Lloyd, *Trial*, supra
note 184, at 2:254–55, where Chase's lead attorney, Robert Goodloe Harper, admits
that certain offenses, such as failing to hold court, might not be indictable, though they
would certainly be grounds for impeachment; Ackerman, *Founding Fathers*, supra
note 11, at 210–11, 356n43 (quoting Harper as evidence that Chase's defense team
"reluctantly conceded that some impeachable offenses might not be indictable").
207. See Ackerman, *Founding Fathers*, supra note 11, at 212 (noting the unusual nature
of Republican votes for Chase's acquittal in light of Chase's questionable conduct
and general party discipline).
208. McDonald, *States' Rights*, supra note 170, at 54 ("[T]o effect repeal, [Republicans]
had to swallow their strict-construction scruples").

209. See supra text accompanying note 200.

210. This is what Keith Whittington calls a constitutional construction. See Keith E. Whittington, "Reconstructing the Federal Judiciary: The Chase Impeachment and the Constitution," *Studs. in Am. Pol. Dev.* 9 (1995): 56–59; see generally Whittington, *Political Foundations*, supra note 112, at 1–27 (describing his "politics of constitutional meaning"). Richard Lillich, one of the most astute chroniclers of the events surrounding Chase's impeachment, makes just this point. Lillich, "Chase Impeachment," supra note 195, at 49 ("In order fully to understand the importance of the Chase impeachment, however, one must appreciate the sense of finality attached to the result in the case. This finality, caused by a complex of the times, the personalities involved, the articles of impeachment, and the conduct of the trial, has given the Chase impeachment proceedings a political stare decisis value far beyond whatever legal issues were resolved").

211. See Rehnquist, *Grand Inquests*, supra note 35, at 125 ("Supreme Court justices sitting on circuit stopped including political harangues in their charges to grand juries"); Lillich, "Chase Impeachment," supra note 195, at 71 ("[F]ederal judges subsequently refrained from active participation in politics"); Whittington, "Reconstructing the Federal Judiciary," supra note 210, at 116 (noting that Chase's impeachment allowed Republicans to "reconstitute the judiciary on more limited and politically neutral grounds").

212. See Rehnquist, *Grand Inquests*, supra note 35, at 130 ("The acquittal of Chase . . . seemed to draw a line as [to] the proper use of the congressional power to impeach and remove a judge from office"); Lillich, "Chase Impeachment," supra note 195, at 71 ("[T]hreats of impeachment were heard no more").

213. Smith and Lloyd, *Trial*, supra note 184, at 1:322 (statement of Rep. Early).

214. Id. at 1:125 (statement of Rep. Randolph).

215. Id. at 1:386 (statement of Rep. Campbell).

216. Id. at 1:354 (statement of Rep. Campbell).

217. *Boston Indep. Chron.*, Apr. 26, 1804, at 1.

218. Smith and Lloyd, *Trial*, supra note 184, at 1:123 (statement of Rep. Randolph).

219. Id. at 2:364 (statement of Rep. Nicholson).

220. Id. at 2:481 (statement of Rep. Randolph).

221. *Richmond Enquirer* (Va.), March 30, 1805, at 3.

222. Letter from Thomas Jefferson to Thomas Ritchie, Dec. 25, 1820, in Ford, *Writings of Thomas Jefferson*, supra note 5, at 10:171.

223. See Whittington, *Reconstructing the Federal Judiciary*, supra note 112, at 88 ("No Federalist congressman ventured to defend a partisan judiciary in 1802"). Whittington deserves credit for the broader point as well. See id. at 93 (noting "the virtual Federalist admission of the inappropriateness of future judicial politicking").

224. *N.Y. Evening Post*, March 3, 1804, at 3.

225. Smith and Lloyd, *Trial*, supra note 184, at 2:326–27 (statement of Mr. Harper).

226. *Wash. Federalist*, Jan. 30, 1805, reprinted in *Boston Gazette*, Feb. 14, 1805, at 2.

227. Smith and Lloyd, *Trial*, supra note 184, at 2:131 (statement of Mr. Lee).

228. Id. at 2:263 (statement of Mr. Harper).

229. Id. at 2:371 (statement of Rep. Rodney).

230. *Memoirs of John Quincy Adams*, ed. Charles Francis Adams (1874), 1:322. The statements attributed to Giles by Adams appear to be paraphrased, not directly quoted.

231. Smith and Lloyd, *Trial*, supra note 184, at 2:141 (statement of Rep. Rodney).

232. Id. at 2:20–21 (statement of Mr. Hopkinson).

233. Id. at 2:371 (statement of Rep. Rodney).

234. *Wash. Federalist*, March 9, 1805, at 3.

235. Annals of Cong., supra note 187, at 14:1213.

236. Id. at 1214.

237. Letter from Samuel Chase to Rufus King, March 13, 1805, in King, *Rufus King*, supra note 201, at 4:446.

238. *Nat'l Intelligencer*, May 6, 1805, at 3, quoted in Ellis, *Jeffersonian Crisis*, supra note 1, at 105.

239. *Nat'l Intelligencer*, Feb. 24, 1814, quoted in Jean Edward Smith, *John Marshall: De-finer of a Nation* (1996), 419.

3: Defiance

1. *Ga. J.*, Aug. 23, 1830, reprinted in *Niles' Reg.*, Sept. 18, 1830, at 69.

2. *Richmond Enquirer*, Dec. 10, 1831, at 1 (reprinting *Augusta Constitutionalist*).

3. See Richard E. Ellis, *The Union at Risk: Jacksonian Democracy, States' Rights and the Nullification Crisis* (1987), 1 (noting the leading constitutional question of country's first century was the "distribution of power between the states and the national government").

4. Amphictyon Essays, letter to the editor, *Richmond Enquirer*, March 30, 1819, reprinted in Gerald Gunther, Introduction to *John Marshall's Defense of* McCulloch v. Maryland, ed. Gerald Gunther (1969), 53, 58.

5. See generally Max Farrand, *Fathers of the Constitution: A Chronicle of the Establishment of the Union* (1921), 81–107; Max Farrand, *The Framing of the Constitution of the United States* (1913), 45–49; Forrest McDonald, *States' Rights and the Union: Imperium in Imperio, 1776–1876* (2000), 8–10, 14–15.

6. Letter from George Washington to James Warren, Oct. 7, 1785, in *The Writings of George Washington*, ed. Jared Spears (1847), 9:139–40; see Farrand, *Framing of the Constitution*, supra note 5, at 3–4, 45–52.

7. See Farrand, *Fathers of the Constitution*, supra note 5, at 81–107; McDonald, *States' Rights*, supra note 5, at 12–15 (describing the states' experiences under the Articles and the pessimism going into the convention).

8. See Farrand, *Fathers of the Constitution*, supra note 5, at 117–18; Farrand, *Framing of the Constitution*, supra note 5, at 68–73; Gordon S. Wood, *The Creation of the American Republic, 1776–1787* (1969), 547–49.

9. Wood, *Creation of the American Republic*, supra note 8, at 525.

10. Letter from George Washington to Congress, Sept. 17, 1787, quoted in Max Farrand, *The Records of the Federal Convention of 1787* (1911), 2:666. For an extended discussion of the difficulty the convention faced in drawing the line between federal and state authority, see Edward A. Purcell, Jr., *Originalism, Federalism, and the American Constitutional Enterprise: A Historical Inquiry* (2007), 21–37.

11. Luther Martin, "Genuine Information," reprinted in Farrand, *Records*, supra note 10, at 3:175.

12. See McDonald, *States' Rights*, supra note 5, at 16–17. On the proposals and debates generally, see Farrand, *Fathers of the Constitution*, supra note 5, at 108–24; Farrand, *Framing of the Constitution*, supra note 5.

13. U.S. Const. art. I, § 8, cl. 18.

14. Letter from George Washington to Congress, Sept. 17, 1787, in Farrand, *Records*, supra note 10, at 2:667; see Lance Banning, "Virginia: Sectionalism and the General Good," in *Ratifying the Constitution*, ed. Michael Allen Gillespie and Michael Lienesch (1989), 277–82; Larry D. Kramer, *The People Themselves: Popular Constitutionalism and Judicial Review.* (2005), 82; Herbert J. Storing, *What the Anti-Federalists Were For* (1981), 10–11 (all discussing the threat "consolidation" was deemed to pose).

15. James Madison, "The Federalist No. 39," in *The Federalist Papers*, ed. Clinton Rossiter (1961), 242–43.

16. See Storing, *Anti-Federalists*, supra note 14, at 9–13, 15–23.

17. Patrick Henry, "Shall Liberty Be Sought," June 5, 1788, quoted in Storing, *Anti-Federalists*, supra note 14, at 24.

18. James Madison, "The Federalist No. 45," in *Federalist Papers*, supra note 15, at 288–89.

19. James Madison, "The Federalist No. 46," in id. at 294, 298.

20. Accord Charles Warren, *The Supreme Court in United States History* (Boston: Little, Brown and Company, 1922), 1:388.

21. Warren, *Supreme Court*, supra note 20, at 2:102; Peter Smith, "Federalism, Instrumentalism, and the Legacy of the Rehnquist Court," *Geo. Wash. L. Rev.* 74 (2006): 907.

22. "Virginia Resolution of 1798, Pronouncing the Alien and Sedition Laws to Be Unconstitutional, and Defining the Rights of the States," Dec. 21, 1798, in *Elliot's Debates*, ed. Jonathan Elliot (1836), 4:528, 529. For the text of the Kentucky Resolution, see "Kentucky Resolution," Nov. 10, 1798, in *Elliot's Debates*, supra, at 4:540–45. See generally Robert A. Burt, *The Constitution in Conflict* (1992), 69–72; Ellis, *Union at Risk*, supra note 3, at 4–5; McDonald, *States' Rights*, supra note 5, at 39–43 (describing the events leading up to the Virginia and Kentucky Resolutions and the introduction of the resolutions). Anxious to keep their identities secret, Jefferson ghost-authored the Kentucky Resolution and Madison did the same for Virginia. Adrienne Koch and Harry Ammon, "The Virginia and Kentucky Resolutions: An Episode in Jefferson and Madison's Defense of Civil Liberties," *Wm. & Mary Q.* 5 (1948): 147–48 (noting Jefferson and Madison remained anonymous for a quarter century).

23. Delaware General Assembly Resolution, Feb. 1, 1799, in *State Documents on Federal Relations*, ed. Herman V. Ames (1906), 16. For the negative responses of the other states, including Rhode Island, Massachusetts, Pennsylvania, New York, Connecticut, New Hampshire, and Vermont, see Ames, *State Documents*, supra, at 16–26; see also McDonald, *States' Rights*, supra note 5, at 43 (quoting various states' responses to the resolutions); Geoffrey R. Stone, *Perilous Times: Free Speech in Wartime from the Sedition Act of 1798 to the War on Terrorism* (2004), 45 (describing and quoting the responses to the resolutions).

24. "New Hampshire to Virginia and Kentucky," June 15, 1799, in Ames, *State Documents*, supra note 23, at 24, 25; see also "Rhode Island to Virginia," Feb. 1799, id., at 17; "Vermont to Virginia," Oct. 30, 1799, id., at 26; "New York to Virginia and Kentucky," March 5, 1799, id., at 23.

25. "Madison's Report on the Virginia Resolutions," in Elliot, *Elliot's Debates*, supra note 22, at 4:546.

26. Hampden (Spencer Roane writing anonymously), letter to the editor, *Richmond Enquirer*, June 11, 1819, in Gunther, *John Marshall's Defense*, supra note 4, at 113.

27. John Lauritz Larson, "Jefferson's Union and the Problem of Internal Improvements," in *Jeffersonian Legacies*, ed. Peter S. Onuf (1993), 356.

28. James M. Banner, Jr., *To the Hartford Convention: The Federalists and the Origins of Party Politics in Massachusetts, 1789–1815* (1970), 111; Warren, *Supreme Court*, supra note 20, at 1:322.

29. See Banner, *Hartford Convention*, supra note 28, at 111; McDonald, *States' Rights*, supra note 5, at 60.

30. Letter from Thomas Jefferson to John B. Colvin, Sept. 20, 1810, in *Thomas Jefferson: Writings*, ed. Merrill D. Peterson (1984), 1231; see generally Larson, "Jefferson's Union," supra note 27, at 340, 358 (noting "that 'orthodox' republican principles—strict construction and majority rule—never yielded that simple clarity of right and wrong that Jeffersonians in opposition described").

31. The measure was justified at different times as preventive and defensive (preserving American men and ships, while avoiding an excuse that would lure the United States into war) and coercive (forcing respect for American shipping rights by denying needed exports). When the inevitable evasion occurred, the policy was strengthened with successively stricter "enforcement" measures. See Dumas Malone, *Jefferson the President: Second Term, 1805–1809* (1974), 483–90; McDonald, *States' Rights*, supra note 5, at 62–64; Bradford Perkins, *Prologue to War* (1961), 150–58.

32. William Edward Buckley, *The Hartford Convention* (1934), 3; McDonald, *States' Rights*, supra note 5, at 64; Warren, *Supreme Court*, supra note 20, at 1:358–60.

33. See Banner, *Hartford Convention*, supra note 28, at 118 (noting that the constitutional arguments against the embargo were "sharply reminiscent" of the Virginia and Kentucky Resolutions); McDonald, *States' Rights*, supra note 5, at 64 (noting the irony that Federalists "rais[ed] the cry of states' rights with a vengeance").

34. "Massachusetts Resolution on the Enforcement Act," Feb. 15, 1809, in Ames, *State Documents*, supra note 23, at 34, 35.

35. "Connecticut General Assembly Resolution," Feb. 23, 1809, in supra note 23, at 40, 42. See generally id., at 38.

36. "'Things Turned Topsy-Turvy,'" *Richmond Enquirer*, Feb. 14, 1809, at 3.

37. For a discussion of the Federalists' positions leading up to and during the War of 1812, see McDonald, *States' Rights*, supra note 5, at 65–67; Lawrence Delbert Cress, "'Cool and Serious Reflection': Federalist Attitudes Toward War in 1812," *J. Early Republic* 7 (1987): 123–45.

38. "Sermon of the Rector of Trinity Church, Boston, Mass.," quoted in Ralph Ketcham, *James Madison: A Biography* (1971), 537.

39. For a discussion on the grievances leading up to the Hartford Convention, see Buckley, *Hartford Convention*, supra note 32, at 3–8; McDonald, *States' Rights*, supra note 5, at 66–69.

40. See Banner, *Hartford Convention*, supra note 28, at 335; Buckley, *Hartford Convention*, supra note 32, at 16–19.

41. See, e.g., Ellis, *Union at Risk*, supra note 3, at 6; Robert Y. Hayne, "Address on the Senate," Jan. 25, 1830, in *The Webster-Hayne Debate on the Nature of the Union*, ed. Herman Belz (2000), 36–37, 67–70 (impeaching Nathan Dane's character by pointing out that Dane attended the Hartford Convention and attacking Webster for representing the state that initiated the convention).

42. On the derision accorded the Hartford commissioners, see Buckley, *Hartford Convention*, supra note 32, at 25–26; Ellis, *Union at Risk*, supra note 3, at 6; Samuel Eliot Morison, *The Life and Letters of Harrison Gray Otis* (1913), 2:171–72. On the convention's decision to reject secession, see "Report of the Hartford Convention," Jan. 6, 1815, quoted and discussed in Morison, *Life and Letters*, supra, at 149–50.

43. All quotations in this paragraph are Gallatin's. See Letter from Albert Gallatin to Matthew Lyon, May 7, 1816, quoted in George Dangerfield, *The Awakening of American Nationalism* (1965), 3–4.

44. Arthur M. Schlesinger, Jr., *The Age of Jackson* (1945), 8–12 (describing the atmosphere of the time and Clay's role in the American System).

45. McDonald, *States' Rights*, supra note 5, at 52, 75.

46. James Madison, "Seventh Annual Message," Dec. 15, 1815, in *The Writings of James Madison*, ed. Gaillard Hunt (1908), 8:342.

47. Schlesinger, *Age of Jackson*, supra note 44, at 19 (depicting Monroe's nearly unanimous election as emblematic of the Era of Good Feelings' lack of political strife). But see Dwight Wiley Jessup, *Reaction and Accommodation: The United States Supreme*

Court and Political Conflict, 1809–1835 (1987), 25–26 (describing the Era of Good Feelings as anything but).

48. See generally Mark A. Graber, "Federalist or Friend of Adams: The Marshall Court and Party Politics," *Studs. in Am. Pol. Dev.* 12 (1998): 230.

49. Martin v. Hunter's Lessee, 14 U.S. (1 Wheat.) 304, 347–48 (1816). The case has a complicated factual and procedural background. See generally Warren, *Supreme Court,* supra note 20, at 1:443–48.

50. Gibbons v. Odgen, 22 U.S. (9 Wheat.) 1, 75 (1824). For a discussion of the case generally, see Jessup, *Reaction and Accommodation,* supra note 47, at 285–92; R. Kent Newmyer, *John Marshall and the Heroic Age of the Supreme Court* (2001), 269, 302–04; R. Kent Newmyer, *The Supreme Court Under Marshall and Taney* (2006), 49–51; Jean Edward Smith, *John Marshall: Definer of a Nation* (1998), 477–81; Warren, *Supreme Court,* supra note 20, at 2:57–71.

51. Warren, *Supreme Court,* supra note 20, at 2:71 (explaining that Marshall's decision did meet wide acclaim although "all his contemporaries did not concur in the general praise"); Smith, *John Marshall,* supra note 50, at 480.

52. John Quincy Adams, Diary Entry, Feb. 13, 1831, quoted in Warren, *Supreme Court,* supra note 20, at 2:212; see also Newmyer, *John Marshall and the Heroic Age,* supra note 50, at 459 (discussing Marshall's legacy).

53. See Ellis, *Union at Risk,* supra note 3, at 6.

54. Edward Everett, "Review of the Memoir of Richard Henry Lee," *N. Am. Rev.* 22 (1826): 374.

55. McCulloch v. Maryland, 17 U.S. (4 Wheat.) 316 (1819). For general discussion of the case, see Richard E. Ellis, *Aggressive Nationalism: McCulloch v. Maryland and the Foundation of Federal Authority in the Young Republic* (2007); Jessup, *Reaction and Accommodation,* supra note 47, at 186–87; Mark Robert Killenbeck, M'Culloch v. Maryland: *Securing a Nation* (2006); Warren, *Supreme Court,* supra note 20, at 1:506–11.

56. On the failed effort to renew the Bank's charter in 1811, see McDonald, *States' Rights,* supra note 5, at 52, 75 (observing that the Second Bank was chartered as the experience in the war with Great Britain indicated the Bank was necessary); see also Warren, *Supreme Court,* supra note 20, at 1:502 (quoting the congressional debates on the Bank in 1811 and 1817). President Madison reconciled his stance on the Bank in 1816 with his earlier position by deferring to "legislative precedent." Letter from James Madison to Jared Ingersoll, June 25, 1831, in *Letters and Other Writings of James Madison* (1867), 4:183–84; see also Ketcham, *James Madison,* supra note 38, at 506 (discussing the need for a bank and Madison's uncomfortable position).

57. Letter from Joseph Story to Stephen White, Mar. 3, 1819, quoted in Ellis, *Aggressive Nationalism,* supra note 55, at 77; see also Killenbeck, M'Culloch v. Maryland, supra note 55, at 96 (describing the argument).

58. McCulloch v. Maryland, 17 U.S. (4 Wheat.) 316, 421 (1819).

59. Id. at 426.

60. Id. at 431.

61. *Nat'l Reg.,* March 6, 1819, at 10.

62. There is some evidence the Court sought out the case to make its point at this moment. Richard Ellis argues that *McCulloch* was a manufactured case rushed through the Maryland court system to serve as a vehicle for the Supreme Court's broad pronouncements regarding federal power. See Ellis, *Aggressive Nationalism,* supra note 55, at 71–73, 123–24, 163.

63. Kramer, *People Themselves*, supra note 14, at 175; McDonald, *States' Rights*, supra note 5, at 72; Warren, *Supreme Court*, supra note 20, at 2:103.

64. *Gen. Advertiser*, March 17, 23, 1819, quoted in Warren, *Supreme Court*, supra note 20, at 1:523.

65. See generally Warren, *Supreme Court*, supra note 20, at 1:519–25 (reprinting newspaper quotes).

66. *Niles' Reg.*, March 13, 1819, at 16; see generally Gunther, *John Marshall's Defense*, supra note 4, at 4; Amphictyon Essays, Apr. 2, 1819, in Gunther, *John Marshall's Defense*, supra note 4, at 72 (arguing that the real issue was the extent of congressional power, not the Bank itself); see also Newmyer, *John Marshall and the Heroic Age*, supra note 50, at 879.

67. See *Niles' Reg.*, March 13, 1819, at 16 ("a total prostration of the State-Rights and the loss of the liberties of the Nation").

68. *Argus of Western Am.* (date uncertain), quoted in Warren, *Supreme Court*, supra note 20, at 1:519.

69. See Amphictyon Essays, March 30, 1819, in Gunther, *John Marshall's Defense*, supra note 4, at 52 (describing Ritchie's relationship with Roane and his role in publishing the letters).

70. Amphictyon Essays, Apr. 2, 1819, in Gunther, *John Marshall's Defense*, supra note 4, at 64.

71. Hampden, June 11, 1819, in id. at 110.

72. Letter from John Marshall to Joseph Story, March 24, 1819, quoted in Jessup, *Reaction and Accommodation*, supra note 47, at 196.

73. Letter from John Marshall to Bushrod Washington, March 27, 1819, quoted in Ellis, *Aggressive Nationalism*, supra note 55, at 104–05.

74. See Gunther, *John Marshall's Defense*, supra note 4, at 1.

75. See G. Edward White, *The Marshall Court and Cultural Change, 1815–1835* (1991), 567.

76. See Jessup, *Reaction and Accommodation*, supra note 47, at 205–08; Warren, *Supreme Court*, supra note 20, at 2:12–19.

77. Letter from James Madison to Spencer Roane, June 29, 1821, in *James Madison's Writings*, ed. Jack N. Rakove (1999), 777.

78. See John Taylor, *New Views of the Constitution of the United States* (1823; repr. 1971); John Taylor, *Tyranny Unmasked*, ed. F. Thornton Miller (1822; repr. 1992); John Taylor, *Construction Construed and Constitutions Vindicated* (1820; repr. 1970).

79. Thomas Ritchie, editor's introduction to Taylor, *Construction Construed*, supra note 78, at iii.

80. Letter from Joseph Story to Brockholst Livingston, June 24, 1822, quoted in Jessup, *Reaction and Accommodation*, supra note 47, at 259.

81. Jessup, *Reaction and Accommodation*, supra note 47, is a chronicle of state defiance during this period. See also Leslie Friedman Goldstein, *Constituting Federal Sovereignty* (2001), 25 (recording instances of state defiance); McDonald, *States' Rights*, supra note 5, at 82–84, 101–02; Newmyer, *John Marshall and the Heroic Age*, supra note 50, at 876.

82. A Friend of the Constitution (John Marshall writing anonymously), letter to the editor, *Alexandria Gazette*, June 30, 1819, in Gunther, *John Marshall's Defense*, supra note 4, at 156.

83. Taylor, *Tyranny Unmasked*, supra note 78, at 207. Taylor was discussing the "incapacity of the Supreme Court to supervise the unconstitutional acts of either the Federal or State governments" with specific reference to the refusal of the New England militias to respond to federal authority during the War of 1812.

84. See, e.g., Fletcher v. Peck, 10 U.S. (6 Cranch) 87 (1810) (striking Georgia's law resolving Yazoo land frauds as unconstitutional); New Jersey v. Wilson, 11 U.S. (7 Cranch) 164, 167 (1812) (holding that the repeal of tax exemption was an unconstitutional impairment of contract); Sturges v. Crowninshield, 17 U.S. (4 Wheat.) 122 (1819) (invalidating application of New York bankruptcy law to certain contracts as impairing an obligation of contract); Green v. Biddle, 21 U.S. (8 Wheat.) 1 (1823) (invalidating Kentucky's "occupying claimant" laws).

85. "State Rights," *City of Wash. Gazette*, Feb. 20, 1821, at 3.

86. Martin Van Buren, "Speech to the Senate," Apr. 7, 1826, quoted in Charles Warren, "Legislative and Judicial Attacks on the Supreme Court of the United States," *Am. L. Rev.* 47 (1913): 31.

87. New Jersey v. Wilson, 11 U.S. (7 Cranch) 164 (1812).

88. Jessup, *Reaction and Accommodation*, supra note 47, at 157–59.

89. McDonald, *States' Rights*, supra note 5, at 77 ("[A]s a practical matter," however, "the Supreme Court decision was simply disregarded, and the state legislature adopted a resolution confirming the court of appeals' decision").

90. See generally Jessup, *Reaction and Accommodation*, supra note 47, at 141; Warren, *Supreme Court*, supra note 20, at 1:374; Kenneth W. Treacy, "The Olmstead Case, 1778–1809," *W. Pol. Q.* 10 (1957): 675–80.

91. Warren, *Supreme Court*, supra note 20, at 1:365; Treacy, "Olmstead Case," supra note 90, at 683–84.

92. Jessup, *Reaction and Accommodation*, supra note 47, at 142; Treacy, "Olmstead Case," supra note 90, at 684–85.

93. United States v. Peters, 9 U.S. 115 (5 Cranch) (1809). See also Albert J. Beveridge, *The Life of John Marshall* (1919), 4:20 ("[T]hese clear strong words were addressed to Massachusetts and Connecticut no less than to Pennsylvania").

94. "Resolution of the Legislature of Pennsylvania," Apr. 3, 1809, quoted in Ames, *State Documents*, supra note 23, at 47.

95. *An Act to Establish the Judiciary Courts of the United States* [Judiciary Act of 1789] (Sept. 24, 1789), *Stats at Large of USA* (Boston: Charles C. Little and James Brown, 1845): 1:73.

96. Treacy, "Olmstead Case," supra note 90, at 696.

97. *New-York Commercial Advertiser*, March 28, 1809, at 2. The copious coverage of events in Pennsylvania is documented in Warren, *Supreme Court*, supra note 20, at 1:367–89.

98. "Resolution of the Legislature of Pennsylvania," Apr. 3, 1809, quoted in Ames, *State Documents*, supra note 23, at 48.

99. Warren, *Supreme Court*, supra note 20, at 1:382 (quoting exchange between Madison and Pennsylvania's Governor Snyder).

100. Id. at 1:381, 385; Treacy, "Olmstead Case," supra note 90, 689–90.

101. Green v. Biddle 21 U.S. (8 Wheat.) 1; see generally Jessup, *Reaction and Accommodation*, supra note 47, at 214–15; McDonald, *States' Rights*, supra note 5, at 79–80; White, *Marshall Court*, supra note 75, at 642.

102. *Argus of Western Am.*, May 12, 1824, quoted in Warren, *Supreme Court*, supra note 20, at 2:100n1.

103. Theodore W. Ruger, "'A Question Which Convulses a Nation': The Early Republic's Greatest Debate About the Judicial Review Power," *Harv. L. Rev.* 117 (2004): 846–48; see also McDonald, *States' Rights*, supra note 5, at 83; Warren, *Supreme Court*, supra note 20, at 2:104–05.

104. McDonald, *States' Rights*, supra note 5, at 83, Warren, *Supreme Court*, supra note 20, at 2:106; Ruger, "Early Republic's Greatest Debate," supra note 103, at 848–51.

105. Governor Joseph Desha, "Message to the Kentucky Legislature," Nov. 7, 1825, quoted in *Niles' Reg.*, Dec. 3, 1825.

106. *Niles' Reg.*, Dec. 10, 1825, quoted in Ames, *State Documents*, supra note 23, at 111.

107. Ruger, "Early Republic's Greatest Debate," supra note 103, at 885 (noting that this was the old Kentucky Court of Appeals acting to regain popular approval).

108. Adrienne Siegel, *The Supreme Court in American Life: The Marshall Court* (1987), 2:139; Warren, *Supreme Court*, supra note 20, at 2:100–01 (describing public perception of the decision); Ruger, "Early Republic's Greatest Debate," supra note 103, at 885. Charles Warren in other places disputes this oft-repeated claim about the Court majority. Four of the seven justices actively participated in deciding *Green v. Biddle*: Washington, Story, Duvall, and Johnson. Justices Todd and Livingston were indisposed at the time, and Marshall recused himself because of family and professional connections with Kentucky land. With almost half the Court absent, Justice Washington's majority opinion officially represented only Justices Story and Duvall in addition to himself. However, this was not simply a situation in which the prevailing rule was supported by only three judges. Although Justice Johnson's separate opinion is generally classified as a dissent, the opinion seems to concur with the result reached by the majority. To complicate matters further, Justice Livingston apparently voiced unofficial agreement with Washington's opinion as well. Thus, Warren says, at least five of the seven justices supported *Green v. Biddle*'s outcome. Warren, "Legislative and Judicial Attacks," supra note 86, at 23; see also Jessup, *Reaction and Accommodation*, supra note 47, at 220; White, *Marshall Court*, supra note 75, at 643.

109. Bodley v. Gaither, 19 Ky. (3 T.B. Mon.) 57 (1825).

110. Hawkins and May v. Barney's Lessee, 30 U.S. (5 Pet.) 457, 466 (1831) (concluding that Kentucky's occupying claimant laws were not prohibited by the compact with Virginia); see Ames, *State Documents*, supra note 23, at 24 (maintaining that Kentucky's defiance ended only with the Court's decision in *Hawkins*). But see McDonald, *States' Rights*, supra note 5, at 84 (stating that Kentucky's defiance ended in 1826, when the state's financial difficulties subsided. Kentucky no longer had a reason to defy and disbanded the new court of appeals.).

111. City of New York v. Miln, 33 U.S. (8 Pet.) 118, 120 (1834) ("The practice of this court is, not (except in cases of absolute necessity) to deliver any judgment in cases where constitutional questions are involved, unless four judges concur in opinion, thus making the decision that of a majority of the whole court").

112. See Jessup, *Reaction and Accommodation*, supra note 47, at 232–33; Warren, *Supreme Court*, supra note 20, at 1:528–30. The original injunction, issued before the seizure, was faulty, but the latter was not. Jessup, *Reaction and Accommodation*, supra note 47, at 233. For the public response to Ohio's tax, see John D. Aiello, "Ohio's War upon the Bank of the United States" (Ph.D. diss., Ohio State University, 1972), 75–81.

113. *Nat'l Reg.*, Oct. 2, 1819, at 8.

114. See Aiello, "Ohio's War," supra note 112, at 67; *Niles' Reg.*, Oct. 30, 1819, at 20 (maintaining that "the case of McCulloch vs. the states of Maryland . . . was a case prepared and submitted to the supreme court of the U, states . . . [t]he doctrines set up by the court, on that occasion, are such as the people of this state . . . cannot recognize as correct)." There is evidence they were correct. See Ellis, *Aggressive Nationalism*, supra note 55, at 71–73, 123–24, 163 (arguing *McCulloch* was a manufactured case designed as an opportunity for the Supreme Court to draw its broad conclusions about federal power).

115. *Niles' Reg.*, Oct. 1819, quoted in Warren, *Supreme Court*, supra note 20, at 1:532.

116. *Niles' Reg.*, Oct. 30, 1819, at 20.

117. Aiello, "Ohio's War," supra note 112, at 96, 112, 119.

118. "Resolutions of Pennsylvania Assembly," Apr. 3, 1809, reprinted in Annals of Cong. (D.C.: Gales and Seaton, 1853): 21:2265–66.

119. "Virginia General Assembly Resolution," Feb. 19, 1821, in Ames, *State Documents*, supra note 23, at 103, 104.

120. Jessup, *Reaction and Accommodation*, supra note 47, at 205; Graber, "Federalist or Friend," supra note 48, at 230; Warren, "Legislative and Judicial Attacks," supra note 86, at 16–17.

121. Annals of Cong. (D.C.: Gales and Seaton, 1855): 38:23. On the proposals generally, see Jessup, *Reaction and Accommodation*, supra note 47, at 300–16; Warren, *Supreme Court*, supra note 20, at 2:114–18.

122. "Remonstrance of the Legislature of Kentucky," Jan. 7, 1824, in Ames, *State Documents*, supra note 23, at 111.

123. See Jessup, *Reaction and Accommodation*, supra note 47, at 314–15.

124. For a discussion of the earlier failed attempts and the circumstances that led to a renewed attack in 1831, see id. at 300–21 (noting resistance to the tariff policy, state defiance, and Jackson's bank veto as contributing to the problem).

125. House Committee on the Judiciary, 21st Cong., 2d Sess., 1831, H.R. Rep. 43, 3–6.

126. Letter from Chief Justice John Marshall to Justice Story, Oct. 15, 1830, quoted in Warren, "Legislative and Judicial Attacks," supra note 86, at 163.

127. Letter from Justice Story to George Ticknor, Jan. 22, 1831, quoted in id. at 163; see also Jessup, *Reaction and Accommodation*, supra note 47, at 346–48 (summarizing and quoting the debates about repealing Section 25 of the Judiciary Act).

128. Quoted in Warren, *Supreme Court*, supra note 20, at 2:196.

129. *Niles' Reg.*, March 31, 1832, at 78.

130. See generally Ellis, *Union at Risk*, supra note 3, at 28; Jessup, *Reaction and Accommodation*, supra note 47, at 355–62; Jill Norgren, *The Cherokee Cases* (1996), 32–39, 46–48; Warren, *Supreme Court*, supra note 20, at 2:189–90; White, *Marshall Court*, supra note 75, at 714–15.

131. *Ga. J.*, reprinted in *Niles' Reg.*, Aug. 18, 1830, at 68.

132. State v. Tassel (1830), in *Niles' Reg.*, Jan. 8, 1831, at 338–39 (reprinting writ); Cherokee Nation v. Georgia, 30 U.S. (5 Pet.) 1 (1831); Worcester v. Georgia, 31 U.S. (6 Pet.) 515 (1832).

133. Ellis, *Union at Risk*, supra note 3, at 29–31; Warren, "Legislative and Judicial Attacks," supra note 86, at 167.

134. Norgren, *Cherokee Cases*, supra note 130, at 53–54 (describing the decision to hire Wirt).

135. Letter from William Wirt to George Gilmer, June 4, 1830, reprinted in *Niles' Reg.*, Sept. 18, 1830, at 69–70.

136. Letter from George Gilmer to William Wirt, June 19, 1830, reprinted in *Niles' Reg.*, Sept. 18, 1830, at 70–71.

137. For a description of the Georgia laws asserting criminal jurisdiction, see Norgren, *Cherokee Cases*, supra note 130, at 58–61. For a discussion of the Corn Tassel case, see Jessup, *Reaction and Accommodation*, supra note 47, at 363–64; Norgren, *Cherokee Cases*, supra note 130, at 95–98 (detailing the arguments made by each side); Warren, *Supreme Court*, supra note 20, at 2:192–93; Warren, "Legislative and Judicial Attacks," supra note 86, at 167. The writ is reprinted in *Niles' Reg.*, Jan. 8, 1831, at 338–39.

138. "Governor Gilmer's Message to the Legislature," Dec. 22, 1830, reprinted in *Niles' Reg.*, Jan. 8, 1831, at 338.

139. "Georgia General Assembly Resolution," Dec. 22, 1830, in Ames, *State Documents*, supra note 23, at 127, 128.

140. "To the Editors of the Georgia Journal," reprinted in the *Richmond Enquirer*, Feb. 5, 1831.

141. Jessup, *Reaction and Accommodation*, supra note 47, at 364; Norgren, *Cherokee Cases*, supra note 130, at 98; Warren, *Supreme Court*, supra note 20, at 2:194.

142. *Richmond Enquirer*, Dec. 10, 1831, at 1 (reprinting *Augusta Constitutionalist*). For a discussion of the public response to the Tassel case, see generally Warren, *Supreme Court*, supra note 20, at 2:194–98 (quoting the responses of many newspapers).

143. *Niles' Reg.*, Jan. 8, 1831, at 838–39 (quoting *United States Telegraph*).

144. Cherokee Nation v. Georgia, 30 U.S. (5 Pet.) at 1. The Court's decision was driven by a conclusion that the Cherokee were not a foreign nation in the constitutional sense but rather a "denominated domestic dependent nation" over which the Supreme Court had no original jurisdiction. Id.

145. Id.

146. Joseph C. Burke, "The Cherokee Cases: A Study in Law, Politics, and Morality," *Stan. L. Rev.* 21 (1969): 516–18 (describing Marshall's unhappiness with the public response to the Court's decision and his out-of-character decision to encourage dissent); Gerard N. Magliocca, "Preemptive Opinions: The Secret History of *Worcester v. Georgia* and *Dred Scott*," *U. Pitt. L. Rev.* 63 (2002): 533 (same); see also Gerard N. Magliocca, *Andrew Jackson and the Constitution: The Rise and Fall of Generational Regimes* (2007), 35 (discussing Marshall's unhappiness with Jackson's policy).

147. Letter from Justice Story to Richard Peters, May 17, 1831, quoted in Burke, "Cherokee Cases," supra note 146, at 516.

148. Ellis, *Union at Risk*, supra note 3, at 30; Burke, "Cherokee Cases," supra note 146, at 518. The dissenting opinion was included in the official reporter. Cherokee Nation v. Georgia, 30 U.S. (5 Pet.) 1, 50 (1831) (Thompson, J., dissenting).

149. For a discussion of the license requirement and the attempt to bring a case to challenge the law, see Jessup, *Reaction and Accommodation*, supra note 47, at 367–68; Norgren, *Cherokee Cases*, supra note 130, at 112–13; Warren, *Supreme Court*, supra note 20, at 2:213–14.

150. Worcester v. Georgia, 31 U.S. (6 Pet.) 515 (1832). For a discussion of the opinion, see Norgren, *Cherokee Cases*, supra note 130, at 117–22 (also discussing Baldwin's dissenting opinion); Warren, *Supreme Court*, supra note 20, at 2:215–16.

151. Warren, *Supreme Court*, supra note 20, at 2:214; see also Jessup, *Reaction and Accommodation*, supra note 47, at 367–68.

152. William Wirt, "Oral Argument Before the Supreme Court," March 1, 1831, quoted in Anton-Hermann Chroust, "Did President Jackson Actually Threaten the Supreme Court of the United States with Nonenforcement of Its Injunction Against the State of Georgia?," *Am. J. Leg. Hist.* 4 (1960): 77 (concluding Wirt's aside is referring to Jackson's asking how the Court will enforce its ruling).

153. Letter from Justice Story to George Ticknor, March 8, 1832, in *The Life and Letters of Joseph Story*, ed. William Waldo Story (1851), 2:83.

154. "Governor Lumpkin's Message to the Georgia Legislature," quoted in Allen Guttmann, *States' Rights and Indian Removal: The Cherokee Nation v. The State of Georgia* (1965), 78.

155. *Macon Advertiser*, March 13, 1832, quoted in Rennard Strickland and William M. Strickland, "A Tale of Two Marshalls: Reflections on Indian Law and Policy, the Cherokee Cases, and the Cruel Irony of Supreme Court Victories," *Okla. L. Rev.* 47 (1994): 114. For additional reactions to the decision, see Warren, *Supreme Court*, supra note 20, at 2:216–21.

156. *Niles' Reg.*, March 31, 1832, at 71.

157. William Wirt, "Oral Argument Before the Supreme Court," March 1, 1831, quoted in Chroust, "Did President Jackson," supra note 152, at 77.

158. *Conn. Mirror*, March 17, 1832; see Warren, *Supreme Court*, supra note 20, at 2:217–21, for a sample of newspaper coverage.

159. See Warren, *Supreme Court*, supra note 20, at 2:217–29 (examples sprinkled throughout).

160. *N.Y. Daily Advertiser*, March 1932 (date uncertain), quoted in Warren, *Supreme Court*, supra note 20, at 2:217.

161. An Act to Provide for Calling Forth the Militia to Execute the Laws of the Union, Suppress Insurrections and Repel Invasions [Militia Act of 1792] (May 2, 1792) (amended 1795), *Stats at Large of USA* (Boston: Charles C. Little and James Brown, 1845): 1:264; Norgren, *Cherokee Cases*, supra note 130, at 123.

162. Norgren, *Cherokee Cases*, supra note 130, at 123 (explaining that the Supreme Court adjourned, perhaps early to avoid conflict, until March 1833). Wirt had expressed concern that even then the order could not be enforced because of a gap in the law. The federal courts lacked jurisdiction to issue writs of habeas corpus for state prisoners, and the Supreme Court could not act in any event unless the state court's order was before it. Burke, "Cherokee Cases," supra note 146, at 526. On the latter score, the Georgia court may have been sufficiently obliging. Although it refused to issue an order, it did allow the lawyers to swear out an affidavit of what occurred. Edwin A. Miles, "After John Marshall's Decision: *Worcester v. Georgia* and the Nullification Crisis," *J. S. Hist.* 39 (1973): 528.

163. *Niles' Reg.*, March 31, 1832, at 44.

164. Letter from Joseph Story to George Ticknor, March 8. 1832, quoted in Norgren, *Cherokee Cases*, supra note 130, at 122.

165. Andrew Jackson, "First Annual Message," Dec. 8, 1829, reprinted in *The Statesman-ship of Andrew Jackson*, ed. Francis Newton Thorpe (1909), 57–58. For a discussion of the removal legislation, see Norgren, *Cherokee Cases*, supra note 130, at 51–55; see also Magliocca, *Andrew Jackson and the Constitution*, supra note 146, at 29 (discussing importance of removal to Jackson).

166. *The Memoirs of John Quincy Adams*, ed. Charles F. Adams (1876), 8:262–63.

167. See Ellis, *Union at Risk*, supra note 3, at 31 (quoting Jackson without citation); Burke, "Cherokee Cases," supra note 146, at 524–25 (explaining that "most [historians] admit that they cannot prove what Jackson said"); Chroust, "Did President Jackson," supra note 152, at 76–78; see also Letter from Andrew Jackson to Col. Anthony Butler, Dec. 8, 1829, quoted in Ellis, *Union at Risk*, supra note 3, at 32 (Jackson saw the *Worcester* case as an effort "to embarrass me").

168. Letter from Andrew Jackson to Brigadier-General John Coffee, Apr. 7, 1832, in *Correspondence of Andrew Jackson*, ed. John Spencer Basset (1929), 4:429–30.

169. See newspapers quoted in Warren, *Supreme Court*, supra note 20, at 2:217–19.

170. Letter from Lewis Williams to William Lenoir, Apr. 9, 1832, quoted in Miles, "After John Marshall's Decision," supra note 162, at 533n32; see also Richard P. Longaker, "Andrew Jackson and the Judiciary," *Pol. Sci. Q.* 71 (1956): 347n13 (claiming that "Jackson did not want to enforce this particular decision and, had he wanted to, his ingenuity would have found a way").

171. See generally Ellis, *Union at Risk*, supra note 3, at 13–15. On Jackson's connection to the people, see Schlesinger, *Age of Jackson*, supra note 44, at 43 ("[T]he secret of his strength: his deep natural understanding of the people"); Harold C. Syrett, *Andrew Jackson* (1953), 26 ("He did not so much direct or form public opinion as stay one step ahead of it"); see also Gerald Leonard, "Party as a 'Political Safeguard of Federalism': Martin Van Buren and the Constitutional Theory of Party Politics," *Rutgers L.*

Rev. 54 (2001): 256–57 ("One could only be a democrat . . . by placing the principle of majority rule above any other principle, especially above any particular substantive policy one might favor").

172. "Second Annual Message," Dec. 6, 1830, reprinted in Thorpe, *Statesmanship of Andrew Jackson*, supra note 165, at 98.

173. See Douglas T. Miller, *Then Was the Future* (1973), 84; Norgren, *Cherokee Cases*, supra note 130, at 67–69; see also Jessup, *Reaction and Accommodation*, supra note 47, at 65–67 (describing the new party system); McDonald, *States' Rights*, supra note 5, at 89–91 (describing the new party system and the democratization that occurred by "expanding the electorate and having candidates compete for popular votes").

174. *Niles' Reg.*, Aug. 29, 1840, quoted in Schlesinger, *Age of Jackson*, supra note 44, at 14. Schlesinger explains that "[p]roperty, in Federalist reflexes, became almost identified with character." Id.

175. Marvin Meyers, *Jacksonian Persuasion: Politics and Belief* (1957), 7–8 ("The political machine reached into every neighborhood. . . . Public opinion was heard with a new sensitivity and addressed with anxious respect"); see also Kramer, *People Themselves*, supra note 14, at 196–200.

176. Schlesinger, *Age of Jackson*, supra note 44, at 51.

177. Letter from Joseph Story to Sarah Waldo Story, March 7, 1829, quoted in Schlesinger, *Age of Jackson,* supra note 44, at 6.

178. Kramer, *People Themselves*, supra note 14 at 196 ("The sole exception to [adherence to the majority] rule was the party's commitment to states' rights, which in the context of Jacksonian America was seen by Democratic leaders as part and parcel of majority rule").

179. Andrew Jackson, "First Inaugural Address," March 4, 1829, reprinted in Thorpe, *Statesmanship of Andrew Jackson*, supra note 165, at 32.

180. Ellis, *Union at Risk*, supra note 3, at 33–37; McDonald, *States' Rights*, supra note 5, at 111; Gerard N. Magliocca, "Veto! The Jacksonian Revolution in Constitutional Law," *Neb. L. Rev.* 78 (1999): 230–31.

181. For a discussion of the veto language and the response to the veto, see McDonald, *States' Rights*, supra note 5, at 112; Schlesinger, *Age of Jackson*, supra note 44, at 89–92; see generally Magliocca, "Veto!," supra note 180.

182. Andrew Jackson, "Bank Veto," July 10, 1832, reprinted in Thorpe, *Statesmanship of Andrew Jackson*, supra note 165, at 162.

183. Nicholas Biddle, "Memorandum of a Conversation with Andrew Jackson (n.d.)," quoted in Ellis, *Union at Risk*, supra note 3, at 34.

184. Schlesinger, *Age of Jackson*, supra note 44, at 89–90 (discussing authorship of the veto message).

185. "Bank Veto," in Thorpe, *Statesmanship of Andrew Jackson*, supra note 165, at 163.

186. 8 Reg. Deb. 1243 (1832) (statement of Sen. White on July 11, 1832, regarding the bank veto); see Martin Van Buren, *An Inquiry into the Origin and Course of Political Parties in the United States* (1867), 329 (Jackson "contented himself with frequent and unreserved expression of concurrence in the views which had been taken of the subject, on the floor of the Senate, by Judge White"); see also Longaker, "Andrew Jackson," supra note 170, at 352.

187. Magliocca, *Andrew Jackson and the Constitution*, supra note 146, at 56–59; Burke, "Cherokee Cases," supra note 146, at 528–29.

188. *Niles' Reg.*, Apr. 14, 1832, at 112 (reprinting an article from the *Utica Observer*), quoted in Burke, "Cherokee Cases," supra note 146, at 528–29.

189. *Nat'l Gazette*, Aug. 28, 1832, quoted in Burke, "Cherokee Cases," supra note 146, at 529.

190. See Warren, *Supreme Court*, supra note 20, at 2:217–19 (quoting news articles and correspondence raising this question).

191. Letter from John C. Calhoun to Virgil Maxcy, Sept. 1, 1831, quoted in Newmyer, *John Marshall and the Heroic Age*, supra note 50, at 353.

192. Daniel Webster, "Address on the Senate Floor," Jan. 26, 27, 1830, in Belz, *Webster-Hayne Debate*, supra note 41, at 125.

193. William W. Freehling, *Prelude to Civil War* (1966), 136–38.

194. Daniel Webster, "Address on the Senate Floor," Jan. 26, 27, 1830, in Belz, *Webster-Hayne Debate,* supra note 41, at 113.

195. Freehling, *Prelude to Civil War*, supra note 193, at 136–40 (explaining the tariff's passage and purported effects on South Carolina).

196. "Exposition Reported by the Special Committee," Dec. 19, 1828, in *The Papers of John C. Calhoun*, ed. Clyde N. Wilson and W. Edwin Hemphill (1977), 10:529, 531. South Carolina's senators presented the protest to the U.S. Senate. *Senate Journal*, 20th Cong., 2d Sess., Feb. 10, 1820, 115–17. On Calhoun's role in drafting, see Ames, *State Documents*, supra note 23, at 152; Ellis, *Union at Risk*, supra note 3, at 7–8; McDonald, *States' Rights*, supra note 5, at 104.

197. For an introduction to Calhoun's career and personality, see Belz, *Webster-Hayne Debate*, supra note 41, at x; Schlesinger, *Age of Jackson*, supra note 44, at 52–54.

198. All quotes from "Exposition Reported by the Special Committee," Dec. 19, 1828, in Wilson and Hemphill, *Papers of John C. Calhoun*, supra note 196, at 10:445–46, 529, 531; see also Freehling, *Prelude to Civil War*, supra note 193, at 154–55, 158–75 (contextualizing and explaining South Carolina's nullification doctrine).

199. Robert Y. Hayne, "Address to the Senate," Jan. 25, 1830, in Belz, *Webster-Hayne Debate*, supra note 41, at 73; see also "Exposition Reported by the Special Committee," Dec. 19, 1828, in Wilson and Hemphill, *Papers of John C. Calhoun*, supra note 196, at 10:469–73 (discussing nullification's roots in the Kentucky and Virginia Resolutions).

200. Merrill D. Peterson, *The Great Triumvirate* (1987), 170, 173 (discussing the potential political alliance between the South and West).

201. Belz, *Webster-Hayne Debate*, supra note 41, at x.

202. Freehling, *Prelude to Civil War*, supra note 193, at 142 (describing southern strategy to form a coalition with the West).

203. See Belz, *Webster-Hayne Debate*, supra note 41, at xi.

204. Robert Y. Hayne, "Address to the Senate," Jan. 25, 1830, in id. at 35.

205. See id. at ix, xvi; Peterson, *Great Triumvirate*, supra note 200, at 179 (on publication). For a description of the circumstances of the debate and the public attention, see Belz, *Webster-Hayne Debate*, supra note 41, at xii; Freehling, *Prelude to Civil War*, supra note 193, at 183–86.

206. Robert Y. Hayne, "Address to the Senate," Jan. 19, 1830, in Belz, *Webster-Hayne Debate*, supra note 41, at 10; see also Robert Y. Hayne, "Address to the Senate," Jan. 25, 1830, in id. at 51.

207. Daniel Webster, "Address to the Senate," Jan. 20, 1830, in id. at 23.

208. Robert Y. Hayne, "Address to the Senate," Jan. 25, 1830, in id. at 73–76.

209. Daniel Webster, "Address to the Senate," Jan. 26, 27, 1830, in id. at 126. These arguments echoed Marshall's opinion in *McCulloch*. See McDonald, *States' Rights*, supra note 5, at 106; White, *Marshall Court*, supra note 75, at 282–83.

210. Daniel Webster, "Address to the Senate," Jan. 26, 27, 1830, in Belz, *Webster-Hayne Debate*, supra note 41, at 125.

211. Robert Y. Hayne, "Address to the Senate," Jan. 25, 1830, in id. at 74 (quoting the Virginia Resolution).

212. Robert Y. Hayne, "Address to the Senate," Jan. 27, 1830, in id. at 182.

213. Id. at 79.
214. Id. at 168–69 (quoting Madison).
215. Id. at 179, 177.
216. Davison M. Douglas, "The Rhetorical Uses of *Marbury v. Madison*: The Emergence of a 'Great Case,'" *Wake Forest L. Rev.* 38 (2003): 381; Daniel A. Farber, "Judicial Review and Its Alternatives: An American Tale," *Wake Forest L. Rev.* 38 (2003): 417. There were few in the 1800s who took the position that judicial review in federalism cases was more acceptable than in separation of powers cases. But see Eakin v. Raub, 12 Serg. & Rawle 330 (Pa. 1825) (Gibson, J., dissenting) (arguing against power of Pennsylvania judges to strike Pennsylvania statutes on basis of the Pennsylvania constitution, but requiring judges to invalidate laws inconsistent with federal law; "By becoming parties to the federal constitution the states have agreed to several limitations of their individual sovereignty"). Gibson later recanted on the power of judicial review generally. See Kramer, *People Themselves*, supra note 14, at 154. Madison arguably is another example, conceding judicial supremacy over the federal branches long after supporting judicial review of state laws. See Kramer, *People Themselves*, supra note 14, at 186–87.
217. Robert Y. Hayne, "Address to the Senate," Jan. 27, 1830, in Belz, *Webster-Hayne Debate*, supra note 41, at 182 (quoting Thomas Jefferson).
218. It was Calhoun who refined this argument. R. Kent Newmyer, "John Marshall, *McCulloch v. Maryland,* and the Southern States' Rights Tradition," *J. Marshall L. Rev.* 33 (2000): 930–31 (noting that Calhoun had done something earlier theorists were unable to do: "a mechanism of implementation, which claimed to be both peaceful and constitutional"). For a description of the inconsistencies in the nullification doctrine and Calhoun's attempts to reconcile them, see Freehling, *Prelude to Civil War*, supra note 193, at 166–73.
219. Robert Y. Hayne, "Address to the Senate," Jan. 27, 1830, in Belz, *Webster-Hayne Debate*, supra note 41, at 173, 175.
220. Daniel Webster, "Address on the Senate Floor," Jan. 26, 27, 1830, in id. at 137.
221. John M. Clayton, "Address on the Senate Floor," March 4, 1830, in id. at 363.
222. Kramer, *People Themselves*, supra note 14, at 189; McDonald, *States' Rights*, supra note 5, at 112; Schlesinger, *Age of Jackson*, supra note 44, at 95–97; Longaker, "Age of Jackson," supra note 170, at 348.
223. "Ordinance of Nullification," Nov. 24, 1832, in William W. Freehling, *Nullification Era: A Documentary Record* (1967), 150–52.
224. Syrett, *Andrew Jackson*, supra note 171, at 31–33, 35–39.
225. Letter from Andrew Jackson to Robert Oliver, Oct. 26, 1830, reprinted in Thorpe, *Statesmanship of Andrew Jackson*, supra note 165, at 17.
226. "Jefferson Dinner," *Norwich Courier*, Apr. 28, 1830, at 2 (printing both quotes; punctuation as it appears in newspaper). For more on the toasts, see Freehling, *Prelude to Civil War*, supra note 193, at 192; White, *Marshall Court*, supra note 75, at 487–88.
227. *United States Telegraph*, Dec. 19, 1832, quoted in Warren, *Supreme Court*, supra note 20, at 2:235. The *Telegraph* continued: "Georgia refuses to obey the decisions of the Federal Judiciary. Not a word is said by the Executive or his minions, except that she is right in doing so. South Carolina says that she will do so at a future period. And the Palace is in arms."
228. "South Carolina's Reply to Jackson's Proclamation," Dec. 20, 1832, in Ames, *State Documents*, supra note 23, at 175.
229. See Miles, "After John Marshall's Decision," supra note 162, at 534.
230. Letter from Wilson Lumpkin to Lewis Cass, Jan. 2, 1833, quoted in Ellis, *Union at Risk*, supra note 3, at 114.

231. *Daily Albany Argus*, Dec. 28, 1832 (reprinting unnamed Savannah newspaper), quoted in Ellis, *Union at Risk*, supra note 3, at 114–15.
232. See generally Ellis, *Union at Risk*, supra note 3, at 114–15 (concluding this is the only difference).
233. In 1831, the Supreme Court upheld a Kentucky act similar to the act at issue in *Green*. Nonetheless, the Court distinguished the more recent act to rule in favor of the state. Hawkins v. Barney's Lessee, 30 U.S. (5 Pet.) 457, 461 (1831). For a brief description of the case and the Court's reversal, see Jessup, *Reaction and Accommodation*, supra note 47, at 328–29.
234. Ky. J. H. 1832–33, at 18–20, 458 (Dec. 4, 1832, Jan. 31, 1833), quoted in Jessup, *Reaction and Accommodation*, supra note 47, at 330.
235. Charles Hammond, *Cincinnati Gazette*, Apr. 1832, quoted in Warren, "Legislative and Judicial Attacks," supra note 86, at 174. For the responses of other states, see Jessup, *Reaction and Accommodation*, supra note 47, at 237.
236. Jessup, *Reaction and Accommodation*, supra note 47, at 346–48 ("[T]he repeal bill was defeated on a motion to reject, 138–51, with all but six of the negative votes coming from Representatives of the South and West"); Warren, "Legislative and Judicial Attacks," supra note 86, at 164.
237. On Madison's shifting views, see generally Kramer, *People Themselves*, supra note 14, at 185–88; Jack N. Rakove, "Judicial Power in the Constitutional Theory of James Madison," *Wm. & Mary L. Rev.* 43 (2002): 1513–48.
238. Letter from James Madison to Thomas Jefferson, June 27, 1823, in Rakove, *James Madison's Writings*, supra note 77, at 800–02.
239. Letter from James Madison to Edward Everett, Aug. 28, 1830, in id. at 847.
240. Andrew Jackson, "Anti-Nullification Proclamation," Dec. 10, 1832, in Thorpe, *Statesmanship of Andrew Jackson*, supra note 165, at 235, 245. For more on Jackson's position, see White, *Marshall Court*, supra note 75, at 283–85.
241. Andrew Jackson, "Anti-Nullification Proclamation," Dec. 10, 1832, in Thorpe, *Statesmanship of Andrew Jackson*, supra note 165, at 243.
242. Letter from Silas Wright, Jr., A. C. Flagg, and John A. Dix to Wilson Lumpkin, Dec. 18, 1832, quoted in Ellis, *Union at Risk*, supra note 3, at 116; see also Miles, "After John Marshall's Decision," supra note 162, at 536. Jackson's Secretary of War wrote Lumpkin confidentially, seeking help and expressing Jackson's approval of the request. He alluded to "other important considerations, which must be apparent to you," making it "peculiarly desirable, that this [release of the missionaries] should be now done." Letter from Lewis Cass to Wilson Lumpkin, Dec. 24, 1832, quoted in Miles, "After John Marshall's Decision," supra note 162, at 537.
243. Miles, "After John Marshall's Decision," supra note 162, at 535.
244. "Notes of Opinions Given & Reasons for Them, at the Meeting of the Prudential Committee in Regard to Advising the Imprisoned Missionaries & the Cherokee Indians," Dec. 25, 1832, quoted in Miles, "After John Marshall's Decision," supra note 162, at 539; see also Ellis, *Union at Risk*, supra note 3, at 115–16.
245. Ellis, *Union at Risk*, supra note 3, at 118.
246. Freehling, *Prelude to Civil War*, supra note 193, at 284–87; McDonald, *States' Rights*, supra note 5, at 109–10.
247. Andrew Jackson, "Anti-Nullification Proclamation," Dec. 10, 1832, in Thorpe, *Statesmanship of Andrew Jackson*, supra note 165, at 218.
248. New jurisdiction was placed in the circuit courts, removal jurisdiction was created for officers of the United States brought into state court in the performance of their revenue collection duties, and the power to grant a writ of habeas corpus to anyone in prison for an act taken pursuant to the law of the United States was bestowed.

See Norgren, *Cherokee Cases*, supra note 130, at 123–24; Burke, "Cherokee Cases," supra note 146, at 531n168.

249. 9 Reg. Deb. 249, 282–300, 317–33, 348–58 (1833); Warren, "Legislative and Judicial Attacks," supra note 86, at 164; see also Jessup, *Reaction and Accommodation*, supra note 47, at 383 (describing large percentage of members of Congress supporting the Court, and quoting John Holmes, Maine's representative, describing Section 25 of the Judiciary Act as essential to the Constitution); Warren, *Supreme Court*, supra note 20, at 2:236 (describing the Court's congressional support as greater than it had been in fifteen years.).

250. *Niles' Reg.*, Feb. 23, 1833, at 429.

251. Ellis, *Union at Risk*, supra note 3, at 166–76; Freehling, *Prelude to Civil War*, supra note 193, at 292–93; Jessup, *Reaction and Accommodation*, supra note 47, at 383.

252. Letter from Catherine Maria Sedgwick to Theodore Sedgwick, Jan. 20, 1833, quoted in Schlesinger, *Age of Jackson*, supra note 44, at 96.

253. See Ellis, *Union at Risk*, supra note 3, at 84–89; Freehling, *Prelude to Civil War*, supra note 193, at 265–67; Jessup, *Reaction and Accommodation*, supra note 47, at 386.

254. Ellis, *Union at Risk*, supra note 3, at 179; Schlesinger, *Age of Jackson*, supra note 44, at 96.

255. Diary Entry of Philip Hone, Dec. 14, 1832, quoted in Ellis, *Union at Risk*, supra note 3, at 89.

256. Letter from Justice Story to Sarah Story, Jan. 27, 1833, quoted in Warren, *Supreme Court*, supra note 20, at 2:237–38. For more on Story's relationship with the President, see Jessup, *Reaction and Accommodation*, supra note 47, at 386–87; Warren, *Supreme Court*, supra note 20, at 2:237–38.

257. Andrew Jackson, "Farewell Address," March 4, 1837, reprinted in Thorpe, *Statesmanship of Andrew Jackson*, supra note 165, at 493, 499.

258. Ellis, *Union at Risk*, supra note 3, at 207n64.

259. See Magliocca, *Andrew Jackson and the Constitution*, supra note 146, at 67–68; Magliocca, "Preemptive Opinions," supra note 146, at 557.

260. Michael J. Klarman, "How Great Were the 'Great' Marshall Court Decisions?," *Va. L. Rev.* 87 (2001): 1181 ("By early 1833 . . . the Court was riding the crest of a nationalist wave produced by the public backlash against nullification"); see also Jessup, *Reaction and Accommodation*, supra note 47, at 382–85.

261. Ellis, *Union at Risk*, supra note 3, at 185–87.

Chapter 4: Control

1. Speech of Stephen Douglas, First Joint Debate at Ottawa, Ill., Aug. 21, 1858, in *The Lincoln-Douglas Debates*, ed. Harold Holzer (1993), 45; speech of Stephen Douglas, Third Joint Debate at Jonesboro, Ill., Sept. 15, 1858, in id. at 140.

2. Speech of Stephen Douglas, Third Joint Debate at Jonesboro, Ill., Sept. 15, 1858, in id. at 140.

3. Dred Scott v. Sandford, 60 U.S. 393 (1857).

4. Frederick Douglass, "The *Dred Scott* Decision: Speech at New York, on the Occasion of the Anniversary of the American Abolition Society," May 11, 1857, reprinted in Paul Finkelman, Dred Scott v. Sandford: *A Brief History with Documents* (1997), 173, 174.

5. "Congress and the Supreme Court—The Great Issue for the Next Presidency," *N.Y. Herald*, Jan. 5, 1867, at 4.

6. Cong. Globe, 40th Cong., 2d Sess. 502 (1867).

7. "The New *Dred Scott*," *Harper's Wkly.*, Jan. 19, 1867, at 34.

8. Notes of James Madison, June 30, 1787, reprinted in Max Farrand, *The Records of the Federal Convention of 1787* (1937), 1:481, 486.

9. Letter from John Caldwell Calhoun to Virgil Maxcy, Sept. 11, 1830, quoted in William M. Meigs, *The Life of John Caldwell Calhoun* (1917), 1:419.

10. See Gerard N. Magliocca, "The Cherokee Removal and the Fourteenth Amendment," *Duke L. J.* 53 (2003): 908–09. For a discussion of the relationship between the Cherokee controversy and abolitionism, see Gerard N. Magliocca, *Andrew Jackson and the Constitution: The Rise and Fall of Generational Regimes* (2007), 87–92.

11. U.S. Const. art. I, § 2, cl. 3.

12. U.S. Const. art. I, § 9.

13. U.S. Const. art. I, § 2.

14. Abraham Lincoln, "Speech at Peoria, Illinois," Oct. 16, 1854, reprinted in *The Collected Works of Abraham Lincoln*, ed. Roy Basler (1953), 2:274.

15. See Don E. Fehrenbacher, *The Dred Scott Case: Its Significance in American Law and Politics* (1978), 107–08.

16. Daniel Webster, "Speech Delivered to the Senate," Jan. 26–27, 1830, reprinted in *The Webster-Hayne Debate on the Nature of the Union*, ed. Herman Belz (2000), 91.

17. Cong. Globe, 29th Cong., 1st Sess. 1217 (1846). On Wilmot and the Mexican-American War, see Fehrenbacher, Dred Scott *Case*, supra note 15, at 128–35. On the opposition of Radical Whigs, see John H. Schroeder, *Mr. Polk's War: American Opposition & Dissent, 1846–1848* (1973), 78–79.

18. Support for the Wilmot Proviso was along sharp sectional lines. Because the House majority was from the North, it passed; however, it died in the Senate each time the proviso was introduced over the course of four years because southern states threatened to secede if it was passed into law. For a general account of the Wilmot Proviso, see Michael F. Holt, *The Political Crisis of the 1850s* (1978), 50–51; see also Harold M. Hyman and William M. Wiecek, *Equal Justice Under Law: Constitutional Development, 1835–1875* (1982), 121–33.

19. See Michael F. Holt, *Political Parties and American Political Development from the Age of Jackson to the Age of Lincoln* (1992), 68–70.

20. Hyman and Wiecek, *Equal Justice Under Law*, supra note 18, at 129 (citing Richard H. Sewell, *Ballots for Freedom: Antislavery Politics in the United States, 1837–1860* (1976), 172–73); see also Arthur M. Schlesinger, Jr., *The Age of Jackson* (1946), 451–52 (arguing that the Wilmot Proviso, even after failing, "formulated and laid before the country" the free-soil issue). Wilmot outlined his reasons for proposing the antislavery bill as political and economical, as opposed to moral: "I make no war upon the South, nor upon slavery in the South. I have no squeamish sensitiveness upon the subject of slavery, no morbid sympathy for the slave. I plead the cause and the rights of white freemen. I would preserve to free white labor a fair country, a rich inheritance, where the sons of toil, of my own race and own color, can live without the disgrace which association with negro slavery brings upon free labor. I stand for the inviolability of free territory. It shall remain free, so far as my voice or vote can aid in the preservation of its character." Appendix to Cong. Globe, 29th Cong., 2d Sess. 317 (1847).

21 . Holt, *Political Parties*, supra note 19, at 69 (quoting letter from David Wilmot to Franklin Pierce, July 13, 1852, on file with N.H. Hist. Soc.); see generally Fehrenbacher, Dred Scott *Case*, supra note 15, at 130; Schlesinger, *Age of Jackson*, supra note 20, at 450–53; Louise Weinberg, "*Dred Scott* and the Crisis of 1860," *Chi.-Kent L. Rev.* 82 (2007): 102–03, 112 (southern objection to Wilmot Proviso was "not about plantations, but about political power," particularly in the Senate).

22. For a general account of Congress's passing the Compromise of 1850, see James M. McPherson, *Battle Cry of Freedom: The Civil War Era* (1988), 70–76; David M. Potter and Don E. Fehrenbacher, *The Impending Crisis, 1848–1861* (1976), 107–10; for the terms of the 1850 fugitive slave legislation, see Robert M. Cover, *Justice Accused: Anti-*

slavery and the Judicial Process (1975), 175; Robert J. Kaczorowski, "Congress's Power to Enforce Fourteenth Amendment Rights: Lessons from Federal Remedies the Framers Enacted," *Harv. J. Legis.* 42 (2005): 196–98.

23. See Potter and Fehrenbacher, *Impending Crisis*, supra note 22, at 131–34; McPherson, *Battle Cry of Freedom*, supra note 22, at 81–82.

24. Abraham Lincoln, "Address to the Republican State Convention at Springfield, Ill.," June 16, 1858 (known as the "A House Divided" speech), reprinted in Basler, *Collected Works of Abraham Lincoln*, supra note 14, at 2:462. For an account of the Kansas-Nebraska Act's passage, see Eric Foner, *Free Soil, Free Labor, Free Men: The Ideology of the Republican Party Before the Civil War* (1995); Holt, *Political Crisis of the 1850s*, supra note 18, at 145–48.

25. Martin Van Buren, *Inquiry into the Origin and Course of Political Parties in the United States* (1867), 355. On this point, historians are united. See, e.g., Foner, *Free Soil*, supra note 24, at 155; Holt, *Political Crisis of the 1850s*, supra note 18, at 148–49.

26. It is undisputed that the Kansas-Nebraska Act was the catalyst for the birth of the Republican Party; however, there is also evidence that two other issues—temperance and immigration—contributed significantly to the party's rise among Whigs and Democrats alike. See Holt, *Political Crisis of the 1850s*, supra note 18, at 153–57.

27. See Holt, *Political Parties*, supra note 19, at 74; Holt, *Political Crisis of the 1850s*, supra note 18, at 148.

28. Holt, *Political Crisis of the 1850s*, supra note 18, at 192.

29. See Joel H. Silbey, *The American Political Nation, 1838–93* (1991), 137; Weinberg, "Dred Scott," supra note 21, at 115.

30. Holt, *Political Crisis of the 1850s*, supra note 18, at 154 (quoting Michigan Republican platform, reprinted in Hans L. Trefousse, *The Republican Party, 1854–1864* (1969), 1185–88). But see Holt, *Political Crisis of the 1850s*, supra note 18, at 188 (showing that several local Republican Party platforms repudiated abolitionism, focusing instead on "the welfare of the white man"). Historians reconcile these contradictory platforms by seeing the early Republican Party as one more favorable to black rights than Democrats, but also somewhat racist and reluctant to interfere with slavery in the South. See Holt, *Political Crisis of the 1850s*, supra note 18, at 188–89.

31. See David Zarefsky, *Lincoln, Douglas, and Slavery: In the Crucible of Public Debate* (1990), 7–8.

32. Holt, *Political Crisis of the 1850s*, supra note 18, at 198. Buchanan garnered only 45 percent of the popular vote.

33. See William E. Gienapp, *Abraham Lincoln and Civil War America* (2002), 56.

34. See, e.g., McPherson, *Battle Cry of Freedom*, supra note 22, at 151 (quoting an old-line Whig as saying, "It was not the attack itself (horrible as that was) that excited me, but the tone of the Southern Press, & the approbation, apparently, of the whole Southern People").

35. See generally William Lasser, *The Limits of Judicial Power: The Supreme Court in American Politics* (1988), 40; Charles Warren, *The Supreme Court in United States History* (Boston: Little, Brown and Company, 1922), 2:487–89. Critics of the push toward a judicial resolution, however, foresaw the devastating effect the policy would have on the Court. "During the long . . . pendency of this question, [the Court] would be incessantly exposed to every adverse influence. Local sympathies, long-cherished prejudices, the predilections of party, the known wishes of the Administration and of the National Legislature, would all conspire to bias the decision; intervening vacancies would be filled with reference to the supposed, perhaps even pledged, opinion of the candidate upon this one question. . . ." Appendix to Cong. Globe, 30th Cong., 1st Sess. 1073 (1848) (statement of Rep. Marsh). "[T]he moral in-

fluence of the Court must be forever destroyed in one section or the other of the Union." Appendix to Cong. Globe, 30th Cong., 1st Sess. 1061 (1848) (statement of Rep. Donnell).

36. Van Buren, *Inquiry into the Origin*, supra note 25, at 362; see generally Mark Graber, *Dred Scott and the Problem of Constitutional Evil* (2006), 33–35.

37. Dred Scott v. Sandford, 60 U.S. 393, 454–55 (1857) (Wayne, J., concurring).

38. Warren, *Supreme Court*, supra note 35, at 2:480 (Court "may be said to have reached its height in the confidence of the people of the country").

39. See Graber, *Problem of Constitutional Evil*, supra note 36, at 36; R. Ken Newmyer, *The Supreme Court Under Marshall and Taney*, 2nd ed. (2006), 113; Robert Green McCloskey, *The American Supreme Court*, 3d ed., rev. Sanford Levinson (2000), 58.

40. McCloskey, *American Supreme Court*, supra note 39, at 54–56; see also James F. Simon, *Lincoln and Chief Justice Taney: Slavery, Secession, and the President's War Powers* (2006), 35–37 (describing support for Taney Court).

41. William Alexander Duer, *A Course of Lectures on the Constitutional Jurisprudence of the United States*, 2d ed. (1856), 46.

42. Potter and Fehrenbacher, *Impending Crisis*, supra note 22, at 271; see *An Act to Establish a Territorial Government for Utah* [Compromise of 1850] (Sept. 9, 1850), *Stats at Large of USA* (Boston: Little, Brown and Company, 1962): 9:455–56 (referring "all cases involving title to slaves . . . without regard to the value of the matter, property, or title in controversy" to local tribunals with right of appeal to the Supreme Court of the United States); *An Act . . . to Establish a Territorial Government for New Mexico* (Sept. 9, 1850), *Stats at Large of USA*, supra, at 9:449–50 (employing same provision).

43. See Warren, *Supreme Court*, supra note 35, at 2:495; Simon, *Lincoln and Chief Justice Taney*, supra note 40, at 99–100. On this question of inviting the Court in, see Graber, *Problem of Constitutional Evil*, supra note 36, at 33–34 (noting that Jacksonians and Whigs alike in all parts of the country "publicly declared" that the regulation of slavery should be decided by the federal judiciary); Wallace Mendelson, "Dred Scott's Case—Reconsidered," *Minn. L. Rev.* 38 (1953): 16–28; Hyman and Wiecek, *Equal Justice Under Law*, supra note 18, at 131.

44. Cong. Globe, 31st Cong., 1st Sess. 1155 (1850).

45. Cong. Globe, 34th Cong., 1st Sess. 796 (1856).

46. Abraham Lincoln, "Speech at Galena, Ill.," July 23, 1856, reprinted in Basler, *Collected Works of Abraham Lincoln*, supra note 14, at 2:354–55; see also Simon, *Lincoln and Chief Justice Taney*, supra note 40, at 133–34.

47. Scott v. Emerson, 15 Mo. 576, 586 (1852). Compare Winny v. Whitesides, 1 Mo. 472 (1824). For a general summary of the Missouri state court decisions, see Finkelman, Dred Scott v. Sandford, supra note 4, at 20–22; on the Missouri Supreme Court's change of heart, see Simon, *Lincoln and Chief Justice Taney*, supra note 40, at 101–02.

48. The suit was filed in federal court as a case of battery and wrongful imprisonment, the defense of which was that Scott was in bondage. See Finkelman, Dred Scott v. Sandford, supra note 4, at 23, 25–26.

49. Dred Scott v. Sandford, 60 U.S. 393, 396–97 (1857) (statement of the case).

50. Finkelman, Dred Scott v. Sandford, supra note 4, at 26.

51. See Carl B. Swisher, *The Oliver Wendell Holmes Devise History of the Supreme Court of the United States*, vol. 5, *The Taney Period, 1863–64*, ed. Paul A. Freund (1974), 614–19.

52. See id. at 610 (noting that both Buchanan and his predecessor Franklin Pierce believed that the election signified that people had rebuked the attempt to sectionalize the country); see also Fehrenbacher, Dred Scott *Case*, supra note 15, at 307.

53. Letter from John Catron to James Buchanan, Feb. 10, 1857, cited in Swisher, *Taney Period*, supra note 51, at 616 (in deciding case, "the positions of the Justices would be highly diverse and would settle nothing"); see also Fehrenbacher, Dred Scott *Case*, supra note 15, at 307.

54. Letter from John Catron to James Buchanan, Feb. 19, 1857, reprinted in *The Works of James Buchanan*, ed. John Bassett Moore (1960), 10:106n1; Fehrenbacher, Dred Scott *Case*, supra note 15, at 309. Buchanan successfully engaged Grier, as instructed: "The great object of my administration will be if possible to destroy the dangerous slavery agitation and thus to restore peace to our distracted country." Draft of Letter from James Buchanan to Robert C. Grier, Nov. 14, 1856, quoted in Swisher, *Taney Period*, supra note 51, at 610. The actual letter from Buchanan no longer exists, though there is no doubt Grier received it. Potter and Fehrenbacher, *Impending Crisis*, supra note 22, at 274. Grier wrote back to the President-elect promptly, stating that he, Wayne, and Taney "fully appreciate and concur in your views as to the desirableness at this time of having an expression of the opinion of the court on this troublesome question. With their concurrence, I will give you in confidence the history of the case before us, with the probable result." Letter from Robert C. Grier to James Buchanan, Feb. 23, 1857, reprinted in Moore, *Works of James Buchanan*, supra, at 10:106n1 (going on to describe the Court's forthcoming resolution of the case). Oddly, the letter as reproduced in this volume lists the author as "D. Grier," a likely typographical error, as the content of the letter makes it clear that it is Justice Grier's.

55. Warren, *Supreme Court*, supra note 35, at 3:19–20 (quoting James Buchanan's Inaugural Address).

56. Graber, *Problem of Constitutional Evil*, supra note 36, at 19 ("precise holding" of case "not entirely clear"); Stanley I. Kutler, *The* Dred Scott *Decision: Law or Politics?* (1967), xiv ("[N]either contemporaries of the event nor subsequent historians have ever concurred as to what a *majority* of the Court agreed upon") (emphasis in original).

57. Timothy Farrar, "The *Dred Scott* Case," review of Benjamin C. Howard, *A Report of the Decision of the Supreme Court of the United States, and the Opinions of the Judges Thereof, in the Case of Dred Scott versus John F. A. Sanford, N. Am. Rev.* 85 (1857): 395. The Chief Justice designated his opinion a "majority" and in an unusual step bypassed the official reporter and wrote the explanatory headnote for the decision himself. See Horace Gray and John Lowell, "The Case of Dred Scott," *Monthly L. Rep.* 10 (1857): 65 (describing the case's headnote as "so widely different from any form of such a note ever seen before, and contain[ing] so many positions not determined by the Court, nor even affirmed by a majority of the judges"). He also broke with protocol and revised his decision in light of the dissents but refused to share the revision before its publication. See Fehrenbacher, Dred Scott *Case*, supra note 15, at 314–21. Reviewers criticized Taney for identifying his opinion as that of the Court. See, e.g., Farrar, "*Dred Scott* Case," supra, at 393 ("[T]he argument of the Chief Justice is called the opinion of the court, for what reason does not appear . . .").

58. Graber, *Problem of Constitutional Evil*, supra note 36, at 19.

59. See id., at 28–29 ("The judicial denial of black citizenship reflected beliefs held by the overwhelming majority of antebellum jurists in both the North and the South"); Fehrenbacher, Dred Scott *Case*, supra note 15, at 437 ("Republican politicians . . . concentrated their attacks on the second half of Taney's opinion, which, after all, was the part that struck directly at the foundations of their party").

60. See Graber, *Problem of Constitutional Evil*, supra note 36, at 60–61.

61. For a further collection of reactions to the *Dred Scott* decision, see Fehrenbacher, Dred Scott *Case*, supra note 15, at 417–48; see also Barry Friedman, "The History of

the Countermajoritarian Difficulty, Part I: The Road to Judicial Supremacy," *N.Y.U. L. Rev.* 73 (1998): 415–19. For an argument that the *Dred Scott* decision had the support of the country's dominant political coalition, and for an engaging discussion of the difficulties posed by slavery's protection in the Constitution, see Graber, *Problem of Constitutional Evil*, supra note 36.

62. "The Latest News," *N.Y. Daily Trib.*, March 7, 1857, at 5.

63. Cong. Globe, 35th Cong., 2d Sess. 1265 (1859) (statement of Sen. John P. Hale).

64. Cong. Globe, 38th Cong., 2d Sess. 1012–13 (1865). For others' opinions of Taney, see generally Swisher, *Taney Period*, supra note 51, at 971–72 (noting that Taney's legacy became inextricably linked with *Dred Scott*, even among his friends).

65. "The *Dred Scott* Case," *Richmond Enquirer*, March 10, 1857, reprinted in Finkelman, Dred Scott v. Sandford, supra note 4, at 129, 130.

66. "Wickedness of the Decision in the Supreme Court Against the African Race," *Indep.*, March 19, 1857, reprinted in Finkelman, Dred Scott v. Sandford, supra note 4, at 151; "The Late Decision of the Supreme Court of the United States," *Zion's Herald & Wesleyan J.*, March 18, 1857, reprinted in Finkelman, Dred Scott v. Sandford, supra note 4, at 153.

67. Holt, *Political Crisis of the 1850s*, supra note 18, at 202; see also Potter and Fehrenbacher, *Impending Crisis*, supra note 22, at 284.

68. Van Buren, *Inquiry into the Origin*, supra note 25, at 375.

69. See Fehrenbacher, Dred Scott *Case*, supra note 15, at 439; Finkelman, Dred Scott v. Sandford, supra note 4, at 36.

70. Mark Graber argues both the *Dred Scott* holdings were acceptable to the dominant Democratic coalition. However, he relies on the statements and actions of public officials and takes little account of the popular reaction. Gerard Magliocca effectively challenges this view, explaining that while *Dred Scott* may have been consistent with an existing coalition, it was inconsistent with a rising one. See Magliocca, *Andrew Jackson and the Constitution*, supra note 10, at 104–06 (Taney defended "Jacksonian generation's values" against critique of "rising generation").

71. Van Buren, *Inquiry into the Origin*, supra note 25, at 359. It is unclear that this necessarily was correct, as only three other justices agreed with Taney's citizenship holding. Graber, *Problem of Constitutional Evil*, supra note 36, at 19.

72. "Extent of the Decision of the *Dred Scott* Case," *N.Y. Evening Post*, March 12, 1857, at 2; see also "The Political Judges and Their Belongings," *N.Y. Daily Trib.*, March 17, 1857, at 5 ("The opinion being outside of the case, or, as the lawyers term it, extrajudicial, has, happily, no legal bearing or control upon the Courts, either State or Federal").

73. Charles W. Smith, Jr., *Roger B. Taney: Jacksonian Jurist* (1973), 173. Maine, Vermont, Ohio, and New York passed such resolutions.

74. Cong. Globe, 35th Cong., 1st Sess. 617 (1858) (statement of Sen. Fessenden).

75. See Larry Kramer, *The People Themselves: Popular Constitutionalism and Judicial Review* (2004), 209.

76. See Marbury v. Madison, 5 U.S. (1 Cranch) 137, 166 (1803) (declaring that where the Constitution gives the executive full discretion to act, the President and his officers are accountable only "to his country . . . and his conscience," never the courts, because "the subject is political," but when the legislature acts to infringe individual rights, officers of the law must answer in court); Luther v. Borden, 48 U.S. (1 How.) 1, 46–47 (1849) (stating that it is beyond the scope of the Court to decide whether the people of a state have abolished or changed their form of government, as a question that belongs in other forums of government).

77. *Abridgment of the Debates of Congress, from 1789 to 1856* (1857), 3:440 (statement of Sen. Hayne).

78. Cong. Globe, 35th Cong., 1st Sess. 1004 (1858) (statement of Sen. Hamlin); "The Supreme Court," *Nat'l Intelligencer*, March 29, 1857; see also "The Decision of the Supreme Court," *N.Y. Daily Trib.*, March 10, 1857, at 6 (noting that "the Court has rushed into politics voluntarily, and without other purpose than to subserve the cause of Slavery").

79. Van Buren, *Inquiry into the Origin*, supra note 25, at 374.

80. See, e.g., *N.Y. Daily Trib.*, March 21, 1857, at 4 (wondering: "[W]hich of the Pro-Slavery Judges, we should like to know, owes his appointment exclusively or in any considerable degree to his eminence as a jurist or to his character as a man?"). Interestingly, despite the charges of slaveholding, David Zarefsky says that none of the Court's members was a slaveholder. See Zarefsky, *Lincoln, Douglas, and Slavery*, supra note 31, at 8 (describing the Court as strongly pro-southern, though not proslavery). As for partisanship, the most famous comment came from the *New York Daily Tribune*: "This decision, we need hardly say, is entitled to just so much moral weight as would be the judgment of a majority of those congregated in any Washington bar-room. It is a dictum proscribed by the stump to the bench—the Bowie-knife sticking in the stump ready for instant use if needed." *N.Y. Daily Trib.*, March 7, 1857, at 4.

81. *N.Y. Daily Trib.*, March 26, 1859, quoted in Stanley I. Kutler, *Judicial Power and Reconstruction* (1968), 16.

82. *N.Y. Daily Trib.*, March 21, 1857, at 4.

83. Van Buren, *Inquiry into the Origin*, supra note 25, at 374.

84. See Fehrenbacher, Dred Scott *Case*, supra note 15, at 314 (discussing the "sinister meaning" that critics of Taney attached to this conversation). See, e.g., Cong. Globe, 35th Cong., 1st Sess. 1004 (1858) (statement of Sen. Hamlin) (referring to their conversation as "political collusion and complicity").

85. *Chi. Trib.*, March 12, 1857, reprinted in Kutler, Dred Scott *Decision*, supra note 56, at 48; see also *N.Y. Daily Trib.*, March 21, 1857, at 4 ("It is certainly a little curious that every measure of legislation which either directly or indirectly seeks to retard the spread of Slavery, is at once discovered by certain people to be unconstitutional. Those india-rubber instruments which we call Constitutions are wonderfully expansive and contractile . . .").

86. Speech of Abraham Lincoln, First Joint Debate at Ottawa, Ill., Aug. 21, 1858, reprinted in Holzer, *Lincoln-Douglas Debates*, supra note 1, at 67; see also Abraham Lincoln, "Address to the Republican State Convention at Springfield, Ill.," June 16, 1858 (known as the "A House Divided" speech), reprinted in Basler, *Collected Works of Abraham Lincoln*, supra note 14, at 2:456–66.

87. For an account of the Republican Party platform after *Dred Scott*, see McPherson, *Battle Cry of Freedom*, supra note 22, at 178–81.

88. Lemmon v. People, 20 N.Y. 562 (N.Y. 1860); see generally McPherson, *Battle Cry of Freedom*, supra note 22, at 180–81.

89. *Harper's Wkly.*, Mar. 28, 1857, reprinted in Kutler, Dred Scott *Decision*, supra note 56, at 50. *Harper's Weekly* was a paper for "Douglas Democrats" in the prewar years and "considered both Northern abolitionists and Southern fire-eaters to be unpatriotic, dangerous radicals." Robert C. Kennedy, "Censorship, Racism, and the Antebellum Press: *Harper's Weekly* Reports Harper's Ferry," in *The Civil War and the Press*, ed. David B. Sachsman et al. (2000), 65. By the postwar period, it had become a "radical" publication. See Foner, *Free Soil*, supra note 24, at 221.

90. Abraham Lincoln, "Address to the Republican State Convention at Springfield, Ill.," June 16, 1858 (known as the "A House Divided" speech), reprinted in Basler, *Collected Works of Abraham Lincoln,* supra note 14, at 2:467.

91. Speech of Stephen A. Douglas, Third Joint Debate at Jonesboro, Ill., Sept. 15, 1858, in Holzer, *Lincoln-Douglas Debates,* supra note 1, at 151.

92. Speech of Stephen A. Douglas at Chi., Ill., July 9, 1858, in *The Political Debates Between Abraham Lincoln and Stephen A. Douglas in the Senatorial Campaign of 1858 in Illinois,* ed. George H. Putnam (1912), 29.

93. Speech of Abraham Lincoln, First Joint Debate at Ottawa, Ill., Aug. 21, 1858, in Holzer, *Lincoln-Douglas Debates,* supra note 1, at 75, 76.

94. Speech of Abraham Lincoln at Chi., Ill., July 10, 1858, in Putnam, *Political Debates,* supra note 92, at 55. Lincoln calls Douglas "Judge" to gibe him because at an earlier point in Illinois history Douglas had voted to reorganize the state supreme court and then taken a seat on the new one. In 1840, Douglas and his Jacksonian supporters in the Illinois legislature passed the Douglas Bill, which substantially reorganized the state judiciary in response to a series of rulings that angered Democrats. The Whigs, including Lincoln, issued a statement following the passage of the law claiming the Douglas Bill had destroyed the independence of the judiciary. Mark A. Graber, "Popular Constitutionalism, Judicial Supremacy, and the Complete Lincoln-Douglas Debates," *Chi.-Kent L. Rev.* 81 (2006): 923–24. Douglas himself was one of the first judges appointed to the reorganized bench. Robert Walter Johannsen, *Stephen A. Douglas* (1973), 95–96.

95. See Robert Justin Lipkin, "Which Constitution? Who Decides?," *Cardozo L. Rev.* 28 (2006): 1092, 1095–96 (criticizing "interpretive equality," wherein the three branches have equal powers in interpreting the Constitution as a "fatally defective" form of departmentalism while admitting that "several important Americans," including Lincoln, "have embraced interpretive equality"); G. Edward White, "The Constitutional Journey of *Marbury v. Madison,*" *Va. L. Rev.* 89 (2003): 1508 (emphasizing that Lincoln's opposition to *Dred Scott* was situated in the context of the Court's striking down congressional action "on an issue that seemed eminently suited to the departmental discretion of other branches"); see also Paul Brest, "Congress' Role and Responsibility in the Federal Balance of Power: Congress as Constitutional Decisionmaker and Its Power to Counter Judicial Doctrine," *Ga. L. Rev.* 21 (1986): 77–78 (noting that while Lincoln allowed *Dred Scott* to be binding on the case at hand, he insisted on the independence and interpretive power of the other branches, claiming that if the Supreme Court were supreme, the people would have "resigned their government" into the hands of the nine judges); Neal Devins and Louis Fisher, "Judicial Exclusivity and Political Instability," *Va. L. Rev.* 84 (1998): 88–89 (arguing that on the basis of the view held by Lincoln, as well as earlier and later American Presidents, each branch is empowered with independent authority to interpret the Constitution, the doctrine of judicial supremacy "is a nonstarter"); Edwin Meese III, "Perspectives on the Authoritativeness of Supreme Court Decisions: The Law of the Constitution," *Tul. L. Rev.* 61 (1987): 985–86 (arguing that all three branches possess an equal share of power in interpreting the Constitution and citing Lincoln as an example of the power of the executive to overturn Supreme Court decisions).

96. Abraham Lincoln, "First Inaugural Address," March 4, 1861, reprinted in Basler, *Collected Works of Abraham Lincoln,* supra note 14, at 4:268.

97. Id.

98. Speech of Abraham Lincoln at Chi., Ill., July 10, 1858, in Putnam, *Political Debates,* supra note 92, at 54–55. Lincoln reiterated this argument in his debate with Douglas

at Quincy. Speech of Abraham Lincoln, Sixth Joint Debate at Quincy Ill., Oct. 13, 1858, in Holzer, *Lincoln-Douglas Debates*, supra note 1, at 291.

99. Speech of Abraham Lincoln at Springfield, Ill., June 26, 1857, reprinted in Basler, *Collected Works of Abraham Lincoln*, supra note 1, at 2:401.

100. Speech of Abraham Lincoln at Chi., Ill., July 10, 1858, in Putnam, *Political Debates*, supra note 92, at 55.

101. Speech of Abraham Lincoln at the Cooper Institute, N.Y., Feb. 27, 1860, reprinted in Basler, *Collected Works of Abraham Lincoln*, supra note 14, at 3:543–44.

102. Speech of Abraham Lincoln at Chi., Ill., July 10, 1858, reprinted in Basler, *Collected Works of Abraham Lincoln*, supra note 14, at 2:495; see also Abraham Lincoln, "First Inaugural Address," March 4, 1861, reprinted in id. at 4:268 ("be over-ruled, and never become a precedent for other cases").

103. See Daniel Farber, *Lincoln's Constitution* (2003), 187 (discussing validity of legislative action, given subsequent legal process).

104. Speech of Abraham Lincoln, Sixth Joint Debate at Quincy, Ill., Oct. 13, 1858, in Holzer, *Lincoln-Douglas Debates*, supra note 1, at 291.

105. Id.

106. Speech of Stephen A. Douglas at Springfield, Ill., July 17, 1858, reprinted in Putnam, *Political Debates*, supra note 92, at 133. For more on Lincoln's nuanced view on the roles of the executive, legislative, and judicial branches in interpreting the Constitution, see generally Geoffrey P. Miller, "The President's Power of Interpretation: Implications of a Unified Theory of Constitutional Law," *Law & Contemp. Probs.* 56 (1993): 43 (discussing, as an example of legislative interpretation of the Constitution, Lincoln's perspective on a fugitive slave law; as a senator he voted for such a law, despite his personal objections, because he felt "compelled by the Constitution"); Richard Murphy, "The Brand X Constitution," *B.Y.U. L. Rev.*, 2007: 1268–69 (explaining that Lincoln justified his objections to *Dred Scott* on the basis that it was a "dubious" decision that overruled past government action and was decided by a "partisan, divided court").

107. See Frank H. Easterbrook, "Presidential Review," *Case W. Res. L. Rev.* 40 (1989–90): 926 (describing Lincoln's response to *Dred Scott* as "nonacquiescence"); Michael Stokes Paulsen, "The Merryman Power and the Dilemma of Autonomous Executive Branch Interpretation," *Cardozo L. Rev.* 15 (1993): 88 (quoting Lincoln's public opposition to *Dred Scott*); Paul L. Colby, "Two Views on the Legitimacy of Nonacquiescence in Judicial Opinions," *Tul. L. Rev.* 61 (1987): 1053 ("Lincoln's opposition . . . charted two fundamental avenues of nonacquiescence. First, the two other branches . . . need not be bound in their own spheres . . . by the rationale of a Supreme Court decision. Secondly, lower-court judges within the federal judiciary and without may also 'nonacquiesce'"). See also Keith Whittington, *Political Foundations of Judicial Supremacy* (2007), 274–75 (situating Lincoln as a reconstructive President who asserted the limited reach of Court decisions and stressed the power of the executive to interpret the Constitution).

108. See *An Act to Secure Freedom to All Persons Within the Territories of the United States* (June 19, 1862), *Stats at Large of USA* (Boston: Little, Brown and Company, 1863): 12:432.

109. See, e.g., Cong. Globe, 37th Cong., 2d Sess. 2067 (1862) (statement of Rep. Fisher) ("If honestly meant, I contend that there is not a single clause in [the act] of the least practical utility"); id. at 2053–54 (statement of Rep. Stevens); id. at 2051 (statement of Rep. Sheffield) ("[W]e might as well undertake to reenact the decalogue as to enact this law"); see also Fehrenbacher, Dred Scott *Case*, supra note 15, at 575 ("sym-

bolic victory"). Slaves in the District of Columbia had been emancipated two months previously. Under the District of Columbia act, loyal slaveholders were compensated for their emancipated slaves. See *An Act for the Release of Certain Persons Held to Service or Labor in the District of Columbia* (Apr. 16, 1862), *Stats at Large of USA*, supra note 108, at 12:376. Speakers in this debate generally took the position that Congress had the power to abolish slavery in the District of Columbia, given its plenary power, so long as compensation was given. See, e.g., Cong. Globe, 37th Cong., 2d Sess. 1495 (1862) (statement of Sen. Sherman) ("We ought now to abolish slavery in this District. We have the right, and it is our duty to do it; and if we had wasted less time in doing it, it would probably be just as well"); see also Cong. Globe, 37th Cong., 2d Sess. 1618 (1862) (statement of Rep. Thomas) ("[T]he power of Congress over slavery in this District is absolute.... All that is requisite ... is just compensation to the master"). But see Cong. Globe, 37th Cong., 2d Sess. 1634–35 (1862) (statement of Rep. Crittenden) (arguing that Congress lacked power to abolish slavery in the District because Virginia and Maryland had not ceded land to the United States with that purpose in mind).

110. Cong. Globe, 37th Cong., 2d Sess. 2044 (1862) (statement of Rep. Diven). The debates were exceedingly odd in that *Dred Scott* was not even mentioned, hardly common for policy makers confronting the decision at the time. Discussion of the Civil Rights Act of 1866 in the House and Senate, comparatively, discussed the constitutional weight of *Dred Scott* quite openly. See, e.g., Cong. Globe, 39th Cong., 1st Sess. 1780 (1866) (statement of Sen. Trumbull) (debating Reverdy Johnson of Maryland over the lingering meaning of the case); Cong. Globe, 39th Cong., 1st Sess. 1120 (1866) (statement of Rep. Rogers) ("[*Dred Scott*] expressly and solemnly decided ... that negroes in this country ... are not citizens or people of the United States.... That cannot [change] until the requisite amendment is made to the Constitution"); Cong. Globe, 39th Cong., 1st Sess. 504 (1866) (statement of Sen. Johnson) ("If the [*Dred Scott*] decision is a binding one and will be followed in the future, this law which we are now about to pass will be held of course to be of no avail, as far as it professes to define what citizenship is"). Most of the discussion of the 1862 measure focused not on the territories at all but upon U.S. military bases.

111. See, e.g., Cong. Globe, 37th Cong., 2d Sess. 2045 (statement of Rep. Arnold) ("Beyond that line [of the Constitution] I would not go; but up to that line squarely would I march"); Cong. Globe, 37th Cong., 2d Sess. 2044 (statement of Rep. Diven) ("[W]e can do it without impairing our constitutional obligations, and without stirring up dissensions"); Cong. Globe, 37th Cong., 2d Sess. 2048 (statement of Rep. Olin) ("[W]hile I should be as glad as any one on this floor to see the institution of slavery at least so crippled that it will never henceforward be a disturbing cause in the administration of the Government, I, for one, will not consent to step an inch beyond the plain guarantees of the Constitution to accomplish even that purpose").

112. Cong. Globe, 37th Cong., 2d Sess. 2044 (statement of Rep. Diven).

113. Cong. Globe, 37th Cong, 2d Sess. 2049 (1862) (statement of Rep. Kelly).

114. See Kramer, *People Themselves*, supra note 75, at 212 (arguing that Lincoln's administration "acted consistently" with his departmental views by "ignoring the Court's opinion" as it recognized black citizenship in a variety of ways), Michael Stokes Paulsen, "The Most Dangerous Branch: Executive Power to Say What the Law Is," *Geo. L. J.* 83 (1994): 274, 276, 334–36 (describing Lincoln's actions, in granting patents and visas to black Americans, as "an act of execution when following judicial precedent would require nonexecution" and citing his belief that judicial decisions are right because judges are experts at legal interpretation; when they are wrong, other branches may "nonacquiesce" in order to reverse the incorrectly decided deci-

sion); see also Graber, *Problem of Constitutional Evil*, supra note 36, at 21n40 (calling the *Dred Scott* decision a "dead letter").

115. 10 Op. Att'y Gen. 382 (1862). The "headnote" to Bates's opinion appears to say a great deal more than the opinion itself. It states: "Free men of color, if born in the United States, are citizens of the United States; and, if otherwise qualified, are competent, according to the Acts of Congress, to be masters of vessels engaged in the coasting trade." Note that the headnote says only "according to Acts of Congress" and is silent about citizenship and competence under the Constitution. But one must read well beyond the headnote to comprehend the clever legal game Bates was playing.

116. Id. at 412.

117. Id. at 410 (quoting plea).

118. Id. at 412.

119. Id.

120. Charles Sumner, *The Works of Charles Sumner* (1874), 5:497–98. Similarly with the issuance of patents, Sumner brought the issue up in Congress, where a committee declined to act, calling it "a matter of interpretation, not of legislation." Id. at 6:144.

121. Abraham Lincoln, "The Emancipation Proclamation," Jan. 1, 1863, reprinted in *Stats at Large of USA*, supra note 108, at 12:1268–69; see also Benjamin R. Curtis, *Executive Power* (1862). Curtis questioned the legitimacy of the proclamation as issued on September 22, 1862. That earlier version announced the intention to free any slave in any Confederate state that did not return to the Union by January 1, 1863. The proclamation as issued at (*Stats at Large of USA* 12:1268–69), made good on that intention, naming the states to which it applied.

122. "[T]he Supreme Court of the United States, by a final decision of surpassing infamy, became the greatest *barracoon* of all. . . . An amendment of the Constitution may do what courts and Congress decline to do, or, even should they act, it may cover their action with its panoply." Cong. Globe, 38th Cong., 1st Sess. 1481–82 (1864) (statement of Sen. Sumner) (referring presumably to *Dred Scott*; "barracoon" refers to an enclosure in which slaves or convicts were confined); see also, e.g., Cong. Globe, 38th Cong., 1st Sess. 1421 (1864) (statement of Sen. Johnson) (without a constitutional amendment, as soon as the war ended most slaves would "be entirely unaffected by the [Emancipation] proclamation and still as much slaves under the Constitution" as before the war); Cong. Globe, 38th Cong., 1st Sess. 1314 (1864) (statement of Sen. Trumbull) ("The only effectual way of ridding the country of slavery . . . is by an amendment. . . . If slavery should now be abolished by act of Congress or proclamation of the President, assuming that either has the power to do it, there is nothing in the Constitution to prevent any state from reestablishing it"). Some even took the remarkable position that the *Dred Scott* decision precluded what became the Thirteenth Amendment. See Cong. Globe, 38th Cong., 2d Sess. 152 (1865) (statement of Rep. Rogers) (arguing that *Dred Scott* "goes clearly to show that there is no authority [to abolish slavery] by amending the Constitution of the country").

123. Cong. Globe, 39th Cong., 1st Sess. 474 (1866) (statement of Sen. Trumbull).

124. Cong. Globe, 39th Cong., 1st Sess. 504 (1866) (statement of Sen. Johnson).

125. Cong. Globe, 39th Cong., 1st Sess. 1117 (1866) (statement of Rep. Wilson); accord Cong. Globe, 39th Cong., 1st Sess. 1124 (1866) (statement of Rep. Cook) ("[C]onstitutional power of Congress to make any men or class of men citizens must be conceded" as beyond "any reasonable doubt").

126. There was one final instance in which the Senate grappled with *Dred Scott*, in the context of seating Hiram Revels, a black man elected to the Senate from Mississippi who arguably had not been a "citizen" long enough to qualify under the Constitution

for the office he had won. In this instance, it is possible some senators purposely defied the *Dred Scott* ruling, admittedly for the purpose of admitting one of their own. Richard Primus deserves credit for unearthing the Revels incident. He provides a thorough account in Richard Primus, "The Riddle of Hiram Revels," *Harv. L. Rev.* 119 (2006): 1680–1734.

127. See Geoffrey Stone, *Perilous Times: Free Speech in Wartime from the Sedition Act of 1798 to the War on Terrorism* (2004), 88–89, 121–23.
128. Abraham Lincoln, "Message to Congress in Special Session," July 4, 1861, reprinted in Basler, *Collected Works of Abraham Lincoln*, supra note 14, at 4:429.
129. Letter from Abraham Lincoln to Hon. Erastus Corning & Others, June 12, 1863, reprinted in id. at 6:267. Somewhat more colorfully, Lincoln doubted that a man "could contract so strong an appetite for emetics during temporary illness, as to persist in feeding upon them through the remainder of his healthful life." Id.
130. For probing examinations of the constitutionality of Lincoln's wartime measures, see Farber, *Lincoln's Constitution*, supra note 103; Stone, *Perilous Times*, supra note 127, at 79–134.
131. See Hyman and Wiecek, *Equal Justice Under Law*, supra note 18, at 241; Swisher, *Taney Period*, supra note 51, at 841, 853, 901–02.
132. Letter from Edward Bates to Edwin M. Stanton, Jan. 31, 1863, cited in Daniel M. Silver, *Lincoln's Supreme Court* (1998), 125; see In re Kemp, 16 Wisc. 359 (1863).
133. In Ex parte Vallandigham, 68 U.S. 243 (1863), for example, the Court claimed no appellate jurisdiction over the proceeding in a military court. After the war was over, however, in 1866, the Court ruled that a similar military trial of an Indiana copperhead was unconstitutional. Ex parte Milligan, 71 U.S. 2 (1866); see also McPherson, *Battle Cry of Freedom*, supra note 22, at 599n17.
134. Samuel W. Pennypacker, *The Pennsylvania Dutchman in Philadelphia* (1897), 130.
135. See Hyman and Wiecek, *Equal Justice Under Law*, supra note 18, at 241; Simon, *Lincoln and Chief Justice Taney*, supra note 40, at 244–46.
136. "Executive Order of Abraham Lincoln to Lieutenant-General Winfield Scott," Apr. 25, 1861, reprinted in *A Compilation of the Messages and Papers of the Presidents*, ed. James D. Richardson (1897), 7:3218–19 (authorizing Scott to suspend the writ if he deemed it advisable "in the extremest necessity" to constrain the Maryland legislature); "Executive Order of Abraham Lincoln to Commanding General of the Army of the United States [Winfield Scott]," Apr. 27, 1861, reprinted in id. at 7:3219 (authorizing Scott or any officer at the scene of armed resistance between Philadelphia and Washington "to suspend the writ of *habeas corpus* for the public safety").
137. U.S. Const. art. I, § 9.
138. Lincoln suspended the writ eight separate times, beginning in Annapolis in April 1861, when the Maryland legislature was about to meet. For a detailed account of Lincoln's suspending the writ of habeas corpus, see Farber, *Lincoln's Constitution*, supra note 103, at 157–63; Stone, *Perilous Times*, supra note 127, at 120; see also McPherson, *Battle Cry of Freedom*, supra note 22, at 221 (reviewing habeas corpus suspension for those actively thwarting draft efforts).
139. Ex parte Merryman, 17 F. Cas. 144, 147 (C.C.D. Md. 1861). For more detail on the *Merryman* case, see Farber, *Lincoln's Constitution*, supra note 103, at 157–63, 188–92; Simon, *Lincoln and Chief Justice Taney*, supra note 40, at 184–97.
140. *Ex parte Merryman*, 17 F. Cas. at 153.
141. Id. (quoting in part U.S. Const. art. II, § 3).
142. See Harold M. Hyman, *A More Perfect Union: The Impact of the Civil War and Reconstruction on the Constitution* (1973), 84n8.

143. See *An Act Relating to Habeas Corpus and Regulating Judicial Proceedings in Certain Cases* [Habeas Corpus Act of 1863] (March 3, 1863), *Stats at Large of USA*, supra note 108, at 12:755, §§ 1, 4 (authorizing the President to suspend the writ "during the present rebellion" but not specifying whether such authority existed before the congressional act; providing indemnification so that "any order of the President, or under his authority, made at any time during the existence of the present rebellion, shall be a defence in all courts to any action or prosecution, civil or criminal . . ."). The common wisdom is that the 1863 act ratified Lincoln's actions. See, e.g., David J. Barron and Martin S. Lederman, "The Commander in Chief at the Lowest Ebb—A Constitutional History," *Harv. L. Rev.* 121 (2008): 1005 (reviewing congressional responses to Lincoln's habeas suspensions and concluding: "For the most part, the [Habeas Corpus] Act ratified what Lincoln had done"); Trevor W. Morrison, "Suspension and the Extrajudicial Constitution," *Colum. L. Rev.* 107 (2007): 1558–60, 1562–64 (discussing congressional debates on the Habeas Corpus Act); see also Mark E. Neely, Jr., *The Fate of Liberty* (1991), 69 (characterizing Habeas Corpus Act as "a model of legislative ambiguity that left it unclear whether the presidential suspensions before the act had always been legal or were legal only now because of congressional approval").

144. Abraham Lincoln, "Message to Congress in Special Session," July 4, 1861, reprinted in Basler, *Collected Works of Abraham Lincoln*, supra note 14, at 4:431.

145. See Norman W. Spaulding, "The Discourse of Law in Time of War: Politics and Professionalism During the Civil War and Reconstruction," *Wm. & Mary L. Rev.* 46 (2005): 2066–67 (describing Bates's "difficult task" and how his opinion was "far from conclusive"); see also Simon, *Lincoln and Chief Justice Taney*, supra note 40, at 197.

146. "Suspension of the Privilege of the Writ of Habeas Corpus," 10 Op. Att'y Gen. 74 (1861).

147. Abraham Lincoln, "Message to Congress in Special Session," July 4, 1861, reprinted in Basler, *Collected Works of Abraham Lincoln*, supra note 14, at 4:430. On Congress's ratification, see Habeas Corpus Act of 1863, supra note 143; see also Stone, *Perilous Times*, supra note 127, at 124.

148. Abraham Lincoln, "Message to Congress in Special Session," July 4, 1861, reprinted in Basler, *Collected Works of Abraham Lincoln*, supra note 14, at 4:430, 431.

149. "The Work Done by Congress," *Harper's Wkly.*, March 14, 1863, at 162.

150. See Letter from Abraham Lincoln to Matthew Birchard and Others, reprinted in Basler, *Collected Works of Abraham Lincoln*, supra note 14, at 6:300–06 (responding to resolution passed by the Ohio Democratic State Convention demanding a relaxation on Lincoln's restrictions of civil liberties); Letter from Abraham Lincoln to Erastus Corning and Others, reprinted in id. at 6:260–69 (responding to roughly the same demands from a group of New York Democrats); see also Neely, *Fate of Liberty*, supra note 143, at 185–209 (detailing flurries of "intense and steady" criticism of Lincoln by Democrats). On Whigs, see, e.g., Curtis, *Executive Power*, supra note 121, at 13–14 (criticizing military commissions).

151. Joel Parker, "Habeas Corpus and Martial Law," *N. Am. Rev.* 93 (1861): 475.

152. Quoted in Warren, *Supreme Court*, supra note 35, at 3:92 (no citation given).

153. See William E. Nelson, *The Fourteenth Amendment: From Political Principle to Judicial Doctrine* (1988), 42–45; see also Ariela Gross, "Slavery, Anti-Slavery, and the Coming of the Civil War" (unpublished manuscript, on file with author), 10–14.

154. For a detailed account of what transpired when the southern delegates were barred from the Senate floor, see William Horatio Barnes, *History of the Thirty-ninth Congress of the United States* (1868), 16–21.

155. Bruce Ackerman, *We the People*, vol. 2: *Transformations* (1998), 167.

156. *Nation*, Dec. 7, 1865, at 710.

157. *An Act to Protect all Persons in the United States in Their Civil Rights, and Furnish the Means of Their Vindication* [Civil Rights Act] (Apr. 9, 1866), *Stats at Large of USA* (Boston: Little, Brown and Company, 1868): 14:27.

158. "[T]he grave question presents itself, whether, when eleven of the thirty-six States are unrepresented in Congress, at this time it is sound policy to make our entire colored population and all other excepted classes citizens of the United States?" Cong. Globe, 39th Cong., 1st Sess. 1679 (1866) (veto message of President Andrew Johnson as read on the Senate floor).

159. *Nation*, Nov. 15, 1866, quoted in Eric Foner, *Reconstruction: America's Unfinished Revolution, 1863–1877* (1988), 267–68; see also Ackerman, *We the People*, vol. 2, supra note 155, at 162–63.

160. Foner, *Reconstruction*, supra note 159, at 269.

161. "A New Secession Impending," *Newark Evening Courier*, Jan. 2, 1867, at 2; "The Judiciary Bill," *Cincinnati Daily Gazette*, Jan. 23, 1867, at 2.

162. Ex parte Milligan, 71 U.S. 2 (1866).

163. He had taken part in conspiracies to release Confederate soldiers being held in prison camps and to foment an uprising in Louisville. Charles Fairman, *The Oliver Wendell Holmes Devise History of the Supreme Court of the United States*, vol. 6, pt. 1, *Reconstruction and Reunion, 1864–88*, ed. Paul A. Freund (1971), 192–96.

164. For a period account illustrating the public importance of the issue of military justice, as well as *Ex parte Merryman*, during Reconstruction, see Edward McPherson, *The Political History of the United States of America During the Period of Reconstruction* (1875).

165. S. M. Johnson, *The Constitution and the Reconstruction Laws: The Policy, Economy, and Justice of Reconstruction* (1868), 2.

166. Cong. Globe, 40th Cong., 2d Sess. 109 (1868) (statement of Sen. Chanler).

167. The majority identified two types of constitutional violations in Milligan's trial. One was based on Article III: "One of the plainest constitutional provisions was, therefore, infringed when Milligan was tried by a court not ordained and established by Congress, and not composed of judges appointed during good behavior." *Ex parte Milligan*, 71 U.S. at 122. The other was based on protections of trial by jury offered by the Fifth and Sixth Amendments. Id. at 122–24.

168. The Court emphasized the loyalty of Indiana, leaving itself some wiggle room to decide differently in cases from the former Confederacy. Id. at 121–22 (noting military jurisdiction inappropriate in loyal states).

169. See Fairman, *Reconstruction and Reunion*, supra note 163, at 232 ("[T]he Republican press every where has denounced the opinion as a second *Dred Scott* opinion . . .") (quoting letter from Justice Davis to Judge Rockwell)); Warren, *Supreme Court*, supra note 35, at 3:154 (describing how the *Milligan* decision was compared with *Dred Scott*); David P. Curie, "The Constitution in the Supreme Court: Civil War and Reconstruction, 1865–73," *U. Chi. L. Rev.* 51 (1984): 144 (noting that "there were those who labeled *Milligan* and the oath cases 'Dred Scott II and III'"). The Democratic press, on the other hand, "found cause for jubilation." See Fairman, *Reconstruction and Reunion*, supra note 163, at 219, 220–21.

170. "The New *Dred Scott*," *Harper's Wkly.*, Jan. 19, 1876, at 34.

171. "Congress and the Supreme Court," *World*, Jan. 21, 1867, at 4 (quoting *Chi. Trib.*).

172. Foner, *Reconstruction*, supra note 159, at 183.

173. Cong. Globe, 38th Cong., 1st Sess. 296 (1864) (statement of Sen. Jacob Howard).

174. Foner, *Reconstruction*, supra note 159, at 60. Somewhere in between were those southerners who had opposed secession but aided the Confederacy once the decision to secede had been made.

175. See Ex parte Garland, 71 U.S. 333 (1866) (invalidating loyalty oath imposed by Congress for service in any federal office or as an attorney in federal courts); Cummings v. Missouri, 71 U.S. 277 (1867) (invalidating similar loyalty oath applied by Missouri Constitution).

176. "Letters from 'Occasional,'" *Daily Morning Chron.*, Jan. 16, 1867, at 1.

177. The Court's breakdown in *Garland* and *Cummings* was similar, but not identical, to the breakdown of the *Milligan* Court. In *Milligan*, Justice Davis authored the opinion for the majority, joined by Justices Nelson, Clifford, Grier, and Field. See *Milligan*, 71 U.S. at 107. Chief Justice Chase authored the narrow concurrence in the judgment for the bloc of Miller, Swayne, and Wayne. *Milligan*, 71 U.S. at 132 (Chase, C. J., concurring). The blocs remained the same in *Cummings* and *Garland*, but for the switch by Justices Davis and Wayne. See *Ex parte Garland*, 71 U.S. at 382 (Miller, J., dissenting); *Cummings*, 71 U.S. at 332 (noting that dissent by Justice Miller in *Ex parte Garland* applied to *Cummings* case as well).

178. Cong. Globe, 39th Cong., 2d Sess. 251 (1867) (statement of Rep. Stevens).

179. "Usurpation," *Harper's Wkly.*, Feb. 9, 1867, at 82.

180. "Impeach! Impeach! Impeach!," *Cairo Democrat*, Jan. 8, 1867, at 2; "The Impeachment of the Supreme Court," *Daily Nat'l Intelligencer*, Dec. 20, 1866. Johnson named the *National Intelligencer* his official organ soon after taking office. Hans L. Trefousse, *Andrew Johnson: A Biography* (1989), 212.

181. *Nation*, Dec. 16, 1869, at 526.

182. See Ackerman, *We the People*, vol. 2, supra note 155, at 161–62; see also Fairman, *Reconstruction and Reunion*, supra note 163, at 108 (describing engagement of people in the South in early 1866); Foner, *Reconstruction*, supra note 159, at 25 (describing how the Civil War mobilized northern reformers).

183. Cong. Globe, 38th Cong., 2d Sess. 252 (1867) (statement of Rep. Stevens).

184. See, e.g., Cong. Globe, 39th Cong., 2d Sess. 501 (1867) (statement of Rep. Bingham) ("But, say some, there are two departments of the Government against this asserted power of the people of the organized States, the executive and judicial. My answer is, neither of these departments has any voice in the matter—no right to challenge the authority of the people").

185. See Walter Dean Burnhams, "The System of 1896: An Analysis," in *The Evolution of American Electoral Systems*, ed. Paul Kleppner et al. (1981), 192–93.

186. Republicans fared well in the 1865 elections. See Foner, *Reconstruction*, supra note 159, at 219. Nonetheless, the failure of referenda on black suffrage measures favored by radicals "emboldened Democrats and the white South, strengthened Johnson's hand, and weakened the Radicals." Id. at 223. However, presidential Reconstruction was dealt a serious blow in the national elections of 1866. Not only did Johnson have few friends going into the election, but his "Swing Around the Circle" campaign tour proved disastrous. Id. at 260, 264. The voters elected a Congress with a sufficient number of Republicans to override presidential vetoes. In state and local elections in 1867, the tide shifted again. "Democrats gained ground dramatically," although the small number of important offices at stake ameliorated any impact of the shift. See id. at 315; Lasser, *Limits of Judicial Power*, supra note 35, at 96. Finally, the Republican Ulysses S. Grant won the election of 1868, but with a surprisingly low margin of the popular vote. See Foner, *Reconstruction*, supra note 159, at 343.

187. See, e.g., "The McCardle Case: Judge Trumbull's Argument in the United States Supreme Court," *Chi. Trib.*, Feb. 12, 1868, at 2 (publishing transcript of Trumbull's argument in support of motion to dismiss McCardle's appeal); "Beginning of the Radical War on the Supreme Court," *World*, Jan. 4, 1867, at 4 (summarizing disparaging statements made by Thaddeus Stevens about the Supreme Court in House of Representatives); "The Southern Cases in the Supreme Court," *Indianapolis J.*, March 28, 1868, at 1; *Nation*, Feb. 13, 1868, at 1 (briefly summarizing Trumbull's argument).

188. Cong. Globe, 40th Cong., 2d Sess. 791 (1868).

189. "The Mississippi Bill," *Phila. Inquirer*, Apr. 15, 1867, at 4.

190. "Trials by Military Commissions—The Supreme Court Decisions," *N.Y. Times*, Jan. 3, 1867, at 4.

191. "The Lesson of the Crisis," *Nation*, Jan. 17, 1867, at 50.

192. See Foner, *Reconstruction*, supra note 159, at 276–77.

193. U.S. Const. amend. XIV, §§ 1, 5.

194. See Fairman, *Reconstruction and Reunion*, supra note 163, at 333–43. This package of laws set out the terms of readmission to the Union and provided for military rule in the South until readmission was accomplished.

195. Id. at 366–67.

196. See Foner, *Reconstruction*, supra note 159, at 314–16; see also Fairman, *Reconstruction and Reunion*, supra note 163, at 403.

197. See Mississippi v. Johnson, 71 U.S. 475 (1867); Georgia v. Stanton, 73 U.S. 50 (1868).

198. Fairman, *Reconstruction and Reunion*, supra note 163, at 420–21.

199. See generally William W. Van Alstyne, "A Critical Guide to *Ex parte McCardle*," *Ariz. L. Rev.* 15 (1973): 229–70.

200. *An Act to Amend "An Act to Establish the Judicial Courts of the United States"* [Habeas Corpus Act] (Feb. 5, 1867), *Stats at Large of USA*, supra note 157, at 14:385.

201. See Lewis Mayers, "The Habeas Corpus Act of 1867: The Supreme Court as Legal Historian," *U. Chi. L. Rev.* 33 (1965): 37. Compare Dallin H. Oaks, "Legal History in the High Court—Habeas Corpus," *Mich. L. Rev.* 64 (1966): 459–61. See generally John Harrison, "State Sovereign Immunity and Congress's Enforcement Powers," *Sup. Ct. Rev.*, 2006: 396–97; Benno C. Schmidt, Jr., "Juries, Jurisdiction, and Race Discrimination: The Lost Promise of *Strauder v. West Virginia*," *Tex. L. Rev.* 61 (1983): 1497.

202. Section 1 of the 1867 jurisdictional statute specifically provided that the Court's jurisdiction would lie "from the judgment of" a "circuit court to the Supreme Court of the United States." Habeas Corpus Act, supra note 200, at 386.

203. Fairman, *Reconstruction and Reunion*, supra note 163, at 449.

204. Id. at 450 (quoting Trumbull's argument before the Court on Jan. 17, 1868). On the other hand, McCardle's lawyer argued that a quick decision was perfectly appropriate for a criminal case: "[H]e wanted to know if the Court would take the responsibility of postponing a decision for three years in a case of such transcendent importance." *Daily Nat'l Intelligencer*, Jan. 18, 1868, quoted in Fairman, *Reconstruction and Reunion*, supra note 163, at 450. There is also some evidence that advancing criminal cases was the usual practice. See Mark A. Graber, "Legal, Strategic or Legal Strategy: Deciding to Decide During the Civil War and Reconstruction," in *The Supreme Court and American Political Development*, ed. Ronald Kahn and Ken I. Kersch (2006), 33, 44.

205. See Fairman, *Reconstruction and Reunion*, supra note 163, at 449–51; Kutler, *Judicial Power*, supra note 81, at 102.

206. See Foner, *Reconstruction*, supra note 159, at 336. Johnson was acquitted by one vote, with seven Republicans crossing the aisle to vote against conviction; however, the margin was not really so close, as a number of senators were ready to switch sides if necessary to prevent Johnson's conviction. Id.

207. See Cong. Globe, 40th Cong., 2d Sess. 478 (1868); see also Fairman, *Reconstruction and Reunion*, supra note 163, at 463.

208. Cong. Globe, 40th Cong., 2d Sess. 108 (1868).

209. See Cong. Globe, 40th Cong., 2d Sess. 478 (1868). Representative Thomas Williams, a Radical Republican lawyer from Pittsburgh, had made the same proposal a year before, after the Court's decision in *Ex parte Garland*. At the time, however, it garnered little support. Fairman, *Reconstruction and Reunion*, supra note 163, at 463.

210. See Fairman, *Reconstruction and Reunion*, supra note 163, at 464; Charles Fairman, *Mr. Justice Miller and the Supreme Court, 1862–1890* (1939), 143.

211. See Fairman, *Reconstruction and Reunion*, supra note 163, at 463–65.

212. See *Indep.* (publication data unknown), quoted in Warren, *Supreme Court*, supra note 35, at 3:189–90; "Supreme Court—The Two-Thirds Provision," *Harper's Wkly.*, Feb. 1, 1868, at 66; "Jurisdiction of the Supreme Court," *Chi. Trib.*, Feb. 4, 1868, at 2; *Chi. Republican*, Jan. 25, 1868, quoted in Warren, *Supreme Court*, supra note 35, at 3:191; see also "The Supreme Court," *N.Y. Times*, Jan. 14, 1868, at 4.

213. See Cong. Globe, 40th Cong., 2d Sess. 1859 (1868).

214. Cong. Globe, 40th Cong., 2d Sess. 2098 (1868) (statement of Sen. Buckalew). There was no record of debate in the Senate of this jurisdiction-stripping provision.

215. Cong. Globe, 40th Cong., 2d Sess. 2094 (1868).

216. "The M'Cardle Case," *Chi. Trib.*, March 3, 1868, at 1 (reporting that many senators and representatives "sought relief from the tedious debates" in Congress by visiting the Court to hear arguments in the case); "The McArdle Case," *N.Y. Times*, Feb. 28, 1868, at 1 (reporting the fairly mundane detail that "Major Enoch Totten . . . has been selected by Secretary Stanton as assistant counsel to defend the Government" in the case); *Springfield Republican*, Jan. 10, 1868, quoted in Warren, *Supreme Court*, supra note 35, at 3:188n1 (reporting "rumor" that Supreme Court planned to invalidate the Reconstruction laws by a vote of 5–3); see generally Warren, *Supreme Court*, supra note 35, at 3:200–02.

217. *Boston Post* (publication data unknown), quoted in Warren, *Supreme Court*, supra note 35, at 3:202n2; *Springfield Republican* (publication data unknown), quoted in Warren, Supreme Court, supra note 35, at 3:202–03; see also Fairman, *Reconstruction and Reunion*, supra note 163, at 479–80 (referring to a letter published in the *National Intelligencer* by James Carlisle, an experienced member of the Supreme Court bar: "[T]he Court has kept itself within the bounds of strict judicial propriety").

218. Cong. Globe, 40th Cong., 2d Sess. 2095 (1868) (statement of Sen. Johnson).

219. *An Act to Amend an Act Entitled "An Act to Amend the Judiciary Act"* (March 27, 1868), *Stats at Large of USA* (Boston: Little, Brown and Company 1869): 15:44 ("That so much of the act approved February [5, 1867] . . . as authorizes an appeal from the judgment of the circuit court to the Supreme Court of the United States, or the exercise of any such jurisdiction by said Supreme Court on appeals which have been or may hereafter by taken, be, and the same is, hereby repealed"); see also Fairman, *Reconstruction and Reunion*, supra note 163, at 459; Van Alstyne, "A Critical Guide," supra note 199, at 239–40.

220. Cong. Globe, 40th Cong., 2d Sess. 2094 (1868) (veto message of President Johnson).

221. His integrity under attack for sneaking the measure through the first time, Representative Robert Schenck of Ohio said, "[I]f I find [the Court] abusing that power by attempting to arrogate to themselves jurisdiction under any statute that happens to be upon the record, from which they claim to derive that jurisdiction, and I can take it away from them by a repeal of that statute, I will do it." Cong. Globe, 40th Cong., 2d Sess. 1883 (1868).

222. Senator Trumbull said of the jurisdiction-stripping bill: "It is a bill of very little importance, in my judgment; and I wish to say to the Senator from Maryland that the Supreme Court has not decided that any case is pending before it under the act of February 5, 1867. No such decision has been made, nor do I believe any such decision ever would be made." Cong. Globe, 40th Cong., 2d Sess. 2096 (1868).

223. Cong. Globe, 40th Cong., 2d Sess. 2096–97 (1868) (statement of Sen. Doolittle).

224. *Indep.* (publication data unknown), quoted in Warren, *Supreme Court,* supra note 35, at 3:199; *Springfield Republican* (publication data unknown), quoted in Warren, *Supreme Court,* supra note 35, at 3:199; see also "The McCardle Case Ended," *Chi. Trib.,* Apr. 1, 1868, at 2 ("This is the end of the famous McCardle case. It will never again be pressed on the Supreme Court"); "Action of the Supreme Court on the M'Ardle Case," *Indianapolis J.,* Apr. 7, 1868, at 1 (arguing Court acted properly in holding off because it "could not possibly have run a race with Congress . . . it would be a ridiculous affectation not to take notice" of Congress's intentions).

225. Fairman, *Reconstruction and Reunion,* supra note 163, at 473–74.

226. Id. at 473.

227. Id. at 473–74. Justice Grier continued, quoting Ovid: "Pudet haec opprobria nobis, Et dici potuisse; et non potuisse refelli" ("I am ashamed that such opprobrium should be cast upon the Court, and that it cannot be refuted"). (Loosely translating Ovid, *Metamorphoses,* bk. 1, lines 758–59).

228. See Fairman, *Reconstruction and Reunion,* supra note 163, at 486, quoting letter from Salmon Chase to John D. Van Buren, Apr. 5, 1868, *Chase Papers,* on file with Hist. Soc. of Pa. ("I had previously proposed an adjournment to June, but met no support").

229. *Georgia v. Grant* was held over because of the inability to deliver personal service of notice to the defendants. Fairman, *Reconstruction and Reunion,* supra note 163, at 470–71. A third unreported case raising the issue, *Ex parte Martin and Gill,* also was held over. See id. at 471–77.

230. Commission on the Bicentennial of the United States Constitution, *The Constitution of the United States* (1988), 26.

231. Ex parte McCardle, 74 U.S. 506, 515 (1869).

232. Warren, *Supreme Court,* supra note 35, at 3:205.

233. Fairman, *Reconstruction and Reunion,* supra note 163, at 478, quoting letter from Jeremiah Black to Howell Cobb, Apr. 1, 1868. Mark Graber offers a somewhat different take on the *McCardle* controversy that is intriguing. He suggests that the Court during Reconstruction was not always wise in protecting itself from political forces and that Congress and the executive at times acted to stop the Court from ruling lest it do itself damage. See Graber, "Legal, Strategic or Legal Strategy," in Kahn and Kersch, *Supreme Court and American Political Development,* supra note 204, at 56–58.

234. See Barry Friedman, "The History of the Countermajoritarian Difficulty, Part II: Reconstruction's Political Court," *Geo. L. J.* 91 (2002): 43; Richard D. Friedman, "The Transformation in Senate Response to Supreme Court Nominations: From Reconstruction to the Taft Administration and Beyond," *Cardozo L. Rev.* 5 (1983): 21 ("In the years following the Civil War, senators demanded that nominees to the Court hold orthodox views on issues relating to Reconstruction"). But see Charles Fairman, "Mr. Justice Bradley's Appointment to the Supreme Court and the Legal Tender Cases," *Harv. L. Rev.* 54 (1941): 1142 ("The word 'pack' had an evil connotation but no precise meaning").

235. Friedman, "Transformation in Senate Response," supra note 234, at 21n114 (quoting Abraham Lincoln's comment in explaining his nomination of Chase in 1864).

236. *An Act to Provide Circuit Courts for the Districts of California and Oregon, and for Other Purposes* (March 3, 1863), *Stats at Large of USA*, supra note 108, at 12:794.
237. *N.Y. Times*, March 4, 1863, quoted in Kutler, *Judicial Power*, supra note 81, at 19.
238. See Ackerman, *We the People*, vol. 2: supra note 155, at 239; Fairman, *Reconstruction and Reunion*, supra note 163, at 168–69; Warren, *Supreme Court*, supra note 35, at 3:145. The measure was passed—with little debate—only after Johnson nominated Attorney General Henry Stanbery to fill a vacancy on the Court. See Charles G. Geyh, "Judicial Independence, Judicial Accountability, and the Role of Constitutional Norms in Congressional Regulation of the Courts," *Ind. L. J.* 78 (2003): 181, 213. After Senator Lyman Trumbull introduced the measure as an amendment to pending legislation on the configuration of the circuits, the Senate approved the measure with no debate on the merits.
239. "Summary of Events," *Am. L. Rev.* 1 (1867): 206.
240. *The Diary of Edward Bates, 1959–1866*, ed. Howard K. Beale (1933), quoted in Kutler, *Judicial Power*, supra note 81, at 63.
241. See Ackerman, *We the People*, vol. 2: supra note 155, at 239; Fairman, *Reconstruction and Reunion*, supra note 163, at 487; Warren, *Supreme Court*, supra note 35, at 3:223.
242. See Felix Frankfurter and James M. Landis, *The Business of the Supreme Court* (1927), 32; Charles G. Geyh and Emily Field Van Tassel, "The Independence of the Judicial Branch in the New Republic," *Chi-Kent L. Rev.* 74 (1998): 57–58. In fact, Lincoln even hesitated to appoint justices during the war to seats that traditionally belonged to the South. See Friedman, "Transformation in Senate Response," supra note 234, at 32n179 (quoting Lincoln as having said, "I have been unwilling to throw all the appointments northward, thus disabling myself from doing justice to the South on the return of peace").
243. Magliocca, *Andrew Jackson and the Constitution*, supra note 10, at 65–69. Twenty of the first thirty-five justices on the Supreme Court were from slave states. Presidents tended to appoint one justice from each of the nine judicial circuits, effectively guaranteeing that the South always had a majority on the Court during the antebellum years. Graber, *Problem of Constitutional Evil*, supra note 36, at 116, 148–49.
244. See Kutler, *Judicial Power*, supra note 81, at 61–62; see also Friedman, "Transformation in Senate Response," supra note 234, at 31–36; Geyh, "Judicial Independence," supra note 238, at 187–88.
245. "Usurpation," *Harper's Wkly.*, Feb. 9, 1867, at 82.
246. "The Last Decision of the Supreme Court on Military Trials During the War," *N.Y. Herald*, Dec. 20, 1866, at 4.
247. Cong. Globe, 40th Cong., 2d Sess. 2127 (1868) (statement of Sen. Buckalew).
248. For a detailed analysis of the Legal Tender Cases, see Friedman, "Reconstruction's Political Court," supra note 234, at 40–44.
249. Hepburn v. Griswold, 75 U.S. 603, 621–22 (1869).
250. Warren, *Supreme Court*, supra note 35, at 3:230–33.
251. "Effect of the Legal Tender Decision," *Daily Morning Chron.*, Feb. 12, 1870, at 2.
252. Knox v. Lee, 79 U.S. 457 (1870).
253. *The New York Times* implored Congress to remedy the situation, stating: "We repeat, therefore, that no duty is more imperative upon the body which advises and consents to appointments, than to be certain that this necessary power in war shall be restored to the Government, and that the Court shall be constructed on a plan which . . . shall discourage personal ambition, and be in strict harmony with the loyalty of the Republic." "Legal Tender—The Supreme Court Decision," *N.Y. Times*, Feb. 12, 1870, at 4; see also "Financial Affairs," *N.Y. Times*, Feb. 10, 1870, at 3 ("The vacancies on the Supreme Bench will soon be filled, and ably filled, and . . . abundant

opportunity will no doubt be afforded for a review of the present Opinion by the full Bench"). The *Times* followed the subsequent appointment process closely. See "The Latest Appointments of Supreme Court Judges," *N.Y. Times*, Feb. 11, 1870, at 1 (reporting likelihood of Strong and Bradley's being confirmed and speculating about their political leanings).

254. "The Legal Tender Decision," *World*, Feb. 8, 1870, at 4; "The Legal Tender Fiasco in the Supreme Court," *World*, Apr. 21, 1870, at 4; "The Legal Tender Question," *Am. L. Rev.* 5 (1870–71): 367.

255. *N.Y. Trib.*, May 2, 1871, at 4.

256. "The Reopening of the Legal-Tender Case," *Nation*, Apr. 7, 1870, at 218.

257. Cong. Globe, 40th Cong., 2d Sess. 483 (1868) (statement of Rep. Bingham).

258. Cong. Globe, 41st Cong., 2d Sess. 94 (1869) (statement of Sen. Edmunds).

259. See Foner, *Reconstruction*, supra note 159, at 245 ("The Civil Rights bill placed an unprecedented—and unrealistic—burden of enforcement on the federal courts"); id. at 243 ("The Civil Rights bill and bill extending the duration and expanding the powers of the Freedmen's Bureau depended upon the judiciary for enforcement"); Kutler, *Judicial Power*, supra note 81, at 143 ("The dominant Republicans regularly turned to the judicial system for protection and enforcement of particular legislation and for fulfillment of their nationalist impulses").

260. Lasser, *Limits of Judicial Power*, supra note 35, at 91–92.

261. See Kutler, *Judicial Power*, supra note 81, at 143. An excellent volume on the reliance on the judiciary to enforce Reconstruction measures is Robert J. Kaczorowski, *The Nationalization of Civil Rights: Constitutional Theory and Practice in a Racist Society, 1866–1883* (1987); see also Robert J. Kaczorowski, "Revolutionary Constitutionalism in the Era of Civil War and Reconstruction," *N.Y.U. L. Rev.* 61 (1986): 863–941. See Chapter 5, infra, for a discussion of how this transfer of jurisdiction affected the judiciary and popular politics in the following generations.

262. *An Act to Determine the Jurisdiction of Circuit Courts of the United States, and to Regulate the Removal of Causes from State Courts, and for Other Purposes* (March 3, 1875), *U.S. Statutes at Large* (1875): 18 pt. 3:470 (conferring general federal question jurisdiction on lower courts), codified at 28 U.S.C. § 1331 (2006). See generally William Wiecek, "The Reconstruction of Federal Judicial Power, 1863–1875," *Am. J. Leg. Hist.* 13 (1969): 333 (describing the expansion of federal court jurisdiction between 1863 and 1875).

263. Cong. Globe, 39th Cong., 2d Sess. 503 (1867) (statement of Rep. Bingham).

264. See Cong. Globe, 40th Cong., 2d Sess. 1859 (1868); see also Fairman, *Reconstruction and Reunion*, supra note 163, at 464. Much was made of this in the debates, and opponents of the jurisdiction-stripping matter noted the irony that an appeal was being taken away in cases involving personal liberty, just as one was added in cases involving money. President Johnson explained in his veto message:

> The first section of the bill meets my approbation, as, for the purpose of protecting the rights of property from erroneous decisions of inferior judicial tribunals, it provides means for obtaining uniformity by appeal to the Supreme Court of the United States in cases which have now become very numerous and of much public interest, and in which such remedy is not now allowed. The second section, however, takes away the right of appeal to that court in cases which involve the life and liberty of the citizen, and leaves them exposed to the judgment of numerous inferior tribunals. It is apparent that the two sections were conceived in a very different spirit. . . ."

Cong. Globe, 40th Cong., 2d Sess. 2094 (1868).

265. Ex parte Milligan, 71 U.S. 2, 109 (1866) (emphasis in original).

Chapter 5: Constituency

1. William M. Meigs, "The Relation of the Judiciary to the Constitution," *Am. L. Rev.* 19 (1885): 191, 198.

2. On the idea of acquiescence, see Mark A. Graber, "The Problematic Establishment of Judicial Review," in *The Supreme Court and American Politics: New Institutionalist Approaches*, ed. Howard Gillman and Cornell W. Clayton (1999), 28; James M. Ashley, "Should the Supreme Court Be Reorganized?," *Arena*, Oct. 1895, at 221; Mark A. Graber, "Naked Land Transfers and American Constitutional Development," *Vand. L. Rev.* 53 (2000): 78; Thomas Speed Mosby, "The Court Is King," *Arena*, Aug. 1906, at 118; Beulah Amidon Ratliff, "Shall We Remake the Supreme Court?," *Nation*, May 21, 1924, at 580.

3. Melville W. Fuller, "Chief Justice Marshall," *Dial*, May 1885, at 10.

4. *An Act to Protect All Citizens in Their Civil and Legal Rights* (March 1, 1875), U.S. *Statutes at Large* (1875): 18 pt. 3:335.

5. *An Act to Determine the Jurisdiction of Circuit Courts of the United States, and to Regulate the Removal of Causes from State Courts, and for Other Purposes* (March 3, 1875), *U.S. Statutes at Large*, supra note 4, at 18 pt. 3:470.

6. Civil Rights Cases, 109 U.S. 3, 13 (1883).

7. James G. Blaine, *Twenty Years of Congress: From Lincoln to Garfield* (1884), 2:467.

8. U.S. Const. amend. XIII, §§ 1–2.

9. Charles Fairman, *The Oliver Wendell Holmes Devise History of the Supreme Court of the United States*, vol. 6, pt. 2, *Reconstruction and Reunion, 1864–88*, ed. Paul A. Freund (1987), 133; Frank J. Scaturro, *The Supreme Court's Retreat from Reconstruction: A Distortion of Constitutional Jurisprudence* (2000), 7–8.

10. Fairman, *Reconstruction and Reunion*, supra note 9, at 132, 133; William E. Nelson, *The Fourteenth Amendment: From Political Principle to Judicial Doctrine* (1988), 46, 48.

11. U.S. Const. amend. XIV, §§ 1, 5; Scaturro, *Supreme Court's Retreat*, supra note 9, at 9.

12. Cong. Globe, 39th Cong., 1st Sess. 249 (1866), quoted in Michael Kent Curtis, *No State Shall Abridge: The Fourteenth Amendment and the Bill of Rights* (1986), 86.

13. Fairman, *Reconstruction and Reunion*, supra note 9, at 133.

14. U.S. Const. amend. XIV, § 2; Fairman, *Reconstruction and Reunion*, supra note 9, at 134; Scaturro, *Supreme Court's Retreat*, supra note 9, at 9.

15. *Nat'l Anti-Slavery Standard*, June 26, 1889, quoted in William Gillette, *Retreat from Reconstruction, 1869–1879* (1979), 19.

16. U.S. Const. amend. XV.

17. Quoted in Gillette, *Retreat from Reconstruction*, supra note 15, at 19.

18. Letter from Hugh L. Bond to Anna Bond, Feb. 9, 1871, quoted in Robert J. Kaczorowski, *The Politics of Judicial Interpretation: The Federal Courts, Department of Justice and Civil Rights, 1866–1876* (1985), 54.

19. Letter from L. B. Eaton to Attorney General, Aug. 12, 1874, quoted in Gillette, *Retreat from Reconstruction*, supra note 15, at 29.

20. Blaine, *Twenty Years of Congress*, supra note 7, at 2:469; see also Fairman, *Reconstruction and Reunion*, supra note 9, at 143–47; Scaturro, *Supreme Court's Retreat*, supra note 9, at 10–11.

21. *An Act to Enforce the Provisions of the Fourteenth Amendment to the Constitution of the United States, and for Other Purposes* (Apr. 20, 1871), *U.S. Statutes at Large* (1873): 17:13, codified at 42 U.S.C. §1985(3) (2006).

22. Ulysses S. Grant, "Second Inaugural Address," March 4, 1873, in James D. Richardson, *A Compilation of the Messages and Papers of the Presidents* (1899), 7:221.

23. 2 Cong. Rec. 4083 (1874), quoted in Fairman, *Reconstruction and Reunion*, supra note 9, at 179.

24. Id.

25. 2 Cong. Rec. at 360–61 app. (1874) (statement of Sen. Morton), quoted in Scaturro, *Supreme Court's Retreat*, supra note 9, at 124; see also Edward S. Corwin, "The Supreme Court and the Fourteenth Amendment," *Mich. L. Rev.* 7 (1908–09): 645 (noting that one theory upon which the act was based was that Section 5 of the Fourteenth Amendment gives Congress the power to pass "affirmative legislation, designed to supply the inadequacies of State legislation and directly impinging upon private individuals"). But see Curtis, *No State Shall Abridge*, supra note 12, at 158 (noting that some members of Congress, Republicans and Democrats alike, believed that the Fourteenth Amendment did not govern the actions of private individuals).

26. Blaine, *Twenty Years of Congress*, supra note 7, at 2:419.

27. George C. Holt, *The Concurrent Jurisdiction of the Federal and State Courts* (1888), 29. Ironically, given *Dred Scott*, the sentence concluded: "except as to the territories and public domain over which Congress has exclusive legislative authority." Id. The Court began by denying Congress the power to regulate slavery in the territories; by the time it was over, the territories were the only place Congress could protect civil rights in the way it chose.

28. Kaczorowski, *Politics of Judicial Interpretation*, supra note 18, at 143.

29. "Monopolies and the Fourteenth Amendment," *Nation*, Dec. 1, 1870, at 361.

30. The Slaughterhouse Cases, 83 U.S. 36, 38 (1872); Kaczorowski, *Politics of Judicial Interpretation*, supra note 18, at 144; Loren P. Beth, "The *Slaughter-House Cases*—Revisited," *La. L. Rev.* 23 (1963): 489; Mitchell Franklin, "The Foundations and Meaning of the *Slaughterhouse Cases*, Part One," *Tul. L. Rev.* 18 (1943–1944): 3–4.

31. Peggy Cooper Davis, "Introducing Robert Smalls," *Fordham L. Rev.* 69 (2000–2001): 1715; Mitchell Franklin, "The Foundations and Meaning of the *Slaughterhouse Cases*, Part Two," *Tul. L. Rev.* 18 (1943–1944): 222–24. Before the Civil War, yellow fever epidemics repeatedly ravaged New Orleans. General Benjamin Butler, the first military governor of the city after the war, virtually eradicated the disease through quarantines and cleanups. Yet after federal troops left the city, the disease quickly regained strength, and epidemics raged once again. Franklin, "Foundations and Meaning, Part Two," supra, at 219–24.

32. Supreme Court Transcript in *Durbridge v. The Slaughterhouse Company*, 409, quoted in Franklin, "Foundations and Meaning, Part One," supra note 30, at 25; see also Kaczorowski, *Politics of Judicial Interpretation*, supra note 18, at 144.

33. For the most complete recent survey of this question, and the most elaborate argument that the Privileges or Immunities Clause was meant to incorporate the Bill of Rights against the states, see Akhil Reed Amar, *The Bill of Rights: Creation and Reconstruction* (1998), 182–85; see also Curtis, *No State Shall Abridge*, supra note 12, at 83–84. Amar's most persuasive evidence may be the words of John Bingham, who actually drafted the Fourteenth Amendment. "The privileges and immunities of citizens of the United States," Bingham said, "are chiefly defined in the first eight amendments to the Constitution of the United States." John Bingham, quoted in Amar, *Bill of Rights*, supra, at 183. In 1949, Charles Fairman laid out a detailed historical case to show that neither the Reconstruction Congress nor the ratifying states understood the Fourteenth Amendment to incorporate the Bill of Rights against the states. Charles Fairman, "Does the Fourteenth Amendment Incorporate the Bill of Rights?," *Stan. L. Rev.* 2 (1949): 5–139. Raoul Berger gave a similar account in his book *Government by Judiciary* in 1977. Fairman's and Berger's accounts, though contradicted by Amar, are still alive as interpretations of the historical record surrounding the Fourteenth Amendment.

34. Relying on another clause of the Constitution, the Due Process Clause, the Supreme Court soon enough would be holding such. See Chapter 6, infra.
35. *Slaughterhouse Cases*, 83 U.S. at 73.
36. Id. at 74.
37. Id. at 79 (quoting Crandall v. Nevada, 73 U.S. (6 Wall.) 36 (1867)).
38. Kaczorowski, *Politics of Judicial Interpretation*, supra note 18, at 159; Beth, "*Slaughter-House Cases*—Revisited," supra note 30, at 488.
39. *Slaughterhouse Cases*, 83 U.S at 129 (Swayne, J., dissenting).
40. Id. at 96 (Field, J., dissenting).
41. Id. at 82 (majority opinion).
42. Id. at 78.
43. Cong. Globe, 39th Cong., 1st Sess. 99 app. (1866) (statement of Sen. Richard Yates), quoted in Curtis, *No State Shall Abridge*, supra note 12, at 55. This is a central issue of William Nelson's book *The Fourteenth Amendment*. He argues that the Court's interpretation of the Fourteenth Amendment in the *Slaughterhouse Cases* was based in the concerns of Congress and the states regarding the federal system. See Nelson, *Fourteenth Amendment*, supra note 10, at 156.
44. Cong. Globe, 39th Cong., 1st Sess. 99 app. (1866), quoted in Curtis, *No State Shall Abridge*, supra note 12, at 55.
45. Cong. Globe, 39th Cong., 1st Sess. 163 (1866) (statement of Sen. Timothy Howe), quoted in Curtis, *No State Shall Abridge*, supra note 12, at 48.
46. *Slaughterhouse Cases*, 83 U.S. at 123, 122 (Bradley, J. dissenting).
47. Fairman, *Reconstruction and Reunion*, supra note 9, at 172.
48. Alfred Kelly, "The Congressional Controversy over School Desegregation, 1867–1875," *Amer. Hist. Rev.* 64 (1959): 553.
49. *Slaughterhouse Cases*, 83 U.S. at 71; see Fairman, *Reconstruction and Reunion*, supra note 9, at 172.
50. Fairman, *Reconstruction and Reunion*, supra note 9, at 226–28; Kaczorowski, *Politics of Judicial Interpretation*, supra note 18, at 200.
51. United States v. Reese, 92 U.S. 214, 217–18, 221 (1875); Kaczorowski, *Politics of Judicial Interpretation*, supra note 18, at 213; Charles Warren, *The Supreme Court in United States History* (Boston: Little, Brown and Company, 1922), 3:324.
52. Kaczorowski, *Politics of Judicial Interpretation*, supra note 18, at 175.
53. Id. at 178. In the first trial, one defendant was acquitted and the jury failed to reach a verdict for the rest. Id. On retrial, three of the nine defendants were found guilty of conspiracy to deprive the victims of their civil rights but not guilty of murder, and the other five were acquitted. Id. The Court "upheld the defense's motion in arrest of judgment," id. at 179, or "dismissed the indictment," id. at 183.
54. United States v. Cruikshank, 92 U.S. 542, 555 (1875); see also Kaczorowski, *Politics of Judicial Interpretation*, supra note 18, at 183.
55. *Cruikshank*, 92 U.S. at 556.
56. Id. at 555; see Kaczorowski, *Politics of Judicial Interpretation*, supra note 18, at 216.
57. Carleton Hunt, "Fifty Years' Experience in Practice at the Bar," address at a meeting of the Louisiana Bar Association, June 6, 1908, quoted in Warren, *Supreme Court*, supra note 51, at 3:330.
58. Quoted in Warren, *Supreme Court*, supra note 51, at 3:329.
59. Civil Rights Cases, 109 U.S. 3, 11 (1883).
60. See Michael J. Klarman, *Unfinished Business: Racial Equality in American History* (2007), 68–69 (discussing Bradley's opinion: "[T]he justices, like most of the country, wished for a return to normalcy").

61. *Civil Rights Cases*, 109 U.S. at 25.
62. Strauder v. West Virginia, 101 U.S. 303 (1879); Michael J. Klarman, "The Plessy Era," *Sup. Ct. Rev.*, 1998: 373, 376; Edward A. Purcell, Jr., "The Particularly Dubious Case of *Hans v. Louisiana*: An Essay on Law, Race, History, and 'Federal Courts,'" *N.C. L. Rev.* 81 (2003): 1990.
63. "The 'Original-Package' Bill," *Chi. Trib.*, July 15, 1890.
64. *Charleston News and Courier*, quoted in Eric Foner, *Reconstruction: America's Unfinished Revolution, 1863–1877* (1988), 570.
65. See Klarman, *Unfinished Business*, supra note 60, at 61–74.
66. "A Pleasant Picture," *Harper's Wkly.*, Sept. 14, 1867, at 579 (quoting correspondence from the *N.Y. Times*).
67. Kaczorowski, *Politics of Judicial Interpretation*, supra note 18, at 93; Scaturro, *Supreme Court's Retreat*, supra note 9, at 11.
68. Foner, *Reconstruction*, supra note 64, at 508.
69. Id. at 502–04, 509–11; Gillette, *Retreat from Reconstruciton*, supra note 15, at 71–72.
70. *The Works of James Abram Garfield*, ed. Burke A. Hinsdale (1883), 1:110–11, quoted in Kaczorowski, *Politics of Judicial Interpretation*, supra note 18, at 163.
71. Letter from James Garfield to R. Folger, Apr. 18, 1870, quoted in Allan Peskin, *Garfield* (1978), 332.
72. Kaczorowski, *Politics of Judicial Interpretation*, supra note 18, at 163.
73. *N.Y. World*, Apr. 16, 1873, quoted in Warren, *Supreme Court*, supra note 51, at 3:265.
74. See Kaczorowski, *Politics of Judicial Interpretation*, supra note 18, at 160–62 (noting a lack of controversy over *Slaughterhouse* decision in newspaper reports as well as support from some Republican papers); Warren, *Supreme Court*, supra note 51, at 3:264–67 (surveying major newspapers and finding them supportive of the Court's decision).
75. "The Right to Confiscate," *Nation*, Sept. 24, 1874, at 200. A mere seven years earlier, *The Nation* had argued that "Congress is directly invested with full power to legislate" to ensure the protection of blacks' civil rights. *Nation*, March 1, 1866, quoted in Kaczorowski, *Politics of Judicial Interpretation*, supra note 18, at 162.
76. *N.Y. Times*, quoted in Warren, *Supreme Court*, supra note 51, at 3:266.
77. *Chi. Trib.*, Apr. 19, 1873, quoted in Warren, *Supreme Court*, supra note 51, at 3:267.
78. Foner, *Reconstruction*, supra note 64, at 523–24.
79. Gillette, *Retreat from Reconstruction*, supra note 15, at 212, 217.
80. Foner, *Reconstruction*, supra note 64, at 523.
81. Letter from James A. Garfield to Julius O. Converse, Jan. 21, 1875, quoted in Gillette, *Retreat from Reconstruction*, supra note 15, at 131.
82. "The Nigger School," *Chi. Trib.*, June 8, 1874, at 4.
83. "The Civil-Rights Bill," *Nation*, Sept. 17, 1874, at 181.
84. 2 Cong. Rec. 5329 (1874), quoted in Gillette, *Retreat from Reconstruction*, supra note 15, at 207.
85. Letter from J. H. Maddox to Benjamin Butler, Jan. 28, 1875, quoted in Gillette, *Retreat from Reconstruction*, supra note 15, at 266; see Gillette, *Retreat from Reconstruction*, supra note 15, at 259–65; see also Heather Cox Richardson, *The Death of Reconstruction* (2001), chapter 4.
86. Gillette, *Retreat from Reconstruction*, supra note 15, at 269.
87. *Am. and Gazette*, March 4, 1875, quoted in Gillette, *Retreat from Reconstruction*, supra note 15, at 295.
88. The role of federalism in ending Reconstruction is a central theme of William Nelson's work on the interpretation of the Fourteenth Amendment. See Nelson, *Fourteenth Amendment*, supra note 10, at 108–09; see also Foner, *Reconstruction*, supra

note 64, at 533. As the balance of this chapter suggests, the Court's fealty to federalist principles yielded in cases protecting the interests of business.

89. On racism in the North and South, see Gillette, *Retreat from Reconstruction*, supra note 15, at 191–96. For an argument that northerners came to see the ex-slaves as a threat to the free labor ideology, see Richardson, *Death of Reconstruction*, supra note 85, at 144–45, 150–53, 183–84.

90. This is the central theme of Robert Kaczorowski's excellent chronicle *The Politics of Judicial Interpretation*. See, e.g., Kaczorowski, *Politics of Judicial Interpretation*, supra note 18, at 27, 51, 60–61, 84–85; see also Gillette, *Retreat from Reconstruction*, supra note 15, at 31 (noting lack of money as one reason the federal government failed to prevent violence against blacks and violations of their civil and political rights). For the estimates on federal spending and the role of nothern capitalists, see Richard Franklin Bensel, *Yankee Leviathan: The Origins of Central State Authority in America, 1859–1877* (1990), 352–53, 361, 365.

91. See Bensel, *Yankee Leviathan*, supra note 90, at 371 (describing the several compromises reached on the occasion of the disputed election, including the withdrawal of federal troops in South Carolina and Louisiana within two months of Hayes's inauguration).

92. Gillette, *Retreat from Reconstruction*, supra note 15, at 166; see also Foner, *Reconstruction*, supra note 64, at 528 (arguing that Grant could not construct a consistent southern policy during his second term).

93. See Kaczorowski, *Politics of Judicial Interpretation*, supra note 18, at 162; James A. Garfield, "A Century of Congress," *Atlantic Monthly*, July 1877, at 49, 64.

94. "The Rights of Negroes," *N.Y. Times*, Oct. 18, 1883, at 4; see also Foner, *Reconstruction*, supra note 64, at 497–99, for a discussion of reformers' losing faith in Reconstruction.

95. 3 Cong. Rec. 1853 (1875), quoted in Gillette, *Retreat from Reconstruction*, supra note 15, at 287.

96. *Springfield Republican*, Jan. 11, 1875, quoted in Gillette, *Retreat from Reconstruction*, supra note 15, at 280.

97. See Purcell, "Particularly Dubious Case," supra note 62, at 2010–21, for an examination of the views of several of the justices who sat on the Reconstruction cases. Purcell may argue the case for racism on the Supreme Court a bit hard, but certainly some of the justices, for a variety of reasons, would have been happy to abandon Reconstruction.

98. Newly appointed in 1870, Bradley had offered a sweeping interpretation of congressional power to regulate even the behavior of private citizens under the Reconstruction amendments. Answering a legal inquiry from a circuit judge, he opined that given Congress's inability to compel state officials, "the only appropriate legislation it can make is that which will operate directly on offenders and offences and protect the rights which the [Fourteenth] Amendment secures." Letter from Justice Joseph P. Bradley to Judge William B. Woods, quoted in Kaczorowski, *Politics of Judicial Interpretation*, supra note 18, at 15. This was the almost universal view of the lower courts prior to the decision in *Slaughterhouse*. See generally Kaczorowski, *Politics of Judicial Interpretation*, supra note 18. Yet, remarkably, Bradley was the author of the Court's decision in the *Civil Rights Cases*, writing: "It is state action of a particular character that is prohibited. Individual invasion of individual rights is not the subject matter of the amendment." *Civil Rights Cases*, 109 U.S. at 11; see Purcell, "Particularly Dubious Case," supra note 62, at 2023–28, for a discussion of Bradley's shifting views; see also Curtis, *No State Shall Abridge*, supra note 12, at 179; John Anthony Scott, "Justice Bradley's Evolving Concept of the Fourteenth Amendment from the *Slaughterhouse Cases* to the *Civil Rights Cases*," *Rutgers L. Rev.* 25 (1971): 552–70. But see William E.

Nelson, *The Roots of American Bureaucracy, 1830–1900* (1982), 70–71 (arguing that Bradley's positions can be reconciled).

99. "Rights of Negroes," supra note 94, at 4.
100. Letter from Rutherford B. Hayes to Morison Waite, July 10, 1882, quoted in Scott, "Justice Bradley's Evolving Concept," supra note 98, at 568; Letter from Morison Waite to Rutherford B. Hayes, July 22, 1882, quoted in Scott, "Justice Bradley's Evolving Concept," supra note 98, at 568.
101. Warren, *Supreme Court*, supra note 51, at 3:335–37.
102. Quoted in id. at 3:335.
103. *Phila. N. Am.*, Oct. 17, 1883, quoted in Fairman, *Reconstruction and Reunion*, supra note 9, at 573.
104. "Rights of Negroes," supra note 94, at 4.
105. Purcell, "Particularly Dubious Case," supra note 62, at 16 (noting the increase in track mileage); Deborah A. Ballam, "The Evolution of the Government-Business Relationship in the United States: Colonial Times to Present," *Am. Bus. L. J.* 31 (1994): 599 (discussing federal land grants); Richard Franklin Bensel, *The Political Economy of American Industrialization, 1877–1900* (2000), 295, 305 (discussing the number of workers and progress in communications).
106. Edward A. Purcell, *Litigation and Inequality: Federal Diversity Jurisdiction in Industrial America, 1870–1958* (1992), 16 (discussing the economic growth rate); Ballam, "Evolution of the Government-Business Relationship," supra note 105, at 599 (noting the use of steel); Bensel, *Political Economy of American Industrialization*, supra note 105, at 303 (on Montgomery Ward).
107. Ballam, "Evolution of the Government-Business Relationship," supra note 105, at 598, 600.
108. Robert H. Wiebe, *The Search for Order, 1877–1920* (1967), xii; see also Purcell, *Litigation and Inequality*, supra note 106, at 16. By the end of World War I, a majority of Americans were living in cities or towns. Ballam, "Evolution of the Government-Business Relationship," supra note 105, at 599.
109. Tony Allen Freyer, *Harmony & Dissonance: The Swift and Erie Cases in American Federalism* (1981), 56.
110. Ballam, "Evolution of the Government-Business Relationship," supra note 105, at 598; see also Purcell, *Litigation and Inequality*, supra note 106, at 16.
111. Allan Nevins, *John D. Rockefeller* (1940), 622, quoted in Wallace Mendelson, *Capitalism, Democracy, and the Supreme Court* (1960), 53; see also Purcell, *Litigation and Inequality*, supra note 106, at 16; Wiebe, *Search for Order*, supra note 108, at 23.
112. Bensel, *Political Economy of American Industrialization*, supra note 105, at 15.
113. Frederick Emory Haynes, "The New Sectionalism," *Q. J. Econ.* 10 (1896): 286.
114. J. P. Dunn, Jr., "The Mortgage Evil," *Pol. Sci. Q.* 5 (1890): 80.
115. Simon Sterne, *Railway Legislation and Management*, quoted in Fairman, *Reconstruction and Reunion*, supra note 9, at 291.
116. "The Railroad Manuals," *Nation*, Sept. 24, 1874, at 206.
117. Richardson, *Death of Reconstruction*, supra note 85, at 44.
118. Edward Chase Kirkland, *Dream and Thought in the Business Community, 1860–1900* (1956), 359–60.
119. *Farmer Discontent, 1865–1900*, ed. Vernon Carstensen (1974), 17.
120. Solon Justus Buck, *The Granger Movement: A Study of Agricultural Organization and its Political, Economic and Social Manifestations, 1870–1880* (1913), 89, 101.
121. Foner, *Reconstruction*, supra note 64, at 512; Gillette, *Retreat from Reconstruction*, supra note 15, at 186; Wiebe, *Search for Order*, supra note 108, at 1.

122. Foner, *Reconstruction*, supra note 64, at 512.

123. "Railroad Manuals," supra note 116, at 206.

124. Ulysses S. Grant, "Sixth Annual Message," Dec. 7, 1874, in Richardson, *Messages and Papers of the Presidents*, supra note 22, at 7:284.

125. Foner, *Reconstruction*, supra note 64, at 583–84; Wiebe, *Search for Order*, supra note 108, at 10.

126. Letter from Ulysses S. Grant to Daniel Ammen, Aug. 28, 1877, quoted in Gillette, *Retreat from Reconstruction*, supra note 15, at 348.

127. See, e.g., Harry N. Scheiber, "Federalism, the Southern Regional Economy, and Public Policy Since 1865," in *Ambivalent Legacy: A Legal History of the South*, ed. David J. Bodenhamer and James W. Ely, Jr. (1984), 82; Tony Allen Freyer, "The Federal Courts, Localism, and the National Economy, 1865–1900," *Bus. Hist. Rev.* 53 (1979): 347–49.

128. William H. Taft, "Charges Against the Federal Judiciary," *Va. L. Reg.* 1 (1896): 397.

129. *Indep.*, May 3, 1883, quoted in Warren, *Supreme Court*, supra note 51, at 3:385. On southern debt repudiation, see John V. Orth, "The Virginia State Debt and the Judicial Power of the United States," in Bodenhamer and Ely, *Ambivalent Legacy*, supra note 127, at 108–19; Charles M. Cameron, "Endogenous Preferences About Courts: A Theory of Judicial State Building in the Nineteenth Century," in *Preferences and Situations: Points of Intersection Between Historical and Rational Choice Institutionalism*, ed. Ira Katznelson and Barry R. Weingast (2005), 204; John J. Gibbons, "The Eleventh Amendment and State Sovereign Immunity: A Reinterpretation," *Colum. L. Rev.* 83 (1983): 1889–2005.

130. Freyer, "Federal Courts," supra note 127, at 347; Harry N. Scheiber, "Xenophobia and Parochialism in the History of American Legal Process: From the Jacksonian Era to the Sagebrush Rebellion," *Wm. & Mary L. Rev.* 23 (1982): 654.

131. Holt, *Concurrent Jurisdiction*, supra note 27, at 169.

132. "Justice Between the East and the West," *Nation*, Aug. 8, 1878, at 79.

133. Dunn, "Mortgage Evil," supra note 114, at 69–70.

134. Id. at 71.

135. Id. at 70, 78–80; see also Bensel, *Political Economy of American Industrialization*, supra note 105, at 57; Freyer, "Federal Courts," supra note 127, at 349.

136. E. Parmalee Prentice and John G. Egan, *The Commerce Clause of the Federal Constitution* (1898), 15.

137. Edward B. Whitney, "Commercial Retaliation Between the States," *Am. L. Rev.* 19 (1885): 67.

138. See generally Stanley C. Hollander, "Nineteenth Century Anti-Drummer Legislation in the United States," *Bus. Hist. Rev.* 38 (1964): 479; Charles W. McCurdy, "American Law and the Marketing Structure of the Large Corporation, 1875–1890," *J. Econ. Hist.* 38 (1978): 636–37.

139. *Proceedings of the Second Annual Meeting of the National Board of Trade, 1869* (1870), quoted in Hollander, "Nineteenth Century Anti-Drummer Legislation," supra note 138, at 488 (speech of Mr. Holton of Milwaukee).

140. Ballam, "Evolution of the Government-Business Relationship," supra note 105, at 605; Freyer, "Federal Courts," supra note 127, at 350; Hollander, "Nineteenth Century Anti-Drummer Legislation," supra note 138, at 483; Scheiber, "Federalism, the Southern Regional Economy," in Bodenhamer and Ely, *Ambivalent Legacy*, supra note 127, at 81–82.

141. *Proceedings of the Second Annual Meeting of the National Board of Trade, Held in Cincinnati*, Dec. 1860, 43, quoted in Scheiber, "Federalism, the Southern Regional Economy," in Bodenhamer and Ely, *Ambivalent Legacy*, supra note 127, at 82.

142. John Norton Pomeroy, "The Supreme Court and State Repudiation," *Am. L. Rev.* 17 (1883): 712, 718–19; see also *Com. & Fin. Chron.*, March 29, 1890, quoted in Bensel, *Political Economy of American Industrialization*, supra note 105, at 335 (discussing "Socialistic legislation"); Taft, "Charges Against the Federal Judiciary," supra note 128, at 396 (commenting on the "socialistic" nature of legislation supported by southern and western farmers).

143. "The Law of Debtor and Creditor in Louisiana," *Hunt's*, July 1846, at 71, quoted in Tony Allen Freyer, *Forums of Order: The Federal Courts and Business in American History* (1979), 11; see also Robert W. Gordon, review of Freyer, *Forums of Order*, *Bus. Hist. Rev.* 54 (1980): 224.

144. See *Railway & Corp. L. J.* 5 (1889): 188; *Railway & Corp. L. J.* 9 (1891): 219–20; see generally Joel H. Silbey, *The American Political Nation, 1838–1893* (1991), 192–93, 227.

145. Jonathan Periam, "The Groundswell: A History of the Origins, Aims, and Progress of the Farmers' Movement" (1874), reprinted in Carstensen, *Farmer Discontent*, supra note 119, at 22.

146. Charles Francis Adams, Jr., "The Granger Movement," *N. Am. Rev.* 20 (1875): 405.

147. Foner, *Reconstruction*, supra note 64, at 516; Ballam, "Evolution of the Government-Business Relationship," supra note 105, at 604; see also Munn v. Illinois, 94 U.S. 113, 115–17 (1876).

148. Adams, "Granger Movement," supra note 146, at 395.

149. "The Granger Decisions," *Chi. Trib.*, March 3, 1877.

150. The constitution was submitted to the people for approval as a whole. The new provisions were also put to a separate vote. The constitution carried the day by a margin of 134,227–35,443. The railroad provision passed 144,750–23,525. The provision authorizing the regulation of warehouse rates passed 143,520–22,702. See Buck, *Granger Movement*, supra note 120, at 131.

151. Freyer, *Forums of Order*, supra note 143, at 128; see also Purcell, *Litigation and Inequality*, supra note 106, at 24.

152. "Current Topics," *Cent. L. J.* 10 (1880): 17. Not only were the jury pools believed better in federal court, but the procedural mechanisms by which federal judges were able to control their juries were also superior. For example, federal judges were allowed to comment on the evidence and direct or set aside verdicts. Purcell, *Litigation and Inequality*, supra note 106, at 24; Howard Gillman, "How Political Parties Can Use the Courts to Advance Their Agendas: Federal Courts in the United States, 1875–1891," *Am. Pol. Sci. Rev.* 96 (2002): 519. By contrast, particularly in the South and the West, many states had statutes of constitutional rules limiting judges' right to comment upon evidence that had evolved in the antebellum years. Renee L. Lerner, "The Transformation of the American Civil Trial: The Silent Judge," *Wm. & Mary L. Rev.* 42 (2000): 220–64.

153. "The Victory in Illinois," *Prairie Wkly.*, June 14, 1873, at 1.

154. "The Defeat of Judge Lawrence," *Chi. Trib.*, June 6, 1873, at 3.

155. Adams, "Granger Movement," supra note 146, at 395. The details of Lawrence's defeat and the Illinois legislation are in Buck, *Granger Movement*, supra note 120, at 84–85, 123–58.

156. "The Grangers and the Judges," *Nation*, June 12, 1873, at 397.

157. See Michael G. Collins, "The Unhappy History of Federal Question Removal," *Iowa L. Rev.* 71 (1986): 739; Gillman, "How Political Parties Can Use the Courts," supra note 152, at 519; Purcell, *Litigation and Inequality*, supra note 106, at 22–27. The federal bench, most of which were pro-business Republicans, shared an ideology in favor of a national economy with the corporations. Gillman, "How Political Parties Can Use the Courts," supra note 152, at 519.

158. Harry N. Scheiber, "Federalism and the American Economic Order, 1789–1910," *L. & Soc. Rev.* 10 (1975): 116.

159. "Current Topics," *Cent. L. J.* 18 (1884): 281.

160. William H. Taft, "Criticisms of the Federal Judiciary," *Am. L. Rev.* 29 (1895): 651.

161. Munn v. Illinois, 94 U.S. 113 (1876).

162. Munn v. People, 69 Ill. 80 (1873).

163. "The Granger Collapse," *Nation*, Jan. 27, 1876, at 57.

164. *Munn*, 94 U.S. at 118–19.

165. *Slaughterhouse Cases*, 83 U.S. at 81.

166. *Slaughterhouse Cases*, 83 U.S. at 87 (Field, J., dissenting).

167. *Munn*, 94 U.S. at 126.

168. *Munn*, 94 U.S. at 141 (Field, J., dissenting).

169. "The Granger Laws," *Chi. Trib.*, March 13, 1877.

170. James Bryce, *The American Commonwealth*, vol. 1, *The National Government—The State Governments* (1914), 274.

171. *Munn*, 94 U.S. at 123, 132–33, 134.

172. Charles C. Marshall, "A New Constitutional Amendment," *Am. L. Rev.* 24 (1890): 931.

173. Pomeroy, "Supreme Court," supra note 142, at 712.

174. "Legislation and Credit," *N.Y. Times*, March 29, 1877, at 4.

175. See Bensel, *Political Economy of American Industrialization*, supra note 105, at xvii, 101–02; Robert D. Marcus, *Grand Old Party: Political Structure in the Gilded Age, 1880–1896* (1971), 5–6. Turnout approached 80 percent in presidential elections from 1876 to 1896. Marcus, *Grand Old Party*, supra, at 5.

176. See generally Silbey, *American Political Nation*, supra note 144.

177. Id. at 157, 211, 219.

178. Matthew Josephson, *The Politicos: 1865–1896* (1938), 422–26.

179. Marcus, *Grand Old Party*, supra note 175, at 50.

180. Pomeroy, "Supreme Court," supra note 142, at 693.

181. Ballam, "Evolution of the Government-Business Relationship," supra note 105, at 596–97. See also Bensel, *Yankee Leviathan*, supra note 90, at 348–65; Morton Keller, *Affairs of State: Public Life in Late Nineteenth Century America* (1977), 85, 161.

182. See Bensel, *Political Economy of American Industrialization*, supra note 105, at xx, 7, 10, 117; Gillman, "How Political Parties Can Use the Courts," supra note 152, at 516; see also Stephen Holmes, *Passions and Constraint: On the Theory of Liberal Democracy* (1995), 165 (discussing Bodin's argument that "if the king exacts penalties personally, he will arouse resentments that will, in turn, weaken his authority"; thus "a clever sovereign" will delegate "to independent magistrates the job of issuing condemnations").

183. See Bensel, *Political Economy of American Industrialization*, supra note 105, at 8–9, 457; Mary R. Dearing, *Veterans in Politics: The Story of the G.A.R.* (1952), vii.

184. The figure appears on the softbound cover of Bensel, *Political Economy of American Industrialization*, supra note 105, attributed to *Judges Mag.*, June 30, 1888; see generally Bensel, *Political Economy of American Industrialization*, supra note 105, at 514.

185. See id., at 515; Mendelson, *Capitalism, Democracy*, supra note 111, at 55–58. The tariff was used to subsidize side payments to farmers and pensions for war veterans. See Bensel, *Political Economy of American Industrialization*, supra note 105, at 8–9; Gillman, "How Political Parties Can Use the Courts," supra note 152, at 516.

186. Bensel, *Political Economy of American Industrialization*, supra note 105, at 7.

187. Letter from Charles Elliot Perkins to J. M. Forbes, Feb. 21, 1894, quoted in Kirkland, *Dream and Thought*, supra note 118, at 135.

188. "Current Topics," supra note 159, at 281.
189. See Kirkland, *Dream and Thought*, supra note 118, at 135; Marcus, *Grand Old Party*, supra note 175, at 50–53, 153, 256–57; Freyer, "Federal Courts," supra note 127, at 345.
190. Letter from Whitelaw Reid to James A. Garfield, Aug. 31, 1880, quoted in Marcus, *Grand Old Party*, supra note 175, at 50; Letter from James A. Garfield to Whitelaw Reid, Sept. 23, 1880, quoted in Marcus, *Grand Old Party*, supra note 175, at 53.
191. See Warren, *Supreme Court*, supra note 51, at 3:344.
192. On Matthews's appointment and confirmation, see Warren, *Supreme Court*, supra note 51, at 3:344. Anti-Monopoly League quote from "The Anti-Monopoly League," *Wash. Post*, May 15, 1881, at 1. James Weaver quote from James Weaver, *A Call to Action*, selections reprinted in *The Populist Mind*, ed. Norman Pollack (1967), 127. Board of Trade quoted in "Opposed to Stanley Matthews," *N.Y. Times*, Feb. 8, 1881, at 1.
193. This is a central thesis of Gillman, "How Political Parties Can Use the Courts," supra note 152.
194. "The President and the Judiciary," *Nation*, Apr. 23, 1885, at 337.
195. Pomeroy, "Supreme Court," supra note 142, at 688.
196. Bensel, *Political Economy of American Industrialization*, supra note 105, at 344–46; Gillman, "How Political Parties Can Use the Courts," supra note 152, at 517–18. President Cleveland appointed Justices Lucius Q. Lamar, Melville Fuller, Edward White, and Rufus Peckham. Bensel, *Political Economy of American Industrialization*, supra note 105, at 345.
197. "Current Topics," supra note 159, at 282.
198. See Warren, *Supreme Court*, supra note 51, at 3:347 (noting that in 1880 the Court began a "distinctly Nationalistic era"); Gillman, "How Political Parties Can Use the Courts," supra note 152, at 518 (detailing the pro-business leanings of the men appointed from 1870 to 1893); Freyer, *Forums of Order*, supra note 143, at 108 (same); Bensel, *Political Economy of American Industrialization*, supra note 105, at 344–47 (same).
199. See Gillman, "How Political Parties Can Use the Courts," supra note 152, at 516 (pointing to the Republican Party's waning interest in protecting civil rights and increasing desire to nationalize the economy).
200. Fred Perry Powers, "Recent Centralizing Tendencies in the Supreme Court," *Pol. Sci. Q.* 5 (1890): 397.
201. The constitutional doctrines of substantive due process, Robert G. McCloskey, *The American Supreme Court*, 2d ed. (1994), 88; Lawrence Friedman, *A History of American Law*, 2d ed. (1985), 521; unconstitutional conditions and the Commerce Clause, Freyer, "Federal Courts," supra note 127, at 352; protected business from state legislation, as did the "general commercial law" that developed after *Swift v. Tyson*, Freyer, "Federal Courts," supra note 127, at 351–52.
202. Prentice and Egan, *Commerce Clause of the Federal Constitution*, supra note 136, at 15.
203. Wabash, St. Louis, & Pac. Ry. Co. v. Illinois, 118 U.S. 557, 571–72 (1886) ("While it [the law regulating railroad rates] purports only to control the carrier when engaged within the state, it must necessarily influence his conduct to some extent in the management of his business through his entire voyage"). The Commerce Clause claim had been a sidelight in *Munn* but had come out the opposite way. Munn v. Illinois, 94 U.S. 113, 135 (1876) (". . . the State may exercise all the powers of government over them [plaintiff's warehouses], even though in so doing it may indirectly operate upon commerce outside its immediate jurisdiction"). Justice Miller, who wrote for the Court in the *Wabash* case, explained away the prior contrary holding by saying the Court simply had not really given the issue sufficient attention. Noting as well the change of mem-

bership on the Court since *Munn*, Miller apologized for the apparent shift, saying he was "prepared to take his share of the responsibility for the language used in [the prior] opinions." *Wabash*, 118 U.S. at 568, 575.

204. "The Week," *Nation*, Oct. 28, 1886, at 339.

205. Chicago, Minneapolis, & St. Paul Ry. Co. v. Minnesota ex rel. R.R. and Warehouse Comm., 134 U.S. 418, 458 (1890).

206. Id. at 462.

207. *Com. & Fin. Chron.*, March 29, 1890, quoted in Bensel, *Political Economy of American Industrialization*, supra note 105, at 335.

208. See Swift v. Tyson, 41 U.S. 1 (1842); Freyer, *Harmony & Dissonance*, supra note 109, at xiii.

209. J. B. Heiskell, "Conflict Between Federal and State Decisions," *Am. L. Rev.* 16 (1882): 759. The *Swift* doctrine gave rise to the highly criticized practice of "forum shopping" by which out-of-state litigants chose to sue in state or federal court depending on which forum's law benefited them, a luxury in-state citizens did not have. Freyer, *Forums of Order*, supra note 143, at 121; see also William B. Hornblower, "Conflict Between Federal and State Decisions," *Am. L. Rev.* 14 (1880): 223 ("What is to be said of a civilized society where, upon precisely the same state of facts, a court on one side of the street will decide in favor of plaintiff, and a court on the other side of the street will decide in favor of defendant?"). The decision also created much uncertainty, for one would be unable to predict what principle of general commercial law a federal judge would choose to apply in a given case. See Hornblower, "Conflict Between Federal and State," supra, at 223. Finally, it was seen as an encroachment on states' rights. See, e.g., Hornblower, "Conflict Between Federal and State," supra, at 224 ("[I]t is *contrary to the spirit of the Constitution.* . . . It necessarily *subverts the true relations of the State and the general government*") (emphasis in original).

210. Compare *Slaughterhouse Cases*, 83 U.S. at 66 ("If any such restraint is supposed to exist in the constitution of the State, the Supreme Court of Louisiana having necessarily passed on that question, it would not be open to review in this court"); see Michael G. Collins, "Before *Lochner*—Diversity Jurisdiction and the Development of General Constitutional Law," *Tul L. Rev.* 74 (2000): 1265.

211. Gelpcke v. City of Dubuque, 68 U.S. 175, 206 (1863).

212. William M. Meigs, "Decisions of the Federal Courts on Questions of State Law," *S. L. Rev.* 8 (1882–1883): 478. Some charged that the judges who decided the case "were guilty of a plain usurpation." William J. Stone, "Notes," *Am. L. Rev.* 27 (1893): 396.

213. Benjamin Curtis, "Notice of the Death of Chief Justice Taney, Proceedings in Circuit Court of the United States for the First Circuit," quoted in Felix Frankfurter and James M. Landis, *The Business of the Supreme Court: A Study in the Federal Judicial System* (1927), 2.

214. Benjamin Robbins Curtis, *Jurisdiction, Practice, and Peculiar Jurisprudence of the Courts of the United States* (1880), 1.

215. Holt, *Concurrent Jurisdiction*, supra note 27, at 1.

216. 2 Cong. Rec. 4303 (1874), quoted in Frankfurter and Landis, *Business of the Supreme Court*, supra note 213, at 67.

217. See Gillman, "How Political Parties Can Use the Courts," supra note 152, at 516–17 ("[T]he main purpose of the Judiciary and Removal Act of 1875 was to redirect civil litigation involving national commercial interests out of state courts and into the federal judiciary"); Stanley I. Kutler, *Judicial Power and Reconstruction Politics* (1968), 157 ("It is clear that the removal legislation involved something more than countering southern obstructionism"); Frankfurter and Landis, *Business of the Supreme Court*,

supra note 216, at 64–65 ("The clash of economic interests in the North, the risks to which absentee capital was exposed in the state legislation of the Granger Movement, furnished new occasions for federal protection against adverse state action").

218. Kutler, *Judicial Power*, supra note 217, at 157.

219. Id. at 154–55.

220. Id. at 156n22, 157.

221. 2 Cong. Rec. 4986 (1874).

222. Santa Clara Co. v. S. Pac. Ry. Co., 118 U.S. 394 (1886); see Ballam, "Evolution of the Government-Business Relationship," supra note 105, at 607; Corwin, "Supreme Court," supra note 25, at 664.

223. *Santa Clara*, 118 U.S. at 396; see also Corwin, "Supreme Court," supra note 25, at 664 (noting that the Chief Justice told counsel during oral argument that the justices had already decided the issue); Arthur Selwyn Miller, *The Supreme Court and American Capitalism* (1968), 54 (same).

224. See Friedman, *A History of American Law*, supra note 201, at 521; see also Ballam, "Evolution of the Government-Business Relationship," supra note 105, at 607.

225. Strawbridge v. Curtis, 7 U.S. 267 (1806).

226. Marshall v. Baltimore & Ohio R.R. Co., 57 U.S. 314, 328 (1853); Louisville, Cincinnati & Charleston R.R. Co. v. Letson, 43 U.S. 497 (1844).

227. Curtis, *Jurisdiction, Practice, and Peculiar Jurisprudence*, supra note 214, at 130.

228. Holt, *Concurrent Jurisdiction*, supra note 27, at 110 (emphasis added); see also Purcell, *Litigation and Inequality*, supra note 106, at 17–18; Freyer, "Federal Courts," supra note 127, at 354.

229. One especially grating aspect of removal involved federal charters. In the *Pacific Railroad Removal Cases*, the Court held that any suit involving a federally chartered corporation—this included most railroads—could be brought in federal court or removed there from the state courts, 115 U.S. 1, 11 (1885); see also *Hart and Wechsler's The Federal Courts and the Federal System*, ed. Richard Fallon et al., 5th ed. (2003), 858; Kutler, *Judicial Power*, supra note 217, at 157; Frankfurter and Landis, *Business of the Supreme Court*, supra note 216, at 69.

230. John Wilder May, *The Law of Insurance, as Applied to Fire, Life, Accident, Guarantee, and Other Non-Maritime Risks* (1882), 886, quoted in Purcell, *Litigation and Inequality*, supra note 106, at 20–21.

231. John Dillon, "Removal of Causes," *S. L. Rev.* 2 (1876–1877): 284.

232. Frankfurter and Landis, *Business of the Supreme Court*, supra note 216, at 60.

233. "The Federal Judiciary," *Wash. Post*, Feb. 5, 1878, at 1.

234. "Book Notices," *Am. L. Rev.* 15 (1881): 271; Meigs, "Decisions of the Federal Courts," supra note 212, at 490.

235. "The Supreme Court," *Am. L. Rev.* 9 (1874–1875): 668; see also Collins, "Unhappy History," supra note 157, at 738 (noting expansion in federal court dockets in the last quarter of the nineteenth century); Gillman, "How Political Parties Can Use the Courts," supra note 152, at 520 (same).

236. Collins, "Unhappy History," supra note 157, at 738–41 (noting the jurisdictional amount increase, elimination of the right of removal, and treatment of corporations as citizens); Freyer, "Federal Courts," supra note 127, at 357–58 (same); Scheiber, "Federalism, the Southern Regional Economy," in Bodenhamer and Ely, *Ambivalent Legacy*, supra note 127, at 75 (describing failed attempts at passing Culberson's bill); Frankfurter and Landis, *Business of the Supreme Court*, supra note 216, at 90, 136 (same). Most corporations got to federal court through diversity of citizenship; treating corporations as citizens of the states in which they did business would have eradi-

cated this option. Freyer, "Federal Courts," supra note 127, at 357; Gillman, "How Political Parties Can Use the Courts," supra note 152, at 517 (actions of Senate).

237. Collins, "Unhappy History," supra note 157, at 739.

238. "Federal Judiciary," supra note 233, at 1.

239. "Current Topics," supra note 159, at 282.

240. 10 Cong. Rec. 817 (1880) (statement of Rep. McMillin), quoted in Scheiber, "Federalism, the Southern Regional Economy," in Bodenhamer and Ely, *Ambivalent Legacy*, supra note 127, at 75.

241. 10 Cong. Rec. 725 (1880) (statement of Rep. Weaver); 10 Cong. Rec. 1015 (1880) (statement of Rep. Waddill).

242. 15 Cong. Rec. 2917 (1884).

243. 10 Cong. Rec. 702 (1880) (statement of Rep. Culberson).

244. See 10 Cong. Rec. 993 (1880) (statement of Rep. Hurd); 10 Cong. Rec. 724 (1880) (statement of Rep. Weaver)

245. See, e.g., Powers, "Recent Centralizing Tendencies," supra note 200, at 402; see also 10 Cong. Rec. 724 (1880) (statement of Rep. Weaver) ("Litigants . . . often yield to the grossest injustice rather than incur the expense and inconvenience of attending court at remote points from their homes").

246. See Purcell, *Litigation and Inequality*, supra note 106, at 90–91.

247. "Federal Judiciary," supra note 233, at 2.

248. Collins, "Unhappy History," supra note 157, at 741–42; Gillman, "How Political Parties Can Use the Courts," supra note 152, at 517; Purcell, *Litigation and Inequality*, supra note 106, at 15. The Senate agreed to the elimination of plaintiff removal, Collins, "Unhappy History," supra note 157, at 741, and a decrease in the time allowed to file a removal petition, Gillman, "How Political Parties Can Use the Courts," supra note 152, at 517.

249. 18 Cong. Rec. 2544 (1880) (statement of Sen. Edmunds).

250. *Railway & Corp. L. J.* 2 (Nov. 1887): 456.

251. At the time the bill passed, Republicans had regained control of the House. Gillman, "How Political Parties Can Use the Courts," supra note 152, at 520. The bill was named after its chief sponsor in the Senate, William Evarts, who had led the fight against restructuring in 1882 but was a convert by 1890. As a private practitioner, he represented mostly railroads and other large commercial interests. See Frankfurter and Landis, *Business of the Supreme Court*, supra note 216, at 98–99; Gillman, "How Political Parties Can Use the Courts," supra note 152, at 520.

252. Gillman, "How Political Parties Can Use the Courts," supra note 152, at 521.

253. Id.

254. Frankfurter and Landis, *Business of the Supreme Court*, supra note 216, at 101–02; Gillman, "How Political Parties Can Use the Courts," supra note 152, at 521.

Chapter 6: Law v. Will

1. Lochner v. New York, 198 U.S. 45 (1905). See Owen M. Fiss, *Troubled Beginnings of the Modern State, 1888–1910* (1993), 4 (describing *Lochner* as "[t]he most notorious decision of" the twentieth century's first decade).

2. William G. Ross, *A Muted Fury: Populists, Progressives, and Labor Unions Confront the Courts, 1890–1937* (1994), 130–31.

3. Theodore Roosevelt, "Nationalism and the Judiciary," pt. 4, *Outlook*, March 18, 1911, at 574.

4. Theodore Roosevelt, "Judges and Progress," *Outlook*, Jan. 6, 1912, at 41.

5. Id.

6. Ross, *A Muted Fury*, supra note 2, at 135–36.

7. Editorial, "The Supreme Court and Partisan Passion," *N.Y. Times*, May 31, 1923, at 14.

8. Am. Fed'n of Labor Executive Council, "Election Circular," Oct. 12, 1908, quoted in Christopher L. Tomlins, *The State and the Unions: Labor Relations, Law, and the Organized Labor Movement in America, 1880–1960* (1985), 66.

9. Theodore Roosevelt, "Nationalism and the Judiciary," pt. 3, *Outlook*, March 11, 1911, at 534.

10. The revisionist movement has attracted scholars from across the ideological spectrum. Conservatives advance revisionist claims, apparently favoring a revitalization of the laissez-faire approach of the *Lochner*-era judges. See, e.g., David E. Bernstein, "*Lochner v. New York*: A Centennial Retrospective," *Wash. U. L.Q.* 83 (2005): 1469; Richard A. Epstein, "The Mistakes of 1937," *Geo. Mason U. L. Rev.*, Winter 1988: 5; Bernard H. Siegan, "Rehabilitating *Lochner*," *San Diego L. Rev.* 22 (1985): 453. Liberals seek to encourage judges to greater judicial activism. See, e.g., Fiss, *Troubled Beginnings*, supra note 1; Rebecca L. Brown, "The Fragmented Liberty Clause," *Wm. & Mary L. Rev.* 41 (1999): 65. Some of the revisionist literature, largely from historians and political scientists, seems less clearly ideological, seeking instead a recovery of what it describes as a lost past. See, e.g., Howard Gillman, *The Constitution Besieged: The Rise and Demise of* Lochner *Era Police Powers Jurisprudence* (1993), 205; Julie Novkov, *Constituting Workers, Protecting Women: Gender, Law, and Labor in the Progressive Era and New Deal Years* (2001); Felice Batlan, "A Reevaluation of the New York Court of Appeals: The Home, the Market, and Labor, 1885–1905," *Law & Soc. Inq.* 27 (2002): 489; Michael Les Benedict, "Laissez-Faire and Liberty: A Re-evaluation of the Meaning and Origins of Laissez-Faire Constitutionalism," *Law & Hist. Rev.* 3 (1985): 293; Charles W. McCurdy, "The Roots of 'Liberty of Contract' Reconsidered: Major Premises in the Law of Employment, 1867–1937," *Sup. Ct. Hist. Soc. Y. B.*, 1984: 20. On revisionism generally, see Gary D. Rowe, "*Lochner* Revisionism Revisited," *L. & Soc. Inquiry* 24 (1999): 221.

11. Oliver Wendell Holmes, Jr., *The Common Law* (1881), 1.

12. See generally David Brody, *Workers in Industrial America: Essays on the Twentieth Century Struggle* (1980), 3–21; Samuel P. Hays, *The Response to Industrialism, 1885–1914*, 2d ed. (1995), 47–68; Richard Hofstadter, *The Age of Reform* (1955), 174–78; John Fabien Witt, *The Accidental Republic: Crippled Workingmen, Destitute Widows, and the Remaking of American Law* (2004), 22–42. There is the argument that conditions in the United States still were better than those left behind or that the hope was of a better life for future generations. Still, working conditions clearly led to serious discontent.

13. James B. Weaver, *A Call to Action* (1892; repr. 1974), 298.

14. Id. at 364.

15. Muller v. Oregon, 208 U.S. 412 (1908).

16. See *N.Y. Times*, Feb. 25, 1908, at 1, discussed in Nancy S. Erickson, "Historical Background of 'Protective' Labor Legislation: *Muller v. Oregon*," in *Property, Family and the Legal Profession*, vol. 2, *Women and the Law: A Social Historical Perspective*, ed. D. Kelly Weisberg (1982), 164.

17. There is, to say the least, an extensive literature on Populism, its antecedents, and its legacy. See John D. Hicks, *The Populist Revolt* (1931; repr. 1981); Randall G. Holcombe, *From Liberty to Democracy* (2002); Robert C. MacMath, *American Populism: A Social History, 1877–1893* (1995); Gretchen Ritter, *Goldbugs and Greenbacks: The Antimonopoly Tradition and the Politics of Finance in America, 1865–1896* (1999); Elizabeth Sanders, *Roots of Reform: Farmers, Workers, and the American State, 1877–1917* (1999).

18. Leon Fink, *Workingmen's Democracy: The Knights of Labor and American Politics* (1983), xii, 18–20; William E. Forbath, *Law and the Shaping of the American Labor Movement* (1991), 13–14; Julie Greene, *Pure and Simple Politics: The American Federation of Labor and Political Activism, 1881–1917* (1998), 31; Leon Fink, "Labor, Liberty, and the Law: Trade Unionism and the Problem of the American Constitutional Order," *J. Am. Hist.* 74 (1987): 912.

19. Fiss, *Troubled Beginnings*, supra note 1, at 39–40; Lawrence Goodwyn, *Democratic Promise: The Populist Moment in America* (1976), 344; Sidney Ratner, *American Taxation: Its History as a Social Force in Democracy* (1942), 164–67; Robert H. Wiebe, *Self-Rule: A Cultural History of American Democracy* (1995), 122–24; see generally Goodwyn, *Democratic Promise*, supra. A succinct and powerful source on the relationship between populists and Supreme Court decisions is Alan Furman Westin, "The Supreme Court, the Populist Movement and the Campaign of 1896," *J. Pol.* 15 (1953): 3.

20. Ray Allen Billington, *Westward Expansion: A History of the American Frontier*, 2d ed. (1960), 743 (quoting Populist Manifesto).

21. Hays, *Response to Industrialism*, supra note 12, at 95–96; Hofstadter, *Age of Reform*, supra note 12, at 131–35, 139–40; Arthur S. Link and Richard L. McCormick, *Progressivism* (1983), 19. A nice review essay on the literature on Progressivism is Daniel T. Rodgers, "In Search of Progressivism," *Rev. Am. Hist.* 10 (1982): 113.

22. Loren P. Beth, *The Development of the American Constitution, 1877–1917* (1971), 90; Hofstadter, *Age of Reform*, supra note 12, at 134, 241–42. On the uneasy relationship between progressives and immigrants, see also Leonard Dinnerstein, *Anti-Semitism in America* (1994), 58–60; Sanders, *Roots of Reform*, supra note 17, at 350.

23. William F. Willoughby, "The Philosophy of Labor Legislation: Presidential Address, American Association for Labor Legislation," *Am. Pol. Sci. Rev.* 8 (1914): 20.

24. See U.S. Const. amend. XVII; Peter H. Argersinger, *Populism and Politics: William Alfred Peffer and the People's Party* (1974), 29, 30, 35, 41, 112, 127; Link and McCormick, *Progressivism*, supra note 21, at 28, 34, 50, 51, 60; Robert H. Wiebe, *The Search for Order: 1877–1920* (1967), 122, 163.

25. Nicholas Murray Butler, *Why Should We Change Our Form of Government?: Studies in Practical Politics* (1912), 5.

26. Elihu Root, "Judicial Decisions and Public Feeling: Address to the New York State Bar Association," Jan. 19, 1912, in *Elihu Root, Addresses on Government and Citizenship*, ed. Robert Bacon and James Brown Scott (1916), 448.

27. See Ratner, *American Taxation*, supra note 19, at 164–67, 172, 178–80, 188; Hicks, *Populist Revolt*, supra note 17, at 443 (reproducing July 1892 Omaha Platform of the People's Party of America, including the "demand [for] a graduated income tax").

28. Gilbert E. Roe, *Our Judicial Oligarchy* (1912), 182–83.

29. Theodore Roosevelt, "A Charter of Democracy: Address to the Ohio Constitutional Convention," *Outlook*, Feb. 24, 1912, at 395.

30. Forbath, *Law and the Shaping*, supra note 18, at 43–44.

31. Link and McCormick, *Progressivism*, supra note 21, at 76, 78.

32. Id. at 80.

33. Henry B. Brown, "The Distribution of Property," *Am. L. Rev.* 27 (1893): 656–57.

34. William H. Taft, "The Right of Private Property," *Mich. L. J.* 3 (1894): 222–23.

35. Brown, "Distribution of Property," supra note 33, at 662–63.

36. See Arnold M. Paul, *Conservative Crisis and the Rule of Law: Attitudes of the Bar and Bench, 1887–1895* (1976), 132–42. On the strike, see David Ray Papke, *The Pullman Case* (1999), 17–19. In part, those like Brown and Taft believed that what was good for the industrialists was also good for the workers—that is, that a rising tide lifts all

boats. See, e.g., Brown, "Distribution of Property," supra note 33, at 662; Taft, "Right of Private Property," supra note 34, at 223.

37. John F. Dillon, "Property—Its Rights and Duties in Our Legal and Social Systems," *Am. L. Rev.* 29 (1895): 163. For an examination of Dillon's speech and his general politics, see Paul, *Conservative Crisis and the Rule of Law*, supra note 36, at 78–79.

38. Butler, *Why Should We Change Our Form of Government?*, supra note 25, at 4.

39. Letter from William Howard Taft, Chief Justice of the United States, to Horace Taft, Nov. 14, 1929, quoted in Henry F. Pringle, *The Life and Times of William Howard Taft* (1964), 2:967.

40. Justice Brewer on "The Nation's Anchor," *Alb. L. J.* 57 (1898): 167; see also "Lincoln Day in Chicago," *N.Y. Times*, Feb. 13, 1898, at 1.

41. George Sutherland, "Private Rights and Government Control: Address of the President, American Bar Association Annual Address," Sept. 4, 1917, in Am. Bar Ass'n, *Report of the Fortieth Annual Meeting of the American Bar Association* (1917), 203.

42. Dillon, "Property—Its Rights and Duties," supra note 37, at 188.

43. "A Century Old To-Day! New York's Splendid Celebration of the United States Judiciary," *N.Y. Mail and Express*, Feb. 4, 1890, quoted in Gillman, *Constitution Besieged*, supra note 10, at 99.

44. On prevailing laissez-faire ideology, see Beth, *Development of the American Constitution*, supra note 22, at 42; Les Benedict, "Laissez-Faire and Liberty," supra note 10, at 303–04.

45. Butler, *Why Should We Change Our Form of Government?*, supra note 25, at xi.

46. Christopher G. Tiedeman, *A Treatise on the Limitations of Police Power in the United States: Considered from Both a Civil and Criminal Standpoint* (1886; repr. 2001), vi.

47. Brown, "Distribution of Property," supra note 33, at 661.

48. John F. Dillon, "Address of the President, American Bar Association Annual Address," Aug. 24, 1892, in Am. Bar Ass'n, *Report of the Fifteenth Annual Meeting of the American Bar Association* (1892), 211.

49. "A Century Old To-Day! New York's Splendid Celebration of the United States Judiciary," *N.Y. Mail and Express*, Feb. 4, 1890, quoted in Gillman, *Constitution Besieged*, supra note 10, at 99.

50. Junius Parker, "The Supreme Court and Its Constitutional Duty and Power," *Am. L. Rev.* 30 (1896): 362.

51. George Sutherland, "The Courts and the Constitution: Address Before the American Bar Association," Aug. 28, 1912, quoted in Samuel R. Olken, "Justice George Sutherland and Economic Liberty: Constitutional Conservatism and the Problem of Factions," *Wm. & Mary Bill Rts. J.* 6 (1997): 54.

52. Christopher G. Tiedeman, *The Unwritten Constitution of the United States: A Philosophical Inquiry into the Fundamentals of American Constitutional Law* (1890; repr. 1974), 163.

53. 47 Cong. Rec. 2793, 2800 (1911) (statement of Sen. Sutherland).

54. Editorial, "The Income Tax Invalid," *N.Y. Daily Trib.*, May 21, 1895, at 6.

55. Tiedeman, *Unwritten Constitution of the United States*, supra note 52, at 163.

56. George W. Alger, *The Old Law and the New Order* (1913), 36. For an engaging doctrinal account of the Supreme Court of the United States' decisions during the *Lochner* era, see John E. Semonche, *Charting the Future: The Supreme Court Responds to a Changing Society, 1890–1920* (1978).

57. See In re Jacobs, 98 N.Y. 98 (1885). The law struck down by the case had provided: "The manufacture of cigars or preparation of tobacco in any form on any floor, or in any part of any floor in any tenement-house is hereby prohibited if such floor or any part of such floor is by any person occupied as a home or residence for the purpose

of living, sleeping, cooking or doing any household work therein." Act of May 12, 1884, ch. 272, sec. 1, 1884 N.Y. Laws 335.

58. William J. Gaynor, "Do Our Courts Stand in the Way of Social and Economic Progress?," *Bench & Bar* 28 (1912): 102–03.

59. *In re Jacobs*, 98 N.Y. at 105, 113. For a detailed treatment of the tenement cigarmaking industry, see Eileen Boris, *Home to Work: Motherhood and the Politics of Industrial Homework in the United States* (1994).

60. "Constitutional Law: Police Regulations for the Protection of Laborers," *Am. L. Rev.* 24 (1890): 328.

61. Godcharles v. Wigeman, 6 A. 354, 356 (Pa. 1886).

62. Pollock v. Farmers' Loan & Trust Co., 157 U.S. 429 (1895), modified on reh'g 158 U.S. 601 (1895).

63. In re Debs, 158 U.S. 564 (1895).

64. United States v. E. C. Knight Co., 156 U.S. 1, 12 (1895) (stating that "[t]he power to regulate commerce is the power to prescribe the rule by which commerce shall be governed, and is a power independent of the power to suppress monopoly").

65. *Pollock*, 157 U.S. at 434n1, modified on reh'g 158 U.S. 601 (1895). See Eric Kades, "Drawing the Line Between Taxes and Takings: The Continuous Burdens Principle, and Its Broader Application," *Nw. U. L. Rev.* 97 (2002): 210–11 (estimating the percentage of Americans taxed by the measure at 0.13 percent; Erik M. Jensen, "The Taxing Power, the Sixteenth Amendment, and the Meaning of 'Incomes,'" *Ariz. St. L. J.* 33 (2001): 107n64 (citing the number of households that earned more than four thousand dollars annually at "well under 1 percent").

66. *Pollock*, 157 U.S. at 531–32, modified on reh'g 158 U.S. 601 (1895) (oral argument by James C. Carter for appellee Continental Trust Company).

67. Id. at 532 (oral argument by Joseph Choate for appellant Pollock).

68. Id. at 553.

69. On the wartime income tax, see Michigan Cent. R.R. Co. v. Slack, 100 U.S. 595 (1879). The U.S. Constitution defines a "Capitation" tax as a direct tax. U.S. Const. art. I, § 2, cl. 3. On capitation taxes, see also Fiss, *Troubled Beginnings*, supra note 1, at 87–88 ("All the justices subscribed to the notion that a tax on real estate was a direct tax"); Ratner, *American Taxation*, supra note 19, at 196–97.

70. *Pollock*, 157 U.S. at 607, modified on reh'g 158 U.S. 601 (1895) (Field, J., concurring).

71. Editorial, "The Last of the Income Tax," *Wash. Post*, May 21, 1895, at 6.

72. Editorial, "The Supreme Court's 'Coach-and-Six,'" *N.Y. Times*, Apr. 9, 1895, at 4; "Income Tax Invalid," supra note 54, at 6.

73. Editorial, "The Income Tax Decision," *Nation*, May 23, 1895, at 394.

74. "Hill Highly Pleased," *Wash. Post*, May 21, 1895, at 1.

75. *Lochner*, 198 U.S. at 45. See Gillman, *Constitution Besieged*, supra note 10, at 1.

76. *Lochner*, 198 U.S. at 58–59 ("There is, in our judgment, no reasonable foundation for holding this to be necessary or appropriate as a health law to safeguard the public health, or the health of the individuals who are following the trade of a baker. . . . We think that there can be no fair doubt that the trade of a baker, in and of itself, is not an unhealthy one to that degree which would authorize the legislature to interfere with the right to labor").

77. See Epstein, "Mistakes of 1937," supra note 10, at 17; Sidney G. Tarrow, "Lochner versus New York: A Political Analysis," *Labor Hist.* 5 (1964): 280–90; see also Barry Friedman, "The History of the Countermajoritarian Difficulty, Part Three: The Lesson of *Lochner*," *N.Y.U. L. Rev.* 76 (2001): 1416–18. Bernstein joins other revisionists in arguing the law invalidated in *Lochner* was motivated by concern about nonunion shops, Bernstein, "Centennial Retrospective," supra note 10, at 1476–86,

but acknowledges the public concerns that ensured the bill's passage, Bernstein, "Centennial Retrospective," supra note 10, at 1479–81.

78. See Paul Kens, *Judicial Power and Reform Politics: The Anatomy of* Lochner v. New York (1990), 51–52 (quoting Edward Marshall, "Bread and Filth Cooked Together," *N.Y. Press*, Sept. 30, 1894, § 4, at 1); accord Batlan, "A Reevaluation of the New York Court of Appeals," supra note 10, at 521–22; Bernstein, "Centennial Retrospective," supra note 10, at 1479–81 (acknowledging public concerns that ensured bill's passage).

79. See Kens, *Judicial Power and Reform Politics*, supra note 78, at 57–59.

80. People v. Lochner, 69 N.E. 373, 382 (N.Y. 1904) (Vann, J., concurring), rev'd, Lochner v. New York, 198 U.S. 45 (1905).

81. "Labor Not Restricted; Contracts Inviolable," *N.Y. Trib.*, Apr. 18, 1905, at 1; see also "Bakery Law Invalid," *Wash. Post*, Apr. 18, 1905, at 1 (describing decision as "based on the ground that the law interferes with the free exercise of the rights of contract between individuals").

82. Editorial, "A Check to Union Tyranny," *Nation*, May 4, 1905, at 346–47.

83. Editorial, "Fussy Legislation," *N.Y. Times*, Apr. 19, 1905, at 10.

84. Editorial, "The Ten Hour Decision," *N.Y. Trib.*, Apr. 19, 1905, at 4.

85. Editorial, "A Notable Opinion," *N.Y. Trib.*, Apr. 23, 1905, at 8.

86. Adair v. United States, 208 U.S. 161 (1908); "Can Discharge Man for Joining Union," *N.Y. Times*, Jan. 28, 1908, at 1.

87. "States' Rights vs. the Nation," *New Republic*, June 15, 1918, at 194; see Hammer v. Dagenhart, 247 U.S. 251 (1918).

88. "Child Labor Law Upset by Court," *N.Y. Times*, June 4, 1918, at 14.

89. See, e.g., Duplex Printing Press Co. v. Deering, 254 U.S. 443 (1921); Truax v. Corrigan, 257 U.S. 312 (1921); see generally Forbath, *Law and the Shaping*, supra note 18, at 157–58; Ross, *A Muted Fury*, supra note 2, at 174–81.

90. Adkins v. Children's Hospital, 261 U.S. 525, 555–56 (1923).

91. See Editorial, "The 'Inalienable Right' to Starve," *Christian Sci. Monitor*, Apr. 11, 1923, at 20; Editorial, "The Minimum Wage Decision," *Wash. Post*, Apr. 10, 1923, at 6; Editorial, "A Merited Rebuke," *L.A. Times*, Apr. 19, 1923, § II, at 4; Thomas L. Stokes, "Plan Legislation to Limit Power Supreme Court," *Atlanta Const.*, Apr. 11, 1923, at 9.

92. "Minimum Wage Decision," supra note 91, at 6.

93. "Death of the Income Tax," *Literary Dig.*, June 1, 1895, at 6 (quoting *St. Louis Post-Dispatch*).

94. See Harry Barnard, *Eagle Forgotten: The Life of John Peter Altgeld* (1938), 338–39.

95. Walter Clark, "The Revision of the Constitution of the United States," *Am. L. Rev.* 32 (1898): 7.

96. See "Persons in the Foreground: The Nine Arbiters of American Destiny," *Current Lit.* 43 (1907): 500–01.

97. Democratic Party platform of 1896, in *National Party Platforms*, ed. Kirk H. Porter (1924), 184. For a narrative of the development of the platform, see Westin, "Campaign of 1896," supra note 19, at 3.

98. Democratic Party platform of 1896, in Porter, *National Party Platforms*, supra note 97, at 185.

99. See Ross, *A Muted Fury*, supra note 2, at 35–37; Westin, "Campaign of 1896," supra note 19, at 33–35.

100. Quoted in Westin, "Campaign of 1896," supra note 19, at 34.

101. See Matthew A. Crenson and Benjamin Ginsberg, *Presidential Power: Unchecked and Unbalanced* (2007), 117; Steven P. Reti, *Silver and Gold: The Political Economy of International Monetary Conferences, 1867–1892* (1998), 148–49; James L. Sundquist,

Dynamics of the Party System: Alignment and Realignment of Political Parties in the United States (1983), 156–57.

102. William M. Meigs, "Some Recent Attacks on the American Doctrine of Judicial Power," *Am. L. Rev.* 40 (1906): 642.
103. Walter Clark, "Is the Supreme Court Constitutional?," *Indep.*, Sept. 26, 1907, at 723.
104. Id. at 724.
105. William Trickett, "Judicial Dispensation from Congressional Statutes," *Am. L. Rev.* 41 (1907): 85 (emphasis in original).
106. Learned Hand, "Due Process of Law and the Eight-Hour Day," *Harv. L. Rev.* 21 (1908): 508.
107. William H. Taft, "Criticisms of the Federal Judiciary," *Am. L. Rev.* 29 (1985): 641.
108. John Henry Wigmore, "Roscoe Pound's St. Paul Address of 1906: The Spark That Kindled the White Flame of Progress," *J. Am. Jud. Soc.* 20 (1937): 177; see also N.E.H. Hull, *Roscoe Pound and Karl Llewellyn: Searching for an American Jurisprudence* (1997), 65.
109. Roscoe Pound, "The Causes of Popular Dissatisfaction with the Administration of Justice: Address Before the Annual Meeting of the American Bar Association," Aug. 29, 1906, in Am. Bar Ass'n, *Report of the Twenty-ninth Annual Meeting of the American Bar Association* (1906), 404, reprinted in *Am. Law.* 14 (1906): 447. For a detailed treatment of Pound, his background, and his controversial speech at the American Bar Association, see Barry Friedman, "Popular Dissatisfaction with the Administration of Justice: A Retrospective (and a Look Ahead)," *Ind. L. J.* 82 (2007): 1193–1214.
110. Theodore Roosevelt, "Eighth Annual Message," Dec. 8, 1908, in *The State of the Union Messages of the Presidents, 1790–1966*, ed. Fred L. Israel (1967), 3:2309.
111. See Roe, *Our Judicial Oligarchy*, supra note 28, at 7–10.
112. *E. C. Knight*, 156 U.S. at 43 (Harlan, J., dissenting).
113. Louis B. Boudin, "Government by Judiciary," *Pol. Sci. Q.* 26 (1911): 267; Louis B. Boudin, *Government by Judiciary* (1932).
114. Charles Grove Haines, *The American Doctrine of Judicial Supremacy* (1914).
115. Charles A. Beard, *An Economic Interpretation of the Constitution of the United States* (1913).
116. In re Jacobs, 98 N.Y. 98 (1885); Ives v. So. Buffalo Ry. Co., 201 N.Y. 271 (1911). Theodore Roosevelt, Introduction to William L. Ransom, *Majority Rule and the Judiciary: An Examination of Current Proposals for Constitutional Change Affecting the Relation of Courts to Legislation* (1912), 6.
117. "Speech of William Howard Taft Accepting the Republican Nomination for President of the United States," Aug. 1, 1912, S. Doc. No. 62–902 (1912), 10, 11.
118. Alger, *Old Law and the New Order*, supra note 56, at 33.
119. Ross, *A Muted Fury*, supra note 2, at 155–59; Gordon E. Sherman, "The Recent Constitutional Amendments," *Yale L. J.* 23 (1913): 129.
120. Four members of the majority (Fuller, Brewer, Peckham, and Brown) had retired by 1912 while only one dissenter (Harlan) had retired by that point. See, e.g., Louis M. Greeley, "The Changing Attitude of the Courts Towards Social Legislation," *Ill. L. Rev.* 5 (1910): 227; see also Fiss, *Troubled Beginnings*, supra note 1, at 36–37.
121. Hammer v. Dagenhart, 247 U.S. 251 (1918).
122. Quoted in "The Child-Labor Defeat," *Literary Dig.*, June 15, 1918, at 16.
123. Editorial, "The Political Function of the Supreme Court," *New Republic*, Jan. 25, 1922, at 236.
124. Thomas Reed Powell, "The Judiciality of Minimum-Wage Legislation," *Harv. L. Rev.* 37 (1924): 572.

125. "Radicals Rally Forces to Curb Supreme Court," *Chi. Daily Trib.*, Apr. 14, 1923, at 7.
126. See Symposium, "Shall We Curb the Supreme Court?," pt. 1, *Forum* 71 (1924): 561; Symposium, "Shall We Curb the Supreme Court?," pt. 2, *Forum* 71 (1924): 841; Symposium, "The Minimum Wage Decision—What Next?," *Survey* 50 (1923): 215.
127. "'Inalienable Right' to Starve," supra note 91, at 20.
128. "14,000 Pack Garden, Cheer La Follette in Attack on Court," *N.Y. Times*, Sept. 19, 1924, at 1; "Full Text of La Follette's Speech Attacking Supreme Court," *N.Y. Times*, Sept. 19, 1924, at 2.
129. "The Supreme Court Under Fire," *Current Opinion* 77 (1924): 556; accord "Our Supreme Court—Tyrant or Protector?," *Literary Dig.*, Sept. 20, 1924, at 12.
130. Albert W. Fox, "Cheer President's Speech as Blow at La Follette Group," *Wash. Post*, Sept. 7, 1924, at 1.
131. "Full Text of La Follette's Speech," supra note 128, at 2.
132. See Charles Warren, "The Progressiveness of the United States Supreme Court," *Colum. L. Rev.* 13 (1913): 294.
133. Charles Warren, *The Supreme Court in United States History* (Boston: Little, Brown and Company, 1922).
134. Warren, "Progressiveness of the United States Supreme Court," supra note 132, at 295. In addition to *Lochner*, Warren points to Connolly v. Union Sewer Pipe Co., 184 U.S. 540 (1902) and Allgeyer v. Louisiana, 165 U.S. 578 (1897). Id.
135. See, e.g., Brown, "Fragmented Liberty Clause," supra note 10, at 86–87; Barry Cushman, "Lost Fidelities," *Wm. & Mary L. Rev.* 41 (1999): 100–02; Michael J. Phillips, "The Progressiveness of the *Lochner* Court," *Denv. U. L. Rev.* 75 (1998): 488–90.
136. Ray A. Brown, "Due Process of Law, Police Power, and the Supreme Court," *Harv. L. Rev.* 40 (1927): 944–45 & n11.
137. Id. at 944.
138. See Felix Frankfurter, *Mr. Justice Holmes and the Supreme Court* (1938), app. at 97 (listing and summarizing cases). It is difficult to arbitrate the numerical dispute, because the counters count different judicial beans. Frankfurter and Warren identify only state, not federal, laws that were invalidated. But Frankfurter listed every case in which state laws were invalidated on any Fourteenth Amendment grounds, not just those state laws that Warren called "'social justice' legislation" and not just those laws invalidated under the amendment's Due Process Clause. Like Warren, Brown examined only "social and economic legislation," but unlike Warren, Brown listed both state and federal cases, and Brown conceived of the "social and economic" category of legislation far less restrictively than Warren. Additionally, each scholar examined a different date range of cases. Frankfurter looked at the years 1877–1938; Warren focused on 1887–1911; and Brown's study encompassed 1896–1927. See Frankfurter, *Mr. Justice Holmes*, supra, at app. at 97; Brown, "Due Process of Law," supra note 136, at 944–45; Warren, "Progressiveness of the United States Supreme Court," supra note 132, at 294–95. In a recent examination of these numbers, Michael Phillips on the whole adopted Frankfurter's approach, adding eight more laws—seven federal and one territorial—to his list. Michael J. Phillips, "How Many Times Was *Lochner*-Era Substantive Due Process Effective?," *Mercer L. Rev.* 48 (1997): 1057–59. Phillips focuses only on cases striking down federal and state laws threatening "the protection of liberty and property against arbitrary government action" under the Due Process Clause of either the Fourteenth or Fifth Amendment and finds that the *Lochner*-era Supreme Court upheld somewhere between three and five times as many laws as it struck down. Phillips, "Progressiveness of the *Lochner* Court," supra note 135, at 463–65, 488–90. Keith Whittington joins other revisionists in arguing that the Court upheld far more than it struck down, Keith E. Whittington, "Con-

gress Before the *Lochner* Court," *B.U. L. Rev.* 85 (2005): 829–32, but contributes to their analysis by arguing that when the Court struck statutes, it often did so with regard to a Congress of the opposing party, frequently out of power, Whittington, "Congress Before the *Lochner* Court," supra, at 834–38. Whittington also argues that most of the measures struck were minor ones. Id., at 834–38.

139. "Future of Labor Laws," *N.Y. Trib.*, Apr. 19, 1905, at 1.

140. Theodore Roosevelt, *Social Justice and Popular Rule* (1926), 197.

141. Frankfurter, *Mr. Justice Holmes*, supra note 138, at 88.

142. Melville Davisson Post, "Recall of Judicial Decisions," *Saturday Evening Post*, Aug. 31, 1912, at 3.

143. Id.

144. "The Election of Federal Judges by a Popular Vote," *Am. L. Rev.* 24 (1890): 479–80.

145. "By the People," *Evening Star*, May 21, 1895, at 1.

146. Weaver, *A Call to Action*, supra note 13, at 71.

147. Walter Clark, "Some Defects in the Constitution of the United States: Address to the Law Department of the University of Pennsylvania," Apr. 27, 1906, reprinted in 47 Cong. Rec. 3374, 3376 (1911).

148. Robert Eugene Cushman, "Non-Partisan Nominations and Elections," *Annals Am. Acad. Pol. & Soc. Sci.* 106 (1923): 83.

149. National Economic League, "Reform in the Administration of Justice," quoted in Herbert Harley, "Taking Judges out of Politics," *Annals Am. Acad. Pol. & Soc. Sci.* 64 (1916): 187.

150. 47 Cong. Rec. 3359, 3359 (1911) (statement of Sen. Owen); see also Ross, *A Muted Fury*, supra note 2, at 114.

151. Roe, *Our Judicial Oligarchy*, supra note 28, at 219.

152. Butler, *Why Should We Change Our Form of Government?*, supra note 25, at 40.

153. George Sutherland, "The Law and the People: Address at the Annual Dinner of the Pennsylvania Society," Dec. 13, 1913, at 5, reprinted in S. Doc. No. 63–328 (1913); see also Rome G. Brown, "The Judicial Recall—A Fallacy Repugnant to Constitutional Government," *Annals Am. Acad. Pol. & Soc. Sci.* 43 (1912): 239; Albert Fink, "The Recall of Judges," *N. Am. Rev.* 193 (1911): 672; James B. McDonough, "The Recall of Decisions—a Fallacy," *Cent. L. J.* 75 (1912): 35; James A. Metcalf, "Dangers That Lurk in the Recall of the Judiciary," *Annals Am. Acad. Pol. & Soc. Sci.* 43 (1912): 278; Wendell P. Stafford, "The Recall of Judges—A Warning," *Cent. L. J.* 75 (1912): 44.

154. "President Vetoes the Statehood Bill," *N.Y. Times*, Aug. 16, 1911, at 3 (reproducing full text of Taft's veto message).

155. Roosevelt, "A Charter of Democracy," supra note 29, at 398; see also William Draper Lewis, "A New Method of Constitutional Amendment by Popular Vote," *Annals Am. Acad. Pol. & Soc. Sci.* 43 (1912): 311–12.

156. Roosevelt, Introduction to Ransom, *Majority Rule and the Judiciary*, supra note 116, at 13–14.

157. Roe, *Our Judicial Oligarchy*, supra note 28, at 219; see also James H. Wolfe, letter to the editor, "Mr. Roosevelt and the Recall," *Nation*, March 28, 1912, at 312–13.

158. See 62 Cong. Rec. 9074, 9081 (1922) (statement of Sen. La Follette).

159. Editorial, "Our Despotic Courts," *Nation*, Sept. 24, 1924, at 300.

160. See, e.g., Chauncey M. Depew, "Depew States the Case for U.S. Supreme Court," *N.Y. Times*, Oct. 12, 1924, § XX, at 12; Donald Ewing, "Guard Our Basic Rights; Maintain Courts—Davis," *Chi. Daily Trib.*, Oct. 5, 1924, at 6; "Women Denounce La Follette Plan," *N.Y. Times*, Oct. 12, 1924, at E4; Paul T. Cheek, letter to the editor, "Attack on the Courts," *Wash. Post*, Oct. 18, 1924, at 6; "J. A. Emery Attacks La Follette Plan," *Wall St. J.*, Jan. 16, 1924, at 9; Editorial, "Destroying the Constitution," *Wash.*

Post, Sept. 13, 1924, at 6; Editorial, "The La Follette Plan," *Wash. Post*, Sept. 19, 1924, at 6.

161. George Wharton Pepper, "Why an Umpire?," *Forum* 71 (1924): 571.

162. Id. at 573.

163. "Borah for Limiting High Court's Veto," *N.Y. Times*, Feb. 6, 1923, at 4; see also Ross, *A Muted Fury*, supra note 2, at 218.

164. William E. Borah, "Five to Four Decisions as Menace to Respect for Supreme Court," *N.Y. Times*, Feb. 18, 1923, § XX, at 1.

165. Editorial, "Supreme Court and Congress," *N.Y. Evening Post*, Feb. 20, 1923, at 8.

166. See Whittington, "Congress Before the *Lochner* Court," supra note 138, at 829 ("If the Court was a countermajoritarian obstacle to progressive reform, then we should want to know how the Court managed to sustain itself against the forces of democracy"); Ross, *A Muted Fury*, supra note 2, at 191, 197–98, 233, 250 (examining this question).

167. See, e.g., Ross, *A Muted Fury*, supra note 2, at 60–61; Louis M. Greeley, "The Changing Attitude of the Courts Towards Social Legislation," *Ill. L. Rev.* 5 (1910): 231–32.

168. Roosevelt, "Judges and Progress," supra note 4, at 41.

169. Ransom, *Majority Rule and the Judiciary*, supra note 116, at ix–x.

170. See, e.g., Editorial, "The Supreme Court and Public Welfare," *Outlook*, June 20, 1923, at 209; Ransom, *Majority Rule and the Judiciary*, supra note 116, at vii–xviii.

171. Roosevelt, "Nationalism and the Judiciary," pt. 4, supra note 3, at 576.

172. Editorial, "Is the Supreme Court Too Supreme?," *Literary Dig.*, July 1, 1922, at 21 (quoting *N.Y. Call*).

173. Ex parte Young, 209 U.S. 123 (1908); Attorney General Edward Young was required to pay a hundred-dollar contempt fine. See Richard C. Cortner, *The Iron Horse and the Constitution: The Railroads and the Transformation of the Fourteenth Amendment* (1993), 176, 196.

174. 45 Cong. Rec. 7256 (1910), quoted in Michael Solimine, "Congress, *Ex Parte Young*, and the Fate of the Three-Judge District Court," *U. Pitt. L. Rev.* 70 (2008): 115.

175. One of the three judges was required to be a Supreme Court justice or (more likely) a circuit court judge. *An Act to Create a Commerce Court, and to Amend the Act Entitled "An Act to Regulate Commerce," Approved February Fourth, Eighteen Hundred and Eighty-seven, as Heretofore Amended, and for Other Purposes* (June 18, 1910), *U.S. Statutes at Large* 36, pt. 1 (1911): 557, codified at § 266 of the 1911 Judicial Code, and as § 2281 of the 1948 Judicial Code; repealed and replaced in 1976 by amended § 2284.

176. Ives v. So. Buffalo Ry. Co., 201 N.Y. 271, 294 (1911).

177. See Felix Frankfurter, "The Business of the Supreme Court of the United States. A Study in the Federal Judicial System, Part IV: Federal Courts of Specialized Jurisdiction," *Harv. L. Rev.* 39 (1926): 1052–53 (noting that it "aroused the fiercest criticism," including within the legal profession).

178. See *An Act to Amend an Act Entitled "An Act to Codify, Revise, and Amend the Laws Relating to the Judiciary," Approved March Third, Nineteen Hundred and Eleven* (Dec. 23, 1914), *U.S. Statutes at Large* 38, pt. 1, bk. 2 (1915): 790, codified as amended at 28 U.S.C. § 1257 (2006); see also Ross, *A Muted Fury*, supra note 2, at 80–81; Walter F. Dodd, "The United States Supreme Court as the Final Interpreter of the Federal Constitution," *Ill. L. Rev.* 6 (1911): 299.

179. George E. Dix, "The Death of the Commerce Court: A Study in Institutional Weakness," *Am. J. Leg. Hist.* 8 (1964): 244–46 (noting that a new federal entity "would necessitate a bothersome readjustment of access" for the railroads, which were already acclimated to regulation under the Interstate Commerce Commission).

180. Frankfurter, "Federal Courts of Specialized Jurisdiction," supra note 177, at 613–14.
181. Even in the states that adopted reforms, the payoff sometimes appeared minimal. Colorado, for example, never actually recalled a decision. Moreover, the provision of Colorado's constitution allowing for the recall of decisions was itself deemed unconstitutional because the people of a single state do not have the power to change the federal Constitution. See Duane A. Smith, "Colorado and Judicial Recall," *Am. J. Leg. Hist.* 7 (1963): 203–08. A California judge was recalled—for setting bail too low in a rape case—but no judges were recalled for overly conservative constitutional decisions. See "A Judge Ousted by Women's Votes," *Literary Dig.*, May 10, 1913, at 1048 (reviewing recall of Charles L. Weller, police magistrate judge in San Francisco, California, and noting that in rape cases "he has repeatedly fixt the bail so low—sometimes at only $50—that the culprit forfeited it and fled"); "Judge Is Recalled," *N.Y. Times*, Apr. 23, 1913, at 1 (noting that Weller lost the recall election by 815 votes out of approximately 61,000 cast). The supermajority voting requirement is the only reform that seems to have affected outcomes in an observable way, and still, the idea never really caught on. See Ross, *A Muted Fury*, supra note 2, at 231–32; W. Rolland Maddox, "Minority Control of Court Decisions in Ohio," *Am. Pol. Sci. Rev.* 24 (1930): 638.

However, this analysis may miss the real impact of these measures. Judges in the states that adopted reforms may have shied away from exercising their power of judicial review as aggressively as they would have absent reforms, obviating the need to discipline them subsequently.
182. The original three states were Ohio, North Dakota, and Nebraska; North Dakota and Nebraska retain a supermajority requirement today. South Carolina also had a supermajority requirement adopted in the late nineteenth century. See Jed Handelsman Shugerman, "A Six–Three Rule: Reviving Consensus and Deference on the Supreme Court," *Ga. L. Rev.* 37 (2003): 954.
183. Ross, *A Muted Fury*, supra note 2, at 152; Smith, "Colorado and Judicial Recall," supra note 181, at 203, 209.
184. These seven states were Oregon, Arizona, California, Colorado, Nevada, Kansas, and Arkansas. The Arkansas provision was declared unconstitutional by that state's supreme court on the ground that the procedure by which it was presented to voters for approval was improper. "Report of the Committee to Oppose Judicial Recall," *A.B.A. J.* 2 (1916): 441–42, 446.
185. See Ross, *A Muted Fury*, supra note 2, at 112–13.
186. Arizona, California, Idaho, Minnesota, Nebraska, North Dakota, Ohio, South Dakota, Washington, Wisconsin, and Wyoming. Cushman, "Non-Partisan Nominations and Elections," supra note 148, at 86, 87n14.
187. See Eileen L. McDonagh, "Race, Class and Gender in the Progressive Era: Restructuring State and Society," in *Progressivism and the New Democracy*, ed. Sidney M. Milkis and Jerome M. Mileur (1999), 147–69 (listing the passage of Progressive Era reforms by state, many of which also passed judicial reforms noted in the previous paragraph).
188. On the effort to restrict suffrage, see Wiebe, *Self-Rule: A Cultural History*, supra note 19, at 135–37; C. Vann Woodward, *Origins of the New South, 1877–1913*, 2d ed. (1971), 275, 338–49; Gabriel J. Chin and Randy Wagner, "The Tyranny of the Minority: Jim Crow and the Counter-Majoritarian Difficulty," *Harv. C. R.-C. L. L. Rev.* 43 (2008): 83–97.
189. See Wiebe, *Self-Rule: A Cultural History*, supra note 19, at 134–35 (noting that turnout declined nationally from around 80 percent of eligible voters in 1896 to 50 percent in 1924, as well as that turnout in New York declined from 88 percent to 55 percent in the same time period, and describing disenfranchisement legislation passed in the

South, including poll taxes, demands for ancestral records, and tests of voters' comprehension of state constitutions); Woodward, *Origins of the New South*, supra note 188, at 327–28 (suggesting that one reason southern states adopted disenfranchising measures was to prevent election fraud, and describing southern blacks as the victims of a struggle among southern whites on "which whites should be supreme").

190. Weaver, *A Call to Action*, supra note 13, at 82. For a leading work expanding on this idea, see Benjamin R. Twiss, *Lawyers and the Constitution: How Laissez Faire Came to the Supreme Court* (1942).

191. Editorial, "The Courts, the Plutocracy and the People; or, the Age-Long Attempt to Bulwark Privilege and Despotism," *Arena* 36 (1906): 87.

192. C. P. Connolly, "Big Business and the Bench," pt. 6, *Everybody's Mag.*, July 1912, at 119.

193. George E. McNeil, "Declaration of the Principles of the K. of L.," in *The Labor Movement: The Problem of To-Day*, ed. George E. McNeil (1891), 488.

194. Roe, *Our Judicial Oligarchy*, supra note 28, at 107.

195. Brooks Adams, *The Theory of Social Revolutions* (1913), 107.

196. Robert Eugene Cushman, "The Social and Economic Interpretation of the Fourteenth Amendment," *Mich. L. Rev.* 20 (1922): 751.

197. Jane Addams, "Discussion," in John R. Commons, "Is Class Conflict in America Growing and Is It Inevitable?," *Am. J. Soc.* 13 (1908): 772.

198. See Barnard, *Eagle Forgotten*, supra note 94, at 338; see also "Olney in Bad Humor," *Chi. Daily Trib.*, Apr. 18, 1895, at 12 (partially quoting Altgeld).

199. Louis D. Brandeis, "The Living Law," *Ill. L. Rev.* 10 (1916): 464.

200. Benjamin N. Cardozo, *The Nature of the Judicial Process* (1921), 166.

201. Dillon, "Property—Its Rights and Duties," supra note 37, at 173.

202. Thomas M. Cooley, *A Treatise on the Constitutional Limitations Which Rest upon the Legislative Power of the States of the American Union* (1868), 393.

203. Weaver, *A Call to Action*, supra note 13, at 27.

204. Edward B. Whitney, "Salutary Results of the Income-Tax Decision," *Forum* 19 (1895): 528.

205. Andrew Alexander Bruce, "The Illinois Ten-Hour Labor Law for Women," *Mich. L. Rev.* 8 (1909): 7.

206. Jesse F. Orton, "An Amendment by the Supreme Court," *Indep.*, Dec. 5, 1912, at 1284.

207. Charles E. Shattuck, "The True Meaning of the Term 'Liberty' in Those Clauses in the Federal and State Constitutions Which Protect 'Life, Liberty, and Property,'" *Harv. L. Rev.* 4 (1891): 392.

208. Hand, "Due Process of Law," supra note 106, at 495.

209. Powell, "Judiciality of Minimum-Wage Legislation," supra note 124, at 555.

210. Trickett, "Judicial Dispensation," supra note 105, at 86.

211. Editorial, "The Court and Public Opinion," *N.Y. Times*, Apr. 10, 1895, at 4.

212. Hand, "Due Process of Law," supra note 106, at 501.

213. T. W. Brown, "Due Process of Law," *Am. L. Rev.* 32 (1898): 20, 30.

214. George W. Alger, "The Courts and Legislative Freedom," *Atlantic Monthly*, March 1913, at 348.

215. Holden v. Hardy, 169 U.S. 366 (1898).

216. Ernst Freund, "Limitation of Hours of Labor and the Federal Supreme Court," *Green Bag* 17 (1905): 413; see also Boudin, "Government by Judiciary," supra note 113, at 268 (noting the laws at issue in *Holden v. Hardy* and *Lochner v. New York* that "[e]ither both laws were constitutional or they were both unconstitutional" under any coherent system of constitutional interpretation).

217. See, e.g., 64 Cong. Rec. 3959 (1923) (statement of Sen. Owen) (introducing into *Congressional Record* letter authored by Senator William E. Borah stating that "[d]uring

the last 30 years there have been some forty-odd exceedingly important cases determined in the Supreme Court by decisions of five to four" and arguing that "neither the will of the people of the State nor the will of the people of the United States should be thwarted upon a decision rendered by a bare majority of the court"); Robert M. La Follette, "Address Before the Annual Convention of the American Federation of Labor," June 14, 1922, reprinted in 62 Cong. Rec. 9077 (1922) (criticizing the fact that "a bare majority of the Court has repeatedly overridden the will of the people as declared by their Representatives in Congress, and has construed the Constitution to mean whatever suited their peculiar economic and political views"). For a discussion of 5–4 decisions by the *Lochner* Court, see Shugerman, "A Six-Three Rule," supra note 182, at 915–17.

218. Editorial, "The Flexibility of Law," *Outlook*, June 20, 1923, at 848.
219. Editorial, "Reckless Criticism," *Wash. Post*, Aug. 12, 1905, at 6.
220. Powell, "Judiciality of Minimum-Wage Legislation," supra note 124, at 548, 549.
221. James B. Thayer, "The Origin and Scope of the American Doctrine of Constitutional Law," *Harv. L. Rev.* 7 (1893): 144, 150.
222. Blaine Free Moore, "The Supreme Court and Unconstitutional Legislation," *Studs. in Hist., Econ., & Pub. L.* 54 (1913): 168 (citing Smyth v. Ames, 169 U.S. 446 (1898)).
223. *Lochner*, 198 U.S. at 56–57.
224. Beulah Amidon Ratliff, "May Congress Limit the Supreme Court?," *Nation*, May 21, 1924, at 580.
225. Beth, *Development of the American Constitution*, supra note 22, at 64; Neil Duxbury, *Patterns of American Jurisprudence* (1995), 9–10; Anthony J. Sebok, *Legal Positivism and American Jurisprudence* (1998), 41. Or so the story goes. For a persuasive contrarian view, see Brian Z. Tamanaha, *Beyond the Formalist-Realist Divide: The Role of Politics in Judging* (2009).
226. Boyd Winchester, "The Judiciary—Its Growing Power and Influence," *Am. L. Rev.* 32 (1898): 806.
227. Morris Raphael Cohen, "The Process of Judicial Legislation," *Am. L. Rev.* 48 (1914): 164.
228. Cushman, "Social and Economic Interpretation," supra note 196, at 744.
229. Oliver Wendell Holmes, Jr., "Privilege, Malice, and Intent," *Harv. L. Rev.* 8 (1894): 7.
230. Id.
231. Gaynor, "Do Our Courts Stand in the Way of Social and Economic Progress?," supra note 58, at 105.
232. "'Inalienable Right' to Starve," supra note 91, at 20.
233. Quoted in Ross, *A Muted Fury*, supra note 2, at 179.
234. Roosevelt, Introduction to Ransom, *Majority Rule and the Judiciary*, supra note 116, at 16.
235. Alger, "Courts and Legislative Freedom," supra note 214, at 348.
236. Gaynor, "Do Our Courts Stand in the Way of Social and Economic Progress?," supra note 58, at 103.
237. "The Ten-Hour Labor Decisions," *Outlook*, Apr. 29, 1905, at 1017.
238. "The New York Labour Law and the Fourteenth Amendment," *L. Q. Rev.* 21 (1905): 212.
239. Editorial, "The Supreme Court Supplants Congress," *Nation*, Apr. 25, 1923, at 485.
240. Roscoe Pound, "Mechanical Jurisprudence," *Colum. L. Rev.* 8 (1908): 609; see Roscoe Pound, "President's Address: Taught Law," *Am. L. Sch. Rev.* 3 (1911–1915): 170; Roscoe Pound, "Chairman's Address: The Need of a Sociological Jurisprudence," *Annual Report A.B.A.* 31 (1907): 915; Roscoe Pound, "The Future of the Common Law," *Neb. L. Bull.* 7 (1927): 122.

241. Roscoe Pound, "Courts and Legislation," *Am. Pol. Sci. Rev.* 7 (1913): 365.

242. Pound, "Mechanical Jurisprudence," supra note 240, at 606.

243. Id. at 609.

244. Oliver Wendell Holmes, Jr., "The Path of the Law," *Harv. L. Rev.* 10 (1897): 469.

245. Roosevelt, "Eighth Annual Message," in Israel, *State of the Union Messages,* supra note 110, at 2309.

246. Felix Frankfurter, "Hours of Labor and Realism in Constitutional Law," *Harv. L. Rev.* 29 (1916): 372.

247. Brief of Appellant Oregon, Muller v. Oregon, 208 U.S. 412 (1908); see also Beth, *Development of the American Constitution,* supra note 22, at 65; Edward A. Purcell, Jr., *Brandeis and the Progressive Constitution: Erie, the Judicial Power, and the Politics of the Federal Courts in Twentieth-Century America* (2000), 166–67; Edward A. Purcell, Jr., *The Crisis of Democratic Theory: Scientific Naturalism & the Problem of Value* (1973), 76–77.

248. Frankfurter, "Hours of Labor and Realism," supra note 246, at 365. On the sexism of Brandeis and Goldmark's approach, see Erickson, "Historical Background of 'Protective' Labor Legislation: *Muller v. Oregon,*" in Weisberg, *Property, Family and the Legal Profession,* Vol. 2, supra note 16, at 175.

249. Morton J. Horwitz, *The Transformation of American Law, 1870–1960: The Crisis of Legal Orthodoxy* (1992), 169–70, 171. Though Karl Llewellyn, a leading legal realist, later denied Roscoe Pound's influence on him, Llewellyn drew early inspiration for his ideas from Pound. See N.E.H. Hull, "Reconstructing the Origins of Realistic Jurisprudence: A Prequel to the Llewellyn-Pound Exchange over Legal Realism," *Duke L. J.,* 1989: 1312, 1334. On realism generally, see Duxbury, *Patterns of American Jurisprudence,* supra note 225, at 48–50; Brian Leiter, *Naturalizing Jurisprudence* (2007), 15–118; Sebok, *Legal Positivism and American Jurisprudence,* supra note 225, at 79–81.

250. Frankfurter, "Hours of Labor and Realism," supra note 246. Morton Horwitz credits Jerome Frank with being the first to employ the phrase "legal realism" itself. See Horwitz, *Crisis of Legal Orthodoxy,* supra note 249, at 175 (citing Jerome Frank, *Law and the Modern Mind* (1930)).

251. Horwitz, *Crisis of Legal Orthodoxy,* supra note 249, at 187.

252. Karl N. Llewellyn, "Some Realism About Realism—Responding to Dean Pound," *Harv. L. Rev.* 44 (1930): 1222.

253. Duxbury, *Patterns of American Jurisprudence,* supra note 225, at 68–69; see also Horwitz, *Crisis of Legal Orthodoxy,* supra note 249, at 169–72.

254. Brown, "Due Process of Law," supra note 213, at 30; see, e.g., Powell, "Judiciality of Minimum–Wage Legislation," supra note 124, at 546 ("The determination of closely-controverted constitutional issues depends . . . in large part upon the composition of the court of last resort at the particular time when the issue comes before it").

Chapter 7: Acceptance

1. "Hoover Declares Party Serves All," *N.Y. Times,* Sept. 28, 1928, at 1 (quoting Hoover's speech to young supporters that "[t]he Republican Party over these many years has been the party of prosperity and progress"); see also William E. Leuchtenburg, *Franklin D. Roosevelt and the New Deal* (1963), 1 (noting that by 1932 this claim was no longer credible).

2. Franklin D. Roosevelt, "A 'Fireside Chat' Discussing the Plan for Reorganization of the Judiciary," March 9, 1937, in *The Public Papers and Addresses of Franklin D. Roosevelt,* vol. 6, *The Constitution Prevails, 1937,* ed. Samuel I. Rosenman (1941), 123.

3. Roosevelt made eight appointments, but to only seven seats. One of his appointees resigned after only one term on the Court. See Peter Charles Hoffer, Williamjames Hull Hoffer, and N.E.H. Hull, *The Supreme Court: An Essential History* (2007), 265–69, 281–87.

4. Clyde P. Weed, *The Nemesis of Reform: The Republican Party During the New Deal* (1994), 19.

5. Leuchtenburg, *FDR and the New Deal*, supra note 1, at 1.

6. *Encyclopedia of the Great Depression*, ed. James Ciment (2001), 1:29, 31.

7. See Leuchtenburg, *FDR and the New Deal*, supra note 1, at 2 (Hoovervilles); Peter H. Irons, *The New Deal Lawyers* (1982), 17 (dumps).

8. Senator William E. Borah, "Address to Brooklyn Republicans," Jan. 28, 1936, reported in *N.Y. Times*, Jan. 29, 1936, at 13.

9. Herbert Stein, *The Fiscal Revolution in America: Policy in Pursuit of Reality* (1996), 10.

10. See Bruce Ackerman, *We the People*, vol. 2: *Transformations* (1998), 281–82; James T. Patterson, *The New Deal and the States: Federalism in Transition* (1969), 32–49.

11. Herbert Hoover, "Public Statement," Feb. 3, 1931, quoted in *The Hoover Administration: A Documented Narrative*, ed. William Starr Myers and Walter H. Newton (1936), 64.

12. Democratic Party platform of 1932, in *National Party Platforms: 1840–1956*, ed. Kirk H. Porter and Donald Bruce Johnson (1956), 331.

13. Id. at 339. In addition to the budget and spending proposal, the Democratic platform called for the preservation of a sound currency. On the other hand, it also advocated greater federal regulation of financial interests, federal assistance to agriculture, and the development of public works programs. See id. at 331–32; see also Ackerman, *We the People*, vol. 2: supra note 10, at 283–84 (describing conflicting and fragmentary nature of Democratic platform though maintaining that "the general direction of Roosevelt's campaign was clear enough—away from limited government and toward the activist regulatory state").

14. Franklin D. Roosevelt, "Radio Address: The 'Forgotten Man' Speech," Apr. 7, 1932, in *The Public Papers and Addresses of Franklin D. Roosevelt*, vol. 1: *The Genesis of the New Deal, 1928–1932*, ed. Samuel I. Rosenman (1938), 626–27; Franklin D. Roosevelt, "Address at Oglethorpe University: The Country Needs, the Country Demands Bold, Persistent Experimentation," May 22, 1932, in Rosenman, *Public Papers of FDR*, vol. 1, supra, at 646.

15. Leuchtenburg, *FDR and the New Deal*, supra note 1, at 17. The congressional results were similarly impressive: "The 1932 landslide swept an unprecedented 310 Democrats into the House, leaving only 117 Republicans; the Senate . . . saw the number of Republicans shrink to 35 from 56." Ackerman, *We the People*, vol. 2: supra note 10, at 286.

16. See Leuchtenburg, *FDR and the New Deal*, supra note 1, at 12. "Insurgents" is the term used by Ronald A. Mulder, *The Insurgent Progressives in the United States Senate and the New Deal, 1933–1939* (1979), ii, 31.

17. Weed, *Nemesis of Reform*, supra note 4, at 29. To support this point, Weed noted that the demographically unrepresentative *Literary Digest* poll predicted the 1932 election accurately.

18. Leuchtenburg, *FDR and the New Deal*, supra note 1, at 39.

19. Franklin D. Roosevelt, "Inaugural Address," March 4, 1933, in *The Public Papers and Addresses of Franklin D. Roosevelt*, vol. 2: *The Year of Crisis, 1933*, ed. Samuel I. Rosenman (1938), 12.

20. The phrase is from his fireside chat on the Court plan. See supra note 2.

21. Franklin D. Roosevelt, "Campaign Address, I Am Waging War in This Campaign Against the 'Four Horsemen' of the Present Republican Leadership—Destruction, Delay, Deceit, Despair," Oct. 25, 1932, in Rosenman, *Public Papers of FDR*, vol. 1, supra note 14, at 837. On the reaction to Roosevelt's speech, see Arthur Krock, "Roosevelt Charged with Court Design in 1932," *N.Y. Times*, Feb. 11, 1937, at 22 (retrospective after Roosevelt announced his plan for the Court); see also William E. Leuchtenburg, *The Supreme Court Reborn* (1995), 83.

22. Joseph Alsop and Turner Catledge, *The 168 Days* (1938), 18.

23. They were nicknamed the Four Horsemen of the Apocalypse because their opinions employed "the logic of would-be": "If this statute were held valid, behold what other measures might be enacted and would have to be upheld." "Notes and Comment," *U.S. L. Rev.* 71 (1937): 65 (on logic of "would-be."). One pundit called this the "argument ad horrendum." Charles P. Curtis, Jr., *Lions Under the Robes* (1947), 128; see also G. Edward White, *The Constitution and the New Deal* (2000), 284–301 (describing both contemporary and retrospective "demonization" of "Four Horsemen").

24. Alsop and Catledge, *168 Days*, supra note 22, at 4–5.

25. Id. at 5; see also Carl Brent Swisher, *American Constitutional Development* (1943), 920. Justice Benjamin Cardozo was a Hoover appointee as well. Hoover made the nomination in light of a substantial political consensus that Cardozo should replace the liberal justice Oliver Wendell Holmes, who had retired. See "Cardozo Is Named to Supreme Court; Nomination Hailed," *N.Y. Times*, Feb. 16, 1932, at 1.

26. Home Bldg. & Loan Ass'n v. Blaisdell, 290 U.S. 398 (1934); Paul L. Murphy, *The Constitution in Crisis Times: 1918–1969* (1972), 110; William L. Prosser, "The Minnesota Mortgage Moratorium," *S. Cal. L. Rev.* 7 (1934): 353.

27. *Blaisdell*, 290 U.S. at 426.

28. Id. at 454–64 (Sutherland, J., dissenting). For a discussion of the inconsistency between Minnesota's law and the intentions of the Constitution's framers, see White, *Constitution and the New Deal*, supra note 23, at 211–15; Sanford Levinson, "Constitutional Norms in a State of Permanent Emergency," *Ga. L. Rev.* 40 (2006): 720–35.

29. *Blaisdell*, 290 U.S. at 449 (Sutherland, J., dissenting).

30. Interview by Richard Friedman with Francis R. Kirkham, Esq., former law clerk to Chief Justice Hughes, Aug. 30, 1976, quoted in Richard D. Friedman, "Switching Time and Other Thought Experiments: The Hughes Court and Constitutional Transformation," *U. Pa. L. Rev.* 142 (1994): 1915–16. Kirkham recited the comment from memory, claiming in a letter that the wording was "about right, but not necessarily exact." Letter from Francis R. Kirkham to Paul A. Freund, May 17, 1962, quoted in Friedman, "Switching Time," supra, at 1916n117.

31. Nebbia v. New York, 291 U.S. 502, 552 (1934) (McReynolds, J., dissenting).

32. Id. at 523, 532, 537 (majority opinion).

33. Dean Alfange, *The Supreme Court and the National Will* (1937), 122.

34. Perry v. United States, 294 U.S. 330 (1935); Nortz v. United States, 294 U.S. 317 (1935); Norman v. Baltimore & Ohio R.R. Co., 294 U.S. 240 (1935). A fourth case, United States v. Bankers' Trust Co., was consolidated with Norman.

35. Robert H. Jackson, *The Struggle for Judicial Supremacy: A Study of a Crisis in American Power Politics* (1999), 102.

36. Arthur Krock, "Roosevelt Speech Was Ready on Gold," *N.Y. Times*, Feb. 21, 1935, at 1; see also Leuchtenburg, *Supreme Court Reborn*, supra note 21, at 87–88 (quoting from draft of Roosevelt's prepared speech).

37. *Perry*, 294 U.S. at 357. In *Norman*, the Court held that Congress's power to coin money and regulate currency provided sufficient authority to take the country off

the gold standard regardless of its impact on private contracts. *Norman*, 294 U.S. at 315–16. The issue of the government's own contractual obligations, at issue in *Perry*, was more complicated. On the oddity of the Court's holding that while Congress had impermissibly abrogated its contractual obligations, no actual damages were incurred, see Henry M. Hart, Jr., "The Gold Clause in the United States Bonds," *Harv. L. Rev.* 48 (1935): 1057 ("Few more baffling pronouncements, it is fair to say, have ever issued from the United States Supreme Court").

38. Alfange, *Supreme Court and the National Will*, supra note 33, at 201.

39. Leuchtenburg, *FDR and the New Deal*, supra note 1, at 144. Because the remarks were extemporaneous and were not officially recorded, there are conflicting accounts. An original source noting language closest to that above is: "Constitution Gone, Says McReynolds," *N.Y. Times*, Feb. 19, 1935, at 1. *The Wall Street Journal* attempted a complete transcript. The language there is slightly different. See "Justice McReynolds' Remarks on Gold Case Decision," *Wall St. J.*, Feb. 23, 1935, at 1 ("The Constitution as many of us have understood it, the Constitution that has meant so much to us, has gone. The guarantees which men and women heretofore have supposed protected them against arbitrary action have been swept away. . . . [T]hat [the ability for the federal government to repudiate its obligations] never was the law. It ought never to be the law and the shame and humiliation of it all no one of us can foresee"); see also "That Golden Ruling," *N.Y. Times*, Feb. 24, 1935, at E1 (noting Justice McReynolds spoke extemporaneously and quoting him as saying it was not too much to say of the Constitution that "it was gone").

40. Panama Refining Co. v. Ryan, 293 U.S. 388 (1935).

41. Jackson, *Struggle for Judicial Supremacy*, supra note 35, at 111.

42. R.R. Ret. Bd. v. Alton R.R. Co., 295 U.S. 330 (1935); Letter from Justice Harlan Fiske Stone to Marshall and Lauson Stone, May 9, 1935, quoted in Leuchtenburg, *Supreme Court Reborn*, supra note 21, at 48.

43. A.L.A. Schechter Poultry Corp. v. United States, 295 U.S. 495 (1935). Also decided against the administration on that day were Humphrey's Executor v. United States, 295 U.S. 602 (1935) (holding that President could not remove Federal Trade Commissioner without cause because the commission was an independent agency serving judicial and legislative functions), and Louisville Joint Stock Land Bank v. Radford, 295 U.S. 555 (1935) (invalidating Frazier-Lemke Farm Mortgage Act as violation of Fifth Amendment guarantee of just compensation). The only major piece of New Deal legislation upheld by the Court, prior to the 1937 switch, was that creating the Tennessee Valley Authority (Ashwander v. Tenn. Valley Auth., 297 U.S. 288 (1936)). Alsop and Catledge, *168 Days*, supra note 22, at 18; Friedman, "Switching Time," supra note 30, at 1927–28.

44. See "Notes and Comment," *U.S. L. Rev.* 67 (1935): 282 (noting that unanimity in *Schechter* was "little anticipated" by either proponents or opponents of the Court's decision); see also Robert K. Carr, *Democracy and the Supreme Court* (1936), 58 (discussing surprise at *Schechter*'s unanimity).

45. "The Supreme Courts," *Law Times*, June 8, 1935, AT 419.

46. "Biggest News Rose in Supreme Court: Editors in Poll on the Year's Leading Stories Vote for Rulings on New Deal," *N.Y. Times*, Dec. 26, 1935, at 19.

47. *Schechter*, 295 U.S. at 507 (argument for Schechter Corp.). The law also was challenged, under *Panama Refining*, as an invalid delegation of power to the President. See id. at 541–42.

48. Id. at 512–14 (argument for the United States).

49. Id. at 528.

50. Id. at 543, 546, 548.

51. Thurman W. Arnold, *The Symbols of Government* (1935), 118 ("William Randolph Hearst, Clarence Darrow, the Chicago Tribune, the American Bar Association, Huey Long, and Senator Borah all thanked God for the Supreme Court, each making the decision a symbol of a different point of view").

52. See George H. Gallup, *The Gallup Poll: Public Opinion 1935–1971* (1972), 1:41, 52 (indicating majority support for NRA revival in polls published on November 29, 1936, and March 14, 1937, respectively); see also Gallup Poll, Feb. 10–15 (1937), available at The Roper Center for Public Opinion Research, University of Connecticut, http://www.ropercenter.uconn.edu/ipoll.html (49 percent yes, 41 percent no, 11 percent no opinion). One unpublished poll in September 1936 showed a majority against, but the question was worded differently (and oddly) as: "Should the NRA, in legal form, be revived?" See Gallup Poll, Sept. 21–26 (1936), available at The Roper Center for Public Opinion Research, University of Connecticut, http://www.ropercenter.uconn.edu/ipoll.html (44 percent yes, 56 percent no). The polls published by Gallup at this time generally excluded the "no opinion" category, basing its percentages only on respondents who expressed opinions. See e-mail from Jeff Jones, managing editor, Gallup Poll, to author, Oct. 8, 2007 (on file with author). This omission turns out to be significant for evaluating public opinion with respect to Roosevelt's Court-packing plan. See infra note 284. Except where specifically indicated, all Gallup figures cited here are percentages only of those offering opinions.

53. *N.Y. Times*, May 28, 1935, at 1 (headline); "Organized Labor, Dazed by NIRA Decision, Fears for Fate of Wagner Bill," *N.Y. Times*, May 28, 1935, at 17.

54. Franklin D. Roosevelt, "The Two Hundred and Ninth Press Conference," May 31, 1935, in *The Public Papers and Addresses of Franklin D. Roosevelt*, vol. 4: *The Court Disapproves, 1935*, ed. Samuel I. Rosenman (1938), 212, 221.

55. Krock, "Roosevelt Charged," supra note 21, at 22.

56. Roosevelt, "The Two Hundred and Ninth Press Conference," in Rosenman, *Public Papers of FDR*, vol. 4, supra note 54, at 221–22.

57. Drew Pearson and Robert S. Allen, *The Nine Old Men* (1936), 31.

58. Letter from Henry Stimson, former Secretary of State, to President Franklin D. Roosevelt, June 10, 1935, quoted in Leuchtenburg, *Supreme Court Reborn*, supra note 21, at 90 ("[The horse-and-buggy comment] was a wrong statement, an unfair statement and, if it had not been so extreme as to be recognizable as hyperbole, a rather dangerous and inflammatory statement").

59. Letter from George Fort Milton to President Franklin D. Roosevelt, June 4, 1935, quoted in Leuchtenburg, *Supreme Court Reborn*, supra note 21, at 90–91.

60. Alsop and Catledge, *168 Days*, supra note 22, at 7.

61. Jackson, *Struggle for Judicial Supremacy*, supra note 35, at 125–26, 128.

62. United States v. Butler, 297 U.S. 1, 65–66, 72 (1936).

63. Id. at 63, 64, 68.

64. See Gallup, *Gallup Poll*, supra note 52, at 1:9; see also Marian C. McKenna, *Franklin Roosevelt and the Great Constitutional War* (2002), 141 (noting majority disapproval of AAA in poll day before *Butler* decision).

65. McKenna, *Great Constitutional War*, supra note 64, at 141; see also Leuchtenburg, *FDR and the New Deal*, supra note 1, at 72–74.

66. Carr, *Democracy and the Supreme Court*, supra note 44, at 71.

67. Arthur Krock, "Supreme Court Moves to the Fore as an Issue," *N.Y. Times*, Jan. 8, 1936, at 18.

68. "Six Supreme Justices Hanged in Effigy in Iowa," *N.Y. Times*, Jan. 8, 1936, at 15. On calls for constitutional amendments, see Barry Cushman, *Rethinking the New Deal*

Court: The Structure of a Constitutional Revolution (1998), 12; William Lasser, *The Limits of Judicial Power: The Supreme Court in American Politics* (1988), 139; Leuchtenburg, *Supreme Court Reborn*, supra note 21, at 96–97.

69. Isidor Loeb, "Constitutional Interpretation in a Transitional Period," *St. Louis L. Rev.* 21 (1936): 105.

70. *Butler*, 297 U.S. at 79 (Stone, J., dissenting). Stone's reasoning is not without its difficulty. The ultimate question ought properly to have been, as Justice Roberts recognized, whether Congress's condition on its spending grant was an exercise of regulatory power outside its delegated authority. Justice Stone went astray by insisting that there could be no "coercion" in offering money to do something. Id. at 86–87. The majority erred, however, in so narrowly conceiving the scope of Congress's delegated powers. See Thomas R. McCoy and Barry Friedman, "Conditional Spending: Federalism's Trojan Horse," *Sup. Ct. Rev.*, 1988: 108–09 (discussing conditional spending grants and *Butler* decision).

71. *Butler*, 297 U.S. at 78, 87 (Stone, J., dissenting). The claim of abuse came in response to the taxing argument. "The suggestion that [the power to tax and spend] must now be curtailed by judicial fiat because it may be abused by unwise use hardly rises to the dignity of argument. So may judicial power be abused." Id. at 87.

72. "Courts Score Guffey Act and RA, Creating Dilemma for New Deal," *Wall St. J.*, May 19, 1936, at 1.

73. Editorial, "Coal and Regulation," *Wall St. J.*, May 19, 1936, at 4.

74. Jackson, *Struggle for Judicial Supremacy*, supra note 35, at 154–55; see also *An Act to Stabilize the Bituminous Coal-mining Industry and Promote Its Interstate Commerce . . .* [Bituminous Coal Conservation Act] (Aug. 30, 1935), *U.S. Statutes at Large* 49, pt. 1 (1936): 992 ("[T]he excessive facilities for the production of bituminous coal and the overexpansion of the industry have led to practices and methods of production, distribution, and marketing of such coal resources of the nation . . . [that] portend the destruction of the industry itself . . .").

75. Carter v. Carter Coal Co., 298 U.S. 238, 282 (1936).

76. Letter from President Franklin D. Roosevelt to Representative Samuel B. Hill, July 5, 1935, reprinted at 79 Cong. Rec. 13449 (1936), quoted in Cushman, *Rethinking the New Deal Court*, supra note 68, at 160.

77. *Carter*, 298 U.S. at 309.

78. Id. at 327 (Cardozo, J., dissenting).

79. Editorial, "Coal and Regulation," supra note 73, at 4.

80. *Carter*, 298 U.S. at 331 (Cardozo, J., dissenting).

81. Id. at 291 (opinion of Hughes, C. J.).

82. Id. at 318.

83. Morehead v. New York ex rel. Tipaldo, 298 U.S. 587, 609 (1936).

84. "A Deplorable Decision," *Commonweal*, June 19, 1936, at 199; see also "Wage Ruling Stirs Indignation in Congress and in Labor Ranks," *N.Y. Times*, June 2, 1936, at 1.

85. *Carter*, 298 U.S. at 308.

86. Franklin D. Roosevelt, "The Three Hundredth Press Conference (Excerpts)," June 2, 1936, in *The Public Papers and Addresses of Franklin D. Roosevelt*, vol. 5: *The People Approve, 1936*, ed. Samuel I. Rosenman (1938), 191–92.

87. Porter and Johnson, *National Party Platforms*, supra note 12, at 367.

88. Merlo J. Pusey, *Charles Evans Hughes* (1951), 2:747.

89. W. Y. Elliott, "Getting a New Constitution," *Annals Am. Acad. Pol. & Soc. Sci.* 185 (1936): 116.

90. Hon. John J. Parker, "The Federal Constitution in a Period of Change, Address Delivered Before the Annual Conference of Referees in Bankruptcy," July 20, 1934, in

Kan. City L. Rev. 3 (1934–1935): 88; see also John J. Parker, "Is the Constitution Passing?," *A.B.A. J.* 19 (1933): 571–72. On Parker's failed nomination, see David A. Yalof, *Pursuit of Justices: Presidential Politics and the Selection of Supreme Court Nominees* (1999), 16, 23–24; "Nominee's Career Assailed," *N.Y. Times*, May 8, 1930, at 1.

91. Donald R. Richberg, "The Constitution and the New Deal," *Annals Am. Acad. Pol. & Soc. Sci.* 185 (1936): 58.

92. Michael Kammen, *A Machine That Would Go of Itself* (1986), 275 (quoting New York attorney in debate with Republican congressman).

93. Ernest M. Patterson, "Foreword," *Annals Am. Acad. Pol. & Soc. Sci.* 185 (1936): xvii–xviii; see also Kammen, *A Machine That Would Go of Itself*, supra note 92, at 276 (describing broadcast over NBC Radio and claiming that "[t]here is abundant evidence that the messages . . . did filter down to reach a wide audience").

94. Scholars debate whether the movement to federal administrative governance of the economy during the Depression was continuous with, or a dislocation from, what had come before. See Larry Kramer, "What's a Constitution For Anyway? Of History and Theory, Bruce Ackerman and the New Deal," *Case W. Res. L. Rev.* 46 (1996): 912–30.

95. See Theda Skocpol, *Protecting Soldiers and Mothers* (1992), 102–51 (on pension system for Civil War veterans); Stephen Skowronek, *Building a New American State: The Expansion of National Administrative Capacities* (1982), 121, 134–38, 171–73 (on railway regulation and movement toward administrative reform and use of government power by Teddy Roosevelt and his successors); Kramer, "What's a Constitution For Anyway?," supra note 94, at 916–17 (noting development of social programs by federal government and enactment of economic and social legislation at state and national levels after Civil War).

96. Felix Frankfurter, *The Public & Its Government* (1930), 22–23, 24–25, 28.

97. William E. Willoughby, "The Philosophy of Labor Legislation: Presidential Address, American Association for Labor Legislation," *Am. Pol. Sci. Rev.* 8 (1914): 16.

98. See David Kennedy, *Over Here: The First World War and American Society* (1980), 93–143 (on increase in federal economic authority during war); Robert C. Post, "Defending the Lifeworld: Substantive Due Process in the Taft Court Era," *B.U. L. Rev.* 78 (1998): 1489–91 (on return to normalcy under Harding).

99. Myers and Newton, *Hoover Administration*, supra note 11, at 65. Hoover's response to the Depression is detailed in Patterson, *New Deal and the States*, supra note 10, at 27–32: In July 1932, with an election pending, Hoover agreed finally to some three hundred million dollars of federal aid, a pittance compared with what Roosevelt would provide, lent to the states as an advance on highway funds.

100. Charles Edward Merriam, *The Written and the Unwritten Attitude* (1931), 27, 31.

101. "Association's 56th Annual Meeting Is Marked by Notable Features," *A.B.A. J.* 19 (1933): 557.

102. Frankfurter, *Public & Its Government*, supra note 96, at 3.

103. Richberg, "Constitution and the New Deal," supra note 91, at 60.

104. Letter from President Franklin D. Roosevelt to David Grey, June 17, 1935, quoted in Patterson, *New Deal and the States*, supra note 10, at 102; see also Franklin D. Roosevelt, "The Two Hundred and Ninth Press Conference," May 31, 1935, in Rosenman, *Public Papers of FDR*, vol. 4, supra note 54, at 216 (doubting "we can go ahead with every possible effort to make national decisions based on the fact that forty-eight sovereignties cannot agree quickly enough or practically enough on any solution for a national economic problem or a national social problem").

105. Alsop and Catledge, *168 Days*, supra note 22, at 2.

106. Representative Bertrand Hollis Snell, "Speech on the House Floor," March 9, 1933, quoted in Mulder, *Insurgent Progressives*, supra note 16, at 41.

107. Parker, "Constitution Passing," supra note 90, at 574; see also Daniel J. Hulsebosch, "The New Deal Court: Emergence of a New Reason," *Colum. L. Rev.* 90 (1990): 1979 (describing Judge Parker's speech to the ABA).

108. R. C. Tway Coal Co. v. Glenn, 12 F. Supp. 570, 595 (D.C. Ky. 1935).

109. Stanley Reed, Solicitor General of the United States, "The Constitution and the Problems of Today, An Address Before the Virginia State Bar Association, at Virginia Beach, Virginia," Aug. 7, 1936, in *Proc. of Va. St. Bar Ass'n* 47 (1936): 278.

110. Editorial, "A Crippling Blow," (London) *Times*, Jan. 7, 1936, at 13.

111. See Leuchtenburg, *FDR and the New Deal*, supra note 1, at 91; George Wolfskill, *The Revolt of the Conservatives: A History of the American Liberty League, 1934–1940* (1962), 10; "Borah Demands a Rebuilt Party," *N.Y. Times*, Nov. 9, 1934, at 2.

112. See Leuchtenburg, *FDR and the New Deal*, supra note 1, at 91 (on American Liberty League formation); Wolfskill, *Revolt of the Conservatives*, supra note 111, at 29 (quoting *Newsweek*).

113. Mulder, *Insurgent Progressives*, supra note 16, at 103 (on Chamber of Commerce, which repudiated in the spring of 1935); Herbert Hoover, *The Challenge to Liberty* (1934), 8.

114. Leuchtenburg, *FDR and the New Deal*, supra note 1, at 116.

115. "Borah Demands a Rebuilt Party," supra note 111, at 2.

116. Leuchtenburg, *FDR and the New Deal*, supra note 1, at 116.

117. Arthur Krock, "Tide Sweeps Nation," *N.Y. Times*, Nov. 7, 1934, at 1.

118. *Stabilization of Bituminous Coal Mining Industry: Hearing on S. 1417 Before the S. Subcomm. of the Comm. on Interstate Commerce*, 74th Cong., 1935, 522–24 (statement of Edward Mahan, president, Southern Coal & Coke Co.). Mr. Mahan did not agree with the Guffey legislation in all particulars.

119. Patterson, *New Deal and the States*, supra note 10, at 90–91.

120. McKenna, *Great Constitutional War*, supra note 64, at 205. See Carter v. Carter Coal Co., 298 U.S. 238, 278 (1936).

121. Barry Cushman argues that the power was there all along to spend federal dollars on relief. Barry Cushman, "Mr. Dooley and Mr. Gallup: Public Opinion and Constitutional Change in the 1930s," *Buff. L. Rev.* 50 (2002): 59–60. But the point here is the will, not the power. This is an apt demonstration of sharp changes in the sentiments of the American people, paralleling those occurring with many aspects of economic administration.

122. Stuart Chase, *Government in Business* (1935), 45, 68.

123. Murphy, *Constitution in Crisis Times*, supra note 26, at 146.

124. Cushman, *Rethinking the New Deal Court*, supra note 68, at 29 (on Republicans); Frances Perkins, "The Social Security Act," *Vital Speeches* (1935): 1:794, reprinted in *The New Deal: A Documentary History*, ed. William Leuchtenburg (1968), 86.

125. James Hart, "A Unified Economy and States' Rights," *Annals Am. Acad. Pol. & Soc. Sci.* 185 (1936): 106. Hart was a political science professor and a regional NRA official. Id. at 114.

126. See Walter F. Dodd, "The Powers of National Government," *Annals Am. Acad. Pol. & Soc. Sci.* 185 (1936): 72.

127. See Wolfskill, *Revolt of the Conservatives*, supra note 111, at 116–17 (describing conservative opposition to centralization of power away from states); William L. Blatt, "Address Before the Forty-fourth Congress of American Industry," Dec. 5, 1939, quoted in Thomas Paul Jenkin, "Reactions of Major Groups to Positive Government in the United States, 1930–1940," *U. Cal. Publications in Pol. Sci.* 1 (1945): 299 ("[R]estrictions of competition, prices and individual judgment are necessary parts of the system of private enterprise. . . . As the state of society grows more complex,

certain undeniable conditions arise that make such additional restrictions imperative. What was considered entirely legal and proper fifty years ago may very well be
against the public interest today"). The relation among industry, commerce, and the
positive role of government is discussed in Jenkin, "Reactions of Major Groups,"
supra, at 298–305.

128. Gallup, *Gallup Poll*, supra note 52, at 1:9, 23. On the AAA, 70 percent of Democrats
were in favor while 92 percent of Republicans opposed. On pensions, both Democrats and Republicans were in favor—94.5 percent and 80 percent, respectively. On
child labor, 61 percent favored a constitutional amendment, with 72 percent of Democrats and 81 percent of socialists in favor, but 54 percent of Republicans opposed;
see also Cushman, "Mr. Dooley and Mr. Gallup," supra note 121, at 39, for a discussion of the poll results pertaining to child labor.

129. See Cushman, "Mr. Dooley and Mr. Gallup," supra note 121, at 40 (citing *Fortune*
magazine survey published in July 1936).

130. Gallup, *Gallup Poll*, supra note 52, at 1:53. The poll of March, 28, 1937, found that
58 percent favored an amendment to the Constitution giving Congress greater power
to regulate industry and agriculture. Interestingly, three months earlier, in mid-
December, a majority opposed "transferring to the Federal Government" authority
over the same, a distinction Barry Cushman attributes, apparently correctly, to the
wording of the questions and perhaps to the timing of the later poll, which was
"taken at the height of the Court-packing crisis." Cushman, "Mr. Dooley and Mr.
Gallup," supra note 121, at 37–38.

131. Gallup, *Gallup Poll*, supra note 52, at 1:14, 41, 52, 60. Concentration of power in
federal government was favored by 56 percent in a January 1936 poll; 72 percent of
Democrats, and even 35 percent of Republicans, were in favor. On wages and hours,
61 percent favored minimum wage regulation in a poll taken in May 1937, while 58
percent favored maximum hours. In September 1936, 51 percent favored revival of
the NRA, while in February 1937, 53 percent favored reenactment.

132. Cushman, "Mr. Dooley and Mr. Gallup," supra note 121, at 50 (citing data from
Gallup and *Fortune* polls indicating widespread agreement across class and geographic
lines that providing for needy was the responsibility of federal government).

133. Democratic Party platform of 1936, in Porter and Johnson, *National Party Platforms*,
supra note 12, at 360, 362.

134. Franklin D. Roosevelt, "Campaign Address at Madison Square Garden, New York
City: We Have Only Just Begun to Fight," Oct. 31, 1936, in Rosenman, *Public Papers
of FDR*, vol. 5, supra note 86, at 568, 571.

135. Ackerman, *We the People*, vol. 2: supra note 10, at 306; Cushman, *Rethinking the New
Deal Court*, supra note 68, at 27–29; Weed, *Nemesis of Reform*, supra note 4, at 101.

136. "Sun Refuses to Support Landon," *Hartford Courant*, Oct. 31, 1936, at 8.

137. Republican Party platform of 1936, in Porter and Johnson, *National Party Platforms*,
supra note 12, at 366–67.

138. Id. at 366.

139. Herbert Hoover, "Address at the Republican National Convention," June 10, 1936,
quoted in Weed, *Nemesis of Reform*, supra note 4, at 97.

140. Editorial, "America's Choice," *L.A. Times*, Nov. 1, 1936, at 1 (first and third quotations); Editorial, *Fullerton Daily News Trib.*, July 1, 1936, at 2, quoted in Robert L.
Pritchard, "Orange County During the Depressed Thirties: A Study in Twentieth-
Century California Local History," in *Hitting Home*, ed. Bernard Sternsher (1970),
260 (middle quotation).

141. *Omaha World Herald*, quoted in Arthur Krock, "Three Democratic Newspapers Debate the Issue," *N.Y. Times*, Sept. 15, 1936, at 28.

142. Ackerman, *We the People*, vol. 2: supra note 10, at 310–11; Mulder, *Insurgent Progressives*, supra note 16, at 158.

143. Michael J. Klarman, *From Jim Crow to Civil Rights* (2004), 111; Leuchtenburg, *FDR and the New Deal*, supra note 1, at 184–89; Mulder, *Insurgent Progressives*, supra note 16, at 161; James T. Patterson, *Congressional Conservatism and the New Deal: The Growth of the Conservative Coalition in Congress, 1933–1939* (1967), 80. For discussion of increasing political influence of African-Americans during this period, see Michael Klarman, "The Puzzling Resistance to Political Process Theory," *Va. L. Rev.* 77 (1991): 799. However, despite the breadth of Roosevelt's coalition, many remained disenfranchised.

144. See Dave Leip, Atlas of U.S. Elections: 1936 Presidential Election Results, http://www.uselectionatlas.org/RESULTS/national.php?f=0&year=1936.

145. Mulder, *Insurgent Progressives*, supra note 16, at 158.

146. Maury Maverick, "The Next Four Years: In Congress," *New Republic*, Nov. 25, 1936, at 100.

147. Editorial, "A Great Personal Triumph," *N.Y. Herald Trib.*, Nov. 4, 1936, at 32; see Walter Lippmann, "Today and Tomorrow: The Election," *Hartford Courant*, Nov. 5, 1936, at 20 (arguing that election landslide resulted from electorate's approval of results of Democratic policies).

148. William Allen White, *Emporia Gazette*, quoted in "Press Comment on Election," *Wash. Post*, Nov. 5, 1936, at X14; see also Franklyn Waltman, "Politics and People: Roosevelt Accorded Greatest Vote of Confidence Since Beginning of Country," *Wash. Post*, Nov. 5, 1936, at X2 ("Honest and sincere conservatives who have found objectionable . . . Mr. Roosevelt's . . . general philosophy must undergo a reorientation of their viewpoints if they desire to be in harmony with the country in which they live").

149. George Creel, "Roosevelt's Plans and Purposes," *Collier's*, Dec. 26, 1936, at 40.

150. See Dean Dinwoodey, "Congress Awaits Next Court Move," *N.Y. Times*, Jan. 24, 1937, at 65; "Many Amendments to Avoid War and Widen Federal Control Will Be Urged in Congress," *N.Y. Times*, Dec. 6, 1936, at N2; see generally Kenneth S. Davis, *FDR: Into the Storm, 1937–1940* (1993), 52; Leuchtenburg, *Supreme Court Reborn*, supra note 21, at 102–03; Howard Gillman, "The Collapse of Constitutional Originalism and the Rise of the Notion of the 'Living Constitution' in the Course of American State-Building," *Studs. in Am. Pol. Dev.* 11 (1997): 232.

151. Merlo J. Pusey, *The Supreme Court Crisis* (1937), 3.

152. Jackson, *Struggle for Judicial Supremacy*, supra note 35, at 178.

153. "A Great Personal Triumph," supra note 147, at 32.

154. Franklin D. Roosevelt, "The Annual Message to Congress," Jan. 6, 1937, in Rosenman, *Public Papers of FDR*, vol. 5, supra note 86, at 638–41.

155. Alsop and Catledge, *168 Days*, supra note 22, at 39–40.

156. Patterson, *Congressional Conservatism*, supra note 143, at 85.

157. See Leuchtenburg, *Supreme Court Reborn*, supra note 21, at 110–11.

158. Creel, "Roosevelt's Plans and Purposes," supra note 149, at 40; see also FDR's explanation after the fight was on: "No amendment which any powerful economic interests or the leaders of any powerful political party have had reason to oppose has ever been ratified within anything like a reasonable time. . . . [T]hirteen states which contain only five percent of the voting population can block ratification even though the thirty-five States with ninety-five percent of the population are in favor of it." Franklin D. Roosevelt, "A 'Fireside Chat' Discussing the Plan for Reorganization of the Judiciary," March 9, 1937, in Rosenman, *Public Papers of FDR*, vol. 6, supra note 2, at 131.

159. *Reorganization of the Federal Judiciary: Hearings on S.1392 Before the Senate Comm. on the Judiciary*, 75th Cong. 2429 (1937) (statement of Robert H. Jackson, Assistant Attorney General of the United States), reprinted in *Congress and the Courts*, ed. Bernard D. Reams, Jr., and Charles R. Haworth (1978), 2343; see also Charles A. Beard, "Rendezvous with the Supreme Court," *New Republic*, Sept. 2, 1936, at 93 (claiming that in view of the Court's recent decisions, justices could be expected to "macerat[e] almost any clarifying amendment").

160. Franklin D. Roosevelt, "Inaugural Address," March 4, 1933, in Rosenman, *Public Papers of FDR*, vol. 2, supra note 19, at 14–15.

161. Creel, "Roosevelt's Plans and Purposes," supra note 149, at 40. The specific clause FDR pointed to at that juncture was the Necessary and Proper Clause, though at other points in time he pointed to other language such as the General Welfare Clause. See, e.g., Franklin D. Roosevelt, "A 'Fireside Chat' Discussing the Plan for Reorganization of the Judiciary," March 9, 1937, in Rosenman, *Public Papers of FDR*, vol. 6: supra note 2, at 132.

162. Samuel Irving Rosenman, *Working with Roosevelt* (1952), 143.

163. See Bruce Ackerman, *We the People*, vol. 1: *Foundations* (1991), 42–43 (describing the modern lawyer's story of the "fall from grace" that began after Reconstruction, "climax[ed]" with the New Deal Court-packing plan, and was finally defeated with Justice Roberts's "switch"); Lawrence Lessig, "Understanding Changed Readings: Fidelity and Theory," *Stan. L. Rev.* 47 (1995): 446 & n220 (explaining that according to "dominant view," post–Court-packing plan jurisprudence "restored the original Constitution, after a period of constitutional usurpation by an activist conservative Court").

164. See White, *Constitution and the New Deal*, supra note 23, at 205–25 (discussing "interpretive revolution" of Constitution); Barry Friedman, "The History of the Countermajoritarian Difficulty, Part Four: Law's Politics," *U. Pa. L. Rev.* 148 (2000): 1012–19 (discussing emergence of view that Constitution was "flexible" and "living"); Gillman, "Collapse of Constitutional Originalism," supra note 150, at 230–46 (making argument that pressures of times led to understanding of Constitution as "living").

165. An extended version of this argument appears in Friedman, "History of the Countermajoritarian Difficulty," supra note 164, at 985–86.

166. James Weaver, *A Call to Action* (1974), 122 (remarks about Granger decisions).

167. Walter Clark, "Law and Human Progress," *Am. L. Rev.* 37 (1903): 512.

168. A. L. Duffus, "Mr. Hughes the Chief Justice Emerges," *N.Y. Times Mag.*, June 28, 1931, at 2.

169. Edwin Borchard, "The Supreme Court and Private Rights," *Yale L. J.* 47 (1938): 1055.

170. Merriam, *Written and the Unwritten Attitude*, supra note 100, at 16–17.

171. Arthur Krock, "Nine Judges–and Nine Men, Too," *N.Y. Times Mag.*, March 29, 1936, at 1.

172. United States v. Butler, 297 U.S. 1, 62 (1936). The opinion "earned him scorching comments from the law journals." Leuchtenburg, *Supreme Court Reborn*, supra note 21, at 96.

173. Krock, "Nine Judges," supra note 171, at 1; see also Peter Irons, *A People's History of the Supreme Court* (1999), 306 (suggesting that Roberts's "mechanistic formula relegate[d] the judge to the role of a carpenter with a T-square"); Charles A. Beard, "The Act of Constitutional Interpretation," *Nat'l L. Guild Q.* 1 (1937–1938): 13 (describing and mocking Roberts's interpretive theory that judges simply "square" statutes with Constitution to determine if "the statute is too long or too short, or just right, or is it straight or crooked"); Charles Grove Haines, "Judicial Review of Acts of Congress and the Need for Constitutional Reform," *Yale L. J.* 45 (1936): 832 ("[Roberts's] lan-

guage is reminiscent of the mechanical approach to law of the late eighteenth and early nineteenth century. . . . Though repeated at various times by justices inclined toward a mechanistic approach to law, its fallacies have been so frequently exposed by the 'realistic' and 'sociological' jurists that it takes considerable temerity to repeat the statement today as an inescapable truism"); A. M. Meyer, "Construction of the Constitution," *Kan. City L. Rev.* 4 (1936): 52 ("It is with his tongue in his cheek, then, that one reads this statement [of Roberts] from the prevailing opinion in United States v. Butler").

174. See Gillman, "Collapse of Constitutional Originalism," supra note 150, for an excellent account of the shift in public thinking in this regard. For examples of contemporary invocations of the "living" Constitution, see, e.g., Elliott, "Getting a New Constitution," supra note 89, at 115 ("[A] constitution must be capable of a living adaptation to a new economic setting if it is not to become the tomb of dead justice . . ."); John G. Winant, "The Constitution and Social Security," *Annals Am. Acad. Pol. & Soc. Sci.* 185 (1936): 22 (describing Constitution as a "living instrument of national government"); "Living Constitution Is Urged by Barkley," *N.Y. Times*, Sept. 17, 1937, at 20 (outlining Kentucky senator's speech claiming that "the surest way to preserve the Constitution" was to "keep it a living, breathing, pulsating instrument"); "Wallace Invokes General Welfare," *N.Y. Times*, Feb. 18, 1937, at 2 (documenting Secretary of Agriculture's argument that Roosevelt's Court plan would increase percentage of men on Court who "would interpret the Constitution as a living document").

175. Frankfurter, *Public & Its Government*, supra note 96, at 75–76 ("As a mere lawyer, Marshall had his superiors among his colleagues. His supremacy lay in his recognition of the practical needs of government. . . . The great judges are those to whom the Constitution is not primarily a text for interpretation but the means of ordering the life of a progressive people"); Franklin D. Roosevelt, "The Annual Message to Congress," Jan. 6, 1937, in Rosenman, *Public Papers of FDR*, vol. 5, supra note 86, at 639 (invoking framers).

176. McCulloch v. Maryland, 17 U.S. (14 Wheat.) 316, 415 (1819).

177. See William A. Roberts, "John Marshall and the New Deal, Address Broadcast over Station WJSV," Feb. 3, 1934, in *Fed. Bar Ass'n J.* 2 (1934): 33–36.

178. Charles A. Beard, "The Constitution in the 20th Century," *Annals Am. Acad. Pol. & Soc. Sci.* 185 (1936): 31.

179. 81 Cong. Rec. 2144 (1937) (statement of Sen. Norris); see also id. at 7379 (statement of Sen. Logan) ("We cannot stand still. Society must move forward. National power must be expanded to meet the exigencies of all occasions, and if the Nation has a Supreme Court that will not allow this, then the Nation must begin to wither and die"). Sometime later Senator Byrnes commented: "The real danger to our constitutional system has not been the readiness of courts to amend their decisions. The real danger has been the tendency of courts to disregard the lessons of experience and the force of better reasoning, and thus to produce hardening of the constitutional arteries. That disease might be fatal to the body politic." James F. Byrnes, "The Constitution and the Will of the People," *A.B.A. J.* 25 (1939): 668.

180. Franklin D. Roosevelt, "The Annual Message to Congress," Jan. 6, 1937, in Rosenman, *Public Papers of FDR*, vol. 5, supra note 86, at 639.

181. S. Rep. No. 75–711, at 15 (1937).

182. Quoted in Leuchtenburg, *Supreme Court Reborn*, supra note 21, at 96–97. Roosevelt was flooded with letters from citizens concerned about the "age problem." Id.

183. Pearson and Allen, *Nine Old Men*, supra note 57.

184. Krock, "Nine Judges," supra note 171, at 1. Hughes's suggestion appears in Charles Evans Hughes, *The Supreme Court of the United States: Its Foundations, Methods*

and Achievements: An Interpretation (1928), 76–77. Hughes's discussion is about the issue of infirmity of old judges, not judicial intransigence.

185. Cushman, "Mr. Dooley and Mr. Gallup," supra note 121, at 72–74. In a Gallup Poll from April 1937, 64 percent of respondents who had formed an opinion favored a constitutional amendment mandating judicial retirement between the ages of seventy and seventy-five. In a subsequent Gallup Poll taken in April 1938, 70 percent of such respondents said that there should be some mandatory retirement age for justices, with a median age of seventy selected. Gallup, *Gallup Poll*, supra note 52, at 1:56, 104. In a *Fortune* survey from July 1937, imposing a mandatory retirement age of seventy was selected as the leading alternative reform to FDR's Court plan. Cushman, "Mr. Dooley and Mr. Gallup," supra note 121, at 73.

186. Memorandum from Homer S. Cummings, Attorney General, to Angus MacLean, Assistant Attorney General, May 11, 1935, quoted in Leuchtenburg, *Supreme Court Reborn*, supra note 21, at 51. William Leuchtenberg, more than anyone else, has detailed the origins of the Court-packing plan. See id. at 82–131.

187. Letter from President Franklin D. Roosevelt to Homer Cummings, Attorney General, Jan. 14, 1936, quoted in id. at 99.

188. See Isidor Feinstein, *The Court Disposes* (1937), 113 (for description of British "New Deal"); Leuchtenburg, *Supreme Court Reborn*, supra note 21, at 95 (on repeated mentioning); see generally Ackerman, *We the People*, vol. 2: supra note 10, at 319.

189. See Robert H. Jackson, Assistant Attorney General, "Statement to Judiciary Committee of the Senate," March 11, 1937, in *"Packing" the Supreme Court and the Judicial Reorganization Bill, January–July 1937*, vol. 1: *Documentary History of the Franklin D. Roosevelt Presidency*, ed. George McJimsey (2001), 345–48.

190. Alsop and Catledge, *168 Days*, supra note 22, at 29; Diary Entry of Harold Ickes, Dec. 27, 1935, in Harold L. Ickes, *The Secret Diary of Harold L. Ickes* (1954), 1:495; Leuchtenburg, *Supreme Court Reborn*, supra note 21, at 118–19.

191. Leuchtenburg, *Supreme Court Reborn*, supra note 21, at 117–19.

192. Id. at 119–20; see also 75 Cong. Rec. 1, 6789 (statement of Sen. Robinson), reprinted in *Franklin D. Roosevelt and the Supreme Court*, ed. Alfred Hains Cope and Fred Krinsky (1952), 83 (raising point in debate over compromise bill).

193. Alsop and Catledge, *168 Days*, supra note 22, at 31–33; Leuchtenburg, *Supreme Court Reborn*, supra note 21, at 124.

194. Franklin D. Roosevelt, "Message to the Congress, The President Presents a Plan for the Reorganization of the Judicial Branch of the Government," Feb. 5, 1937, in Rosenman, *Public Papers of FDR*, vol. 6, supra note 2, at 52.

195. Id. at 51–66. For the draft of the proposed bill, see id. at 63. Presentation and supporting documents are also available in Cope and Krinsky, *FDR and the Supreme Court*, supra note 192, at 17–27.

196. Leuchtenburg, *Supreme Court Reborn*, supra note 21, at 134.

197. Letter from Harold Ickes, Secretary of Interior, to William Allen White, editor of *Emporia Gazette*, Feb. 25, 1937, quoted in Patterson, *Congressional Conservatism*, supra note 143, at 88. Ickes continued: "All that is left is to do now is to declare that [the Court] is infallible, that it is the spiritual descendent of Moses and that the number Nine is three times three, and three stands for the Trinity."

198. Editorial, "Striking at the Roots," *N.Y. Herald Trib.*, Feb. 6, 1937, at 1.

199. *The Supreme Court Issue and the Constitution: Comments Pro and Con by Distinguished Men*, ed. William R. Barnes and A. W. Littlefield (1937), 34.

200. Franklin D. Roosevelt, "The Three Hundred and Forty-second Press Conference," Feb. 5, 1937, in Rosenman, *Public Papers of FDR*, vol. 5, supra note 86, at 43–44.

201. Sen. Alben W. Barkley, "Keynote Speech at Democratic National Convention," June 23, 1936, quoted in "The Keynote Speech," *N.Y. Times*, June 24, 1936, at 1; see also Beard, "Rendezvous with the Supreme Court," supra note 159, at 92–93, for a discussion of this speech.

202. "Another 5–4 Conservative Decision," *N.Y. Daily News*, June 2, 1936, quoted in McKenna, *Great Constitutional War*, supra note 64, at 214; see also H. L. Mencken, "Burying the Dead Horse," Aug. 17, 1936, quoted in Ackerman, *We the People*, vol. 2: supra note 10, at 313 (claiming Roosevelt's reelection would "set off the most violent attack upon the Constitution ever made").

203. "Lowden Pictures Crisis," *N.Y. Times*, June 11, 1935, at 1 (quoting former governor Frank O. Lowden of Illinois).

204. Republican Party platform of 1936, in Porter and Johnson, *National Party Platforms*, supra note 12, at 365–66.

205. Governor Alfred M. Landon, "Campaign Address at Madison Square Garden, New York City," Oct. 29, 1936, in "The Texts of Governor Landon's Addresses at Madison Square Garden and over the Radio," *N.Y. Times*, Oct. 30, 1936, at 16.

206. Alan Brinkley, *The End of Reform: New Deal Liberalism in Recession and War* (1995), 17.

207. Edward A. Purcell, Jr., *The Crisis of Democratic Theory: Scientific Naturalism & the Problem of Value* (1973), 137.

208. Recall that during the Gold Clause controversy, Roosevelt was prepared to defy the Court, privately floating the suggestion after *Butler*. Leuchtenburg, *Supreme Court Reborn*, supra note 21, at 101 (on post-*Butler* suggestion). He also harbored a sort of grudge at the Court for not playing along. After his election in 1932, Roosevelt apparently dropped hints that he would like to consult with the Court from time to time on how to achieve his objectives, a suggestion that obviously was not taken up. Alsop and Catledge, *168 Days*, supra note 22, at 16; Pusey, *Charles Evans Hughes*, supra note 88, at 2:733.

209. See White, *Constitution and the New Deal*, supra note 23, at 102–08. The first administrative law casebook was published in the early 1930s by Felix Frankfurter and J. Forrester Davison. Id. at 106. In 1938, James Landis published his classic *The Administrative Process*, seeking to justify the use of administrative agencies. James K. Landis, *The Administrative Process* (1938). For contemporary discussions of the legitimacy of the growing administrative state, see Carr, *Democracy and the Supreme Court*, supra note 44, at 7 and Frankfurter, *Public & Its Government*, supra note 96, at 157–59.

210. Mulder, *Insurgent Progressives*, supra note 16, at 210–13.

211. See Barry Dean Karl, *Executive Reorganization and Reform in the New Deal: The Genesis of Administrative Management, 1900–1939* (1963), 256. Accounts of the executive reorganization effort are full of references to concern about Roosevelt's acquiring dictatorial power. See id. at 248; Richard Polenberg, *Reorganizing Roosevelt's Government* (1966), vii.

212. "Texas Legislature Fights Court Plan," *N.Y. Times*, Feb. 10, 1937, at 1.

213. Editorial, "Not Safe for Democracy," *Des Moines Reg.*, Feb. 6, 1937, in "Opinions of the Nation's Press on Court Plan," *N.Y. Times*, Feb. 6, 1937, at 10; see also "Striking at the Roots," supra note 198, at 1 ("[Roosevelt] would strike at the roots of [the] equality of the three branches of government upon which the nation is founded, and centralize in himself the control of judicial as well as executive functions"); Editorial, "The Proposal to 'Pack' the Supreme Court," *Hartford Courant*, Feb. 6, 1937, at 10 (claiming plan was Roosevelt's way of "seeking power and still more power, of substituting himself for both the legislative and judicial branches of the Government and of making him the repository of all government functions"); Editorial, *Cleveland*

Plain Dealer, Feb. 6, 1937, quoted in "Press of Nation Comments on President's Proposal," *L.A. Times*, Feb. 6, 1937, at 6 (arguing that plan's major purpose was to bend "the Supreme Court to the will of a popular Executive, backed by a Congress inclined to subservience"); Franklyn Waltman, "Politics and People: Roosevelt Fails to Conceal That Real Objective Is a Supreme Court Amenable to His Will," *Wash. Post*, Feb. 6, 1937, at 2 (criticizing alleged justification for plan as specious).

214. "Strawn Scores Proposal," *N.Y. Times*, Feb. 6, 1937, at 10.

215. H. L. Mencken, "A Constitution for the New Deal," *Am. Mercury*, June 1937, at 131.

216. "The Big Debate," *Time*, March 1, 1937, at 10.

217. Quoted in Bernard DeVoto, "The Easy Chair: Desertion from the New Deal," *Harper's Mag.*, Oct. 1937, at 558.

218. S. Rep. No. 75-711, at 15 (1937).

219. Alsop and Catledge, *168 Days*, supra note 22, at 262.

220. "The People's Liberties in Jeopardy," *Chi. News*, Jan. 23, 1937, reprinted in McKenna, *Great Constitutional War*, supra note 64, at 110.

221. Feinstein, *Court Disposes*, supra note 188, at 99 ("The Court can scent communism several centuries down wind, in a federal income tax or in a minimum wage for chambermaids. We suspect that it will be less alert to the menace of fascism").

222. Louis P. Goldberg and Eleanore Levenson, *Lawless Judges* (1935), 231.

223. Leuchtenburg, *Supreme Court Reborn*, supra note 21, at 135 (on Maverick's rushing down aisle); Letter from Representative Maury Maverick to John I. Palmer, Jan. 18, 1937, quoted in id. at 291n25.

224. Roger N. Baldwin, "Personal Liberty," *Annals Am. Acad. Pol. & Soc. Sci.* 185 (1936): 164.

225. Felix Frankfurter, unsigned editorial, "The Red Terror of Judicial Reform," *New Republic*, Oct. 1, 1924, reprinted in *Felix Frankfurter on the Supreme Court*, ed. Philip B. Kurland (1970), 158–59.

226. Quoted in Steven F. Lawson, "Progressives and the Supreme Court: A Case for Judicial Reform in the 1920s," *Historian* 42 (1980): 432.

227. Felix Frankfurter, unsigned editorial, "Red Terror of Judicial Reform," reprinted in Kurland, *Felix Frankfurter*, supra note 225, at 160.

228. H. L. Mencken, "The Supreme Court," *Evening Sun*, Nov. 19, 1923, at 17.

229. This history is recounted in David M. Rabban, *Free Speech in Its Forgotten Years* (1997), 342–80, and Geoffrey R. Stone, *Perilous Times: Free Speech in Wartime from the Sedition Act of 1798 to the War on Terrorism* (2004), 236–38.

230. Gitlow v. New York, 268 U.S. 652, 666 (1925).

231. Stromberg v. California, 283 U.S. 359 (1931); Near v. Minnesota, 283 U.S. 697 (1931); see also Murphy, *Constitution in Crisis Times*, supra note 26, at 120 (discussing both cases); "Frees Convicted Girl Red," *N.Y. Times*, May 19, 1931, at 5 (reporting decision in flag case).

232. "The Supreme Court's Shift to Liberalism," *Literary Dig.*, June 13, 1931, at 8; D. E. Wolf, "The Supreme Court in a New Phase," *Current Hist.*, July 1931, at 590; see also Murphy, *Constitution in Crisis Times*, supra note 26, at 121 (discussing impact of decisions).

233. "Supreme Court's Shift to Liberalism," supra note 232, at 8.

234. Grosjean v. Am. Press Co., 297 U.S. 233 (1936).

235. Meyer v. Nebraska, 262 U.S. 390 (1923).

236. Pierce v. Society of Sisters, 268 U.S. 510 (1925).

237. See "Oregon School Law Declared Invalid by Supreme Court," *N.Y. Times*, June 2, 1925, at 1 ("Charges that the law was backed by the Ku Klux Klan and was aimed at the Roman Catholic Church have been heard on every side since the statute was en-

acted"); see also Barry Cushman, "The Secret Lives of the Four Horsemen," *Va. L. Rev.* 83 (1997): 581 ("The Horsemen unanimously repelled the monoculturalist Ku Klux Klan's attack on parochial education in Pierce v. Society of Sisters . . .").

238. Lawson, "Progressives and the Supreme Court," supra note 226, at 431–32.

239. Editorial, "The Oregon and Nebraska Acts," *Chi. Daily Trib.*, Oct. 19, 1924, at 8.

240. Buchanan v. Warley, 245 U.S. 60 (1917); Nixon v. Herndon, 273 U.S. 536 (1927). For a discussion of these cases, see Klarman, *From Jim Crow*, supra note 143, at 62, 80–81, 135–37; Murphy, *Constitution in Crisis Times*, supra note 26, at 94; David E. Bernstein, "Philip Sober Controlling Philip Drunk: *Buchanan v. Warley* in Historical Perspective," *Vand. L. Rev.* 51 (1998): 797–880.

241. Moore v. Dempsey, 261 U.S. 86 (1923); see generally Klarman, *From Jim Crow*, supra note 143, at 98–99, 117–21; Murphy, *Constitution in Crisis Times*, supra note 26, at 95.

242. Klarman, *From Jim Crow*, supra note 143, at 123.

243. Powell v. Alabama, 287 U.S. 45, 57 (1932); Editorial, "The Scottsboro Case," *Wash. Post*, Nov. 8, 1932, at 6; see also Klarman, *From Jim Crow*, supra note 143, at 99, 117, 123–25 (describing case and Court's rationale).

244. Norris v. Alabama, 294 U.S. 587 (1935); see generally Klarman, *From Jim Crow*, supra note 143, at 99, 117, 125–27.

245. Brown v. Mississippi, 297 U.S. 278 (1936); see generally Klarman, *From Jim Crow*, supra note 143, at 99, 117, 128–29; Murphy, *Constitution in Crisis Times*, supra note 26, at 125.

246. See, e.g., James Truslow Adams, historian, "Radio Address," March 1937, quoted in Brinkley, *End of Reform*, supra note 206, at 20 ("If a President tries to take away our freedom of speech, if a Congress takes away our property unlawfully, if a State legislature, as in the recent case of Louisiana under the dictatorship of Huey Long, takes away the freedom of the press, who is to save us except the Courts?"); Frank Gannett, president and publisher of the twenty Gannett newspapers, "The People's Fight, National Broadcast from the National Committee to Uphold Constitutional Government," Feb. 21, 1937, in McJimsey, *"Packing" the Supreme Court*, supra note 189, at 316 ("The Court stands as a defender of all classes, all creeds and all races"); Pusey, *Supreme Court Crisis*, supra note 151, at 46 ("We do not need to imagine what conditions some parts of the country would face if no independent tribunal could set constitutional rights above legislative whims"); Ignatius M. Wilkinson, "The President's Plan Respecting the Supreme Court," *Fordham L. Rev.* 6 (1937): 184–85 ("There are many decisions of the Supreme Court where we find it standing as the sole guardian of persons, often poor and insignificant in themselves, whose natural rights . . . were in danger of being destroyed because of an objective which was thought to be desirable by a majority").

247. Frank Gannett, "People's Fight," in McJimsey, *"Packing" the Supreme Court*, supra note 189, at 316.

248. S. Rep. No. 75-711, at 19–23 (1937).

249. Memorandum from Joseph P. Lash, "Answer to the Argument That the Proposal Will Lead to a Deprivation of Civil Liberties," March 3, 1937, in McJimsey, *"Packing" the Supreme Court*, supra note 189, at 290.

250. Franklin D. Roosevelt, "A 'Fireside Chat' Discussing the Plan for Reorganization of the Judiciary," March 9, 1937, in Rosenman, *Public Papers of FDR*, vol. 6, supra note 2, at 132.

251. See Senator Burton Wheeler, "Address Before the Fourth Annual Woman Congress," March 10, 1937, quoted in "President Accused of 'Haste and Hate,'" *N.Y. Times*, March 11, 1937, at 8 ("Create now a political court to echo the ideas of the Executive

and you have created a weapon; a weapon which in the hands of another President could well be an instrument of destruction; a weapon that . . . can extinguish your right of liberty of speech, of thought, of action and of religion; a weapon whose use is only dictated by the conscience of the wielder"); Senator Henrik Shipstead, "News Conference Address," May 11, 1937, quoted in Mulder, *Insurgent Progressives*, supra note 16, at 206 ("What you can do today for a good purpose, some one else could do for a bad purpose tomorrow").

252. Alsop and Catledge, *168 Days*, supra note 22, at 10.

253. Pusey, *Supreme Court Crisis*, supra note 151, at 2.

254. "Court Impasse," *N.Y. Times*, Feb. 21, 1937, at 49.

255. Quoted in Alsop and Catledge, *168 Days*, supra note 22, at 67.

256. Id. at 69.

257. Id. at 72.

258. Leuchtenburg, *Supreme Court Reborn*, supra note 21, at 137.

259. Patterson, *Congressional Conservatism*, supra note 143, at 95–99. Among other things, southerners were unhappy the administration was not taking a stronger position on sit-down strikes being staged by labor; they also feared a liberalized Supreme Court would endanger Jim Crow. Id. Senator Carter Glass of Virginia gave an impassioned radio address against the plan in which he dwelt at length on the Supreme Court and issues of race. See Senator Carter Glass, "Radio Address," March 29, 1937, in *Vital Speeches* (1937): 3:386. See also Kevin J. McMahon, *Reconsidering Roosevelt on Race: How the Presidency Paved the Road to* Brown (2004), 79–86 (discussing Senator Glass's speech and analyzing the racial politics that were part of the debate over the Court plan).

260. Alsop and Catledge, *168 Days*, supra note 22, at 162–76.

261. Id. at 97; Patterson, *Congressional Conservatism*, supra note 143, at 109.

262. See Letter from Representative James W. Wadsworth to Thomas E. Broderick, Feb. 11, 1937, quoted in Patterson, *Congressional Conservatism*, supra note 143, at 109 (arguing that because Republicans would have to rely on Democratic votes to defeat Court plan, they should "refrain from taking a united party action . . . lest by putting a partisan tinge on the issue we [Republicans] drive reluctant Democrats back into Roosevelt's arms").

263. "John Doe Also Speaks Mind on President's Proposal," *Newsweek*, Feb. 20, 1937, at 17.

264. Mulder, *Insurgent Progressives*, supra note 16, at 177–79.

265. Quoted in Patterson, *Congressional Conservatism*, supra note 143, at 116. For a discussion of Wheeler's preferred amendment alternative, see Ackerman, *We the People*, vol. 2: supra note 10, at 321.

266. Arthur Krock, "Two Results of Supreme Court Argument," *N.Y. Times*, Feb. 10, 1937, at 22.

267. K. N. Llewellyn, "A United Front on the Court," *Nation*, March 13, 1937, at 288; see also Heywood Broun, "Some Sleeping Beauties," *Nation*, June 26, 1937, at 730 (arguing that "Mr. Roosevelt's plan . . . may have its faults, but it is the only one available" and that "liberals are constantly being used to help the purposes of sinister groups" serving "as shock troops by the Old Guard").

268. Cushman, *Rethinking the New Deal Court*, supra note 68, at 15. Apparently understanding that at least two of the justices were reluctant to leave without such security, Sumners had pushed such a measure in the past. Alsop and Catledge, *168 Days*, supra note 22, at 41. These justices apparently were concerned in light of what had happened to Justice Oliver Wendell Holmes, Jr., upon his retirement. He had left the bench relying on a congressional promise not to cut the sala-

ries of judges over seventy who had ten years of service, and then Congress did cut the salary Holmes earned. See Pusey, *Charles Evans Hughes*, supra note 88, at 2:760.

269. "Opposition Grows," *N.Y. Times*, Feb. 9, 1937, at 1.

270. Quoted in Alsop and Catledge, *168 Days*, supra note 22, at 71.

271. "Roosevelt Prepares 'an Infusion of New Blood' and the Republicans Prepare for 'the Beginning of the End,'" *Newsweek*, Feb. 13, 1937, at 9.

272. Franklin D. Roosevelt, "Address at the Democratic Victory Dinner: If We Would Make Democracy Succeed, I Say We Must Act—NOW!," March 4, 1937, in Rosenman, *Public Papers of FDR*, vol. 5, supra note 86, at 121, 116.

273. Franklin D. Roosevelt, "A 'Fireside Chat' Discussing the Plan for Reorganization of the Judiciary," March 9, 1937, in Rosenman, *Public Papers of FDR*, vol. 6: supra note 2, at 123.

274. Alsop and Catledge, *168 Days*, supra note 22, at 88–89.

275. See Leuchtenburg, *Supreme Court Reborn*, supra note 21, at 141 (on short case); Alsop and Catledge, *168 Days*, supra note 22, at 121–23 (on Ashurst not liking haste); Cushman, *Rethinking the New Deal Court*, supra note 68, at 21 (on end date).

276. Leuchtenburg, *Supreme Court Reborn*, supra note 21, at 134.

277. See, e.g., Alfange, *Supreme Court and the National Will*, supra note 33, at ix ("[T]he work is intended primarily for nonprofessional readers . . ."); Morris L. Ernst, *The Ultimate Power* (1937), xiv–xv ("[T]his volume was not designed for lawyers. . . . I think the time is ripe for the non-lawyers to reassert their earnest disrespect for what lawyers and judges have done to us all"); Feinstein, *Court Disposes*, supra note 188, at 12 ("This is a book by a layman for laymen").

278. Cartoon, "Wherever Two or Three Gather," *Richmond-Times Dispatch*, reprinted in James Truslow Adams, "The Court Issue: Is Democracy Menaced?," *N.Y. Times*, Feb. 21, 1937, at 113.

279. Leuchtenburg, *Supreme Court Reborn*, supra note 21, at 139–40 (discussing strategy of noncommittal by many Democratic senators); Patterson, *Congressional Conservatism*, supra note 143, at 99n76 (discussing evidence that opposition in Senate reflected constituent wishes); "John Doe Also Speaks," supra note 263, at 17 (discussing members of Congress's refusing to commit themselves in light of divergent public opinion).

280. "John Doe Also Speaks," supra note 263, at 17.

281. Raymond Moley, "Today in America: 'The Fear of Fear,'" *Newsweek*, Feb. 27, 1937, at 5; see also "Congress Snowed Under by Mail," *N.Y. Times*, Feb. 21, 1937, at 51 (stating that early mail, though heartfelt, was likely from the "higher economic brackets").

282. "Senate Spars for Time on Reform Bill Until Word Arrives from 'Little Fellow' Back Home," *Newsweek*, Feb. 27, 1937, at 10.

283. Editorial, "Unpacking the Supreme Court," *N.Y. Post*, Feb. 8, 1937, reprinted in Barnes and Littlefield, *Supreme Court Issue and the Constitution*, supra note 199, at 92.

284. Two polls at the end of March (which Gallup for some reason did not publish) indicated narrow plurality support. See Gallup Poll, March 20–25 (1937), available at The Roper Center for Public Opinion Research, University of Connecticut. http://www.ropercenter.uconn.edu/ipoll.html (Responding to the question "Are you in favor of President Roosevelt's proposal regarding the Supreme Court": 46 percent yes; 45 percent no; 9 percent no opinion); Gallup Poll, March 24–29 (1937), available at The Roper Center for Public Opinion Research, University of Connecticut. http://www.ropercenter.uconn.edu/ipoll.html (44 percent yes; 43 percent no; 13 percent

no opinion). Gallup gave "yes," "no," and "no opinion" as the choice, but when one observes the movement of respondents *in and out* of the "no opinion" category, it seems apparent that at least some of this group was informed but undecided. Indeed, "no opinion" was by far the most volatile opinion group during the "Court fight." See Frank V. Cantwell, "Public Opinion and the Legislative Process," *Am. Pol. Sci. Rev.* 40 (1946): 926–31, 934 chart 1. This suggests that the "no opinion" category, which Gallup then excluded from its published reports, is actually critical to understanding the public's shifting positions on Roosevelt's Court plan and perhaps even the plan's chance of success at the time. Though the plurality support for the plan was admittedly thin, the poll data suggest that public opinion had not genuinely settled and thus that the plan may have had a legitimate chance at public acceptance at this point. One commentator has downplayed this genuine uncertainty. Cushman, "Mr. Dooley and Mr. Gallup," supra note 121, at 69n339 (arguing that despite few polls indicating plurality support after Roosevelt's fireside chat, both the published polls and the unpublished surveys showed "persistent opposition" by the public to the plan).

 Gregory Caldeira's article on public opinion and the Court plan, infra, note 285, is often cited approvingly in the legal literature. See Ackerman, *We the People*, vol. 2: supra note 10, at 324 (suggesting it should be "required reading"); see also Friedman, "History of the Countermajoritarian Difficulty," supra note 164, at 977–78n24 (discussing Caldeira's article). For an analysis of events, Frank Cantwell's 1946 piece is even more valuable. Cantwell offers a track of polling data week to week, running alongside major news events. See Cantwell, "Public Opinion and the Legislative Process," supra. Caldeira performs a regression analysis to determine which events affected support for the plan and by what amount. It is unclear what Caldeira's regression adds, but it is clear he omitted an event that plainly was consequential, though the tracking polls indicate it only affected the no vote (albeit sharply): the opening of the Senate case against the plan, highlighted by the Chief Justice's letter against it.

285. For the relevant poll data, see Gallup, *Gallup Poll*, supra note 52, at 1:50–51, 53–55, 58–59, 69; see also Gregory A. Caldeira, "Public Opinion and the U.S. Supreme Court: FDR's Court-Packing Plan," *Am. Pol. Sci. Rev.* 81 (1987): 1146–47; Cantwell, "Public Opinion and the Legislative Process," supra note 284, at 926–31, 934; Cushman, "Mr. Dooley and Mr. Gallup," supra note 121, at 69–70, 69n339.

286. Roosevelt's electorate included a large number of immigrants, African-Americans, and the poorer economic stratum, including those on relief. See Cushman, "Mr. Dooley and Mr. Gallup," supra note 121, at 15n35, 82–83 & n399. The failure to poll these groups explains the *Literary Digest* debacle in the 1936 election. See id., at 79–83. Gallup did better, of course. But it still was coming up short on FDR's support, and this likely remains the reason why. See id. at 15n35 (quoting Gallup offering this explanation). Gallup's elimination of mail ballots was an attempt to deal with the sampling problems that plagued the *Literary Digest* poll. Id. at 82–83. Still, there is evidence that when answering the questions of those more educated, respondents would withhold truthful answers. Id. at 95n443. Also, some pollsters at the time eliminated southern blacks and the poor from polls that involved "political issues." This was a reaction to the widespread disenfranchisement of southern blacks and the use of the poll tax, which limited the ability for members of these groups to vote and led pollsters to exclude them from cross sections of the voting population. Id. at 89–90.

287. Gallup, *Gallup Poll*, supra note 52, at 1:51–55 (on Democrats' support); Cushman, "Mr. Dooley and Mr. Gallup," supra note 121, at 15 ("In the 1936 election, Gallup un-

derpredicted Roosevelt's 60.7 percent nationwide popular vote total by 6.9 percent; the average state-by-state error was 6 percent. Following the election, Gallup made some technical refinements that appear to have improved the performance of subsequent polls").

288. Cartoon, "All the King's Horses and All the King's Men," *L.A. Times*, March 29, 1937, at A4.

289. West Coast Hotel v. Parrish, 300 U.S. 379 (1937); Jackson, *Struggle for Judicial Supremacy*, supra note 35, at 207–13.

290. *Parrish*, 300 U.S. at 389. The Court explained that in *Tipaldo*, New York had not urged overruling *Adkins*, but only "distinguishing" it, and for this reason the Court had not taken up the question of overruling *Adkins*.

291. Alsop and Catledge, *168 Days*, supra note 22, at 145.

292. Washington, Virginia & Maryland Coach Co. v. NLRB, 301 U.S. 142 (1937), was unanimous in upholding the act. The four divided cases were: Associated Press v. NLRB, 301 U.S. 103 (1937); NLRB v. Friedman–Harry Marks Clothing Co., 301 U.S. 58 (1937); NLRB v. Fruehauf Trailer Co., 301 U.S. 49 (1937); and NLRB v. Jones & Laughlin Steel Corp., 301 U.S. 1 (1937) itself.

293. Carter v. Carter Coal Co., 298 U.S. 238, 317–18 (1936) (Hughes, C. J., concurring).

294. *Jones & Laughlin Steel Corp.*, 301 U.S. at 41–42.

295. Quoted in Irons, *New Deal Lawyers*, supra note 7, at 287.

296. *Jones & Laughlin Steel Corp.*, 301 U.S. at 87 (McReynolds, J., dissenting).

297. National Labor Relations Board v. Friedman–Harry Marks Clothing Co., 301 U.S. 58, 74 (1937).

298. Alsop and Catledge, *168 Days*, supra note 22, at 153.

299. "Supreme Court Upholds Wagner Labor Act in Series of 5 Decisions, 4 of Them 5 to 4," *Atlanta Const.*, Apr. 13, 1937, at 1 (headline); "Democrats Laud Court's Decision," *Atlanta Const.*, Apr. 13, 1937, at 8 (separate coverage).

300. Turner Catledge, "Split on Court Bill," *N.Y. Times*, Apr. 13, 1937, at 1.

301. Alsop and Catledge, *168 Days*, supra note 22, at 152.

302. "Roosevelt Still Determined to Reorganize Court; New Wage and Hour Bills Planned Immediately," *Atlanta Const.*, Apr. 14, 1937, at 1.

303. Quoted in Alsop and Catledge, *168 Days*, supra note 22, at 153.

304. Pusey, *Charles Evans Hughes*, supra note 88, at 2:760.

305. Id. at 2:760–61.

306. Steward Machine Co. v. Davis, 301 U.S. 548 (1937). All Four Horsemen would have struck down the provision of the Social Security Act at issue in the case on the ground that it invaded the powers reserved to the states under the Tenth Amendment. However, Justices Sutherland and Van Devanter objected only to the act's administrative provisions, arguing they invaded the administrative powers of the state. They agreed with the majority that the act had otherwise been validly passed pursuant to Congress's spending power. *Davis*, 301 U.S. at 609 (Sutherland, J., dissenting).

307. "Farewell Appearance," *Time*, June 7, 1937, at 13.

308. Pusey, *Supreme Court Crisis*, supra note 151, at 103.

309. Compare Gallup Poll, June 3–8 (1937), available at The Roper Center for Public Opinion Research, University of Connecticut, http://www.ropercenter.uconn.edu/ipoll.html (33 percent yes; 48 percent no; 18 percent no opinion), with Gallup Poll, May 12–17 (1937), available at The Roper Center for Public Opinion Research, University of Connecticut, http://www.ropercenter.uconn.edu/ipoll.html (39 percent yes; 46 percent no; 15 percent no opinion). For an overview of this shift at the

time of Van Devanter's retirement, see Caldeira, "Public Opinion and the U.S. Supreme Court," supra note 285, at 1148. Cantwell presents a more nuanced explanation. He suggests that in the months preceding Van Devanter's retirement (when it was rumored that Van Devanter as well as Justice Brandeis might retire), there was a significant dip in the yes vote, with people moving into the no opinion category. After the retirement decision was announced, opinion crystallized. The no opinion vote sank rapidly, with these people moving into the no side, which moved up to 50 percent. See Cantwell, "Public Opinion and the Legislative Process," supra note 284, at 930–31, 934 chart 2.

310. S. Rep. No. 75-711 (1937); see also Alsop and Catledge, *168 Days*, supra note 22, at 228–29; Leuchtenburg, *Supreme Court Reborn*, supra note 21, at 146.

311. S. Rep. No. 75-711, at 3, 23 (1937).

312. Leuchtenburg, *Supreme Court Reborn*, supra note 21, at 148.

313. Ackerman, *We the People*, vol. 2: supra note 10, at 292; Pusey, *Charles Evans Hughes*, supra note 88, at 2:761.

314. Alsop and Catledge, *168 Days*, supra note 22, at 208–16.

315. One of these would not be until 1938. Under the proposed compromise, Roosevelt would be able to appoint one new judge per calendar year for each sitting judge over the age of seventy-five. On the basis of the Court's composition, this would have allowed an additional appointment for both 1939 and 1940 as well. Leuchtenburg, *Supreme Court Reborn*, supra note 21, at 148.

316. Alsop and Catledge, *168 Days*, supra note 22, at 241–42; Arthur Krock, "One Result of the Jefferson Islands Picnic," *N.Y. Times*, June 29, at 20. Views on the efficacy of this rally differ considerably. Compare Alsop and Catledge, *168 Days*, supra note 22, at 242 ("[N]o one was conciliated, no one was charmed out of rebellion . . ."), with Krock, "One Result of the Jefferson Islands Picnic," supra (claiming that the hearts of many party members "melted in sympathy" when meeting with Roosevelt during the picnic and suggesting growing belief "that a compromise may be achieved" on the Court bill).

317. Leuchtenburg, *Supreme Court Reborn*, supra note 21, at 149.

318. Alsop and Catledge, *168 Days*, supra note 22, at 245–46, 248.

319. Id. at 263, 267.

320. Quoted in Turner Catledge, "Want Bill Dropped," *N.Y. Times*, July 15, 1937, at 1.

321. Mulder, *Insurgent Progressives*, supra note 16, at 200.

322. Pusey, *Supreme Court Crisis*, supra note 151, at 52–53.

323. See Ackerman, *We the People*, vol. 2: supra note 10, at 279–382; Cushman, *Rethinking the New Deal Court*, supra note 68; Leuchtenburg, *Supreme Court Reborn*, supra note 21, at 132–62; White, *Constitution and the New Deal*, supra note 23, at 198–236.

324. See generally Stephen M. Griffin, "Constitutional Theory Transformed," *Yale L. J.* 108 (1999): 2115–64 (attempting to debunk "restorationist" theories of New Deal constitutional change and advancing own institution-based theory); Laura Kalman, "Law, Politics, and the New Deal(s)," *Yale L. J.* 108 (1999): 2165–214 (asserting continued importance of externalist politics–based theory for explaining New Deal constitutional change); William E. Leuchtenburg, "When the People Spoke, What Did They Say?: The Election of 1936 and the Ackerman Thesis," *Yale L. J.* 108 (1999): 2077–114 (arguing that Roosevelt opponents made constitutional change dominant election issue in 1936 and that people, while probably not consciously amending Constitution, were ratifying significant change in governing philosophy).

325. See Ackerman, *We the People*, vol. 2: supra note 10, at 346 (recognizing that New Deal revolution was memorialized by judges and lawyers through judicial decisions, though ultimately finding this acceptable); David A. Pepper, "Against Legalism: Re-

NOTES TO PAGE 230   499

butting an Anachronistic Account of 1937," *Marq. L. Rev.* 82 (1998): 64 (arguing historical debate over New Deal switch has been so important because the "Court's status vis-à-vis popular politics" and "deeper questions of constitutional and democratic theory" hinge on the effect of political influence); William Wayne Justice, "The Two Faces of Judicial Activism," *Geo. Wash. L. Rev.* 61 (1992): 5 (identifying the "wholesale rejection" of legal precedents by the New Deal Court as an example of jurisprudential activism because it was dramatic Court-initiated constitutional change even though "the words of the Constitution did not change in 1937"); see also Jed Rubenfeld, *Freedom and Time: A Theory of Constitutional Self-Government* (2001), 172 ("If constitutional commitments are not to give way to governance by present political will, the power to interpret them must be assigned to a body insulated from that will").

326. Roberts asserted that he voted against the minimum wage law at issue in *Tipaldo*, because in that case the state of New York did not come right out and ask the Court to overrule *Adkins*, instead claiming that 1923 decision against the District of Columbia's minimum wage law was distinguishable. Roberts's memorandum implies that if New York had explicitly asked the Court to overturn *Adkins* in *Tipaldo*, he would have done so and upheld the minimum wage at that time. But because New York attempted to defend its law by distinguishing *Adkins* in a way Roberts thought "disingenuous," he instead voted to strike down New York's law. See Felix Frankfurter, "Mr. Justice Roberts," *U. Pa. L. Rev.* 104 (1955): 314–15.

    The majority opinion in *Tipaldo* does state this reason of Roberts's as one of its two grounds for ruling against the New York law. Morehead v. New York ex rel. Tipaldo, 298 U.S. 587, 604–05 (1936). Chief Justice Hughes's opinion in *West Coast Hotel* explains things this way also. West Coast Hotel v. Parrish, 300 U.S. 379, 388–90 (1937). However, Justice Roberts's memory was faulty on two critical points. Contrary to his assertion, New York's petition did ask the Court to reconsider *Adkins*. It did not stress the argument, but it made it. So, technically there was no technicality in the way. See Michael Ariens, "A Thrice-Told Tale, or Felix the Cat," *Harv. L. Rev.* 107 (1994): 638n105. In addition, at the time Roberts voted to hear *West Coast Hotel*, he could not possibly have known from filed court papers what arguments were being advanced regarding *Adkins*. Id. at 641–42. The petition for review filed in *West Coast Hotel* was by the employer, not the state, and the employer would not have wanted to have *Adkins* overruled. See Cushman, *Rethinking the New Deal Court*, supra note 68, at 97 (noting state of Washington was appellee rather than appellant in case). In fact, as Roberts reveals in his memorandum, his conservative colleagues could not comprehend his vote to hear the *West Coast Hotel* case. He overheard one of the Horsemen say, referring to the oddity of his having voted against New York's law in *Tipaldo*, then voting to hear another similar case, "What is the matter with Roberts?" Frankfurter, "Mr. Justice Roberts," supra, at 315.

327. Owen J. Roberts, *The Court and the Constitution* (1951), 61.

328. Hughes admitted to having delayed the release of *West Coast Hotel* (though he says this was to avoid its looking as if there were any connection with the plan, this hope itself seems ephemeral). Cushman, *Rethinking the New Deal Court*, supra note 68, at 18. As it turns out, Hughes also had planned the Wagner Act cases to come down the same day as *West Coast Hotel*, this but a week after Hughes's letter was made public at the Judiciary Committee hearings. The idea failed to come to fruition because of the time it took Justice McReynolds to draft his dissent. Barry Cushman, "Clerking for Scrooge," review of *The Forgotten Memoir of John Knox: A Year in the Life of a Supreme Court Clerk in FDR's Washington*, ed. David J. Garrow and Denis J. Hutchinson, *U. Chi. L. Rev.* 70 (2003): 722, 731 (noting that the time McReynolds

took in drafting dissent delayed release of opinion that "could have been read from the bench at the March 29 opinion day had Justice McReynolds completed his assignment").

329. For accounts of the origins of the letter, its effects, and the criticism surrounding Hughes's failure to notify the other justices, see Alsop and Catledge, *168 Days*, supra note 22, at 125–27; Leonard Baker, *Back to Back: The Duel Between FDR and the Supreme Court* (1967), 153–63; Pusey, *Charles Evans Hughes*, supra note 88, at 2:754–57. A copy of the letter is available in S. Rep. No. 75-711, app. C (1937).

330. Robert S. Allen, "Hughes Checkmates the President," *Nation*, May 29, 1937, at 610.

331. See Alsop and Catledge, *168 Days*, supra note 22, at 206 ("The thing [Van Devanter's retirement announcement] was planned in the utmost detail. At the senators' [Wheeler and Borah's] slightly devilish prompting, Van Devanter even decided to send his letter of resignation to the President on the very day of the Judiciary Committee's preordained unfavorable vote on the court bill").

332. "Minimum Wage Law Unconstitutional: Switch Due to Roberts," *N.Y. Times*, March 30, 1937, at 1 (headline); see also "Supreme Court Backs Women's Minimum Pay," *L.A. Times*, March 30, 1937, at 1 ("Tribunal Reverses Self"); Arthur Krock, "Flexibility of Constitution Conceded by High Court," *N.Y. Times*, March 30, 1937, at 22 (arguing that to "laymen" the different questions presented in *Parrish* and *Tipaldo* "will seem a fine point, indeed virtually invisible beside the fact that the Supreme Court today, because Justice Roberts joined the four dissenters[,] . . . validated . . . what it had previously invalidated").

333. "Roberts Goes over to Side of Liberals," *Hartford Courant*, March 30, 1937, at 1.

334. "Chambermaid's Day," *Time*, Apr. 5, 1937, at 12.

335. Quoted in Leuchtenburg, *Supreme Court Reborn*, supra note 21, at 143.

336. Letter from Felix Frankfurter to Justice Harlan Fiske Stone, March 30, 1937, quoted in Michael E. Parrish, *Felix Frankfurter and His Times: The Reform Years* (1982), 271.

337. "Senate Hears Robinson Roar with Delight at Supreme Court's Reversal in *Adkins* Case," *Wash. Post*, March 30, 1937, at 1.

338. Alsop and Catledge, *168 Days*, supra note 22, at 145.

339. Thomas Reed Powell, "The Next Four Years: The Constitution," *New Republic*, Jan. 13, 1937, at 319.

340. There were five cases: NLRB v. Jones & Laughlin Steel Corp., 301 U.S. 1 (1937); NLRB v. Fruehauf Trailer Co., 301 U.S. 49 (1937); NLRB v. Friedman–Harry Marks Clothing Co., 301 U.S. 58 (1937); Associated Press v. NLRB, 301 U.S. 103 (1937); and Wash., Va. and Md. Coach Co. v. NLRB, 301 U.S. 142 (1937). Two court of appeals decisions unanimously sustained the Wagner Act, but in those cases it seemed pretty apparent interstate commerce was involved under any definition. See NLRB v. Associated Press, 85 F.2d 56 (2d Cir. 1936) (affirming act as applied to sale of news stories in interstate commerce); Wash., Va. & Md. Coach Co. v. NLRB, 85 F.2d 990 (4th Cir. 1936) (affirming act as applied to interstate bus company). In fact, in the *Washington, Virginia and Maryland Coach* case, the Supreme Court unanimously sustained the Wagner Act; even the Four Horsemen saw there was no argument. In the other three cases, including *Jones & Laughlin Steel* itself, the courts of appeals were unanimous in striking down the Wagner Act on the authority of *Schechter* and *Carter Coal*. See NLRB v. Friedman–Harry Marks Clothing Co. 85 F.2d 1, 1 (2d Cir. 1936) (citing *Carter Coal* and *Schechter* and holding that "[t]he relations between the employer and its employees in this manufacturing industry were merely incidents of production. . . . [R]espondent was in no way engaged in interstate commerce, nor did its labor practices so directly affect interstate commerce as to come within the

federal commerce power"); NLRB v. Jones & Laughlin Steel Co., 83 F.2d 998, 999 (5th Cir. 1936) (holding that under *Carter Coal*, "[t]he order we are asked to enforce is not shown to be one authorized to be under the authority of Congress"); Fruehauf Trailer Co. v. NLRB, 85 F.2d 391, 392 (6th Cir. 1936) ("[S]ince, under the ruling of *Carter*, the Congress has no authority or power to regulate or control . . . relations between the trailer company and its employees, the National Labor Relations Board was without authority to issue the order").

341. *Atlanta Const.*, Apr. 13, 1937, at 1.

342. Arthur Krock, "Why the Manufacturing Decisions Were Unexpected," *N.Y. Times*, Apr. 14, 1937, at 24.

343. "Four 5–4; One 9–0," *Time*, Apr. 19, 1937, at 15.

344. Letter from Thurman Arnold to Fred S. Caldwell, May 17, 1937, quoted in Leuchtenburg, *Supreme Court Reborn*, supra note 21, at 143.

345. Professor Philip Bobbitt and Roosevelt biographer Kenneth S. Davis credit Thomas Reed Powell with this phrase. See Philip Bobbitt, *Constitutional Fate* (1982), 39; Davis, *Into the Storm*, supra note 150, at 81. At least three other variations exist. Joseph Alsop takes credit for the phrase "a switch in time saves nine." Alsop and Catledge, *168 Days* supra note 22, at 135. Leonard Baker credits Abe Fortas with the expression "the switch in time that serves nine." Baker, *Back to Back*, supra note 329, at 174 (citing "High Court Assailed at Labor Institute," *N.Y. Times*, June 15, 1937, at 19). Laurence Tribe credits Fortas with the more familiar "the switch in time that saved the nine." Laurence H. Tribe, *God Save This Honorable Court* (1985), 66. *The Oxford Dictionary of American Legal Quotations* quotes the phrase as "[t]he switch in time that saved the Nine." Fred R. Shapiro, *The Oxford Dictionary of American Legal Quotations* (1993), 393. It does not identify the origin of the expression.

346. Raymond Moley, "After the Wagner Decisions," *Newsweek*, Apr. 24, 1937, at 48.

347. Quoted in *The Making of the New Deal: The Insiders Speak*, ed. Katie Loucheim (1983), 96.

348. Letter from Charles Wyzanski to Felix Frankfurter, Apr. 14, 1937, quoted in Irons, *New Deal Lawyers*, supra note 7, at 289.

349. Henry Steele Commager, "Constitutional History and the Higher Law," in *The Constitution Reconsidered*, ed. Conyers Read (1938), 238–39.

350. Howard Brubaker, "Of All Things," *New Yorker*, Apr. 10, 1937, at 34.

351. "Four 5–4; One 9–0," supra note 343, at 14.

352. *N.Y. Herald Trib.*, March 31, 1937, at 1.

353. *N.Y. Evening J.*, Feb. 11, 1937, quoted in McKenna, *Great Constitutional War*, supra note 64, at 326–27.

354. Cantwell, "Public Opinion and the Legislative Process," supra note 284, at 928, 931.

355. Id. at 929.

356. See id. at 929–30 ("The reversal of opinion can be traced to the fact that the Administration immediately made capital of the two successive favorable decisions of the Court . . . maintaining that the two decisions proved the point that the Court was actually composed of human beings who were subject to error and could see the error of their ways").

357. Alsop and Catledge, *168 Days*, supra note 22, at 142.

358. Robert S. Allen, "Roosevelt's Defeat— the Inside Story," *Nation*, July 31, 1937, at 123.

359. See Hoffer, Hoffer and Hull, *Essential History*, supra note 3, at 281–87 (describing Stone Court and succession of Roosevelt appointments).

360. See Leuchtenburg, *Supreme Court Reborn*, supra note 21, at 184–99 for detailed discussion of Black's nomination process.

361. Frank Hogan, "Important Shifts in Constitutional Doctrines," *A.B.A. J.* 25 (1939): 636.
362. Frank W. Grinnell, "The New Guesspotism," *A.B.A. J.* 30 (1944): 507.
363. Smith v. Allwright, 321 U.S. 649, 669 (1944) (Roberts, J., dissenting).
364. Leuchtenburg, *Supreme Court Reborn*, supra note 21, at 234.
365. This is not to say that economic issues disappeared entirely. Issues regarding state authority in a national economy retained some prominence. See C. Herman Pritchett, *The Roosevelt Court: A Study in Judicial Politics and Values, 1937–1947* (1963), 81–90 (discussing Commerce Clause and state tax issues of period); Robert E. Cushman, "Constitutional Law in 1939–1940," *Am. Pol. Sci. Rev.* 35 (1941): 279–82 (discussing decisions affecting state taxation); see also Earl M. Maltz, "The Impact of the Constitutional Revolution of 1937 on the Dormant Commerce Clause—a Case Study in the Decline of State Autonomy," *Harv. J. L. & Pub. Pol'y* 19 (1995): 127 (observing period as turning point in the subjects of Supreme Court concern).
366. Wickard v. Filburn, 317 U.S. 111, 114–15, 120, 128–29 (1942).
367. Barry Cushman gets all the credit for locating these sources. See Cushman, *Rethinking the New Deal Court*, supra note 68, at 215–18 (discussing Jackson papers); White, *Constitution and the New Deal*, supra note 23, at 230–32 & n88, n90, n92–95 (citing Cushman and discussing papers). On Jackson's succession to Stone's vacated seat, see Hoffer, Hoffer and Hull, *Essential History*, supra note 3, at 282.
368. Cushman, *Rethinking the New Deal Court*, supra note 68, at 303–04 & n75; see also White, *Constitution and the New Deal*, supra note 23, at 231.
369. Cushman, *Rethinking the New Deal Court*, supra note 68, at 217–18.
370. Editorial, "Of Many Minds," *N.Y. Times*, Jan. 15, 1937, at 20.
371. S. Rep. No. 75-711, at 14 (1937).
372. Editorial, "Another Vacant Seat," *N.Y. Times*, Jan. 6, 1938, at 18.
373. Editorial, "Objectives and Methods," *N.Y. Times*, Aug. 9, 1939, at 13 (quoting Franklin D. Roosevelt and criticizing his remarks).

Chapter 8: Limitations

1. "The Warren Court: Fateful Decade," *Newsweek*, May 11, 1964, at 24.
2. Philip B. Kurland, "The Supreme Court, 1963 Term—Foreword, Equal in Origin and Equal in Title to the Legislative and Executive Branches of the Government," *Harv. L. Rev.* 78 (1964): 143. In truth, Kurland was talking about a slightly longer period, reaching back to the late 1940s, but the real work of that period was done during Warren's tenure. Id.; see also Lucas A. Powe, Jr., *The Warren Court and American Politics* (2000), 485 ("Then and now when supporters and critics alike are asked for a neutral adjective to describe the Warren Court's work, revolutionary is the overwhelming choice").
3. See, e.g., Robert H. Bork, *The Tempting of America: The Political Seduction of the Law* (1990), 348 (arguing that "the increasingly political nature of the Supreme Court . . . reached its zenith with the Warren Court"); Morton J. Horwitz, *The Warren Court and the Pursuit of Justice* (1998), 3 ("[T]he Warren Court is increasingly recognized as having initiated a unique and revolutionary chapter in American constitutional history"); Cass R. Sunstein, *Radicals in Robes* (2005), 36 (arguing that the "perfectionism" of the Warren Court "left a large mark on the law," to the annoyance of modern conservatives); Mark Tushnet, "The Warren Court as History: An Interpretation," in *The Warren Court in Historical and Political Perspective*, ed. Mark Tushnet (1993), 34 (noting that "[t]he Warren Court seems to have taught the [current] justices that the Supreme Court could help shape public policy"); Owen Fiss, "A Life Lived Twice," *Yale L. J.* 100 (1991): 1118 (acknowledging role of execu-

tive and legislative branches but concluding that "the truth of the matter is that it was the Warren Court that spurred the great changes to follow, and inspired and protected those who sought to implement them").

Other academic commentators have recognized the limits of the Warren Court's influence and the important roles played by other institutional actors in the legislative and executive branches. See, e.g., Michael J. Klarman, *From Jim Crow to Civil Rights* (2004), 449; Powe, *Warren Court and American Politics*, supra note 2, at 501; Gerald N. Rosenberg, *The Hollow Hope* (1991), 156; Corinna Barrett Lain, "Countermajoritarian Hero or Zero? Rethinking the Warren Court's Role in the Criminal Procedure Revolution," *U. Pa. L. Rev.* 152 (2004): 1451.

4. Anthony Lewis, "Historic Change in the Supreme Court," *N.Y. Times Mag.*, June 17, 1962, at 7.

5. Id. at 38.

6. Id. at 7.

7. Anthony Lewis, "Public Mood Plays Big Role in Court Rulings; Decisions Running Counter to the Broad Consensus Do Not Last; Implementation of Decisions Can Rest on Reaction of Public," *N.Y. Times*, June 23, 1963, at 148.

8. C. Herman Pritchett, *The Roosevelt Court: A Study in Judicial Politics and Values, 1937–1947* (1948), 92; Paul A. Freund, "The Supreme Court and Civil Liberties," *Vand. L. Rev.* 4 (1951): 535; see generally Powe, *Warren Court and American Politics*, supra note 2, at 5–7.

9. Norman Silber and Geoffrey Miller, "Toward 'Neutral Principles' in the Law: Selections from the Oral History of Herbert Wechsler," *Colum. L. Rev.* 93 (1993): 924 (quoting Herbert Wechsler).

10. Henry Steele Commager, *Majority Rule and Minority Rights* (1943), 66.

11. Arthur M. Schlesinger, Jr., "The Supreme Court: 1947," *Fortune*, Jan. 1947, at 73, 201. The economic issues that remained on the Court's plate involved the residual authority of the states to regulate in what was now conceded to be a national economy. See Pritchett, *Roosevelt Court*, supra note 8, at 81–90 (discussing Commerce Clause and state tax and regulation issues of time); Robert E. Cushman, "Constitutional Law in 1939–1940," *Am. Pol. Sci. Rev.* 35 (1941): 279–82 (discussing Supreme Court decisions affecting state taxation); see generally Earl M. Maltz, "The Impact of the Constitutional Revolution of 1937 on the Dormant Commerce Clause—a Case Study in the Decline of State Autonomy," *Harv. J. L. & Pub. Pol'y* 19 (1995): 121 (heralding period as a turning point in these economic areas).

12. Felix Frankfurter, "John Marshall and the Judicial Function," *Harv. L. Rev.* 69 (1955): 230 ("Yesterday the active area . . . was concerned with 'property.' Today it is 'civil liberties.' Tomorrow it may again be 'property'"). Frankfurter actually rued that the Fourteenth Amendment had been adopted, given the difficulty it posed for judges trying to reconcile judicial power with democratic will. Writing his longtime ally Judge Learned Hand, who shared his view, Frankfurter said, "I once shocked Cardozo by saying that I would favor the repeal of that Amendment—and had wished that only the XIII and XV had issued from the Civil War. But since we have it, we have it—and I literally go through torture, from time to time." Letter from Felix Frankfurter to Learned Hand, June 25, 1954, in *Hand Papers*, Folder #20 (Harvard Law School Library), quoted in Morton J. Horwitz, *The Transformation of American Law, 1870–1960* (1992), 259.

13. West Virginia State Bd. of Educ. v. Barnette, 319 U.S. 624, 649 (1943).

14. Eugene V. Rostow, *The Sovereign Prerogative: The Supreme Court and the Quest for Law* (1962), xxxiv; see also Walton H. Hamilton and George D. Braden, "The Special

Competence of the Supreme Court," *Yale L. J.* 50 (1941): 1331 ("[I]t sets down no clear line of demarcation of functions").

15. See, e.g., Alexander M. Bickel, *The Supreme Court and the Idea of Progress* (1970), 33–34 (lauding Frankfurter for *Sweezy v. New Hampshire*, while noting that Frankfurter "never successfully identified sources from which this judgment was to be drawn that would securely limit as well as nourish it"); see also H. N. Hirsch, *The Enigma of Felix Frankfurter* (1981), 193 (Frankfurter's opinion in *Illinois ex rel. McCollum v. Board of Education* "violated nearly every assumption upon which his system of judicial belief supposedly rested"); Wallace Mendelson, "The Influence of James B. Thayer upon the Work of Holmes, Brandeis, and Frankfurter," *Vand. L. Rev.* 31 (1978): 79–82 (discussing tension between Frankfurter's liberalism and judicial philosophy).

16. U.S. v. Carolene Prods. Co., 304 U.S. 144 (1938). See Hamilton and Braden, "Special Competence," supra note 14, at 1354 ("most articulate").

17. The full text of Footnote Four reads:

> There may be narrower scope for operation of the presumption of constitutionality when legislation appears on its face to be within a specific prohibition of the Constitution, such as those of the first ten amendments, which are deemed equally specific when held to be embraced within the Fourteenth.
>
> It is unnecessary to consider now whether legislation which restricts those political processes which can ordinarily be expected to bring about repeal of undesirable legislation, is to be subjected to more exacting judicial scrutiny under the general prohibitions of the Fourteenth Amendment than are most other types of legislation.
>
> Nor need we enquire whether similar considerations enter into the review of statutes directed at particular religious, or national, or racial minorities: whether prejudice against discrete and insular minorities may be a special condition, which tends seriously to curtail the operation of those political processes ordinarily to be relied upon to protect minorities, and which may call for a correspondingly more searching judicial inquiry.

> *Carolene Prods.*, 304 U.S. at 152–53n4 (citations omitted).
> For a discussion by one of Stone's clerks of the framing of Footnote Four, including how Stone added the first criterion at the behest of Chief Justice Hughes, see Louis Lusky, "Footnote Redux: A *Carolene Products* Reminiscence," *Colum. L. Rev.* 82 (1982): 1096–1100.

18. Minersville Sch. Dist. v. Gobitis, 310 U.S. 586 (1940). Because of a clerical error, the Gobitas name was incorrectly entered as Gobitis. See Vincent Blasi and Seana V. Shiffrin, "The Story of *West Virginia State Board of Education v. Barnette*: The Pledge of Allegiance and the Freedom of Thought," in *Constitutional Law Stories*, ed. Michael C. Dorf (2004), 436n14.

19. *Barnette*, 319 U.S. 624 (1943).

20. Pritchett, *Roosevelt Court*, supra note 8, at 95 ("[T]his decision came in June, 1940, at a time when the Germans were overrunning France and the Low Countries, and American security was challenged as it had not been for 125 years").

21. Id.; see Richard M. Fried, *Nightmare in Red* (1990), 49–51 (discussing American fears of a fifth column of Nazi and Communist sympathizers within the country); Geoffrey R. Stone, *Perilous Times: Free Speech in Wartime, from the Sedition Act of 1798 to the War on Terrorism* (2004), 251 ("The shocking fall of France . . . triggered a sense of alarm and vulnerability in the United States"). Indeed, Frankfurter wrote to Stone that "time and circumstances are surely not irrelevant considerations in resolving the conflicts that we do have to resolve in this particular case." Letter from Justice

Frankfurter to Justice Stone, May 27, 1940, quoted in Alpheus Thomas Mason, *Security Through Freedom: American Political Thought and Practice* (1955), 217–20.

22. Alpheus Thomas Mason, *Harlan Fiske Stone: Pillar of the Law* (1956), 532.

23. "Frankfurter v. Stone," *New Republic*, June 24, 1940, at 843.

24. See Schlesinger, "Supreme Court: 1947," supra note 11, at 206 (describing critics' views).

25. *Barnette*, 319 U.S. at 646 (Frankfurter, J., dissenting).

26. Id. at 661, 667 (Frankfurter, J., dissenting).

27. Id. at 646–47 (Frankfurter, J., dissenting).

28. Id. at 638 (majority opinion).

29. Id. at 642.

30. John P. Frank, "Court and Constitution: The Passive Period," *Vand. L. Rev.* 4 (1951): 400.

31. Truman's four appointees were Justice Burton (in 1945), Chief Justice Vinson (1946), Justice Clark (in 1949), and Justice Minton (also in 1949). See Henry J. Abraham, *Justice and Presidents: A Political History of Appointments to the Supreme Court* (1974), 224 ("[Truman] was also given to extravagant notions of loyalty that prompted him to make many a 'crony' appointment. . . . [I]t was a mediocre group"); Eugene Gressman, "The Tragedy of the Supreme Court," *New Republic*, Sept. 3, 1951, at 10 (arguing Truman's appointees have brought Court "down to its old-time level of mediocrity"); Fred Rodell, "Our Not So Supreme Supreme Court," *Look*, July 31, 1951, at 60 (arguing jurisprudence of Truman's "old cronies" has been "mediocre to miserable"); see generally David A. Yalof, *Pursuit of Justices: Presidential Politics and the Selection of Supreme Court Nominees* (1999), 20–40.

32. Stone, *Perilous Times*, supra note 21, at 312.

33. Frank, "Court and Constitution," supra note 30, at 403 (internal citation omitted).

34. Edwin A. Falk, "In Time of Peace Prepare for War," *Rec. Ass'n B. City N.Y.* 1 (1946): 251–52.

35. Id. at 245.

36. S.J. Res. 44, 83d Cong. (1954); see Walter F. Murphy, *Congress and the Court* (1962), 78 (discussing amendment). Edwin A. Falk, the author of *In Time of Peace Prepare for War*, assisted Butler in preparing the amendment; he sat in the Senate gallery the day it passed. 100 Cong. Rec. 6347 (1954). The American Bar Association also actively supported the amendment. 100 Cong. Rec. 6347 (remarks by Senator Jenner thanking ABA for support); "Report of the Standing Committee on Jurisprudence and Law Reform," in *Annual Report A.B.A.* 78 (1953): 235.

37. See Murphy, *Congress and the Court*, supra note 36, at 78 (discussing House support for amendment).

38. Brown v. Bd. of Educ., 347 U.S. 483 (1954).

39. See, e.g., Alexander M. Bickel, *The Least Dangerous Branch* (1962), 246; Richard Kluger, *Simple Justice* (1976; repr. 1977), 746–47; Horwitz, *Pursuit of Justice*, supra note 3, at 15; see also George W. Bush, "Remarks at the Opening of the *Brown v. Board of Education* National Historic Site in Topeka, Kansas," May 17, 2004, in *Public Papers of the Presidents of the United States: George W. Bush, 2004*, bk. 1 (2007), 891.

Recent scholarship about *Brown* minimizes the Supreme Court's "heroic" role, favoring a more pragmatic approach that recognizes the limited part the Court can play on its own and the essential role Congress and the President played in desegregating southern schools. Michael Klarman's remarkable *From Jim Crow to Civil Rights* is the most thorough telling of this story. See Klarman, *From Jim Crow*, supra note 3, at 3–7; see also Mary L. Dudziak, *Cold War Civil Rights: Race and the Image of American Democracy* (2000), 15–16; Rosenberg, *Hollow Hope*, supra note 3, at 42–71; Derrick A. Bell, Jr., "*Brown v. Board of Education* and the Interest-Convergence Dilemma," *Harv. L. Rev.* 93 (1980): 523–26.

40. Plessy v. Ferguson, 163 U.S. 537 (1896); see also J. Harvie Wilkinson III, *From* Brown *to* Bakke, *The Supreme Court and School Integration: 1954–1978* (1979), 17–20 (describing *Plessy* and its role in segregation).

41. *Plessy*, 163 U.S. at 544–45, 550–51.

42. See Mark V. Tushnet, *The NAACP's Legal Strategy Against Segregated Education, 1925–1950* (1987), 21–22 (clarifying that equal facilities technically were required only by the Louisiana statute, not by the Court's interpretation of the Constitution).

43. See id. at 1–6 (describing origins of NAACP). Between 1882 and 1968, at least forty-seven hundred blacks were lynched in the United States. Horwitz, *Pursuit of Justice*, supra note 3, at 17; see also *To Secure These Rights: The Report on the President's Committee on Civil Rights* (1947), 20–25 (discussing lynchings from 1936 to 1947).

44. See Tushnet, *NAACP's Legal Strategy*, supra note 42, at 106–15; see also Kluger, *Simple Justice*, supra note 39, at 290–94.

45. See generally Horwitz, *Pursuit of Justice*, supra note 3, at 18; Klarman, *From Jim Crow*, supra note 3, at 173–85.

46. See Paul G. Kauper, *Frontiers of Constitutional Liberty* (1956), 210 ("A nation at war with Hitler's Germany could not reconcile racism with its democratic credo . . .").

47. Walter White, "People, Politics and Places," *Chi. Defender*, Feb. 9, 1946, at 15 (quoting Judge Thurman Clark).

48. See Dudziak, *Cold War Civil Rights*, supra note 39, at 23; Klarman, *From Jim Crow*, supra note 3, at 185.

49. See Horwitz, *Pursuit of Justice*, supra note 3, at 19; Klarman, *From Jim Crow*, supra note 3, at 168.

50. Gunnar Myrdal, *An American Dilemma: The Negro Problem and Modern Democracy* (1962), 26 (emphasis in original).

51. See Klarman, *From Jim Crow*, supra note 3, at 173–74; Tushnet, *NAACP's Legal Strategy*, supra note 42, at 116.

52. See Dudziak, *Cold War Civil Rights*, supra note 39, at 23–24. The report of that commission, *To Secure These Rights*, is a record of the appalling inequality in America in the late 1940s. It found wide disparities in education, housing, and basic human services. Even more troubling, the report began with an extensive and disturbing portrait of an America in which African-Americans were neither free from state-sanctioned violence nor permitted to exercise fundamental political rights. No part of the country was spared reproach, but in text as well as vivid graphics the report's obvious villain was the South. See *To Secure These Rights*, supra note 43, at 23–29, 35–40, 62–79; accord Kluger, *Simple Justice*, supra note 39, at 253; Tushnet, *NAACP's Legal Strategy*, supra note 42, at 116–17.

53. See Dudziak, *Cold War Civil Rights*, supra note 39, at 83–87; Horwitz, *Pursuit of Justice*, supra note 3, at 19–20; C. Vann Woodward, *The Strange Career of Jim Crow*, 2d ed. (1966), 136–38.

54. See Robert A. Caro, *The Years of Lyndon Johnson: Master of the Senate* (2002), 92–94, 215–18 (describing South's use of filibuster to block civil rights legislation). Truman's acts alienated southerners who, in the presidential election of 1948, bolted to the Dixiecrat Party, running South Carolinian Strom Thurmond for President. Without the South, Truman still squeaked out a win. See Kluger, *Simple Justice*, supra note 39, at 255. Other scholars suggest that supporting civil rights won Truman far more support in the North than he lost in the South. See Dudziak, *Cold War Civil Rights*, supra note 39, at 25–26; Klarman, *From Jim Crow*, supra note 3, at 180–81, 186.

55. Sweatt v. Painter, 339 U.S. 629 (1950); McLaurin v. Okla. St. Regents for Higher Educ., 339 U.S. 637 (1950).

56. *Sweatt*, 339 U.S. at 633–34; see also *McLaurin*, 339 U.S. at 641 (finding restrictions on appellant "impair and inhibit his ability to study, to engage in discussions and exchange views with other students, and, in general, to learn his profession").

57. Arthur Krock, "An Historic Day in the Supreme Court," *N.Y. Times*, June 6, 1950, at 28; see also Klarman, *From Jim Crow*, supra note 3, at 208.

58. See Bernard Schwartz, *Super Chief* (1983), 104–06.

59. Klarman, *From Jim Crow*, supra note 3, at 298; Dennis J. Hutchinson, "Unanimity and Desegregation: Decisionmaking in the Supreme Court, 1954–1958," *Geo. L. J.* 68 (1979): 32.

60. Hutchinson, "Unanimity and Desegregation," supra note 59, at 36n284 and accompanying text; see Klarman, *From Jim Crow*, supra note 3, at 293–98 (describing Court's conference following oral arguments); Kluger, *Simple Justice*, supra note 39, at 587–614 (same). Historians are not entirely in accord on how the justices were inclining. Compare Klarman, *From Jim Crow*, supra note 3, at 298 (arguing that Black, Burton, Douglas, and Minton were pro striking down segregation, with Vinson and Reed contra, and Frankfurter, Jackson, and Clark ambivalent), and Powe, *Warren Court and American Politics*, supra note 2, at 23 (arguing same split, with Clark inclined toward Vinson/Reed camp, Jackson ambivalent about racial issues but concerned with judicial overreach, and Frankfurter worried about Court's reputation), with Schwartz, *Super Chief*, supra note 58, at 75 (stating that five or more justices were leaning toward repudiating *Plessy*).

61. Klarman, *From Jim Crow*, supra note 3, at 302 (quoting Frankfurter calling this "the first indication I have ever had that there is a God"); Hutchinson, "Unanimity and Desegregation," supra note 59, at 38.

62. Klarman, *From Jim Crow*, supra note 3, at 301–03; Powe, *Warren Court and American Politics*, supra note 2, at 24, 27–28; Hutchinson, "Unanimity and Desegregation," supra note 59, at 39.

63. See Klarman, *From Jim Crow*, supra note 3, at 183; see also Bell, "Interest-Convergence Dilemma," supra note 39, at 524 (noting role of Cold War in aligning interests of white Americans with *Brown* decision).

64. See Dudziak, *Cold War Civil Rights*, supra note 39, at 26–27; Klarman, *From Jim Crow*, supra note 3, at 182–84; Woodward, *Strange Career*, supra note 53, at 131–32.

65. Letter from Dean Acheson, Acting Secretary of State, to Fair Employment Practice Committee, May 8, 1946, in *To Secure These Rights*, supra note 43, at 146. The Committee on Civil Rights quoted this letter in support of its argument that domestic discrimination had a significant impact on American foreign relations. See id. at 146–48.

66. Mary Dudziak's *Cold War Civil Rights* is a compendium of historical data on this point, from the world over. See, e.g., Dudziak, *Cold War Civil Rights*, supra note 39, Chapter 1.

67. Id. at 44 (quoting NAACP petition).

68. Id. at 43; Klarman, *From Jim Crow*, supra note 3, at 182–83.

69. Brief for the United States as Amicus Curiae at 6, Brown v. Bd. of Educ., 347 U.S. 483 (1954) (Nos. 1, 2, 3, 4, 5).

70. See Klarman, *From Jim Crow*, supra note 3, at 310 (citing George H. Gallup, *The Gallup Poll: Public Opinion, 1935–1971* (1972), 2:1249–50); Lloyd M. Wells, "The Supreme Court and Public Opinion, 1937–1957," in *The Politics of Judicial Review, 1937–1957*, ed. John M. Claunch (1957), 36.

71. See "N.A.A.C.P. Sets Advanced Goals; Officials Say They Will Drive for End of Residential and Job Discrimination," *N.Y. Times*, May 18, 1954, at 16.

72. See Dudziak, *Cold War Civil Rights*, supra note 39, at 107.

73. Roscoe Drummond, "The End of Segregation 'Perfects' America Democracy," *The* (Nashville) *Tennessean*, May 19, 1954, at 9.
74. "The School Decision," *Christian Century*, June 2, 1954, at 662.
75. "To All on Equal Terms," *Time*, May 24, 1954, at 21.
76. See Kluger, *Simple Justice*, supra note 39, at 710; Powe, *Warren Court and American Politics*, supra note 2, at 38–39.
77. William White, "Ruling to Figure in '54 Campaign; Decision Tied to Eisenhower—Russell Leads Southerners in Criticism of Court," *N.Y. Times*, May 18, 1954, at 1 (quoting Senator Eastland).
78. See Kluger, *Simple Justice*, supra note 39, at 711; Powe, *Warren Court and American Politics*, supra note 2, at 37–38; Schwartz, *Super Chief*, supra note 58, at 110–11.
79. "Black Day of Tragedy," quoted in "Editorial Excerpts on School Bias Ruling," *N.Y. Times*, May 19, 1954, at 20.
80. See, e.g., Drummond, "End of Segregation," supra note 73; "Court Said to End 'A Sense of Guilt,' Virginia School Head Asserts U.S. Prestige Will Rise as Result of Anti-Bias Ruling," *N.Y. Times*, May 18, 1954, at 18.
81. Brown v. Bd. of Educ., 349 U.S. 294 (1955) (Brown II).
82. Schwartz, *Super Chief*, supra note 58, at 93 (quoting Black, J.); see also Michael J. Klarman, *Unfinished Business: Racial Equality in American History* (2007), 153 (discussing justices' motives).
83. Klarman, *From Jim Crow*, supra note 3, at 314 (quoting Black, J.).
84. Id. (quoting Minton, J.).
85. Bickel, *Idea of Progress*, supra note 15, at 6 (quoting Frankfurter, J.).
86. "The Segregation Issue," *Time*, Dec. 22, 1952, at 12.
87. Id. at 13.
88. Schwartz, *Super Chief*, supra note 58, at 113–14. According to Schwartz, Rogers, while demanding that "honest" be removed, raised his forefinger toward the bench. Warren took offense to this. He was "quite flushed" in his response, and it looked to onlookers that he might decide to hold Rogers in contempt. Id. at 114; see also Kluger, *Simple Justice*, supra note 39, at 731–32.
89. John N. Popham, "South Is Divided on Court's Order; Some Call Decision 'Best We Could Hope For'—Reaction of Leadership Is Temperate," *N.Y. Times*, June 1, 1955, at 29; see also Powe, *Warren Court and American Politics*, supra note 2, at 57–58 (describing initial reaction to *Brown II*).
90. Jim Thomasson, "Decree Gratifies Both Sides; Left to District Courts: Some Officials Say Ruling Allows Indefinite Segregation; NAACP Declares No Desegregation Delay," *The* (Nashville) *Tennessean*, June 1, 1955, at 1; accord Klarman, *From Jim Crow*, supra note 3, at 318; Klarman, *Unfinished Business*, supra note 82, at 153; Powe, *Warren Court and American Politics*, supra note 2, at 56; Vincent Blasi, "A Requiem for the Warren Court," *Tex. L. Rev.* 48 (1970): 615 ("Whatever the Court meant by [all deliberate speed], Southern school districts read it as a license for inertia").
91. See Wilkinson, *From Brown to Bakke*, supra note 40, at 82–84; J. Patrick White, "The Warren Court Under Attack: The Role of the Judiciary in a Democratic Society," *Md. L. Rev.* 19 (1959): 184. These measures had broad popular support in the South: in 1956, over 80 percent of southern whites opposed desegregated public schools. See Powe, *Warren Court and American Politics*, supra note 2, at 67.
92. See Powe, *Warren Court and American Politics*, supra note 2, at 164; see also Wilkinson, *From Brown to Bakke*, supra note 40, at 65 ("As late as 1962, not a single Negro attended white schools or colleges in Mississippi, Alabama or South Carolina. By 1964 . . . a scant 2.3 percent of southern blacks were enrolled in desegregated

schools") (internal footnote omitted). By 1969, 20.3 percent of black children in the South attended schools with whites; in Alabama, the figure was 7.4 percent. See Bickel, *Idea of Progress*, supra note 15, at 127.

93. Woodward, *Strange Career*, supra note 53, at 156 (quoting Virginia senator Harry F. Byrd, Sr.).

94. See Powe, *Warren Court and American Politics*, supra note 2, at 58–60 (discussing Kilpatrick's theory); Woodward, *Strange Career*, supra note 53, at 156–58 (detailing laws passed by Alabama, Georgia, Mississippi, South Carolina, and Virginia).

95. "Text of 96 Congressmen's Declaration on Integration," *N.Y. Times*, March 12, 1956, at 19; see also Powe, *Warren Court and American Politics*, supra note 2, at 60–62 (discussing Southern Manifesto).

96. James F. Byrnes, "The Supreme Court Must Be Curbed," *U.S. News & World Rep.*, May 18, 1956, at 56.

97. Eisenhower was to say privately that the Court had "set back progress in the South at least 15 years." Klarman, *From Jim Crow*, supra note 3, at 325 (quoting Eisenhower). Eisenhower apparently told Earl Warren at one point that the southerners "are not bad people. All they are concerned about is to see that their sweet little girls are not required to sit in school alongside some big overgrown Negroes." Earl Warren, *The Memoirs of Earl Warren* (1977), 291 (quoting Eisenhower). Warren believed that had Eisenhower stepped behind the Court, "we would have been relieved . . . of many of the racial problems which have continued to plague us." Warren, *Memoirs*, supra, at 291.

98. Klarman, *From Jim Crow*, supra note 3, at 326 (quoting Eisenhower's announcement).

99. See Wilkinson, *From* Brown *to* Bakke, supra note 40, at 88–90.

100. See Dudziak, *Cold War Civil Rights*, supra note 39, at 127–28.

101. "Eisenhower Address on Little Rock Crisis," *N.Y. Times*, Sept. 25, 1957, at 14.

102. Cooper v. Aaron, 358 U.S. 1 (1958).

103. *Cooper*, 358 U.S. at 18.

104. See Klarman, *From Jim Crow*, supra note 3, at 349–63; Rosenberg, *Hollow Hope*, supra note 3, at 70–71 (arguing that while the *Brown* decision may have had important indirect effects, "before Congress and the executive branch acted, courts had virtually *no direct effect* on ending discrimination . . ."); see generally Rosenberg, *Hollow Hope*, supra note 3, at 1–169 (discussing the ability of courts to bring about social change).

105. See Dudziak, *Cold War Civil Rights*, supra note 39, at 157; Klarman, *From Jim Crow*, supra note 3, at 373.

106. See Woodward, *Strange Career*, supra note 53, at 171–72.

107. See Dudziak, *Cold War Civil Rights*, supra note 39, at 157–58; Klarman, *From Jim Crow*, supra note 3, at 373–74.

108. See Powe, *Warren Court and American Politics*, supra note 2, at 217–18; Woodward, *Strange Career*, supra note 53, at 174–75.

109. See Klarman, *From Jim Crow*, supra note 3, at 433–35; Powe, *Warren Court and American Politics*, supra note 2, at 223–25.

110. John F. Kennedy, "Radio and Television Report to the American People on Civil Rights," June 11, 1963, in *Public Papers of the Presidents of the United States: John F. Kennedy, 1963* (1964), 468, 469; see also Jennifer L. Hochschild, *The New American Dilemma: Liberal Democracy and School Desegregation* (1984), 15.

111. See Woodward, *Strange Career*, supra note 53, at 180–81.

112. See Dudziak, *Cold War Civil Rights*, supra note 39, at 187–89; Powe, *Warren Court and American Politics*, supra note 2, at 226–27.

113. Lyndon B. Johnson, "Address Before a Joint Session of the Congress," Nov. 27, 1963, in *Public Papers of the Presidents of the United States: Lyndon B. Johnson, 1963–64*, bk. 1 (1965), 9.
114. See Powe, *Warren Court and American Politics*, supra note 2, at 232–34.
115. See id. at 233–34; Wilkinson, *From* Brown *to* Bakke, supra note 40, at 103–04.
116. Heart of Atlanta Motel, Inc. v. United States, 379 U.S. 241 (1964); Katzenbach v. McClung, 379 U.S. 294 (1964); see also Powe, *Warren Court and American Politics*, supra note 2, at 234–36 (discussing constitutional challenges to Civil Rights Act).
117. See Klarman, *From Jim Crow*, supra note 3, at 363.
118. Griffin v. County Sch. Bd., 377 U.S. 218, 234 (1964). After Prince Edward closed its public schools in 1959, a private group, the Prince Edward School Foundation, formed to operate private schools for white children. Although initially privately funded, by the 1960–1961 school year state and county tuition grants were the "major source" of funding for the foundation. Id. at 223. The Court found that these actions were undertaken "for one reason, and one reason only: to ensure . . . that white and colored children in Prince Edward County would not, under any circumstances, go to the same school." Id. at 231. Accordingly, the Court upheld an injunction that prohibited giving tuition grants and tax credits to private schools as long as the county's public schools remained closed. Id. at 233. In addition, the Court authorized the district court to require the county to levy taxes in order to reopen the public schools "if necessary to prevent further racial discrimination." Id.
119. Green v. County Sch. Bd., 391 U.S. 430, 439 (1968) (emphasis added).
120. Naim v. Naim, 87 S.E.2d 749 (Va. 1956) (holding that antimiscegenation statute was supported by legitimate state purposes).
121. See Klarman, *From Jim Crow*, supra note 3, at 321; see also Powe, *Warren Court and American Politics*, supra note 2, at 69 (noting that first national poll on interracial marriage revealed 4 percent of white respondents approving).
122. Hutchinson, "Unanimity and Desegregation," supra note 59, at 62–63.
123. Id. at 63 (quoting Burton's law clerk).
124. Id. at 64 (quoting Frankfurter, J.).
125. Loving v. Virginia, 388 U.S. 1 (1967).
126. "The Temple Builder," *Time*, July 1, 1957, at 11.
127. Dennis v. United States, 341 U.S. 494 (1951) (plurality opinion); see generally Arthur J. Sabin, *In Calmer Times: The Supreme Court and Red Monday* (1999), 31–90 (discussing *Dennis*); Stone, *Perilous Times*, supra note 21, at 395–407 (same).
128. *Dennis*, 341 U.S. at 579 (Black, J., dissenting); see also Sabin, *In Calmer Times*, supra note 127, at 40.
129. The Court purported to apply the First Amendment test, which permitted punishing defendants' speech only if it posed a "clear and present danger." *Dennis*, 341 U.S. at 505 (plurality opinion). Despite history's longest criminal trial to date, the record was rather sparse on this point. See Stone, *Perilous Times*, supra note 21, at 396. The Court was forced to fall back upon what the dissent disparagingly labeled its own "judicial notice" of the threat posed by the worldwide Communist conspiracy. See *Dennis*, 341 U.S. at 588–89 (Douglas, J., dissenting). As Justice Douglas pointed out, however, the question was the "strength and tactical position of petitioners and their converts in this country," not elsewhere in the world. "Communism in the world scene is no bogey-man; but Communism as a political faction or party in this country plainly is." *Dennis*, 341 U.S. at 588 (Douglas, J., dissenting). History's judgment of *Dennis* has not been kind. See, e.g., Stone, *Perilous Times*, supra note 21, at 410 ("Over time, the Court and the nation came to regard *Dennis* as an embarrassment, or worse").

130. See generally Stone, *Perilous Times*, supra note 21, at 323–30 (discussing Red scare from 1945 to 1950); Sabin, *In Calmer Times*, supra note 127, at 31–39 (same).

131. Winston Churchill, "Sinews of Peace," March 5, 1946, in *Winston S. Churchill: His Complete Speeches*, ed. Robert R. James (1974), 7:7290.

132. Harry S. Truman, "Special Message to the Congress on Greece and Turkey: The Truman Doctrine," March 12, 1947, in *Public Papers of the Presidents of the United States: Harry S. Truman, 1947* (1963), 176; see also Dudziak, *Cold War Civil Rights*, supra note 39, at 27.

133. See Richard Crockatt, *The Fifty Years War* (1995), 80; Fried, *Nightmare in Red*, supra note 21, at 87–90, 113–14; Stone, *Perilous Times*, supra note 21, at 330, 334.

134. See Fried, *Nightmare in Red*, supra note 21, at 17–23; Stone, *Perilous Times*, supra note 21, at 328–31.

135. This quotation comes from the version of the speech that McCarthy later read into the *Congressional Record*. See 96 Cong. Rec. 1954–57 (1950). Different accounts of the speech, which he gave in Wheeling, West Virginia, have him claiming different numbers of Communists. See Fried, *Nightmare in Red*, supra note 21, at 123–24.

136. See Stone, *Perilous Times*, supra note 21, at 334.

137. *Dennis*, 341 U.S. at 581 (Black, J., dissenting); see also William O. Douglas, *The Court Years 1939–1975: The Autobiography of William O. Douglas* (1980), 92 ("In the 1950s, when the Cold War flourished, the resulting climate of opinion made the dispensation of justice very unlikely when one was merely charged with being a Communist . . .").

138. Editorial, "'A Clear and Present Danger,'" *L.A. Times*, June 6, 1951, at A4; Editorial, "The Smith Act Upheld," *N.Y. Times*, June 5, 1951, at 30; see also Sabin, *In Calmer Times*, supra note 127, at 86–87 (discussing media reaction to *Dennis*).

139. See Fried, *Nightmare in Red*, supra note 21, at 130; Thomas C. Reeves, *The Life and Times of Joe McCarthy* (1982), 334–46. Both sources note, however, that contemporary estimates of McCarthy's influence on the election were exaggerated.

140. *Dennis*, 341 U.S. at 581 (Black, J., dissenting).

141. See Fried, *Nightmare in Red*, supra note 21, at 137–43, 178–82; Stone, *Perilous Times*, supra note 21, at 413.

142. Sabin, *In Calmer Times*, supra note 127, at 136 (quoting Hearst).

143. See id. at 136.

144. This shift, however, was by no means immediate, as some would have liked. See Powe, *Warren Court and American Politics*, supra note 2, at 80 (noting that in 1954, while McCarthy "was self–destructing on national television . . . the Court was deciding cases by exactly the same voting patterns . . . as it did prior to Warren's taking his seat").

145. Earl Warren, "The Law and the Future," *Fortune*, Nov. 1955, at 226, 229, 230.

146. Pennsylvania v. Nelson, 350 U.S. 497 (1956) (reversing sedition conviction of Communist Party member on the ground that state sedition law was preempted by the Smith Act); Slochower v. Bd. of Educ., 350 U.S. 551 (1956) (holding that a public college could not summarily fire a professor for invoking the Fifth Amendment during a congressional hearing).

147. Philip P. Frickey, "Getting from Joe to Gene (McCarthy): The Avoidance Canon, Legal Process Theory, and Narrowing Statutory Interpretation in the Early Warren Court," *Cal. L. Rev.* 93 (2005): 420.

148. Quoted in David Riesman, "New Critics of the Court," *New Republic*, July 29, 1957, at 11.

149. Watkins v. United States, 354 U.S. 178 (1957); Sweezy v. New Hampshire, 354 U.S. 234 (1957); Yates v. United States, 354 U.S. 298 (1957); Service v. Dulles, 354 U.S. 363 (1957).

150. "The Court, Congress, Chaos," *Newsweek*, July 1, 1957, at 20.

151. Sabin, *In Calmer Times*, supra note 127, at 1 (calling Hoover "livid").
152. Chief Justice Warren was appointed in 1954, Justice Harlan in 1955, Justice Brennan in 1956, and Justice Whittaker in 1957 (Whittaker participated only in one of the decisions, *Service v. Dulles*, 354 U.S. 363 (1957), in which he joined the majority). Historians have pointed to these shifts in personnel to explain the decisions. See Fried, *Nightmare in Red*, supra note 21, at 184 (discussing appointments of Brennan and Warren); Murphy, *Congress and the Court*, supra note 36, at 98–99 (highlighting Brennan's immediate impact); Powe, *Warren Court and American Politics*, supra note 2, at 82, 88–89 (noting Warren's shift leftward and Brennan's replacement of the more conservative Minton); Frickey, "Getting from Joe to Gene (McCarthy)," supra note 147, at 420n120 ("Not coincidentally, [1956] was Justice Brennan's first term on the Court . . ."); compare C. Herman Pritchett, *Congress versus the Supreme Court, 1957–1960* (1961), 10 (noting "Eisenhower's appointees were largely responsible for swinging the Court's balance back toward a more liberal orientation"). However, some recent scholars have persuasively argued that membership alone cannot account for the Court's dramatic shift. Sabin, *In Calmer Times*, supra note 127, at xiii ("More than a change in Court personnel was involved; the nation itself had changed by 1957"); Stone, *Perilous Times*, supra note 21, at 413 (attributing shift to both changes in Court and changed political circumstances).
153. No more than three justices dissented in any of the twelve cases, and eight of the cases were either unanimous or had only one dissenter. See Watkins v. United States, 354 U.S. 178 (1957) (6–1 for Watkins); Sweezy v. New Hampshire, 354 U.S. 234 (1957) (6–3 for Sweezy); Yates v. United States, 354 U.S. 298 (1957) (6–1 for Yates); Service v. Dulles, 354 U.S. 363 (1957) (8–0 for Service); United States v. Witkovich, 353 U.S. 194 (1957) (6–2 for Witkovich); Schware v. Bd. of Bar Exam'rs, 353 U.S. 232 (1957) (8–0 for Schware); Konigsberg v. State Bar, 353 U.S. 252 (1957) (5–3 for Konigsberg); Mesarosh v. United States, 352 U.S. 1 (1956) (6–3 for Mesarosh); Jencks v. United States, 353 U.S. 657 (1957) (7–1 for Jencks); Amalgamated Meat Cutters v. NLRB, 352 U.S. 153 (1956) (9–0 for Amalgamated Meat Cutters); Leedom v. Int'l Union of Mine, Mill & Smelter Workers, 352 U.S. 145 (1956) (9–0 for Union); Gold v. United States, 352 U.S. 985 (1957) (6–3 for Gold).

   Four justices who were in the majority in *Dennis* were members of the Court during at least part of the 1956 term: Reed, Burton, Frankfurter, and Minton. Reed participated in four of the twelve decisions and voted against the government in three of them. Burton participated in eleven, voting against the government in seven, and Frankfurter participated in all twelve, voting against the government in ten. Minton participated in one, *Mesarosh*, and voted against the government; he was still on the bench when the per curiam opinion granting a new trial and the dissenting opinion calling for remand were issued, but he had left office before the majority considered and drafted an extended opinion. *Mesarosh*, 352 U.S. at 3n1.
154. Walter Lippman, "Today and Tomorrow . . . Back Toward the Constitution," *Wash. Post & Times Herald*, June 25, 1957, at A15.
155. "The Temple Builder," supra note 126, at 12–13.
156. Editorial, "A Day for Freedom," *N.Y. Times*, June 18, 1957, at 32, quoted in Powe, *Warren Court and American Politics*, supra note 2, at 98.
157. "Blow to Random Inquiry," *Wash. Post & Times Herald*, June 19, 1957, at A12.
158. Thomas L. Stokes, "High Court Writes Witch-Hunt Epitaph," *Atlanta Const.*, June 20, 1957, at 4.
159. See Powe, *Warren Court and American Politics*, supra note 2, at 85–86, 100–02; Frickey, "Getting from Joe to Gene (McCarthy)," supra note 147, at 426; White, "Warren Court Under Attack," supra note 91, at 189.

160. Riesman, "New Critics of the Court," supra note 148, at 11 (quoting the *State*).
161. "U.S. Press Comment on Decisions in *Watkins*, *Smith* Cases," *N.Y. Times*, June 19, 1957, at 19 (quoting *Chi. Trib.*).
162. Id. (quoting *Plain Dealer*).
163. Edward Corwin, letter to the editor, *N.Y. Times*, March 16, 1958, at E10.
164. Allen Drury, "Martin Assails High Court; Controversial Term Ending; Inquiry Curbs Decried," *N.Y. Times*, July 1, 1957, at 1; "Jenner Would Curb High Court's Power," *N.Y. Times*, July 27, 1957, at 21.
165. Congress quickly enacted one measure addressing one of the Court decisions. See Murphy, *Congress and the Court*, supra note 36, at 182; Pritchett, *Congress versus the Supreme Court*, supra note 152, at 35. In a 1957 domestic security case, *Jencks v. United States*, the Court held that defendants in criminal trials were entitled to see the police statements of witnesses against them. 353 U.S. 657, 667–68 (1957). The decision caused an uproar over opening police files to suspects and their lawyers. See Murphy, *Congress and the Court*, supra note 36, at 128–31 (describing press and government reaction to *Jencks* decision); Sabin, *In Calmer Times*, supra note 127, at 147–48. *The New York Times* expressed concern about "the nightmare of accused Communists, tax evaders or kidnappers sitting down for a long, leisurely perusal of J. Edgar Hoover's carefully guarded library." Editorial, "The Court and the F.B.I.," *N.Y. Times*, June 30, 1957, at 140. Hoover and his FBI led a lobbying campaign to modify the rule. See Murphy, *Congress and the Court*, supra note 36, at 139–41; Clifford M. Lytle, "Congressional Response to Supreme Court Decisions in the Aftermath of the School Segregation Cases," *J. Pub. L.* 12 (1963): 301–02. Liberals, realizing the size of the storm coming their way, seized control of the bill.
    The law as passed largely adopted the *Jencks* rule. See Murphy, *Congress and the Court*, supra note 36, at 131–53 (describing passage of *Jencks* statute); Sabin, *In Calmer Times*, supra note 127, at 149–51 (same). Commentators then and now could not agree on whether that law ratified what the Court had done or vilified the justices. Compare Philip B. Kurland, *Politics, the Constitution, and the Warren Court* (1970), 28; Murphy, *Congress and the Court*, supra note 36, at 152–53; Powe, *Warren Court and American Politics*, supra note 2, at 101; Sabin, *In Calmer Times*, supra note 127, at 151; Frickey, "Getting from Joe to Gene (McCarthy)," supra note 147, at 428.
166. S. 2646, 85th Cong., 1st Sess. (1957); see Powe, *Warren Court and American Politics*, supra note 2, at 130–31.
167. Pennsylvania v. Nelson, 350 U.S. 497 (1956).
168. See Murphy, *Congress and the Court*, supra note 36, at 91–95; Powe, *Warren Court and American Politics*, supra note 2, at 87–88.
169. See, e.g., Sabin, *In Calmer Times*, supra note 127, at 132 (noting that H.R. 3 "became a rallying point for action against the Court"); "Jenner Would Curb," supra note 164 (quoting Senator Jenner's explanation that he proposed the legislation because the Court was "undermining efforts of the peoples' [sic] representatives at both the national and state levels to meet and master the Communist plot").
170. See Caro, *Master of the Senate*, supra note 54, at 1031; Murphy, *Congress and the Court*, supra note 36, at 199–202.
171. See Caro, *Master of the Senate*, supra note 54, at 1031–32 (describing vote counting of bills' opponents); Murphy, *Congress and the Court*, supra note 36, at 206 (describing Johnson's changing strategy); Pritchett, *Congress versus the Supreme Court*, supra note 152, at 35–36 (same).
172. Murphy, *Congress and the Court*, supra note 36, at 208; White, "Warren Court Under Attack," supra note 91, at 194.

173. He actually moved to adjourn; the motion passed by a wide margin. Interestingly, this move was apparently suggested to the flustered Johnson by Richard Russell, a conservative senator from the South. Caro, *Master of the Senate*, supra note 54, at 1031; Murphy, *Congress and the Court*, supra note 36, at 211–12. One might have thought that a southerner would have favored an immediate vote. This fact leads Walter Murphy to suggest that conservatives did not so much want to discipline the court as send it a clear message. See Murphy, *Congress and the Court*, supra note 36, at 258–61. See Murphy, *Congress and the Court*, supra note 36, at 214–17 (describing dramatic final vote on H.R. 3). Walter Murphy suggests that though Nixon would have voted no, a vote either way would not have solved Nixon's dilemma, since the Republican Party was split on the bill. Id. at 216.

175. White, "Warren Court Under Attack," supra note 91, at 194 (quoting Sen. Douglas). Where the broader public stood precisely in all this is anyone's guess. The communism issue was cooling down; Democrats did well in the midterm congressional elections three months later. LBJ was a savvy politician who had gained his congressional seat supporting Roosevelt's Court-packing plan, and it was his judgment that the politically astute thing to do was oppose the legislation. Thus there is reason to think that despite the aggressive efforts of congressional anti-Communists and segregationists, the legislative effort did not muster majority sentiment in the country. But that remains conjecture. The fact is that the House was (and even afterward remained) in favor of some, if not all, of the legislation, and the margins in the Senate were much closer than LBJ anticipated. See Murphy, *Congress and the Court*, supra note 36, at 252–56.

176. See Sabin, *In Calmer Times*, supra note 127, at 192 (quoting Eric Sevareid to the effect that the Court had "checkmate[d]" the House Un-American Activities Committee (HUAC) and emerged "as the leading champion of civil liberties"). *Newsweek* opined that now "it may be so difficult to convict a man under the Smith Act [that] the law could become a dead letter." "Four Major Decisions—and What They Mean for the Future," *Newsweek*, July 1, 1957, at 20; see also Sabin, *In Calmer Times*, supra note 127, at 186–92 (describing media reaction to Red Monday decisions). The Justice Department itself apparently believed that Smith Act prosecutions were no longer viable. After 1957, it stopped initiating prosecutions under the "advocacy" clause of the act, and brought only "a few" more cases under the act's "membership" clause. Sabin, *In Calmer Times*, supra note 127, at 11.

177. It is very difficult to reconcile the Court's legislative investigation decisions *Watkins* and *Barenblatt*. Both cases involved witnesses in HUAC hearings who refused to answer questions regarding communism, declined to invoke the Fifth Amendment's protection against self-incrimination, and instead claimed that the questions violated their rights under the First Amendment. In *Watkins*, the Court admonished Congress that it had no power "to expose for the sake of exposure." Watkins v. United States, 354 U.S. 178, 200 (1957). However, rather than decide the case on First Amendment grounds, the Court reversed Watkins's conviction on the ground that Watkins had been unable to know what questions were pertinent to the committee's work. *Watkins*, 354 U.S. at 209. In *Barenblatt*, the Court reached the opposite result. On the First Amendment issue, the Court backed off from the "exposure for exposure's sake" language of *Watkins*, finding it inappropriate for judges to inquire into the "true objective" of congressional hearings. Barenblatt v. United States, 360 U.S. 109, 142 (1959). The Court also reversed course on the issue of pertinency, finding that the questions in Barenblatt's hearing *were* pertinent, since Barenblatt (unlike Watkins) had refused to testify about his own involvement with the party and since "the subject matter of the inquiry" had been clearly identified "at the com-

mencement of the investigation as Communist infiltration into the field of education." *Barenblatt*, 360 U.S. at 124–25.

A stronger case can be made for the consistency of the Court's Smith Act decisions. *Dennis* and *Yates* were both brought under the act's advocacy clause, which
criminalized the advocacy of overthrowing the government by force. The post-1957
decisions *Scales* and *Noto*, in contrast, involved prosecutions under the act's membership clause, which criminalized knowingly becoming a member in an organization advocating violent overthrow of the government. Although the two sets of decisions are distinguishable in this regard, it can nonetheless be argued that the
Court's approach in *Scales* and *Noto* is generally consistent with *Yates* and *Dennis*.
In each pair, the Court rejected constitutional challenges while construing the
statute itself narrowly. Thus *Dennis* rejected First Amendment challenges to the
advocacy clause, while *Yates* construed the clause to permit conviction only upon
"advocacy of action." Yates v. United States, 354 U.S. 298, 324 (1957). The evidentiary bar established by *Yates* proved so high that the Justice Department "dropped
the charges against the remaining defendants in *Yates*," "dismissed its pending
charges" in a number of cities, and never again filed another prosecution under the
membership clause. Stone, *Perilous Times*, supra note 21, at 415. Similarly, *Scales*
rejected due process and First Amendment challenges to the membership clause.
Scales v. United States, 367 U.S. 203, 224–30 (1961). At the same time, *Scales* read
the Smith Act narrowly to apply only to "active" membership in an organization
engaging in "advocacy of violent overthrow." *Scales*, 367 U.S. at 207–08. Applying
this higher evidentiary burden, the Court reversed Noto's conviction. Noto v.
United States, 367 U.S. 290, 291 (1961). Thus the result of *Noto* was very similar to
the result of *Yates*: indictments under the membership clause were dismissed, and
convictions with appeals pending were reversed. Sabin, *In Calmer Times*, supra note
127, at 203.

178. Letter from Justice Frankfurter to Justice Brennan, Jan. 7, 1959, quoted in Sabin, *In
Calmer Times*, supra note 127, at 207. Beginning in 1959, Frankfurter voted for the
government in Barenblatt v. United States, 360 U.S. 109 (1959); Uphaus v. Wyman,
360 U.S. 72 (1959); Vitarelli v. Seaton, 359 U.S. 535 (1959); Flemming v. Nestor, 363
U.S. 603 (1960); Braden v. United States, 365 U.S. 431 (1961); Wilkinson v. United
States, 365 U.S. 399 (1961); Konigsberg v. State Bar, 366 U.S. 36 (1961); In re Anasta-
plo, 366 U.S. 82 (1961); Scales v. United States, 367 U.S. 203 (1961); Deutch v. United
States, 367 U.S. 456 (1961); Cafeteria Workers v. McElroy, 367 U.S. 886 (1961); and
Communist Party v. SACB, 367 U.S. 1 (1961). He voted against it in four cases: Noto
v. United States, 367 U.S. 290 (1961); Cramp v. Bd. of Public Instruction, 368 U.S. 278
(1961); Raley v. Ohio, 360 U.S. 423 (1959); and Greene v. McElroy, 360 U.S. 474 (1959).
Those four cases all were decided either unanimously or with only one dissenter.

179. Roger K. Newman, "The Warren Court and American Politics: An Impressionistic
Appreciation," review of Powe, *Warren Court and American Politics*, *Const. Comment.*
18 (2001): 677 (quoting Drew Pearson's diary).

180. Powe, *Warren Court and American Politics*, supra note 2, at 95; Sabin, *In Calmer
Times*, supra note 127, at 160.

181. From 1959 until 1962, Harlan voted against the government in only five cases, all but
one of which were decided unanimously or with only one dissenter. See Noto v.
United States, 367 U.S. 290 (1961); Cramp v. Bd. of Public Instruction, 368 U.S.
278 (1961); Raley v. Ohio, 360 U.S. 423 (1959); and Greene v. McElroy, 360 U.S. 474
(1959). The exception was Vitarelli v. Seaton, 359 U.S. 535 (1959), which was, as
Professor Powe notes, "a nonconsequential, nonconstitutional case." Powe, *Warren
Court and American Politics*, supra note 2, at 142.

Harlan's retreat is particularly striking since he wrote the decision invalidating the convictions of lower-tier Communist officials in *Yates* and joined Warren's strongly worded attack on congressional investigations in *Watkins*. Watkins v. United States, 354 U.S. 178 (1957). Though *Watkins* was decided on the ground that the pertinence of the unanswered committee questions was insufficiently clear, Warren delivered a strong denunciation of "exposure for the sake of exposure." Id. at 199. After the fight, though, Harlan wrote the decision in Barenblatt v. United States, 360 U.S. 109 (1959), explaining that the pertinence point was central to *Watkins* and discounting the exposure point entirely. See Powe, *Warren Court and American Politics*, supra note 2, at 93–96, 143–45 (discussing decisions).

182. Editorial, "A Regrettable Decision," *N.Y. Times*, March 2, 1960, at 36.

183. "Understanding the Court," *Wash. Post & Times Herald*, June 19, 1959, at A14; Monroe W. Karmin, "High Court's Course," *Wall St. J.*, June 19, 1959, at 6 ("The Supreme Court appears to be readjusting its philosophy along more conservative lines").

184. Editorial, "The Bane of Small Minds," *Chi. Daily Trib.*, June 28, 1959, at 12 ("[T]he court has, in effect reversed positions adopted in 1956 and 1957 . . .").

185. Even some of the Court-curbing bills' supporters welcomed the bills' defeat. See, e.g., Powe, *Warren Court and American Politics*, supra note 2, at 140–41 (quoting California Republican Thomas Kuchel, saying that anti-Court bills had gone down to a "well-deserved death").

186. The assault took even the most astute commentators by surprise. After the Senate Judiciary Committee released the Jenner-Butler bill in May 1958, Anthony Lewis reported, "As recently as a month ago most observers refused to take the Congressional critics of the Supreme Court seriously." Anthony Lewis, "High Court Attacked for 'Liberalism' Now; Unusual Congressional Alliance Drives to Curb Its Powers," *N.Y. Times*, May 4, 1958, at E10. For the Court to switch, it needed cases before it in which to signal the shift. In 1958, while the fight was on, and at the very end of its term, the Court issued two decisions, Lerner v. Casey, 357 U.S. 468 (1958), and Beilan v. Bd. of Public Educ., 357 U.S. 399 (1958), that signaled capitulation by gutting Slochower v. Bd. of Educ., 350 U.S. 551 (1956), a decision in which the Court had held invalid the city of New York's dismissal of an employee for exercising his Fifth Amendment rights in a HUAC hearing. *Lerner* and *Beilan* both involved government employees who had been fired after "taking the Fifth" when asked by their employers about their membership in the Communist Party. The government employers claimed that the employees were not fired for invoking their Fifth Amendment rights. Rather, the employers claimed that the employees' refusal to testify indicated "incompetence" and "doubtful trust and reliability." This was a highly dubious distinction, but the Court bought it and sustained the dismissals. See Powe, *Warren Court and American Politics*, supra note 2, at 137–38. Although these decisions signaled that the Court was retreating, by the time they were released in June 1958 it was too late to avert Congress's reaction.

187. See, e.g., Murphy, *Congress and the Court*, supra note 36, at 246–47; Powe, *Warren Court and American Politics*, supra note 2, at 141–42 (congressional attack caused Frankfurter to end "his dalliance with the four liberals").

188. Powe, *Warren Court and American Politics*, supra note 2, at 140 (noting that "seven Republican senators who had supported one or more of the anti-Court bills either retired or went down to defeat").

189. See Murphy, *Congress and the Court*, supra note 36, at 235–37.

190. "What 36 State Chief Justices Said About the Supreme Court," *U.S. News & World Rep.*, Oct. 3, 1958, at 102.

191. Id. at 101. The chief justices criticized the Supreme Court for using the Fourteenth Amendment to "cut down State action" in cases involving state legislative investigations, public employment, admission to the bar, and state administration of criminal law. Id. at 97–99.
192. "Justices in Judgment," *Time*, Sept. 1, 1958, at 15.
193. See Murphy, *Congress and the Court*, supra note 36, at 118–19; Powe, *Warren Court and American Politics*, supra note 2, at 99–100.
194. 105 Cong. Rec. A14780–81 (daily ed. Feb. 25, 1999) (reprinting ABA report).
195. *A.B.A. J.* 45 (1959): 409–10.
196. Erwin Griswold, "Morrison Lecture, Delivered Before the State Bar of California at Coronado, California," Oct. 9, 1958, in *Mass. L.Q.* 43 (1958): 101.
197. Paul A. Freund, "The Supreme Court Crisis," *N.Y. St. Bar Bulletin* 31 (1959): 66.
198. Edward A. Purcell, Jr., "Learned Hand: The Jurisprudential Trajectory of an Old Progressive," review of Gerald Gunther, *Learned Hand: The Man and the Judge*, *Buff. L. Rev.* 43 (1995): 918 (quoting Gunther, *Learned Hand: The Man and the Judge* (1994), ix–x).
199. See Griswold, "Morrison Lecture," supra note 196 (remarking that Hand's message was "far from clear").
200. Frankfurter had lobbied for Hand vociferously in the 1940s, perhaps so much so that Roosevelt, wanting a sure liberal and justifiably suspicious of Frankfurter's judicial politics, ultimately demurred. See Purcell, "Learned Hand," supra note 198, at 914–16.
201. Learned Hand, *The Bill of Rights* (1958), 15.
202. Id. at 42.
203. Id. at 54–55, 73. Hand had been egged on behind the scenes by Frankfurter. See Gunther, *Learned Hand*, supra note 198, at 671.
204. Herbert Wechsler, "Toward Neutral Principles of Constitutional Law," *Harv. L. Rev.* 73 (1959): 12, 34.
205. Anthony Lewis, "The Supreme Court and Its Critics," *Minn. L. Rev.* 45 (1961): 319.
206. Bickel, *Idea of Progress*, supra note 15, at 47; Erwin N. Griswold, "The Supreme Court, 1959 Term—Foreword, Of Times and Attitudes: Professor Hart and Judge Arnold," *Harv. L. Rev.* 74 (1960): 94; Lewis, "Supreme Court and Its Critics," supra note 205, at 322 (noting that "[w]orkmanship is a word heard often from the academic critics").
207. Bernard Schwartz, "Felix Frankfurter and Earl Warren: A Study of Deteriorating Relationship," *Sup. Ct. Rev.*, 1980: 115, 137; Melvin I. Urofsky, *Division and Discord: The Supreme Court Under Stone and Vinson, 1941–1953* (1997), 45.
208. See Horwitz, *Pursuit of Justice*, supra note 3, at 11; compare "Warren Court: Fateful Decade," supra note 1, at 25 (describing Warren's bench questions).
209. Philip B. Kurland, "The Supreme Court, 1963 Term—Foreword," supra note 2, at 176.
210. Alexander M. Bickel, "Mr. Justice Black: The Unobvious Meaning of Plain Words," *New Republic*, March 14, 1960, at 13; see also Philip B. Kurland, "The Supreme Court and Its Judicial Critics," *Utah L. Rev.* 6 (1959): 460 (academic criticism "tends to fall on ears that are deaf to the bases of the criticisms and hear only the condemnation of the Court").
211. "Is the Supreme Court Reaching for Too Much Power?," *U.S. News & World Rep.*, Oct. 7, 1963, at 64.
212. "Warren Court: Fateful Decade," supra note 1, at 24.
213. See United States Senate, *Limitation of Appellate Jurisdiction of the United States Supreme Court: Hearings Before the Subcomm. on the Judiciary to Investigate the*

Administration of the Internal Security Act and Other International Security Laws of the Comm. on the Judiciary, 85th Cong. (1958) (giving statements of members of Congress relying on Hand); 104 Cong. Rec. S18673 (1958) (quoting letter from Hand); see Gunther, *Learned Hand*, supra note 198, at 660–61 (describing statements by members of Congress relying on Hand, as well as Hand's reaction).

214. Ralph T. Catterall, "Judicial Self-Restraint: The Obligation of the Judiciary," *A.B.A. J.* 42 (1956): 832–33 (asserting that a lack of judicial restraint leads to judicial despotism, such as that exemplified in the *Brown* decision); Robert H. Bork, "The Supreme Court Needs a New Philosophy," *Fortune*, Dec. 1968, at 168 ("Restraint entails not so much a reduced as a different role for the Court, one better suited to a democratic society than the role now played by the Warren Court").

215. Lawrence Van Gelder, "Alexander M. Bickel Dies; Constitutional Law Expert," *N.Y. Times*, Nov. 8, 1974, at 42.

216. Bickel, *Least Dangerous Branch*, supra note 39, at 16–18.

217. V. O. Key, Jr., *Politics, Parties, and Pressure Groups* (1943), 5; see also H. B. Mayo, *An Introduction to Democratic Theory* (1960), 87–94 (arguing that elections do not ascertain popular will); Joseph A. Schumpeter, *Capitalism, Socialism and Democracy* (1942; repr. 1976), 250–56 (attacking notions of the common good and will of the people); David B. Truman, *The Governmental Process: Political Interests and Public Opinion* (1958), 23 (treating groups as "basic social units" because of the "uniformities of behavior produced through them"); see generally Edward A. Purcell, Jr., *The Crisis of Democratic Theory: Scientific Naturalism & the Problem of Value* (1973), 254 (describing resurgence of group theory of politics in 1950s America); Darryl Baskin, "American Pluralism: Theory, Practice, and Ideology," *J. Pol.* 32 (1970) (summarizing main tenets and major criticisms of pluralist theory).

218. Jack W. Peltason, *Federal Courts in the Political Process* (1955), 2.

219. Robert A. Dahl, *Pluralist Democracy in the United States* (1967), 168; see also Robert A. Dahl, *A Preface to Democratic Theory* (1963), 132 (arguing that elections create "minorities rule" and not minority or majority rule). On Dahl's influence, see Horwitz, *Transformation of American Law*, supra note 12, at 256; Purcell, *Crisis of Democratic Theory*, supra note 217, at 260.

220. *Carolene Prods.*, 304 U.S. at 152–53n4.

221. Powe, *Warren Court and American Politics*, supra note 2, at 233 (noting that from 1938 to 1963, Senator Richard Russell of Georgia led eleven successful filibusters against civil rights bills).

222. Lewis, "Historic Change," supra note 4, at 7.

223. Kenneth Crawford, "Reaction's Refuge," *Newsweek*, June 3, 1963, at 31.

224. Frankfurter and his followers remained willfully blind to the fact that even their patron saint of judicial restraint, James Bradley Thayer, would not have applied the rule when courts were reviewing state (as opposed to congressional) legislation. See Charles L. Black, Jr., "The Supreme Court, 1966 Term—Foreword, 'State Action,' Equal Protection, and California's Proposition 14," *Harv. L. Rev.* 81 (1967): 104 & n124; Purcell, "Learned Hand," supra note 198, at 886–88.

225. "Should the Supreme Court's Power Be Curbed?," *Senior Scholastic*, March 4, 1966, at 7 (reprinting *Washington Star* cartoon).

226. Bickel, *Idea of Progress*, supra note 15, at 7 (quoting Jackson).

227. Alpheus Thomas Mason, "The Supreme Court Under Fire Again," *Reporter*, Sept. 24, 1964, at 45; see also J. Skelly Wright, "The Role of the Supreme Court in a Democratic Society—Judicial Activism or Restraint?," *Cornell L. Rev.* 54 (1968): 6 ("All too often . . . the practical choice has been between the Court doing the job as best it can and no one doing it at all").

228. Theodore Lowi, *The End of Liberalism* (1969); see also Ronald Kahn, *The Supreme Court & Constitutional Theory, 1953–1993* (1994), 184 (discussing Lowi's criticism of the "control of public policies by bureaucracies, subcommittees in Congress, and private interest group clienteles").

229. E. E. Schattschneider, *The Semi-Sovereign People* (1960), 35.

230. Robert L. Rabin, "Lawyers for Social Change: Perspectives on Public Interest Law," *Stan. L. Rev.* 28 (1976): 225.

231. See id. at 208, 224–25.

232. See Tushnet, *NAACP's Legal Strategy*, supra note 42, at xii (describing the NAACP's campaign as a "precursor" to "institutional reform litigation"); Rabin, "Lawyers for Social Change," supra note 230, at 210 (noting influence of the ACLU and NAACP on the "budding public interest law movement").

233. Rabin, "Lawyers for Social Change," supra note 230, at 228–29.

234. Kahn, *Supreme Court & Constitutional Theory*, supra note 228, at 250–51.

235. Charles L. Black, Jr., "The Supreme Court and Democracy," *Yale Rev.* 50 (1961): 199.

236. See Peltason, *Federal Courts*, supra note 218, at 51–52.

237. Professor Powe attributes the development of "the Court the public currently identifies as 'the Warren Court'" to President Kennedy's appointment of Arthur Goldberg in 1962 to replace Felix Frankfurter. Powe, *Warren Court in American Politics*, supra note 2, at 209, 211; see also Horwitz, *Pursuit of Justice*, supra note 3, at 12 (noting that "after Justice Goldberg was appointed in 1962, the Court at last had a liberal majority"); Tushnet, "Warren Court as History," in Tushnet, *Warren Court*, supra note 3, at 7; Anthony Lewis, "New Judges and Doctrines Alter Character of Supreme Court; Decisions Stress Personal Rights; Goldberg Most Frequently Completes the Majority in Shifts During Term," *N.Y. Times*, June 23, 1963, at 64 (contemporary account of Goldberg's impact during 1962 term). However, political scientists Jeffrey Segal and Harold Spaeth have questioned Goldberg's influence, noting that his "vote was crucial to the Court's majority in the 1962 term, but not in the 1963 or 1964 terms," when there were few 5–4 splits in civil liberties cases. They conclude that "[t]he liberal reputation of the 1961 through 1968 Warren Court would be unchanged had Goldberg never served on the Court." Jeffrey A. Segal and Harold J. Spaeth, "Decisional Trends on the Warren and Burger Courts," *Judicature* 73 (1989): 104.

    While Goldberg certainly had some influence on the balance of power on the Court, there are two problems with the theory of his influence. First, several major liberal decisions were handed down before his arrival, including Baker v. Carr, 369 U.S. 186 (1962); Mapp v. Ohio, 370 U.S. 421 (1962); and Engel v. Vitale, 367 U.S. 643 (1961). Second, it is important not to lose sight of the historical context of Goldberg's appointment. He joined the Court at a time when "it was one institution in a unified government dominated in both Congress and the presidency by liberal Democrats." Tushnet, "Warren Court as History," in Tushnet, *Warren Court*, supra note 3, at 12–13. McCarthyism was also fading as a national political force, relieving some of the pressure the Court had felt during the late 1950s. See Sabin, *In Calmer Times*, supra note 127, at 204. Moreover, the Court was not the only branch of the federal government to tilt noticeably leftward around 1962. See Dudziak, *Cold War Civil Rights*, supra note 39, at 201 (discussing President Kennedy's civil rights stance in 1963).

238. Stephen J. Whitfield, *The Culture of the Cold War* (1991), 83.

239. Id. at 88 (quoting Eisenhower conversation with Billy Graham).

240. Id. at 88–89.

241. For a discussion of the revival's relationship to the Cold War, see id. at 77–100.

242. Purcell, *Crisis of Democratic Theory*, supra note 217, at 241 (quoting Robert I. Gannon, president of Fordham University).

243. Whitfield, *Culture of the Cold War*, supra note 238, at 77 (quoting Graham's remarks at a 1949 revival).

244. Everson v. Bd. of Educ., 330 U.S. 1, 18 (1947).

245. *Everson*, 330 U.S. at 19 (Jackson, J., dissenting).

246. Illinois ex rel. McCollum v. Bd. of Educ., 333 U.S. 203 (1948). The dissenter was Justice Reed.

247. Zorach v. Clauson, 343 U.S. 306, 308–09, 315 (1952).

248. Id. at 325 (Jackson, J., dissenting).

249. Id. at 317 (Black, J., dissenting).

250. Id. at 325 (Jackson, J., dissenting).

251. Mary Hornaday, "Backing for School Prayer Marks Gains in New York," *Christian Sci. Monitor*, Dec. 4, 1951, at 10; "Pastors Endorse School Prayers; State Regents Board Proposal Called 'Freedom Protection' by Dutch Reformed Pastor," *N.Y. Times*, Dec. 3, 1951, at 31.

252. "School Prayers Backed; Catholic Education Official Here Terms Regents' Proposal Just," *N.Y. Times*, Dec. 4, 1951, at 35.

253. Hornaday, "Backing for School Prayer," supra note 251 (quoting Ruth Farbman, president of the United Parents Association).

254. Engel v. Vitale, 370 U.S. 421 (1962).

255. Id. at 434, 424.

256. Id. at 425.

257. Id. at 445 (Stewart, J., dissenting). Neither Justice Frankfurter nor Justice White participated in deciding the case. Id. at 436.

258. Anthony Lewis, "Supreme Court Outlaws Official School Prayers in Regents Case Decision; Ruling is 6 to 1; Suit Was Brought by 5 L.I. Parents Against Education Board," *N.Y. Times*, June 26, 1962, at 1 (quoting Rep. George Andrews of Alabama).

259. "Byrd Leads Picnic in Prayer Barred by 'Warren Court,'" *N.Y. Times*, Aug. 26, 1962, at 43 (quoting Sen. Harry F. Byrd, Sr.).

260. Anthony Lewis, "Court Again Under Fire; Politics Seen Behind Much of Criticism on Prayer Decision but Scholars Also Voice Objections," *N.Y. Times*, July 1, 1962, at 10.

261. Anthony Lewis, "Both Houses Get Bills to Lift Ban on School Prayer; Southerners Lead Attack on Supreme Court's Edict in New York Case; Amendments Proposed; Dirksen Doubts Constitution Will Be Modified—Celler Terms Ruling Correct," *N.Y. Times*, June 27, 1962, at 1.

262. Philip B. Kurland, "The Regents' Prayer Case: 'Full of Sound and Fury, Signifying . . . ,'" *Sup. Ct. Rev.*, 1962: 2; see also Powe, *Warren Court and American Politics*, supra note 2, at 188.

263. "The Court Decision—and the School Prayer Furor," *Newsweek*, July 9, 1962, at 43; "To Stand as a Guarantee," *Time*, July 6, 1962, at 7.

264. Gallup, *Gallup Poll*, supra note 70, at 3:1779.

265. The poll also gauged reaction to the 1963 case *Sch. Dist. v. Schempp*, which banned Bible reading in public schools. See id. at 3:1837 (reporting that in June 1963, when asked the question "The United States Supreme Court has ruled that no state or local government may require the reading of the Lord's Prayer or Bible verses in public schools. What are your views on this?," 70 percent of respondents indicated disapproval); see also Alison Gash and Angelo Gonzales, "School Prayer," in *Public Opinion and Constitutional Controversy*, ed. Nathaniel Persily et al. (2008), 68 (noting consistent pattern from 1960s through 2004 that "rates of support for school prayer . . . exceeded rates of disapproval of the Supreme Court's decisions"); Louis Harris & Assocs., "Harris 1966 Election Survey, No. 1643," Sept. 1966, distributed

by Odum Institute at http://www.irss.unc.edu/data_archive/pollsearch.html (reporting that in 1966, when asked the question "Another decision of the U.S. Supreme Court was to rule that children could not be required to recite a prayer in school. Do you personally think that decision of the U.S. Supreme Court was right or wrong?," 65.5 percent of respondents said it was wrong).

266. Kenneth M. Dolbeare and Phillip E. Hammond, "Inertia in Midway: Supreme Court Decisions and Local Responses," *J. Leg. Educ.* 23 (1970): 28 (quoting GPO); see also Powe, *Warren Court and American Politics*, supra note 2, at 187.

267. Nancy E. Musala, letter to the editor, *Newsweek*, July 23, 1962, at 2.

268. "To Stand as a Guarantee," supra note 263, at 7 (quoting Judge Adams).

269. For example, unlike the majority opinion by Justice Black, which focused solely on school prayer, Justice Douglas's concurrence went out of its way to declare that financing "religious exercise" is "an unconstitutional undertaking whatever form it takes." *Engel*, 370 U.S. at 437 (Douglas, J., concurring).

270. See Gash and Gonzales, "School Prayer," in Persily et al., *Public Opinion*, supra note 265, at 76; Powe, *Warren Court and American Politics*, supra note 2, at 358.

271. See Gash and Gonzales, "School Prayer," in Persily et al., *Public Opinion*, supra note 265, at 74; Powe, *Warren Court and American Politics*, supra note 2, at 361; James O'Gara, "Religion and the Court," *Commonweal*, July 5, 1963, at 391.

272. See Powe, *Warren Court and American Politics*, supra note 2, at 190.

273. James E. Clayton, *The Making of Justice* (1964), 21.

274. Id. at 22 (quoting Justice Clark); see also Schwartz, *Super Chief*, supra note 58, at 442 ("Warren and the Justices were both surprised and pained by the reaction to their decision").

275. Schwartz, *Super Chief*, supra note 58, at 442 (quoting Earl Warren, Jr.).

276. Sch. Dist. v. Schempp, 374 U.S. 203 (1963).

277. Raymond Moley, "God, Man, and Liberty," *Newsweek*, July 23, 1962, at 76.

278. See Clayton, *Making of Justice*, supra note 273, at 22.

279. Lewis, "New Judges and Doctrines," supra note 237.

280. See "To Stand as a Guarantee," supra note 263, at 7 (quoting Atlanta clergyman who said the decision was "'the most terrible thing that's ever happened to us'—then admitted he did not really know what the decision said").

281. John F. Kennedy, "President's News Conference," June 27, 1962, in *Public Papers of the Presidents of the United States: John F. Kennedy, 1962* (1963), 509, 510–11.

282. Lewis, "Public Mood Plays Big Role," supra note 7.

283. Clayton, *Making of Justice*, supra note 273, at 275 (quoting United Press International wire); see also Powe, *Warren Court and American Politics*, supra note 2, at 361 ("Mainstream Protestants rushed to the Court's defense"); O'Gara, "Religion and the Court," supra note 271, at 391 ("Most Protestant and all Jewish opinion I have seen upholds the Court's decision, though I suspect more Protestant rank-and-file disquiet than shows in the official statements"). In 1964, when congressional hearings were held on a proposed constitutional amendment to undo the prayer decisions, the National Council of Churches, the Baptists, Lutherans, Presbyterians, Seventh-day Adventists, Unitarians, and the United Church of Christ all expressed their opposition. Powe, *Warren Court and American Politics*, supra note 2, at 362.

284. Editorial, "Prayer Is Personal," *N.Y. Times*, June 27, 1962, at 34.

285. J. Gordon Chamberlin, letter to the editor, "Boon to Churches and Schools," *N.Y. Times*, June 29, 1962, at 26; see also Thomas G. Sanders, "The Court Expands a Concept," *Nation*, July 13, 1963, at 25 (calling the prayer decisions "a significant affirmation of minority rights in a religiously pluralistic society").

286. Robert G. McCloskey, "Principles, Powers, and Values: The Establishment Clause and the Supreme Court," in *Religion and the Public Order: An Annual Review of Church and State*, ed. Donald A. Ginnella (1964), 3:28.

287. "A Tide Reversed," *Time*, June 19, 1964, at 62, 65; see also Powe, *Warren Court in American Politics*, supra note 2, at 362 ("[I]nstead of showing opposition to the Court, the hearings demonstrated that the Court could muster influential religious and academic support against a constitutional amendment").

288. Alexander Burnham, "Court's Decision Stirs Conflict," *N.Y. Times*, July 27, 1962, at 1.

289. Powe, *Warren Court and American Politics*, supra note 2, at 362 (noting that "classroom devotions virtually vanished in the East and the West" following the decisions); Dolbeare and Hammond, "Inertia in Midway," supra note 266, at 32 (noting that the East reduced the practice of homeroom prayers by 87 percent, the West by 64 percent, the Midwest by 45 percent, and the South by only 26 percent).

290. Dolbeare and Hammond, "Inertia in Midway," supra note 266, at 5–6, 72–93.

291. Id. at 10.

292. See Dean Johnson, "Cities Outvoted by Rural Areas in Many Legislatures," *Wash. Post & Times Herald*, July 20, 1959, at A9 (describing failure by state legislatures, including Mississippi, to reapportion); see also Powe, *Warren Court and American Politics*, supra note 2, at 245 (same in Vermont); Gladwin Hill, "California Faces Rural-City Fight; Reapportionment Struggle Threatens New Program for Water Resources," *N.Y. Times*, Dec. 6, 1959, at 53 (same in California); "Vote for Inequality," *Wash. Post & Times Herald*, Feb. 26, 1960, at 14 (same in Maryland).

293. Colegrove v. Green, 328 U.S. 549, 556 (1946).

294. Baker v. Carr, 369 U.S. 186 (1962) (holding that plaintiffs had standing, that district court had jurisdiction over plaintiffs' federal constitutional claims, and that plaintiffs' allegations of a denial of equal protection constituted a justiciable cause of action).

295. See id. at 187–88, 197–98, 237.

296. Id. at 267, 270 (Frankfurter, J., dissenting).

297. See Powe, *Warren Court and American Politics*, supra note 2, at 205, 209–10.

298. Wesberry v. Sanders, 376 U.S. 1, 7–8, 18 (1964).

299. See, e.g., Brief and Argument for Appellees at 8, Baker v. Carr, 369 U.S. 186 (1962) (No. 6) ("As every student knows, the population concept was compromised and found inadequate by the framers of the Constitution who adopted a different formula for selecting United States Senators").

300. 110 Cong. Rec. at 16,061 (1964) (statement of Oct. 29, 1948, read into the *Congressional Record*, July 8, 1964); see also Jim Newton, *Justice for All: Earl Warren and the Nation He Made* (2006), 388.

301. Reynolds v. Sims, 377 U.S. 533, 562–63 (1964).

302. *Wesberry*, 376 U.S. at 6–8.

303. See Andrew Hacker, "One Man, One Vote—Yes or No?," *N.Y. Times Mag.*, Nov. 8, 1964, at 31.

304. Strom Thurmond, "The Federal Judiciary: The Usurpation of Power—Speech Delivered to Joint Meeting of the Greenville County Medical Association and the Greenville County Bar Association," July 3, 1964, in *Vital Speeches of the Day*, Aug. 15, 1964, at 667.

305. Everett McKinley Dirksen, "The Supreme Court Is Defying the People," *Sat. Evening Post*, Sept. 12, 1964, at 10.

306. Robert Dixon, Jr., *Democratic Representation: Reapportionment in Law and Politics* (1968), 394–97 (discussing legislative history of and public reaction to the two bills); Hacker, "One Man, One Vote," supra note 303, at 31.

307. Editorial, "Low Blow at the Supreme Court," *N.Y. Times*, July 6, 1964, at 28; Walter F. Murphy, "Deeds Under a Doctrine," *Am. Pol. Sci. Rev.* 59 (1965): 64.

308. See Clayton, *Making of Justice*, supra note 273, at 138.

309. Raymond Moley, "Reapportionment Mess," *Newsweek*, June 21, 1965, at 104.

310. James Reston, "Rural Areas Facing Loss of Political Dominance; Court Ruling Expected to Bring Gradual Shift of Power to Suburbs and Cities and to Strengthen the Democrats; Rural Blocs Face Political Losses," *N.Y. Times*, March 27, 1962, at 1.

311. Herbert Wechsler, *The Nationalization of Civil Liberties and Civil Rights* (1968), 25.

312. "The Supreme Court Draws the Line," *Newsweek*, March 2, 1964, at 16 (describing Bickel's views).

313. "Bigger Voice for Big Cities," *Newsweek*, Apr. 9, 1962, at 32 (quoting Rep. Thomas B. Curtis of Missouri).

314. Wechsler, *Nationalization of Civil Liberties*, supra note 311, at 25; see also Richard C. Cortner, *The Apportionment Cases* (1970), 253 (noting that by 1968, legislatures in forty-nine states had been reapportioned, and only "Oregon's legislature, the upper house in Massachusetts, and the lower houses in Alaska, Hawaii, and South Carolina remained untouched by the reapportionment revolution").

315. Phil C. Neal, "*Baker v. Carr*: Politics in Search of Law," *Sup. Ct. Rev.*, 1962: 253; see also Cortner, *Apportionment Cases*, supra note 314, at 222 ("Reapportionment under federal and state judicial supervision which followed the Court's decision in *Baker v. Carr* had gone surprisingly smoothly . . .").

316. See Powe, *Warren Court and American Politics*, supra note 2, at 203–04 (describing reaction to *Baker v. Carr*); William G. Ross, "Attacks on the Warren Court by State Officials: A Case Study of Why Court-Curbing Movements Fail," *Buff. L. Rev.* 50 (2002): 606 ("[O]pinion polls indicated that the Court's decision in Reynolds . . . received far more approval than disapproval"). Polls did show a wide gap of approval over disapproval, though the "not sure" segment also was quite high. See, e.g., Gallup, *Gallup Poll*, supra note 70, at 3:1897 (reporting that in response to the question "As you know, the United States Supreme Court has ruled that the number of representatives of both the lower house and the Senate in all state legislatures must be in proportion to population. In most states, this means reducing the number of legislators from the rural areas and increasing the number from urban areas. Do you approve or disapprove of this ruling?," 47 percent approved, 30 percent disapproved, and 23 percent had no opinion); Louis Harris & Assocs., "Harris 1966 Election Survey," supra note 265 (reporting that in response to the question "Another decision of the U.S. Supreme Court was to rule all Congressional Districts had to have an equal number of people in them so each person's vote would count equally. Do you personally think that decision of the Supreme Court was right or wrong?," 57 percent thought the decision was right, 18.6 percent thought it was wrong, and 24.4 percent were not sure).

317. Louis L. Jaffe, "Was Brandeis an Activist? The Search for Intermediate Premises," *Harv. L. Rev.* 80 (1967): 991.

318. Alexander M. Bickel, "Reapportionment and the Courts," *New Republic*, June 27, 1964, at 7; see also Arthur J. Goldberg, "Equality and Governmental Action," *N.Y.U. L. Rev.* 39 (1964): 216 ("The storm that broke over the Court following *Baker v. Carr* was, on the whole, one of applause"); Robert G. McCloskey, "The Supreme Court, 1961 Term—Foreword, The Reapportionment Case," *Harv. L. Rev.* 76 (1962): 59 (early reactions to *Baker* "may warrant the conjecture that the Court here happened to hit upon what the students of public opinion might call a latent consensus").

319. Holman Harvey and Kenneth O. Gilmore, "Reapportionment: Shall the Court or the People Decide?," *Reader's Dig.*, March 1965, at 113 (quoting statement made prior to the reapportionment decisions).

320. See Hill, "California Faces Rural-City Fight," supra note 292 (noting "sparsely pop-
ulated 'cow counties'" threatening a "$1,750,000,000 water resources development
program, which is generally considered vital to the state's development"); Johnson,
"Cities Outvoted," supra note 292 (noting numerous legislatures dominated by rural
interests).
321. See Clarence Petersen, "Discouraging Story of Politics Is Told," *Chi. Daily Trib.*,
Jan. 6, 1961, at B9 (describing CBS report).
322. Brief for the United States as Amicus Curiae on Reargument at 9, Baker v. Carr,
369 U.S. 186 (1962) (No. 6).
323. Schwartz, *Super Chief*, supra note 58, at 425 (quoting Kennedy).
324. *Baker*, 369 U.S. at 258–59 (Clark, J., concurring).
325. Richard L. Strout, "The Tennessee Case," *Christian Sci. Monitor*, Dec. 24, 1959, at 20.
326. Powell v. Alabama, 287 U.S. 45, 49–58 (1932); Brown v. Mississippi, 297 U.S. 278,
281–82 (1936).
327. *To Secure These Rights*, supra note 43, at 27.
328. Barron v. Baltimore, 32 U.S. 243 (1833) (holding that the provisions of the Fifth Amendment were "intended solely as a limitation on the exercise of power by the government of the United States, and are not applicable to the legislation of the states").
329. Adamson v. California, 332 U.S. 46, 70–75 (1947); see also Powe, *Warren Court and
American Politics*, supra note 2, at 11 (discussing Black's theory). The three justices
who joined Black's opinion were Murphy, Rutledge, and Douglas. Murphy (joined
by Rutledge) wrote a separate dissent agreeing with Black's total incorporation theory
but adding that in situations where a specific provision of the Bill of Rights did not
apply, he would still use the Fourteenth Amendment's Due Process Clause to protect
"fundamental standards of procedure." *Adamson*, 332 U.S. at 123–24 (Murphy, J.,
dissenting). Black's argument engendered controversy then and thereafter from historians. Compare Charles Fairman, "Does the Fourteenth Amendment Incorporate
the Bill of Rights? The Original Understanding," *Stan. L. Rev.* 2 (1949): 139 (concluding that "the record of history is overwhelmingly" against Black), with Akhil
Reed Amar, *The Bill of Rights* (1998), 183–206 (arguing against Fairman).
330. Griswold, "Morrison Lecture," supra note 196, at 106.
331. Herbert L. Packer, "Policing the Police: Nine Men Are Not Enough," *New Republic*,
Sept. 4, 1965, at 19.
332. Fred P. Graham, *The Self-Inflicted Wound* (1970), 4–5.
333. Mapp v. Ohio, 367 U.S. 643 (1961).
334. Olmstead v. United States, 277 U.S. 438, 485 (1928) (Brandeis, J., dissenting).
335. People v. Defore, 150 N.E. 585, 587 (N.Y. 1926).
336. It was anticipated that the Court would extend the exclusionary rule to the states in
some case, though perhaps not in *Mapp*'s. Mapp's primary claim had been that her
rights under the First Amendment were violated. The constitutionality of the exclusionary rule was neither raised nor briefed in *Mapp*, other than in a single stray reference in the ACLU's amicus brief. Indeed, when Mapp's lawyer was asked during oral
argument whether he wanted the Court to consider the issue, he declined. The dissenting justices chastised the majority for "reaching out" to decide the issue in that
case. See Lain, "Countermajoritarian Hero or Zero?," supra note 3, at 1376–77.
337. Weeks v. United States, 232 U.S. 383 (1914).
338. See Lain, "Countermajoritarian Hero or Zero?," supra note 3, at 1381–82 & n117.
339. *Mapp*, 367 U.S. at 648 (quoting Silverthorne Lumber Co. v. United States, 251 U.S.
385, 392 (1920) (Holmes, J.)); id. at 656.
340. Yale Kamisar, "When *Wasn't* There a 'Crime Crisis'?," *F.R.D.* 39 (1965): 458–59.

341. Lewis, "Historic Change," supra note 4, at 7, 38; see also Editorial, "The Individual's Rights," *N.Y. Times*, June 22, 1961, at 30 (supporting "historic" *Mapp* decision); Lain, "Countermajoritarian Hero or Zero?," supra note 3, at 1379–81 (arguing that "the Supreme Court's decision in *Mapp* coincided with an emerging national consensus on the exclusionary rule, albeit at its early stages").

342. Gideon v. Wainwright, 372 U.S. 335 (1963).

343. Powell v. Alabama, 287 U.S. 45 (1932).

344. Betts v. Brady, 316 U.S. 455 (1942). The special circumstances formulation did not appear in the decision but was read into it by later decisions. See, e.g., Bute v. Illinois, 333 U.S. 640, 677 (1948).

345. Clayton, *Making of Justice*, supra note 273, at 235; Yale Kamisar, "The Right to Counsel and the Fourteenth Amendment: A Dialogue on 'The Most Pervasive Right' of an Accused," *U. Chi. L. Rev.* 30 (1962): 17–19 (surveying state practices); Lain, "Countermajoritarian Hero or Zero?," supra note 3, at 1392.

346. See Yale Kamisar, "How Earl Warren's Twenty-two Years in Law Enforcement Affected His Work as Chief Justice," *Ohio St. J. Crim. L.* 3 (2005): 21 (noting that "in practice the courts in the states that followed the 'special circumstances' rule rarely, if ever[,] bothered to find out whether the circumstances were 'special'"); Lain, "Countermajoritarian Hero or Zero?," supra note 3, at 1391 & n159.

347. Anthony Lewis, *Gideon's Trumpet* (1964), 38.

348. See id. at 47–49; Lain, "Countermajoritarian Hero or Zero?," supra note 3, at 1391.

349. See Lewis, *Gideon's Trumpet*, supra note 347, at 141–48; Lain, "Countermajoritarian Hero or Zero?," supra note 3, at 1392.

350. Lewis, *Gideon's Trumpet*, supra note 347, at 145 (quoting Mondale).

351. Gideon v. Wainwright, 372 U.S. 335, 344 (1963).

352. Lewis, *Gideon's Trumpet*, supra note 347, at 204 (quoting Gideon).

353. Anthony Lewis, "Supreme Court Ruling Steps Up Legal Aid for Poor Defendants; Legislatures, Tribunals and Bar Groups of Many States Are Meeting or Going Beyond Decision to Provide Lawyers," *N.Y. Times*, June 30, 1963, at 39.

354. See Lewis, *Gideon's Trumpet*, supra note 347, at 201–02.

355. Id. at 203 (quoting Howard McDonnell).

356. Id. at 206 (quoting Chief Justice Carleton Harris of Arkansas).

357. Id. at 202 (quoting Governor Farris Bryant of Florida).

358. See id. at 223–38 (discussing retrial).

359. In 1936, the Court had unanimously reversed the convictions of three black defendants who confessed after being savagely whipped by the police. See Brown v. Mississippi, 297 U.S. 278 (1936). The Court later extended protections against psychological coercion, deeming inadmissible confessions obtained through sleep deprivation and threats of physical violence. See Chambers v. Florida, 309 U.S. 227 (1940); see also Klarman, *From Jim Crow*, supra note 3, at 227–29 (discussing *Chambers* and other 1940s coercion cases). Professor Klarman argues that despite *Chambers* and other criminal procedure cases, the police in the Jim Crow South continued to "habitually coerce[] confessions from black suspects." Klarman, *From Jim Crow*, supra note 3, at 282.

360. Walter V. Schaefer, "Federalism and State Criminal Procedure," *Harv. L. Rev.* 70 (1956): 10.

361. J. Edward Lumbard, "The Administration of Criminal Justice," *N.Y. St. Bar J.*, Oct. 1963, at 366.

362. "Concern About Confessions," *Time*, Apr. 29, 1966, at 53 ("Without tapes, films or neutral witnesses, judges have no way of determining whether a suspect really

talked freely or was tricked or bullied into 'waiving' his right to silence, or even into confessing falsely—a not unknown reaction to the sinister air of the police station").

363. The voluntariness standard originated in *Brown v. Mississippi*, where the Court invalidated a confession obtained through physical violence. Brown v. Mississippi, 297 U.S. 278 (1936). As Professor Lain points out, by the time of *Miranda*, the Court "had developed a long list of factors (thirty-some in all) relevant to the determination" of voluntariness. "None proved to be particularly helpful," and "state courts continued to affirm convictions based on confessions obtained under dubious circumstances." Thus the Court "needed a more definitive rule." Lain, "Countermajoritarian Hero or Zero?," supra note 3, at 1401–02.

364. Miranda v. Arizona, 384 U.S. 436, 444–45 (1966).

365. *Miranda*, 384 U.S. at 500 (Clark, J., dissenting).

366. Fred P. Graham, "Leary Says Court Decision Will Hurt 'Law and Order'; General Reaction Is Mild—Crime Unit Aide Sees No Major Changes," *N.Y. Times*, June 15, 1966, at 1.

367. Editorial, "Freely and Voluntarily," *N.Y. Times*, June 15, 1966, at 46.

368. For example, a Philadelphia detective declared that the decision "puts the police . . . out of business." The executive director of the International Association of Chiefs of Police snidely observed, "[W]e'll have to supply all squad cars with attorneys," and the New York City police commissioner called the decision "sophisticated law for an immature society." "Rewriting the Rules," *Newsweek*, June 27, 1966, at 22 (quoting police officials); see also "New Rules for Police Rooms," *Time*, June 24, 1966, at 54 ("It's the damnedest thing I ever heard—we may as well close up shop") (quoting Texas police chief).

369. "New Rules for Police Rooms," supra note 368, at 53.

370. Eugene H. Methvin, "Let's Have Justice for Non-Criminals, Too!," *Reader's Dig.*, Dec. 1966, at 53.

371. "New Rules for Police Rooms," supra note 368, at 54 (reprinting cartoons from *St. Louis Globe-Democrat*, *L.A. Times*, and *N.Y. Daily News*); see also Powe, *Warren Court and American Politics*, supra note 2, at 399–400 (describing reaction to *Miranda*).

372. See Powe, *Warren Court and American Politics*, supra note 2, at 392–93 (describing ALI proposal); Graham, *Self-Inflicted Wound*, supra note 332, at 61–63 (describing prominent lower-court judges' concerns about dampening other reform efforts); Lain, "Countermajoritarian Hero or Zero?," supra note 3, at 1409–11 (describing proposal).

373. See Lain, "Countermajoritarian Hero or Zero?," supra note 3, at 1410–12. Lain argues persuasively that *Miranda* should not have been a particularly unwelcome or surprising decision, given national sentiment regarding police conduct and actions being taken to address it. See id. at 1409–18.

374. Brief of the State of New York et al. as Amici Curiae at 36–38, Miranda v. Arizona, 384 U.S. 436 (1966).

375. *The Kerner Report: The 1968 Report of the National Advisory Commission on Civil Disorders* (1968; repr. 1988), 36–38.

376. See Thomas Byrne Edsall with Mary D. Edsall, *Chain Reaction: The Impact of Race, Rights, and Taxes on American Politics* (1992), 58–59 (describing rise of black militancy, including formation of Panthers).

377. *Kerner Report*, supra note 375, at ix, 69.

378. See id. at 107 (noting that 1967 riot left forty-three dead and caused more than thirty-two million dollars in damages); Powe, *Warren Court and American Politics*, supra note 2, at 275 (calling Detroit's "the worst riot in a century").

379. Edsall and Edsall, *Chain Reaction*, supra note 376, at 51 (quoting Gerald Ford). In April 1965, only 28 percent of survey respondents said that the government was pushing racial integration "too fast." By September 1966, after Watts but before the 1967 Newark and Detroit riots, 52 percent thought the government was pushing civil rights too hard. Id. at 59.

380. See Graham, *Self-Inflicted Wound*, supra note 332, at 11, 69–71 (describing controversy and emerging consensus on crime rates).

381. Lewis F. Powell, Jr., "An Urgent Need: More Effective Criminal Justice," *A.B.A. J.* 51 (1965): 438.

382. Graham, *Self-Inflicted Wound*, supra note 332, at 11.

383. Warren E. Burger, "Address at Ripon College," reprinted in *U.S. News & World Rep.*, Aug. 7, 1967, at 70; Bob Woodward and Scott Armstrong, *The Brethren: Inside the Supreme Court* (2005), 6–7 (noting that Nixon told Burger he had used arguments made in the Ripon speech in a campaign address).

384. Stephen Lewin, Preface to *Crime and Its Prevention*, ed. Stephen Lewin (1968), 3 (noting study of two cities that found that 45 percent of respondents feared going out at night and 35 percent had stopped speaking to strangers).

385. Lyndon B. Johnson, "Remarks at the Swearing In of Ramsey Clark as Attorney General," March 10, 1967, in *Public Papers of the Presidents of the United States: Lyndon B. Johnson, 1967*, bk. 1 (1968), 312, 313.

386. Edward M. Kennedy, "A Plan of Action," *Sat. Evening Post*, Feb. 11, 1967, at 28.

387. "Crime and Lawlessness: Who's to Blame, the Police or the Public?," *Senior Scholastic*, Feb. 15, 1968, at 7.

388. See Graham, *Self-Inflicted Wound*, supra note 332, at 8 (citing Gallup Polls, including 1968 poll in which two of three persons surveyed thought the Supreme Court had erred in restricting the police's ability to question suspects and obtain confessions). Corinna Lain argues that many of the post-*Miranda* polls misstated the decision and so are problematic. See Lain, "Countermajoritarian Hero or Zero?," supra note 3, at 1421–24.

389. Edsall and Edsall, *Chain Reaction*, supra note 376, at 74 ("Race, the Vietnam War, student protests, the rights revolution, and what was seen by many as a rapid disintegration of the traditional social order, had produced deep fissures in the Democratic coalition, making the party vulnerable to challenge from the right"); Alexander M. Bickel, "Crime, the Courts, and the Old Nixon," *New Republic*, June 15, 1968, at 8 (noting the increase in crime and Nixon's "demagogic" attempt to use crime as the "communism issue of 1968").

390. Graham, *Self-Inflicted Wound*, supra note 332, at 15 (quoting Richard Nixon).

391. Hubert Humphrey, "Democratic Candidate for President Acceptance Speech, Delivered Before the Democratic National Convention," Aug. 29, 1968, in *Vital Speeches of the Day*, Sept. 15, 1968, at 708; Graham, *Self-Inflicted Wound*, supra note 332, at 10 (quoting George Wallace).

392. See Graham, *Self-Inflicted Wound*, supra note 332, at 12; Powe, *Warren Court and American Politics*, supra note 2, at 408–10.

393. S. Rep. No. 90–1097, at 40 (1968), reprinted in 1968 U.S.C.C.A.N. 2112, 2126.

394. Graham, *Self-Inflicted Wound*, supra note 332, at 12; Powe, *Warren Court and American Politics*, supra note 2, at 409.

395. Terry v. Ohio, 392 U.S. 1, 10, 12, 14n11 (1968) (quoting the President's Commission on Law Enforcement and Administration of Justice's finding that "[i]n many communities, field interrogations are a major source of friction between the police and minority groups").

396. See Isidore Silver, "Eroding the Fourth Amendment: Stop and Frisk," *Commonweal*, July 12, 1968, at 455–56.

397. *Terry*, 392 U.S. at 27. Corinna Lain makes the point that no one was arguing one side of the dilemma Warren framed: that the strictures of the Fourth Amendment did not apply at all in stop and frisk situations. Thus the decision was not a compromise, as legal academics have often portrayed it, but "a profoundly pro–law enforcement decision that gave to the police almost all they had asked of the Court." Lain, "Countermajoritarian Hero or Zero?," supra note 3, at 1440–44 & n396.

398. Silver, "Eroding the Fourth Amendment," supra note 396, at 456; see also Powell, *Warren Court and American Politics*, supra note 2, at 407 (wondering "if *Terry* would have been similarly decided two years earlier"); Kamisar, "How Earl Warren's Twenty-two Years," supra note 346, at 31 ("The person who wrote *Terry* seems to be quite different from the person who wrote *Miranda* . . ."); William J. Stuntz, "Local Policing After the Terror," *Yale L. J.* 111 (2002): 2152n43 ("One cannot read [*Miranda* and *Terry*] without sensing that something in [Warren's] thinking changed between 1966 and 1968").

399. See Laura Kalman, *Abe Fortas: A Biography* (1990), 359–70; Powe, *Warren Court and American Politics*, supra note 2, at 467–73, 477–81.

400. "Furor over Supreme Court," *U.S. News & World Rep.*, May 26, 1969, at 31.

401. Linda Greenhouse, *Becoming Justice Blackmun: Harry Blackmun's Supreme Court Journey* (2005), 6, 63.

402. Writing in 1970, political scientist Martin Shapiro described "impact studies" as "a body of literature reporting on the compliance of public officials to specific Supreme Court mandates." Martin Shapiro, "The Impact of the Supreme Court," *J. Leg. Educ.* 23 (1970): 77. Shapiro noted that "the bulk of the classic impact studies have concerned themselves with the response of school authorities to Supreme Court decisions on religious instruction, prayers and bible reading in the schools." Id. at 78 (citing studies); see also Arthur Miller, "On the Need for Impact Analysis of Supreme Court Decisions," *Geo. L. J.* 53 (1965): 365–402 (calling for scholars to analyze the actual impact of Supreme Court decisions).

403. Today the most noted of all impact studies is Gerald Rosenberg's *The Hollow Hope*. The book's gloomy title perhaps overstated matters. What Rosenberg documented (albeit not uncontroversially) is a point history has proven time and again: courts make headway when other political actors support them; they fail when they are opposed. See Rosenberg, *Hollow Hope*, supra note 3.

404. Blasi, "A Requiem for the Warren Court," supra note 90, at 610; e-mail from Vincent Blasi, Corliss Lamont Professor of Civil Liberties, Columbia Law School, to author, May 15, 2006, 12:18 EST (on file with author) (describing composition of "Requiem").

405. Blasi, "A Requiem for the Warren Court," supra note 90, at 620.

406. Bickel, *Idea of Progress*, supra note 15, at 92–94, 173.

407. Anthony Lewis, "The Heavenly City of Professor Bickel," *N.Y. Times*, Oct. 10, 1969, at 46.

Chapter 9: Interpretation

1. "Changes Nixon May Make in Federal Courts," *U.S. News & World Rep.*, Dec. 2, 1968, at 42; see also Richard Nixon, "Conversation with Newsmen on the Nomination of the Chief Justice of the United States," May 22, 1969, in *Public Papers of the Presidents of the United States: Richard Nixon, 1969* (1971), 392 ("I happen to believe that the Constitution should be strictly interpreted").

2. Ronald Reagan, "Remarks Announcing the Nomination of Robert H. Bork to Be an Associate Justice of the Supreme Court of the United States," July 1, 1987, in *Public Papers of the Presidents of the United States: Ronald Reagan, 1987*, bk. 1 (1989), 736.

3. Robert H. Bork, "The Supreme Court Needs a New Philosophy," *Fortune*, Dec. 1968, at 140–41.

4. Robert H. Bork, "The Crisis in Constitutional Theory: Back to the Future, Address to the Philadelphia Society," Apr. 3, 1987, in *The Supreme Court of the United States: Hearings and Reports on Successful and Unsuccessful Nominations of Supreme Court Justices by the Senate Judiciary Committee: 1916–1987*, ed. Roy M. Mersky and J. Myron Jacobstein (1990), 14:834.

5. Ronald Dworkin, *Taking Rights Seriously* (1977), 137.

6. Ronald Dworkin, *Law's Empire* (1986), 378.

7. Ronald Brownstein, "Justices from Lobbies and Chambers; The Inside-Outside Battle About Seating Judge Bork," *L.A. Times*, Oct. 4, 1987, pt. 5, at 1.

8. Quoted in Maggie Gallagher, "For Want of a Nail," *Nat'l Rev.*, Nov. 20, 1987, at 32.

9. Leonard W. Levy, *Against the Law* (1974), xiv.

10. See "President Nixon Addresses the Supreme Court as Chief Justice Warren Retires," *A.B.A. J.* 55 (1969): 864–65; Alexander M. Bickel, "Close of the Warren Era," *New Republic*, July 12, 1969, at 12.

11. See John W. Dean, *The Rehnquist Choice: The Untold Story of the Nixon Appointment That Redefined the Supreme Court* (2001), 2–12, 24–28. Dean details Nixon's efforts to derail the Fortas nomination as well as drive him off the bench because of financial impropriety. Nixon tried to do the same with Douglas but was unsuccessful. Still, the sudden resignations of Justices Black and Harlan because of ill health afforded him two additional nominations. Id. at 31–43.

12. See, e.g., "Address to the Nation Announcing Intention to Nominate Lewis F. Powell, Jr., and William H. Rehnquist to Be Associate Justices of the Supreme Court of the United States," Oct. 21, 1971, in *Public Papers of the Presidents of the United States: Richard Nixon, 1971* (1972), 1053 ("[I]t is the duty of a judge to interpret the Constitution and not to place himself above the Constitution or outside the Constitution"); "Changes Nixon May Make," supra note 1, at 42; Louis M. Kohlmeter, "Nixon Still Wants 'Strict Constructionist' for High Court, but Rules Out Southerner," *Wall St. J.*, Apr. 10, 1970, at 2.

13. "Conversation with Newsmen on the Nomination of the Chief Justice of the United States," in *Public Papers: Richard Nixon, 1969*, supra note 1, at 392.

14. Levy, *Against the Law*, supra note 9, at 31.

15. Philip B. Kurland, "1970 Term: Notes on the Emergency of the Burger Court," *Sup. Ct. Rev.*, 1971: 265.

16. "Chief Justice Scores Constructionist Label," *Wash. Post*, Jan. 28, 1973, at A24.

17. See John P. MacKenzie, "A Bible Between Them," *Wash. Post*, Jan. 20, 1969, at B6; Robert B. Semple, Jr., "Warren E. Burger Named Chief Justice by Nixon; Now on Appeals Bench; A Critic of Court," *N.Y. Times*, May 22, 1969, at 36; see generally Brad Snyder, "How the Conservatives Canonized *Brown v. Board of Education*," *Rutgers L. Rev.* 52 (2000): 415.

18. See Donald T. Critchlow, *Phyllis Schlafly and Grassroots Conservatism: A Woman's Crusade* (2005), 191; Thomas Byrne Edsall with Mary D. Edsall, *Chain Reaction: The Impact of Race, Rights, and Taxes on American Politics* (1991), 75–76; Snyder, "How the Conservatives Canonized," supra note 17, at 415.

19. "Strict Constructionism," *Chi. Daily Defender*, Apr. 22, 1970, at 15.

20. Ethan Bronner, *Battle for Justice: How the Bork Nomination Shook America* (1989), 117; Snyder, "How the Conservatives Canonized," supra note 17, at 425, 429.

21. Quoted in Michael J. Gerhardt, "The Rhetoric of Judicial Critique: From Judicial Restraint to the Virtual Bill of Rights," *Wm. & Mary Bill Rts. J.* 10 (2002): 627n212.

22. Quoted in id. (citation omitted in original).

23. Richard L. Stout, "Key Appointments Will Extend Nixon Influence," *Christian Sci. Monitor*, May 12, 1969, at 5.

24. James Jackson Kilpatrick, "A Very Different Constitution," *Nat'l Rev.*, Aug. 12, 1969, at 800.

25. Fred P. Graham, *The Self-Inflicted Wound* (1970), 305.

26. See, e.g., id. at 302; Yale Kamisar, "The Warren Court (Was It Really So Defense-Minded?), the Burger Court (Is It Really So Prosecution-Oriented?), and Police Investigatory Practices," in *The Burger Court: The Counter-Revolution That Wasn't*, ed. Vincent Blasi (1983); Louis Michael Seidman, "Factual Guilt and the Burger Court: An Examination of Continuity and Change in Criminal Procedure," *Colum. L. Rev.* 80 (1980): 436; Stephen L. Wasby, "Certain Conservatism or Mixed Surprise? Civil Liberties in the Burger Court, 1976–77," *Civil Liberties Rev.*, Nov.–Dec. 1977, at 48. But see Stephen A. Saltzburg, "Forward: The Flow and Ebb of Constitutional Criminal Procedure in the Warren and Burger Courts," *Geo. L. J.* 69 (1980) (arguing that Burger Court decisions have not substantially undercut the decisions of the Warren Court).

27. Levy, *Against the Law*, supra note 9, at 422.

28. "Surprises in the High Court: New Attitudes, New Concerns," *U.S. News & World Rep.*, July 14, 1975, at 39.

29. "The Extraordinary Burden Borne by Nine Ordinary Men," *Economist*, Feb. 16, 1980, at 31, 34.

30. Blasi, *Burger Court*, supra note 26. See, e.g., Lawrence Baum, "Explaining the Burger Court's Support for Civil Liberties," *PS* 20 (1987): 21; "Extraordinary Burden," supra note 29, at 31, 34 ("[T]he constitutional revolution of the Warren years has not been undone"); Harry Kalven, Jr., "The Supreme Court, 1970 Term—Foreword, Even When a Nation Is at War," *Harv. L. Rev.* 85 (1971): 5; "The Nixon Radicals," *Time*, June 5, 1972, at 65; Mark Tushnet, "The U.S. Constitution and the Intent of the Framers," *Buff. L. Rev.* 36 (1987): 31 ("[T]he period from 1969 to 1986 saw the Court slowly shifting from the premises of the Warren Court but never fully repudiating them").

31. Gene R. Nichol, Jr., "An Activism of Ambivalence," review of *The Burger Court: The Counter-Revolution That Wasn't*, ed. Vincent Blasi, *Harv. L. Rev.* 98 (1984): 319; see also Norman Dorsen, "The United States Supreme Court: Trends and Prospects," *Harv. C.R.-C.L. L. Rev.* 21 (1986): 13.

32. Paul Bender, "The Techniques of Subtle Erosion," *Harper's Mag.*, Dec. 1972, at 18–19.

33. Vincent Blasi, "The Rootless Activism of the Burger Court," in Blasi, *Burger Court*, supra note 26, at 206–07; Dorsen, "United States Supreme Court," supra note 31, at 13–14.

34. Kalven, "Supreme Court, 1970 Term—Foreword," supra note 30, at 15; see N.Y. Times Co. v. United States, 403 U.S. 713 (1971).

35. Blasi, "Rootless Activism," in Blasi, *Burger Court*, supra note 26, at 201; see United States v. Nixon, 418 U.S. 683 (1974).

36. Buckley v. Valeo, 424 U.S. 1 (1976).

37. INS v. Chadha, 462 U.S. 919, 956–59 (1983); id. at 967 (White, J., dissenting); "Supreme Court Decision That Stunned Congress," *U.S. News & World Rep.*, July 4, 1983, at 14.

38. "The Court Is Supreme," *Economist*, July 2, 1983, at 16.

39. Bernard Schwartz, *The Ascent of Pragmatism: The Burger Court in Action* (1990), 408.

40. Anthony Lewis, Foreword to Blasi, *Burger Court*, supra note 26, at ix.

41. See Furman v. Georgia, 408 U.S. 238, 240 (1972). All four Nixon appointees—Burger, Blackmun, Powell, and Rehnquist—dissented in separate opinions.

42. "Mixed Reviews," *New Republic*, July 15, 1972, at 7; Michael Meltsner, *Cruel and Unusual: The Supreme Court and Capital Punishment* (1973), 290.

43. Stuart Banner, *The Death Penalty: An American History* (2002), 258; see also Bob Woodward and Scott Armstrong, *The Brethren: Inside the Supreme Court* (2005), 255 (reporting that Brennan said to his clerks, "Boys, it is a surprise to me, but the death cases seem to be coming out 5 to 4 against the death penalty").

44. Furman v. Georgia, 408 U.S. 238, 417 (1972) (Powell, J., dissenting).

45. McGautha v. California, 402 U.S. 183 (1971).

46. *Furman*, 408 U.S. at 299 (Brennan, J., concurring) ("The progressive decline in, and the current rarity of, the infliction of death demonstrate that our society seriously questions the appropriateness of this punishment today"); accord id. at 360 (Marshall, J., concurring).

47. See Banner, *Death Penalty*, supra note 43, at 230, 246–47; Corinna Barrett Lain, "*Furman* Fundamentals," *Wash. L. Rev.* 82 (2007): 19; see also Lee Epstein and Joseph F. Kobylka, *The Supreme Court and Legal Change: Abortion and the Death Penalty* (1992), 37.

48. Banner, *Death Penalty*, supra note 43, at 240; Epstein and Kobylka, *Supreme Court and Legal Change*, supra note 47, at 44–47.

49. See Banner, *Death Penalty*, supra note 43, at 240–44; Epstein and Kobylka, *Supreme Court and Legal Change*, supra note 47, at 58–59; Meltsner, *Cruel and Unusual*, supra note 42, at 107.

50. See Banner, *Death Penalty*, supra note 43, at 230; Epstein and Kobylka, *Supreme Court and Legal Change*, supra note 47, at 48–52.

51. See *Furman*, 408 U.S. at 448–50 (Powell, J., dissenting); id. at 310 (Stewart, J., concurring); id. at 257 (Douglas, J., concurring).

52. See Banner, *Death Penalty*, supra note 43, at 230.

53. Nicholas DeB. Katzenbach, "The Chairman of the National Crime Commission Answers Some Tough Questions About Crime," *Look*, March 7, 1967, at 104.

54. *Furman*, 408 U.S. at 311–12 (White, J., concurring).

55. *Furman*, 408 U.S. at 309 (Stewart, J., concurring).

56. "Death Rows Cheer Ruling," *Chi. Trib.*, June 30, 1972, at C16; Morton Mintz, "Joy on Death Row; Praise, Scorn on Hill," *Wash. Post*, June 30, 1972, at A13; see generally Lain, "*Furman* Fundamentals," supra note 47, at 47–48 (chronicling the backlash in the states to the *Furman* decision).

57. Herbert H. Haines, *Against Capital Punishment: The Anti–Death Penalty Movement in America, 1972–1994* (1996), 45; Tom Wicker, "Death Again in California," *N.Y. Times*, Nov. 12, 1972, at E11.

58. Epstein and Kobylka, *Supreme Court and Legal Change*, supra note 47, at 84–85.

59. David Mutch, "Many States Are Trying to Revive Death Penalty for Certain Crimes," *Christian Sci. Monitor*, Jan. 20, 1973, at 1.

60. Banner, *Death Penalty*, supra note 43, at 270.

61. "Death to the Death Penalty?," *Chi. Trib.*, July 3, 1972, at 12.

62. Lesley Oelsner, "Court to Review Death Penalty Issue," *N.Y. Times*, Jan. 23, 1976, at 20.

63. Oral Argument of Robert H. Bork, Esq., Amicus Curiae, Jurek v. Texas, 428 U.S 262 (1976) and Roberts v. Louisiana, 428 U.S. 325 (1976), in *Landmark Briefs and Arguments of the Supreme Court of the United States: Constitutional Law*, ed. Philip B. Kurland and Gerhard Casper (1976): 90:18.

64. Woodson v. North Carolina, 428 U.S. 280 (1976); Coker v. Georgia, 433 U.S. 584 (1977).

65. Gregg v. Georgia, 428 U.S. 153, 193–95 (1976) (plurality opinion); see also Epstein and Kobylka, *Supreme Court and Legal Change*, supra note 47, at 40 (describing

the ALI's suggestion for bifurcation and for cabining discretion with "aggravating" circumstances).

66. *Gregg*, 428 U.S. at 195.

67. Id. at 179.

68. Id. at 226 (White, J., concurring).

69. C. Robert Zelnick, "Supreme Court Refines Its Death Penalty Stand," *Christian Sci. Monitor*, July 6, 1976, at 4.

70. Julia Malone, "Burger Court: 'Liberal' Women's Rights Record," *Christian Sci. Monitor*, Dec. 3, 1980, at 8.

71. For commentary on the relationship between the ERA and the Supreme Court's interpretation of the Equal Protection Clause, see Reva Siegel, "Constitutional Culture, Social Movement Conflict and Constitutional Change: The Case of the De Facto ERA," *Cal. L. Rev.* 94 (2006): 1324; David A. Strauss, "The Irrelevance of Constitutional Amendments," *Harv. L. Rev.* 114 (2001): 1476–77.

72. See Erwin Chemerinsky, *Constitutional Law: Principles and Policies*, 2d ed. (2002), 643–47.

73. Reed v. Reed, 404 U.S. 71, 76 (1971).

74. Gerald Gunther, "The Supreme Court, 1971—Foreword: In Search of Evolving Doctrine on a Changing Court: A Model for a Newer Equal Protection," *Harv. L. Rev.* 86 (1972): 34.

75. Chemerinsky, *Constitutional Law*, supra note 72, at 728 ("The framers of the Fourteenth Amendment meant only to outlaw race discrimination").

76. Quoted in Ruth B. Cowan, "Women's Rights Through Litigation: An Examination of the American Civil Liberties Union Women's Rights Project, 1971–1976," *Colum. Hum. Rts. L. Rev.* 8 (1976): 380.

77. Lauren Katzowitz, summary of Ruth Bader Ginsburg and Jane Picker, "Discussion of the Equal Rights Amendment at the Ford Foundation," May 22, 1972, 12.

78. Bradwell v. Illinois, 83 U.S. 130, 141 (1872) (Bradley, J., concurring).

79. Goesaert v. Cleary, 335 U.S. 464, 465 (1948).

80. Hoyt v. Florida, 368 U.S. 57, 62 (1961).

81. Ruth Bader Ginsburg, "Gender in the Supreme Court: The 1973 and 1974 Terms," *Sup. Ct. Rev.*, 1975: 2n10.

82. Quoted in Jean A. Briggs, "How You Going to Get 'Em Back in the Kitchen? (You Aren't)," *Forbes*, Nov. 15, 1977, at 177.

83. Ruth Rosen, *The World Split Open: How the Modern Women's Movement Changed America* (2000), 25.

84. Id. at 78–79.

85. Betty Friedan, *The Feminine Mystique* (1997), 18.

86. Id. at 253.

87. See Title VII of the *Civil Rights Act of 1964* (July 2, 1964), *U.S. Statutes at Large* 78 (1965): 255, codified as amended at 42 U.S.C. § 2000e (2006).

88. See Mary Frances Berry, *Why ERA Failed: Politics, Women's Rights, and the Amending Process of the Constitution* (1986), 61; Barbara Sinclair Deckard, *The Women's Movement: Political, Socioeconomic, and Psychological Issues*, 2d ed. (1979), 345.

89. Quoted in Rosen, *World Split Open*, supra note 83, at 72.

90. See Cynthia Harrison, *On Account of Sex: The Politics of Women's Issues, 1845–1968* (1988), 192–96 (describing the formation of NOW in 1966 in part as a reaction to the "EEOC's cavalier attitude toward sex discrimination").

91. See id. at 117–19; Deckard, *Women's Movement*, supra note 88, at 459–61.

92. Jo Freeman, *The Politics of Women's Liberation* (1975), 148 ("The women's liberation movement 'took off' in 1970").

93. Id. at 147.
94. See Friedan, *Feminine Mystique*, supra note 85, at 390, 392; see also Siegel, "Constitutional Culture," supra note 71, at 1373–74.
95. See "Very Volcanic," *Newsweek*, Aug. 31, 1970, at 47 (displaying a strike poster slogan "Don't Iron While the Strike Is Hot"); "Women on the March," *Time*, Sept. 7, 1970, at 12.
96. "Women on the March," supra note 95, at 12.
97. Rosen, *World Split Open*, supra note 83, at 311.
98. "Women on the March," supra note 95, at 12.
99. Quoted in Rosen, *World Split Open*, supra note 83, at 296.
100. Frontiero v. Richardson, 411 U.S. 677, 688 (1973) (plurality opinion).
101. *Frontiero*, 411 U.S. at 692 (Powell, J., concurring) ("I cannot join the opinion of Mr. Justice Brennan, which would hold that all classifications based upon sex, 'like classifications based on race, alienage and national origin,' are 'inherently suspect and must therefore be subjected to close judicial scrutiny'").
102. See Serena Mayeri, "Constitutional Choices: Legal Feminism and the Historical Dynamics of Change," *Cal. L. Rev.* 92 (2004): 762 (describing how American feminism had been divided since the early 1920s into two opposing camps, one insisting that the ERA was needed to secure women's equal status and the other opposing any formal equality measures to protect labor).
103. Berry, *Why ERA Failed*, supra note 88, at 63; Jane J. Mansbridge, *Why We Lost the ERA* (1986), 8–9; Gilbert Y. Steiner, *Constitutional Inequality: The Political Fortunes of the Equal Rights Amendment* (1985), 7; Katzowitz, "Discussion of the Equal Rights Amendment," supra note 77, at 2.
104. *President's Commission on the Status of Women, American Women* (1963), 44, quoted in Mary Eastwood, "The Double Standard of Justice: Women's Rights Under the Constitution," *Val. U. L. Rev.* 5 (1971): 283.
105. See Mayeri, "Constitutional Choices," supra note 102, at 798.
106. Memorandum from Pauli Murray to Edith Green, March 12, 1963, quoted in id. at 764–65.
107. Id. at 799.
108. Mary Eastwood, "Proposal for NOW," Jan. 1, 1967, quoted in id. at 795.
109. Carol Felsenthal, *The Sweetheart of the Silent Majority: The Biography of Phyllis Schlafly* (1981), 234–35.
110. Katzowitz, "Discussion of the Equal Rights Amendment," supra note 77, at 1.
111. Berry, *Why ERA Failed*, supra note 88, at 66.
112. Phyllis Schlafly, "What's Wrong with 'Equal Rights' for Women?," 1972, quoted in Critchlow, *Phyllis Schlafly*, supra note 18, at 217.
113. Berry, *Why ERA Failed*, supra note 88, at 66.
114. *U.S.L.W.*, July 17, 1973, at 3057.
115. *Frontiero*, 411 U.S. at 692 (Powell, J., concurring).
116. Memorandum from William J. Brennan, Jr., associate justice, Supreme Court of the United States, to Lewis F. Powell, Jr., associate justice, Supreme Court of the United States, March 6, 1973, quoted in Lee Epstein and Thomas G. Walker, "Positive Political Theory and the Study of U.S. Supreme Court Decision Making: Understanding the Sex Discrimination Cases," *N.Y. City L. Rev.* 1 (1996): 188.
117. Id.
118. See, e.g., Berry, *Why ERA Failed*, supra note 88, at 80 (noting a statewide poll in North Carolina showing a 2–1 support for the ERA); Steiner, *Constitutional Inequality*, supra note 103, at 27.
119. Berry, *Why ERA Failed*, supra note 88, at 83.

120. See Friedan, *Feminine Mystique*, supra note 85, at 392; *National Party Platforms: 1840–1972*, ed. Donald Bruce Johnson and Kirk H. Porter (1973), 791–92, 876–77.

121. Deckard, *Women's Movement*, supra note 88, at 366–68.

122. Proclamation No. 4147, Aug. 26, 1972, *Weekly Comp. Pres. Doc.* 8, 1286–87, quoted in Siegel, "Constitutional Culture," supra note 71, at 1375n138.

123. Mansbridge, *Why We Lost the ERA*, supra note 103, at 13 ("Alabama, Arizona, Arkansas, Florida, Georgia, Illinois, Louisiana, Mississippi, Missouri, Nevada, North Carolina, Oklahoma, Utah, and Virginia had not ratified").

124. 116 Cong. Rec. H7984–85 (daily ed. Aug. 10, 1970), quoted in Eastwood, "Double Standard of Justice," supra note 104, at 282.

125. Equal Rights for Men and Women, S. Rep. No. 92-689, at 7 (1972).

126. Note, "Sex Discrimination and Equal Protection: Do We Need a Constitutional Amendment?," *Harv. L. Rev.* 84 (1971): 1502; see also *Frontiero*, 411 U.S. at 686 (citing Kristen Amundsen, *The Silenced Majority: Women and American Democracy* (1971); *The President's Task Force on Women's Rights and Responsibilities, A Matter of Simple Justice* (1970)).

127. Craig v. Boren, 429 U.S. 190, 190 (1976).

128. Id. at 197.

129. Miss. Univ. for Women v. Hogan, 458 U.S. 718, 724 (1982) (citations omitted); see also Mark Gitenstein, *Matters of Principle: An Insider's Account of America's Rejection of Robert Bork's Nomination to the Supreme Court* (1992), 149 ("Most gratifying to the feminists, O'Connor seized upon the Court's language in one of its earlier cases interpreting *Craig v. Boren* and required the state to establish an 'exceedingly persuasive justification' for gender discrimination").

130. "Great Changes, New Chances, Tough Choices," *Time*, Jan. 5, 1976, at 6.

131. Deckard, *Women's Movement*, supra note 88, at 406.

132. See Janet Boles, "The Equal Rights Movement as a Non-Zero-Sum Game," in *Rights of Passage: The Past and Future of the ERA*, ed. Joan Hoff-Wilson (1986), 57–58 (reporting that in 1970 the poll showed 42 percent in favor, 41 percent opposed, but by 1981 that had changed to 67 percent in favor and 29 percent opposed).

133. The methodology of this paragraph follows the approach of Siegel, "Constitutional Culture," supra note 71, at 1405–07.

134. Critchlow, *Phyllis Schlafly*, supra note 18, at 225; see generally Robert Post and Reva Siegel, "Roe Rage: Democratic Constitutionalism and Backlash," *Harv. C.R.-C.L. L. Rev.* 42 (2007): 418–20 (linking women's rights with homosexuality and abortion); Lisa Cronin Wohl, "Phyllis Schlafly: The Sweetheart of the Silent Majority," *Ms. Mag.*, March 1974, at 57. For a nice evocative summary of the claims against the ERA, see Jane DeHart-Matthews and Donald Matthews, "The Cultural Politics of the ERA's Defeat," in Hoff-Wilson, *Rights of Passage*, supra note 132, at 46–51.

135. See DeHart-Matthews and Matthews, "Cultural Politics," in Hoff-Wilson, *Rights of Passage*, supra note 132, at 53; see also Mansbridge, *Why We Lost the ERA*, supra note 103, at 22 (explaining broad support for equality in the abstract: "Americans can favor abstract rights even when they oppose substantive change").

136. DeHart-Matthews and Matthews, "Cultural Politics," in Hoff-Wilson, *Rights of Passage*, supra note 132, at 53; see generally Boles, "Equal Rights Movement," in id. at 54–61 (explaining that the fight over ERA "was accompanied by a virtual revolution in public opinion on the proper role and rights of women in society").

137. 118 Cong. Rec. 8, 9566 (1972) (statement of Sen. Ervin).

138. Rosemary Thomson, *A Christian View of the Equal Rights Amendment*, 1975, quoted in Critchlow, *Phyllis Schlafly*, supra note 18, at 235.

139. See, e.g., Fred Barbash, "Draft Registration of Women Tops Supreme Court Lineup," *Wash. Post*, Oct. 5, 1980, at C1.

140. Rostker v. Goldberg, 453 U.S. 57 (1980).

141. See Wohl, "Phyllis Schlafly," supra note 134, at 55 (giving Schlafly's suggestion that the ERA would decriminalize rape).

142. Michael M. v. Superior Court of Sonoma County, 450 U.S. 464 (1982).

143. Fred Barbash, "Draft Registration, Gender Distinction, and the Honk and Holler Case," *Wash. Post*, March 23, 1981, at A4.

144. Roe v. Wade, 410 U.S. 113 (1973).

145. Ruth Bader Ginsburg, "Some Thoughts on Autonomy and Equality in Relation to *Roe v. Wade*," *N.C. L. Rev.* 63 (1985): 376 (contrasting *Roe* with the gender discrimination cases that "in the main, have not provoked large controversy").

146. See Epstein and Kobylka, *Supreme Court and Legal Change*, supra note 47, at 187–88 (providing polling statistics on how Americans were split on the abortion issue).

147. Linda Greenhouse, "Constitutional Question: Is There a Right to Abortion?," *N.Y. Times Mag.*, Jan. 25, 1970, at 30. She continued in part: "The very phrase rings of the rhetoric of a Women's Liberation meeting."

148. Lawrence Lader, *Abortion* (1966), 1.

149. Tom C. Clark, "Religion, Morality, and Abortion: A Constitutional Appraisal," *Loy. L.A. L. Rev.* 2 (1969): 1.

150. See, e.g., James C. Mohr, *Abortion in America: The Origins and Evolution of National Policy, 1800–1900* (1978) (providing a detailed account of the history of abortion in America); John T. Noonan, Jr., *A Private Choice: Abortion in America in the Seventies* (1979), 5–6; Brief of the Association for Public Justice and the Value of Life Committee, Inc., as Amici Curiae in support of Appellants, Webster v. Reproductive Health Services, 492 U.S. 490 (1989) (No. 88-605), at 3–22 (providing a long and detailed history of abortion).

151. See Noonan, A Private Choice, supra note 150, at 5–6; Eva R. Rubin, *Abortion, Politics, and the Courts:* Roe v. Wade *and Its Aftermath* (1982), 9–10.

152. See Mohr, *Abortion in America*, supra note 150, at 47; Rubin, *Abortion, Politics, and the Courts*, supra note 151, at 10.

153. Rubin, *Abortion, Politics, and the Courts*, supra note 151, at 13–14; Brief of the Association for Public Justice and the Value of Life Committee, Inc., supra note 150, at 19–22. Kentucky was the exception.

154. See Barbara Hinkson Craig and David M. O'Brien, *Abortion and American Politics* (1993), 231 (quoting Frank Susman's oral argument in *Webster* that "[t]hirty percent of pregnancies in this country today terminate in abortion. . . . It is a rate that sometimes astounds people, but it is a rate that has not changed one whit from the time the Constitution was enacted through the 1800's and through the 1900's"); Mark A. Graber, *Rethinking Abortion: Equal Choice, The Constitution, and Reproductive Politics* (1996), 42–43 ("Scholars estimate that one of every three to five pregnancies in the United States was aborted during the first seventy years of the twentieth century"); Graber, *Rethinking Abortion*, supra (discussing rates of injury and death from illegal abortions); Rubin, *Abortion, Politics, and the Courts*, supra note 151, at 15 ("Estimates of the total number of illegal abortions were not accurate and varied considerably, ranging from two hundred thousand to 1.2 million a year.").

155. See Craig and O'Brien, *Abortion and American Politics*, supra note 154, at 41–42; Rubin, *Abortion, Politics, and the Courts*, supra note 151, at 17; Lawrence Tribe, *Abortion: The Clash of Absolutes* (1990), 39.

156. Tribe, *Abortion: The Clash of Absolutes*, supra note 155, at 39.

157. Id. at 41.
158. See Craig and O'Brien, *Abortion and American Politics*, supra note 154, at 41; Lader, *Abortion*, supra note 148, at 10–16 (chronicling the Finkbine story); Rubin, *Abortion, Politics, and the Courts*, supra note 151, at 21; Tribe, *Abortion: The Clash of Absolutes*, supra note 155, at 37–38.
159. See Rubin, *Abortion, Politics, and the Courts*, supra note 151, at 22.
160. Epstein and Kobylka, *Supreme Court and Legal Change*, supra note 47, at 142.
161. Craig and O'Brien, *Abortion and American Politics*, supra note 154, at 74; David J. Garrow, *Liberty and Sexuality: The Right to Privacy and the Making of* Roe v. Wade (1994), 616–17. At least thirteen states had by 1970 joined California in following the American Law Institute model. See Jimmye Kimmey, "How the Abortion Laws Happened," *Ms. Mag.*, Apr. 1973, at 48, 50; see also Rubin, *Abortion, Politics, and the Courts*, supra note 151, at 22.
162. Clark, "Religion, Morality, and Abortion," supra note 149, at 6.
163. Alan F. Guttmacher, *Babies by Choice or by Chance* (1959), 178, quoted in Graber, *Rethinking Abortion*, supra note 154, at 52.
164. Lader, *Abortion*, supra note 148, at 66.
165. Keith Monroe, "How California's Abortion Law Isn't Working," *N.Y Times*, Dec. 29, 1968, at SM10.
166. Jack Rosenthal, "Survey Finds Majority, in Shift, Now Favors Liberalized Laws," *N.Y. Times*, Aug. 25, 1972, at 1.
167. Linda Greenhouse, *Becoming Justice Blackmun: Harry Blackmun's Supreme Court Journey* (2005), 91.
168. Garrow, *Liberty and Sexuality*, supra note 161, at 605–06.
169. Roe v. Wade, 410 U.S. 113, 143 (1973); Tribe, *Abortion: The Clash of Absolutes*, supra note 155, 38.
170. See *Roe*, 410 U.S. at 144–45.
171. Fred P. Graham, "Bar Group Supports Eased Abortions," *N.Y. Times*, Feb. 8, 1972, at 37.
172. See Elizabeth Adell Cook, Ted G. Jelen, and Clyde Wilcox, *Between Two Absolutes: Public Opinion and the Politics of Abortion* (1992), 37; Craig and O'Brien, *Abortion and American Politics*, supra note 154, at 249–50; Judith Blake, "Abortion and Public Opinion: The 1960–1970 Decade," *Science, New Series* 171 (1971): 541–42.
173. Tribe, *Abortion: The Clash of Absolutes*, supra note 155, at 50; Roberta Brandes Gratz, "Never Again," *Ms. Mag.*, Apr. 1973, at 46.
174. See *Roe*, 410 U.S. at 164.
175. See Warren Weaver Jr., "National Guidelines Set by 7-to-2 Vote," *N.Y. Times*, Jan. 23, 1973, at 1; Greenhouse, *Becoming Justice Blackmun*, supra note 167, at 96–97 (describing negotiations among justices behind the *Roe* decision).
176. See Kristin Luker, *Abortion and the Politics of Motherhood* (1984), 144; Nancy Stearns, "Commentary, *Roe v. Wade*: Our Struggle Continues," *Berkeley Women's L. J.* 4 (1989): 6 ("Too many of us thought we had won the fight with Roe v. Wade and went on to other issues, or just went home"); Jeffrey A. Tannenbaum, "A New Cause: Many Americans Join Move to Ban Abortion; Legislatures Take Note," *Wall St. J.*, Aug. 2, 1973, at 1.
177. See Craig and O'Brien, *Abortion and American Politics*, supra note 154, at 84–91; Rubin, *Abortion, Politics, and the Courts*, supra note 151, at 117, 125–26, 130; Albert M. Pearson and Paul M. Kurtz, "The Abortion Controversy: A Study in Law and Politics," *Harv. J. L. & Pub. Pol'y* 8 (1985): 430–43.
178. Quoted in Rubin, *Abortion, Politics, and the Courts*, supra note 151, at 149.
179. "The High Court's Grand Finale," *Newsweek*, July 14, 1980, at 23.

180. See Pearson and Kurtz, "Abortion Controversy," supra note 177, at 430–33; Craig and O'Brien, *Abortion and American Politics*, supra note 154, at 84–91.

181. "The Battle over Abortion," *Time*, Apr. 6, 1981, at 20.

182. Greenhouse, "Constitutional Question," supra note 147, at 30.

183. Oral Argument of Sarah Weddington, Roe v. Wade, 410 U.S. 113 (1973), in Kurland and Casper, *Landmark Briefs and Arguments*, supra note 63, at 75:788.

184. Id. at 75:810.

185. Skinner v. Oklahoma, 316 U.S. 535, 541 (1942).

186. Griswold v. Connecticut, 381 U.S. 479, 485 (1965).

187. Eisenstadt v. Baird, 405 U.S. 438, 453 (1971).

188. *Griswold*, 381 U.S. at 484–85.

189. *Roe*, 410 U.S. at 152–53.

190. *Griswold*, 381 U.S. at 500 (Harlan, J., concurring); see also Poe v. Ullman, 367 U.S. 497, 542 (1961) (Harlan, J., dissenting).

191. *Griswold*, 381 U.S. at 481–82.

192. See, e.g., George C. Christie, "A Model of Judicial Review of Legislation," *S. Cal. L. Rev.* 48 (1975): 1329 (quoting Blackmun's conclusion, above, and stating, "Unquestionably, statements like this have contributed to the almost universal conclusion that the reasoning in *Roe v. Wade* is simply unconvincing").

193. John Hart Ely, "The Wages of Crying Wolf: A Comment on *Roe v. Wade*," *Yale L. J.* 82 (1973): 923, 927, 936, 947 (emphasis in original); see Greenhouse, *Becoming Justice Blackmun*, supra note 167, at 136 (explaining that "Wages" was destined to become one of the most cited law review articles in the second half of the twentieth century).

194. Michael J. Perry, "'Interpreting' the Constitution," in *The Constitution, the Courts, and the Quest for Justice*, ed. Robert A. Goldwin and William A. Schambra (1989), 70.

195. Gary L. McDowell, "The Politics of Original Intention," in id. at 2.

196. Thomas C. Grey, "Do We Have an Unwritten Constitution?," *Stan. L. Rev.* 27 (1975): 709; Terrance Sandalow, "Constitutional Interpretation," *Mich. L. Rev.* 79 (1981): 1033–72.

197. Sandalow, "Constitutional Interpretation," supra note 196, at 1033.

198. McDowell, "Politics of Original Intention," in Goldwin and Schambra, *Quest for Justice*, supra note 194, at 5–6.

199. J. Clifford Wallace, "The Jurisprudence of Judicial Restraint: A Return to the Moorings," *Geo. Wash. L. Rev.* 50 (1981): 14.

200. William H. Rehnquist, "The Notion of a Living Constitution," *Tex. L. Rev.* 54 (1976): 693 (emphasis in original).

201. Pauli Murray and May O. Eastwood, "Jane Crow and the Law: Sex Discrimination and Title VII," *Geo. Wash. L. Rev.* 34 (1965): 237; see also Linda K. Kerber, *No Constitutional Right to Be Ladies: Women and the Obligations of Citizenship* (1998), 193.

202. Quoted in Bronner, *Battle for Justice*, supra note 20, at 10.

203. Grey, "Unwritten Constitution," supra note 196, at 711–13.

204. Id. at 707–08.

205. Paul Brest, "The Misconceived Quest for the Original Understanding," *B.U. L. Rev.* 60 (1980): 222–24.

206. Grey, "Unwritten Constitution," supra note 196, at 703, 715; Suzanna Sherry, "The Founders' Unwritten Constitution," *U. Chi. L. Rev.* 54 (1987): 1127–77.

207. Brest, "Misconceived Quest," supra note 205, at 226.

208. See Gary L. McDowell, *Curbing the Courts: The Constitution and the Limits of Judicial Power* (1988), 14 (citing Ronald Dworkin, *Taking Rights Seriously*, supra note 5, at 149) (explaining that the "current generation of legal scholars has taken as a

nearly unquestioned truth" Dworkin's view that there must be a "fusion of constitutional law and moral theory").

209. Dworkin, *Taking Rights Seriously*, supra note 5, at 137, 147.

210. McDowell, "Politics of Original Intention," in Goldwin and Schambra, *Quest for Justice*, supra note 194, at 2 (emphasis in original).

211. John B. McArthur, "Abandoning the Constitution: The New Wave in Constitutional Theory," *Tul. L. Rev.* 59 (1984): 280.

212. Robert H. Bork, Foreword to Gary L. McDowell, *The Constitution and Contemporary Constitutional Theory* (1985), v.

213. Edwin Meese III, "Toward a Jurisprudence of Original Intent," *Harv. J. L. & Pub. Pol'y* 11 (1988): 5.

214. Bork, Foreword to McDowell, *Constitution and Contemporary Constitutional Theory*, supra note 212, at v.

215. Kurt Anderson, "To the Right, March!," *Newsweek*, Sept. 14, 1981, at 26 ("According to a survey for the National Republican Committee, 25 percent of the U.S. agrees with New Right positions on four or five of the main 'social issues': abortion, capital punishment, busing, ERA and homosexual rights. A Gallup Poll in June found that one-third of Americans consider themselves at least 'moderately' right-wing").

216. See "No Hiding Place This Term," *Newsweek*, Oct 10, 1983, at 61 (reporting conservatives' disappointment over Burger Court decisions).

217. Quoted in "The 1970s," *U.S. News & World Rep.*, July 2, 1970, at 18.

218. See Critchlow, *Phyllis Schlafly*, supra note 18, at 221.

219. Rosen, *World Split Open*, supra note 83, at 292–93.

220. Berry, *Why ERA Failed*, supra note 88, at 68; Felsenthal, *Sweetheart of the Silent Majority*, supra note 109, at 290 (reporting "Mother Nature Is a Lesbian" buttons at the convention).

221. See Critchlow, *Phyllis Schlafly*, supra note 18, at 246–47 (describing Schlafly's counter-rally).

222. See Janis Johnson, "Bishops Begin Anti-Abortion Drive," *Wash. Post*, Nov. 21, 1975, at A1; Paul J. Weber, "Bishops in Politics: The Big Plunge," *Am. Mag.*, March 20, 1976.

223. Luker, *Abortion and the Politics of Motherhood*, supra note 176, at 126.

224. See id. at 145.

225. See Charles Fried, *Order and Law: Arguing the Reagan Revolution* (1991), 19 ("The religious right . . . had a quite explicit and demanding agenda that included severely restricting the availability of abortions, allowing spoken prayer in the public schools").

226. Quoted in "Mobilizing the Moral Majority," *Conservative Dig.*, Aug. 1979, at 14. On the creation of the Moral Majority, see Gitenstein, *Matters of Principle*, supra note 129, at 164–65.

227. See Craig and O'Brien, *Abortion and American Politics*, supra note 154, at 50, 52; Rubin, *Abortion, Politics, and the Courts*, supra note 151, at 110–11; "Mobilizing the Moral Majority," supra note 226, at 15.

228. "Lobbying for Christ: Evangelical Conservatives Move from Pews to Polls, but Can They Sway Congress?" *CQ Wkly. Rep.*, Sept. 6, 1980, at 2627, 2630.

229. William Billings, *The Christian's Political Action Manual* (1980), iii; see also Senator Gordon J. Humphrey, introduction to id. at iv ("In a decade when Godly virtues and traditional Judeo-Christian values have been, for the most part, thrown out and replaced by the doctrines of secular humanism, it is strange to see so many Christians still sitting on the sidelines of politics").

230. Robert G. Marshall, *Bayonets and Roses: Comprehensive Pro-Life Political Action Guide* (1976), 262.

231. Critchlow, *Phyllis Schlafly*, supra note 18, at 264.

232. Ronald Reagan, "Speech Before the American Conservative Union," Feb. 1977, quoted in Edsall and Edsall, *Chain Reaction*, supra note 18, at 141 ("[*sic*]" removed).

233. Critchlow, *Phyllis Schlafly*, supra note 18, at 265–66.

234. See Edsall and Edsall, *Chain Reaction*, supra note 18, at 21–22, 134 (noting that although many people were disillusioned with Carter's promise to manage the economy, "in the South, the realignment of white fundamentalist Christians between the elections of 1970 and 1980 transformed the presidential election outcome in 1980 in at least seven states").

235. "Jimmy Carter's Betrayal of the Christian Voter," *Conservative Dig.*, Aug. 1979, at 15. Reagan's victory in 1980 is best explained by a confluence of factors. However, it cannot be denied that certain segments of the electorate turned from Carter to Reagan because of Reagan's conservative positions on social issues. See Walter Dean Burnham, "The 1980 Earthquake: Realignment, Dealignment, or What?," in *The Hidden Election: Politics and Economics in the 1980 Presidential Campaign*, ed. Thomas Ferguson and Joel Rogers (1981), 125; see also Edsall and Edsall, *Chain Reaction*, supra note 18, at 21–22.

236. Critchlow, *Phyllis Schlafly*, supra note 18, at 266 (reporting that Republicans had gained control of the Senate and after winning thirty-three seats in the House left the Democrats with only a "thin margin of control"); Herman Schwartz, *Packing the Courts: The Conservative Campaign to Rewrite the Constitution* (1988), 18 (describing how the Republicans took control of the Senate).

237. See Anderson, "To the Right, March!," supra note 215, at 24; see also Edsall and Edsall, *Chain Reaction*, supra note 18, at 134.

238. David M. Halpern with John J. Lindsay, Mary Lord, and Howard Fineman, "The Attack on Abortion," *Newsweek*, Apr. 6, 1981, at 38.

239. Id.

240. Schwartz, *Packing the Courts*, supra note 236, at 19.

241. James McClellan, "A Lawyer Looks at Rex Lee," *Benchmark*, March–Apr., 1984.

242. See Steven M. Teles, *The Rise of the Conservative Legal Movement: The Battle for Control of the Court* (2008), 2 ("If [conservatives] were to have any chance of influencing the development of the law, conservatives would have to compete directly with liberals at the level of organizational, and not simply electoral, mobilization"). On the strategic use of the language of originalism by the conservative movement, see Robert Post and Reva Siegel, "Originalism as a Political Practice: The Right's Living Constitution," *Fordham L. Rev.* 75 (2006): 545–74.

243. Quoted in Bronner, *Battle for Justice*, supra note 20, at 120.

244. City of Akron v. Akron Ctr. for Reprod. Health, 462 U.S. 416, 423 & nn5–6 (1983).

245. See id.; Douglas W. Kmiec, *The Attorney General's Lawyer: Inside the Meese Justice Department* (1992), 73–77; Jonathan O'Neill, *Originalism in American Law and Politics: A Constitutional History* (2005), 149.

246. Greenhouse, *Becoming Justice Blackmun*, supra note 167, at 143.

247. See *City of Akron*, 462 U.S. at 453.

248. Quoted in Kmiec, *Attorney General's Lawyer*, supra note 245, at 144.

249. *City of Akron*, 462 U.S. at 420 & n1.

250. Lewis, Foreword to Blasi, *Burger Court*, supra note 26, at viii; see also Blasi, "Rootless Activism," in id. at 208 ("[O]ne element in the philosophy of judicial restraint is respect for precedent, even activist precedent"); Woodward and Armstrong, *Brethren*, supra note 43, at 133–34 (discussing Justice Harlan's views on *Miranda*).

251. McClellan, "A Lawyer Looks," supra note 241, at 4, 12.

252. Wallace, "Jurisprudence of Judicial Restraint," supra note 199, at 15.

253. Stephen Wermiel, "Reagan Names Fried to Become Solicitor General," *Wall St. J.*, Sept. 26, 1985, at 64; see also Epstein and Kobylka, *Supreme Court and Legal Change*, supra note 47, at 253 ("Meese would not nominate Fried until he filed the *Thornburgh* brief"). But see Fried, *Order and Law*, supra note 225, at 33 ("But the pressure on me to file a brief in the case was neither excessive nor improper").

254. See Teles, *Rise of the Conservative Legal Movement*, supra note 242, at 137–39 (describing early Federalist Society meetings at Yale Law School); see also O'Neill, *Originalism in American Law*, supra note 245, at 148 (quoting Charles Cooper, assistant attorney general for the Office of Legal Counsel) ("[The Federalist Society] was to the Reagan Administration a philosophical supporter and intellectual resource").

255. See Teles, *Rise of the Conservative Legal Movement*, supra note 242, at 139–41 (describing the formation of the Federalist Society); see also Jonathan Mahler, "The Federalist Capers: Inside Ken Starr's Intellectual Auxiliary," *Lingua Franca*, Sept. 1998, at 39–47.

256. See Cornell W. Clayton, *The Politics of Justice: The Attorney General and the Making of Legal Policy* (1992), 151 (describing Meese's Department of Justice as under the "influence of New Right" groups and discussing personnel).

257. "Judge Scalia's Cheerleaders," *N.Y. Times*, July 23, 1986, at B6.

258. Edwin Meese III, "The Supreme Court of The United States: Bulwark of a Limited Constitution," *Tex. L. Rev.* 27 (1986): 465.

259. Kmiec, *Attorney General's Lawyer*, supra note 245, at 18, 21.

260. See, e.g., McDowell, "Politics of Original Intention," in Goldwin and Schambra, *Quest for Justice*, supra note 194; Daniel A. Farber, "The Originalism Debate: A Guide for the Perplexed," *Ohio St. L. J.* 49 (1989): 1085–1106; Arthur Schlesinger Jr., "On 'Original Intent,'" *Wall St. J.*, Jan. 17, 1986, at 18; Stephen Wermeil, "Nation's Charter," *Wall St. J.*, May 20, 1987 at 1.

261. William J. Brennan, Jr., "The Constitution of the United States: Contemporary Ratification," *U.C. Davis L. Rev.* 19 (1985): 4–5; see also John Paul Stevens, "Construing the Constitution," *U.C. Davis L. Rev.* 19 (1985): 20.

262. Thornburgh v. Am. College of Obstetricians and Gynecologists, 476 U.S. 747, 789 (1986) (White, J., dissenting).

263. The literature on originalism is voluminous. See, e.g., Randy Barnett, *Restoring the Lost Constitution: The Presumption of Liberty* (2004); Brest, "Misconceived Quest," supra note 205; Brennan, "Constitution of the United States," supra note 261; Farber, "Originalism Debate," supra note 260; H. Jefferson Powell, "The Original Understanding of Original Intent," *Harv. L. Rev.* 98 (1985): 885–948; Antonin Scalia, "Originalism: The Lesser Evil," *U. Cin. L. Rev.* 57 (1989): 849–66; Tushnet, "Intent of the Framers," supra note 30.

264. See Powell, "Original Understanding," supra note 263. Of course, even this had its riposte: "the obvious logical problem of how those who deny the possibility of knowing original intention can thus claim it was part of the original intention not to use original intention." McDowell, "Politics of Original Intention," in Goldwin and Schambra, *Quest for Justice*, supra note 194, at 5; see also Charles A. Lofgren, "The Original Understanding of Original Intent?," *Const. Comment.* 5 (1988): 77 (responding to Professor Powell by arguing that the original intent of the ratifiers, and not that of the framers, should guide constitutional interpretation).

265. Accord Post and Siegel, "Originalism as a Political Practice," supra note 242, at 549 ("The current ascendancy of originalism does not reflect the analytic force of its jurisprudence, but instead depends upon its capacity to fuse aroused citizens, government officials, and judges into a dynamic and broad-based political movement").

266. Meese, "Bulwark of a Limited Constitution," supra note 258, at 457.

267. Quoted in David M. O'Brien, "Meese's Agenda for Ensuring the Reagan Legacy," *L.A. Times*, Sept. 28, 1986, at 3.

268. Quoted in id.

269. See Philip Bobbitt, *Constitutional Fate: Theory of the Constitution* (1982), 7–8 (describing the "historical" and "doctrinal" modalities of constitutional interpretation).

270. See Edwin Meese III, "Construing the Constitution," *U.C. Davis L. Rev.* 19 (1985): 26–27; Meese, "Jurisprudence of Original Intent," supra note 213, at 10; Office of Legal Policy, U.S. Dept. of Justice, "Report to the Attorney General, Original Meaning Jurisprudence: A Sourcebook" (1987), 9 ("The goal is to determine the meaning of the constitutional language at issue to the society that adopted it"); see also Thomas Colby and Peter J. Smith, "Originalism's Living Constitution" (GWU Leg. Studs. Res. Paper No. 393, 2008), available at http://papers.ssrn.com/sol3/papers.cfm?abstract_id=1090282. On the change in focus from original intent to original understanding in response to critiques, see Larry Kramer, "Two (More) Problems with Originalism," *Harv. J. Law & Pub. Pol'y* 31 (2008): 909–10.

271. Quoted in Teles, *Rise of the Conservative Legal Movement*, supra note 242, at 145.

272. Quoted in id. at 144.

273. "Address by the Hon. Edwin Meese, III, 75th Attorney General of the United States," in *Originalism: A Quarter-Century of Debate*, ed. Steven G. Calabresi (2007), 327.

274. See Office of Legal Policy, "Original Meaning Jurisprudence," supra note 270, at i ("Original meaning jurisprudence has been the dominant form of constitutional interpretation during most of our nation's history"); see also Teles, *Rise of the Conservative Legal Movement*, supra note 242, at 145.

275. See Robert H. Bork, *The Tempting of America: The Political Seduction of the Law* (1990), 216 ("[T]he consolidation of all power at the federal level is too firmly entrenched . . . to be undone"). But see Douglas H. Ginsburg, "On Constitutionalism, B. Kenneth Simon Lecture in Constitutional Thought," Sept. 17, 2002, in *Cato Sup. Ct. Rev.*, 2002–2003: 7 (criticizing the Court's expansive reading of the Commerce Clause and urging the revival of the nondelegation doctrine); see also Barnett, *Restoring the Lost Constitution*, supra note 263.

276. See Bork, *Tempting of America*, supra note 275, at 168.

277. Office of Legal Policy, "Original Meaning Jurisprudence," supra note 270, at 5.

278. Brown v. Bd. of Educ. of Topeka, 347 U.S. 483 (1954).

279. See McDowell, *Curbing the Courts*, supra note 208, at xiv (expressing the author's "special debt" to Berger); O'Neill, *Originalism in American Law*, supra note 245, at 129–32 (describing how Berger's originalism appealed to Reagan and the new conservative coalition).

280. See Raoul Berger, *Government by Judiciary: The Transformation of the Fourteenth Amendment*, 2d ed. (1997), 457 ("The historical records all but incontrovertibly establish that the framers of the Fourteenth Amendment excluded both suffrage and segregation from its reach"); see "Fie on the Fourteenth," *Time*, Nov. 14, 1977, at 101 ("Berger's conclusion: virtually every major judicial advance of the past quarter century, from desegregation to reapportionment, was based on unconstitutional usurpation of the power by the courts and their misuse of the vague Due Process and Equal Protection guarantees of the 14th Amendment").

281. Michael J. Perry, *The Constitution, the Courts, and Human Rights: An Inquiry into the Legitimacy of Constitutional Policymaking by the Judiciary* (1982), 1–2. But see Michael W. McConnell, "Originalism and the Desegregation Decisions," *Va. L. Rev.*

81 (1995): 953 (arguing that the original understanding of the Fourteenth Amendment supports the result in *Brown*). In response to McConnell's claim, see Michael J. Klarman, "*Brown*, Originalism, and Constitutional Theory: A Response to Professor McConnell," *Va. L. Rev.* 81 (1995): 1883 (refuting McConnell's argument that *Brown* is correct on originalist grounds).

282. See generally Bork, *Tempting of America*, supra note 275, at 149 ("[A] judge should state the principle at the level of generality that the text and historical evidence warrant"); Tribe, *Abortion: The Clash of Absolutes*, supra note 155, at 100–01 (describing how Bork and Scalia define the generality of a right).

283. See Bork, *Tempting of America*, supra note 275, at 113 (arguing that the Constitution protects some aspects of privacy and freedom from government interference, but that abortion is not included); see also id. at 149–50 (making generality point about affirmative action).

284. Id. at 82.

285. Paul Brest, "The Fundamental Rights Controversy: The Essential Contradictions of Normative Constitutional Scholarship," *Yale L. J.* 90 (1981): 1091; see also Ronald Dworkin, "The Bork Nomination," *Cardozo L. Rev.* 9 (1987): 106–07.

286. Robert H. Bork, "The Constitution, Original Intent, and Economic Rights," *San Diego L. Rev.* 23 (1986): 828.

287. See, e.g., Tribe, *Abortion: The Clash of Absolutes*, supra note 155, at 100–01; Dworkin, "Bork Nomination," supra note 285, at 104–08.

288. See "Judging the Judges: The First Two Years of the Reagan Bench," *Benchmark*, July–Oct. 1984, at 2; Office of Legal Policy, "Original Meaning Jurisprudence," supra note 270, at 49. On the use of originalism to justify departures from precedent, see Post and Siegel, "Originalism as a Political Practice," supra note 242, at 560. This debate has continued to the present. See Steven G. Calabresi, "The Tradition of the Written Constitution: Text, Precedent, and Burke," *Ala. L. Rev.* 57 (2006): 637 (arguing that the text of the Constitution as originally understood should trump precedent); Gary Lawson, "The Constitutional Case Against Precedent," *Harv. J. L. & Pub. Pol'y* 17 (1994): 23–34. But see Henry Paul Monaghan, "Stare Decisis and Constitutional Adjudication," *Colum. L. Rev.* 88 (1988) : 724, 772–73 (concluding that originalist interpretations of Constitution must occasionally give way to stare decisis); see also Thomas W. Merrill, "Bork v. Burke," *Harv. J. L. & Pub. Pol'y* 19 (1996): 509–24 (arguing that attention to precedent is justified on conservative grounds).

289. Quoted in Bronner, *Battle for Justice*, supra note 20, at 258–59.

290. Wallace, "Jurisprudence of Judicial Restraint," supra note 199, at 15.

291. McDowell, "Politics of Original Intention," in Goldwin and Schambra, *Quest for Justice*, supra note 194, at 18.

292. Bork, *Tempting of America*, supra note 275, at 155.

293. Quoted in Wermeil, "Nation's Charter," supra note 260, at 1–2.

294. See Craig and O'Brien, *Abortion and American Politics*, supra note 154, at 174; O'Neill, *Originalism in American Law*, supra note 245, at 146; Jeffrey Toobin, *The Nine: Inside the Secret World of the Supreme Court* (2007), 17.

295. "A Reagan Court? The Justices Give the Conservatives a Split Decision," *Newsweek*, July 15, 1985, at 69.

296. Terry Eastland, "Reagan Justice: Combating Excess, Strengthening the Rule of Law," *Pub. Affairs*, Fall 1988, at 21.

297. Id.

298. Quoted in David M. O'Brien, "If the Bench Becomes a Brawl: Reagan's Legacy for U.S. Courts," *L.A. Times*, Aug. 23, 1987, at 1.

299. See Bronner, *Battle for Justice*, supra note 20, at 40–41; David M. O'Brien, *Judicial Roulette: Report on the Twentieth Century Fund Task Force on Judicial Selection* (1988), 61–63; Schwartz, *Packing the Courts*, supra note 236, at 100–01.

300. Nadine Cohodas, "Conservatives Pressing to Reshape Judiciary," *CQ Wkly.*, Sept. 7, 1985 at 2.

301. Quoted in O'Brien, *Judicial Roulette*, supra note 299, at 62.

302. Quoted in id. at 61–62.

303. Craig and O'Brien, *Abortion and American Politics*, supra note 154, at 166–67.

304. Ronald Reagan, "Remarks by Telephone to the Annual Convention of the Knights of Columbus in Chicago, Illinois," Aug. 5, 1986, in *Public Papers of the Presidents of the United States: Ronald Reagan, 1986*, bk. 2 (1989), 1055; see also Craig and O'Brien, *Abortion and American Politics*, supra note 154, at 177 (describing Reagan campaigning for Republicans in the Senate).

305. Howard Kurtz, "Amid Many Failures, Meese Makes a Mark," *Wash. Post*, July 13, 1987, at A1.

306. See Bronner, *Battle for Justice*, supra note 20, at 120; Cohodas, "Conservatives Pressing to Reshape Judiciary," supra note 300, at 1759.

307. Quoted in Earl M. Maltz, *The Chief Justiceship of Warren Burger, 1969–1986* (2000), 25.

308. See Craig and O'Brien, *Abortion and American Politics*, supra note 154, at 179–80 (describing how Democrats strongly opposed Rehnquist because they believed that he was too extreme in his judicial views, especially with respect to race, women's rights, freedom of speech, and the separation of church and state).

309. See "Supreme Court: Memo from Rehnquist," *Newsweek*, Dec. 13, 1971, at 32; 117 Cong. Rec. 45,440 (1971), quoted in Snyder, "How the Conservatives Canonized," supra note 17, at 442 (quoting a Rehnquist letter that claimed the memorandum was written as a statement of Justice Jackson's view).

310. See Craig and O'Brien, *Abortion and American Politics*, supra note 154, at 180.

311. "Supreme Court Shows Independent Streak," *U.S. News & World Rep.*, July 15, 1985, at 43.

312. Stuart Taylor, "To Reagan's Consternation, Brennan Leads Court in Big Cases," *N.Y. Times*, March 30, 1987, at A10.

313. Jacob V. Lamar Jr., "Advise and Dissent," *Time*, Sept. 21, 1987, at 12.

314. Richard Lacayo, "The Battle Begins," *Time*, July 13, 1987, at 10.

315. Patrick B. McGuigan and Dawn M. Weyrich, *Ninth Justice: The Fight for Bork* (1990), 9.

316. See "A Reagan Court?," supra note 295, at 69.

317. See Wygant v. Jackson Bd. of Educ., 476 U.S. 267 (1986); United States v. Paradise, 480 U.S. 149 (1987). Another affirmative action case in which Powell cast a crucial vote was on court-ordered remedies. See Local 28, Sheet Metal Workers' Int'l Ass'n v. EEOC, 478 U.S. 421 (1986).

318. Thornburgh v. Am. Coll. of Obstetricians and Gynecologists, 476 U.S. 747 (1986).

319. Quoted in Epstein and Kobylka, *Supreme Court and Legal Change*, supra note 47, at 260.

320. Ronald Reagan, "Remarks Announcing the Nomination of Robert H. Bork to Be an Associate Justice of the United States," July 1, 1987, in *Public Papers: Ronald Reagan, 1987*, supra note 2, at 736.

321. 133 Cong. Rec. S9188–S9189 (daily ed. July 1, 1987) (statement of Sen. Kennedy), quoted in Bork, *Tempting of America*, supra note 275, at 268, 282; Bronner, *Battle for Justice*, supra note 20, at 100.

322. James Reston, "Kennedy and Bork," *N.Y. Times*, July 5, 1987, at E15.

323. Quoted in Michael Pertschuk and Wendy Schaetzel, *The People Rising: The Campaign Against the Bork Nomination* (1989), 27.

324. Quoted in id.

325. Quoted in Victoria Irwin, "Grass-roots Groups in Frenzy over Bork," *Christian Sci. Monitor*, Sept. 2, 1987, at 6.

326. Bronner, *Battle for Justice*, supra note 20, at 197–98. The speaker was John Bolton, later the United States' ambassador to the United Nations.

327. Quoted in Lamar, "Advise and Dissent," supra note 313, at 14.

328. See McGuigan and Weyrich, *Ninth Justice*, supra note 315, at 26–27.

329. See, e.g., Bronner, *Battle for Justice*, supra note 20, at 147–48, 160; Pertschuk and Schaetzel, *People Rising*, supra note 323, at 134,146–47, 257.

330. Quoted in Pertschuk and Schaetzel, *People Rising*, supra note 323, at 34. When the Democrats retook the Senate in 1986, Senator Kennedy offered Biden the chair of the Senate Judiciary Committee. Biden reluctantly accepted, fearing it would interfere with his presidential bid. The reasons for his switch on Bork are still murky, though most likely it stemmed from the early liberal opposition to Bork and the pressures he felt as a presidential candidate to take a strong stand. See Bronner, *Battle for Justice*, supra note 20, at 139, 211–12.

331. "Bork: Overqualified?," *Wall St. J.*, Sept. 15, 1987, at 32 (emphasis in original).

332. Quoted in McGuigan and Weyrich, *Ninth Justice*, supra note 315, at 8.

333. See, e.g., Lou Cannon and Edward Walsh, "Reagan Nominates Appeals Judge Bork to Supreme Court," *Wash. Post*, July 2, 1987, at A1 ("Bork's position on abortion is likely to be a particular lightning rod for opposition to his nomination"); E. J. Dionne, "Abortion, Bork and the '88 Campaign," *N.Y. Times*, July 8, 1987, at A20 (explaining that the Bork nomination "is pushing the abortion issue back to the center stage of American politics"); Stephen Wermiel, "Bork's Abortion Views Looming Large as Problem in High Court Confirmation," *Wall St. J.*, July 6, 1987, at 2.

334. Bronner, *Battle for Justice*, supra note 20, at 160 (reporting that the opposition avoided the "A word": abortion); Epstein and Kobylka, *Supreme Court and Legal Change*, supra note 47, at 263 (describing how both camps played down the abortion issue); Pertschuk and Schaetzel, *People Rising*, supra note 323, at 257 (describing the opposition's strategy to use "privacy" instead of "abortion").

335. See Griswold v. Connecticut, 381 U.S. 479 (1965).

336. See Bork, *Tempting of America*, supra note 275, at 95–97; Pertschuk and Schaetzel, *People Rising*, supra note 323, at 257–58.

337. See Pertschuk and Schaetzel, *People Rising*, supra note 323, at 173 (quoting *Commentary*, Jan. 1988) (describing a television advertisement stating that "[Bork] defended poll taxes and literacy tests, which kept many Americans from voting. He opposed the civil rights law that ended 'whites only' signs at lunch counters"). As for his personal conduct, twice in his life Bork had gone out of the way to remedy discrimination he encountered. See Bronner, *Battle for Justice*, supra note 20, at 64–65, 82–83.

338. See Bronner, *Battle for Justice*, supra note 20, at 66–68.

339. See Bolling v. Sharpe, 347 U.S. 497 (1954); Bronner, *Battle for Justice*, supra note 20, at 232–33.

340. See Bronner, *Battle for Justice*, supra note 20, at 225.

341. See id. at 254.

342. Quoted in McGuigan and Weyrich, *Ninth Justice*, supra note 315, at 40.

343. See Bronner, *Battle for Justice*, supra note 20, at 220 ("Polls taken by the major media showed the nation to be evenly divided on his nomination").

344. See id. at 300–01.

345. Suzanne Garment, "The War Against Robert H. Bork," *Commentary*, Jan. 1988, at 21.

346. Bronner, *Battle for Justice*, supra note 20, at 242.

347. See id. at 254.

348. O'Brien, *Judicial Roulette*, supra note 299, at 102–03.

349. Bronner, *Battle for Justice*, supra note 20, at 246–47, 251.

350. Epstein and Kobylka, *Supreme Court and Legal Change*, supra note 47, at 263 ("But by late September 1987, Louis Harris reported that 57 percent of Americans opposed Bork's confirmation, whereas only 29 percent supported it").

351. Dale Russakoff, "How the South Was Swayed," *Wash. Post*, Oct. 8, 1987, at A1; see also Bork, *Tempting of America*, supra note 275, at 310.

352. Bronner, *Battle for Justice*, supra note 20, at 314.

353. Quoted in id. at 320.

354. Stuart Taylor, "Tuning Out the White House," *N.Y. Times*, Sept. 11, 1988, at SM38.

355. Stuart Taylor, "Of Bork and Tactics: The Issue Is No Longer Confirmation but Rather the Confirmation Process," *N.Y. Times*, Oct. 21, 1987, at A23.

356. Quoted in Pertschuk and Schaetzel, *People Rising*, supra note 323, at 241.

357. "Justice Bork or Ukase?," *Wall St. J.*, July 8, 1987, at 18.

358. Ronald Reagan, "Radio Address to the Nation on the Supreme Court Nomination of Robert H. Bork," Oct. 10, 1987, in *Public Papers: Ronald Reagan, 1987*, bk. 2, supra note 304, at 1164.

359. Garment, "War Against Robert H. Bork," supra note 345, at 26.

360. Quoted in Bronner, *Battle for Justice*, supra note 20, at 208.

361. "The Bork Nomination," *Wash. Post*, July 2, 1987, at A20.

362. "The Bork Nomination," *Wash. Post*, Oct. 5, 1987, at A14.

363. "The Bork Disinformers," *Wall St. J.*, Oct. 5, 1987, at 22.

364. Quoted in Pertschuk and Schaetzel, *People Rising*, supra note 323, at 242.

365. Bronner, *Battle for Justice*, supra note 20, at 348.

366. Linda Greenhouse, "The Bork Battle: Visions of the Constitution," *N.Y. Times*, Oct. 4, 1987, at E1.

367. Accord Bronner, *Battle for Justice*, supra note 20, at 347; see also Christopher L. Eisgruber, *The Next Justice: Repairing the Supreme Court Appointments Process* (2007), 154 (hearings focused on Bork's judicial philosophy, and Senate rejected him because he was "not a moderate"); Toobin, *Nine*, supra note 294, at 19 ("More than anything, the fight over Bork's nomination illustrated that Meese and his allies had done a better job of persuading themselves of the new conservative agenda than they had of convincing the country at large").

368. Stephen Carter, "The Confirmation Mess," *Harv. L. Rev.* 101 (1988): 1192–93.

369. Russakoff, "South Was Swayed," supra note 351, at A1.

370. Quoted in McGuigan and Weyrich, *Ninth Justice*, supra note 315, at 167; see also Gitenstein, *Matters of Principle*, supra note 129, at 287 ("A Roper poll, which had been circulated in the Southern delegation . . . showed overall opposition in the South at 51 percent against and 31 percent for, and with Southern whites the number was a startling 46 percent to 42 percent against").

371. Quoted in Bronner, *Battle for Justice*, supra note 20, at 291.

372. Terry Eastland, "What Next for Justice Department?," *Legal Times*, Oct. 31, 1988, at 18.

373. Quoted in Bronner, *Battle for Justice*, supra note 20, at 275.

374. "Bork Nomination," supra note 362, at A14; see also Bronner, *Battle for Justice*, supra note 20, at 276 ("Bork himself seemed to be confirming what people had been told to fear about him: The bearded egghead from Yale just wanted to play with ideas. He didn't understand that beyond those elegant intellectual constructs, the lives of real people hung in the balance"); Bronner, *Battle for Justice*, supra note 20, at 337

(contrasting Bork with Justice Anthony Kennedy, who answered questions in his confirmation hearing with more human compassion: "Compassion, warmth, sensitivity, and an unyielding insistence on justice are the attributes of every good judge").

375. McGuigan and Weyrich, *Ninth Justice*, supra note 315, at 209.
376. Id. at 218.
377. See Greenhouse, *Becoming Justice Blackmun*, supra note 167, at 42.
378. See Bronner, *Battle for Justice*, supra note 20, at 332–33.
379. Quoted in id. at 337.
380. "Nomination of Anthony M. Kennedy to Be Associate Justice of the Supreme Court of the United States: Hearings Before the S. Comm. on the Judiciary," S. Hrg. 100–1037, 100th Cong. (1987), reprinted in *The Supreme Court of the United States Nominations: 1916–1987* (1991), 15:415, 428, 457.
381. Quoted in Bronner, *Battle for Justice*, supra note 20, at 337.
382. "Nomination of Anthony M. Kennedy" in *Supreme Court Nominations*, supra note 380, at 15:139, 141.
383. Id. at 15:140.
384. Id. at 15:139, 183.
385. Id. at 15:183.
386. Id. at 15:86.
387. Stuart Taylor, "Judge Kennedy: Tilting Right but Not Far," *N.Y. Times*, Nov. 15, 1987, at 1.
388. Stephen Wermeil, "Nominee Kennedy Is a Conservative, but Not like Bork," *Wall St. J.*, Nov. 12, 1987, at 28.
389. Al Kamen, "Kennedy Confirmed, 97–0," *Wash. Post*, Feb. 4, 1988, at A1.

Chapter 10: Activism

1. See Bowers v. Hardwick, 478 U.S. 186 (1986); Lawrence v. Texas, 539 U.S. 558 (2003) (overturning *Bowers*).
2. See Planned Parenthood of Southeastern Pennsylvania v. Casey, 505 U.S. 833 (1992).
3. See Grutter v. Bollinger, 539 U.S. 306 (2003).
4. See Bush v. Gore, 531 U.S. 98 (2000) (per curiam).
5. See Lori A. Ringhand, "The Rehnquist Court," *U. Pa. J. Const. L.* 9 (2007): 1033–81 (statistical analysis of Rehnquist Court decisions).
6. Mark R. Levin, *Men in Black: How the Supreme Court Is Destroying America* (2005), 11; Cass R. Sunstein, *Radicals in Robes: Why Extreme Right Wing Courts Are Wrong for America* (2005).
7. See Martin Garbus, *Courting Disaster: The Supreme Court and the Unmaking of American Law* (2002); Pat Robertson, *Courting Disaster: How the Supreme Court Is Usurping the Power of Congress and the People* (2004).
8. See William Rehnquist, 2004 Year-end Report on the Federal Judiciary, released Jan. 1, 2005, available at http://www.supremecourtus.gov/publicinfo/year-end/2004year-endreport.pdf, at 5.
9. Professor Thomas Merrill dubbed the Court thus and explained its characteristics in an incisive piece, using social science analysis to explain what he called the "second Rehnquist Court." See Thomas W. Merrill, "The Making of the Second Rehnquist Court: A Preliminary Analysis," *St. Louis U. L. J.* 47 (2003): 570.
10. In 1986, Rehnquist replaced Burger as Chief Justice and Justice Scalia joined the Court. In 1987, Justice Kennedy replaced Justice Powell. In 1990, Justice Souter replaced Justice Brennan. In 1991, Justice Thomas replaced Justice Marshall. See id. at 578.

11. See id. at 570 (dating the first Rehnquist Court from October 1986 to July 1994).

12. See id.

13. See R. Lacayo and J. Cramer, "A Blank Slate," *Time*, Aug. 6, 1990, at 16 ("Facing these polarized options, the President . . . select[ed] a Stealth candidate"); id. (quoting one senior Republican: "There's been a lot of wink-wink, nod-nod among conservatives who think Souter . . . can be trusted"); Stephen Wermiel and David Shribman, "Bush's Choice: High Court Nominee Is Conservative but Isn't Seen as an Ideologue," *Wall St. J.*, July 24, 1990, at A1 ("President Bush . . . struck quickly by choosing a conservative jurist with no paper trail on abortion").

14. William Raspberry, Editorial, "What Manner of Man, Clarence Thomas?," *Wash. Post*, July 3, 1991, at A19; Julia Malone, "Clarence Thomas: Nominee Under Scrutiny," *Atlanta J. and Const.*, July 3, 1991, at A5.

15. See John W. Mashek and Ethan Bronner, "Thomas, a Conservative, Nominated to High Court; Confirmation Fight Expected," *Boston Globe*, July 2, 1991, at 1; Raspberry, "Manner of Man," supra note 14; A. L. May and Bob Dart, "Nunn Lends Support to Thomas as House Foes Step Up Criticism," *Atlanta J. and Const.*, July 17, 1991, at E1.

16. See David G. Savage, *Turning Right: The Making of the Rehnquist Supreme Court* (1992; repr. 1993).

17. James F. Simon, *The Center Holds: The Power Struggle Inside the Rehnquist Court* (1995), 11.

18. Id. at 12. Even Savage conceded that by the time the Democrat Bill Clinton won the White House in 1992, "the sharp turn to the right had been halted." See Savage, *Turning Right*, supra note 16, at 473.

19. Linda Greenhouse summed up the early Rehnquist Court: "There is no doubt that in decisions ranging from school prayer to habeas corpus to property rights to federalism, the Court adopted a more modulated approach" than most had predicted. Linda Greenhouse, "A Telling Court Opinion," *N.Y. Times*, July 1, 1992, at A1. For a different take on the first Rehnquist Court, see Mark Tushnet, *A Court Divided: The Rehnquist Court and the Future of Constitutional Law* (2005), 69–70 (arguing that "O'Connor and Kennedy were conservatives, but of a different stripe from Scalia and Thomas" because they were more interested in the size of government than in social issues).

20. See Editorial, "A Monumental, Fragile Mandate," *N.Y. Times*, Nov. 4, 1992, at A30.

21. See Adam Clymer, "The 1994 Elections: Congress—the Overview; G.O.P. Celebrates Its Sweep to Power; Clinton Vows to Find Common Ground," *N.Y. Times*, Nov. 10, 1994, at A1.

22. Adarand Constructors, Inc. v. Pena, 515 U.S. 200, 224 (1995). Previously the Court had subjected state and local laws to strict scrutiny but had been more deferential to Congress. Compare City of Richmond v. J. A. Croson, 488 U.S. 469 (1989) with Metro Broadcasting, Inc. v. F.C.C., 497 U.S. 547 (1990) (overruled by *Adarand*).

23. *Adarand*, 551 U.S. at 237 (concluding with "if it satisfies the 'narrow tailoring' test this Court has set out in previous cases").

24. See id. at 239 (Scalia, J., concurring) ("[G]overnment can never have a 'compelling interest' in discriminating on the basis of race in order to 'make up' for past racial discrimination in the opposite direction"); id. at 240 (Thomas, J., concurring) ("In my mind, government-sponsored racial discrimination based on benign prejudice is just as noxious as discrimination inspired by malicious prejudice. In each instance, it is racial discrimination, plain and simple").

25. Linda Greenhouse, "In Step on Racial Policy," *N.Y. Times*, June 14, 1995, at A1.

26. See Dan T. Carter, *From George Wallace to Newt Gingrich: Race in the Conservative Counterrevolution* (1996), xiv; Thomas Byrne Edsall with Mary D. Edsall, *Chain*

Reaction (1991), 177; Nicholas Laham, *The Reagan Presidency and the Politics of Race* (1998), 9.

27. Bill Clinton, "Address to the Democratic National Committee," Sept. 20, 1991, in Stanley B. Greenberg, *Middle Class Dreams: The Politics and Power of the New American Majority* (1995; repr. 1996), 212.

28. Quoted in Terry H Anderson, *The Pursuit of Fairness* (2004), 233–34; Republican Party platform of 1992, adopted Aug. 17, 1992, http://presidency.ucsb.edu/showplatforms.php?platindex=R1992, at 23 ("[W]e reject efforts to replace equal rights with quotas or other preferential treatment").

29. "Clinton Scrutinizes Affirmative Action, He Seeks Full Review of Programs," *St. Louis Post-Dispatch*, Feb. 25, 1995, at 1A .

30. William J. Clinton, "Remarks on Affirmative Action at the National Archives and Records Administration," July 19, 1995, in *Public Papers of the Presidents of the United States: William J. Clinton, 1995*, bk. 2 (1996), 1113.

31. See Anderson, *Pursuit of Fairness*, supra note 28, at 245 (discussing the split in Republican ranks); Kevin Merida, "Senate Rejects Gramm Bid to Bar Affirmative Action Set-Asides," *Wash. Post*, July 21, 1995, at A13 (reporting Senate votes).

32. "Senate Rejects Gramm Bid," supra note 31.

33. Quoted in Lydia Chávez, *The Color Bind: The Campaign to End Affirmative Action* (1998), 109.

34. See Jonathan Tilove, "Divided They Stand: Affirmative Action; GOP Pulls Back on Delicate Issue," *Atlanta J. and Const.*, March 3, 1996, at C2; Bill McAllister, "No Push by GOP to End Affirmative Action," *L.A. Times*, July 15, 1996, at 18.

35. Quoted in Faye M. Anderson, "Washington Report," *Headway*, Apr. 30, 1997, at 28; see also Jennifer L Hochschild, "The Strange Career of Affirmative Action," *Ohio St. L. J.* 59 (1998): 1021–22 (collecting Gingrich's conflicting statements about affirmative action); Christopher Caldwell, "The Meritocracy Dodge: Defenders of Affirmative Action Go On the Attack," *Wkly. Standard*, July 14, 1997, at 23 (quoting Gingrich as saying, "We need 80 percent of our effort on proving we have found a better way to solve the problem and 20 percent of our effort on ending affirmative action").

36. Lee v. Weisman, 505 U.S. 577 (1992).

37. See, e.g., Allegheny v. ACLU, Greater Pittsburgh Chapter, 492 U.S. 573 (1989) (Kennedy, J., concurring in judgment in part and dissenting in part) (arguing that crèche display is as constitutional as Christmas tree and menorah displays upheld by the majority); Lynch v. Donnelly, 465 U.S. 668 (1984) (upholding the constitutionality of a crèche display as part of a larger Christmas display that included secular elements such as a cutout elephant).

38. See *Lee*, 505 U.S. at 593 (describing the pressure to signify ambiguously either respect or adherence to the views expressed in the prayer as "subtle and indirect, [but potentially] as real as any overt compulsion").

39. See Kirk W. Elifson and C. Kirk Hadaway, "Prayer in Public Schools," *Pub. Opinion Q.* 49 (1985): 321 (reporting a 1980 poll showing 72.1 percent believing schools should be allowed to start the day with a prayer); John C. Green and James L. Guth, "The Missing Link," *Pub. Opinion Q.* 53 (1989): 41–42 (reporting that the figure remained at 71.5 percent four years later and that "[i]n 1983 Gallup found 81 percent of the 'aware' public favoring a constitutional amendment allowing voluntary school prayer").

40. The American Jewish National Congress, American Jewish Committee, and National Council of Churches of Christ in the U.S.A., among others, filed amici briefs in support of the ACLU in *Allegheny*, 492 U.S. 573, whereas the National Legal Foundation, a nonprofit Christian law firm filed an amicus brief in support of Allegheny

County. See Brief Amici Curiae of the Am. Jewish Cong. on Behalf of Itself and the Nat'l Jewish Cmty. Relations Advisory Council in Support of Respondents, 492 U.S. 573 (1989) (Nos. 87–2050, 88–90, 88–96); Brief of the Am. Jewish Comm. et al. as Amici Curiae in Support of Respondents, 492 U.S. 573 (1989) (Nos. 87–2050, 88–90, 88–96); Brief of the Nat'l Legal Found. Amicus Curiae, in Support of Petitioners, County of Allegheny v. ACLU Greater Pittsburgh Chapter, 492 U.S. 573 (1989) (Nos. 87–2050, 88–90, 88–96). In Wallace v. Jaffree, 472 U.S. 38 (1985), the American Jewish Congress again filed against school prayer, while the Christian Legal Society and National Association of Evangelicals filed in support. See Brief of the Christian Legal Soc'y et al. as Amici Curiae Supporting Appellants, Wallace v. Jaffree, 472 U.S. 38 (1985) (No. 83–812); Brief Amici Curiae of the Am. Jewish Cong. et al. as Amici Curiae Supporting Appellees, Wallace v. Jaffree, 472 U.S. 38 (1985) (No. 83–812). See Elifson and Hadaway, "Prayer in Public Schools," supra note 39, at 325 (noting that "Jews oppose [both nonsectarian and, specifically, Christian] prayer in the schools much more so than Catholics or Protestants"); Green and Guth, "Missing Link," supra note 39, at 45 (finding school prayer is strongly backed by "active church members and sectarian Protestants. Catholics and mainline Protestants are less supportive, while liberal Protestants, Jews, and those with no preference are strongly opposed").

41. See, e.g., Allen D. Hertzke, *Representing God in Washington: The Role of Religious Lobbies in the American Polity* (1988), 121; John C. Jeffries, Jr., and James E. Ryan, "A Political History of the Establishment Clause," *Mich. L. Rev.* 100 (2001): 325; "A Tide Reversed," *Time*, June 19, 1964, at 60 ("[C]hurch leaders . . . now overwhelmingly agree that the court has affirmed the essential meaning of the First Amendment: it protects all religions by establishing none").

42. The Court had ruled against a moment of silence law in Wallace v. Jaffree, 472 U.S. 38 (1985), but largely on the ground that the legislative motive was plainly to advance religion. As of 2009, the Court had yet to rule on a "true" or "pure" moment of silence statute. On popular preferences, see Mariana Servin-Gonzales and Oscar Torres-Reyna, "The Polls—Trends: Religion and Politics," *Pub. Opinion Q.* 63 (1999): 599–600 (reporting that polls ten years apart show a consistent majority preferring a moment of silence to organized prayer and that when informed on the state of the jurisprudence, about 60 percent said that organized prayer was "not the 'kind of issue' for which they would change the Constitution"); Alison Gash and Angelo Gonzales, "School Prayer," in *Public Opinion and Constitutional Controversy*, ed. Nathaniel Persily et al. (2008), 69–70 ("[I]n 1986, respondents [in a survey] were given the choice between silent prayer, general prayer, Christian prayer and no prayer. . . . [T]he combined support for allowing some form of prayer was actually more than 80 percent—with half of respondents typically expressing a preference for silent prayer. Opinion remained at similar levels over the next twelve years"); David W. Moore, "Public Favors Voluntary Prayer for Public Schools," Gallup News Serv., Aug. 26, 2005, http://www.gallup.com/poll/18136/Public-Favors-Voluntary-Prayer-Public-Schools .aspx (finding that despite 76 percent support for a constitutional amendment to allow "voluntary prayer in public schools . . . only 23 percent of Americans prefer some type of spoken prayer, while 69 percent favor a moment of silence for contemplation or silent prayer. These views are essentially the same as those expressed a decade ago in a similar poll").

43. Quoted in Bruce J. Dierenfield, "'Somebody Is Tampering with America's Soul': Congress and the Prayer Debate," *Congress & the Presidency* 24 (1997): 196.

44. Quoted in Richard L. Berke, "G.O.P. Governors Caution Congress on Social Agenda," *N.Y. Times*, Nov. 21, 1994, at A1.

45. Quoted in id.

46. Quoted in Dierenfield, "Congress and the Prayer Debate," supra note 43, at 196.

47. Webster v. Reprod. Health Servs., 492 U.S. 490 (1989).

48. Transcript of Oral Argument, Webster v. Reprod. Health Servs., 492 U.S. 490 (1989) (No. 88–605), available at http://www.oyez.org/cases/1980–1989/1988/1988_88_605/argument/, at 6, 8.

49. Webster, 492 U.S. at 518. Rehnquist declined to overturn Roe in the case at hand, noting that the facts in the two cases were not similar enough to do so. See id. at 518–19. Justice Scalia disagreed, urging the Court to use Webster as an opportunity to overturn Roe, rather than "be run into a corner before we grudgingly yield up our judgment." Id. at 535 (Scalia, J., concurring).

50. See Webster, 492 U.S. at 526 (O'Connor, J., concurring in part and in the judgment).

51. Margaret Carlson, "The Battle over Abortion," Time, July 17, 1989, at 62.

52. See Steve Marshall and Leslie Phillips, "Abortion March Draws 300,000," USA Today, Apr. 10, 1989, at 3A (reporting that more than three hundred thousand people had marched in support of abortion rights on April 9, with the oral argument scheduled for April 26).

53. See Barbara Hinkson Craig and David M. O'Brien, Abortion and American Politics (1993), 296; Mark A. Graber, Rethinking Abortion (1999), 131.

54. Laurence H. Tribe, Abortion: The Clash of Absolutes (1990), 180.

55. In the New Jersey race, a CBS poll found 22 percent of voters "considered abortion the 'most important' issue in the campaign," and they voted for the pro-choice candidate "by a margin of two to one." In Virginia, 71 percent said that abortion was "somewhat or very important to them," and 62 percent of those people voted for the pro-choice candidate. See id. at 189. See Craig and O'Brien, Abortion and American Politics, supra note 53, at 298.

56. Irving Kristol, "What Won, and What Lost, in 1990," Wall St. J., Nov. 16, 1990, at A1 (predicting this would occur by 1992).

57. Quoted in Craig and O'Brien, Abortion and American Politics, supra note 53, at 300; see generally Mark A. Graber, "The Non-Majoritarian Difficulty," Studs. in Am. Pol. Dev. 7 (1993): 60 (discussing Republican officials' attempts to "remov[e] abortion from national politics").

58. See Lacayo and Cramer, "A Blank Slate," supra note 13.

59. Richard L. Berke, "Groups Backing Abortion Rights Ask Court to Act," N.Y. Times, Nov. 8, 1991, at A1.

60. See Casey, 505 U.S. at 902 (appendix to opinion of O'Connor, Kennedy, and Souter, JJ.).

61. Roe v. Wade, 410 U.S. 113, 163 (1973); see also Akron v. Akron Ctr. for Reprod. Health, 462 U.S. 416, 442 (1983) (striking down a requirement that the physician provide information about fetal development); id. at 449–50 (striking down a twenty-four-hour waiting period); Planned Parenthood of Cent. Missouri v. Danforth, 428 U.S. 52, 70 (1978) (striking down a spousal consent requirement).

62. Petition for Writ of Certiorari, Planned Parenthood of Southeastern Pennsylvania v. Casey, 505 U.S. 833 (1992), (No. 91–744), at i; see also Tushnet, A Court Divided, supra note 19, at 209 (discussing Planned Parenthood petition).

63. See Casey, 503 U.S. at 944 (Rehnquist, C. J., concurring in part and dissenting in part) ("We believe that Roe was wrongly decided, and that it can and should be overruled . . ."); id. at 979 (Scalia, J., concurring in part and dissenting in part) ("The States may, if they wish, permit abortion on demand, but the Constitution does not require them to do so.").

64. See Casey, 505 U.S. at 912 (Stevens, J., concurring in part and dissenting in part)

("The Court is unquestionably correct in concluding that the doctrine of *stare decisis* has controlling significance in a case of this kind . . ."); id. at 923 (Blackmun, J., concurring in part and dissenting in part) (praising the joint opinion for reaffirming the "essential holding" of *Roe*).

65. *Casey*, 505 U.S. at 877 (joint opinion).

66. Id. at 880–901.

67. Id. at 869.

68. Greenhouse, "A Telling Court Opinion," supra note 19.

69. See Thomas M. Keck, *The Most Activist Supreme Court in History: The Road to Modern Judicial Conservatism* (2004), 2; Ringhand, "Rehnquist Court," supra note 5, at 1035–36 (comparing the Rehnquist Court, which invalidated thirty-four federal statutes, with the Warren and Burger Courts, which invalidated only twenty-one and nineteen, respectively).

70. United States v. Lopez, 514 U.S. 549 (1995).

71. In 1991, in *Gregory v. Ashcroft*, the Court held that absent a clear statement regarding intent to alter the federal-state balance, Congress would not be presumed to have intended to subject state judges to the requirements of the federal Age Discrimination in Employment Act. Gregory v. Ashcroft, 501 U.S. 452, 470 (1991). In 1992, the Court held Congress could not "commandeer" state legislative authority, in *New York v. United States*. See New York v. United States, 505 U.S. 144 (1992). Although these cases attracted notice, it was nothing like the flood of commentary that followed *Lopez*.

72. *Lopez*, 514 U.S. at 561.

73. See id. at 618–19 (Breyer, J., dissenting); Brief for the United States, United States v. Lopez, 514 U.S. 549 (1995) (No. 93–1260), at 9, 20–22.

74. *Lopez*, 514 U.S. at 631 (appendix to opinion of Breyer, J).

75. Id. at 564 (majority opinion).

76. Nina Totenberg, "Supreme Court Strikes Down Guns near School Law," *All Things Considered*, NPR, Apr. 26, 1995.

77. See, e.g., Printz v. United States, 521 U.S. 898, 935 (1997) (holding that Congress cannot bypass prohibition against compelling states to enact federal programs by "conscripting" state law enforcement officials directly); Seminole Tribe of Fla. v. Florida, 517 U.S. 44 (1996) (holding that Congress lacked the requisite power under the Indian Commerce Clause to deprive states of their sovereign immunity).

78. United States v. Morrison, 529 U.S. 598 (2000).

79. "Activism in Different Robes," *Economist*, July 3, 1999, at 22.

80. Anthony Lewis, "The Supreme Power," *N.Y. Times*, June 29, 1999, at A19.

81. Symposium, "Activism," *U. Colo. L. Rev.* 73 (2002): 1139–416.

82. Cass R. Sunstein, Op-Ed, "Tilting the Scales Rightward," *N.Y. Times*, Apr. 26, 2001, at A23.

83. Linda Greenhouse, "The High Court's Target: Congress," *N.Y. Times*, Feb. 25, 2001, § 4, at 3.

84. Ruth Colker and James J. Brudney, "Dissing Congress," *Mich. L. Rev.* 100 (2001): 80–144.

85. Herman Schwartz, "Supreme Court: Assault on Federalism Swipes at Women," *L.A. Times*, May 21, 2000, at 1.

86. David G. Savage, "Rulings Give States Broad Immunity Against Lawsuits," *L.A. Times*, June 24, 1999, at 1.

87. Editorial, "The High Court Loses Restraint," *N.Y. Times*, Apr. 29, 1995, at A22; Linda Greenhouse, "Justices Curb Federal Power to Subject States to Lawsuits," *N.Y. Times*, March 28, 1996, at A1; see also Linda Greenhouse, "High Court Kills Law

Banning Guns in a School Zone," *N.Y. Times*, Apr. 27, 1995, at A1 ("The Supreme Court today dealt a stinging blow to the Federal Government's ability to move into the realm of local law enforcement . . .").

88. For a summary of the decisions by the various courts, see Bush v. Gore (*Bush II*), 531 U.S. 98, 100–03 (2000) (per curiam). For a collection of contemporary news articles detailing the history, see Correspondents of *The New York Times*, 36 *Days: The Complete Chronicle of the 2000 Presidential Election Crisis* (2001). For a bare chronology, see Richard A. Posner, *Breaking the Deadlock: The 2000 Election, the Constitution and the Courts* (2001), xiii–xiv. For a narrative retold after the fact, see Political Staff of *The Washington Post*, *Deadlock: The Inside Story of America's Closest Election* (2001).

89. See Douglas Brinkley, Introduction to Correspondents of *The New York Times*, 36 *Days*, supra note 88, at xi, xv; Posner, *Breaking the Deadlock*, supra note 88, at 6.

90. See *Bush II*, 531 U.S. at 100–01 (per curiam) (putting the gap at 1,784 votes out of 5,816,486 cast); Political Staff of *The Washington Post*, *Deadlock*, supra note 88, at vii; Posner, *Breaking the Deadlock*, supra note 88, at vii.

91. Linda Greenhouse, "Learning to Live with *Bush v. Gore*," *Green Bag 2d* 4 (2001): 384 (taking the phrase of "several observers").

92. See Political Staff of *The Washington Post*, *Deadlock*, supra note 88, at vii (reporting concession and retraction); Kevin Sack and Frank Bruni, "How Gore Stopped Short on His Way to Concede," in Correspondents of *The New York Times, 36 Days*, supra note 88, at 3, 4 (quoting Gore).

93. During the election itself there were reports of voter harassment and intimidation. Then it appeared that the peculiar design of Palm Beach County's "butterfly" ballot had led many Gore voters mistakenly to vote for third-party candidate Patrick Buchanan. See Brinkley, Introduction to Correspondents of *The New York Times*, 36 *Days*, supra note 88, at xvi; Political Staff of *The Washington Post*, *Deadlock*, supra note 88, at 70; Don Van Natta, Jr., "For Democrats, Problems All Across Florida," in Correspondents of *The New York Times*, 36 *Days*, supra note 88, at 17, 19; see also Posner, *Breaking the Deadlock*, supra note 88, at 7.

94. See Political Staff of *The Washington Post*, *Deadlock*, supra note 88, at 117.

95. See id. at 156.

96. The certification date was extended to the eighteenth for overseas ballots. See Posner, *Breaking the Deadlock*, supra note 88, at 8.

97. See Bush v. Palm Beach County Canvassing Bd. (*Bush I*), 531 U.S. 70, 73–78 (2000) (per curiam); Palm Beach County Canvassing Bd. v. Harris (*Harris II*), 772 So. 2d 1273, 1290 (Fla. 2000) (per curiam) (reinstating the November 26 deadline); Palm Beach County Canvassing Bd. v. Harris (*Harris I*), 772 So. 2d 1220, 1240 (Fla. 2000) (per curiam) (ordering an extension until November 26).

98. 3 U.S.C. § 5 (2007); see Posner, *Breaking the Deadlock*, supra note 88, at 114.

99. See Political Staff of *The Washington Post*, *Deadlock*, supra note 88, at 156–57.

100. Posner, *Breaking the Deadlock*, supra note 88, at 9; Dana Milbank and Jo Becker, "Controversy Swirls Around Harris; Florida Secretary of State Seen as Partisan Figure with Strong Republican Ties," *Wash. Post*, Nov. 14, 2000, at A22; Ronald Brownstein, "Political Stakes Prompt Partisan Pressure," *Pittsburgh Post-Gazette*, Nov. 15, 2000, at A7.

101. See *Bush II*, 531 U.S. at 101 (per curiam), Political Staff of *The Washington Post*, *Deadlock*, supra note 88, at xii.

102. See Gore v. Harris, 772 So. 2d 1243 (Fla. 2000); see also *Bush II*, 531 U.S. at 100 (per curiam) (describing the result in the Florida court).

103. See *Bush II*, 531 U.S. at 100 (per curiam) (describing the series of events).

104. See id. at 103 (per curiam).
105. See id. at 134 (Souter, J., dissenting); id. at 145 (Breyer, J., dissenting).
106. See id. at 110 (per curiam). There is agreement that as a strictly legal matter, the Gore team could have returned to the Florida Supreme Court and that grounds remained under which that court could have restarted the vote count. However, the Gore camp determined this was not a politically feasible or desirable outcome. See Political Staff of *The Washington Post*, *Deadlock*, supra note 88, at 234 ("Could they fight on? Sure, [Gore's lawyer David Boies said]. Should they? 'It is not just making a decision of whether this is viable or sensible. . . . It is whether the viability of it or the sensibility of it [is] great enough to consider it. It is not just a legal question.' It was a question about a divided country, and about the future of Al Gore"); Nelson Lund, "The Unbearable Rightness of *Bush v. Gore*," *Cardozo L. Rev.* 23 (2001): 1277 ("Gore's lawyers reportedly recognized that the Florida Supreme Court had been left free to order a new recount, but decided on political grounds not to request one").
107. Quoted in Political Staff of *The Washington Post*, *Deadlock*, supra note 88, at 239.
108. Richard L. Hasen, "A Critical Guide to *Bush v. Gore*," *Ann. Rev. Polit. Sci.* 7 (2004): 297. For a brief discussion of the defenders of the Court, see Greenhouse, "Learning to Live," supra note 91, at 382 (identifying only Nelson Lund and Michael McConnell as defenders of the Court's legal analysis).
109. See, e.g., Jack M. Balkin, "*Bush v. Gore* and the Boundary Between Law and Politics," *Yale L. J.* 110 (2001): 1407 (comparing Justice Thomas's claim, shortly after *Bush v. Gore*, that "he believed that the work of the Court was not in any way influenced by politics or partisan considerations" with a belief in Santa Claus or the Easter Bunny); Samuel Issacharoff, "Political Judgments," *U. Chi. L. Rev.* 68 (2001): 650 (describing the Court's attempt to limit the reach of its equal protection instruction as "either meaningless or reveal[ing] the new equal protection argument as a cynical vessel used to engage in result-oriented judging by decree"); David A. Strauss, "*Bush v. Gore*: What Were They Thinking?," *U. Chi. L. Rev.* 68 (2001): 737–38 (concluding that "several members of the Court—perhaps a majority—were determined to overturn any ruling of the Florida Supreme Court . . . if that ruling significantly enhanced the Vice President's chances of winning the election"); Cass R. Sunstein, "Order Without Law," *U. Chi. L. Rev.* 68 (2001): 758 ("[T]he Court's rationale was not only exceedingly ambitious but also embarrassingly weak").
110. Lund, "Unbearable Rightness," supra note 106, at 1219n2.
111. U.S. Const. art. II, § 1, cl. 2.
112. Eric Foner, *Reconstruction: America's Unfinished Revolution, 1863–1877* (2002), 579–80.
113. Act of Feb. 3, 1887, ch. 90, 24 Stat 373 (codified as amended at 3 U.S.C. §§ 5–6, 15–18 [2008]).
114. 3 U.S.C. § 15.
115. See Posner, *Breaking the Deadlock*, supra note 88, at 140.
116. 3 U.S.C. § 15.
117. Posner, *Breaking the Deadlock*, supra note 88, at 140.
118. Counting of Electoral Votes, 17 *Cong. Rev.* S 817–18 (Jan., 21, 1886) (Sen. Sherman), quoted in Issacharoff, "Political Judgments," supra note 109, at 72.
119. Several scholars criticized the Court's equal protection argument for being a decision without foundation in precedent. See Peter M. Shane, "Disappearing Democracy: How *Bush v. Gore* Undermined the Federal Right to Vote for Presidential Electors," *Fla. St. U. L. Rev.* 29 (2002): 536 ("[N]one of the practices being challenged amounted, under anyone's account, to a form of explicit or otherwise intentional discrimination against Bush voters—the sort of harm typically addressed through an equal protection

rubric"); Sunstein, "Order Without Law," supra note 109, at 758 ([T]he Court's rationale was not only exceedingly ambitious but also embarrassingly weak. . . . [I]ts equal protection holding had no basis in precedent or history."); David G. Savage, "The Vote Case Fallout," *A.B.A. J.*, Feb. 2001, at 32 (quoting Professor A. E. Dick Howard: "This is a remarkable use of the Equal Protection Clause. It is not consistent with anything they have done in the past 25 years").

    More consistently, scholars criticized the practical implications of the Court's decision and its attempt to limit that holding to the case at hand. See Issacharoff, "Political Judgments," supra note 109, at 650; Pamela S. Karlan, "Unduly Partial: The Supreme Court and the Fourteenth Amendment in *Bush v. Gore*," *Fla. St. U. L. Rev.* 29 (2001): 587–602; Akhil Reed Amar, Op-Ed, "Supreme Court: Should We Trust Judges?," *L.A. Times*, Dec. 17, 2000, at M1.

120. *Bush II*, 531 U.S. at 104–05 (per curiam).
121. Id. at 109 (per curiam).
122. See id. at 111 (per curiam).
123. The dissenting Supreme Court justices all made the point that there was nothing sacrosanct about December 12, and that later dates—certainly the December 18 date for casting electoral votes, but perhaps even as late as January 5—might have been equally permissible. See id. at 124 (Stevens, J., dissenting); id. at 130 (Souter, J., dissenting); id. at 143–44 (Ginsburg, J., dissenting); id. at 146–47 (Breyer, J., dissenting).
124. Michael W. McConnell, Op-Ed, "A Muddled Ruling," *Wall St. J.*, Dec. 14, 2000, at A26. Expanding upon his argument in a subsequent article, he complained that "the Court accepted the Florida Supreme Court's premise that a manual recount was necessary, but then invoked a questionable reading of state law to say that no such recount could even be attempted." Michael W. McConnell, "Two-and-a-Half Cheers for *Bush v. Gore*," in *The Vote*, ed. Cass R. Sunstein and Richard A. Epstein (2001), 98, 102.
125. See Kermit Roosevelt III, *The Myth of Judicial Activism: Making Sense of Supreme Court Decisions* (2006), 193 ("The more common explanation [of the decision] is that the Court felt it had to act to avert a constitutional crisis"); Greenhouse, "Learning to Live," supra note 91, at 382 (describing the significant group of legal scholars who believed that "the Court took a bullet for the country"); William P. Marshall, "The Supreme Court, *Bush v. Gore* and Rough Justice," *Fla. St. U. L. Rev.* 29 (2001): 789 (arguing that "rough justice" required that if the Court believed that a constitutional crisis would result from congressional resolution, that the Gore camp was improperly manipulating the vote count, or that the Florida Supreme Court was being improperly partisan, then intervention would be justified even "if its decision were not based in legal principle" (emphasis removed)); David G. Savage and Henry Weinstein, "The Presidential Transition: High Court in Awkward Spot over Equal Protection Ruling," *L.A. Times*, Dec. 16, 2000, at A1 (quoting liberal Cass Sunstein: "The good thing you can say about this case is that it settled things in the least messy way. But as a matter of law it is a real embarrassment").
126. Charles Krauthammer, "The Winner in *Bush v. Gore*," *Time*, Dec. 18, 2000, at 104.
127. Posner, *Breaking the Deadlock*, supra note 88, at 147.
128. See *Bush II*, 531 U.S. at 155 (Breyer, J., dissenting) ("Given this detailed comprehensive scheme for counting electoral votes [in 3 U.S.C. § 15], there is no reason to believe that federal law either foresees or requires resolution of such a political issue by this Court. . . . However awkward or difficult it may be for Congress to resolve difficult electoral disputes, Congress, being a political body, expresses the people's will far more accurately than does an unelected Court. And the people's will is what elections are about"); see also Issacharoff, "Political Judgments," supra note 109, at 651 (noting that 3 U.S.C. § 15 deliberately left the resolution of election disputes to the

care of political branches and arguing that "[i]n Election 2000, that would have meant Florida's governor and its legislature and the newly-elected members of Congress"); Shane, "Disappearing Democracy," supra note 119, at 584 ("[The Court] could have deferred to Congress under the political question doctrine . . . the final resolution of the question whether any state has properly administered its appointment of presidential electors").

129. See Scott v. Sandford, 60 U.S. 393 (1856).
130. Joan Biskupic, "Election Still Splits Court," *USA Today*, Jan. 22, 2001, at 1A.
131. See Howard Gillman, *The Votes that Counted* (2001), 174; id. at 189 ("The five justices in the *Bush v. Gore* majority are thus the only judges involved in this election dispute who fall uniquely within the category that is most indicative of a partisan justice: they made a decision that was consistent with their political preferences but inconsistent with precedent and inconsistent with what would have been predicted given their views in other cases"); Roosevelt, *Myth of Judicial Activism*, supra note 125, at 194 (defending, in a qualified way, the "constitutional crisis" theory, but wondering whether "if Gore had been ahead and Bush the one seeking recounts, would the same five justices have intervened to stop them? In all fairness, I think the answer to this question has to be no"); Amar, "Should We Trust Judges?," supra note 119 ("When my students ask about the case, I will tell them that we should and must accept it. But we need not, and should not, respect it"); Ronald Dworkin, "A Badly Flawed Election," *N.Y. Rev. of Books*, Jan. 11, 2001, at 53 ("The conservatives stopped the democratic process in its tracks, with thousands of votes yet uncounted, first by ordering an unjustified stay of the statewide recount of the Florida vote that was already in progress, and then declaring, in one of the least persuasive Supreme Court opinions that I have ever read, that there was no time left for the recount to continue"); Editorial, "Judges' Ideology," *Boston Globe*, June 28, 2001, at A14 ("That decision, widely derided for its flimsy legal underpinnings, was clearly driven by ideology"); Neal Kumar Katyal, Op-Ed, "Politics over Principle," *Wash. Post*, Dec. 14, 2000, at A35 (predicting that the Court's "lawless and unprecedented" ruling would be seen as "Exhibit A in a new academic movement dedicated to exposing the Supreme Court's political biases").
132. Mortimer B. Zuckerman, "A Time for Healing," *U.S. News & World Rep.*, Dec. 25, 2000, at 88.
133. Maureen Dowd, Op-Ed., "The Bloom Is Off the Robe," *N.Y. Times*, Dec. 13, 2000, at A35.
134. Michael S. Greve, "The Real Division in the Court," *Wkly. Standard*, Dec. 25, 2000, at 28.
135. See Biskupic, "Election Still Splits Court," supra note 130 ("[T]he decision was particularly uncomfortable for O'Connor because she, along with Chief Justice Rehnquist . . . have considered retirement"); Sanford Levinson, "Return of Legal Realism," *Nation*, Jan. 8–15, 2001, at 8 ("Bush v. Gore is all too easily explainable as the decision of five conservative Republicans—at least two of whom are eager to retire and be replaced by Republicans nominated by a Republican President"); see also Jack M. Balkin and Sanford Levinson, "Understanding the Constitutional Revolution," *Va. L. Rev.* 87 (2001): 1083 ("It is perfectly normal for Presidents to entrench members of their party in the judiciary. . . . It is quite another matter for members of the federal judiciary to select a president who will entrench like-minded colleagues in the judiciary").
136. Zuckerman, "A Time for Healing," supra note 132.
137. Bruce Ackerman, "The Court Packs Itself," *Am. Prospect*, Feb. 12, 2001, at 48.
138. Id.

139. Id.

140. Jeffrey Rosen, "Disgrace: The Supreme Court Commits Suicide," *New Republic*, Dec. 25, 2000, at 18.

141. Reported in John C. Yoo, "In Defense of the Court's Legitimacy," in Sunstein and Epstein, *The Vote*, supra note 124, at 223, 224. The ad read, "[W]hen a bare majority of the U.S. Supreme Court halted the recount of ballots under Florida law, the five justices were acting as political proponents for candidate Bush, not as judges." Id.

142. Savage, "Vote Case Fallout," supra note 119, at 33 (quoting Cass Sunstein); see also Linda Greenhouse, "The Legal Spectacle: Divining the Consequences of a Court Divided," *N.Y. Times*, Dec. 17, 2000, § 4, at 1.

143. Gary Kamiya, "Supreme Court to Democracy: Drop Dead," *Slate*, Dec. 14, 2000, http://archive.salon.com/politics/feature/2000/12/14/bush/index.html.

144. Rosen, "Disgrace," supra note 140, at 20.

145. Larry D. Kramer, Op-Ed, "No Surprise, It's an Activist Court," in Correspondents of *The New York Times*, *36 Days*, supra note 88, at 317.

146. Calvin Trillin, "What Must Have Happened to Create the Supreme Court Decision in *Bush v. Gore*," *Nation*, Jan. 8–15, 2001, at 8.

147. Linda Greenhouse gets the credit for calling this the third Rehnquist Court. Linda Greenhouse, "The Third Rehnquist Court," Foreword to Craig Bradley, *The Rehnquist Legacy* (2005), xiii–xiv. See Jan Crawford Greenburg, *Supreme Conflict: The Inside Story of the Struggle for Control of the United States Supreme Court* (2007), 162 (identifying the 1992 term as the one in which Justice Kennedy began to vote with the "more liberal wing" on some of the Court's more "divisive" cases); J. Harvie Wilkinson III, "The Rehnquist Court at Twilight," *Stan. L. Rev.* 58 (2006): 1970–71 ("At the beginning of the twenty-first century, almost as if on cue, something happened. The Rehnquist Court shifted course").

148. See Hamdan v. Rumsfeld, 548 U.S. 557 (2006); Hamdi v. Rumsfeld, 542 U.S. 507 (2004).

149. See Grutter v. Bollinger, 539 U.S. 306 (2003) (upholding affirmative action admissions process at the University of Michigan Law School); Lawrence v. Texas, 539 U.S. 558 (2003) (holding a Texas law banning consensual same-sex sodomy unconstitutional).

150. Michael S. Greve, "The Term the Constitution Died," July 25, 2003, http://www.aei.org/include/pub_print.asp?pubID=18112.

151. See Stuart Taylor, Jr., "Veering Left: The Art of Judicial Evolution," *Nat'l J.* 35 (2003): 2154 (noting that on issues of racial preferences, abortion, and gay rights, conservatives claimed that "Supreme Court justices are overly attentive to elite opinion"); see, e.g., Lino A. Graglia, "It's Not Constitutionalism, It's Judicial Activism," *Harv. J. L. & Pub. Pol'y* 19 (1996): 298 ("[T]he effect of rulings of unconstitutionality over the past four decades has been to enact the policy preferences of the cultural elite on the far left of the American political spectrum"); Robert H. Bork, Op-Ed, "American Conservatism: The Soul of the Law," *Wall St. J.*, Jan. 20, 2003, at A14 (criticizing the Court's increased reference of international law in decisions, such as *Lawrence*, instead of reliance on constitutional text and noting that "[t]he tendency, therefore, is to develop a universal 'constitutional' law which, as in America, is a product of the opinions of an international intellectual elite"); Jonah Goldberg, "It's Alive!: Why the Constitution Should Remain Dead," *Nat'l Rev. Online*, July 8, 2003, http://www.nationalreview.com/goldberg/goldberg070803.asp ("The fact is that the Court rarely reflects popular opinion so much as elite opinion. . . . For example, the Court recently upheld racial preferences even though a large majority of Americans consistently oppose them. The Court based its ruling not on what Americans *want* but on

what it thinks Americans *need* . . ."); John O'Sullivan, "Affirmative Action Forever?," *Nat'l Rev.*, July 28, 2003, at 14 (arguing that "passionate" support from the elite, not "consistent public hostility to racial preferences," won out in the affirmative action decisions).

152. See Greenburg, *Supreme Conflict*, supra note 147, at 161 (attributing the term to Judge Laurence Silberman).

153. This was no new idea. The references below stretch back into the 1980s and are merely illustrative. See Robert H. Bork, *The Tempting of America: The Political Seduction of the Law* (1990), 135, 243; William Bradford Reynolds, "Renewing the American Constitutional Heritage," *Harv. J. L. & Pub. Pol'y* 8 (1985): 228, 233.

154. See *Grutter*, 539 U.S. at 350 (Thomas, J., concurring in part and dissenting in part) ("The majority upholds the Law School's racial discrimination not by interpreting the people's Constitution, but by responding to a faddish slogan of the cognoscenti").

155. *Lawrence*, 539 U.S. at 602 (Scalia, J., dissenting).

156. See Bowers v. Hardwick, 478 U.S. 186, 187–88 (1986). For an account of the facts underlying *Bowers*, see William N. Eskridge, Jr., *Dishonorable Passions: Sodomy Laws in America, 1861–2003* (2008), 233–37.

157. *Bowers*, 478 U.S. at 194.

158. Id. at 200 (Blackmun, J., dissenting); see also William N. Eskridge, Jr., "Some Effects of Identity-Based Social Movements on Constitutional Law in the Twentieth Century," *Mich. L. Rev.* 100 (2002): 2182 ("White's obsessive focus on 'homosexual sodomy,' notwithstanding the statute's inclusion of sodomy of all kinds, exposed the Court to criticism that it was not treating gay people impartially").

159. *Bowers*, 478 U.S. at 200–01 (Blackmun, J., dissenting) (arguing that the privacy claim "does not depend in any way on [plaintiff's] sexual orientation").

160. See George J. Church, "Knocking on the Bedroom Door," *Time*, July 4, 1986; John Rechy, Op-Ed, "A High Court Decision and a Sense of Betrayal," *L.A. Times*, July 6, 1986, at 1.

161. Curtis J. Sitomer, "Private Lives, Public Law," *Christian Sci. Monitor*, July 17, 1986, at 23; see also Mike Royo, "Is Your Neighbour a 'Sex Criminal'?," *Chi. Trib.*, July 2, 1986, at 3 (mocking the criminalization of sodomy).

162. Larry Rohter, "Friend and Foe See Homosexual Defeat," *N.Y. Times*, July 1, 1986, at A19 (quoting, additionally, a New York City Council member calling *Bowers* "the best decision ever made").

163. Lawrence v. Texas, 539 U.S. 558 (2003). The facts underlying the case are recounted in Eskridge, *Dishonorable Passions*, supra note 156, at 299–301.

164. See Greenburg, *Supreme Conflict*, supra note 147, at 37.

165. *Lawrence*, 539 U.S. at 578.

166. Id. at 567.

167. Justice O'Connor would not have overruled *Bowers*. Id. at 579 (O'Connor, J., concurring).

168. "Evangelist Calls for New Court," *N.Y. Times*, July 16, 2003, at A12.

169. Mitchell Landsberg and John M. Glionna, "High Court Term Ends: Sodomy Ruling Fuels the Culture War," *L.A. Times*, June 27, 2003, at A31; see also *Lawrence*, 539 U.S. at 590 (Scalia, J., dissenting); Landsberg and Glionna, "High Court Term Ends," supra.

170. Christopher Heredia, "Conservatives Condemn 'Error of Biblical Proportions,'" *San Fran. Chron.*, June 27, 2003, at A6.

171. Dahlia Lithwick, "The Ghost of the Warren Court Past," *Slate*, June 26, 2003, http://www.slate.com/id/2084657/entry/2084901/.

172. See Gratz v. Bollinger, 539 U.S. 244, 254 (2003).
173. See Grutter v. Bollinger, 539 U.S. 306, 315 (2003) (listing soft variables, such as the "enthusiasm of recommenders" and the "quality of the undergraduate institution") (citation omitted).
174. See *Grutter*, 539 U.S. at 328.
175. *Gratz*, 539 U.S. at 271 (discussing the test set forth by Justice Powell in Regents Univ. Cal. v. Bakke, 438 U.S. 265, 318 (1978)).
176. Compare *Gratz*, 539 U.S. at 255 (granting twenty points to any member of an "underrepresented racial or ethnic minority group" in an index where one hundred points guarantee admission) with *Grutter*, 539 U.S. at 316 (singling out race as a soft factor of particular importance).
177. See *Grutter*, 539 U.S. at 349 (Scalia, J., dissenting) ("The Constitution proscribes government discrimination on the basis of race, and state-provided education is no exception"); id. at 353 (Thomas, J., dissenting) ("The Constitution abhors classifications based on race, not only because those classifications can harm favored races or are based on illegitimate motives, but also because every time the government places citizens on racial registers and makes race relevant to the provision of burdens or benefits, it demeans us all").
178. See *Grutter*, 539 U.S. at 378 (Rehnquist, C. J., dissenting) (taking sole issue with the narrow tailoring prong of the test and criticizing the majority's acceptance of the university's claims as "unprecedented in . . . deference"); id. at 389 (Kennedy, J., dissenting) (concurring with Chief Justice Rehnquist and further arguing that the realities of the law school plan involve making race outcome determinative for many members of the 15 to 20 percent of the class admitted for reasons other than high Law School Admission Test scores and grades).
179. Charles Lane, "Affirmative Action for Diversity Is Upheld," *Wash. Post*, June 24, 2003, at A1.
180. Cynthia L. Estlund, "Putting *Grutter* to Work: Diversity, Integration, and Affirmative Action in the Workplace," *Berkeley J. Emp. & Lab. L.* 26 (2005): 2.
181. See "Anyone for a Bit of Legal Fudge?," *Economist*, June 28, 2003, at 57; "The Wrong Decision, Poorly Made," *Economist*, June 28, 2003, at 14; see also Editorial, "Court Gives Confusion the Nod," *Denver Post*, June 24, 2003, at B06 ("How can you give minority applicants an 'edge' without allowing race to be 'the determining factor'? Isn't that like telling people it's fine to go singing in the rain so long as no one gets wet?").
182. "Bit of Legal Fudge," supra note 181.
183. Peter Berkowitz, "Dubious Diversity," *Wkly. Standard*, July 17, 2003, at 16.
184. Jim Sleeper, Op-Ed, "Countermeasures Against Racism Have Gone Too Far for Much Too Long," *L.A. Times*, June 24, 2003, at B15.
185. Quoted in Anderson, *Pursuit of Fairness*, supra note 28, at 272; see also *Gratz*, 539 U.S. at 304 (Ginsburg, J., dissenting) ("[I]nstitutions of higher education may resort to camouflage"). Not all liberals were much happier with the decisions. See Roosevelt, *Myth of Judicial Activism*, supra note 125, at 183 ("[The Court] grant[s] different measures of deference to different kinds of discrimination. . . . From this perspective, strict scrutiny for affirmative action is illegitimate"); Richard Cohen, Editorial, "Confused O'Connor," *Wash. Post*, June 26, 2003, at A29 (calling the university's argument as accepted in O'Connor's opinion "total nonsense—and insulting to blacks and Hispanics who are not mere condiments recruited to add spice to an otherwise bland law school class").
186. See Nev. Dept. of Human Res. v. Hibbs, 538 U.S. 721 (2003) (concerning the Family and Medical Leave Act, 29 U.S.C. §§ 2601–54, 2617(a) (2008)); Tennessee v.

Lane, 541 U.S. 509 (2004) (concerning Title II of the Americans with Disabilities Act, 42 U.S.C. §§ 12131–165, § 12132 (2008)).

187. Warren Richley, "States' Rights Momentum on Court May Be Waning," *Christian Sci. Monitor*, May 19, 2004, at 2.

188. Quoted in Warren Richley, "Court Boosts Civil Rights Law for Disabled," *Christian Sci. Monitor*, May 18, 2004, at 1.

189. Gonzales v. Raich, 545 U.S. 1 (2005).

190. See Dahlia Lithwick, "Dude, Where's My Integrity?," *Slate*, Nov. 29, 2004, http://www.slate.com/id/2110204/ ("[S]hould the court's staunchest conservatives get away with being for states' rights only when the state in question isn't California? No. Will they? Oh, you can bet your bong on it"); see also Ann Althouse, "The Marijuana Case: A Great Test of Law and Politics," blog post, Nov. 28, 2004, 09:32 CST, http://althouse.blogspot.com/2004/11/marijuana-case-great-test-of-law-and.html.

191. Justice Kennedy did not author a separate opinion in *Raich*, but Justice Scalia felt the need to explain why his holding was consistent with *Lopez*. See *Raich*, 545 U.S. at 37 (Scalia, J., concurring) ("Congress may regulate even noneconomic local activity if that regulation is a necessary part of a more general regulation of interstate commerce").

192. Editorial, "High on the Commerce Clause," *Wall St. J.*, June 8, 2005, at A14.

193. "Up in Smoke: States' Rights," *Economist*, June 11, 2005, at 49; see also Ilya Somin, "*Gonzales v. Raich*: Federalism as a Casualty of the War on Drugs," *Cornell J. L. & Pub. Pol'y* 15 (2006): 1; Ernest A. Young, "Just Blowing Smoke? Politics, Doctrine, and the Federalist Revival after *Gonzales v. Raich*," *Sup. Ct. Rev.*, 2005: 3; Nick Gillespie, "What Were the Judges Smoking?," *Cincinnati Post*, June 8, 2005, at A8.

194. See David W. Moore, "Public Overwhelmingly Backs Bush in Attacks on Afghanistan," Gallup News Serv., Oct. 8, 2001, http://www.gallup.com/poll/4966/Public-Overwhelmingly-Backs-Bush-Attacks-Afghanistan.aspx; Richard L. Berke and Janet Elder, "Poll Finds Strong Support for U.S. Use of Military Force," *N.Y. Times*, Sept. 16, 2001, § 1, at 6; Jeanne Cummings et al., "Three Challenges: Bush Looks to Rally Politicians and Allies and a Shaken Public," *Wall St. J.*, Sept. 13, 2001, at A1.

195. See Neil A. Lewis and Eric Schmitt, "Inquiry Finds Abuses at Guantanamo Bay," *N.Y. Times*, May 1, 2005, § 1, at 35; Douglas Jehl, "C.I.A. Is Seen as Seeking New Role on Detainees," *N.Y. Times*, Feb. 16, 2005, at A16; Bob Herbert, Editorial, "Our Friends, the Torturers," *N.Y. Times*, Feb. 18, 2005, at A27; Ian Fisher, "Reports of Secret U.S. Prisons in Europe Draw Ire and Otherwise Red Faces," *N.Y. Times*, Dec. 1, 2005, at A14; see also William N. Eskridge, Jr., and John Ferejohn, *America's Statutory Constitution* (forthcoming), at Chapter 9 at 22–23 (discussing the Bush administration's development of interrogation practices after Sept. 11, 2001).

196. See Hamdan v. Rumsfeld, 548 U.S. 557 (2006) (holding that the military commissions established at Guantanamo Bay were procedurally deficient); Hamdi v. Rumsfeld, 542 U.S. 507 (2004) (holding that due process required that U.S. citizens held as enemy combatants be given a meaningful chance to contest the factual basis for their detention). For a discussion of the public events leading up to the Court's *Hamdi* decision, which included the Solicitor General's urging the Court to "trust the executive" in times of war, the controversy surrounding the U.S. Bybee-Yoo torture memorandum, and the uncovering of the prisoner abuse at Abu Ghraib prison, see Eskridge and Ferejohn, *America's Statutory Constitution*, supra note 195, at Chapter 9 at 23–26.

197. Levin, *Men in Black*, supra note 6, at 12.

198. See Dickerson v. United States, 530 U.S. 428 (2000); Miranda v. Arizona, 384 U.S. 436 (1966).

199. See Joan Biskupic, "Rehnquist Shifts on Miranda with Little Warning," *USA Today*, June 27, 2000, at 4A; Jan Crawford Greenburg, "High Court Upholds *Miranda* Warnings; Once a Critic Himself, Rehnquist Rebuffs Ruling's Challengers," *Chi. Trib.*, June 27, 2000, at 1; see also Paul G. Cassell, "The Paths Not Taken," *Mich. L. Rev.* 99 (2001): 900.

200. See Atkins v. Virginia, 536 U.S. 304 (2002); Roper v. Simmons, 543 U.S. 551 (2005).

201. Douglas H. Ginsburg, "On Constitutionalism," *Cato Sup. Ct. Rev.*, 2002–2003: 19.

202. Although the references to international consensus are undeniable, the tiny part they play in the decisions and the fact that they tend to be illustrative rather than logical preconditions for the decision argue against the vehemence of the reaction. See *Atkins*, 536 U.S. at 316n21 ("Moreover, within the world community, the imposition of the death penalty for crimes committed by mentally retarded offenders is overwhelmingly disapproved"); *Lawrence*, 539 U.S. at 572 (rebutting the claim in *Bowers* by Chief Justice Burger that sodomy cut against Western civilization and Judeo-Christian moral and ethical standards, the Court mentions a 1957 committee advice to the British Parliament and a decision of the European Court of Human Rights); *Roper*, 543 U.S. at 575 ("Our determination that the death penalty is disproportionate punishment for offenders under 18 finds confirmation in the stark reality that the United States is the only country in the world that continues to give official sanction to the juvenile death penalty. This reality does not become controlling . . .").

203. Edwin Meese III, Afterword to Levin, *Men in Black*, supra note 6, at 209, 211; see also Fox News, "DeLay Rips Justice Kennedy," Apr. 20, 2005, http://www.foxnews.com/story/0,2933,154009,00.html (quoting House Majority Leader Tom DeLay: "We've got Justice Kennedy writing decisions based upon international law, not the Constitution of the United States. That's just outrageous . . .").

204. Levin, *Men in Black*, supra note 6, at 11–12; James Taranto, "James Dobson Imitates Ted Kennedy," *Wall St. J. Best of the Web Today*, Apr. 12, 2005, http://www.opinionjournal.com/best/?id=110006548.

205. Phyllis Schlafly, *The Supremacists: The Tyranny of Judges and How to Stop It* (2004), vii.

206. Robertson, *Courting Disaster*, supra note 7, at xxiv.

207. See Mike Allen, "GOP Seeks More Curbs on Courts," *Wash. Post*, May 12, 2005, at A03.

208. See Debra Rosenberg, "The War on Judges," *Newsweek*, Apr. 25, 2005, at 23 (reporting that O'Connor also had a private lunch with Rep. Steve King of the House Judiciary Committee).

209. See Caprice L. Roberts, "In Search of Judicial Activism: Dangers in Quantifying the Qualitative," *Tenn. L. Rev.* 74 (2007): 570 (discussing difficulties with defining activism).

210. Keck, *Most Activist Supreme Court in History*, supra note 69, at 7.

211. Graglia, "It's Not Constitutionalism," supra note 151, at 296.

212. Sunstein, *Radicals in Robes*, supra note 6, at 42–43 ("This is the value neutral definition of activism. It doesn't say whether activism is good or bad"); see also Levin, *Men in Black*, supra note 6, at 13 ("[J]udicial activist[s] . . . substitute their will for the judgment of deliberative bodies").

213. Adam Cohen, Editorial, "Psst . . . Justice Scalia . . . You Know, You're an Activist Judge, Too," *N.Y. Times*, Apr. 19, 2005, at A20.

214. Keck, *Most Activist Supreme Court in History*, supra note 69, at 286; see also Balkin and Levinson, "Understanding the Constitutional Revolution," supra note 135, at 1045 ("In the past year the Supreme Court of the United States has decided an election and installed a president. In the past ten years it has produced fundamental changes in American constitutional law. These two phenomena are related").

215. Michael S. Greve, "A Conservative View of the Court," *Nat'l Rev.*, July 16, 2003, at 35.

216. Jeffrey Rosen, "The Unregulated Offensive," *N.Y. Times Mag.*, Apr. 17, 2005, at 46.
217. See Keck, *Most Activist Supreme Court in History*, supra note 69, at 181.
218. See W. John Moore, "A Little Group Makes Big Law," *Nat'l J.* 29 (1997): 2323.
219. See Keck, *Most Activist Supreme Court in History*, supra note 69, at 181–82.
220. See Peggy Walsh-Sarnecki, "The Men Who Would End Affirmative Action," *Detroit Free Press*, Aug. 25, 1998, at 1A (quoting William Alpert).
221. Keck, *Most Activist Supreme Court in History*, supra note 69, at 8 (attributing the sentiment to Justices Scalia and Thomas).
222. Antonin Scalia, *A Matter of Interpretation: Federal Courts and the Law* (1997), 23.
223. See "Are Judges Thwarting the Will of the People?," *CNN Crossfire*, CNN, Dec. 28, 1999. Hutchinson's comment about "interpreting the Constitution" followed a comment from David Corn, former editor of *The Nation*, in which Corn noted that protection of states from monetary damages is nowhere mentioned in the text of the Tenth Amendment or the Constitution. Corn makes a point akin to that made here, saying, "The thing that bugs me about your position . . . is that you think this only happens in the liberal end of the spectrum, that judicial activism is a buzzword for liberal judges." Id. The case that drove this discussion was Alden v. Maine, 527 U.S. 706 (1999), which held that Congress could not subject states to suits for monetary damages without state consent.
224. See Benjamin Wittes, *Confirmation Wars: Preserving Independent Courts in Angry Times* (2006), 23; id. at 24 (acknowledging the Republicans' like failure).
225. Nina Totenberg, "Looking Back at This Term's Decisions by the U.S. Supreme Court," *Talk of the Nation*, NPR, July 8, 2003.
226. Jon Stewart et al., *America (the Book): A Citizen's Guide to Democracy Inaction* (2004), 82.
227. Jeffrey Rosen, "The New Look of Liberalism on the Court," *N.Y. Times Mag.*, Oct. 5, 1997, at 62 ("The liberal Justices, Ginsburg most of all, have become the partisans of judicial restraint").
228. See Cass R. Sunstein, "Interest Groups in American Public Law," *Stan. L. Rev.* 38 (1985): 30 (arguing that the Equal Protection Clause of the Fourteenth Amendment and judicial interpretation of the Administrative Procedure Act represent judicial protection against governments being captured by factions); Cass R. Sunstein, "Naked Preferences and the Constitution," *Colum. L. Rev.* 84 (1984): 1691–92 (arguing that the Constitution contains, and the Court should enforce, prohibitions against interest groups capturing legislatures).
229. See Cass R. Sunstein, *One Case at a Time: Judicial Minimalism on the Supreme Court* (1999); Sunstein, *Radicals in Robes*, supra note 6, at xiii ("I argue for minimalism in this book").
230. Sunstein, *Radicals in Robes*, supra note 6, at 35.
231. See Mark V. Tushnet, *Taking the Constitution Away from the Courts* (1999), 154 ("Doing away with judicial review would have one clear effect: It would return all constitutional decision-making to the people acting politically").
232. See, e.g., Rachel E. Barkow, "More Supreme Than Court?," *Colum. L. Rev.* 102 (2002): 336; Stephen M. Griffin, "Judicial Supremacy and Equal Protection in a Democracy of Rights," *U. Pa. J. Const. L.* 4 (2002): 282; Larry D. Kramer, "The Supreme Court, 2000 Term—Foreword, We the Court," *Harv. L. Rev.* 115 (2001): 14; Robert C. Post and Reva B. Siegel, "Equal Protection Law: Federal Antidiscrimination Legislation After *Morrison* and *Kimel*," *Yale L. J.* 110 (2000): 444; see generally Barry Friedman, "The Cycles of Constitutional Theory," *Law & Contemp. Probs.* 67 (2004): 149–74 (analyzing the cyclical shifts in liberal and conservative critiques of Supreme Court decisions).
233. Greve, "A Conservative View," supra note 215, at 35.

234. See Gonzales v. Oregon, 546 U.S. 243 (2006).

235. Editorial, "Federalism, à la Carte," *Wall St. J.*, Jan. 18, 2006, at A10.

236. Editorial, "Unconstitutional Cannabis," *L.A. Times*, June 7, 2005, at B12.

237. Bork, *Tempting of America*, supra note 153, at 3.

238. Quoted in Victoria Sackett and Wendy Benedetto, "The Experts Look at Souter— and Wonder," *USA Today*, July 24, 1990, at 9A .

239. Linda Greenhouse, "The Decision: A Nominee Deemed Politic, Not Political," *N.Y. Times*, May 14, 1994, § 1, at 10 (noting the strong bipartisan support Breyer received); see also Henry J. Reske, "Ginsburg Gains Easy Confirmation," *A.B.A. J.*, Sept. 1993, at 18; Pamela Constable, "Breyer Wins Senate Confirmation," *Boston Globe*, July 20, 1994, at 3 (noting that members on both sides of the aisle "hailed" Breyer's "intellectual abilities, his moderate judicial approach and potential as a consensus builder on the court"); "Breyer Already in 'Moderate' Sync," *Cincinnati Post*, Aug. 12, 1994, at 2A.

240. For a discussion of the resistance to Thomas's appointment and the strength of opposition that followed the allegations of sexual harassment, see generally Jane Mayer and Jill Abramson, *Strange Justice: The Selling of Clarence Thomas* (1995); Paul Simon, *Advice & Consent: Clarence Thomas, Robert Bork and the Intriguing History of the Supreme Court's Nomination Battles* (1992), 76–131.

241. See Ken Foskett, *Judging Thomas: The Life and Times of Clarence Thomas* (2004), 3 (calling the Thomas confirmation "the most racially and sexually charged Supreme Court drama in American history"); R. W. Apple, Jr., "The Thomas Confirmation," *N.Y. Times*, Oct. 16, 1991, at A1 (describing the 52–48 vote as "one of the narrowest margins in history").

242. See Sunstein, *Radicals in Robes*, supra note 6, at 14–15 (describing Justices Ginsburg and Breyer as "exceptionally distinguished choices," who "because of their centrism . . . cannot be seen as ideological counterweights to Justices Antonin Scalia and Clarence Thomas").

243. Charles E. Schumer, Op-Ed, "Judging by Ideology," *N.Y. Times*, June 26, 2001, at A19.

244. Patrick J. Buchanan, *Where the Right Went Wrong* (2004), 225–26.

245. See Duane Murray Oldfield, *The Right and the Righteous: The Christian Right Confronts the Republican Party* (1996), 101 (discussing Focus on the Family's sizable budget and operation); Elisabeth Bumiller, "War Rooms (and Chests) Ready for a Court Vacancy," *N.Y. Times*, June 20, 2005, at A13 (reporting that activists are on "code red" for a vacancy); Gail Russell Chaddock, "Court Nominees Will Trigger Rapid Response," *Christian Sci. Monitor*, July 7, 2005, at 2 (describing a "more agile and better financed" body of activists poised for confirmation fights); Bob Davis and Robert S. Greenberger, "Objection! Two Old Foes Plot Tactics in Battle over Judgeships," *Wall St. J.*, March 2, 2004, at A1 (describing People for the American Way's large budget and staff); Robert Deutsch, Rehnquist's Appearance Spurs Speculation About Court Vacancy, *USA Today*, Jan. 21, 2005, at http://www.usatoday.com/news/washington/2005–01–21-rehnquist_x.htm?loc=interstitialskip (discussing war rooms and funding); Michael A. Fletcher and Charles Babington, "Partisans Gear Up for High Court Fight Ahead," *Wash. Post*, March 13, 2005, at A5 (noting preparations of more than 185 progressive organizations); Robert Novak, "Compiling Profiles of Judicial Nominees Plows New Ground," *Chi. Sun-Times*, May 16, 2005, at 45 (reporting on investigators hired to look into potential court nominees).

246. See generally Catherine Fisk and Erwin Chemerinsky, "The Filibuster," *Stan. L. Rev.* 49 (1997): 181–254 (summarizing the development and practices involved in the filibuster).

247. Neil A. Lewis, "Mixed Results for Bush in Battles over Judges," *N.Y. Times*, Oct. 22, 2004, at A1 (discussing the Democrats' new strategy to oppose even those Republi-

can judicial nominees with "strong credentials and no embarrassing flaws"). Bruce Ackerman may have been the genesis of this idea. See Levin, *Men in Black*, supra note 6, at 177 (quoting Ackerman after *Bush v. Gore*: "The first step should be a moratorium on Supreme Court appointments until the American people return to the polls in 2004. Under present rules, it only takes forty senators to block any appointment to the Court").

248. Quoted in Eleanor Clift, "Nuclear Option," *Newsweek*, April 8, 2005, http://www .msnbc.msn.com/id/7430895/site/newsweek/page/o/ (web-exclusive commentary).

249. Quoted in Carl Hulse, "Frist Warns on Filibuster over Bush Nominees," *N.Y. Times*, Nov. 12, 2004, at A21; see also Terry Eastland, "If You Were a Democrat," *Wkly. Standard*, March 28, 2005, at 7 ("No Senate minority ever before had made routine use of the filibuster to bloc judicial nominees who would have enjoyed majority Senate support").

250. Quoted in Duncan Currie, "A New Weapon in the Judges' War," *Wkly. Standard*, Dec. 6, 2004, at 11 (claiming Republicans were "crying wolf" that Democrats were filibustering circuit court nominees).

251. Chuck Raasch, "Trent Lott Looks Back on Leadership," Gannett News Serv., Aug. 18, 2005, at 1 (quoting Trent Lott); see also David D. Kirkpatrick, "Frist Set to Use Religious Stage on Judges Issue," *N.Y. Times*, Apr. 15, 2005, at A1 (quoting Senator McCain: "When Bill Clinton was president, we, effectively, in the Judiciary Committee blocked a number of his nominees"). But see Charles Babington, "Frist Urges End to Nominee Filibusters," *Wash. Post*, Apr. 25, 2005, at A01 (reporting that Republicans claimed their strategy of "bottling up nominations in committee" was "less drastic" than filibusters).

252. See Clift, "Nuclear Option," supra note 248; Currie, "New Weapon," supra note 250 (referring to Republican attempts to stymie the Democratic filibuster as a "nuclear option" that could "take several shapes").

253. See Holly Yeager, "Judgment Day Approaches," *Fin. Times*, May 10, 2005, at 17.

254. Sheryl Gay Stolberg, "As Vote on Filibuster Nears, G.O.P. Senators Face Mounting Pressure," *N.Y. Times*, Apr. 20, 2005, at A19; see also Carl Hulse and Linda Greenhouse, "Republicans May Hasten Showdown on Judicial-Nomination Filibusters," *N.Y. Times*, Apr. 13, 2005, at A15; Currie, "New Weapon," supra note 250 ("It's called the 'nuclear option' because I think the Senate would literally melt down. . . . The Democrats would simply grind the Senate to a halt") (quoting Erwin Chemerinsky, professor of law, Duke University School of Law).

255. See David D. Kirkpatrick and Albert Salvato, "In Telecast, Frist Defends His Efforts to Stop Filibusters," *N.Y. Times*, Apr. 25, 2005, at A14 (reporting that MoveOn.org alone was planning to spend $700,000).

256. See David Schuster, "Ad Wars," *MSNBC*, May 19, 2005, http://www.msnbc.msn .com/id/7764695/ (describing the Vader ad); Kirkpatrick and Salvato, "In Telecast, Frist Defends His Efforts," supra note 255 (describing the elephant ad).

257. David D. Kirkpatrick, "Lobbying Heats Up on Filibuster Rule Change," *N.Y. Times*, Apr. 3, 2005, § 1, at 26.

258. Babington, "Frist Urges End," supra note 251.

259. Quoted in "Republicans May Hasten Showdown," supra note 254.

260. "Text of Senate Compromise on Nominations of Judges," *N.Y. Times*, May 24, 2005, at A18.

261. Howard Kurtz, "The Gang of 14, Blogged Down in the Middle," *Wash. Post*, May 29, 2005, at D1.

262. See David D. Kirkpatrick, "Deal Draws Criticism from Left and Right," *N.Y. Times*, May 24, 2005, at A18.

263. See Editorial, "Senate Charade," *Wall St. J.*, May 25, 2005, at A12; Tony Blankley, "A Senate Regency," *Wash. Times*, May 25, 2005, at A19.

264. Kramer, "Supreme Court, 2000 Term—Foreword," supra note 232, at 13 (emphasis added).

265. See Barkow, "More Supreme Than Court?," supra note 232; see also Stephen M. Griffin, *American Constitutionalism* (1996), 208 ("The opinion [in *Casey*] thus asserts that the Court is at the center of the American constitutional universe; that its actions best embody the essence of American constitutionalism").

266. Larry D. Kramer, "Popular Constitutionalism, circa 2004," *Cal. L. Rev.* 92 (2004): 960; see also Larry D. Kramer, *The People Themselves: Popular Constitutionalism and Judicial Review* (2004). Others advanced similar ideas—if under different labels—arguing that constitutional interpretation was better accomplished through channels more democratic than the judiciary. See, e.g., Jamin B. Raskin, *Overruling Democracy: The Supreme Court vs. The American People* (2004), 242 ("[T]he Supreme Court is systematically obstructing the channels of democracy. . . . It's time to reassert our popular sovereignty and reclaim our rightful democratic destiny as the true authors of America"); Tushnet, *Taking the Constitution*, supra note 231; William E. Forbath, "Popular Constitutionalism in the Twentieth Century: Reflections on the Dark Side, the Progressive Constitutional Imagination, and the Enduring Role of Judicial Finality in Popular Understandings of Popular Self-Rule," *Chi.-Kent L. Rev.* 81 (2006): 967 (extending Kramer's historical analysis and argument into the Progressive Era); Griffin, "Judicial Supremacy," supra note 232, at 295 (arguing that in a three-branch government where all branches are obligated to enforce the Constitution, the supremacy of the judiciary "no longer makes sense"); Robert C. Post and Reva B. Siegel, "Legislative Constitutionalism and Section Five Power," *Yale L. J.* 112 (2003): 2059 (advocating a "departmentalism" model that would "permit Congress to serve the function of articulating popular understandings of the Constitution" without robbing the judiciary of its "ability to safeguard constitutional rights"); Jeremy Waldron, "The Core of the Case Against Judicial Review," *Yale L. J.* 115 (2006): 1348 (arguing that judicial review of congressional action is "inappropriate as a mode of final decisionmaking in a free and democratic society"); Keith E. Whittington, "Extrajudicial Constitutional Interpretation: Three Objections and Responses," *N.C. L. Rev.* 80 (2002): 786 (responding to "objections that would displace the authority of nonjudicial actors" to interpret the Constitution and "recognizing a relatively strong authority for extrajudicial constitutional interpretation"); compare Stephen Breyer, *Active Liberty: Interpreting Our Democratic Constitution* (2005), 15 ("[I]t should be possible to trace without much difficulty a line of authority for the making of governmental decisions back to the people themselves. . . . And this authority must be broad. The people must have room to decide and leeway to make mistakes"); Breyer, *Active Liberty*, supra, at 107–08 (describing courts as "ill equipped to make the investigations which should precede most legislation" and concluding that a judge "is not to substitute even his juster will for that of the people" (internal quotations omitted). The concept spawned symposia. See, e.g., "Symposium: The People Themselves: Popular Constitutionalism and Judicial Review," *Chi.-Kent. L. Rev.* 81 (2006): 809–1275; "Symposium: Theories of Taking the Constitution Seriously Outside the Courts," *Fordham L. Rev.* 73 (2005): 1341–476. The critics of popular constitutionalism and the movement away from judicial supremacy were numerous. See, e.g., Larry Alexander and Frederick Schauer, "Defending Judicial Supremacy: A Reply," *Const. Comment.* 17 (2000): 480; Larry Alexander and Lawrence B. Solum, "Popular? Constitutionalism?," *Harv. L. Rev.* 118 (2005): 1629; Daniel A. Farber, "Judicial Review and Its Alternatives: An American Tale," *Wake*

Forest L. Rev. 38 (2003): 449 (arguing that only the judiciary is capable of preserving and enforcing individual rights); Erwin Chemerinsky, "In Defense of Judicial Review: A Reply to Professor Kramer," *Cal. L. Rev.* 92 (2004):1013; Doni Gewirtzman, "Glory Days: Popular Constitutionalism, Nostalgia, and the True Nature of Constitutional Culture," *Geo. L. J.* 93 (2005): 897 (questioning whether the lack of public participation and interest in politics and government can support a system that relies on citizen involvement for constitutional interpretation); Frederick Schauer, "Judicial Supremacy and the Modest Constitution," *Cal. L. Rev.* 92 (2004): 1046 (defending judicial supremacy as the "natural partner of constitutionalism, itself").

267. Kramer, "Supreme Court, 2000 Term—Foreword," supra note 232, at 163.

268. See, e.g., Roberts, "In Search of Judicial Activism," supra note 209; Schlafly, *Tyranny of Judges*, supra note 205; Robert C. Post and Reva B. Siegel, "Popular Constitutionalism, Departmentalism, and Judicial Supremacy," *Cal. L. Rev.* 92 (2004): 1027–44; Editorial, "The Court's Good Week," *Wall St. J.*, June 30, 1997, at A14; "DeLay Rips Justice Kennedy," supra note 203; Tim Jones, "Activists Put Heat on Judges," *Chi. Trib.*, Dec. 5, 2005, at 1 (discussing host of politicians and citizens criticizing judges for a lack of accountability to the people, and the impact on state judge elections); Newt Gingrich, Reviews Written, http://www.amazon.com/gp/cdp/member-reviews/A27WFYW9ZJ5DN1?ie=UTF8&display=public&sort%5Fby=MostRecentReview&page=3.

269. Writing on Amazon.com, Gingrich gave the book five stars and called it "[a] book that will change history" because it "explains what we can do about" the "relentless drive by a liberal establishment toward a secular, multicultural, values-neutral and historically ignorant country at odds with the values of the vast majority of Americans." Newt Gingrich, Reviews Written, http://www.amazon.com/gp/cdp/member-reviews/A27WFYW9ZJ5DN1?ie=UTF8&display=public&sort%5Fby=MostRecentReview&page=3; see also Scott D. Gerber, "The Court, the Constitution, and the History of Ideas," *Vand. L. Rev.* 61 (2008): 1077 ("Robert Bork could have written Larry Kramer's book").

270. Levin, *Men in Black*, supra note 6, at 195.

271. See Schlafly, *Tyranny of Judges*, supra note 205.

272. Buchanan, *Where the Right Went Wrong*, supra note 244, at 224.

273. Robertson, *Courting Disaster*, supra note 7, at xxiv.

274. See Dana Milbank, "And the Verdict on Justice Kennedy Is: Guilty," *Wash. Post*, Apr. 9, 2005, at A3 (reporting on a conference called "Confronting the Judicial War on Faith" in which Schlafly, among others, said, "Congress ought to talk about impeachment" for Justice Kennedy); Robertson, *Courting Disaster*, supra note 7, at xxiv (calling on the "black-robed tyrants" who had "shredded the moral fabric of this nation" to "step down").

275. Rehnquist, 2004 *Year-end Report*, supra note 8, at 7, 8.

276. Robertson, *Courting Disaster*, supra note 7, at 15.

277. "Court's Good Week," supra note 268.

278. Kramer, "Supreme Court, 2000 Term—Foreword," supra note 232, at 169 (concluding his essay).

279. "On His High Horse—George Bush's Progress," *Economist*, Nov. 9, 2002, at 23; see also Morris P. Fiorina et al., *Culture War?* (2005), 49.

280. See Fiorina et al., *Culture War?*, supra note 279, at 14–16. For a gauge of the popular consensus that there are "red" and "blue" states, see "Red States and Blue States," Wikipedia, http://en.wikipedia.org/wiki/Red_states_and_blue_states.

281. Quoted in William Martin, *With God on Our Side: The Rise of the Religious Right in America* (1996), 344 (questioning if the political process could resolve the extensive ideological divide in the country).

282. Quoted in Fiorina et al., *Culture War?*, supra note 279, at 6 (explaining why Bush had not attempted to expand his voter base).

283. Robertson, *Courting Disaster*, supra note 7, at xxiii (adding that this group also "wants to overthrow Christian values by a majority of nonelected judges who serve for life and answer to no one").

284. More than 30 percent of both red and blue staters placed themselves at a four. The next most common identification for both groups is six, followed by five and then three. See Fiorina et al., *Culture War?*, supra note 279, at 28 (Figure 2.2); see also Mary McIntosh, "Understanding the Public's Relationship to Government," in Annenberg Democracy Project, *A Republic Divided* (2007), 55, 65 (reporting that only 50 percent of the country believes that "high-level government officials understand what the public thinks about issues facing the country" and that 48 percent believes that they do not).

285. Geoffrey Layman, *The Great Divide* (2001), 14.

286. Annenberg Democracy Project, *A Republic Divided*, supra note 284, at xvi.

287. Id. at xxi.

288. More than 40 percent of both red and blue staters placed the Democrats at two, and more than 50 percent of both placed the Republicans at six. While Americans consider *themselves* slightly right-leaning but mostly centrist, they view their political parties as noncentrist. Fiorina et al., *Culture War?*, supra note 279, at 28–29 (Figures 2.2 and 2.3); see also Jacob S. Hacker and Paul Pierson, *Off Center: The Republican Revolution and the Erosion of American Democracy* (2005), 9–10 (arguing that the Republican Party's "most committed, mobilized, and deep-pocketed supporters" increasingly pull politicians away from the center); Hacker and Pierson, *Off Center*, supra, at 110–11 (explaining that moderate Republican politicians adopt increasingly conservative agendas to satisfy the "hard Right").

289. See Robert D. Putnam, *Bowling Alone: The Collapse and Revival of American Communities* (2000), 342 ("Americans at the political poles are more engaged in civic life, whereas moderates have tended to drop out"); Layman, *Great Divide*, supra note 285, at 328 ("Even if society has not become more culturally divided, the parties surely have").

290. See Fiorina et al., *Culture War?*, supra note 279, at 116–17 ("[L]egal and pragmatic changes have reduced the discretion of public officials to reward the individuals and groups who support them and punish those who oppose them").

291. Quoted in Martin, *God on Our Side*, supra note 281, at 332.

292. Fiorina et al., *Culture War?*, supra note 279, at 141.

293. See Layman, *Great Divide*, supra note 285, at 151 (Figure 4.4).

294. See Samuel Issacharoff, "Collateral Damage: The Endangered Center in American Politics," *Wm. & Mary L. Rev.* 46 (2004): 422–23.

295. See, e.g., Fiorina et al., *Culture War?*, supra note 279, at 167; Tom Hamburger and Peter Wallsten, *One Party Country: The Republican Plan for Dominance in the 21st Century* (2006), 38–41; Issacharoff, "Collateral Damage," supra note 294, at 428 ("[D]istricts are intentionally constructed to be noncompetitive, removing the power of centrist voters"); Issacharoff, "Collateral Damage," supra note 294, at 29 ("In 2000, 98.5% of incumbents won their elections . . ."); Samuel Issacharoff and Jonathan Nagler, "Protected from Politics: Diminishing Margins of Electoral Competition in U.S. Congressional Elections," *Ohio St. L. J.* 68 (2007): 1126 (documenting that the 1994 and 2006 elections were outliers and noting that "[t]he effect of single-party control of a congressional district is to transform a two-stage equilibrium into a one-stage game").

296. Howard Fineman, "Ready to Blow," *Newsweek*, May 23, 2005, at 28.

297. Fiorina et al., *Culture War?*, supra note 279, at ix.

298. Quoted in Ethan Bronner, "Polls Indicate Most Are of Two Minds on Abortion," *Boston Globe*, Apr. 19, 1989, at 3.

299. William A. Galston and Elaine C. Kamarck, Third Way, *The Politics of Polarization* (2005), http://www.third-way.com/products/16, at 37.

300. See Thomas B. Edsall, *Building Red America* (2006), 52 (discussing the return to wedge issues and Karl Rove's focus on social issues); Hamburger and Wallsten, *One Party Country*, supra note 295, at 97 ("[T]he White House sought to drive a wedge between two core Democratic constituencies: the teachers' unions . . . and the African American and Latino parents who were desperate over the condition of their children's schools").

301. Quoted in Edsall, *Building Red America*, supra note 300, at 64.

302. See id. at 53. Indeed, polls showed that voters consistently ranked gay rights as being among the most divisive and most important political issues to them, even where other issues might have more tangible effects on their lives. See id. at 87 (discussing the disproportionate focus on homosexuality as compared with other relevant family-based issues, like divorce, that have a greater national impact); Fiorina et al., *Culture War?*, supra note 279, at 21 (noting that though the difference in acceptance of homosexuality is only 10 percent, this is still the widest opinion gap between red states and blue states on the issue of religion and morality). While issues such as the death penalty reveal a 7-point split between red and blue states, issues like gays in the military (16-point split), discrimination on the basis of sexual orientation (11-point split), and adoption by homosexuals (12-point split) proved more divisive. Fiorina et al., *Culture War?*, supra note 279, at 25.

 Abortion too was a divisive issue among the more ideological crowd. The ideological divide between red and blue states on abortion grew more than any other issue between 1972 and 1996. See Layman, *Great Divide*, supra note 285, at 110; see also Fiorina et al., *Culture War?*, supra note 279, at 25 (noting an 11-point split between red and blue states on the issue of abortion).

303. See Craig and O'Brien, *Abortion and American Politics*, supra note 53, at 326–27 (quoting Sarah Weddington, the lawyer for Roe in *Roe*, calling the decision "[p]atronizing" and characterizing the ruling as saying that "you people in the legislature can erect hurdles and roadblocks so that only women who are the most determined, who have the most money, who are the most sophisticated [can get an abortion]"; Tom Jipping, a lawyer for a conservative group, saying the pro-choice people "got exactly what they wanted"; Andrea Shelton, of another conservative group, saying, "These women will never be happy until they have everything. They won. They know they won"; Ruth Jones, a pro-choice advocate, saying "*Roe v. Wade* was dismantled"); Tony Mauro, "Future of 'Roe' Hangs by One Vote," *USA Today*, June 30, 1992, at 1A (quoting James Bopp, Jr., of the National Right to Life Committee, saying, "We lost 95% today," and Marcia Greenberger, of the National Women's Law Center, describing the consequences of the decision as "frightening").

304. "Abortion: From Legal Battle to Political Wars," *Nightline*, ABC, June 30, 1992.

305. Paul M. Barrett, "Split Decision: Supreme Court Curbs, but Won't Overrule, Right to Abortion," *Wall St. J.*, June 30, 1992, at A1.

306. Clift, "Nuclear Option," supra note 248; see also Matt Bai, *The Argument: Billionaires, Bloggers, and the Battle to Remake Democratic Politics* (2007), 88 ("To the rest of the country, this probably sounded like a silly fracas over *Robert's Rules of Order*, but in Washington it was all people could talk about, because people understood that it was really about the Supreme Court").

307. Layman, *Great Divide*, supra note 285, at 14 (referring to noncultural issues); see also Frederick Schauer, "The Supreme Court, 2005 Term—Foreword, The Court's

Agenda—and the Nation's," *Harv. L. Rev.* 120 (2006): 16–20 (collecting surveys of what the country cares about and finding issues such as Iraq, Social Security, the economy/jobs, and health care, not "social" issues, to be more salient to the public).

308. Fiorina et al., *Culture War?*, supra note 279, at 152; see also Schauer, "Supreme Court, 2005 Term—Foreword," supra note 307, at 23–24 ("[The usual list of major social issues] are issues about which Americans are deeply divided . . . but they are persistently less important to Americans than issues of foreign policy, the economy, and personal well being"); John Brennan, "Most Take Middle Ground on Abortion Issues," *L.A. Times*, Aug. 6, 1992, at 6 (making the point that polls showed abortion "well down on the list of things voters find compelling").

309. Tushnet, *A Court Divided*, supra note 19, at 10. Tushnet's view differs somewhat from the social trends argument above in that he ties Rehnquist Court decisions to the ascendancy of economic over cultural conservativism on the Court and in the country. Id.

310. The level of support for *Roe v. Wade* held steady at around 65 percent from 1992 until 2002. See Fiorina et al., *Culture War?*, supra note 279, at 54 (Figure 4.1). Even for so-called soft reasons, support for abortion was surprisingly high. In 1989, support for legalized abortion in cases of poverty ranged from 60 percent in California and Florida to 47 percent in Texas; in cases where the mother was a high school student, from 56 percent in California and Florida to 46 percent in Ohio and Texas. See Elizabeth Adell Cook et al., *Between Two Absolutes: Public Opinion and the Politics of Abortion* (1992), 43 (Table 2.1); see also Fiorina et al., *Culture War?*, supra note 279, at 55–56 (reporting that bare majorities sometimes expressed support for legalized abortions even under circumstances where "the family has low income and cannot afford any more children," or "she is not married and does not want to marry the man," or "she is married and does not want any more children").

311. See Fiorina et al., *Culture War?*, supra note 279, at 65 (Table 4.2). Ninety-one percent favored counseling on dangers and alternatives; 77 percent supported requirements of parental permission. See id. (Table 4.3). A N.Y. *Times*/CBS poll in Sept. 1989 found that 70 percent favored parental consent laws and 65 percent favored viability testing. "Weighing Abortion Restrictions," *N.Y. Times*, Sept. 29, 1989, at A13.

312. These sentiments were echoed everywhere. See Brennan, "Most Take Middle Ground," supra note 308 ("Despite attempts of militants to portray them otherwise, polls show most Americans somewhere in the middle when asked their views on abortion").

313. Mimi Hall, "Activists Aside, Justices' Ruling Pleases Many," *USA Today*, July 1, 1992, at 3A.

314. See Frank Newport and Leslie McAneny, "Whose Court Is It Anyhow?: O'Connor, Kennedy, Souter Position Reflects Abortion Views of Most Americans," *Gallup Poll Monthly*, July 1992, at 51. The one exception here was the Court's decision to strike the spousal notification requirement as unconstitutional. A Gallup Poll taken just months before the Court's decision showed that 73 percent of the population supported a restriction requiring a woman to obtain spousal consent prior to obtaining an abortion. Id.

315. E. J. Dionne, Jr., "Justices' Abortion Ruling Mirrors Public Opinion," *Wash. Post*, July 1, 1992, at A4; see also Aaron Epstein, "Women's Right to Abortion Weakened by Top U.S. Court," *Toronto Star*, June 30, 1992, at A1 ("[The Court's] views mirror polls indicating that most Americans favor abortion rights, but oppose making abortions easy to obtain"); Hall, "Activists Aside," supra note 313 ("Both activists who oppose and who favor abortion rights called the decision a defeat for their side. But polls say the ruling mirrored public opinion"); Marsha Ingewerson and Clara Germani,

"Supreme Court Treads in Middle on Abortion," *Christian Sci. Monitor*, July 1, 1992, at 1 ("The decision appears to closely mirror public opinion: The majority of Americans give high importance to both freedom of individual choice and the sanctity of individual life"). Writing one year after the fact, Craig and O'Brien noted that "the decision reached in *Casey* virtually mirrored opinion polls. . . . The vast majority of Americans support legalized abortion while also favoring restrictions"). Craig and O'Brien, *Abortion and American Politics*, supra note 53, at 327.

316. Barrett, "Split Decision," supra note 305.

317. Eleanor Clift, "'One Justice Away:' The Political Fallout," *Newsweek*, July 13, 1992, at 18.

318. Less elaborate versions of this argument are presented in Neal Devins, "Congress as Culprit," *Duke L. J.* 51 (2001): 436; Christopher H. Schroeder, "Causes of the Recent Turn in Constitutional Interpretation," *Duke L. J.* 51 (2001): 311; Keith E. Whittington, "Taking What They Give Us: Explaining the Court's Federalism Offensive," *Duke L. J.* 51 (2001): 479.

319. Richard Milhous Nixon, "Annual Message to the Congress on the State of the Union," Jan. 22, 1971, in *Public Papers of the Presidents of the United States: Richard Milhous Nixon, 1971* (1972), 3.

320. See id. at 54.

321. Nat'l League of Cities v. Usery, 426 U.S. 833 (1976) (ruling that the minimum wage and maximum hours provisions of the Fair Labor Standards Act could not be applied to the states or their subdivisions).

322. See John Kincaid, "Foreword: The New Federalism Context of the New Judicial Federalism," *Rutgers L. J.* 26 (1995): 915 ("This 'increasingly conservative federal judiciary' was a product of President Nixon's New Federalism").

323. Ronald Reagan, "Inaugural Address," Jan. 20, 1981, in *Public Papers of the Presidents of the United States: Ronald Reagan, 1981* (1982), 2.

324. Russell Baker, Op-Ed, "The Heat Is Off," *N.Y. Times*, Aug. 1, 1981, § 1, at 25.

325. See Demetrios Caraley, "Changing Conceptions of Federalism," *Pol. Sci. Q.* 101 (1986): 294 ("[B]oth Democratic and Republican governors and mayors communicated strong opposition to . . . members of Congress over the prospect of having to assume major new funding responsibilities. Consequently no specific . . . draft legislation was ever sent by President Reagan to Congress"); David S. Broder, "White House Is Warned on Its Federalism Plans," *Wash. Post*, July 29, 1982, at A10 (reporting that the chair of the Senate Subcommittee on Intergovernmental Relations, the incoming chair of the National Governors Association, and several state legislators told Reagan's top negotiator on the federalism initiative "that there was no sound philosophical basis for sending the largest cash welfare program back to the states").

326. Quoted in David Broder and Herbert H. Denton, "Huge 'Sorting Out' of Federal Role," *Wash. Post*, Jan. 27, 1982, at A1.

327. Garcia v. San Antonio Transit Auth., 469 U.S. 528 (1985).

328. For an account of the failure of the block grant program and the fact that federalism seemed not to be the major motivator it once had, see Michael W. McConnell, "The Politics of Returning Power to the States," *Harv. J. L. & Pub. Pol'y* 6 (1982): 103–18. Even prior to the overturning of *Usery*, people seemed skeptical that the Reagan program would deliver much in the way of states' rights. See id. at 106 ("The general consensus of the speakers seemed to be that *Usery* was a fluke and that it will not be germinating much in the way of further practical limitations on federal power over the States").

329. Rochelle L. Stanfield, "The New Federalism," *Nat'l J.* 27 (1995): 226.

330. Jeffrey B. Gayner, "The Contract with America: Implementing New Ideas in the U.S.," Heritage Lecture No. 549, Oct. 12, 1995, http://www.heritage.org/Research/PoliticalPhilosophy/HL549.cfm.

331. Quoted in Elizabeth Drew, *Showdown* (1996), 26.

332. John Kincaid, "The Devolution Tortoise and the Centralization Hare," *New Eng. Econ. Rev.*, May–June 1998, at 14 (likening devolution to other "related buzz words—decentralization, deregulation, delegation, deconcentration"); Elliot Krieger, "GOP's Contract," *Providence J.-Bulletin*, April 16, 1995, at 1C ("[T]he Contract with America is largely about devolution. . . . That theory leads to replacing federal welfare regulations and crime-prevention programs with block grants to the states, to cuts in both deferral spending and federal taxes, and to the scaling back of federal environmental and health regulations"); see also Editorial, "Festival of Federalism," *Providence J.*, Apr. 13, 1995, at A16 ("Speaker Gingrich and his colleagues are examining the premises of our national government—what is it doing, and should it be doing it?—and have sought to reinvigorate state and local government").

333. Kincaid, "Devolution Tortoise," supra note 332.

334. Quoted in Drew, *Showdown*, supra note 331, at 86.

335. See Kincaid, "Devolution Tortoise," supra note 332, at 27 (referencing Exec. Order 12875, 58 Fed. Reg. 58093 (Oct. 28, 1993)).

336. William J. Clinton, "Address Before a Joint Session of the Congress on the State of the Union," Jan. 23, 1996, in *Public Papers of the Presidents of the United States: William J. Clinton, 1996*, bk. 1 (1997), 79.

337. In 1995, data published by the Roper Center in *The Public Perspective* showed that 78 percent of Americans favored shifting more control over crime prevention to the states. "How Much Government-Devolution," data essay, *Pub. Persp.* 6 (Apr.–May 1995); see also Editorial, "The Ex-Federalists: Whatever Happened to Returning Power to the States?," *Houston Chron.*, May 26, 1996, at 2 ("On issue after issue, from tort reform to . . . the prosecution and punishment of crime, congressional Republicans have supported legislation that would usurp powers held by the states . . ."); Jeffrey Rosen, "Fed Up," *New Republic*, May 22, 1995, at 13 (noting the "mindless impulse to federalize crimes that the states are prosecuting perfectly well on their own").

338. Nina Bernstein, "An Accountability Issue," *N.Y. Times*, Apr. 1, 1996, at A1.

339. Joan Biskupic, "High Court Bolsters State Rights," *Wash. Post*, March 28, 1996, at A1.

340. See Tushnet, *A Court Divided*, supra note 19, at 277 ("Not a single central feature of the New Deal's regulatory regime was overturned in that revolution, nor were central elements of the Great Society's programs displaced"); Neal Devins, "The Federalism-Rights Nexus," *U. Colo. L. Rev.* 73 (2002): 1315–16 ("[M]ost of these decisions have been narrow in scope . . .").

341. Ann Devroy and Al Kamen, "Clinton Says Gun Ruling Is a Threat," *Wash. Post*, Apr. 30, 1995, at A1.

342. Editorial, "A Shot Across Congress' Bow," *Chi. Trib*, Apr. 30, 1995, at 2.

343. Editorial, "States' Business," *Wash. Post*, May 16, 2000, at A20; accord Editorial, "High Court Wisely Keeps Limits on Federal Authority," *Atlanta J.*, May 17, 2000, at A14 (stating that the decision "reaffirmed something that, in the long run, is far more beneficial to all Americans . . . the principle that America is a republic, with much governmental authority remaining at the state and local levels . . ."); Editorial, "Turning Back a Federal Intrusion," *Chi. Trib.*, May 16, 2000, at 14 ("Is violence against women a national problem? Of course. . . . But not every national problem warrants a federal solution"). Even Anthony Lewis, seething about much of the federalism jurisprudence, admitted *Morrison* was "a close case." Anthony Lewis, "Court and Congress," *N.Y. Times*, May 20, 2000, at A15.

344. Kathleen M. Sullivan, Op-Ed, "Federal Power, Undimmed," *N.Y. Times*, July 27, 1999, § 4, at 17 ("[T]he striking feature of these rulings is how little they challenged the Federal Government's substantive power to make labor, patent and trademark law").

345. ANES Guide to Public Opinion and Electoral Behavior, http://www.electionstudies .org/nesguide/toptable/tab5a_1.htm. In response to the question "How much of the time do you think you can trust the government in Washington to do what is right?," 14 percent said "just about always," and 62 percent "most of the time." A further 22 percent said "some of the time." In 1994, the relevant numbers were 2 percent, 19 percent, and 74 percent, respectively. The year 1994 was something of a nadir. In 1992 the numbers were 3 percent, 26 percent, and 68 percent, and in 1996 they were 3 percent, 30 percent, and 66 percent. Id.

346. See Neal Devins, "The Majoritarian Rehnquist Court," *L. & Contemp. Probs.* 67 (2004): 66 (internal quotations omitted).

347. See Kincaid, "Devolution Tortoise," supra note 332, at 17 (study performed by Princeton Survey Research Associates).

348. Quoted in Stanfield, "New Federalism," supra note 329.

349. "How Much Government-Devolution," supra note 337, at 29. While 22 percent said the federal government should have more responsibility for public education, 72 percent said the state governments should. The respective numbers for reducing crime were 24 percent and 68 percent; for providing job training, 31 percent and 55 percent; for protecting the environment, 50 percent and 38 percent; for protecting civil rights, 67 percent and 26 percent; and for strengthening the economy, 64 percent and 24 percent. Id.

350. Keith E. Whittington, "Dismantling the Modern State?," *Hastings Const. L.Q.* 25 (1998): 483.

351. See Sanford Levinson, "*Bush v. Gore* and the French Revolution," *L. & Contemp. Probs.*, Summer 2002, at 36 ("[T]he greatest issue facing America, at least if one took the campaign speeches of Bush and Gore at all seriously, was the specific policy by which prescription drugs would be made available to older Americans. . . . Neither candidate had anything remotely cogent to say about foreign policy, an issue of almost no concern to Americans at the time").

352. "Florida Recount Controversy from the Public's Perspective," Gallup News Serv., Dec. 22, 2000, http://institution.gallup.com/content/default.aspx?ci=2176, at 1.

353. This, despite the fact that 30 percent of adults nationwide, admittedly overwhelmingly composed of Gore voters, said that the decision caused them to lose confidence in the Supreme Court. See id.

354. Kramer, *People Themselves*, supra note 266, at 231.

355. Polling done in June 2001 showed overall approval figures almost identical to results in August and September 2000. Herbert M. Kritzer, "The Impact of *Bush v. Gore* on Public Perceptions and Knowledge of the Supreme Court," *Judicature* 85 (July–Aug. 2001): 38; see also James L. Gibson, Gregory A. Caldeira, and Lester Kenyatta Spence, "The Supreme Court and the U.S. Presidential Election of 2000: Wound, Self-Inflicted or Otherwise?," *Brit. J. Pol. Sci.* 33 (2003): 543 (noting that when those polled were asked if they would support limiting the jurisdiction of the Court, "if anything, support for the Court *increased*," from 49 percent in 1987 to 62.8 percent in 2001).

356. See Editorial, "Presidents in Waiting," *N.Y. Times*, Dec. 3, 2000, § 4, at 18.

357. Of adults nationwide, 51 percent said the justices were being influenced by their personal political views, compared with 42 percent saying they were not. Jeffrey M. Jones, "Public Willing to Accept Supreme Court as Final Arbiter of Election Dispute," Gallup News Serv., Dec. 12, 2000, http://institution.gallup.com/content/default

.aspx?ci=2224 (study conducted before the decision). Following the Court's decision, 54 percent said the U.S. Supreme Court was fair in deciding the case, compared with 38 percent saying it was not. "Florida Recount Controversy," supra note 352. These later numbers show a sharp drop from before the decision, when 72 percent said they expected the Court to be fair and 17 percent said they expected an unfair decision. Jones, "Public Willing," supra.

358. See, e.g., Gregory A. Caldeira and James L. Gibson, "The Etiology of Public Support for the Supreme Court," *Am. J. Pol. Sci.* 36 (1992): 640 (examining diffuse support for the Court and finding that a majority of people are dedicated to preserving the Court's role); Barry Friedman, "Mediated Popular Constitutionalism," *Mich. L. Rev.* 101 (2003): 2596–636 (discussing diffuse support in the context of more theoretical judicial legitimacy); Stephen P. Nicholson and Robert M. Howard, "Framing Support for the Supreme Court in the Aftermath of *Bush v. Gore*," *J. Pol.* 65 (2003): 676 (analyzing the impact of *Bush v. Gore* on diffuse and specific support for the Supreme Court).

359. See Isabel Hilton, "Overdue Process: Part 3 of 4," *Fin. Times*, Aug. 28, 2004, at 16 ("[T]he Abu Ghraib photographs . . . [were] the best hope for the people in Guantanamo. . . . After all, we weren't saying these people were innocent, but we were saying you shouldn't sodomise them" (quoting Stafford Smith, counsel for the defendant)); Mark Helm, "Prison Abuse Scandal Could Sway High Court," *Times-Union* (Albany), May 16, 2004, at A10 (reporting that the Abu Ghraib photographs were broadcast by CBS eight hours after the Court heard oral arguments and quoting James Fitzpatrick, author of an amicus brief supporting the defendants, saying, "The administration's main argument, which boiled down to 'Trust us,' just doesn't hold water after the revelations of prisoner abuse in Iraq").

360. See Eskridge and Ferejohn, *America's Statutory Constitution*, supra note 195, at Chapter 8 at 2 ("It is true that the very conservative Rehnquist Court set forth some Constitutional limits on the state's ability to treat sexual minorities as outlaws—but that Large 'C' Constitutional development followed the small 'c' constitutional disentrenchment of the old norm [of compulsory heterosexuality]").

361. Bowers v. Hardwick, 478 U.S. 186 (1986). The boom in gay rights organizations occurred particularly after the Stonewall riots of 1969. See John D'Emilio, *Sexual Politics, Sexual Communities* (1983), 237–38; "Gays Gain in Fight for Rights," *Hartford Courant*, Aug. 22, 1976 ("So far, 17 states have repealed their sodomy laws . . . and similar legislation has been introduced in most of the others"); Bill Peterson, "Gay Rights Law Loses 2–1 in Miami," *Wash. Post*, June 8, 1977, at A1 ("Thirty-six other cities [aside from Miami, which just repealed its antidiscrimination ordinance by popular vote] . . . have ordinances similar to the one repealed here"). For a general discussion of the organization and tactics of the gay rights movement, which focused on administrative and legislative reform—as opposed to the judicial route taken by the NAACP—see Eskridge and Ferejohn, *America's Statutory Constitution*, supra note 195, at Chapter 8; Eskridge, "Some Effects of Identity-Based Social Movements," supra note 158, at 2159–79.

362. Peterson, "Gay Rights Law Loses," supra note 361; see also John D'Emilio, "Cycles of Change, Questions of Strategy," in *The Politics of Gay Rights*, ed. Craig A. Rimmerman et al. (2000), 31, 37 ("The further repeal of sodomy statutes virtually stopped in the 1980s, and the passage of civil rights protections for homosexuals slowed as well").

363. Support for legalization grew steadily from 1977 to 1983 and then dropped sharply following 1985 (from 44 percent support to 32 percent). Support remained in the low to mid-30s until 1989, when it jumped up to 47 percent. See Frank Newport, "Six in 10 Americans Agree that Gay Sex Should Be Legal," Gallup News Serv., June 27,

2003, http://www.gallup.com/poll/8722/Six-Americans-Agree-Gay-Sex-Should-Legal
.aspx; Eskridge, *Dishonorable Passions*, supra note 156, at 267 (providing a vivid history of antihomosexual sodomy laws in the United States).

364. Quoted in Randy Shilts, *And the Band Played On: Politics, People and the AIDS Epidemic* (1988), 311.

365. See Martin, *With God on Our Side*, supra note 281, at 243 ("[A]s late as 1988 . . .
forty-five percent of the general population and fifty-seven percent of fundamental-
ists favored a quarantine of people with AIDS"). Suggestions from the far right for
containing the epidemic went beyond the mere quarantine of AIDS victims. Some
called for a quarantine of "all homosexual establishments," while others suggested
"that all AIDS sufferers be given a readily identifiable tattoo, to protect others." Id.
(internal citations omitted).

366. Lisa Leff, "Gay Cause Is Gaining Attention, Leaders Say," *Wash. Post*, Aug. 26, 1986,
at A4; see also Eskridge, "Some Effects of Identity-Based Social Movements," supra
note 158, at 2183 ("In a twisted way, [*Bowers*] was (in part) a boon to lesbigay rights
as a social movement, for the court's openly antigay opinion not only reinforced les-
bigays as a 'marked' minority group, but also rallied lesbigay attorneys out of their
closets in record numbers and attracted moderate allies"); Eskridge and Ferejohn,
America's Statutory Constitution, supra note 195, at Chapter 8 at 30–31 ("*Bowers* was
a Second Stonewall, a display of antihomosexual spleen that fueled public responses
from gay people and their growing number of allies").

367. See Joyce Murdoch and Deb Price, *Courting Justice: Gay Men and Lesbians v. the
Supreme Court* (2001), 334 ("Hardwick had hit with explosive force . . . instantly
radicalizing many [gay Americans] who'd never been politically active"); John Robinson, "Gay Leaders Urge Others to 'Come Out,'" *Boston Globe*, Oct. 10, 1988, at 1
(documenting National Coming Out Day); Lena Williams, "200,000 March in Capital to Seek Gay Rights and Money for AIDS," *N.Y. Times*, Oct. 12, 1987, at A1 (documenting a two hundred thousand–strong march for gay rights in 1987).

368. Jonathan Yardley, "The March of Time," *Wash. Post*, Dec. 9, 1996, at E2.

369. See Audrey Barrick, "Gay Tolerance in U.S. Reaching Record Marks," *Christian
Post*, May 29, 2007, http://www.christianpost.com/article/20070529/27674_Poll:_Gay_
Tolerance_Reaching_Record_Marks_in_America.htm (reporting 60 percent support
for the legality of homosexual relations in May 2003); Joan Biskupic, "For Gays,
Tolerance Translates to Rights," *Wash. Post*, Nov. 5, 1999, at A01; Chris Bull, "Firm
Partnerships," *Advocate*, May 23, 2000, at 66; see also Eskridge and Ferejohn, *America's
Statutory Constitution*, supra note 195, at Chapter 8 at 31 ("By 1993, the coming-out-
of-the-closet backlash against *Bowers*, the efflorescence of family-affirming stories
about lesbian and gay families, and the abatement of the AIDS epidemic and its dis-
association with gay sex, all contributed to a modest sea change in America's attitudes about homosexuals and homosexual sodomy laws").

370. See Tom Teepen, Editorial, "Clinton Adds Weight to Gay Rights Debate," *Atlanta
J. and Const.*, Nov. 12, 1997, at A13 (further reporting that 70 percent had no idea
that such discrimination was lawful to begin with).

371. Quoted in Bill Nichols, "Clinton Criticized for Gay Group Talk," *USA Today*, Nov.
10, 1997, at 7A; see Teepen, "Clinton Adds Weight," supra note 370 (reporting that
Clinton spoke to the Human Rights Campaign); "Clinton Favors Partial Ban on Gays,"
Boston Herald, July 17, 1993, at 1.

372. Romer v. Evans, 517 U.S. 620 (1996); Editorial, "Rethinking Equality," *Wall St. J.*,
May 22, 1996, at A22.

373. Editorial, "Sodomy and Sneakers," *Wall St. J. Europe*, June 30, 2003, at A12.

374. *Lawrence*, 539 U.S. at 573.

375. Prior to the Court's decision, even traditionalists had begun to question the practicality of criminalizing such an "increasingly visible" portion of the population. By the time the case was before the Court, a "rainbow coalition of moderate and traditionalist perspectives" had filed as amici in favor of the petitioner. Eskridge and Ferejohn, *America's Statutory Constitution*, supra note 195, at Chapter 8 at 31, 35 (noting that twenty-eight churches and faith groups filed in support of Lawrence, while "no denomination filed in support of the Texas Homosexual Conduct Law—not the Roman Catholic Church, not the Southern Baptist Convention, not the Church of Jesus Christ of Latter Day Saints").

376. "Below the Fold," *Fox News Sunday*, Fox, June 29, 2003. Former Republican representative and host of Fox News' *Scarborough Country* Joe Scarborough recognized that many of his friends agreed with Justice Scalia, though he did not. "Maybe it's a generational thing. Or maybe it's just because I don't want the feds kicking down doors. . . . [C]onservatives may actually look back on the court's decision today and be glad that at least one branch of our federal government dared to restrain an ever-expanding police state." Joe Scarborough, *Scarborough Country*, MSNBC, June 26, 2003.

377. *Late Edition with Wolf Blitzer*, CNN, June 29, 2003.

378. George W. Bush, "Address Before a Joint Session of the Congress on the State of the Union," Jan. 20, 2004, in *Public Papers of the Presidents of the United States: George W. Bush, 2004*, bk. 1 (2007), 88.

379. California's and Washington's "preference" initiatives passed with 54.6 percent and 58.22 percent of the vote, respectively. This in the context of some polls indicating opposition as high as 90 percent among whites to preferences in hiring and promotion in jobs. See Gail L. Heriot, "Strict Scrutiny, Public Opinion, and Affirmative Action on Campus: Should the Courts Find a Narrowly Tailored Solution to a Compelling Need in a Policy Most American Oppose?," *Harv. J. on Legis.* 40 (2003): 225–26. In Houston, the city council had a "tumultuous" debate over the wording despite the fact that the legal result was the same either way. Polls showed that a measure banning "preferential treatment" would have passed, but the measure banning "affirmative action" failed by 55 percent to 45 percent. See Sam Howe Verhovek, "Referendum in Houston Shows Complexity of Preferences Issue," *N.Y. Times*, Nov. 6, 1997, at A1; see also Loan Le and Jack Citrin, "Affirmative Action," in Persily et al., *Public Opinion*, supra note 42, at 163 ("Illustrating the ambiguity of the term, a *Newsweek* poll conducted in January 2003 found that 38% of the sample said they thought of affirmative action as setting quotas for minorities, whereas 44% said they perceived it as increasing outreach efforts to find qualified minorities"); id. at 171–73 (dividing affirmative action into three types: "[S]pecial [E]fforts," which received 59 percent support in 2005; "Quotas," which received only 26 percent support in 2001 if "lower standards for racial minorities were permitted"; and "Preferences," which was treated similarly to quotas); Marsha King, "Debate over Affirmative Action Moves to This State," *Seattle Times*, Nov. 13, 1997, at A1 (reporting that language may have strongly affected the votes and that roughly 29 percent of people who said they favored California's referendum prohibiting preferential treatment on the basis of race or gender also favored affirmative action).

380. Le and Citrin, "Affirmative Action," in Persily et al., *Public Opinion*, supra note 42, at 175.

381. See "Complete Results: *N.Y. Times*/CBS Poll," Jan. 24, 2003, http://www.nytimes.com/packages/html/politics/20030124POLL_RESULTS.html (46 percent said "very important"; 33 percent, "somewhat important").

382. See Pew Research Center, "Conflicted Views of Affirmative Action," May 14, 2003, http://people-press.org/reports/display.php3?ReportID=184.

383. See Hamburger and Wallsten, *One Party Country*, supra note 295, at 55 ("No Republican leader in the years after 1992 did more than George and Jeb Bush to turn the GOP around on the issue of race").

384. See id. at 77.

385. See id. at 72; see also Patrick Healy, "Texas Plan for College Diversity Draws Fire," *Boston Globe*, Aug. 22, 2000, at A1; Clarence Page, "Jeb Bush Wrestles with Race," *Cincinnati Post*, Apr. 28, 2000, at 22A.

386. Out of twenty-four appointments in his first term, Bush named five women, four African-Americans, three Hispanics, and two Asian-Americans to his cabinet. He appointed two African-Americans to lead the State Department and a Hispanic to lead the Justice Department. See Terry M. Neal, "Diversity and the Bush Cabinet," *Wash. Post* online, Dec. 23, 2004, http://www.washingtonpost.com/wp-dyn/articles/A22082-2004Dec23.html.

387. Forty-one amici briefs were filed on behalf of the respondents, fifteen on behalf of petitioners and two supporting neither party. For a listing of the briefs filed in each case, see "Briefs and Other Related Documents," Gratz v. Bollinger, 539 U.S. 244 (2003); Grutter v. Bollinger, 539 U.S. 306 (2003), available on Westlaw.

388. See Brief for 65 Leading American Businesses as Amici Curiae Supporting Respondents, Grutter v. Bollinger, 539 U.S. 306 (2003) (Nos. 02–241, 02–516) (including American Airlines, American Express, Boeing, Chevron, Coca-Cola, DaimlerChrysler, General Electric, Fannie Mae, Intel, Johnson & Johnson, Kellogg, Kraft, Microsoft, Nike, PepsiCo, Pfizer, PricewaterhouseCoopers, and Shell among many others). Other companies, such as General Motors, filed briefs separately. See Brief of General Motors Corporation as Amicus Curiae in Support of Respondents, Grutter v. Bollinger, 539 U.S. 306 (2003) (Nos. 02–241, 02–516).

389. See Brief for 65 Leading American Businesses, *Grutter*, supra note 388, at 2 ("Diversity in higher education is therefore a compelling government interest not only because of its positive effects on the educational environment itself, but also because of the crucial role diversity in higher education plays in preparing students to be the leaders this country needs in business, law, and all other pursuits that affect the public interest").

390. See Consolidated Brief of Lt. Gen. Julius W. Becton et al. as Amici Curiae on behalf of Respondents, Grutter v. Bollinger, 539 U.S. 306 (2003) (Nos. 02–241, 02–516), at 5 ("Based on decades of experience, *amici* have concluded that a highly qualified, racially diverse officer corps educated and trained to command our nation's racially diverse enlisted ranks is essential to the military's ability to fulfill its principal mission to provide national security"); see also Jeffrey Toobin, *The Nine: Inside the Secret World of the Supreme Court* (2007), 219 (discussing the uniquely prominent role that the U.S. military amicus brief played during oral argument).

391. See Brief for the United States as Amicus Curiae Supporting Petitioner, Gratz v. Bollinger, 539 U.S. 244 (2003) (No. 02–516), 17 (defending Texas's percentage-based program).

392. See "Remarks on the Michigan Affirmative Action Case," Jan. 15, 2003, in *Public Papers of the Presidents of the United States: George W. Bush, 2003*, bk. 1 (2007), 56.

393. Rachel Hartigan-Shea, "Split Decision," *U.S. News and World Rep.*, June 23, 2003, at 1.

394. David Von Drehle, "Court Mirrors Public Opinion," *Wash. Post*, June 24, 2003, at A1.

395. *Late Edition*, CNN, supra note 377.

396. Von Drehle, "Court Mirrors," supra note 394; see also Toobin, *The Nine*, supra note 390, at 225 (arguing that O'Connor "picked a result, and reached a compromise, that was broadly acceptable to most Americans").

397. See Graber, "Non-Majoritarian Difficulty," supra note 57, at 42 ("[T]he eventual judicial decision will rarely, if ever, curtail public debate on crosscutting issues. Federal justices, after all, have no particular ability to find compromises that have eluded mainstream politicians").

398. Tom Wicker, "Reflections of a Court Watcher," Foreword to *The Rehnquist Court*, ed. Herman Schwartz (2002), 12 ("[W]hatever rulings a Court at any given moment may render, the public is likely to accept both the Court and its decisions—with screams of agony, perhaps, as after *Brown* in the fifties, but without challenging a decision or causing effective political reprisal against the institution or the justices").

399. Charles Lane, "Polls: Americans Say Court Is 'About Right,'" *Wash. Post*, July 7, 2003, at A15.

400. Devins, "Majoritarian Rehnquist Court," supra note 346, at 76. Poll results six months after *Bush v. Gore* reported support for the Court at 81 percent.

401. About 75 percent said they trusted the Supreme Court to operate in the best interests of the American people, and 70 percent said they trusted the judicial branch. The President/executive branch got about 55 percent, and Congress got about 50 percent. See Annenberg Democracy Project, *A Republic Divided*, supra note 284, at 216 (Figure 1).

402. When the public was asked if it trusted government institutions to operate in the best interests of the American people, Congress's scorecard fell from around 57 percent to 40 percent between 2005 and 2006. For the same period, the President fell from about 57 percent to about 43 percent and the Supreme Court gained from about 60 percent to about 61 percent. See id. at 218 (Figure 2).

403. Jeffrey M. Jones, "Supreme Court Approval Rating Best in Four Years," Gallup News Serv., Sept. 29, 2006, http://institution.gallup.com/content/default.aspx?ci=24802.

404. Id.

405. Kelo v. City of New London, 545 U.S. 469 (2005).

406. David G. Savage, "Even a Supreme Court Loss Can Propel a Cause," *L.A. Times*, Jan. 3, 2007, at A10 (reporting that the "political earthquake" led to thirty-four states' tightening their laws between the decision in June 2005 and Dec. 18, 2006, making "it harder for city officials to take private property for development"). For a sampling of the national response, see Avi Salzman, "Homeowners Shown the Door," *N.Y. Times*, July 3, 2005, at CT1; Elizabeth Mehren, "Eminent Domain Plaintiff Will Keep Her House," *L.A. Times*, July 1, 2006, at A15 (reporting that despite the ruling, Ms. Kelo would keep her house and that President Bush banned the federal government from exercising eminent domain save for public projects such as hospitals); Craig Gilbert, "Public-Use Ruling Has Political Backlash," *Milwaukee J. Sentinel*, Aug. 7, 2005, at A1 (quoting House Majority Leader Tom DeLay calling the decision "horrible" and Ralph Nader calling it "unconscionable").

407. Sheryl Gay Stolberg, "Republican Lawmakers Fire Back at Judiciary," *N.Y. Times*, July 1, 2005, at A10.

408. Roosevelt, *Myth of Judicial Activism*, supra note 125, at 135; see also Janice Nader et al., "Government Takings of Private Property," in Persily et al., *Public Opinion*, supra note 42, at 304 ("Unlike other controversial court decisions involving abortion, gay marriage, and school integration, where courts have overturned legislative action, in *Kelo* the Court endorsed local and state control, and it was the Court's *failure* to intervene that has upset the public").

409. Savage, "Even a Supreme Court Loss," supra note 406.
410. Nader et al., "Government Takings," in Persily et al., *Public Opinion*, supra note 42, at 304 (evaluating the host of data concerning the public's opposition to the Court's *Kelo* decision and noting that they demonstrate, among other values, disillusionment with "the expectation that the Supreme Court will protect ordinary citizens from overreaching governmental power"). Polls following the decision showed that 81 percent polled disagreed with the Court's decision. Sixty-nine percent favored legislation restricting the government's ability to seize land under eminent domain. Id.
411. See, e.g., Devins, "Majoritarian Rehnquist Court," supra note 346 (arguing that the Court is finely attuned and responsive to the signals sent by Congress and the people); Barry Friedman, "Dialogue and Judicial Review," *Mich. L. Rev.* 91 (1993): 577 (challenging the notion of the counter-majoritarian difficulty as premised on faulty assumptions regarding the nature of the Court and the American public and arguing instead that the Court is engaged in a dialogue with the other branches as to the shape of constitutional law); Graber, "Non-Majoritarian Difficulty," supra note 57; Griffin, "Judicial Supremacy," supra note 232, at 112 (arguing that "[t]o achieve a better understanding" of judicial review than can be provided by considering the court as a counter-majoritarian force, "we must situate judicial review in its political context"); Michael J. Klarman, "Rethinking the Civil Rights and Civil Liberties Revolutions," *Va. L. Rev.* 82 (1996): 1 (arguing that neither the counter-majoritarian arguments nor the non-counter-majoritarian arguments are completely right and that the truth is in the middle). The idea was not original; important scholarship in the mid-century made the same point. See Robert A. Dahl, "Decision Making in a Democracy," *J. Pub. L.* 6 (1957): 279 (originating the idea); Robert G. McCloskey, *The American Supreme Court* (1960), 246 ("[I]t is hard to find a single historical instance when the court has stood firm for very long against a really clear wave of public demand").
412. *This Week with David Brinkley*, ABC, Apr. 30, 1995.
413. "Roundtable," *Fox Special Report with Brit Hume*, Fox, June 26, 2003.
414. Toobin, *The Nine*, supra note 390, at 340.
415. See Jeffrey Rosen, "Answer Key," *New Republic*, Nov. 21, 2005, at 16 ("By splitting every difference, she [Justice O'Connor] aggrandized her own power at the expense of Congress and the states"); Jeffrey Rosen, *The Most Democratic Branch: How the Courts Serve America* (2006).
416. See Wilkinson, "Rehnquist Court at Twilight," supra note 147, at 1978.
417. See id. at 1982, 1983.
418. Rosen, "Answer Key," supra note 415, at 16.
419. Wilkinson, "Rehnquist Court at Twilight," supra note 147, at 1987.
420. David A. Strauss, "The Modernizing Mission of Judicial Review," Jan. 16, 2007 (unpublished draft available at http://www.law.virginia.edu/pdf/workshops/0607/strauss.pdf used with permission), 52 (arguing for "something closer to the *Carolene Products* approach" to judicial involvement in the democratic process, "which . . . identifies the protection of certain minorities as a central feature of the judicial role" and serves as a "path of somewhat greater resistance for the courts").
421. Wilkinson, "Rehnquist Court at Twilight," supra note 147, at 1996; see also Kramer, *People Themselves*, supra note 266, at 231 ("[A] people that acceded to the Court's pretensions in this respect [as the sole arbiter of the Constitution] will permit the Justices to go farther and do more than a people that does not. . . . It could well be that a majority of the country presently supports what the Rehnquist Court is doing. That still does not explain why all those who disagree, and disagree strongly, nevertheless feel constrained passively to accept the Court's rulings . . .").

Conclusion: What History Teaches

1. Stephen Holmes acknowledges the tension but sees the Constitution as empowering popular rule. See Stephen Holmes, *Passions and Constraint: On the Theory of Liberal Democracy* (1995), 134–77.

2. Stephen Holmes argues that the framers' design allowed for, if not invited, constitutional change. Holmes, *Passions and Constraint*, supra note 1, at 161 ("To satisfy rival interests and muster majority support, participants at the Federal Convention incorporated conflicting and ambiguous provisions into the Constitution, thus delegating essential discretionary powers to their descendants").

3. According to the journalist Jan Crawford Greenburg, the Chief Justice persuaded O'Connor to step down. He wanted to serve an additional year but did not want two vacancies on the Court at one time. Jan Crawford Greenberg, *Supreme Conflict: The Inside Story of the Struggle for Control of the United States Supreme Court* (2007), 18–19. Jeffrey Toobin tells a slightly different story, agreeing that Rehnquist told O'Connor that he would not step down in 2005 but asserting that it was O'Connor who objected to leaving the Court with two simultaneous vacancies. Jeffrey Toobin, *The Nine: Inside the Secret World of the Supreme Court* (2007), 252.

4. Richard W. Stevenson, "President Names Roberts as Choice for Chief Justice," *N.Y. Times*, Sept. 5, 2005, at A1.

5. Sheryl Gay Stolberg, "Panel Approves Roberts 13–5, as 3 of 8 Democrats Back Him," *N.Y. Times*, Sept. 23, 2005, at A1.

6. Quoted in Joan Biskupic, "Roberts, Rehnquist Compel Comparisons: Close Relationship Underscores Transition," *USA Today*, Sept. 7, 2005, at A12; see also Warren Richey and Gail Russell Chaddock, "Roberts Tapped for Higher Court Calling," *Christian Sci. Monitor*, Sept. 6, 2005, at 1 (nominating Roberts to replace Rehnquist "maintains the rough balance of power that existed on the high court prior to the chief justice's death").

7. Charles Babington and Peter Baker, "Roberts Confirmed as 17th Chief Justice: Senate Republicans Are Unanimous, Democrats Evenly Split," *Wash. Post*, Sept. 30, 2005, at A1.

8. Sheryl Gay Stolberg and Elisabeth Bumiller, "Senate Confirms Roberts as 17th Chief Justice," *N.Y. Times*, Sept. 30, 2005, at A1.

9. Quoted in Babington and Baker, "Roberts Confirmed as 17th Chief Justice," supra note 7.

10. Jeffrey Rosen, "A Majority of One," *N.Y. Times Mag.*, June 3, 2001, at 32.

11. Linda Greenhouse, "Consistently, a Pivotal Role," *N.Y. Times*, July 2, 2005, at A1 ("The last such defining moment occurred with the retirement in 1987 of Justice Lewis F. Powell Jr., whose position on the court then resembled Justice O'Connor's today"); see also Peter Baker, "Bork's Shadow Looms over Court Opening: Defeat of '87 Nomination a Model for Liberals, a Lesson for Conservatives," *Wash. Post*, July 12, 2005, at A1.

12. See generally Toobin, *Nine*, supra note 3, at 288–97.

13. Norman Dorsen, "The Selection of U.S. Supreme Court Justices," *Int'l J. Const. L.* 4 (2006): 655; see also Terry Eastland, "A Faith-Based Nomination: In Making the Case for Harriet Miers, the White House Is Emphasizing Her Religious Views," *Wkly. Standard*, Oct. 17, 2005, at 28.

14. Jeanne Cummings and Jess Bravin, "New Round: Choice of Alito for High Court Sets Stage for Ideological Battle—Jurist's Many Cases Provide Fodder for Senate Fight; Pivotal Role for 'Gang of 14'—Husband's Rights in Abortion," *Wall Street J.*, Nov. 1, 2005, at A1.

15. Andrew M. Siegel, "Nice Disguise," *New Republic*, Nov. 14, 2005, at 20.

16. David D. Kirkpatrick, "One Nominee, Two Very Different Portraits in a New Round of Ads," *N.Y. Times*, Nov. 18, 2005, at A26 (discussing television ad opposing Alito's nomination); Sheryl Gay Stolberg, "Internet Ads Back Nominee on Search Case," *N.Y. Times*, Dec. 14, 2005, at A31 (describing Internet ad supporting Alito's nomination).

17. Charles Babington, "Alito Is Sworn In on High Court: Senators Confirm Conservative Judge Largely on Party Lines," *Wash. Post*, Feb. 1, 2006, at A1 ("By the narrowest margin since Clarence Thomas's 1991 nomination, the Senate voted 58 to 42, largely along party lines, to confirm Alito. . . . Four Democratic senators voted for Alito, and one Republican—Lincoln D. Chafee, who faces a tough reelection battle this year in Democratic-leaning Rhode Island—voted against him").

18. Steven Lubet, Editorial, "The Alito Confirmation: How Democrats Lost the Political Battle," *San Diego Union-Trib.*, Feb. 1, 2006, at B7.

19. David D. Kirkpatrick, "Alito Sworn In as Justice After Senate Gives Approval," *N.Y. Times*, Feb. 1, 2006, at A21.

20. David D. Kirkpatrick, "In Alito, G.O.P. Reaps Harvest Planted in '82," *N.Y. Times*, Jan. 30, 2006, at A1 (quoting Douglas W. Kmiec).

21. See, e.g., Linda Greenhouse, "Roberts Is at Court's Helm, but He Isn't Yet in Control," *N.Y. Times*, July 2, 2006, § 1, at 1 (observing that the 2005–2006 term of the Roberts Court ruled more moderately than anticipated because of the effect of Justice Kennedy's swing vote); Edward Lazarus, "Under John Roberts, Court Re-Rights Itself," *Wash. Post*, July 1, 2007, at B1 (describing the 2006–2007 term as a "nearly unmitigated disaster for progressives"); Robert Barnes, "Justices Show Ability to Move to the Center," *Wash. Post*, May 29, 2008, at A2 (concluding that the 2007–2008 term returned to a more moderate posture).

22. See, e.g., Gilbert E. Roe, *Our Judicial Oligarchy* (1912), 197 (claiming that the *Lochner*-era conservative judiciary opposed "the public will" and was "building an oligarchy"); Robert H. Bork, "The Supreme Court Needs a New Philosophy," *Fortune*, Dec. 1968, at 138 (protesting that the liberal Warren Court was "overriding the policies of the elected representatives of the people").

23. See, e.g., Arnold M. Paul, *Conservative Crisis and the Rule of Law: Attitudes of Bar and Bench, 1887–1895* (1960), 229 (explaining that conservatives in the 1890s believed that "in a time of social crisis, when rampant populism might threaten the established order, the Supreme Court must act as counterweight to election returns, as defender of minority rights against majority rule"); Philip B. Kurland, "Toward a Political Supreme Court," *U. Chi. L. Rev.* 37 (1969): 45 (defending the Warren Court by claiming that the Court's primary function is to "protect the individual against the Leviathan of government and to protect minorities against oppression by majorities").

24. Alexander M. Bickel, *The Least Dangerous Branch: The Supreme Court at the Bar of Politics* (1962), 16.

25. Id. at 16–23; see also Christopher Eisgruber, *Constitutional Self-Government* (2001); John Hart Ely, *Democracy and Distrust: A Theory of Judicial Review* (1980), 73–105; Bruce Ackerman, "Constitutional Politics/Constitutional Law," *Yale L. J.* 99 (1989): 643; Frank Michelman, "Law's Republic," *Yale L. J.* 97 (1988): 1531–32; Lawrence G. Sager, "Justice in Plain Clothes: Reflections on the Thinness of Constitutional Law," *Nw. U. L. Rev.* 88 (1993): 410–35.

26. See, e.g., Charles L. Black, Jr., *The People and the Court* (1960), 166 (identifying the possibility of counter-majoritarian action by the Court as "the chief cause of scholarly and professional dubiety as to the Court's role"); Robert H. Bork, "Neutral Principles and Some First Amendment Problems," *Ind. L. J.* 47 (1971): 1 (presuming that courts are not only able to, but also likely to thwart the popular will: "[W]e have come to expect that the nature of the Constitution will change, often quite dramati-

cally, as the personnel of the Supreme Court changes. . . . In the present state of affairs that expectation is inevitable, but it is nevertheless deplorable").

27. See Michael J. Klarman, *From Jim Crow to Civil Rights: The Supreme Court and the Struggle for Racial Equality* (2004), 6 (arguing that courts generally protect civil rights of minority groups only when doing so is in the interest of the political majority); Derrick A. Bell, Jr., "*Brown v. Board of Education* and the Interest-Convergence Dilemma," *Harv. L. Rev.* 93 (1980): 518–33; Mary L. Dudziak, "Desegregation as a Cold War Imperative," *Stan. L. Rev.* 41 (1988): 61–120.

28. Joseph Alsop and Turner Catledge, *The 168 Days* (1938), 10.

29. Dean Alfange, *The Supreme Court and the National Will* (1937), ix, 40, 235.

30. See, e.g., Larry Kramer, *The People Themselves: Popular Constitutionalism and Judicial Review* (2004), 227–28 (claiming that the founding generation would view the "activism" of the modern Court as being so distant from their conception of democracy as to be unrecognizable as "the kind of democracy Americans had fought and died and struggled to create"); see also Mark R. Levin, *Men in Black: How the Supreme Court Is Destroying America* (2005), 195 ("The Supreme Court is abusing and subverting its constitutional role. It has chosen to become the unelected, unassailable social engineer of American society. The sad truth is that the other branches of government have become complicit in the Court's power grab"); see generally supra Chapter 10.

31. United States v. Morrison, 529 U.S. 598, 616n7 (2000); see also Kimel v. Fla. Bd. of Regents, 528 U.S. 62, 81 (2000) ("The ultimate interpretation and determination of the Fourteenth Amendment's substantive meaning remains the province of the Judicial Branch"); City of Boerne v. Flores, 521 U.S. 507, 523–24 (1997) ("The design of the Fourteenth Amendment has proved significant also in maintaining the traditional separation of powers between Congress and the Judiciary. . . . The power to interpret the Constitution in a case or controversy remains in the Judiciary").

32. Quoted in Jeffrey Rosen, "Rehnquist the Great?: Even Liberals May Come to Regard William Rehnquist as One of the Most Successful Chief Justices of the Century," *Atlantic Monthly*, Apr. 2005, at 84–86.

33. Sandra Day O'Connor, "Public Trust as a Dimension of Equal Justice: Some Suggestions to Increase Public Trust," *Ct. Rev.* 36 (1999): 13. For evidence that Justice Kennedy shares these concerns, see Mark V. Tushnet, *A Court Divided: The Rehnquist Court and the Future of Constitutional Law* (2005), 177–78 ("[Kennedy's] years of teaching constitutional law taught him about the limits on the role of judges. The limits were practical; if judges went too far, the political system would slap them down").

34. See Kramer, *People Themselves*, supra note 30, at 227 ("The acceptance of judicial authority is most apparent, however, in the all-but-complete disappearance of public challenges to the Justices' supremacy over constitutional law. Apart from a few academic dissidents, everyone nowadays seems willing to accept the Court's word as final—and to do so, moreover, regardless of the issue, regardless of what the Justices say, and regardless of the Court's political complexion"); see also J. Harvie Wilkinson III, "The Rehnquist Court at Twilight: The Lures and Perils of Split-the-Difference Jurisprudence," *Stan. L. Rev.* 58 (2006): 1996 ("The ideal of courts as bodies of law, and of democracy as a robust arbiter of differences, began to slip slowly from America. Without these values, there can be neither lasting liberty nor lasting order. Americans should not need to ask their Court the question posed by freedom fighters everywhere: You rule, but by what right?")

35. Justices O'Connor and Breyer spoke out defending judicial independence at a conference at Fordham University in April 2008. Dorothy Smalls, "The Selling of the

Judiciary: Campaign Cash 'in the Courtroom,'" *N.Y. Times*, Apr. 15, 2008, at A22. For an example of earlier speeches on this topic by O'Connor, see Dahlia Lithwick, "Courting Attention," *Wash. Post*, Apr. 9, 2006, at B2. O'Connor has also taken to defending judicial independence in the newspaper editorial pages. See Sandra Day O'Connor, "The Threat to Judicial Independence," *Wall Street J.*, Sept. 27, 2006, at A18 ("[W]hile scorn for certain judges is not an altogether new phenomenon, the breadth and intensity of rage currently being leveled at the judiciary may be unmatched in American history").

36. Press Release, New York University, "Law Schools' Deans Challenge Congressional Attack on the Judiciary," May 10, 2005, available at http://www.nyu.edu/public.affairs/releases/detail/647.

37. Gallup polling conducted September 8–11, 2008, indicates that while public trust in the executive and legislative branches of government fell to near-record lows (42 percent reporting a "great deal or fair amount of trust in the executive branch" and 47 percent for the legislative branch), public trust of the judicial branch remains relatively high at 69 percent. Jeffrey M. Jones, "Trust in Government Remains Low," Gallup, Sept. 18, 2008, available at http://www.gallup.com/poll/110458/Trust-Government-Remains-Low.aspx; see also Benjamin Wittes, *Confirmation Wars: Preserving Independent Courts in Angry Times* (2007), 5 ("In Gallup polling over many years, strong majorities have expressed confidence in the judicial branch, and a plurality has regarded it as neither too liberal nor too conservative").

38. David Strauss, "The Modernizing Mission of Judicial Review" (2007, unpublished manuscript, on file with author), 49, 52 ("[I]t does not follow that judges and justices should self-consciously seek to anticipate the movement of public opinion and align their decisions accordingly. . . . Perhaps modernization prescribes a too-quick, or at least too-complete, judicial acquiescence in the democratic process"); see also L. A. Powe, Jr., "Are 'the People' Missing in Action (and Should Anyone Care)?," *Tex. L. Rev.* 83 (2005): 866–84 (documenting seven problematic instances in which the public seemed to control the direction of constitutional law).

39. Greg Robinson, *By Order of the President: FDR and the Internment of Japanese Americans* (2001), 127.

40. David J. O'Brien and Stephen Fugita, *The Japanese American Experience* (1991), 45 ("[T]he definitive Munson report, which was prepared several months before the attack on Pearl Harbor and found no danger of collaboration between Japanese Americans and the Japanese [in either Hawaii or on the West Coast] was suppressed until after the war"). Greg Robinson argues that though evidence of the risk of Japanese sabotage on the West Coast was exaggerated and distorted in its presentation to President Roosevelt, the President's support for internment was primarily influenced by "an implacable belief that Japanese Americans—Issei and Nisei alike—were dangerous and foreign." Robinson, *By Order of the President*, supra note 39, at 72.

41. But see Michelle Malkin, In *Defense of Internment: The Case for "Racial Profiling" in World War II and the War on Terror* (2004), 16–20 (arguing that because of the well-known cases of clandestine enemy infiltration in both Europe and Pacific islands during the Second World War as well as Japanese imperialist propaganda within the mainland United States, civilian Japanese-American internment was a justified military precaution; to pretend otherwise "would have been foolish"); Eric A. Posner and Adrian Vermeule, *Terror in the Balance: Security, Liberty, and the Courts* (2007), 112–13 (contesting the notion that racism in a time of military emergency alone can account for the Japanese-American internment, arguing that different treatment of German- and Italian-Americans could be better explained through geographic and demographic trends).

42. Mark A. Graber, *Dred Scott and the Problem of Constitutional Evil* (2006), 30–36. See also Samuel Issacharoff and Richard H. Pildes, "Emergency Contexts Without Emergency Powers: The United States' Constitutional Approach to Rights During Wartime," *I. CON* 2 (2004): 311–12 (arguing *Korematsu* best understood in light of decision in *Ex parte Endo*, handed down that same day).

43. Korematsu v. United States, 323 U.S. 214 (1944). See Michael J. Klarman, *Unfinished Business: Racial Equality in American History* (2007), 144 ("Given the tenor of the times, there is reason to doubt" that disclosure to justices of information indicating Japanese sabotage risks were slight would have made difference in outcome). Jeffrey Rosen theorizes that the Court's opinion in Ex parte Endo, 323 U.S. 283 (1944), handed down the same day as *Korematsu*, was an attempt by the Court's liberal justices to minimize the appearance of racism by holding that internment was not constitutional as applied to an individual whose loyalty was unquestioned even by the government. See Jeffrey Rosen, *The Supreme Court: The Personalities and Rivalries That Defined America* (2007), 151–52.

44. Racial antipathy toward the Japanese population along the West Coast was cited by the government as necessitating the relocation and internment program, but historians question whether this public hysteria predated the relocation order or arose only after the order was issued on February 19, 1942. Compare Department of the Interior, *WRA: A Story of Human Conservation* (1946), 10 (claiming that "throughout January, the rising tide of emotional fury and violence spread from one end of the State [of California] to the other"), with Robinson, *By Order of the President*, supra note 39, at 101–02 (pointing to official government opinion surveys conducted in the last week in January indicating only minority support for further government intervention).

45. Robinson, *By Order of the President*, supra note 39, at 126, cites the dearth of press coverage of the evacuation and the inability of Congressman John Tolan to produce much testimony opposing the internment in his February 1942 fact-finding hearings.

46. Gallup Poll (Poll No. 285, Questions QN16A, QN16B), conducted Dec. 2, 1942, available at www.gallup.com.

47. Hirabayashi v. United States, 320 U.S. 81 (1943). See "Supreme Court Speaks Plainly on Jap Exclusion," *L.A. Times*, June 22, 1943, at A4.

48. For sources discussing the roots of social science study of the Supreme Court, see Lawrence Baum, "C. Herman Pritchett, Innovator with an Ambiguous Legacy," in *Pioneers of Judicial Behavior*, ed. Nancy Maveety (2003), 57; see also Sara C. Benesh, "Harold J. Spaeth: The Supreme Court Computer," in id. at 116; Lee Epstein and Jack Knight, "Walter F. Murphy: The Interactive Nature of Judicial Decision Making," in id. at 197; Nancy Maveety and John Anthony Maltese, "J. Woodford Howard Jr.: Fluidity, Strategy, and Analytical Synthesis in Judicial Studies," in id. at 228.

49. See, e.g., David G. Barnum, *The Supreme Court and American Democracy* (1993), 287–99 (following public opinion polling trends in issues of free speech, race relations, contraception, and criminal justice and finding the trends mirrored in Supreme Court decisions); Barry Friedman, "The Politics of Judicial Review," *Tex. L. Rev.* 84 (2005): 257–337; Barry Friedman, "Mediated Popular Constitutionalism," *Mich. L. Rev.* 101 (2003): 2596–636; William Mishler and Reginald S. Sheehan, "The Supreme Court as a Countermajoritarian Institution? The Impact of Public Opinion on Supreme Court Decisions," *Am. Pol. Sci. Rev.* 87 (1993): 90–96; Terri Peretti, "A Normative Appraisal of Social Scientific Knowledge Regarding Judicial Independence," *Ohio St. L. J.* 64 (2003): 349–69 (exploring the limits, causes, and uses of judicial independence).

50. For examples of works examining this question, see Richard Posner, *How Judges Think* (2008), 238–39; Lawrence Baum, "What Judges Want: Judges' Goals and Judicial Behavior," *Pol. Res. Q.* 47 (1994): 760; Richard Posner, "What Do Judges Maximize? (The Same Thing Everybody Else Does)," *S. Ct. Econ. Rev.* 3 (1993): 1–41; see also Terri Jennings Peretti, *In Defense of a Political Court* (1999), 80–160.

51. See Charles M. Cameron, Albert D. Cover, and Jeffrey A. Segal, "Senate Voting on Supreme Court Nominees: A Neoinstitutional Model," *Am. Pol. Sci. Rev.* 84 (1990): 525; see also John Anthony Maltese, *The Selling of Supreme Court Nominees* (1998), 150–51.

52. Christopher L. Eisgruber, *The Next Justice: Repairing the Supreme Court Appointments Process* (2007), 132–33 (accounting for all so-called surprises to the Court in the latter twentieth century as situations where the nominating President knew he was taking a gamble); Lawrence Tribe, *God Save This Honorable Court: How the Choice of Supreme Court Justices Shapes Our History* (1985), 50–76 (explaining that Presidents have better accuracy in predicting nominees' ideology than is commonly believed).

53. We have not had many Democratic Presidents in recent years. Bill Clinton's freedom of movement with regard to his nominees was constrained by a hostile Senate. Republican Presidents have done their best to appoint justices acceptable to the right wing of their party, though they too have faced constraints. Eisgruber, *Next Justice*, supra note 52, at 126; see also David Alistair Yalof, *Pursuit of Justices* (1999), 144.

54. See Steven G. Calabresi and James Lindgren, "Term Limits for the Supreme Court: Life Tenure Reconsidered," *Harv. J. L. & Pub. Pol.* 29 (2006): 778–89.

55. See Lee Epstein et al., "Ideological Drift Among Supreme Court Justices: Who, When, and How Important?," *Nw. U. L. Rev.* 101 (2007): 1504–19.

56. See William H. Rehnquist, "Remarks of the Chief Justice: My Life in the Law Series," *Duke L. J.* 52 (2003): 793 (recounting Justice Chase's political ambition); William O. Douglas, *An Almanac of Liberty*, (1954), vi (Justice Douglas describing his own legal philosophy as reflecting "more the small town than the city; more free enterprise than big business; more the man who risks his life than he who risks his dollar; more the farmer than the middleman; more the cooperative than the cartel").

57. See, e.g., Cliff Carruba, Barry Friedman, Andrew Martin, and Georg Vanberg, "Does the Median Justice Control the Content of Supreme Court Opinions?," Oct. 25, 2007 (unpublished manuscript, on file with author); Tom S. Clark and Charles M. Cameron, "The Macro-Politics of the Supreme Court," Second Annual Conference on Empirical Legal Studies Paper (2007); Thomas H. Hammond, Chris W. Bonneau, and Reginald S. Sheehan, *Strategic Behavior and Policy Choice on the U.S. Supreme Court* (2005); see also Jeffrey R. Lax and Charles M. Cameron, "Bargaining and Opinion Assignment on the U.S. Supreme Court," *J. L. Econ. & Org.* 23 (2007): 276–302; Lee Epstein and Tonja Jacobi, "Super Medians," 61 *Stan. L. Rev.* 37 (2008).

58. See Keith Whittington, *Political Foundations of Judicial Supremacy: The Presidency, the Supreme Court, and Constitutional Leadership in U.S. History* (2007), 19–27 (exploring the political interplay among the presidency, Congress, and the Court); Lee Epstein, Jack Knight, and Andrew D. Martin, "The Supreme Court as a Strategic National Policymaker," *Emory L. J.* 50 (2001): 585 (focusing on the "institutional constraints imposed on the Court" by the other branches rather than by popular will).

59. See Anna Harvey and Barry Friedman, "Pulling Punches: Congressional Constraints on the Supreme Court's Constitutional Rulings, 1987–2000," *Legis. Stud. Q.* 31 (2006): 537 (finding evidence that Court certiorari decisions are constrained by congressional and presidential ideology). But see Jeffrey A. Segal and Harold J. Spaeth, *The Supreme Court and the Attitudinal Model Revisited* (2002), 111 (arguing that "the justices need

not respond to public opinion, Congress or the President" and "may freely implement their personal policy preferences").

60. Joseph P. Kalt and Mark A. Zupan, "The Apparent Ideological Behavior of Legislators: Testing for Principal-Agent Slack in Political Institutions," *J. L. & Econ.* 33 (1990): 128 (testing ideological slack in senatorial voting behavior); see also David Epstein and Sharyn O'Halloran, "Legislative Organization Under Separate Powers," *J. L. Econ. & Org.* 17 (2002): 373–75 (describing legislative committees' oversight function in keeping administrative agencies in line with constituent preferences); Keith Krehbiel, *Pivotal Politics: A Theory of U.S. Lawmaking* (1998).

61. Alexis de Tocqueville, *Democracy in America*, tr. George Lawrence (2000), 150.

62. James Bryce, *The American Commonwealth* (1995), 1:242–43.

63. Kramer, *People Themselves*, supra note 30, at 231–33 (arguing that neither Congress nor the President has made overt punitive threats against the Court since Roosevelt's Court-packing plan); see also John A. Ferejohn and Larry D. Kramer, "Independent Judges, Dependent Judiciary: Institutionalizing Judicial Restraint," *N.Y.U. L. Rev.* 77 (2002): 978 ("The only means by which Congress can penalize a particular judge's errant behavior is through impeachment, a largely toothless threat used in practice to remove judges only when extreme misconduct can be proved").

64. In response to the Court's decision in Hamdan v. Rumsfeld, 548 U.S. 557 (2006), holding that the administration's Guantánamo Bay military commissions lacked congressional authorization, the Senate initially considered several different legislative responses. See Michael John Garcia, "The War Crimes Act: Current Issues," *CRS Report for Congress* (2007), 5–6, available at http://www.fas.org/sgp/crs/intel/RL33662.pdf. However, in a "last-ditch effort to retain control of Congress" in the 2006 midterm elections, Bush administration officials "pushed" forward the Military Commissions Act of 2006, P.L. 109–366, 120 Stat. 2636, which attempted to further strip federal courts of the jurisdiction to hear habeas corpus petitions from Guantánamo detainees. Julian E. Barnes, "Guantanamo Detainees' Trial Rules Set: The Pentagon Plans to Charge 60 to 80 Under Its Guidelines, Which Have Renewed Debate on Harsh Treatment," *L.A. Times*, Jan. 19, 2007, at A11. These further efforts at jurisdiction stripping, however, were rejected by the Court in June 2008 in Boumediene v. Bush, 128 S. Ct. 2229, 2277 (2008), again holding that "petitioners may invoke the fundamental procedural protections of habeas corpus."

65. In a related vein, see generally Charles Gardner Geyh, *When Courts and Congress Collide: The Struggle for Control of America's Judicial System* (2008), 51–111 (discussing evolution in the relationship of Congress and the courts).

66. Accord Jeffrey Rosen, *The Most Democratic Branch: How the Courts Serve America* (2006), 185 (explaining that "on the rare occasions that [the Court] has been even modestly out of line with popular majorities, it has gotten into trouble").

67. See William N. Eskridge and Philip P. Frickey, "Foreword: Law as Equilibrium," *Harv. L. Rev.* 108 (1994): 28–29 (describing how the Court negotiates its policy goals "but only as that vision can be achieved within a complex, interactive setting in which each organ of government is both cooperating with and competing with the other organs"); Geyh, *When Courts and Congress Collide*, supra note 65, at 258–60 (discussing "dynamic equilibrium" between Congress and the courts).

68. Peretti, *In Defense of a Political Court*, supra note 50, at 100; see also Eskridge and Frickey, "Law as Equilibrium," supra note 67, at 36–39 (describing the "anticipated response" of the Court's modifying its decisions to avoid sanction); Mishler and Sheehan, "Supreme Court as a Countermajoritarian Institution," supra note 49, at 91–96 (noting a close correlation between public opinion and judicial opinions); James A. Stimson, Michael B. Mackuen, and Robert S. Erikson, "Dynamic Represen-

tation" *Am. Pol. Sci. Rev.* 89 (1995): 544–45 (referring to the phenomenon as "rational anticipation").

69. Almost four decades after ruling prayer in public schools unconstitutional in Engel v. Vitale, 370 U.S. 421 (1962), the Supreme Court upheld its ban on school prayer in Santa Fe Indep. Sch. Dist. v. Doe, 530 U.S. 290 (2000), despite opinion polls showing that at least 75 percent of the country favors allowing school prayer. See David Klinghoffer, "Give Us This Day," *Baltimore Sun*, Dec. 29, 1994, at 15A. In the 1989 case of Texas v. Johnson, 491 U.S. 397 (1989), the Court held flag burning to be expression protected by the First Amendment, a ruling that continues to stand despite strong public opposition. See David D. Kirkpatrick, "Congress Again Debates Protecting the Flag," *N.Y. Times*, June 22, 2005, at A15 (citing opinion polls ranging from 65 percent to 80 percent support for outlawing flag burning).

70. Andrew D. Martin and Christina Wolbrecht, "Partisanship and Pre-Floor Behavior: The Equal Rights and School Prayer Amendments," *Pol. Res. Q.* 53 (2000): 721 (explaining that Celler's House Judiciary Committee eventually blocked sixty-nine separate versions of the school prayer amendment beginning in 1962).

71. The phrase "gridlock interval" was coined in Krehbiel, *Pivotal Politics*, supra note 60, at 34–38 (explaining the phenomenon of the gridlock interval, in which a majority of a legislature may support a change in the status quo, yet no change occurs because of supermajority requirements to overcome either filibuster or veto threats). For some of the precursors of this work, see, e.g., John A. Ferejohn, "Incumbent Performance and Electoral Control," *Pub. Choice* 50 (1986); John Ferejohn and Charles Shipan, "Congressional Influence on Bureaucracy," *J. L. Econ. & Org.* 6 (1990): 1–20; Barry R. Weingast, "The Congressional-Bureaucratic System: A Principal-Agent Perspective (with Applications to the SEC)," *Pub. Choice* 44 (1984).

72. Krehbiel, *Pivotal Politics*, supra note 60, at 65–71 (noting that the gridlock interval shrinks after moments of popular elections, especially in the face of broad electoral mandates).

73. Celler bent to pressure to hold hearings only after two years and a sustained letter-writing campaign by motivated constituents. Michal R. Belknap, *The Supreme Court Under Earl Warren, 1953–1969* (2005), 145.

74. See Jeffrey Rosen, "Supreme Court Inc.," *N.Y. Times Mag.*, March 16, 2008, at 38.

75. See Robert Barnes, "High Court Upholds Curb on Abortion: 5–4 Vote Affirms Ban on 'Partial-Birth' Procedure," *Wash. Post*, Apr. 19, 2007, at A1 (reporting on abortion case Gonzales v. Carhart, 550 U.S. 124 (2007)); Linda Greenhouse, "Justices, Ruling 5–4, Endorse Personal Right to Own Gun," *N.Y. Times*, June 27, 2008, at A1 (discussing gun control case District of Columbia v. Heller, 128 S.Ct. 2783 (2008)); Jeffrey Rosen, "Can a Law Change Society?," *N.Y. Times*, July 1, 2007, § 4, at 1 (discussing the future of affirmative action in the wake of Parents Involved in Community Schs. v. Seattle Sch. Dist. No. 1, 127 S.Ct. 2738 (2007)).

76. Kelo v. City of New London, Conn., 545 U.S. 469 (2005). For analysis of public response to *Kelo*, see, e.g., Judy Coleman, "The Powers of a Few, the Anger of the Many," *Wash. Post*, Oct. 9, 2005, at B2.

77. See Michael J. Klarman, "What's So Great About Constitutionalism?," *Nw. U. L. Rev.* 93 (1998): 189 (arguing that "judicial review is systematically biased in favor of culturally elite values").

78. See, e.g. Charles A. Radin, "Scalia Gesture Not Obscene, Court Rep Says," *Boston Globe*, March 28, 2006, at B2 (analyzing press reaction to a "Sicilian gesture" of dismissal Scalia made to a reporter who approached him unsolicited); Editorial, "The over-the-Top Justice," *N.Y. Times*, Apr. 2, 2006, § 4, at 11 (cataloging Scalia's actions that indicate disregard for press approval).

79. See Robert Barnes, "Federalists Relish Well-Placed Friends: President, Several Justices Help Celebrate Legal Society's 25 Years of Conservatism," *Wash. Post*, Nov. 16, 2007, at A3; Richard Leiby, "The Reliable Source," *Wash. Post*, Nov. 16, 2004, at C3 (describing Scalia as "the godfather of the Federalist Society").

80. See, e.g., praise heaped on the Court after striking down the Communications Decency Act of 1996. "The Court Rules for Freedom," *Chi. Trib.*, June 29, 1997, at C16 ("That ruling was one of the most welcome and significant defenses of free speech the court has ever issued"); "Three Welcome Rulings from the High Court," *San Fran. Chron.*, June 27, 1997, at A26 ("The justices took the unpopular—but constitutionally correct—course of striking down the 1996 Communications Decency Act").

81. See Stephen J. Choi and G. Mitu Gulati, "Trading Votes for Reasoning: Covering in Judicial Opinions," *S. Cal. L. Rev.* 81 (2008): 757 (finding First Amendment cases the most likely to be covered by *The New York Times* over a four-year period from 1993 to 1997); Lee Epstein and Jeffrey A. Segal, "Measuring Issue Salience," *Am. J. Pol. Sci.* 44 (2000): 74.

82. See generally Richard A. Posner, "Pragmatic Adjudication," *Cardozo L. Rev.* 18 (1996): 11 (discussing various approaches believed to be taken by judges in deciding novel cases).

83. There was more than one Japanese internment case, but still the justices had to deal with them within a span of eighteen months. The first of the three cases, Hirabayashi v. United States, 320 U.S. 81 (1943), was decided on June 21, 1943, and the final internment case, Ex parte Endo, 323 U.S. 214 (1943), was decided on December 18, 1944 (the same day as *Korematsu*).

84. See David Easton, *A Systems Analysis of Political Life* (1965) (introducing the terms "diffuse support" and "specific support"; Gregory A. Caldeira and James L. Gibson, "The Etiology of Public Support for the Supreme Court," *Am. J. Pol. Sci.* 36 (1992): 639–49 (applying the terms and measuring diffuse and specific support for the Supreme Court); see generally Friedman, "Mediated Popular Constitutionalism," supra note 49, at 2616–20.

85. See Easton, *A Systems Analysis of Political Life*, supra note 84, at 273 ("[Specific support] flows from the favorable attitudes and predisposition stimulated by outputs that are perceived by members to meet their demands as they arise or in anticipation").

86. See id. ("[Diffuse support creates] a reservoir of favorable attitudes or good will that helps [the public] to accept or tolerate outputs to which they are opposed or the effects of which they see as damaging to their wants").

87. James L. Gibson, Gregory A. Caldeira, and Vanessa A. Baird, "On the Legitimacy of National High Courts," *Am. Pol. Sci. Rev.* 92 (1998): 346–52.

88. See J. Mark Ramseyer, "The Puzzling (In)Dependence of Courts: A Comparative Approach," *J. Leg. Stud.* 23 (1994): 722 (highlighting two necessary factors for politicians to accept an independent judiciary: "[a] whether they expect elections to continue indefinitely, and [b] if elections will continue, whether they expect to continue to win them indefinitely"); Matthew C. Stephenson, "'When the Devil Turns . . .': The Political Foundations of Independent Judicial Review," *J. Leg. St.* 32 (2003): 63–64 (theorizing that the existence of judicial independence arises from stable competition between political parties). Larry Kramer argues that the judiciary fight of 1801 surrounding *Marbury v. Madison* was the result of a breakdown in this kind of politically competitive compromise. Kramer, *People Themselves*, supra note 30, at 116–22.

89. James L. Gibson, Gregory A. Caldeira, and Lester Kenyatta Spence, "The Supreme Court and the US Presidential Election of 2000: Wounds, Self-Inflicted or Otherwise?," *British J. Pol Sci.* 33 (2003): 538 (describing a national poll conducted within

three months of *Bush v. Gore* that showed "only slightly less confidence [in the Court] than the results of a comparable survey conducted at the beginning of 2000").

90. Caldeira and Gibson, "Etiology of Public Support" supra note 84, at 641; Gibson et al., "On the Legitimacy of National High Courts," supra note 87, at 348.

91. Greg Caldeira and James Gibson have done more than any others to study the phenomenon of diffuse support. They describe the concept as "resistant to empirical investigation" within the United States. Gibson et al., "On the Legitimacy of National High Courts," supra note 87, at 345.

92. See, e.g., Republican Party of Minnesota v. White, 536 U.S. 765, 798 (2002) (Stevens, J., dissenting) ("There is a critical difference between the work of the judge and the work of other public officials. In a democracy, issues of policy are properly decided by majority vote; it is the business of legislators and executives to be popular. But in litigation, issues of law or fact should not be determined by popular vote; it is the business of judges to be indifferent to unpopularity"); Don Herzog, *Happy Slaves: A Critique of Consent Theory* (1989), 129 ("[J]urors should ignore the government's desires in deliberating and ruling"); Robert Post and Reva Siegel, "*Roe* Rage: Democratic Constitutionalism and Backlash," *Harv. C.R.-C.L. L. Rev.* 42 (2007): 375 ("Judges regularly assert the authority of their constitutional judgments by invoking the distinction between law and politics. They rely on professional legal reason to separate law from politics. If judges appear to yield to political pressure, the public may lose confidence in the authority of courts to declare constitutional law").

93. John H. Cushman, Jr., "Bush Talks in Gentler Tone to Abortion Foes in Capital," *N.Y. Times*, Jan. 23, 1990, at A18; Manny Fernandez, "Abortion Protest Draws Thousands; Marchers Brave Cold to Speak Out Against 1973 *Roe v. Wade* Decision," *Wash. Post*, Jan. 23, 2004, at B1.

94. Planned Parenthood of Southeastern Pennsylvania v. Casey, 505 U.S. 833, 861, 865 (1992); see also id. at 866 ("[T]he Court's legitimacy depends on making legally principled decisions under circumstances in which their principled character is sufficiently plausible to be accepted by the Nation").

95. Id. at 1000 (Scalia, J., concurring in the judgment in part and dissenting in part); see also Webster v. Repro. Health Servs., 492 U.S. 490, 535 (1989) (Scalia, J., concurring in part and concurring in the judgment) ("We can now look forward to at least another Term with carts full of mail from the public, and streets full of demonstrators, urging us—their unelected and life-tenured judges who have been awarded those extraordinary, undemocratic characteristics precisely in order that we might follow the law despite the popular will—to follow the popular will").

96. Steven B. Burbank and Barry Friedman, "Reconsidering Judicial Independence," in *Judicial Independence at the Crossroads: An Interdisciplinary Approach*, ed. Steven B. Burbank and Barry Friedman (2002), 27–28 (analyzing the influence of community pressures on the independence of southern trial judges during the civil rights movement).

97. See Deborah Goldberg, "Interest Group Participation in Judicial Elections," in *Running for Judge: The Rising Political, Financial, and Legal Stakes of Judicial Elections*, ed. Matthew Streb (2007), 76 (reporting that prisoners convicted of first-degree murder in a judge's election year were 15 percent more likely to be sentenced to death than in nonelection years); Melinda Gann Hall, "Justices as Representatives: Elections and Judicial Politics in the American States," *Am. Pol. Res.* 23 (1995): 495–97 (finding that elected judges in the last two years of their terms are more likely to uphold death sentences).

98. Learned Hand, *The Spirit of Liberty: Papers and Addresses of Learned Hand*, ed. Irving Dillard (1952), 189.

99. Accord Rosen, *Most Democratic Branch*, supra note 66, at 198 ("[T]he Court should defer to the national majority's constitutional views, not its political views"); id. at 200 (arguing that judges are better suited to preserving past constitutional consensus than anticipating future consensus).

100. Woodrow Wilson, *Constitutional Government in the United States* (1908), 172; Theodore Roosevelt, "Nationalism and the Judiciary," *Outlook* 97 (1911): 384–85.

101. See Barry Friedman, "Dialogue and Judicial Review," *Mich. L. Rev.* 91 (1993): 653–80 (describing the dialogic process of constitutional interpretation through the example of abortion cases).

102. Bruce A. Ackerman, *We the People*, vol. 2: *Transformations* (2000), 315 (arguing that by acquiescing as quickly as it did, the Court unnecessarily directed the process of constitutional change away from more direct and explicit paths such as the Article V amendment process or Roosevelt's unconventional Court-packing proposal. "If, however, the President, Congress, and the country were doing quite well confronting the crisis without the Court's assistance, we must ask a different question: Did the Court retreat too soon?"); Larry D. Kramer "The Supreme Court, 2000 Term—Foreword, We the Court," *Harv. L. Rev.* 115 (2001): 121–28 (describing the collision between the Court and New Dealers that led to a "chastened" Court and a new and lasting settlement between popular constitutionalism and judicial supremacy).

103. See Eisgruber, *Constitutional Self-Government*, supra note 25, at 14–78 (reviewing criticisms of judicial review in a constitutional system that includes the Article V super-majoritarian amendment process); Sager, "Justice in Plain Clothes," supra note 25, at 423–25 (advocating judicial "underenforcement" of constitutional justice issues to encourage legislative solutions and prevent the premature restriction of political compromise); see also Lawrence G. Sager, "The Incorrigible Constitution," *N.Y.U. L. Rev.* 65 (1990): 901 ("Unlike ordinary legislation, the Constitution is not freely amendable by elected governmental officials. Rather, it is clear that the Framers did not want the Constitution to be easily amended, and, in practice, it has been almost impossible to rewrite").

104. See Michael J. Klarman, "*Brown* and *Lawrence* (and *Goodridge*)," *Mich. L. Rev.* 104 (2005): 473–82 (highlighting constitutional decisions on school desegregation and same-sex marriage that produced popular backlash and forced longer-term democratic responses).

105. See Klarman, *From Jim Crow to Civil Rights*, supra note 27, at 464–66 (discussing the causes of famous twentieth-century backlashes, hypothesizing that such backlashes occur when a court ruling interferes with ongoing legislative negotiations); Jack M. Balkin, "Original Meaning and Constitutional Redemption," *Const. Comment.* 24 (2007): 515 (arguing that even long before theories of originalism or living constitutionalism, the Supreme Court has always interpreted the Constitution in light of "changing political and social mobilizations"); William N. Eskridge, Jr., "Some Effects of Identity-Based Social Movements on Constitutional Law in the Twentieth Century," *Mich. L. Rev.* 100 (2002): 2064 ("[M]ost twentieth century changes in the constitutional protection of individual rights were driven by or in response to the great identity-based social movements ("IBSMs") of the twentieth century"); William E. Forbath, "Popular Constitutionalism in the Twentieth Century: Reflections on the Dark Side, the Progressive Constitutional Imagination, and the Enduring Role of Judicial Finality in Popular Understandings of Popular Self-Rule," *Chi.-Kent L. Rev.* 81 (2006): 988–90 (claiming that in the second half of the twentieth century, pressure from social movements in reaction to adverse constitutional decisions helped alter constitutional understanding and led to accommodation by the Court); Robert C. Post, "Foreword: Fashioning the Legal Constitution: Culture,

Courts, and Law," *Harv. L. Rev.* 117 (2003): 104–06 (exploring how the Court's "dialectical relationship" with the social movements shapes doctrinal choices); Reva B. Siegel, "Constitutional Culture, Social Movement Conflict and Constitutional Change: The Case of the De Facto ERA," *Cal. L. Rev.* 94 (2006): 1324 (arguing that social movements in response to the proposed Equal Rights Amendment and subsequent Fourteenth Amendment sex discrimination cases helped forge political consensus).

106. Ruth Bader Ginsburg, "Speaking in a Judicial Voice," *N.Y.U. L. Rev.* 67 (1992): 1198.
107. Sandra Day O'Connor, *The Majesty of the Law: Reflections of a Supreme Court Justice* (2003), 166.
108. Owen J. Roberts, *The Court and the Constitution* (1951), 61.
109. James Bradley Thayer, "The Origin and Scope of the American Doctrine of Constitutional Law," in *Legal Essays* (1908), 39.

ACKNOWLEDGMENTS

This book had a long gestation period, during which I accumulated many debts. In a sense, the project began over fifteen years ago, while I was a scholar at the Rockefeller Foundation's glorious refuge in Bellagio, Italy. I had intended then to begin writing a very different book, one about the proper use of the power of judicial review. Instead, I realized I could not move forward until I understood when, and why, Americans (and particularly legal academics) became obsessed with the notion that judicial review was necessarily juxtaposed with the will of popular majorities. I thought this was a question that would take me a short while to answer; instead, it began the journey that took me to this volume.

I am lucky to be part of an extraordinary academic community. Few outside of the academy can possibly understand how almost unfailingly gracious academics are with their time and energies when it comes to the shared collaborative scholarly effort. Bill Nelson and Dan Hulsebosch were extraordinary colleagues throughout this process. Not only did they welcome me time and again to the NYU School of Law's Legal History Colloquium, but they were the ones who most helped me excavate the precise story I had to tell. The two of them taught me a lot about being a historian. Rachel Barkow read more than anyone else, always with a smile and a keen eye for what was working and what was not. She is a paragon of positive reinforcement. Jack Rakove shared his usual great wisdom; he also put his wonderful editor's pen to the whole manuscript. Mark Graber was tireless with his help. Daryl Levinson gave a vacation over to reading the manuscript. I thank him for forcing me to confront the hard questions. And then there is Michael Klarman. At just the moment when I thought I was making progress, he graced me with a seventy-page single-spaced memo about everything I had done wrong. Suffice it to say that my appreciation for his memo increased gradually over time. Michael, who has always been ridiculously generous with his time, not only taught me a great deal, he did more to save me from abject humiliation than any other person who helped.

Many people read all or part of the manuscript, in one of its many iterations. With fear that I am missing someone, my deep thanks to: Bruce Ackerman, Jill Anton, Saul

Anton, Jenna Bednar, Richard Bensel, Richard Bernstein, Noam Bramson, Steve Burbank, Bethany Chaney, Barry Cushman, Tabatha El-haj, Bill Eskridge, Ben Friedman, Patrick Garlinger, Howard Gillman, Michael Greve, Ariela Gross, Susan Haar, Anna Harvey, Sam Issacharoff, Robert Kaczorowski, Laura Kalman, Maggie Lemos, Alan Lequire, Andree Lequire, Renee Lerner, Bill Leuchtenberg, Elizabeth McCallum, John McGinnis, Robert Post, Kenny Pringle, Ed Purcell, Lori Ringhand, Gary Rowe, Seana Shiffrin, Jed Shugerman, Reva Siegel, Peter Smith. In addition, a lot of other folks helped with advice at crucial moments, including Derrick Bell, David Bernstein, Steve Calabresi, Peggy Davis, Ariela Dubler, Noah Feldman, Dedi Felman, Willy Forbath, David Golove, Risa Goluboff, Sally Gordon, John Harrison, Larry Kramer, Sandy Levinson, Serena Mayeri, Bill Novak, Rick Pildes, John Reid, Cristina Rodriguez, Steve Teles, Keith Whittington, John Witt, and Kenji Yoshino.

I presented portions of the project in many places and always benefited from the comments and thoughts I received as I traveled. I am grateful for the help I received at faculty workshops at the law schools at the University of Southern California, Stanford, the University of Chicago, the University of Texas, the University of Virginia, Vanderbilt, and Washington University in St. Louis. I also had profitable encounters with legal historians in the District of Columbia at a gathering organized by Maeva Marcus and the Institute for Constitutional Studies, at a legal history class at Harvard Law School, and at a legal history workshop at Yale Law School. I abused my colleagues at the NYU School of Law repeatedly in summer and term-time faculty workshops, and particularly in the Legal History Colloquium.

Legions of research assistants have helped to bring this book to fruition. To those who worked on the original articles on the counter-majoritarian difficulty that led me to this project, you were acknowledged at the time but I want to salute you again here. For their labor on the book in particular, I want to thank Joanne Albertson, Kevin Arlyck, Talia Barsam, Jim Beha, Jeff Benjamin, Chris Bradley, Brian Burgess, Adan Canizales, Heather Childs, Michael Connelly, Alicia D'addario, Dan Deacon, Leslie Dubeck, Russell Ferri, Brooke Grossman, Matt Haggans, Ilana Haramati, Craig Heeren, Taja-nia Henderson, Adam Hill, Jacob Kreutzer, Greg Larkin, Josh Libling, Jessica Lonergan, Andrew Long, Gina Magel, AJ Martinez, Ashley Miller, Sean Nutall, Deanna Oswald, Ravi Rajendra, Nicholas Sage, Ian Samuel, Greg Scanlon, Delci Winders, Lindsey Weinstock, David Wake, Xin Yu, and Laura Zuckerwise.

This book would not exist were it not for the extraordinary assistance of many librarians. My great appreciation to the library staffs at Vanderbilt Law School and the New York University School of Law, with special shout-outs to Gretchen Feltes and Howard Hood. I can never thank my special library pal Jay Shuman enough for making this work possible: he labored under a flood of numbered lists and pleas to have obscure sources "as soon as possible!" and never pushed back. Well, okay—once. Maybe twice.

Then there are the people who exist in their own categories of thanks. To say that New York University School of Law has been a nurturing environment is to engage in vast understatement. The truth of that rests in the relentless support of its remarkable deans, John Sexton and Ricky Revesz. Ricky in particular found it impossible ever to say no to anything I needed for this book; his friendship, collegiality, and support have been a constant beacon. Lisa Koederitz managed my library "annex," helped with the manuscript, and did much more. Lillian Zalta performed miracles to make sure I had a library annex in the first place. Sara Lewin made it possible for me to finish this book while being Vice Dean and a new parent, and still maintain some (paltry) semblance of a life; more important, she kept me smiling. Jenny Bindel, in her low-key efficient way, sailed this ship into port; at the very time when I dreaded most what was coming next, her work on final production somehow left me free to relax on deck. I've promised myself all along that I'd thank Andrea Bocelli, Michael Cormican, John Griffin, and Adam Steinlauf when the time came for doing their parts. Abby Cope and Eva Scrivo made the photo shoot for the book jacket a special pleasure. Tom Foreman, whom I've never met, performed a random act of kindness.

With a tip of the hat to Jack Rakove, Donald Lamm appeared at my door one hot and humid New York day and told me I needed an agent. Then, in his typical no-nonsense way, he took matters in hand, as he apparently has for many fortunate others. He put me in the good care of Christy Fletcher of Fletcher & Company, my agent and my friend. Christy has done many things for me, but perhaps none more important than ushering me to the tutelage of my editor, Eric Chinski, at Farrar, Straus and Giroux. Eric is an amazing reader; he saw in the manuscript what the book could be and pushed me to make it so. He is also unflappable, a trait any author cherishes. To the rest of the wonderful, professional team at FSG—Eugenie Cha, the ever-present and ever-thoughtful Susan Goldfarb, Judy Kiviat, Debra Helfand, Jeff Seroy, and Laurel Cook—as well as to my copyeditor, Pearl Hanig, I know this was not your easiest project, and I thank you for all you did to help it along.

Much of this book was researched and written late at night and into the morning hours. Whenever I was fatigued, bored, fretting, or just in need of a break, I amused myself by reading the acknowledgments written by authors of my source materials. Inevitably, the author was nurtured by loving parents. He or she was fortunate to have a giving and talented spouse. It was a miracle the work got done with the small children scampering about and tearing things up, but life would be oh-so-much-more impoverished without them. Strangely, now here I am, though that was hardly where I stood when this project was conceived. My parents, Sally and Benjamin Friedman, have given much to me, as parents are wont to do; I never fully appreciated that until I had my own children, but now I do. My wonderful in-laws, Gloria and Saul Anton, were hugely supportive. Throughout, I took special sustenance in the deep joy my father experienced in watching this manuscript come to fruition.

I am prepared to state unequivocally that no author was ever cared for—or fed, for that matter—better than I have been by my incredibly talented wife, Jill Anton. Nonetheless, she regularly delighted in pointing out to me all who have managed to begin and complete their own book projects while I plodded along with mine. Among the many things Jill has done with and for me, nothing begins to compare to the extraordinary joy I draw from our two remarkable children, Samara and Simon. They are the light of my life. My daughter, Samara, is the only person in the world who fully understands what it means when my study door is closed, and yet feels entitled to walk in when she wishes and demand my attention. (I regret to say that when pressed, she insists she must "do a little work" and "take some notes"). I hope that never, ever changes. Her brother, Simon, is just now at the charming stage of locomoting on his own to my office to empty out my desk drawers on the floor. His smile upon seeing me compensates for the chore of putting all those binder clips back in their place, and for much else. When someone actually asked in public to whom the book would be dedicated, Jill—who is reticent by nature—shocked me by declaring forcefully and unequivocally that it had better be her. Although I am not someone who unthinkingly follows direction, I trust Jill understands there never was, and never could have been, any other choice. She is my joy; she is what keeps me going.

GREENWICH VILLAGE
February 2009

INDEX

Social Security Act (1935), 209, 213, 227, 497*n*306
Souter, David, 325, 329, 330, 334, 346, 380, 546*n*10, 547*n*13
South Carolina Ordinance of Nullification, 99
Southern Manifesto, 247
sovereign immunity, 331–32, 356, 551*n*77
Spaeth, Harold J., 519*n*237, 583*n*59
Spaight, Richard, 24, 28, 30, 39–41, 398*n*110, 401*n*160
Specter, Arlen, 352
Spence, Lester Kenyatta, 586*n*89
Spock, Benjamin, 294
Stalin, Joseph, 251
Stamp Act (1765), 27–28, 395*n*64
Stanbery, Henry, 451*n*238
Stanford University, 301, 303, 337, 350; Law School, 357
Stanton, Edward, 122, 449*n*216
stare decisis, doctrine of, 307, 542*n*188, 551*n*64
Starr, Kenneth, 360, 362
State Department, U.S., 575*n*386
Stearns, Nancy, 536*n*176
Stephens, Alexander, 125
Stephenson, Matthew C., 586*n*88
Stevens, John Paul, 288, 309, 329, 551*n*64, 587*n*92
Stevens, Thaddeus, 125, 127, 128, 139, 448*n*187
Stewart, John, 345
Stewart, Potter, 263, 286–88
Stewart, Roy, 275
Stimson, Henry, 482*n*58
Stimson, James A., 584*n*68
Stone, Frederick, 131
Stone, Geoffrey R., 512*n*152
Stone, Harlan Fiske, 198, 200, 203, 230, 234, 240, 260, 483*n*70, 504*nn*17, 21
Stone, I. F., 220
Story, Joseph, 80–83, 88, 90, 91, 93, 103, 425*n*108
Strauss, David A., 365, 553*n*109, 577*n*420, 581*n*38
strict scrutiny, 289, 291–95, 326, 547*n*22, 558*n*185
Strong, William, 452*n*253
Stuart v. Laird (1803), 59, 61–63, 412*n*130, 413*n*147, 414*n*158
Stuntz, William J., 528*n*398
Sturges v. Crowninshield (1819), 424*n*84
Sullivan, Kathleen M., 357, 571*n*344
Sumner, Charles, 109–10, 113, 120, 143, 147, 443*n*120
Sumners, Hatton, 223, 224, 227, 494*n*268
Sunstein, Cass, 323, 331, 337, 343, 345, 346, 502*n*3, 553*n*109, 554*n*125, 556*n*141, 560*n*212, 561*n*228, 229, 562*n*242
Supremacy Clause, 35–36, 42, 78, 98, 101, 398*n*108

Susman, Frank, 535*n*154
Suspension Clause, 122, 123
Sutherland, George, 172, 173, 198, 199, 203–205, 215, 227, 236, 480*n*23, 493*n*237, 497*n*306, 500*n*340
Swayne, Noah, 142, 447*n*177
Sweatt v. Painter (1950), 244
Sweezy v. New Hampshire (1957), 504*n*15, 512*n*153
Swift v. Tyson (1842), 162, 462*n*201, 463*n*209
Swift, Zephaniah, 39–41
Syrett, Harold C., 428*n*171

Taft, William Howard, 152, 155, 171, 172, 178, 180, 183, 186, 192, 206, 221, 467*n*36
Talleyrand-Périgord, Charles Maurice de, 47
Tallmadge, Benjamin, 44–45
Talmadge, Herman, 246
Taney, Roger, 103, 110, 113–16, 121–24, 134, 162, 437*n*54, 57, 59, 438*n*70, 71
Taylor, John, 67, 83, 403*n*4, 423*n*83
Taylor, Stuart, Jr., 556*n*151
Teepen, Tom, 573*nn*370, 371
Teles, Steven M., 539*n*242
Tennessee Valley Authority (TVA), 481*n*43
Tenth Amendment, 497*n*306, 561*n*223
Texas, University of, Law School, 278
Terry v. Ohio (1968), 277, 527*n*395, 528*n*398
Texas House of Representatives, 225
Texas v. Johnson (1989), 585*n*69
Thayer, James Bradley, 191, 384–85, 518*n*224
Third Way, 352
Thirteenth Amendment, 120, 121, 124, 139, 443*n*122, 503*n*12
Thomas, Clarence, 325, 326, 340, 346, 546*n*10, 547*n*19, 24, 553*n*109, 557*n*154, 558*n*177, 562*n*240–42, 579*n*17
Thompson, Dorothy, 219
Thompson, Frank, Jr., 417*n*201
Thompson, Philip, 57
Thompson, Smith, 90
Thornburgh v. American College of Obstetricians and Gynecologists (1986), 315, 540*n*253
Thurman, Allen G., 141
Thurmond, Strom, 268, 506*n*54
Ticknor, George, 91, 92
Tiedeman, Christopher, 172–73
Tilden, Samuel J., 148, 358
Tocqueville, Alexis de, 17, 375–77
Todd, Thomas, 425*n*108
Tolan, John, 582*n*45
Toobin, Jeffrey, 364, 575*n*390, 578*n*3
Torres-Reyna, Oscar, 549*n*42
Totenberg, Nina, 319, 321, 331, 345
Totten, Major Enoch, 449*n*216
Tracy, Uriah, 66, 409*n*92
Treasury, U.S., 46
Treaty of Peace (1783), 26, 27